Introduction to Management Accounting and Financial Management

Introduction to Management Accounting and Financial Management

Compiled from:

Management Accounting for Decision Makers
Eighth Edition
Peter Atrill and Eddie McLaney

Financial Management for Decision Makers
Eighth Edition
Peter Atrill

Pearson

Harlow, England • London • New York • Boston • San Francisco • Toronto • Sydney • Dubai • Singapore • Hong Kong
Tokyo • Seoul • Taipei • New Dehli • Cape Town • São Paulo • Mexico City • Madrid • Amsterdam • Munich • Paris • Milan

Pearson
KAO Two
KAO Park
Harlow
Essex CM17 9NA

And associated companies throughout the world

Visit us on the World Wide Web at:
www.pearson.com/uk

Compiled from:

Management Accounting for Decision Makers
Eighth Edition
Peter Atrill and Eddie McLaney
978-1-292-07243-2

Financial Management for Decision Makers
Eighth Edition
Peter Atrill
978-1-292-13433-8

ISBN 978-1-78726-405-2

Printed and bound in Great Britain by CPI Group.

Contents

Part One

Management Accounting

Chapter 1

INTRODUCTION TO MANAGEMENT ACCOUNTING

INTRODUCTION

Welcome to the world of management accounting! In this introductory chapter, we examine the role of management accounting within a business. To understand the context for management accounting we begin by examining the nature and purpose of a business. Thus, we first consider what businesses seek to achieve, how they are organised and how they are managed. Having done this, we go on to explore how management accounting information can be used within a business to improve the quality of managers' decisions. We also identify the characteristics that management accounting information must possess to fulfil its role. Management accounting has undergone many changes in response to developments in the business environment and to the increasing size and complexity of businesses. In this chapter we shall discuss some of the more important changes that have occurred.

Learning outcomes

When you have completed this chapter, you should be able to:

- Identify the purpose of a business and discuss the ways in which a business may be organised and managed.
- Discuss the issues to be considered when setting the long-term direction of a business.
- Explain the role of management accounting within a business and describe the key qualities that management accounting information should possess.
- Explain the changes that have occurred over time in both the role of the management accountant and the type of information provided by management accounting systems.

WHAT IS THE PURPOSE OF A BUSINESS?

Peter Drucker, an eminent management thinker, has argued that '*The purpose of business is to create and keep a customer*' (see reference 1 at the end of the chapter). Drucker defined the purpose of a business in this way in 1967, at a time when most businesses did not adopt this strong customer focus. His view therefore represented a radical challenge to the accepted view of what businesses do. Almost fifty years later, however, his approach has become part of the conventional wisdom. It is now widely recognised that, in order to succeed, businesses must focus on satisfying the needs of the customer.

Although the customer has always provided the main source of revenue for a business, this has often been taken for granted. In the past, too many businesses assumed that the customer would readily accept whatever services or products were on offer. When competition was weak and customers were passive, businesses could operate under this assumption and still make a profit. However, the era of weak competition has passed. Today, customers have much greater choice and are much more assertive concerning their needs. They now demand higher quality services and goods at cheaper prices. They also require that services and goods be delivered faster with an increasing emphasis on the product being tailored to their individual needs. If a business cannot meet these needs, a competitor often can. Thus the business mantra for the current era is '*the customer is king*'. Most businesses now recognise this fact and organise themselves accordingly.

Real World 1.1 discusses how this mantra applies to business schools offering programmes for business executives.

Real World 1.1

The customer is king

For corporations, there is just one message to come out of the recession about business school executive development programmes: it is a buyers' market where the customer is king. And for most business schools, there is also only a single message: rethink your business model if you want to survive.

Customer responsiveness, total quality management and global sensitivity – all topics on which business professors can expound at length – now have to be part of what business schools practise as well as what they preach. Gone are the days when a business school could run a course because it had a professor who understood the subject; customer need has now become paramount.

With both training companies and management consultancies encroaching on the patch of the traditional business education providers, schools have seen two to three years of painful decline in revenues from executive education programmes. Now they hope that business is returning.

Where business is returning, demand has clearly changed. Companies – which pay on average $1,000 per person per day for business school programmes – are putting themselves squarely in the driving seat in the design and delivery of programmes. They are demanding the kinds of performance measures that inform other aspects of their businesses.

Business schools have talked for years about the best ways of measuring corporate return on investment for short business school programmes, and concluded that it could not really be appraised. Now some companies have decided to impose their own measurement systems, and are withholding payment for programmes until they are convinced that they have been successful.

Corporate clients are also less likely to fly their managers to overseas business schools, now requiring the professors to travel instead. In both open-enrolment and customised programmes, the schools that are proving their worth are those that are prepared to take the programmes to the clients. Even Harvard Business School, the doyen of the industry, now teaches programmes in China and India.

Technology is also much in demand, to save time and money. 'Money is an issue,' says Prof Valor (IESE Business School). 'But time is money, too.' Companies are increasingly replacing elements of classroom programmes with internet-based sessions – web seminars and online study groups or learning tools.

FT *Source*: Adapted from Bradshaw, D. (2011) Business school strategy: customer becomes king, *Financial Times*, 9 May.

HOW ARE BUSINESSES ORGANISED?

Nearly all businesses that involve more than a few owners and/or employees are set up as limited companies. Finance will come from the owners (shareholders) both in the form of a direct cash investment to buy shares (in the ownership of the business) and through the shareholders allowing past profits, which belong to them, to be reinvested in the business. Finance will also come from lenders (banks, for example) as well as through suppliers providing goods and services on credit.

In larger limited companies, the owners (shareholders) tend not to be involved in the daily running of the business; instead they appoint a board of directors to manage the business on their behalf. The board is charged with three major tasks:

1 setting the overall direction for the business;
2 monitoring and controlling the activities of the business; and
3 communicating with shareholders and others connected with the business.

Each board has a chairman, elected by the directors, who is responsible for the smooth running of the board. In addition, each board has a chief executive officer (CEO) who is responsible for running the business on a day-to-day basis. Occasionally, the roles of chairman and CEO are combined, although it is usually considered to be good practice to separate them and so to prevent a single individual having excessive power.

The board of directors represents the most senior level of management. Below this level, managers are employed, with each manager being given responsibility for a particular part of the business's operations.

Activity 1.1

Why are larger businesses *not* managed as a single unit by just one manager?

Three common reasons are:

- The sheer volume of activity or number of employees makes it impossible for one person to manage them.
- Certain business operations may require specialised knowledge or expertise.
- Geographical remoteness of part of the business operations may make it more practical to manage each location as a separate part, or set of separate parts.

The operations of a business may be divided for management purposes in different ways. For smaller businesses offering a single product or service, separate departments are often created. Tasks are grouped according to functions (such as marketing, human resources and finance) with each department responsible for a particular function. The managers of each department will then be accountable to the board of directors. In some cases, a departmental manager may also be a board member. A typical departmental structure, organised along functional lines, is shown in Figure 1.1.

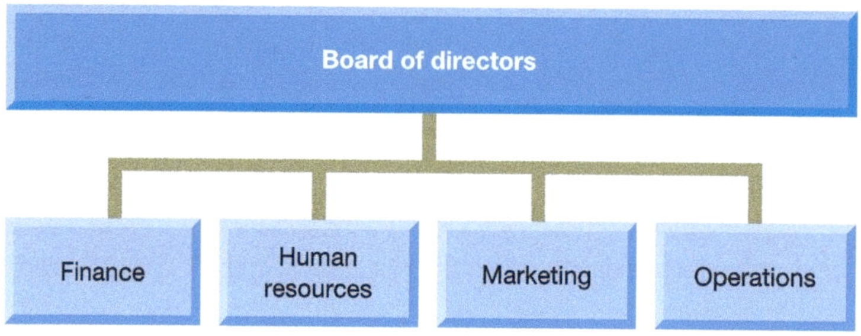

This is a typical departmental structure organised according to business functions.

Figure 1.1 A departmental structure organised according to business functions

Departments based around functions allow for greater specialisation, which, in turn, can promote greater efficiency. The departmental structure, however, can sometimes become too rigid. This can result in poor communication between departments and, perhaps, a lack of responsiveness to changing market conditions.

The structure set out in Figure 1.1 may be adapted according to the particular needs of the business. Where, for example, a business has few employees, the human resources function may not form a separate department but rather form part of another department. Where business operations are specialised, separate departments may be created to deal with each specialist area. Example 1.1 illustrates how Figure 1.1 may be modified to meet the needs of a particular business.

Example 1.1

Supercoach Ltd owns a small fleet of coaches that it hires out with drivers for private group travel. The business employs about sixty people. It could be departmentalised as follows:

- *Marketing department*, dealing with advertising, dealing with enquiries from potential customers, maintaining good relationships with existing customers and entering into contracts with customers.
- *Routing and human resources department*, responsible for the coach drivers' routes, schedules, staff duties and rotas and problems that arise during a particular job or contract.
- *Coach maintenance department*, looking after repair and maintenance of the coaches, buying spares, and giving advice on the need to replace old or inefficient coaches.
- *Finance department*, responsible for managing cash flows, costing business activities, pricing new proposals, measuring financial performance, preparing budgets, borrowing, paying wages and salaries, billing and collecting amounts due from customers, and processing and paying invoices from suppliers.

For large businesses that have a diverse geographical spread and/or a wide product range, the simple departmental structure set out in Figure 1.1 will usually have to be adapted. Separate divisions are often created for each geographical area and/or major product group. Each division will be managed separately and will usually enjoy a degree of autonomy. This can result in much greater responsiveness to changing market conditions. Within each division, however, departments are often created and organised along functional lines. Certain functions providing support across the various divisions, such as human resources, may be undertaken at head office to avoid duplication. The managers of each division will be accountable to the board of directors. In some cases, individual board members may also be divisional managers.

A typical divisional organisational structure is set out in Figure 1.2. Here the main basis of the structure is geographical. North division deals with production and sales in the north and so on.

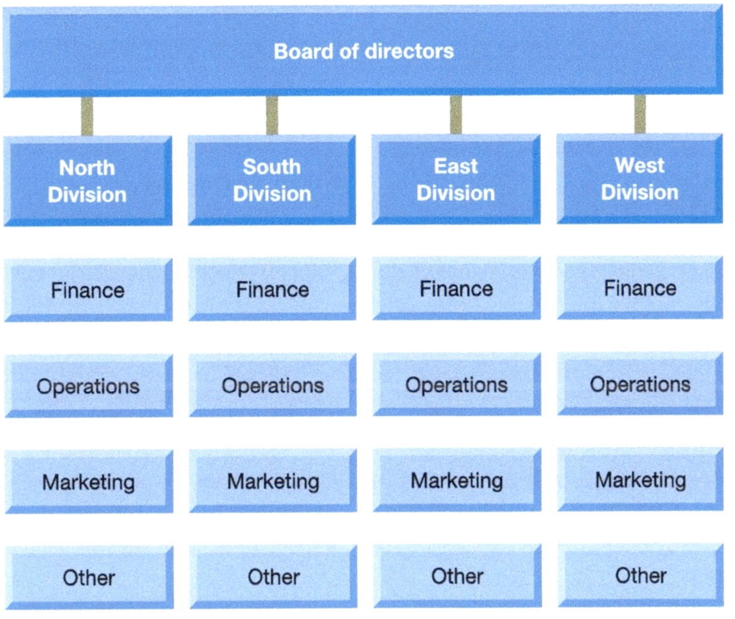

This is a typical organisational structure for a business that has been divided into separate operating divisions.

Figure 1.2 A divisional organisational structure

Once a particular divisional structure has been established, it need not be permanent. Successful businesses are likely to be innovative and constantly seeking to improve their operations. This may well extend to revising their divisional structure. Take for example the business whose structure is depicted in Figure 1.2. At some stage, senior management may conclude that the needs of customers and/or operational efficiency would be better served by having a structure that was based on product lines rather than on geography. This may result in reorganising so that there is a separate division for each product, irrespective of where production takes place or where customers are based.

Real World 1.2 provides an example of a reorganisation at a well-known business. In this case, the ultimate goal was to allow the business to respond more effectively to customer needs in a fast-changing environment.

Real World 1.2

Installing updates now

Microsoft chief executive Steve Ballmer has announced an operational realignment and a reshuffle of top management in a fresh attempt to remake the software company for an era in which the rules are set by rivals such as Apple and Google. The changes are meant to position the company better to come up with new computing experiences that take advantage of the mobile devices and services that are defining the way technology is now delivered, Mr Ballmer said in an email to employees.

The shake-up includes an attempt to break down the walls between the large operating divisions that have long kept Microsoft employees in carefully defined silos. These have been blamed by many observers and former executives for holding back new ideas that span the range of Microsoft's activities. It also marks a complete reversal of the structure Mr Ballmer put in place in 2005, when he created a cadre of powerful and autonomous divisional business leaders. The earlier approach, intended to copy the success of companies such as General Electric, had left Microsoft ill-prepared for the fast-moving technology world, said Rob Helm, an analyst at Directions on Microsoft.

In particular, a desire to defend earnings from the Windows PC operating system, the main profit generator, has long been seen as a drag on innovation. The influence of Windows has waned as growth in personal computing has moved to smartphones and tablets dominated by software made by Apple and Google. One person familiar with the company's thinking said the reorganisation was not expected to be enough, on its own, to revive Microsoft's prospects, and that attention was also being given to important areas such as senior executive talent and strategy. Realigning the company was overdue, but still made sense given the new market environment Microsoft is facing, this person added.

Under Mr Ballmer's latest plan, Microsoft's engineers will be pooled in four groups, for instance bringing together all of those working on operating systems for products such as PCs, mobile devices and the Xbox games console who were previously in different divisions. That should make it easier for Microsoft to come up with a single software platform that operates across all devices, making it more competitive with Apple's iOS and Google's Android software, according to analysts. 'This is something they had to solve; they had to remove internal friction to actually deliver it,' said Al Hilwa, an analyst at IDC.

Alongside the engineering groups, Mr Ballmer has centralised marketing and business development functions under new executives reporting to him, eating away at the divisional business fiefdoms.

FT *Source*: Adapted from Waters, R. (2013) Steve Ballmer shakes up Microsoft structure in battle to compete, ft.com, 11 July.

In the Microsoft example, we can see that the existing divisional structure was seen as being too rigid. A looser structure was, therefore, put in place. We shall explore the benefits and problems of divisionalisation in some detail in Chapter 10.

While both divisional and departmental structures are very popular in practice, other organisational structures may also be found.

HOW ARE BUSINESSES MANAGED?

Over the past three decades, the environment in which businesses operate has become increasingly turbulent and competitive. Various reasons have been identified to explain these changes, including:

- the increasing sophistication of customers (as we have seen);
- the development of a global economy where national frontiers have become less important;
- rapid changes in technology;
- the deregulation of domestic markets (for example, electricity, water and gas);
- increasing pressure from owners (shareholders) for competitive economic returns; and
- the increasing volatility of financial markets.

The effect of these environmental changes has been to make the role of managers more complex and demanding. This, along with the increasing size of many businesses, has led managers to search for new ways to manage their businesses. One important tool that has been developed in response to managers' needs is **strategic management**. This is concerned with establishing the long-term direction for the business. It involves setting long-term goals and then ensuring that they are implemented effectively. To enable the business to develop a competitive edge, strategic management focuses on doing things differently rather than simply doing things better.

Strategic management aims to provide a business with a clear sense of purpose along with a series of steps to achieve that purpose. The steps taken should link the internal resources of the business to the external environment of competitors, suppliers, customers and so on. This must be done in such a way that any business strengths, such as having a skilled workforce, are exploited and any weaknesses, such as being short of investment finance, are not exposed. To achieve this requires the development of strategies and plans that take account of the business's strengths and weaknesses, as well as the opportunities offered and threats posed by the external environment. Access to a new, expanding market is an example of an opportunity; the decision of a major competitor to reduce prices is an example of a threat.

Real World 1.3 provides an indication of the extent that strategic planning is carried out in practice.

Real World 1.3

Strategic planning high on the list

A recent survey investigated the use of various management tools throughout the world. It found that strategic planning is used by 43 per cent of those businesses that took part. This made it the joint most popular management tool. The survey, which is conducted annually, has placed strategic planning in first position for three of the last five years and in second position for two of those years.

The survey results were based on interviews with 1,208 senior executives throughout the world.

Source: Rigby, D. and Bilodeau, B. (2013) *Management Tools and Trends 2013*, Bain and Company.

The strategic management process can be approached in different ways. One well-established approach, involving five steps, is described below.

1 Establish mission, vision and objectives

The first step is to establish the mission of a business, which may be set out in the form of a **mission statement**. This is a concise declaration of the overriding purpose of the business.

It addresses the question *'What business are we in?'* To answer this question, managers should focus on those customer needs that the business seeks to satisfy rather than on the products currently produced. Thus, a publisher of novels might, for example, conclude that it is really in the entertainment business. The **vision statement** is closely connected to the mission statement and declares the business's aspirations. It addresses the question *'What do we want to achieve?'* Once again, it should be in as concise a form as possible. By answering both questions, managers should be provided with a clear focus for decision making.

Activity 1.2

Can you think why mission statements and vision statements should be concise?

Having to produce concise statements forces managers to think carefully about the essential nature of their business and the aspirations that they have for it. In practice, this can prove more difficult than it may sound. Concise statements have the added advantages that they are easier to remember and to communicate to employees, owners and others.

The mission and vision of a business will often adorn its website. **Real World 1.4** provides examples of both types of strategic statement for one large business.

Real World 1.4

Power trip

Aggreko plc provides power generation and temperature control solutions to customers who need them quickly or for a short period of time. Its mission is:

> **To offer specialist energy solutions that are delivered by our high-quality people in such a way that we continually grow our global list of satisfied and long-term customers.**

Its stated vision is:

> **To be the leading global player in the specialist energy marketplace.**

Source: www.aggreko.com, accessed 8 February 2014.

Having established the purpose and aspirations of the business, objectives must then be developed to translate these into specific commitments for the forthcoming period. Objectives are designed to introduce real discipline into the strategy process. They should provide clear targets, or outcomes, which are both challenging and achievable and which can provide a basis for assessing actual performance. Quantifiable objectives provide the clearest targets; however, some areas of performance, such as employee satisfaction, may only be capable of partial quantification. Other areas, such as business ethics, may be impossible to quantify.

In practice, the objectives set by a business are likely to range across all key areas and might include a commitment to achieve:

- a specified percentage share of the market in which the business competes;
- a high level of customer satisfaction;
- a high degree of employee involvement;
- a specified percentage of sales revenue being generated from newly-developed products;
- high standards of ethical behaviour in business dealings;

- a specified percentage operating profit margin (operating profit as a percentage of sales revenue);
- a specified percentage return on capital employed.

Businesses tend not to make their statement of objectives public, often because they do not wish to make their intentions clear to their competitors.

2 Undertake a position analysis

With the **position analysis**, the business seeks to discover how, given its attributes, it is placed in relation to its environment (customers, competitors, suppliers, technology, the economy, political climate and so on). This will be done in the context of its mission, vision and objectives. This is often approached within the framework of an analysis of the business's strengths, weaknesses, opportunities and threats (a **SWOT analysis**). A SWOT analysis involves identifying the business's strengths and weaknesses as well as the opportunities provided and threats posed by the world outside the business. Strengths and weaknesses are internal factors that are attributes of the business, whereas opportunities and threats are factors expected to be present in the environment in which the business operates.

Activity 1.3

Ryanair Holdings plc is a highly successful 'no-frills' airline. Can you suggest some factors that could be strengths, weaknesses, opportunities and threats for this business? Try to think of two for each of these (eight in all).

Strengths could include such things as:

- a strong, well-recognised brand name;
- a modern fleet of aircraft requiring less maintenance;
- reliable customer service concerning punctuality and baggage loss; and
- an internet booking facility used by virtually all passengers, which reduces administration costs.

Weaknesses might include:

- limited range of destinations;
- use of secondary airports situated some distance from city centres;
- poor facilities at secondary airports; and
- poor customer service concerning complaints.

Opportunities might include:

- new destinations becoming available, particularly in eastern Europe;
- increasing acceptance of 'no-frills' air travel among business travellers; and
- the development of new fuel-efficient aircraft.

Threats to the business might come from:

- increased competition – either new low-fare competitors entering the market or traditional airlines reducing fares to compete;
- increases in fuel prices and airport charges;
- increasing congestion at airports, making it more difficult to turn aircraft around quickly;
- changes in the regulatory environment (for example, changes in EU laws concerning the maximum monthly flying hours for a pilot) making it harder to operate; and
- vulnerability to a downturn in economic conditions.

You may have thought of others.

The SWOT framework is not the only possible approach to undertaking a position analysis, but it seems to be a very popular one. A 2009 survey of businesses in a wide range of business sectors, geographical locations and sizes found that about 65 per cent of those businesses use the SWOT approach (see reference 2 at the end of the chapter).

3 Identify and assess the strategic options

This involves attempting to identify possible courses of action. Each of those identified should enable the business to reach its objectives by using its strengths to exploit opportunities while not exposing its weaknesses to threats. The strengths, weaknesses, opportunities and threats are, of course, those identified by the SWOT analysis. Having identified the available options, each will then be assessed according to agreed criteria.

4 Select strategic options and formulate plans

The business will select what appears to be the best of the courses of action or strategies (identified in Step 3) available. When doing this, the potential for the selected strategies to achieve the mission, vision and objectives must be the key criterion. While the strategies selected provide a general road map, a more detailed plan is required to specify the particular actions to be taken. This overall plan will normally be broken down into a series of plans, one for each aspect of the business.

In an effort to match the chosen strategies with the opportunities available, a business may decide to acquire other businesses. **Real World 1.5** provides an example of acquisitions that were made because of their 'strategic fit'.

Real World 1.5

Fit for purpose

Zoopla Property Group, the company behind property websites Zoopla.co.uk and PrimeLocation.com, has acquired four property portals from Trinity Mirror as it seeks to challenge the market-leader Rightmove. The deal will consolidate Zoopla's position as the second-biggest operator of UK property websites, which have become a key channel for residential property purchases and lettings.

Zoopla, which is controlled by media group DMGT, paid £3.3m for the websites, the biggest of which is SmartNewHomes.co.uk, a portal dedicated to new homes. The deal comes as the number of new homes being built in England rose 6 per cent in the three months to June from the previous quarter, boosted by the government's Help to Buy scheme. Alex Chesterman, founder and chief executive of Zoopla Property Group, said that Zoopla had 'led the consolidation in the online property sector' since it launched in 2008 and was pursuing a strategy to develop niche digital property brands alongside its core national brand Zoopla.co.uk.

SmartNewHomes was an 'excellent strategic fit', he added.

In addition to SmartNewHomes.co.uk, Zoopla has acquired HomesOverseas.co.uk, a portal dedicated to overseas property listings; Email4Property.co.uk, an estate agent directory and lead generation website, and Zoomf.com.

Combined, the websites had revenues of £2.9m and made an operating profit of £0.5m for the year to December 2012.

FT *Source*: Cookson, R. (2013) Zoopla buys property websites from Trinity Mirror for £3.3m, ft.com, 4 September.

When Alex Chesterman said that Zoopla's acquisition was an 'excellent strategic fit', he was making the point that, given Zoopla's position and ambitions, the acquisition represented better value to Zoopla than it might have done to a similar investor, paying the same price, but for whom the strategic fit was not as good.

5 Perform, review and control

Finally, the business must implement the plans derived in Step 4. The actual outcome will be monitored and compared with the plans to see whether things are progressing satisfactorily. Steps should be taken to exercise control where actual performance does not appear to be matching earlier planned performance.

Figure 1.3 shows the strategic management framework in diagrammatic form. This framework will be considered further in subsequent chapters. We shall see, for example, how the business's mission and vision links, through objectives and long-term plans, to detailed budgets, in Chapters 6 and 7.

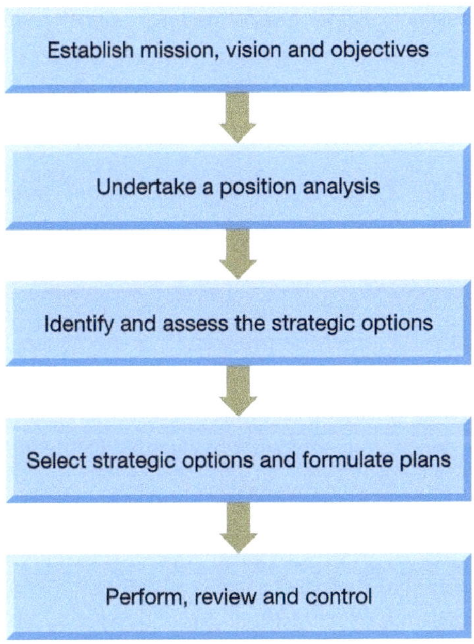

The business should set out its mission, vision and objectives and then develop plans in a systematic manner to achieve them.

Figure 1.3 The strategic management framework

THE CHANGING BUSINESS LANDSCAPE

Factors such as increased global competition and advances in technology, mentioned earlier, have had a tremendous impact on the kind of businesses that survive and prosper. They have also had an impact on the kind of business structures and processes adopted. Examples of the changes that have occurred in many countries in recent years, including the UK, are:

- *The growth of the service sector.* This includes businesses such as financial services, communications, tourism, transportation, consultancy, leisure and so on. This growth of the service sector has been matched by the decline of the manufacturing and extractive (for example, coal mining) sectors.

- *The emergence of new industries.* This includes science-based industries such as genetic engineering and biotechnology.
- *The growth of e-commerce.* Consumers are increasingly drawn to buying a wide range of goods including groceries, books, music and computers online. Businesses also use e-commerce to order supplies, monitor deliveries and distribute products.
- *Automated manufacturing.* Many manufacturing processes are now fully automated and computers are used to control the production process.
- *Lean manufacturing.* This involves a systematic attempt to identify and eliminate waste, surplus production, delays, defects and so on in the production process.
- *Greater product innovation.* There is much greater pressure to produce new, innovative products. The effect has been to increase the range of products available and to shorten the life cycles of many products.
- *Faster response times.* There is increasing pressure on businesses to develop products more quickly, to produce products more quickly and to deliver products more quickly.

These changes have presented huge challenges for the management accountant. New techniques have been developed and existing techniques adapted to try to ensure that management accounting retains its relevance. These issues are considered in more detail as we progress through the book.

WHAT IS THE FINANCIAL OBJECTIVE OF A BUSINESS?

A business is normally created to enhance the wealth of its owners. Throughout this book we shall assume that this is its main objective. This may come as a surprise, as there are other objectives that a business may pursue that are related to the needs of others associated with the business.

Activity 1.4

Can you think of two examples of what these objectives may be?

A business may seek to:

- provide good working conditions for its employees;
- conserve the environment for the local community;
- develop safer products for its customers; and
- offer fair trading terms to suppliers in underdeveloped countries.

You may have thought of others.

While a business may pursue these objectives, it is normally set up primarily with a view to increasing the wealth of its owners. In practice, the behaviour of businesses over time appears to be consistent with this objective.

Within a market economy there are strong competitive forces at work that ensure that failure to enhance owners' wealth will not be tolerated for long. Competition for the funds provided by the owners and competition for managers' jobs will normally mean that the owners' interests will prevail. If the managers do not provide the expected increase in ownership wealth, the owners have the power to replace the existing management team with a new team that is more responsive to owners' needs. Does this mean that the needs of other groups associated with the business (employees, customers, suppliers, the community and so on) are not really important? The answer to this question is almost certainly no, if the business wishes to survive and prosper over the longer term.

Satisfying the needs of other groups is usually consistent with increasing the wealth of the owners over the longer term. Disaffected customers, for example, may turn to another supplier, resulting in a loss of shareholder wealth for the original supplier. A dissatisfied workforce may result in low productivity, strikes and so forth, which will in turn have an adverse effect on owners' wealth. Similarly, a business that upsets the local community by unacceptable behaviour, such as polluting the environment, may attract bad publicity, resulting in a loss of customers and heavy fines. **Real World 1.6** provides an example of how two businesses responded to potentially damaging allegations.

Real World 1.6

The price of clothes

US clothing and sportswear manufacturers Gap and Nike have many of their clothes produced in Asia where labour tends to be cheap. However, some of the contractors that produce clothes on behalf of the two companies have been accused of unacceptable practices. Campaigners visited the factories and came up with damaging allegations. The factories were employing minors, they said, and managers were harassing female employees.

Nike and Gap reacted by allowing independent inspectors into the factories. They promised to ensure their contractors obeyed minimum standards of employment. Earlier this year, Nike took the extraordinary step of publishing the names and addresses of all its contractors' factories on the internet. The company said it could not be sure all the abuse had stopped. It said that if campaigners visited its contractors' factories and found examples of continued malpractice, it would take action.

Nike and Gap said the approach made business sense. They needed society's approval if they were to prosper. Nike said it was concerned about the reaction of potential US recruits to the campaigners' allegations. They would not want to work for a company that was constantly in the news because of the allegedly cruel treatment of those who made its products.

Source: Adapted from Skapinker, M. (2005) Fair shares?, *Financial Times*, 11 June.

We should be clear that generating wealth for the owners is not the same as seeking to maximise the current year's profit. Wealth creation is concerned with the longer term. It relates not only to this year's profit but to that of future years as well. In the short term, corners can be cut and risks taken that improve current profit at the expense of future profit. **Real World 1.7** provides some examples of how emphasis on short-term profit can be damaging.

Real World 1.7

Short-term gains, long-term problems

For many years, under the guise of defending capitalism, we have been allowing ourselves to degrade it. We have been poisoning the well from which we have drawn wealth. We have misunderstood the importance of values to capitalism. We have surrendered to the idea that success is pursued by making as much money as the law allowed without regard to how it was made.

Thirty years ago, retailers would be quite content to source the shoes they wanted to sell as cheaply as possible. The working conditions of those who produced them was not their concern. Then headlines and protests developed. Society started to hold them responsible for previously invisible working conditions. Companies like Nike went through a transformation. They realised they were polluting their brand. Global sourcing became visible. It was no longer viable to define success simply in terms of buying at the lowest price and selling at the highest.

Financial services and investment are today where footwear was thirty years ago. Public anger at the crisis will make visible what was previously hidden. Take the building up of huge portfolios of loans to poor people on US trailer parks. These loans were authorised without proper scrutiny of the circumstances of the borrowers. Somebody else then deemed them fit to be securitised and so on through credit default swaps and the rest without anyone seeing the transaction in terms of its ultimate human origin.

Each of the decision makers thought it okay to act like the thoughtless footwear buyer of the 1970s. The price was attractive. There was money to make on the deal. Was it responsible? Irrelevant. It was legal, and others were making money that way. And the consequences for the banking system if everybody did it? Not our problem.

The consumer has had a profound shock. Surely we could have expected the clever and wise people who invested our money to be better at risk management than they have shown themselves to be in the present crisis? How could they have been so gullible in not challenging the bankers whose lending proved so flaky? How could they have believed that the levels of bonuses that were, at least in part, coming out of their savings could have been justified in 'incentivising' a better performance? How could they have believed that a 'better' performance would be one that is achieved for one bank without regard to its effect on the whole banking system? Where was the stewardship from those exercising investment on their behalf?

The answer has been that very few of them do exercise that stewardship. Most have stood back and said it doesn't really pay them to do so. The failure of stewardship comes from the same mindset that created the irresponsible lending in the first place. We are back to the mindset that has allowed us to poison the well: never mind the health of the system as a whole, I'm making money out of it at the moment. Responsibility means awareness for the system consequences of our actions. It is not a luxury. It is the cornerstone of prudence.

FT *Source*: Adapted from Goyder, M. (2009) How we've poisoned the well of wealth, *Financial Times*, 15 February. We would like to thank Mark Goyder, Founder Director of Tomorrow's Company for permission to quote his article 'How we've poisoned the well of wealth' as published in the *Financial Times*.

BALANCING RISK AND RETURN

All decision making involves the future. Financial decision making is no exception. The only thing certain about the future, however, is that we cannot be sure what will happen. Things may not turn out as planned and this risk should be carefully considered when making financial decisions.

As in other aspects of life, risk and return tend to be related. Evidence shows that returns relate to risk in something like the way shown in Figure 1.4.

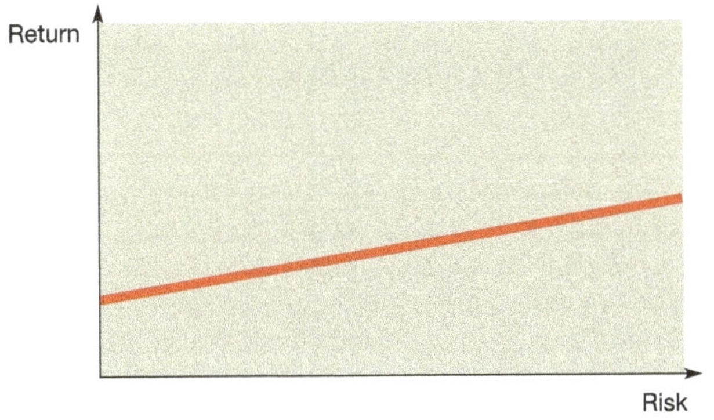

Even at zero risk a certain level of return will be required. This will increase as the level of risk increases.

Figure 1.4 Relationship between risk and return

Activity 1.5

Look at Figure 1.4 and state, in broad terms, where an investment in

(a) a UK government savings account, and
(b) a lottery ticket

should be placed on the risk–return line.

A UK government savings account is normally a very safe investment. Even if the government were in financial difficulties, it might well be able to print more money to repay investors. Returns from this form of investment, however, are normally very low.

Investing in a lottery ticket runs a very high risk of losing the whole amount invested. This is because the probability of winning is normally very low. However, a winning ticket can produce enormous returns.

Thus, the government savings account should be placed towards the far left of the risk–return line and the lottery ticket towards the far right.

This relationship between risk and return has important implications for setting financial objectives for a business. The owners will require a minimum return to induce them to invest at all, but will require an additional return to compensate for taking risks; the higher the risk, the higher the required return. Managers must be aware of this and must strike the appropriate balance between risk and return when setting objectives and pursuing particular courses of action.

The recent turmoil in the banking sector has shown, however, that the right balance is not always struck. Some banks have taken excessive risks in pursuit of higher returns and, as a consequence, have incurred massive losses. They are now being kept afloat with taxpayers' money. **Real World 1.8** discusses the collapse of one leading bank, in which the UK government took a majority stake, and argues that the risk appetite of banks must now change.

Real World 1.8

Banking on change

The taxpayer has become the majority shareholder in the Royal Bank of Scotland (RBS). This change in ownership, resulting from the huge losses sustained by the bank, will shape the future decisions made by its managers. This does not simply mean that it will affect the amount that the bank lends to homeowners and businesses. Rather it is about the amount of risk that it will be prepared to take in pursuit of higher returns.

In the past, those managing banks such as RBS saw themselves as producers of financial products that enabled banks to grow faster than the economy as a whole. They did not want to be seen as simply part of the infrastructure of the economy. It was too dull. It was far more exciting to be seen as creators of financial products that created huge profits and, at the same time, benefited us all through unlimited credit as low rates of interest. These financial products, with exotic names such as 'collateralised debt obligations' and 'credit default swaps', ultimately led to huge losses that taxpayers had to absorb in order to prevent the banks from collapse.

Now that many banks throughout the world are in taxpayers' hands, they are destined to lead a much quieter life. They will have to focus more on the basics such as taking deposits, transferring funds and making simple loans to customers. Is that such a bad thing?

The history of banks has reflected a tension between carrying out their core functions and the quest for high returns through high risk strategies. It seems, however, that for some time to come they will have to concentrate on the former and will be unable to speculate with depositors' cash.

Source: Based on information in Peston Robert (2008) We own Royal Bank, BBC News, 28 November, www.bbc.co.uk.

WHAT IS MANAGEMENT ACCOUNTING?

Having considered what businesses are and how they are organised and managed, we can now turn our attention to the role of **management accounting**. A useful starting point for our discussion is to understand the general role of accounting, which is to help people make informed business decisions. All forms of accounting, including management accounting, are concerned with collecting and analysing financial information and then communicating this information to those making decisions. This decision-making perspective of accounting provides the theme for the book and shapes the way that we deal with each topic.

For accounting information to be useful for decision making, the accountant must be clear about *for whom* the information is being prepared and *for what purpose* it will be used. In practice there are various groups of people (known as 'user groups') with an interest in a particular organisation, in the sense of needing to make decisions about that organisation. For the typical private sector business, the most important of these groups of users of accounting information are shown in Figure 1.5. Each of these groups will have different needs.

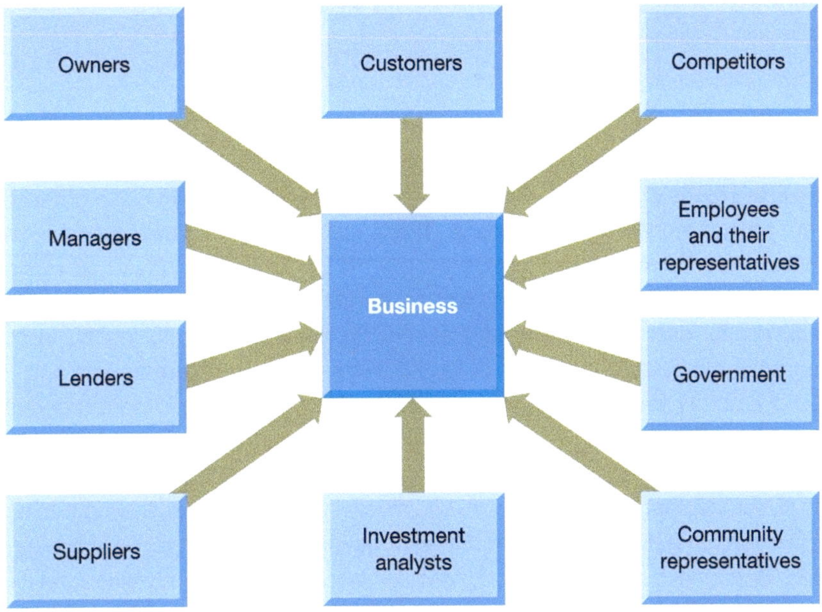

Several user groups have an interest in accounting information relating to a business. The majority of these are outside the business but, nevertheless, have a stake in it. This is not meant to be an exhaustive list of potential users; however, the groups identified are normally the most important.

Figure 1.5 Main users of accounting information relating to a business

This book is concerned with providing accounting information for only one of the groups identified – the managers. This, however, is a particularly important user group. Managers are responsible for running the business and their decisions and actions play a vital role in determining its success. Planning for the future and exercising day-to-day control over a business involves a wide range of decisions being made. For example, managers may need to decide whether to:

- develop new products or services (as with a computer manufacturer developing a new range of computers);
- increase or decrease the price or quantity of existing products or services (as with a telecommunications business changing its mobile phone call and text charges);
- increase or decrease the operating capacity of the business (as with a beef farming business reviewing the size of its herd);
- change the methods of purchasing, production or distribution (as with a clothes retailer switching from local to overseas suppliers).

The accounting information provided should help in identifying and assessing the financial consequences of the kind of decisions listed above. In later chapters, we shall consider each of the types of decisions in the list and see how their financial consequences can be assessed.

HOW USEFUL IS MANAGEMENT ACCOUNTING INFORMATION?

There are arguments and convincing evidence that managers regard management accounting information as useful. There have been numerous research surveys that have asked managers to rank the importance of management accounting information, in relation to other sources of information, for decision-making purposes. These studies have almost invariably found that managers rank accounting information very highly. It is also worth noting that businesses of any size will normally produce management accounting information even though there is no legal compulsion for businesses to do so. Presumably, the cost of producing this information is justified on the grounds that managers believe it to be useful. Such arguments and evidence, however, leave unanswered the question as to whether the information produced is *actually* useful for decision-making purposes: that is, does it really affect managers' behaviour?

It is impossible to measure just how useful management accounting information is to managers. We should remember that such information would usually represent only one input to a particular decision. The precise weight attached to that information by the manager, and the benefits that flow as a result, cannot be accurately assessed. We shall shortly see, however, that it is at least possible to identify the kinds of qualities that accounting information must possess in order to be useful. Where these qualities are lacking, the usefulness of the information will be undermined.

PROVIDING A SERVICE

One way of viewing management accounting is as a form of service. Management accountants provide economic information to their 'clients', the managers. The quality of the service provided would be determined by the extent to which the managers' information needs have been met. It is generally accepted that, to be useful, management accounting information should possess certain key qualities, or characteristics. In particular, it must be relevant and it must faithfully represent what it is supposed to represent. These two qualities, which are regarded as fundamental qualities, are now explained in more detail.

- **Relevance**. Management accounting information should make a difference. That is, it should be capable of influencing managers' decisions. To do this, it must help to *predict future events* (such as predicting the next year's profit), or help to *confirm past events* (such as establishing the previous year's profit), or do both. By confirming past events, managers can check on the accuracy of their earlier predictions. This can, in turn, help them to improve the ways in which they make predictions in the future.

  To be relevant, management accounting information must cross a threshold of **materiality**. An item of information should be considered material, or significant, if its omission or misstatement could alter the decisions that managers make.

Activity 1.6

Do you think that information that is material for one business will also be material for all other businesses?

No. It will often vary from one business to the next. What is material will normally depend on factors such as the size of the business, the nature of the information and the amounts involved.

If a piece of information is not material, it should not be included within the management accounting reports. It will merely clutter them up and, perhaps, interfere with the managers' ability to interpret them.

- **Faithful representation**. Management accounting information should represent what it is supposed to represent. To do this, the information should be *complete.* In other words it should reflect all of the information needed to understand what is being portrayed. It should also be *neutral*, which means that the information should be presented and selected without bias. Finally, it should be *free from error*. This is not the same as saying that it must always be perfectly accurate; this is not really possible. Estimates may have to be made which eventually turn out to be inaccurate. It does mean, however, that there should be no errors in the way in which the estimates are prepared and described. In practice, a piece of management accounting information may not reflect perfectly these three aspects of faithful representation. It should aim to do so, however, insofar as possible.

Management accounting information must contain *both* of these fundamental qualities if it is to be useful. There is little point in producing information that is relevant, but which lacks faithful representation, or producing information that is irrelevant, even if it is faithfully represented.

Further qualities

Where management accounting information is both relevant and faithfully represented, there are other qualities that, if present, can *enhance* its usefulness. These are comparability, verifiability, timeliness and understandability. Each of these qualities is now considered.

- **Comparability**. When using management accounting information, managers often want to make comparisons. They may want to compare performance of the business over time (for example, profit this year compared to last year). They may also want to compare certain aspects of business performance to those of similar businesses (such as the level of sales achieved during the year). Better comparisons can be made where the management accounting system treats items that are basically the same in the same way and where policies for measuring and presenting management accounting information are made clear.
- **Verifiability**. This quality provides assurance to users that the management accounting information provided faithfully represents what it is supposed to represent. Management accounting information is verifiable where different, independent experts would be able to agree that it provides a faithful portrayal. Verifiable information tends to be supported by evidence, such as an invoice stating the cost of some item of inventories.
- **Timeliness**. Management accounting information should be produced in time for managers to make their decisions. A lack of timeliness will undermine the usefulness of the information. Normally, the later management accounting information is produced, the less useful it becomes.
- **Understandability**. Management accounting information should be set out as clearly and concisely as possible so as to help those managers at whom it is aimed to understand it.

Activity 1.7

Do you think that management accounting reports should be understandable to those who have not studied management accounting?

It would be very helpful if everyone could understand management accounting reports. This, however, is unrealistic, as it is not normally possible to express complex financial events and transactions in simple, non-technical terms. Any attempts to do so are likely to provide a distorted picture of reality.

It is probably best that we regard management accounting reports in the same way that we regard a report written in a foreign language. To understand either of these, we need to have had some preparation. When management accounting reports are produced, it is normally assumed that the relevant manager not only has a reasonable knowledge of business and accounting but is also prepared to invest some time in studying the reports. Nevertheless, the onus is clearly on management accountants to provide information in a way that makes it as understandable as possible to non-accountants. This is an extremely important aspect of the accountant's role.

It is worth emphasising that the four qualities just discussed cannot make management accounting information useful. They can only enhance the usefulness of information that is already relevant and faithfully represented.

WEIGHING UP THE COSTS AND BENEFITS

Even though a piece of management accounting information may have all the qualities described, it does not automatically mean that it should be collected and reported to users. There is still one more hurdle to jump. Consider Activity 1.8.

Activity 1.8

Suppose an item of information is capable of being provided. It is relevant to a particular decision and can be faithfully represented. It is also comparable, verifiable and timely, and could be understood by the manager.

Can you think of a good reason why, in practice, you might decide not to produce the information?

You may judge the cost of doing so to be greater than the potential benefit of having the information. This cost–benefit issue will limit the amount of management accounting information provided.

In theory, a particular item of management accounting information should only be produced if the costs of providing it are less than the benefits, or value, to be derived from its use. Figure 1.6 shows the relationship between the costs and value of providing additional management accounting information.

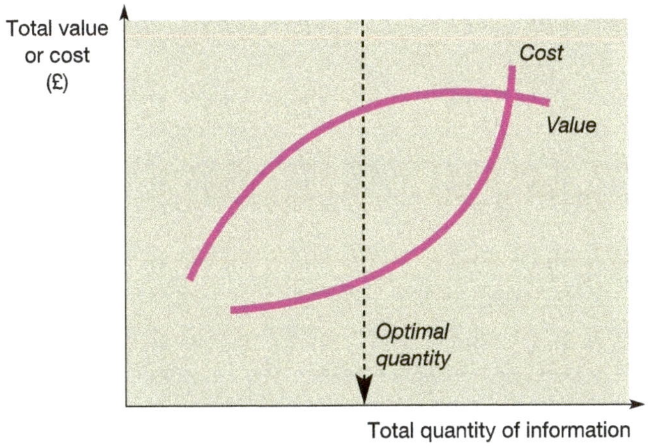

The benefits of management accounting information eventually decline. The cost of providing the information, however, will rise with each additional piece of information. The optimal level of information provision is where the gap between the value of the information and the cost of providing it is at its greatest.

Figure 1.6 Relationship between the cost and value of providing additional management accounting information

The figure shows how the total value of information received by the manager eventually begins to decline. This is, perhaps, because additional information becomes less relevant, or because of the problems that a manager may have in processing the sheer quantity of information provided. The total cost of providing the information, however, will increase with each additional piece of information. The broken line indicates the point at which the gap between the value of information and the cost of providing that information is at its greatest. This represents the optimal amount of information that can be provided. Beyond this optimal level, each additional piece of information will cost more than the value of having it. This theoretical model, however, poses a number of problems in practice, which we shall now discuss.

To illustrate the practical problems of establishing the value of information, let us assume that when parking our car, we dented one of the doors and scraped the paintwork. We want to have the dent taken out and the door resprayed at a local garage. We have discovered that the nearest garage would charge £350 but we believe that other local garages may offer to do the job for a lower price. The only way of finding out the prices at other garages is to visit them, so that they can see the extent of the damage. Visiting the garages will involve using some fuel and will take up some of our time. Is it worth the cost of finding out the price for the job at the various local garages? The answer, as we have seen, is that if the cost of discovering the price is less than the potential benefit, it is worth having that information.

To identify the various prices for the job, there are several points to be considered, including:

- How many garages shall we visit?
- What is the cost of fuel to visit each garage?
- How long will it take to make all the garage visits?
- At what price do we value our time?

The economic benefit of having the information on the price of the job is probably even harder to assess, in advance. The following points need to be considered:

- What is the cheapest price that we might be quoted for the job?
- How likely is it that we shall be quoted a price cheaper than £350?

As we can imagine, the answers to these questions may be far from clear – remember that we have only contacted the local garage so far. When assessing the value of accounting information we are confronted with similar problems.

Producing management accounting information can be very costly. The costs, however, are often difficult to quantify. Direct, out-of-pocket costs, such as salaries of accounting staff, are not usually a problem, but these are only part of the total costs involved. There are other costs such as the cost of users' time spent on analysing and interpreting the information provided.

Activity 1.9

What about the economic benefits of producing management accounting information? Do you think it is easier, or harder, to assess the economic benefits of management accounting information than to assess the costs of producing it?

It is normally much harder to assess the benefits. We saw earlier that, even if we could accurately measure the economic benefits arising from a particular decision, we must bear in mind that management accounting information will be only one factor influencing that decision. Other factors will also be taken into account. Furthermore, the precise weight attached to the management accounting information by the decision maker cannot normally be established.

There are no easy answers to the problem of weighing costs and benefits. Although it is possible to apply some 'science' to the problem, a lot of subjective judgement is normally involved.

The qualities, or characteristics, influencing the usefulness of management accounting information that have been discussed above are summarised in Figure 1.7.

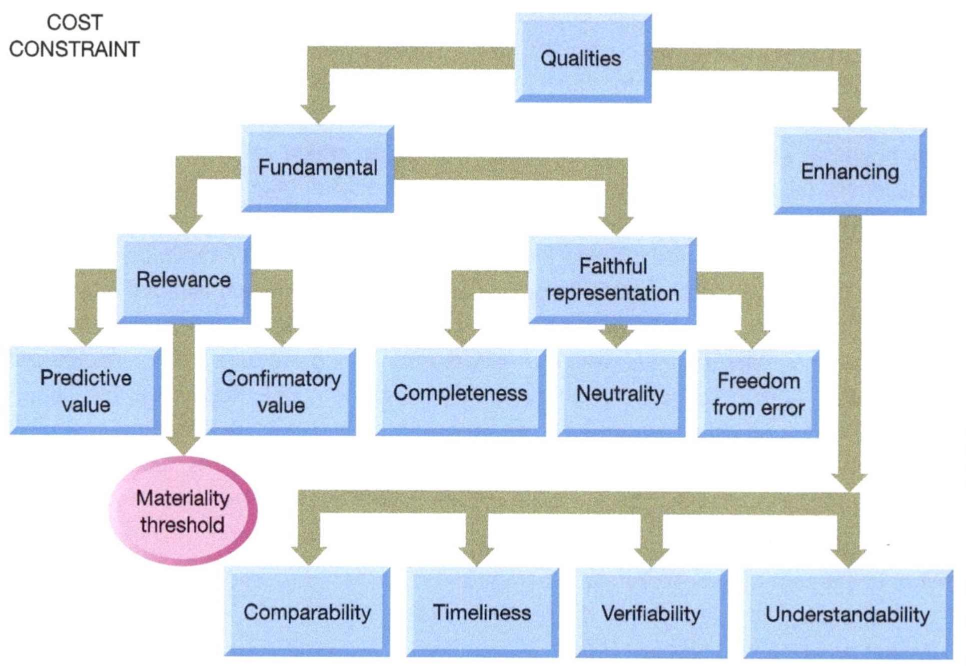

There are two fundamental qualities that determine the usefulness of accounting information. In addition, there are four qualities that enhance the usefulness of accounting information. The benefits of providing the information, however, should outweigh the costs.

Figure 1.7 The qualities that influence the usefulness of accounting information

MANAGEMENT ACCOUNTING AS AN INFORMATION SYSTEM

We have already seen that management accounting can be seen as the provision of a service to its 'clients', the managers. Another way of viewing management accounting is as a part of the business's total information system. Managers have to make decisions concerning the allocation of scarce economic resources. To ensure that these resources are efficiently allocated, managers often require economic information on which to base their decisions. It is the role of the management accounting system to provide that information.

The **management accounting information system** has certain features that are common to all information systems within a business. These are:

- identifying and capturing relevant information (in this case economic information);
- recording the information collected in a systematic manner;
- analysing and interpreting the information collected; and
- reporting the information in a manner that suits the needs of individual managers.

The relationship between these features is set out in Figure 1.8.

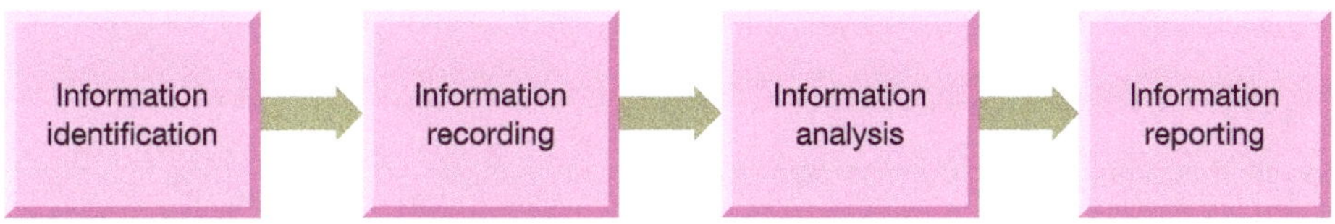

There are four sequential stages of a management accounting information system. The first two stages are concerned with preparation, whereas the last two stages are concerned with using the information collected.

Figure 1.8 The management accounting information system

Given the decision-making emphasis of this book, we shall be concerned primarily with the last two elements of the process – the analysis and reporting of management accounting information. We shall consider the way in which information is used by, and is useful to, managers rather than the way in which it is identified and recorded.

Efficient management accounting systems are an essential ingredient of an efficient business. When accounting systems fail, the results can be disastrous. **Real World 1.9** provides an example of a systems failure. It arose from the failure to integrate two separate accounting systems following the merger of two businesses.

Real World 1.9

Blaming the system

Peter Long, chief executive of TUI Travel, said the tour operator had suffered 'a blot on the copybook' after an accounting blunder cost the chief financial officer his job and forced it to restate its 2009 results to the tune of £117m. Paul Bowtell announced his resignation after the group wrote off an additional £88m on top of the £29m writedown announced in August. The City reacted by pushing shares in TUI down 11 per cent, or 25.4p, to close at 205p on Thursday.

The cause of the errors lies in TUI's use of two separate computer systems in its business after its merger with First Choice in 2007. One system is used by TUI's retail division to make customer bookings, while the other is used by tour operators working for TUI. Initial customer bookings were registered by both systems. However, subsequent changes to customers' holidays – such as discounts or other small-fee items – were only registered in the retail booking system and not the tour operator system, creating discrepancies.

Mr Long, who described Mr Bowtell's offer to resign as honourable, said he had discussed the blunder with major investors. 'At the end of the day, it's a blot on the copybook and I will make amends so that we can build and grow their company for them,' he said. He described the blunder as the result of 'inherent weaknesses in the system', which post-merger reviews could have identified earlier.

TUI estimated that these discrepancies have existed for four or five years, but were too small to have been noticed. It was only in the 2009 season, when travel operators were forced into heavy promotions to entice recession-fearing European consumers, that the discounts became large enough to be noticed.

FT *Source*: Adapted from Blitz, R. and O'Doherty, J. (2010) TUI chief contrite at accounting blunder, ft.com, 21 October.

IT'S JUST A PHASE

Although management accounting has always been concerned with helping managers to manage, the information provided has undergone profound changes over the years. This has been in response to changes in both the business environment and in business methods. The development of management accounting can be seen as having four distinct phases.

Phase 1

Until 1950, or thereabouts, businesses enjoyed a fairly benign economic environment. Competition was weak and, as products could easily be sold, there was no pressing need for product innovation. The main focus of management attention was on the internal processes of the business. In particular, there was a concern for determining the cost of goods and services produced and for exercising financial control over the relatively simple production processes that existed during that period. In this early phase, management accounting information was not a major influence on decision making. Although cost and budget information was produced, it was not widely supplied to managers at all levels of seniority.

Phase 2

During the 1950s and 1960s management accounting information remained inwardly focused; however, the emphasis shifted towards producing information for short-term planning and control purposes. Management accounting came to be seen as an important part of the system of management control and of particular value in controlling the production and other internal processes of the business. The controls developed, however, were largely reactive in nature. Problems were often identified as a result of actual performance deviating from planned performance. Only then would corrective action be taken.

Phase 3

During the 1970s and early 1980s the world experienced considerable upheaval as a result of oil price rises and economic recession. This was also a period of rapid technological change and increased competition. These factors conspired to produce new techniques of production, such as robotics and computer-aided design. These new techniques led to a greater concern for controlling costs, particularly through waste reduction. Waste arising from delays, defects, excess production and so on was identified as a non-value-added activity – that is, an activity that increases costs, but does not generate additional revenue. Various techniques were developed to reduce or eliminate waste. To compete effectively, managers and employees were given greater freedom to make decisions and this in turn has led to the need for management accounting information to be made more widely available. Advances in computing, such as the personal computer, changed the nature, amount and availability of management accounting information. Increasing the volume and availability of information to managers meant that greater attention had to be paid to the design of management accounting information systems.

Phase 4

During the 1990s and 2000s advances in manufacturing technology and in information technology, such as the World Wide Web, continued unabated. This further increased the level of competition which, in turn, led to a further shift in emphasis. Increased competition provoked a concern for the more effective use of resources, with particular emphasis on creating value for shareholders by understanding customer needs (see reference 3 at the end of the chapter). This change resulted in management accounting information becoming more outwardly focused. The attitudes and behaviour of customers have become the object of much information gathering. Increasingly, successful businesses are those that are able to secure and maintain competitive advantage over their rivals through a greater understanding of customer needs. Thus, information that provides details of customers and the market has become vitally important. Such information might include customers' evaluation of services provided (perhaps through the use of opinion surveys) and data on the share of the market enjoyed by the particular business.

It must be emphasised that the effect of these four phases is cumulative. That is to say that each successive phase built on what already existed as common practice, rather than replacing it. For example, the activities of Phase 1 (principally, cost determination) remain an important part of the work of the management accountant during Phase 4.

Figure 1.9 summarises the four phases in the development of modern management accounting.

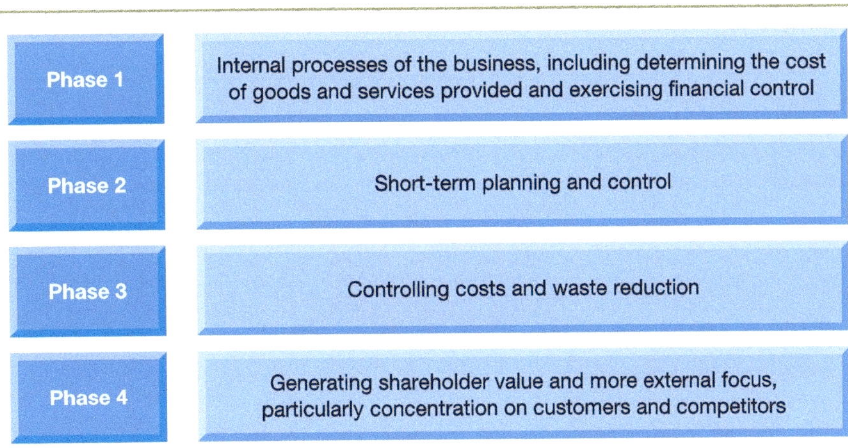

Modern management accounting has developed by passing through four phases. Each of these adds to, rather than replaces, the previous phase. Thus, determining the cost of output, which was the main focus of the first phase, still plays an important role in management accounting today.

Figure 1.9 The four phases in the development of management accounting

WHAT INFORMATION DO MANAGERS NEED?

We have seen that management accounting can be regarded as a form of service where managers are the 'clients'. This raises the question, however, as to what kind of information these 'clients' require. It is possible to identify four broad areas of decision making where management accounting information is required:

- *Developing objectives and plans.* We have seen that managers are responsible for establishing the objectives of the business and then developing appropriate strategies to achieve them. Management accounting information can help in developing objectives and in identifying the various strategies available. It can also generate financial plans to reveal likely outcomes from implementing the various strategies identified. These plans should help managers to evaluate each strategy and to select the most appropriate.
- *Performance evaluation and control.* Management accounting information can help in reviewing the performance of the business against agreed criteria. Controls need to be in place to try to ensure that actual performance conforms to planned performance. Actual outcomes will, therefore, be compared with plans to see whether the performance is better or worse than expected. Where there is a significant difference, some investigation should be carried out and corrective action taken where necessary.
- *Allocating resources.* Resources available to a business are limited and it is the duty of managers to ensure that they are used as efficiently and effectively as possible. Management accounting information can play a key role in carrying out this duty. Thus, decisions such as the optimum level of output, the appropriate location for production facilities, the optimum mix of products and the appropriate type of investment in new equipment tend to rely heavily on management accounting information.
- *Determining costs and benefits.* Many management decisions require knowledge of the costs and benefits of pursuing a particular course of action such as providing a service, producing a new product or closing down a department. The decision will involve weighing the costs against the benefits. The management accountant can help managers by providing details of particular costs and benefits. In some cases, costs and benefits may be extremely difficult to quantify; however, some approximation is usually better than nothing at all.

These areas of management decision making are set out in Figure 1.10.

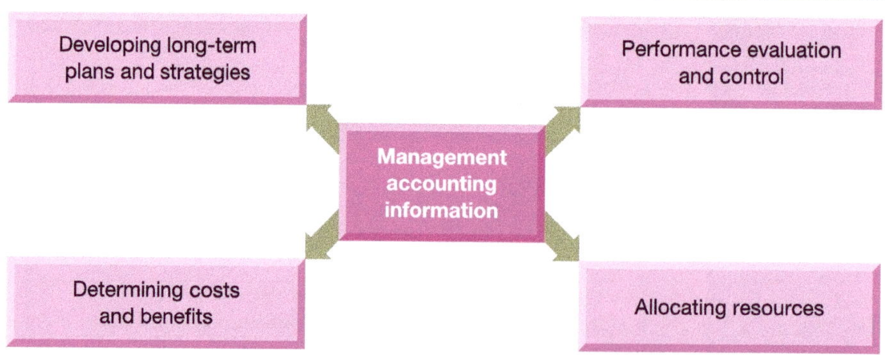

Management accounting information helps managers to make decisions in four broad areas: developing long-term plans and strategies, performance evaluation and control, allocating resources and determining costs and benefits.

Figure 1.10 Decisions requiring management accounting information

REPORTING NON-FINANCIAL INFORMATION

Adopting a more strategic and customer-focused approach to running a business has highlighted the fact that many factors, which are often critical to success, cannot be measured in purely financial terms. Many businesses have developed **key performance indicators (KPIs)**. These include the traditional financial measures, such as return on capital employed. However, KPIs often include a significant proportion of non-financial indicators to help assess the prospects of long-term success. As the traditional provider of decision-making information, the management accountant has increasingly shouldered responsibility for reporting non-financial measures regarding quality, product innovation, product cycle times, delivery times and so on.

Activity 1.10

It can be argued that non-financial measures, such as those mentioned above, do not, strictly speaking, fall within the scope of accounting information and, therefore, could (or should) be provided by others. What do you think?

It is true that others could collect this kind of information. However, management accountants are major information providers to managers and usually see it as their role to provide a broad range of information for decision making.

The boundaries of accounting are not fixed and it is possible to argue that management accountants should collect this kind of information as it is often linked inextricably to financial outcomes. They may, therefore, be best placed to explain the relationship between financial and non-financial results.

Activity 1.11 considers the kind of information that may be expressed in non-financial terms and which the management accountant may provide for an airline business.

Activity 1.11

Imagine that you are the chief executive of the 'no-frills' airline Ryanair Holdings plc. What kinds of non-financial information (that is, information not containing monetary values) may be relevant to help you evaluate the performance of the business for a particular period? Try to think of at least six.

Here are some possibilities, although there are many more that might have been chosen:

- volume of passengers transported to various destinations;
- average load factor (that is, percentage of total passenger seats occupied) per trip;
- market share of air passenger travel;
- number of new routes established by Ryanair;
- percentage of total passenger volume generated by these new routes;
- aircraft turnaround times at airports;
- punctuality of flights;
- levels of aircraft utilisation;

→

- number of flight cancellations;
- percentage of baggage losses;
- levels of customer satisfaction;
- levels of employee satisfaction;
- percentage of bookings made over the internet;
- maintenance hours per aircraft.

In Chapter 10 we shall look at some of the financial and non-financial KPIs that are used in practice.

INFLUENCING MANAGERS' BEHAVIOUR

We have seen that management accounting information is provided to improve the quality of managers' decisions. In other words, it is intended to have an effect on the behaviour of managers. It aims to influence their actions and those of other employees in such a way as to contribute more fully towards achieving the business objectives. In some cases, however, the change in behaviour caused by management accounting may not be beneficial.

One potential problem is that managers and employees will focus their attention and efforts on those aspects of the business that are being measured and will ignore other aspects. Often, the aspects being measured are those that are used to evaluate performance. Managers and employees may therefore conclude that 'the things that count are the things that get counted'. Such a narrow focus, however, can have undesirable consequences for the business.

Activity 1.12

A departmental manager has been given responsibility for controlling departmental costs and this forms an important part of her annual performance appraisal. The manager is allocated an amount of money to spend on staff training each year. How might the manager's focus on 'the things that get counted' result in undesirable consequences?

To demonstrate cost consciousness, the manager may underspend during the year by cutting back on staff training. Although this may help to exert control over costs, staff morale and longer-term profitability may be adversely affected. These adverse effects may go unrecognised, at least in the short term, as cost control will be the focus of attention.

There is also the potential problem that a particular measure will be manipulated. Where, for example, profit is seen as important, a manager may attempt to boost this measure by continuing to use old, fully depreciated, pieces of equipment in order to keep depreciation charges low. This may be done despite the fact that the purchase of new equipment would produce higher quality products and would help the business to flourish over the longer term. The incentive for such behaviour is often linked to managers' rewards. Thus, in the case just described, annual, profit-related bonuses may be the key motivation behind the manager's actions.

A further potential problem is that the targets against which performance is measured become the objects of manipulation. A sales manager, for example, may provide a deliberately low forecast of the size of the potential market for the next period if it is believed that this forecast will form the basis of future sales targets. The incentive to do this may again be related to management rewards, for example where bonuses are given for exceeding sales targets. It may, however, be done to ensure that future sales targets can be achieved with relatively little effort.

The management accountant must be aware of the impact of accounting measures of performance on human behaviour. When designing accounting measures, it is important to try to ensure that all key aspects of performance are taken into account, even though certain aspects may be difficult to measure. Furthermore, when operating an accounting measurement system, the management accountant must be alert to behaviour aimed at manipulating particular measures rather than achieving the goals to which they relate.

REAPING THE BENEFITS OF INFORMATION TECHNOLOGY

The impact of information technology (IT) on the development of management accounting is difficult to overstate. The ability of computers to process large amounts of information means that routine reports can be produced quickly and accurately. Indeed, certain reports may be produced on a daily, or even real-time, basis. This can be vital to businesses operating in a highly competitive environment, which risk the loss of competitive advantage from making decisions based on inaccurate or out-of-date reports. IT has also enabled information to be more widely spread throughout the business. Increasingly, through their personal computers, employees at all levels can gain access to relevant information and reports to guide their decisions and actions.

IT has allowed management reports to be produced in greater detail and in greater variety than could be contemplated under a manual system. In addition, it has allowed sophisticated measurement systems to be provided at relatively low cost. Managers can use IT to help assess proposals by allowing variables (such as product price, output, product cost and so on) to be changed easily. With a few keystrokes, managers can increase or decrease the size of key variables to create a range of possible scenarios.

In recent years, Enterprise Resource Planning (ERP) systems have been developed. These provide an integrated suite of applications, or modules, to track resources across the whole of the business. They operate in real time and offer modules covering a range of business functions including accounting, manufacturing, marketing and sales, human resources and project management. The benefits include greater timeliness and accuracy of reporting and the opportunity to generate a wealth of data relating to the business. Thus, managers become even better placed to plan and to exert greater control. ERP systems have accelerated changes to the role of the management accountant that first began with the introduction of IT. These changes will be discussed in the next section.

The IT revolution is gathering pace, which suggests that IT will continue to play an influential role in shaping the nature of management accounting. Of particular interest are advances made in the evaluation of financial and non-financial information. Computers are developing the ability to make the kind of sophisticated judgements that once only humans were considered able to make. This, and other advances in IT, could provide a future source of competitive advantage for a business.

FROM BEAN COUNTER TO TEAM MEMBER

Given the changes described above, it is not surprising that the traditional role of the management accountant within a business has changed. IT has released the management accountant from much of the routine work associated with preparation of management accounting reports. This has allowed more time to focus on the analysis and interpretation of the information produced. It has also provided the opportunity for the management accountant to take a more proactive role within the business.

Increasingly, management accountants are seen as part of the management team. In addition to providing advice and guidance, they often take a lead in the design of new information systems and become directly involved in planning and decision making. By participating in this way, as well as providing management accounting information for planning and decision making, the management accountant plays a key role in achieving the objectives of the business. It is, therefore, a role that should add value to the business and improve its competitive position.

This new and enhanced role for the management accountant has implications for the kind of skills required to operate effectively. Increasingly, 'soft' skills such as interpersonal skills for collaborating across boundaries and for working as part of an effective team are required. There is also a need for communication skills to influence the behaviour of others and to assist in providing advice. For being part of the management team, leadership skills as well as a high level of awareness of how the business operates are required. Finally, strong analytical skills are needed to be able to interpret the plethora of financial and non-financial data generated by modern businesses.

Changes to the role of the management accountant should benefit the development of management accounting as a discipline. While working as part of a cross-functional team, the management accountant should gain a greater awareness of strategic and operational matters, an increased understanding of the information needs of managers and a deeper appreciation of the importance of value creation. This is likely to have a positive effect on the design and development of management accounting systems. As a consequence, we should see increasing evidence that management accounting systems are being designed to fit the particular structure and processes of the business rather than the other way round.

REASONS TO BE ETHICAL

The way in which individual businesses operate in terms of the honesty, fairness and transparency with which they treat their stakeholders (customers, employees, suppliers, the community, the shareholders and so on) has become a key issue. There have been many examples of businesses, some of them very well known, acting in ways that most people would regard as unethical and unacceptable. Examples of such actions include:

- paying bribes to encourage employees of other businesses to reveal information about the employee's business that could be useful;
- oppressive treatment of suppliers, for example, making suppliers wait excessive periods before payment; and
- manipulating the financial statements to mislead users of them, for example, to overstate profit so that senior managers become eligible for performance bonuses (known as 'creative accounting').

Despite the many examples of unethical acts that have attracted publicity over recent years, it would be very unfair to conclude that most businesses are involved in unethical activities. Nevertheless, revelations of unethical practice can be damaging to the entire business community. Lying, stealing and fraudulent behaviour can lead to a loss of confidence in business and the imposition of tighter regulatory burdens. In response to this threat, businesses often seek to demonstrate their commitment to acting in an honest and ethical way.

One way in which this can be done is to produce, and adhere to, a code of ethics concerning business behaviour. **Real World 1.10** provides some interesting food for thought on this topic. It is concerned with a research study which compared two groups of businesses.

Real World 1.10

Honesty is the best policy

Some of the largest UK businesses were divided into two groups: those that had published a code of ethics for their business and those that had not. The commercial success of these two groups of business was then assessed over the five consecutive years ending in 2005. Commercial success was measured by four factors, two linked to the financial (accounting) results and two related to the performance of the businesses' shares on the Stock Exchange.

Overall the businesses with a published ethical statement performed better than the group without such a statement. Of course, it may simply be that the better-organised businesses produce both the statement and better performances, but nevertheless it is an interesting finding.

Source: Information taken from Ugoji, K., Dando, N. and Moir, L. (2007) *Does Business Ethics Pay? – Revisited*, Institute of Business Ethics.

Management accountants are likely to find themselves at the forefront with issues relating to business ethics. In the three examples of unethical business activity listed above, a management accountant would probably have to be involved either in helping to commit the unethical act or in covering it up. Management accountants are, therefore, particularly vulnerable to being put under pressure to engage in unethical acts. Some businesses recognise this risk and produce an ethical code for their accounting staff. **Real World 1.11** provides an example of one such code.

Real World 1.11

The only way is ethics

The Helphire Group plc provides various forms of assistance to motorists involved in accidents that were not their fault. It has an ethical policy which exhorts all employees to act honestly, to comply with legal requirements, to treat others with respect and so on. In addition, it has the following ethical policy aimed at its accounting staff.

> The Group's financial records should be complete and accurate so that they reflect the true state of the business and disclose the true nature of disbursements and transactions. All the Group's books, records, accounts and financial statements must be maintained in reasonable detail using standard Group systems; must appropriately reflect the Group's transactions; must conform both to applicable legal requirements and generally accepted accounting principles and to existing systems of internal control. In particular it is prohibited to undertake transactions that contravene tax laws, legal regulations and/or policy or procedural requirements of the Group including:

→

> Making any payment arrangement which is not disclosed to the Group's solicitors or fails to comply with Group Policy on Anti Money Laundering.
>
> Making or approving any payment with the understanding that any part of such payment is to be used for any purpose other than that recorded in the Group's books of account and by the documents supporting the payment.
>
> Establish undisclosed funds or assets or to make false or misleading entries in any books of accounts or accounting documents or to destroy accounting records and supporting documents within required statutory retention periods.
>
> Use Group funds or assets for any unlawful purpose.
>
> Knowingly make false or inaccurate statements in the Group's risk assessment returns and declarations to the Group Finance Department.
>
> Knowingly make any false or inaccurate statements to any of the internal or external Auditors carrying out periodic reviews of the Group's accounting records and internal controls.
>
> *Source*: Helphire Group plc website (www.helphire.co.uk), accessed 6 February 2014.

MANAGEMENT ACCOUNTING AND FINANCIAL ACCOUNTING

Management accounting is one of two main strands in accounting; the other strand is **financial accounting**. The difference between the two is based on the user groups to which each is addressed. Management accounting seeks to meet the needs of managers, whereas financial accounting seeks to meet the accounting needs of the other users that were identified earlier in Figure 1.5 (see p. 17).

The difference in their targeted user groups has led to each strand of accounting developing along different lines. The main areas of difference are as follows:

- *Nature of the reports produced*. Financial accounting reports tend to be general-purpose. Although they are aimed primarily at providers of finance such as owners and lenders, they contain financial information that will be useful for a broad range of users and decisions. Management accounting reports, on the other hand, are often specific-purpose reports. They are designed with a particular decision in mind and/or for a particular manager.
- *Level of detail*. Financial accounting reports provide users with a broad overview of the performance and position of the business for a period. As a result, information is aggregated (that is, added together) and detail is often lost. Management accounting reports, however, often provide managers with considerable detail to help them with a particular operational decision.
- *Regulations*. The financial accounting reports of many businesses are subject to regulations imposed by the law and by accounting rule makers. These regulations often require a standard content and, sometimes, a standard format to be adopted. As management accounting reports are for internal use only, there are no regulations from external sources concerning their content and form. They can be designed to meet the needs of particular managers.
- *Reporting interval*. For most businesses, financial accounting reports are produced on an annual basis, although some large businesses produce half-yearly reports and a few produce quarterly ones. Management accounting reports will be produced as frequently as is needed. A sales manager, for example, may require routine sales reports on a daily, weekly or monthly basis so as to monitor performance closely. Special-purpose reports can also be prepared when the occasion demands: for example, where an evaluation is required of a proposed investment in new equipment.

- *Time orientation*. Financial accounting reports reveal the performance and position of a business for the past period. In essence, they are backward-looking. Management accounting reports, on the other hand, often provide information concerning future performance as well as past performance. It is an oversimplification, however, to suggest that financial accounting reports never incorporate expectations concerning the future. Occasionally, businesses will release forward-looking information to other users in an attempt to raise finance or to fight off unwanted takeover bids. Even preparation of financial accounting reports for the past period typically requires making some judgements about the future, for example the residual value of a depreciating asset.
- *Range and quality of information*. Two key points are worth mentioning here. Firstly, financial accounting reports concentrate on information that can be quantified in monetary terms. Management accounting also produces such reports, but is also more likely to produce reports that contain information of a non-financial nature, such as physical volume of inventories, number of sales orders received, number of new products launched, physical output per employee and so on. Secondly, financial accounting places greater emphasis on the use of objective, verifiable evidence when preparing reports. Management accounting reports may use information that is less objective and verifiable, but nevertheless provide managers with the information they need.

We can see from this that management accounting is less constrained than financial accounting. It may draw from a variety of sources and use information that has varying degrees of reliability. The only real test to be applied when assessing the value of the information produced for managers is whether or not it improves the quality of the decisions made.

The main differences between financial accounting and management accounting reports are summarised in Figure 1.11.

	Management accounting	*Financial accounting*
Nature of the reports produced	Tend to be specific-purpose	Tend to be general-purpose
Level of detail	Often very detailed	Usually broad overview
Regulations	Unregulated	Usually subject to accounting regulation
Reporting interval	As short as required by managers	Usually annual or bi-annual
Time orientation	Often based on projected future information as well as past information	Almost always historical
Range and quality of information	Tend to contain financial and non-financial information, often use information that cannot be verified	Focus on financial information, great emphasis on objective, verifiable evidence

Although management and financial accounting are closely linked and have broadly common objectives, they differ in emphasis in various aspects.

Figure 1.11 Management and financial accounting reports compared

The differences between management accounting and financial accounting reports suggest differences in the information needs of managers and those of other users. While differences undoubtedly exist, there is also a good deal of overlap between the information needs of both.

Activity 1.13

Can you think of any areas of overlap between the information needs of managers and those of other users? (*Hint*: Think about the time orientation and the level of detail of accounting information.)

Two points that spring to mind are:

- Managers will, at times, be interested in receiving a historical overview of business operations of the sort provided to other users.
- Other users would be interested in receiving detailed information relating to the future, such as the planned level of profits, and non-financial information, such as the state of the sales order book and the extent of product innovations.

To some extent, differences between the two strands of accounting reflect differences in access to financial information. Managers have much more control over the form and content of the information that they receive. Other users have to rely on what managers are prepared to provide or what financial reporting regulations insist must be provided. Although the scope of financial accounting reports has increased over time, fears concerning loss of competitive advantage and user ignorance about the reliability of forward-looking data have meant that other users do not receive the same detailed and wide-ranging information as that available to managers.

In the past it has been argued that accounting systems are biased in favour of providing information for external users. Financial accounting requirements have been the main priority and management accounting has suffered as a result. More recent survey evidence suggests, however, that this argument has lost its force. Nowadays, management accounting systems will usually provide managers with information that is relevant to their needs rather than that determined by external reporting requirements. External reporting cycles, however, retain some influence over management accounting. Managers tend to be aware of external users' expectations (see reference 4 at the end of the chapter).

NOT-FOR-PROFIT ORGANISATIONS

Although the focus of this book is management accounting as it relates to private sector businesses, there are many organisations that do not exist mainly for the pursuit of profit yet produce management accounting information for decision-making purposes. Examples of such organisations include charities, clubs and associations, universities, national and local government authorities, churches and trades unions. Managers need accounting information about these types of organisation to help them to make decisions. In essence, the nature and scope of management accounting information used by private sector, profit-seeking businesses is much the same as is needed by not-for-profit bodies. This means that, although the emphasis of this book is on the private sector business, the principles apply equally well to the non-profit-seeking sector.

Activity 1.14

'A not-for-profit organisation is normally unconcerned with the creation of wealth.' Do you agree?

Although these organisations will not be concerned with the creation of wealth *for owners (shareholders)*, they will normally be very interested in creating wealth for the achievement of their particular missions.

Not-for-profit organisations are not exempt from the changes that have taken place in the world. They too must be 'customer' orientated and are under increasing pressure to deliver value for money in the manner in which they operate. This means allocating scarce resources carefully and monitoring fundraising activities closely. To operate in this environment, management accountants will often need excellent communication skills as levels of financial awareness among trustees and managers tend to be lower than in the private business sector.

Real World 1.12 provides an example of the importance of accounting to relief agencies, which are, of course, not-for-profit organisations.

Real World 1.12

Accounting for disasters

In the aftermath of the Asian tsunami more than £400 million was raised from charitable donations. It was important that this huge amount of money for aid and reconstruction was used as efficiently and effectively as possible. That did not just mean medical staff and engineers. It also meant accountants.

The charity that exerts financial control over aid donations is Mango: Management Accounting for Non-Governmental Organisations (NGOs). It provides accountants in the field and it provides the backup, such as financial training and all the other services that should result in really robust financial management in a disaster area.

The world of aid has changed completely as a result of the tsunami. According to Mango's director, Alex Jacobs, 'Accounting is just as important as blankets. Agencies have been aware of this for years. But when you move on to a bigger scale there is more pressure to show the donations are being used appropriately.'

More recently, the earthquake in Haiti led to a call from Mango for French-speaking accountants to help support the relief programme and to help in the longer-term rebuilding of Haiti.

Sources: Adapted from Bruce, Robert (2005) Tsunami: finding the right figures for disaster relief, ft.com, 7 March; and Bruce, Robert (2006) The work of Mango: Coping with generous donations, ft.com, 27 February; Grant, Paul (2010) Accountants needed in Haiti, *Accountancy Age*, 5 February.

SUMMARY

The main points of this chapter may be summarised as follows:

What is the purpose of a business?

- To create and keep a customer.

How are businesses organised and managed?

- Most businesses of any size are set up as limited companies.
- A board of directors is appointed by shareholders to oversee the running of the business.
- Businesses are often divided into departments and organised along functional lines; however, larger businesses may be divisionalised along geographical and/or product lines.

Strategic management

- The development of strategic management is in response to changes in the competitive environment and to the increase in size of many businesses.
- Strategic management involves five steps:
  1. Establish mission, vision and objectives.
  2. Undertake a position analysis (for example, a SWOT analysis).
  3. Identify and assess strategic options.
  4. Select strategic options and formulate plans.
  5. Perform, review and control.

The changing business landscape

- Increased competition and advances in technology have changed the business landscape.
- There have been changes in the kind of businesses in existence as well as changes in business structures and processes.

Setting financial aims and objectives

- A key financial objective for a business is to enhance the owners' (shareholders') wealth.
- When setting financial objectives the right balance must be struck between risk and return.

Management accounting and user needs

- For management accounting to be useful, it must be clear *for whom* and *for what purpose* the information will be used.
- Managers are an important type of user of financial information concerning the business but there are several others including owners, employees, lenders and government.

Providing a service

- Management accounting can be viewed as a form of service as it involves providing information to its 'clients' – the managers.

- To provide a useful service, management accounting information must possess certain qualities, or characteristics. The fundamental qualities are relevance and faithful representation. Other qualities that enhance the usefulness of accounting information are comparability, verifiability, timeliness and understandability.
- Providing a service to managers can be costly and information should be produced only if the cost of providing the information is less than the benefits gained.

Management accounting as an information system

- Management accounting is part of the total information system within a business. It shares the features that are common to all information systems within a business, which are the identification, recording, analysis and reporting of information.

What information do managers need?

- To meet managers' needs, information relating to the following broad areas is required:
  - developing objectives and plans
  - performance evaluation and control
  - allocating resources
  - determining costs and benefits.
- Providing non-financial information has become an increasingly important part of the management accountant's role.

Influencing managers' behaviour

- The main purpose of management accounting is to affect people's behaviour.
- Doing so, however, is not always beneficial and may have unintended consequences.

Reaping the benefits of IT

- IT has had a major effect on the ability to provide accurate, detailed and timely information.
- Developments in IT have enabled information and reports to be more widely disseminated throughout the business.
- IT has had a profound impact on the role of the management accountant.

Changing role of the management accountant

- Management accounting has changed over the years in response to changes in the business environment (including the IT revolution) and in business methods.
- Less time is spent preparing reports and more time is spent on analysis and on providing business advice.
- The management accountant is often a key member of the management team, which requires greater interpersonal, leadership and management skills.
- This new dimension to the management accountant's role should benefit the design of more relevant management accounting information systems.

Ethical behaviour

- Management accountants may be put under pressure to commit unethical acts.
- Many businesses now publish a code of ethics governing the behaviour of accounting staff.

→

Management accounting and financial accounting

- Accounting has two main strands – management accounting and financial accounting.
- Management accounting seeks to meet the needs of the business's managers, and financial accounting seeks to meet the needs of providers of finance but will also be of use to other user groups.
- These two strands differ in terms of the types of reports produced, the level of reporting detail, the time orientation, the degree of regulation and the range and quality of information provided.

Not-for-profit organisations

- Not-for-profit organisations also require management accounting information for decision-making purposes.

KEY TERMS

For definitions of these terms, see Appendix A.

Strategic management
Mission statement
Vision statement
Position analysis
SWOT analysis
Management accounting
Relevance
Materiality
Faithful representation
Comparability
Verifiability
Timeliness
Understandability
Management accounting information system
Key performance indicators (KPIs)
Financial accounting

REFERENCES

1 Drucker, P. (1967) *The Effective Executive*, Heinemann.

2 Chartered Institute of Management Accounting (2009) *Management Accounting Tools for Today and Tomorrow*, CIMA.

3 Abdel-Kader, M. and Luther, R. (2008) The impact of firm characteristics on management accounting practices: a UK-based empirical analysis, *British Accounting Review*, March.

4 Dugdale, D., Jones, C. and Green, S. (2006) *Contemporary Management Accounting Practices in UK Manufacturing*, Elsevier.

FURTHER READING

If you would like to explore the topics covered in this chapter in more depth, we recommend the following:

Atkinson, A., Kaplan, R., Matsamura, E. and Young, S.M. (2011) *Management Accounting: Information for Decision Making and Strategy Execution*, 6th edn, Pearson, Chapter 1.

Bhimani, A., Horngren, C., Datar, S. and Rajan, M. (2012) *Management and Cost Accounting*, 5th edn, Financial Times Prentice Hall, Chapter 1.

Hilton, R. and Platt, D. (2014) *Managerial Accounting*, 10th edn, McGraw-Hill Higher Education, Chapter 1.

Hopper, T., Scapens, R. and Northcott, D. (2007) *Issues in Management Accounting*, 3rd edn, FT Prentice Hall, Chapter 6.

Johnson, G., Whittington D., and Scholes, K. (2011) *Exploring Strategy: Text and Cases*, 9th edn, Financial Times Prentice Hall, Chapters 1–3.

REVIEW QUESTIONS

Solutions to these questions can be found in Appendix C.

1.1 Identify the main users of accounting information for a university. For what purposes would different user groups need information? Would these groups use the accounting information in a different way from the equivalent groups in private sector businesses?

1.2 Management accounting has been described as 'the eyes and ears of management'. What do you think this expression means?

1.3 Assume that you are a manager considering the launch of a new service. What accounting information might be useful to help in making a decision?

1.4 'Management accounting information should be understandable. As some managers have a poor knowledge of accounting we should produce simplified financial reports to help them.' To what extent do you agree with this view?

EXERCISES

Exercise 1.2 is more advanced than 1.1. Both have solutions given in Appendix D.

1.1 You have been speaking to a friend who owns a small business and she has said that she has read something about strategic management and that no modern business can afford not to get involved with it. Your friend has little idea what strategic management involves.

Required:
Briefly outline the steps in strategic management, summarising what each step involves.

1.2 Jones Dairy Ltd (Jones) operates a 'doorstep' fresh milk delivery service. Two brothers carry on the business that they inherited from their father in the early 1970s. They are the business's only directors. The business operates from a yard on the outskirts of Trepont, a substantial town in mid Wales.

Jones expanded steadily from when the brothers took over until the early 1980s, by which time it employed 25 full-time rounds staff. This was achieved because of four factors: (1) some expansion of the permanent population of Trepont, (2) expanding Jones's geographical range to the villages surrounding the town, (3) an expanding tourist trade in the area and (4) a positive attitude to 'marketing'.

As an example of the marketing effort, when new residents move into the area, the member of the rounds staff concerned reports this back. One of the directors immediately visits the potential customer with an introductory gift, usually a bottle of milk, a bottle of wine and a bunch of flowers. He then attempts to obtain a regular milk order. Similar methods are used to persuade existing residents to place orders for delivered milk.

By the mid 1980s Jones had a monopoly of doorstep delivery in the Trepont area. A combination of losing market share to Jones and the town's relative remoteness had discouraged the national doorstep suppliers. The little locally-based competition there once was had gone out of business.

Supplies of milk come from a bottling plant, owned by one of the national dairy businesses, which is located 50 miles from Trepont. The bottlers deliver nightly, except Saturday nights, to Jones's depot. Jones delivers daily, except on Sundays.

Profits, after adjusting for inflation, have fallen since the early 1980s. Sales volumes have fallen by about a third, compared with a decline of about 50 per cent for doorstep deliveries nationally over the same period. New customers are increasingly difficult to find, despite a continuing policy of encouraging them. Many existing customers tend to have less milk delivered. A sufficient profit has been made to enable the directors to enjoy a reasonable income compared with their needs, but only by raising prices. Currently Jones charges 72p for a standard pint, delivered. This is fairly typical of prices for milk delivered to the doorstep around the UK. The Trepont supermarket, which is located in the centre of town, charges 50p a pint and other local stores charge between 55p and 60p.

Currently Jones employs 15 full-time rounds staff, a van maintenance mechanic, a secretary/bookkeeper and the two directors. Jones is regarded locally as a good employer. Regular employment opportunities in the area are generally few. Rounds staff are expected to, and generally do, give customers a friendly, cheerful and helpful service.

The two brothers continue to be the only shareholders and directors and comprise the only level of management. One of the directors devotes most of his time to dealing with the supplier and with issues connected with details of the rounds. The other director looks after administrative matters, such as the accounts and human resources issues. Both directors undertake rounds to cover for sickness and holidays.

Required:

As far as the information given in the question will allow, undertake an analysis of the strengths, weaknesses, opportunities and threats (a SWOT analysis) of the business.

Chapter 2

RELEVANT COSTS AND BENEFITS FOR DECISION MAKING

INTRODUCTION

This chapter considers the identification and use of costs in making management decisions. These decisions should be made in a way that will promote the business's achievement of its objectives. We shall see that not all of the costs and benefits that appear to be linked to a particular business decision are relevant to it. It is important to distinguish carefully between the costs and benefits that are relevant and those that are not. Failure to do this could well lead to bad decisions being made. The principles outlined here will provide the basis for much of the rest of the book.

Learning outcomes

When you have completed this chapter, you should be able to:

- Define and distinguish between relevant costs, outlay costs and opportunity costs.
- Identify and quantify the costs and benefits that are relevant to a particular decision.
- Use relevant costs and benefits to make decisions.
- Set out relevant costs and benefits analysis in a logical form so that the conclusion may be communicated to managers.

COST–BENEFIT ANALYSIS

Managers tend to spend much of their time making plans and decisions. As part of this process, they must try to assess the likely outcome from each course of action being considered. This involves a careful weighing of the prospective **benefits** against the **costs** involved. Benefits are those outcomes, resulting from a course of action, that help a business to achieve its objectives. Costs, on the other hand, represent the sacrifice of resources needed to achieve those benefits. For a proposed plan, or decision, to be worthwhile, the likely benefits should exceed the associated costs.

Real World 2.1 provides an interesting example of where **cost–benefit analysis** was used to evaluate a possible course of action designed to solve a serious problem faced by many businesses.

Real World 2.1

Stocktaking

Light-fingered employees are a problem for all employers; however, the issue is particularly severe in the retail trade. Tatiana Sandino, an associate professor in accounting and management at Harvard Business School, and co-author Clara Xiaoling Chen, an assistant professor of accountancy at the University of Illinois at Urbana-Champaign, cite figures from the National Retail Security survey in the US which says that employee theft of inventories contributed to a loss of $15.9bn in 2008.

To try to discover what might dissuade employees from stealing, the two academics wondered if higher remuneration might help. They hypothesised that higher wages might encourage employees to feel more warmly towards their employers, that these employees – if they were paid more – would be less inclined to steal because they would not want to lose their jobs and paying a larger sum in the first place would attract more honest employees.

Using two data sets and including factors such as workers' different socio-economic environments and how many people the stores employed, the authors found that paying a larger salary caused a drop in employee theft and could, in certain circumstances, make fiscal sense.

A cost–benefit analysis found that what an employer saved in cash and inventories theft covered about 39 per cent of the cost of the wage increase. 'Our study suggests that an increase in wages will decrease theft, but won't fully pay off,' says Prof Sandino. The pair suggests that raising salaries might be the right course of action if other benefits – such as reduced employee turnover or higher employee productivity – account for at least 61 per cent of the wage increase.

Source: Adapted from Anderson, L. (2012) Something for the weekend, ft.com, 16 November.

To help weigh costs and benefits arising from a particular decision, it would be useful if both could be measured in monetary terms (as they were in the example discussed in Real World 2.1). This would then provide a common denominator for cost–benefit analysis. Some costs and benefits, however, may elude attempts to place a reliable monetary value on them. Take, for example, the likely problems of trying to measure the costs, in terms of loss of reputation, incurred by selling customers faulty products or the benefits accruing from steps taken to lift morale among the workforce. To make things worse, the timing and duration of these costs and benefits may be difficult to estimate. Nevertheless, they can have a significant effect on the ability of a business to meet its objectives. They should not, therefore, be ignored or given less weight when making decisions. There is always a risk that managers will take too narrow a view and act on the basis that 'the things that count are the things that get counted'. This is to say that attention is paid to those aspects on which it is easy to place a monetary value, but aspects that are difficult to value are ignored. This will inevitably lead to bad decision making. We shall return to this point a little later in the chapter.

WHAT IS MEANT BY 'COST'?

The term 'cost' is a slippery concept. Although a very broad description was given earlier when discussing cost–benefit analysis, it can be defined in different ways. Managers therefore need to be clear what it means in the context of decision making. This is an important issue to which we now turn.

Identifying and measuring cost may seem, at first sight, to be pretty straightforward: it is simply the amount paid for the goods supplied or the service provided. When measuring cost *for decision-making purposes*, however, things are not quite that simple. The following activity illustrates why this is the case.

Activity 2.1

You own a motor car, for which you paid a purchase price of £5,000 – much below the list price – at a recent car auction. You have just been offered £6,000 for this car.

What is the cost to you of keeping the car for your own use? *Note*: Ignore running costs and so on; just consider the 'capital' cost of the car.

By retaining the car, you are forgoing a cash receipt of £6,000. Thus, the real sacrifice, or cost, incurred by keeping the car for your own use is £6,000. Any decision that you make with respect to the car's future should logically take account of this figure. This cost is known as the 'opportunity cost' since it is the value of the opportunity forgone in order to pursue the other course of action. (In this case, the other course of action is to retain the car.)

We can see that the cost of retaining the car is not the same as the purchase price. In one sense, of course, the cost of the car in Activity 2.1 is £5,000 because that is how much was paid for it. However, this cost, which for obvious reasons is known as the **historic cost**, is only of academic interest. It cannot logically ever be used to make a decision on the car's future. If we disagree with this point, we should ask ourselves how we should assess an offer of £5,500, from another person, for the car. The answer is that we should compare the offer price of £5,500 with the **opportunity cost** of £6,000. This should lead us to reject the offer as it is less than the £6,000 opportunity cost. In these circumstances, it would not be logical to accept the offer of £5,500 on the basis that it was more than the £5,000 that we originally paid. The only other figure that should concern us is the value to us, in terms of pleasure, usefulness and so on, of retaining the car. If we valued this more highly than the £6,000 opportunity cost, we should reject both offers.

We may still feel, however, that the £5,000 is relevant here because it will help us in assessing the profitability of the decision. If we sold the car, we should make a profit of either

£500 (£5,500 – £5,000) or £1,000 (£6,000 – £5,000) depending on which offer we accept. Since we should seek to make the higher profit, the right decision is to sell the car for £6,000. However, we do not need to know the historic cost of the car to make the right decision. What decision should we make if the car cost us £4,000 to buy? Clearly we should still sell the car for £6,000 rather than for £5,500 as the important comparison is between the offer price and the opportunity cost. We should reach the same conclusion whatever the historic cost of the car.

To emphasise the above point, let us assume that the car cost £10,000. Even in this case the historic cost would still be irrelevant. Had we just bought a car for £10,000 and found shortly after that it is only worth £6,000, we might well be fuming with rage at our mistake, but this does not make the £10,000 a **relevant cost**. The only relevant factors, in a decision on whether to sell the car or to keep it, are the £6,000 opportunity cost and the value of the benefits of keeping it. Thus, the historic cost can never be relevant to a future decision.

To say that historic cost is an **irrelevant cost** is not to say that *the effects of having incurred that cost* are always irrelevant. The fact that we own the car, and are thus in a position to exercise choice as to how to use it, is not irrelevant. It is highly relevant.

Opportunity costs are rarely taken into account in the routine accounting processes, such as recording revenues, expenses, assets and claims. This is because they do not involve any out-of-pocket expenditure. It seems that they are only calculated where they are relevant to a particular management decision. Historic costs, on the other hand, do involve out-of-pocket expenditure and are recorded. They are used in preparing the annual financial statements, such as the statement of financial position and the income statement. This is logical, however, since these statements are intended to be accounts of what has actually happened and are drawn up after the event.

Real World 2.2 gives an example of how perceptions of the worth of an asset can alter as circumstances alter. When News Corp bought the social networking site MySpace in 2005, it judged that the benefits of ownership were worth $580 million. By 2011, this judgement had altered drastically. When the decision to sell for $35 million was being made, the fact that MySpace had a historic cost of $580 million was presumably ignored. Only the future benefits of ownership were weighed against the $35 million.

Real World 2.2

No space for MySpace

After a drawn-out sales process and a saga that Rupert Murdoch, its chairman, would probably rather forget, News Corp has found a buyer for MySpace, agreeing to sell the loss-making social network to Specific Media in a $35 million deal.

The move, first reported by News Corp's *All Things D* website, brings to an end a turbulent episode that initially reignited Mr Murdoch's interest in the internet, with his company briefly capitalising on a website that, in its heyday, was one of the world's hottest internet properties. But years of management mistakes, the rise of Facebook and clashes between the News Corp hierarchy and MySpace managers led to Mr Murdoch's dream of a dominant global social network turning to dust.

Under the terms of the deal, News Corp will receive a small cash payment and a minority stake in Specific Media in return for MySpace, which it acquired in 2005 for $580 million. Specific Media, a California-based online advertising network founded by the Vanderhook brothers, will control the company.

MySpace had been steadily losing money in the period leading up to the sale. The News Corp division including the site is expected to post close to $500 million in operating losses this fiscal year, according to people familiar with the situation. That did not deter Specific Media, which enlisted Justin Timberlake to back its bid.

At its peak, MySpace employed 1,400 people but that number has fallen to 400 through waves of cost cutting: about 200 will leave the company following the sale, according to a person close to the situation. Specific Media saw off interest from Chris DeWolfe, a former MySpace chief executive, and private equity firms, including Golden Gate Capital. But the deal's price represents a steep loss for News Corp. Its ownership of MySpace had started off so promisingly in 2005. The purchase of a fast-growing company with genuine cachet among young internet users re-invented Mr Murdoch as a 21st century news media mogul.

Shortly after the acquisition, MySpace struck a $900 million three-year advertising deal with Google, which depended on strict traffic targets being met. MySpace revenues leapt from $1 million a month to $50 million a month, and Mr Murdoch confidently predicted the site would generate $1 billion in advertising revenues by the end of 2008. But then things took a turn for the worse. MySpace became cluttered with unappealing ads, Mr DeWolfe departed after clashes with News Corp management and users began to leave in droves. A move by MySpace and other News Corp digital businesses into the biggest new office development in Los Angeles was scrapped – after the $350 million, 12-year lease had been signed – leaving the company paying more than $1 million a month for an empty building.

The site shed users while Facebook was adding them in their millions. MySpace then revealed it had missed its Google targets and the management turmoil continued with two other chief executives leaving.

Mr Murdoch's frustration about the site's performance was evident. Relaunches of MySpace failed, culminating in the decision to seek a buyer. Mr Murdoch, who is spending more of his time these days looking at opportunities in the education industry, did not comment on the sale – and it is unclear whether he still has the same enthusiasm he once did for online social networking.

Source: Garrahan, M. (2011) Murdoch's MySpace dream turns to dust, ft.com, 30 June.

RELEVANT COSTS: OPPORTUNITY AND OUTLAY COSTS

We have just seen that, when we are making decisions concerning the future, **past costs** (that is, historic costs) are irrelevant. It is future opportunity costs and future **outlay costs** that are of concern. An opportunity cost can be defined as the value, in monetary terms, of being deprived of the next best opportunity in order to pursue the particular objective. An outlay cost is an amount of money that will have to be spent to achieve an objective. We shall shortly meet plenty of examples of both of these types of future cost.

To be relevant to a particular decision, a future outlay cost, or opportunity cost, must satisfy all three of the following criteria:

1 *It must relate to the objectives of the business.* Most businesses have enhancing owners' (shareholders') wealth as their key strategic objective. That is to say, they are seeking to become richer (see Chapter 1). Thus, to be relevant to a particular decision, a cost must have an effect on the wealth of the business.
2 *It must be a future cost.* Past costs cannot be relevant to decisions being made about the future.
3 *It must vary with the decision.* Only costs that are different between outcomes can be used to distinguish between them. Take, for example, a road haulage business that has decided that it will buy a new additional lorry and the decision lies between two different models.

The load capacity, the fuel and maintenance costs are different for each lorry. The potential costs and benefits associated with these are relevant items. The lorry will require a driver, so the business will need to employ one, but a suitably qualified driver could drive either lorry equally well, for the same wage. The cost of employing the driver is thus irrelevant to the decision as to which lorry to buy. This is despite the fact that this cost is a future one.

Activity 2.2

If the decision did not concern a choice between two models of lorry but rather whether to operate an additional lorry or not, would the cost of employing the additional driver be relevant?

Yes – because it would then be a cost that would vary with the decision.

Figure 2.1 shows a decision flow diagram for deciding which costs are relevant.

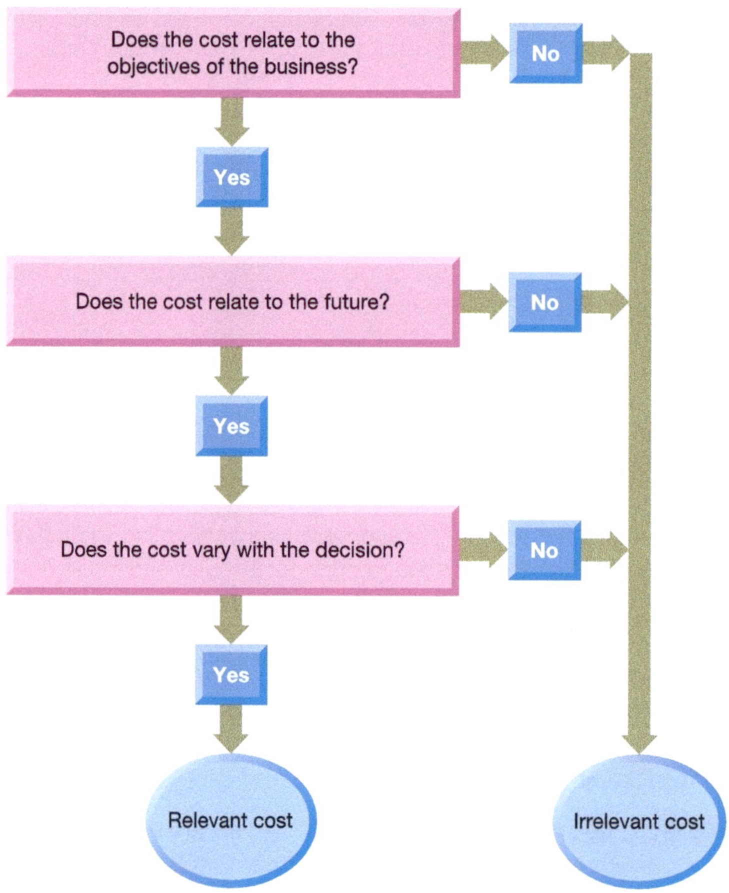

To be relevant to a particular decision, a cost must satisfy all three criteria.

Figure 2.1 A decision flow diagram for identifying relevant costs

To be relevant to a particular decision, the benefits must also satisfy all three criteria mentioned. That is, they should relate to the objectives of the business, they should relate to the future and they should vary with the decision.

Activity 2.3

A garage business has an old car that it bought several months ago. The car needs a replacement engine before it can be driven. It is possible to buy a reconditioned engine for £300. This would take seven hours to fit by a mechanic who is paid £15 an hour. At present the garage is short of work, but the owners are reluctant to lay off any mechanics or even to cut down their basic working week because skilled labour is difficult to find and an upturn in repair work is expected soon.

The garage paid £3,000 to buy the car. Without the engine it could be sold for an estimated £3,500. What is the minimum price at which the garage should sell the car with a reconditioned engine fitted?

The minimum price is the amount required to cover the relevant costs of the job. At this price, the benefits will exactly equal the costs and so neither a profit nor loss is made. Any price that is lower than this amount will mean that the wealth of the business is reduced. Thus, the minimum price is:

	£
Opportunity cost of the car	3,500
Cost of the reconditioned engine	300
Total	3,800

Labour paid irrespective

The original cost of the car is irrelevant for reasons that have already been discussed. It is the opportunity cost of the car that concerns us. The cost of the new engine is relevant because, if the work is done, the garage will have to pay £300 for the engine; but the garage will pay nothing if the job is not done. The £300 is an example of a future outlay cost.

The labour cost is irrelevant because the same cost will be incurred whether the mechanic undertakes the engine-replacement work or not. This is because the mechanic is being paid to do nothing if this job is not undertaken; thus the additional labour cost arising from this job is zero.

It should be emphasised that the garage will not seek to sell the car with its reconditioned engine for £3,800; it will attempt to charge as much as possible for it. Any price above the £3,800, however, will make the garage better off financially than it would be if it did not undertake the engine replacement.

Activity 2.4

Assume exactly the same circumstances as in Activity 2.3, except that the garage is quite busy at the moment. If a mechanic is to be put on the engine-replacement job, it will mean that other work that the mechanic could have done during the seven hours, all of which could be charged to a customer, will not be undertaken. The garage's labour charge is £60 an hour, though the mechanic is only paid £15 an hour.

What is the minimum price at which the garage should sell the car, with a reconditioned engine fitted, under these altered circumstances?

The minimum price is:

	£
Opportunity cost of the car	3,500
Cost of the reconditioned engine	300
Labour cost (7 × £60)	420
Total	4,220

→

We can see that the opportunity cost of the car and the cost of the engine are the same as in Activity 2.3, but now a charge for labour has been added to obtain the minimum price. The relevant labour cost here is that which the garage will have to sacrifice in making the time available to undertake the engine-replacement job. During the time that the mechanic is working on this job, the garage is losing the opportunity to do work for which a customer would pay £420. Note that the £15 an hour mechanic's wage is still not relevant. The mechanic will be paid £15 an hour irrespective of whether it is the engine-replacement work or some other job that is undertaken.

Activity 2.5

A business is considering making a bid to undertake a contract. Fulfilment of the contract will require the use of two types of raw material. Quantities of both of these materials are held by the business. If it chose to, the business could sell the raw materials in their present state. All of the inventories of these two raw materials will need to be used on the contract. Information on the raw materials concerned is as follows:

Inventories item	*Quantity (units)*	*Historic cost (£/unit)*	*Sales value (£/unit)*	*Replacement cost (£/unit)*
A1	500	5	3	6
B2	800	7	8	10

Inventories item A1 is in frequent use in the business on a variety of work.

The inventories of item B2 were bought a year ago for a contract that was abandoned. It has recently become obvious that there is no likelihood of ever using this raw material unless the contract currently being considered proceeds.

Management wishes to deduce the minimum price at which the business could undertake the contract without reducing its wealth as a result (that is, the price at which the costs are exactly equal to the benefits). This can be used as the baseline in deducing the bid price.

How much should be included in the minimum price in respect of the two inventories items detailed above?

The minimum price must cover the relevant costs. The costs to be covered by the minimum price are:

	Inventories item
A1	£6 × 500 = £3,000
B2	£8 × 800 = £6,400

We are told that the item A1 is in frequent use and so, if it is used on the contract, it will need to be replaced. Sooner or later, the business will have to buy 500 units (currently costing £6 a unit) additional to those which would have been required had the contract not been undertaken.

Item B2 will never be used by the business unless the contract is undertaken. Thus, if the contract is not undertaken, the only reasonable thing for the business to do is to sell the B2. This means that if the contract is undertaken and the B2 is used, it will have an opportunity cost equal to the potential proceeds from disposal, which is £8 a unit.

Note that the historic cost information about both materials is irrelevant. This will always be the case.

Activity 2.6

HLA Ltd is in the process of preparing a quotation for a special job for a customer. The job will have the following material requirements:

Material	*Units required*	*Units currently held in inventories*			*Replacement cost (£/unit)*
		Quantity held (units)	*Historic cost (£/unit)*	*Sales value (£/unit)*	
P	400	0	–	–	40
Q	230	100	62	50	64
R	350	200	48	23	59
S	170	140	33	12	49
T	120	120	40	0	68

Material Q is used consistently by the business on various jobs.

The business holds materials R, S and T as the result of previous overbuying. No other use (apart from this special job) can be found for R, but the 140 units of S could be used in another job as a substitute for 225 units of material V that are about to be purchased at a price of £10 a unit. Material T has no other use, it is a dangerous material that is difficult to store and the business has been informed that it will cost £160 to dispose of the material currently held.

If it chose to, the business could sell the raw materials Q, R and S already held in their present state.

What is the relevant cost of the materials for the job specified above?

The relevant cost is as follows:

	£
Material P	
This will have to be purchased at £40 a unit (400 × £40)	16,000
Material Q	
Those units already held will have to be replaced and the remaining 130 units will have to be purchased, therefore the relevant price is (230 × £64)	14,720
Material R	
200 units of this are held and these could be sold. The relevant price of these is the sales revenue forgone (200 × £23)	4,600
The remaining 150 units of R would have to be purchased (150 × £59)	8,850
Material S	
This could be sold or used as a substitute for material V. The existing inventories could be sold for £1,680 (that is, 140 × £12); however, the saving on material V is higher and therefore should be taken as the relevant amount (225 × £10)	2,250
The remaining units of material S must be purchased (30 × £49)	1,470
Material T	
A saving on disposal will be made if material T is used	(160)
Total relevant cost	47,730

Real World 2.3 discusses the opportunity cost of holding gold.

Real World 2.3

A golden opportunity cost

During the recession, which began in 2008, many investors bought gold in an attempt to protect their wealth in the face of declining investment returns. This had the effect of increasing the cost of gold. Clearly, gold offers no interest or dividend payments, but because these have typically been low, investors have not incurred a very high opportunity cost.

The recent upturn in the US economy had led to expectations of increases in both dividend and interest rates. This, in turn, has had an adverse effect on the price of gold. As a *Financial Times* article put it:

> This year it benefited from the fall in US real yields, a measure of the opportunity cost of holding lumps of metal. Believers in a stronger US economy, and so higher rates, should not touch gold.

FT *Source*: Mackintosh, J. (2014) Gold! Always believe in your soul, ft.com, 5 February.

SUNK COSTS AND COMMITTED COSTS

A **sunk cost** is simply another way of referring to a past cost and so the terms 'sunk cost' and 'past cost' can be used interchangeably. A **committed cost** arises where an irrevocable decision has been made to incur the cost because, for example, a business has entered into a binding contract. As a result, it is effectively a past cost despite the fact that the cash may not be paid until some point in the future. Since the business must eventually pay, a committed cost can never be a relevant cost for decision-making purposes.

It is important to remember that, to be relevant, a cost must be capable of varying according to the decision made. If the business is already committed by a legally-binding contract to a cost, that cost cannot vary with the decision.

Activity 2.7

Past costs are irrelevant costs. Does this mean that what happened in the past is irrelevant?

No, it does not mean this. The fact that the business has an asset that it can deploy in the future is highly relevant. What is not relevant is how much it cost to acquire that asset. This point was examined in the discussion that followed Activity 2.1.

Another reason why the past is not irrelevant is that it generally – though not always – provides us with our best guide to the future. Suppose that we need to estimate the cost of doing something in the future to help us to decide whether it is worth doing. In these circumstances our own experience, or that of others, on how much it has cost to do the thing in the past may provide us with a valuable guide to how much it is likely to cost in the future.

NON-MEASURABLE COSTS AND BENEFITS

It was mentioned at the beginning of the chapter that certain costs and benefits may defy measurement in monetary terms. These costs and benefits often have a broader, but less immediate, impact on the business. Ultimately, however, they are likely to affect the ability of a business to achieve its objectives.

Activity 2.8

Activity 2.4 was concerned with the cost of putting a car into a marketable condition. Apart from whether the car could be sold for more than the relevant cost of doing this, are there any other costs or benefits that may be difficult to quantify but should, nevertheless, be taken into account in making a decision as to whether to do the work?

We can think of three:

- Turning away another job in order to do the engine replacement may lead to customer dissatisfaction.
- Having the car available for sale may be useful commercially for the garage, beyond the profit that can be earned from that particular car sale. For example, having a good range of second-hand cars for sale may attract potential customers wanting to buy a car.
- It has been assumed that the only opportunity cost concerns labour (the charge-out rate for the seven hours concerned). In practice, most car repairs involve the use of some materials and spare parts. These are usually charged to customers at a profit to the garage. Any such profit from a job turned away would be lost to the garage. This lost profit would be an opportunity cost of the engine replacement. It should, therefore, be included in the calculation of the minimum price to be charged for the sale of the car.

You may have thought of additional points.

These 'qualitative' costs and benefits should provide a further input to the final plans or decisions. To do this, managers must rely on judgement when applying weightings to them. By taking account of these other costs and benefits the final plans, or decisions, may run counter to that indicated by the quantifiable costs and benefits.

To end the chapter, **Real World 2.4** describes another case where the decision makers, quite correctly, ignored past costs and just concentrated on future options for the business concerned. It also highlights how two sets of managers can take quite different views of the worth of an investment, presumably based on similar sources of information.

Real World 2.4

Delivering for £1

In April 2013 Better Capital PCC Ltd, a private equity business, paid £1 to buy City Link, the delivery and courier business, from Rentokil Initial plc, the pest control and hygiene business.

Rentokil had bought City Link as part of the takeover of Target Express in 2006, but had never been able to make a success of its acquisition. An analyst at Espirito Santo, the investment bank, said 'City Link has been a persistent thorn in the side of [Rentokil's] management's efforts to deliver a turnround at Rentokil and has assumed both significant financial cost and management focus, detracting from the core of the business'. The

→

management at Rentokil was clearly very pleased to rid itself of City Link without incurring further losses.

Better Capital could obviously see a brighter future for City Link and committed £40 million to fund additional working capital and restructuring, including the acquisition of new delivery vehicles and expanding the number of staff.

Better Capital is no stranger to deals done for £1. In February 2014, it sold Readers Digest, a publishing business, for that sum. It had bought the business for £14 million in 2010 and subsequently invested £9 million in it.

Sources: Based on City Link (2014) City Link reaps benefits of Better Capital investment, www.city-link.co.uk/press/2014/news, January; Wembridge, M. (2013) Rentokil Initial sells City Link to John Moulton's buyout group, ft.com, 29 April; Armstrong, A. (2014) Reader's Digest sold for £1 by Better Capital, *Daily Telegraph*, 16 February.

Self-assessment question 2.1

JB Limited is a small specialist manufacturer of electronic components. Makers of aircraft, for both civil and military purposes, use much of its output. One of the aircraft makers has offered a contract to JB Limited for the supply, over the next twelve months, of 400 identical components. The data relating to the production of each component are as follows:

- *Material requirements*:
  3 kg of Material M1 (see Note 1 below)
  2 kg of Material P2 (see Note 2 below)
  1 bought-in component (part number 678) (see Note 3 below)

  Note 1: Material M1 is in continuous use by the business; 1,000 kg are currently held by the business. The original cost was £4.70/kg, but it is known that future purchases will cost £5.50/kg.

  Note 2: 1,200 kg of Material P2 are currently held. The original cost of this material was £4.30/kg. The material has not been required for the last two years. Its scrap value is £1.50/kg. The only foreseeable alternative use is as a substitute for Material P4 (in constant use) but this would involve further processing costs of £1.60/kg. The current cost of Material P4 is £3.60/kg.

  Note 3: It is estimated that the components (part number 678) could be bought in for £50 each.

- *Labour requirements*: Each component would require five hours of skilled labour and five hours of semi-skilled. A skilled employee is available and is currently paid £14/hour. A replacement would, however, have to be obtained at a rate of £12/hour for the work that would otherwise be done by the skilled employee. The current rate for semi-skilled work is £10/hour and an additional employee could be appointed for this work.
- *General manufacturing costs*: It is JB Limited's policy to charge a share of the general costs (rent, heating and so on) to each contract undertaken at the rate of £20 for each machine hour used on the contract. If the contract is undertaken, the general costs are expected to increase as a result of undertaking the contract by £3,200.

Spare machine capacity is available and each component would require four machine hours. A price of £200 a component has been offered by the potential customer.

Required:

(a) Should the contract be accepted? Support your conclusion with appropriate figures to present to management.

(b) What other factors ought management to consider that might influence the decision?

The solution to this question can be found in Appendix B.

SUMMARY

The main points of this chapter may be summarised as follows:

Cost–benefit analysis

- Involves a careful weighing of the costs and benefits of plans and decisions.
- To be worthwhile, benefits should exceed the associated costs.
- Not all costs and benefits can be measured in monetary terms.

Relevant and irrelevant costs

- Relevant costs must:
  - relate to the objective being pursued by the business;
  - be a future cost;
  - vary with the decision.
- Relevant costs therefore include:
  - opportunity costs;
  - differential future outlay costs.
- Irrelevant costs therefore include:
  - all past (or sunk) costs;
  - all committed costs;
  - non-differential future outlay costs.

Non-measurable costs and benefits

- Should provide an input to the final plans or decisions.
- Managers must rely on judgement when applying weights to these items.

KEY TERMS

For definitions of these terms, see Appendix A.

Benefit
Cost
Cost–benefit analysis
Historic cost
Opportunity cost
Relevant cost
Irrelevant cost
Past cost
Outlay cost
Sunk cost
Committed cost

FURTHER READING

If you would like to explore the topics covered in this chapter in more depth, we recommend the following:

Drury, C. (2012) *Management and Cost Accounting*, 8th edn, Cengage Learning, Chapter 9.

Hilton, R. (2011) *Managerial Accounting*, 9th edn, McGraw-Hill Higher Education, Chapter 14.

Horngren, C., Datar, S. and Rajan, M. (2012) *Cost Accounting: A Managerial Emphasis*, 14th edn, Prentice Hall International, Chapter 11.

Kaplan, R., Atkinson, A., Matsumura, E. and Young, S.M. (2011) *Management Accounting*, 6th edn, Prentice Hall, Chapter 3.

REVIEW QUESTIONS

Solutions to these questions can be found in Appendix C.

2.1 To be relevant to a particular decision, a cost must have three attributes. What are they?

2.2 Distinguish between a sunk cost and an opportunity cost.

2.3 Define the word 'cost' in the context of management accounting.

2.4 What is meant by the expression 'committed cost'? How do committed costs arise?

EXERCISES

Exercises 2.1, 2.2 and 2.3 are basic level, 2.4 and 2.5 are intermediate level and 2.6, 2.7 and 2.8 are advanced level. Those with coloured numbers have solutions given in Appendix D.

2.1 Lombard Ltd has been offered a contract for which there is available production capacity. The contract is for 20,000 identical items, manufactured by an intricate assembly operation, to be produced and delivered in the next few months at a price of £80 each. The specification for one item is as follows:

Assembly labour	4 hours
Component X	4 units
Component Y	3 units

There would also be the need to hire equipment, for the duration of the contract, at an outlay cost of £200,000.

The assembly is a highly skilled operation and the workforce is currently underutilised. It is the business's policy to retain this workforce on full pay in anticipation of high demand next year, for a new product currently being developed. There is sufficient available skilled labour to undertake the contract now under consideration. Skilled workers are paid £15 an hour.

Component X is used in a number of other sub-assemblies produced by the business. It is readily available. 50,000 units of Component X are currently held in inventories. Component Y was a special purchase in anticipation of an order that did not in the end materialise. It is, therefore, surplus to requirements and the 100,000 units that are currently held may have to be sold at a loss. An estimate of various values for Components X and Y provided by the materials planning department is as follows:

Component	*X*	*Y*
	£/unit	*£/unit*
Historic cost	4	10
Replacement cost	5	11
Net realisable value	3	8

It is estimated that any additional relevant costs associated with the contract (beyond the above) will amount to £8 an item.

Required:

Analyse the information and advise Lombard Ltd on the desirability of the contract.

2.2 The local authority of a small town maintains a theatre and arts centre for the use of a local repertory company, other visiting groups and exhibitions. Management decisions are taken by a committee that meets regularly to review the financial statements and to plan the use of the facilities.

The theatre employs a full-time, non-performing staff and a number of artistes at total costs of £9,600 and £35,200 a month, respectively. The theatre mounts a new production every month for 20 performances. Other monthly costs of the theatre are as follows:

	£
Costumes	5,600
Scenery	3,300
Heat and light	10,300
A share of the administration costs of the local authority	16,000
Casual staff	3,520
Refreshments	2,360

On average the theatre is half full for the performances of the repertory company. The capacity and seat prices in the theatre are:

200 seats at £24 each
500 seats at £16 each
300 seats at £12 each

In addition, the theatre sells refreshments during the performances for £7,760 a month. Programme sales cover their costs, and advertising in the programme generates £6,720 a month.

The management committee has been approached by a popular touring group, which would like to take over the theatre for one month (25 performances). The group is prepared to pay the local authority half of its ticket income as a fee for the use of the theatre. The group expects to fill the theatre for 10 nights and achieve two-thirds capacity on the remaining 15 nights. The prices charged are £2 less than normally applies in the theatre.

The local authority will, as normal, pay for heat and light costs and will still honour the contracts of all artistes and pay the non-performing employees who will sell refreshments, programmes and so on. The committee does not expect any change in the level of refreshments or programme sales if they agree to this booking.

Note: The committee includes the share of the local authority administration costs when making profit calculations. It assumes occupancy applies equally across all seat prices.

Required:

(a) On financial grounds should the management committee agree to the approach from the touring group? Support your answer with appropriate workings.

(b) What other factors may have a bearing on the decision by the committee?

2.3 Andrews and Co. Ltd has been invited to tender for a contract. It is to produce 10,000 metres of an electrical cable in which the business specialises. The estimating department of the business has produced the following information relating to the contract:

- *Materials*: The cable will require a steel core, which the business buys in. The steel core is to be coated with a special plastic, also bought in, using a special process. Plastic for the covering will be required at the rate of 0.10 kg/metre of completed cable.
- *Direct labour*:

Skilled:	10 minutes/metre
Unskilled:	5 minutes/metre

The business already holds sufficient of each of the materials required to complete the contract. Information on the cost of the inventories is as follows:

	Steel core *£/metre*	*Plastic* *£/kg*
Historic cost	1.50	0.60
Current buying-in cost	2.10	0.70
Scrap value	1.40	0.10

The steel core is in constant use by the business for a variety of work that it regularly undertakes. The plastic is a surplus from a previous contract where a mistake was made and an excess quantity ordered. If the current contract does not go ahead, this plastic will be scrapped.

Unskilled labour, which is paid at the rate of £7.50 an hour, will need to be taken on specifically to undertake the contract. The business is fairly quiet at the moment which means that a pool of skilled labour exists that will still be employed at full pay of £12 an hour to do nothing if the contract does not proceed. The pool of skilled labour is sufficient to complete the contract.

Required:

Indicate the minimum price at which the contract could be undertaken, such that the business would be neither better nor worse off as a result of doing it.

2.4 SJ Services Ltd has been asked to quote a price for a special contract to render a service that will take the business one week to complete. Information relating to labour for the contract is as follows:

Grade of labour	*Hours required*	*Basic rate/hour*
Skilled	27	£12
Semi-skilled	14	£9
Unskilled	20	£7

A shortage of skilled labour means that the necessary staff to undertake the contract would have to be moved from other work that is currently yielding an excess of sales revenue over labour and other costs of £8 an hour.

Semi-skilled labour is currently being paid at semi-skilled rates to undertake unskilled work. If the relevant members of staff are moved to work on the contract, unskilled labour will have to be employed for the week to replace them.

The unskilled labour actually needed to work on the contract will be specifically employed for the week of the contract.

All labour is charged to contracts at 50 per cent above the rate paid to the employees, so as to cover the contract's fair share of the business's general costs (rent, heating and so on). It is estimated that these general costs will increase by £50 as a result of undertaking the contract.

Undertaking the contract will require the use of a specialised machine for the week. This machine is currently being hired out to another business at a weekly rental of £175 on a week-by-week contract.

To derive the above estimates, the business has had to spend £300 on a specialised study. If the contract does not proceed, the results of the study can be sold for £250.

An estimate of the contract's fair share of the business's rent is £150 a week.

Required:

Deduce the minimum price at which SJ Services Ltd could undertake the contract such that it would be neither better nor worse off as a result of undertaking it.

2.5 A business in the food industry is currently holding 2,000 tonnes of material in bulk storage. This material deteriorates with time. In the near future, it will, therefore, be necessary for it to be repackaged for sale or sold in its present form.

The material was acquired in two batches: 800 tonnes at a price of £40 a tonne and 1,200 tonnes at a price of £44 a tonne. The current market price of any additional purchases is £48 a tonne. If the business were to dispose of the material, in its present state, it could sell any quantity but for only £36 a tonne; it does not have the contacts or reputation to command a higher price.

Processing this material may be undertaken to develop either Product A or Product X. No weight loss occurs with the processing, that is, 1 tonne of the material will make 1 tonne of A or X. For Product A, there is an additional cost of £60 a tonne, after which it will sell for £105 a tonne. The marketing department estimates that a maximum of 500 tonnes could be sold in this way.

With Product X, the business incurs additional costs of £80 a tonne for processing. A market price for X is not known and no minimum price has been agreed. The management is currently engaged in discussions over the minimum price that may be charged for Product X in the current circumstances. Management wants to know the relevant cost per tonne for Product X so as to provide a basis for negotiating a profitable selling price for the product.

Required:
Identify the relevant cost per tonne for Product X, given sales volumes of X of:

(a) up to 1,500 tonnes
(b) over 1,500 tonnes, up to 2,000 tonnes
(c) over 2,000 tonnes.

Explain your answer.

2.6 A local education authority is faced with a predicted decline in the demand for school places in its area. It is believed that some schools will have to close in order to remove up to 800 places from current capacity levels. The schools that may face closure are referenced as A, B, C and D. Their details are as follows:

- *School A* (capacity 200) was built 15 years ago at a cost of £1.2 million. It is situated in a 'socially disadvantaged' community area. The authority has been offered £14 million for the site by a property developer.
- *School B* (capacity 500) was built 20 years ago and cost £1 million. It was renovated only two years ago at a cost of £3 million to improve its facilities. An offer of £8 million has been made for the site by a business planning a shopping complex in this affluent part of the area.
- *School C* (capacity 600) cost £5 million to build five years ago. The land for this school is rented from a local business for an annual cost of £300,000. The land rented for School C is based on a 100-year lease. If the school closes, the property reverts immediately to the owner. If School C is not closed, it will require a £3 million investment to improve safety at the school.
- *School D* (capacity 800) cost £7 million to build eight years ago; last year £1.5 million was spent on an extension. It has a considerable amount of grounds, which is currently used for sporting events. This factor makes it attractive to developers, who have recently offered £9 million for the site. If School D is closed, it will be necessary to pay £1.8 million to adapt facilities at other schools to accommodate the change.

In its accounting system, the local authority depreciates non-current assets based on 2 per cent a year on the original cost. It also differentiates between one-off, large items of capital expenditure or revenue, on the one hand, and annually recurring items, on the other.

The local authority has a central staff, which includes administrators for each school costing £200,000 a year for each school, and a chief education officer costing £80,000 a year in total.

Required:

(a) Prepare a summary of the relevant cash flows (costs and revenues, relative to not making any closures) under the following options:
(1) closure of D only
(2) closure of A and B
(3) closure of A and C.
Show separately the one-off effects and annually recurring items, rank the options open to the local authority and, briefly, interpret your answer. *Note*: Various approaches are acceptable provided that they are logical.

(b) Identify and comment on any two different types of irrelevant cost contained in the information given in the question.

(c) Discuss other factors that might have a bearing on the decision.

2.7 Rob Otics Ltd, a small business that specialises in manufacturing electronic-control equipment, has just received an enquiry from a potential customer for eight identical robotic units. These would be made using Rob Otics's own labour force and factory capacity. The product specification prepared by the estimating department shows the following:

- Material and labour requirements for each robotic unit:

Component X	2 per unit
Component Y	1 per unit
Component Z	4 per unit
Assembly labour	25 hours per unit (but see below)
Inspection labour	6 hours per unit

As part of the costing exercise, the business has collected the following information:

- *Component X.* This item is normally held by the business as it is in constant demand. There are 10 units currently held which were bought for £150 a unit. The sole supplier of Component X has announced a price rise of 20 per cent, effective immediately, for any further supplies. Rob Otics has not yet paid for the items currently held.
- *Component Y.* 25 units are currently held. This component is not normally used by Rob Otics but the units currently held are because of a cancelled order following the bankruptcy of a customer. The units originally cost the business £4,000 in total, although Rob Otics has recouped £1,500 from the liquidator of the bankrupt business. As Rob Otics can see no use for these units (apart from the possible use of some of them in the order now being considered), the finance director proposes to scrap all 25 units (zero proceeds).
- *Component Z.* This is in regular use by Rob Otics. There is none in inventories but an order is about to be sent to a supplier for 75 units, irrespective of this new proposal. The supplier charges £25 a unit on small orders but will reduce the price to £20 a unit for all units on any order over 100 units.
- *Other items.* These are expected to cost £250 in total.

Assembly labour is currently in short supply in the area and is paid at £10 an hour. If the order is accepted, all necessary labour will have to be transferred from existing work. As a result, other orders will be lost. It is estimated that for each hour transferred to this contract £38 will be lost (calculated as lost sales revenue £60, less materials £12 and labour £10). The production director suggests that, owing to a learning process, the time taken to make each unit will reduce, from 25 hours to make the first one, by one hour a unit made. (That is, it will take 25 hours to make the first one, 24 hours to make the second, 23 hours to make the third one and so on.)

Inspection labour can be provided by paying existing personnel overtime which is at a premium of 50 per cent over the standard rate of £12 an hour.

When the business is working out its contract prices, it normally adds an amount equal to £20 for each assembly labour hour to cover its general costs (such as rent and electricity). To the resulting total, 40 per cent is normally added as a profit mark-up.

Required:

(a) Prepare an estimate of the minimum price that you would recommend Rob Otics Ltd to charge for the proposed contract such that it would be neither better nor worse off as a result. Provide explanations for any items included.

(b) Identify any other factors that you would consider before fixing the final price.

2.8 A business places substantial emphasis on customer satisfaction and, to this end, delivers its product in special protective containers. These containers have been made in a department within the business. Management has recently become concerned that this internal supply of containers is very expensive. As a result, outside suppliers have been invited to submit tenders for the provision of these containers. A quote of £250,000 a year has been received for a volume that compares with current internal supply.

An investigation into the internal costs of container manufacture has been undertaken and the following emerges:

(a) The annual cost of material is £120,000, according to the stores records, maintained at actual historic cost. Three-quarters (by cost) of this represents material that is regularly stocked and replenished. The remaining 25 per cent of the material cost is a special foaming chemical. This chemical is not used by the business for any other purpose than making the containers. There are 40 tonnes of this chemical currently held. It was bought in bulk for £750 a tonne. Today's replacement price for this material is £1,050 a tonne but it is unlikely that the business could realise more than £600 a tonne if it had to be disposed of owing to the high handling costs and special transport facilities required.

(b) The annual labour cost is £80,000 for this department. Most of this cost, however, relates to casual employees or recent starters. If an outside quote were accepted, therefore, little redundancy would be payable. There are, however, two long-serving employees who would each accept as a salary £15,000 a year until they reached retirement age in two years' time.

(c) The department manager has a salary of £30,000 a year. The closure of this department would release him to take over another department for which a vacancy is about to be advertised. The salary, status and prospects are similar.

(d) A rental charge of £9,750 a year, based on floor area, is allocated to the containers department. If the department were closed, the floor space released would be used for warehousing and, as a result, the business would give up the tenancy of an existing warehouse for which it is paying £15,750 a year.

(e) The plant cost £162,000 when it was bought five years ago. Its market value now is £28,000 and it could continue for another two years, at which time its market value would have fallen to zero. (The plant depreciates evenly over time.)

(f) Annual plant maintenance costs are £9,900 and allocated general administrative costs £33,750 for the coming year.

Required:

Calculate the annual cost of manufacturing containers for comparison with the quote using relevant figures for establishing the cost or benefit of accepting the quote. Indicate any assumptions or qualifications you wish to make.

Chapter 3

COST–VOLUME–PROFIT ANALYSIS

INTRODUCTION

This chapter is concerned with the relationship between the volume of activity, cost and profit. Broadly, cost can be analysed between an element that is fixed, irrespective of the volume of activity, and an element that varies with the volume of activity. We shall consider how knowledge of this relationship can be used to make decisions and to assess risk, particularly in the context of short-term decisions.

The theme of Chapter 2 concerning relevant costs is further developed in this chapter. We shall examine situations where a whole class of cost – fixed cost – can be treated as irrelevant for decision-making purposes.

Learning outcomes

When you have completed this chapter, you should be able to:

- Distinguish between fixed cost and variable cost and use this distinction to explain the relationship between cost, volume and profit.
- Prepare a break-even chart and deduce the break-even point for some activity.
- Discuss the weaknesses of break-even analysis.
- Demonstrate the way in which marginal analysis can be used when making short-term decisions.

COST BEHAVIOUR

We saw in the previous chapter that cost represents the resources sacrificed to achieve benefits. Costs incurred by a business may be classified in various ways and one useful way is according to how they behave in relation to changes in the volume of activity. Costs may be classified according to whether they

- remain constant (fixed) when changes occur to the volume of activity; or
- vary according to the volume of activity.

These are known as **fixed costs** and **variable costs** respectively. Thus, in the case of a restaurant, the manager's salary would normally be a fixed cost while the cost of the unprepared food would be a variable cost.

As we shall see, knowing how much of each type of cost is associated with a particular activity can be of great value to the decision maker.

FIXED COST

The way in which a fixed cost behaves can be shown by preparing a graph that plots the fixed cost of a business against the level of activity, as in Figure 3.1. The distance 0F represents the amount of fixed cost, and this stays the same irrespective of the volume of activity.

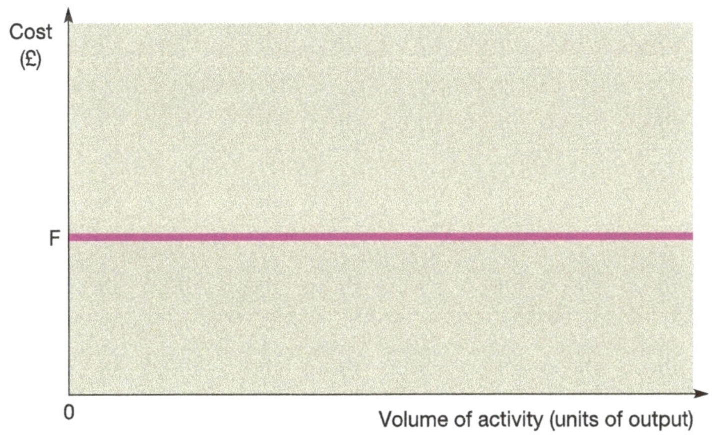

As the volume of activity increases, the fixed cost stays exactly the same (0F).

Figure 3.1 Graph of fixed cost against volume of activity

Activity 3.1

Can you give some examples of items of cost that are likely to be fixed for a hairdressing business?

We came up with the following:

- rent;
- insurance;
- cleaning cost; and
- staff salaries.

These items of cost are likely to be the same irrespective of the number of customers having their hair cut or styled.

Staff salaries (or wages) are often assumed to be a variable cost but in practice they tend to be fixed. Members of staff are not normally paid according to the volume of output and it is unusual to dismiss staff when there is a short-term downturn in activity. Where there is a long-term downturn, or at least it seems that way to management, redundancies may occur with fixed-cost savings. This, however, is true of all types of fixed cost. For example, management may also decide to close some branches to make rental cost savings.

There are circumstances in which the labour cost is variable (for example, where staff are paid according to how much output they produce), but this is unusual. Whether labour cost is fixed or variable depends on the circumstances in the particular case concerned.

It is important to be clear that 'fixed', in this context, means only that the cost is unaffected by changes in the volume of activity. Fixed cost is likely to be affected by inflation. If rent (a typical fixed cost) goes up because of inflation, a fixed cost will have increased, but not because of a change in the volume of activity.

Similarly, the level of fixed cost does not stay the same irrespective of the time period involved. Fixed cost elements are almost always *time-based*: that is, they vary with the length of time concerned. The rental charge for two months is normally twice that for one month. Thus, fixed cost normally varies with time, but (of course) not with the volume of output. This means that when we talk of fixed cost being, say, £1,000, we must add the period concerned, say, £1,000 a month.

Activity 3.2

Does fixed cost stay the same irrespective of the volume of output, even where there is a massive rise in that volume? Think in terms of the rent cost for the hairdressing business.

In fact, the rent is only fixed over a particular range (known as the 'relevant' range). If the number of people wanting to have their hair cut by the business increased, and the business wished to meet this increased demand, it would eventually have to expand its physical size. This might be achieved by opening an additional branch, or perhaps by moving the existing business to larger accommodation. It may be possible to cope with relatively minor increases in activity by using existing space more efficiently, or by having longer opening hours. If activity continued to expand, however, increased rent charges would seem inevitable.

In practice, the situation described in Activity 3.2 would look something like Figure 3.2.

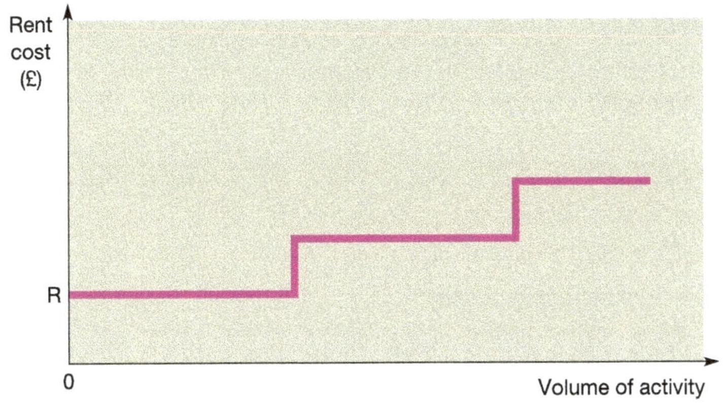

As the volume of activity increases from zero, the rent (a fixed cost) is unaffected. At a particular point, the volume of activity cannot increase further without additional space being rented. The cost of renting the additional space will cause a 'step' in the rent cost. The higher rent cost will continue unaffected if volume rises further until eventually another step point is reached.

Figure 3.2 Graph of rent cost against the volume of activity

At lower volumes of activity, the rent cost shown in Figure 3.2 would be 0R. As the volume of activity expands, the accommodation becomes inadequate and further expansion requires an increase in the size of the accommodation and, therefore, its cost. This higher level of accommodation provision will enable further expansion to take place. Eventually, additional cost will need to be incurred if further expansion is to occur. Elements of fixed cost that behave in this way are often referred to as **stepped fixed costs**.

VARIABLE COST

We saw earlier that variable cost varies with the volume of activity. In a manufacturing business, for example, this would include the cost of raw materials used.

Variable cost can be represented graphically as in Figure 3.3. At zero volume of activity, the variable cost is zero. It then increases in a straight line as activity increases.

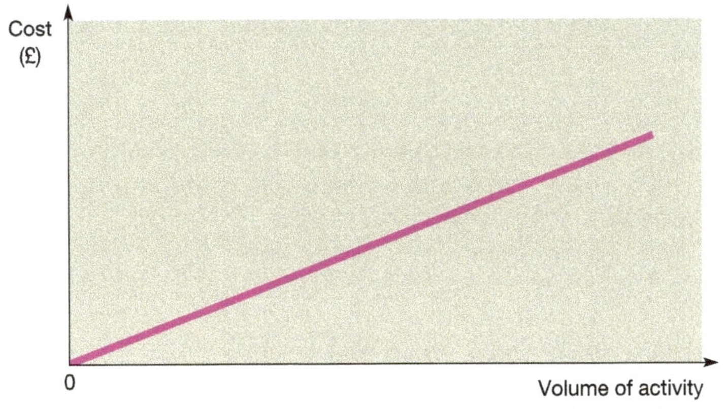

At zero activity, there is no variable cost. However, as the volume of activity increases, so does the variable cost.

Figure 3.3 Graph of variable cost against the volume of activity

Activity 3.3

Can you think of some examples of cost elements that are likely to be variable for a hairdressing business?

We can think of a couple:

- lotions, sprays and other materials used; and
- laundry cost to wash towels used.

You may have thought of some others.

As with many types of business activity, the variable cost incurred by hairdressers tends to be low in comparison with the fixed cost: that is, fixed cost tends to make up the bulk of total cost.

The straight line for variable cost on this graph implies that this type of cost will be the same per unit of activity, irrespective of the volume of activity. We shall consider the practicality of this assumption a little later in this chapter.

SEMI-FIXED (SEMI-VARIABLE) COST

In some cases, a particular cost has an element of both fixed and variable cost. These can be described as **semi-fixed (semi-variable) costs**. An example might be the electricity cost for the hairdressing business. Some of this will be for heating and lighting, and this part is probably fixed, at least until the volume of activity expands to a point where longer opening hours or larger accommodation is necessary. The other part of the cost will vary with the volume of activity. Here we are talking about such things as power for hairdryers.

Activity 3.4

Can you suggest another cost for a hairdressing business that is likely to be semi-fixed (semi-variable)?

We thought of telephone charges for landlines. These tend to have a rental element, which is fixed, and there may also be certain calls that have to be made irrespective of the volume of activity involved. However, increased business would probably lead to the need to make more telephone calls and so to increased call charges.

Analysing semi-fixed (semi-variable) costs

The fixed and variable elements of a particular cost may not always be clear. Past experience, however, can often provide some guidance. Let us again take the example of electricity. If we have data on what the electricity cost has been for various volumes of activity, say the relevant data over several three-month periods (electricity is usually billed by the quarter), we can estimate the fixed and variable elements. The easiest way to do this is to use the **high-low method**. This method involves taking the highest and lowest total electricity cost figures from the range of past quarterly data available. An assumption is then made that the difference between these two quarterly figures is caused entirely by the change in variable cost.

Example 3.1 demonstrates how the fixed and variable elements of electricity cost may be estimated using this method.

Example 3.1

Davos Ltd collected data relating to its electricity cost and volume of activity over several quarters and found the following:

	Lowest quarterly activity	*Highest quarterly activity*
Volume of activity	100,000 units	180,000 units
Total electricity cost	£80,000	£120,000

We can see that an increase in activity of 80,000 units (that is, from 100,000 to 180,000 units) led to an increase in total electricity cost of £40,000 (that is from £80,000 to £120,000). As it is assumed that this increase is caused by an increase in variable cost, the variable cost per unit of output must be £40,000/80,000 = £0.50 per unit.

The breakdown in total electricity cost for the highest and lowest quarters will therefore be as follows:

	Lowest quarterly activity	*Highest quarterly activity*
Volume of activity	100,000 units	180,000 units
	£	£
Variable cost		
100,000 × £0.50	50,000	
180,000 × £0.50		90,000
Fixed cost (balancing figure)	30,000	30,000
Total electricity cost	80,000	120,000

Activity 3.5

What is the weakness of using the high-low approach?

The weakness of this method is that it relies on only two points in a range of information relating to quarterly electricity charges. It ignores all other information.

A more reliable estimate of the fixed and variable cost elements can be made if the full range of electricity cost for each quarter is used in the analysis. By plotting total electricity cost against the volume of activity for each quarter, a graph that looks like the one shown in Figure 3.4 may be produced.

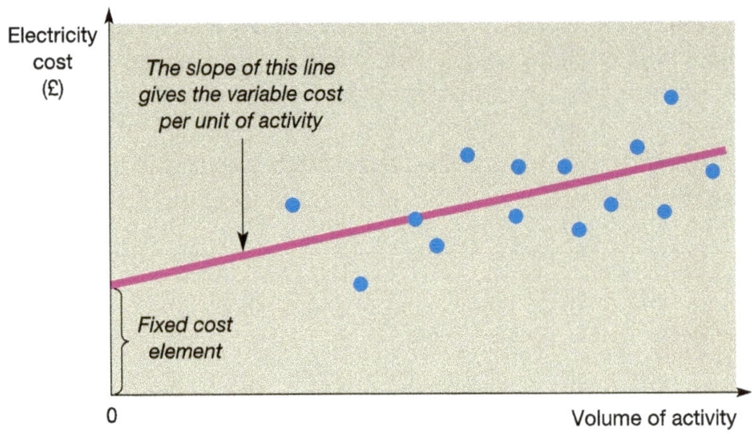

Here the electricity bill for a time period (for example, three months) is plotted against the volume of activity for that same period. This is done for a series of periods. A line is then drawn that best 'fits' the various points on the graph. From this line we can then deduce both the cost at zero activity (the fixed element) and the slope of the line (the variable element).

Figure 3.4 Graph of electricity cost against the volume of activity

Each of the dots in Figure 3.4 is the electricity charge for a particular quarter plotted against the volume of activity (probably measured in terms of sales revenue) for the same quarter. The diagonal line on the graph is the *line of best fit*. This means that this was the line that best seemed (to us, at least) to represent the data. A better estimate can usually be made using a statistical technique (*least squares regression*), which does not involve drawing graphs and making estimates. In terms of accuracy, however, there is probably little practical difference between the two approaches.

From the graph we can say that the fixed element of the electricity cost is the amount represented by the vertical distance from the origin at zero (bottom left-hand corner) to the point where the line of best fit crosses the vertical axis of the graph. The variable cost per unit is the amount that the graph line rises for each increase in the volume of activity.

Armed with knowledge of how much each element of cost represents for a particular product or service, it is possible to make predictions regarding total and per-unit cost at various projected levels of output. Such information can be very useful to decision makers. Much of the rest of this chapter will be devoted to seeing how it can be useful, starting with **break-even analysis**.

FINDING THE BREAK-EVEN POINT

If, for a particular product or service, we know the fixed cost for a period and the variable cost per unit, we can produce a graph like the one shown in Figure 3.5. This graph shows the total cost over the possible range of volume of activity.

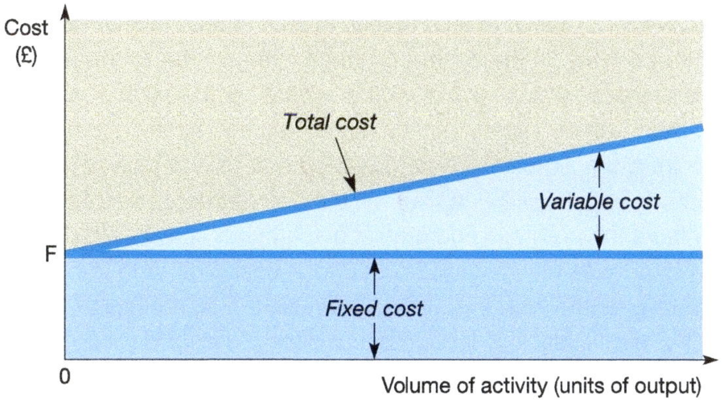

The bottom part of the graph represents the fixed cost element. To this is added the wedge-shaped top portion, which represents the variable cost. The two parts together represent total cost. At zero activity, the variable cost is zero, so total cost equals fixed cost. As activity increases so does total cost, but only because variable cost increases. We are assuming that there are no steps in the fixed cost.

Figure 3.5 Graph of total cost against volume of activity

The bottom part of Figure 3.5 shows the fixed cost area. Added to this is the variable cost, the wedge-shaped portion at the top of the graph. The uppermost line represents the total cost over a range of volume of activity. For any particular volume, the total cost can be measured by the vertical distance between the graph's horizontal axis and the relevant point on the uppermost line.

Logically, the total cost at zero activity is the amount of the fixed cost. This is because, even where there is nothing happening, the business will still be paying rent, salaries and so on, at least in the short term. As the volume of activity increases from zero, the fixed cost is augmented by the relevant variable cost to give the total cost.

If we take this total cost graph in Figure 3.5, and superimpose on it a line representing total revenue over the range of volume of activity, we obtain the **break-even chart**. This is shown in Figure 3.6.

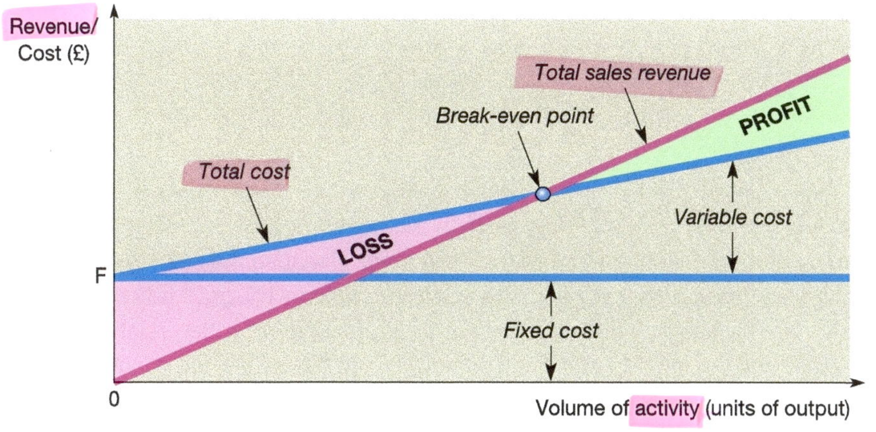

The sloping line starting at zero represents the sales revenue at various volumes of activity. The point at which this finally catches up with the sloping total cost line, which starts at F, is the break-even point (BEP). Below this point a loss is made, above it a profit.

Figure 3.6 Break-even chart

Note in Figure 3.6 that, at zero volume of activity (zero sales), there is zero sales revenue. The profit (loss), which is the difference between total sales revenue and total cost, for a particular volume of activity, is the vertical distance between the total sales revenue line and the total cost line at that volume of activity. Where there is no vertical distance between these two lines (total sales revenue equals total cost) the volume of activity is at **break-even point (BEP)**. At this point there is neither profit nor loss; that is, the activity *breaks even*. Where the volume of activity is below BEP, a loss will be incurred because total cost exceeds total sales revenue. Where the business operates at a volume of activity above BEP, there will be a profit because total sales revenue will exceed total cost. The further the volume of activity is below BEP, the higher the loss: the further above BEP it is, the higher the profit.

Deducing BEPs graphically is a laborious business. Since, however, the relationships in the graph are all linear (that is, the lines are all straight), it is easy to calculate the BEP.

We know that at BEP (but not at any other volume of activity)

Total sales revenue = Total cost

(At all other volumes of activity except the BEP, either total sales revenue will exceed total cost or the other way round. Only at BEP are they equal.) The above formula can be expanded so that

Total sales revenue = Fixed cost + Variable cost

If we call the number of units of output at BEP *b*, then

$$b \times \text{Sales revenue per unit} = \text{Fixed cost} + (b \times \text{Variable cost per unit})$$

so

$$(b \times \text{Sales revenue per unit}) - (b \times \text{Variable cost per unit}) = \text{Fixed cost}$$

and

$$b \times (\text{Sales revenue per unit} - \text{Variable cost per unit}) = \text{Fixed cost}$$

giving

$$b = \frac{\textbf{Fixed cost}}{\textbf{Sales revenue per unit} - \textbf{Variable cost per unit}}$$

If we look back at the break-even chart in Figure 3.6, this formula seems logical. The total cost line starts off at point F, higher than the starting point for the total sales revenues line (zero) by amount F (the amount of the fixed cost). Because the sales revenue per unit is greater than the variable cost per unit, the sales revenue line will gradually catch up with the total cost line. The rate at which it will catch up is dependent on the relative steepness of the two lines. Bearing in mind that the slopes of the two lines are the variable cost per unit and the selling price per unit, the above equation for calculating *b* looks perfectly logical.

Though the BEP can be calculated quickly and simply without resorting to graphs, this does not mean that the break-even chart is without value. The chart shows the relationship between cost, volume and profit over a range of activity and in a form that can easily be understood by non-financial managers. The break-even chart can therefore be a useful device for explaining this relationship.

Example 3.2

Cottage Industries Ltd makes baskets. The fixed cost of operating the workshop for a month totals £500. Each basket requires materials that cost £2 and takes one hour to make. The business pays the basket makers £10 an hour. The basket makers are all on contracts such that if they do not work for any reason, they are not paid. The baskets are sold to a wholesaler for £14 each.

What is the BEP for basket making for the business?

Solution

The BEP (in number of baskets) is:

$$\text{BEP} = \frac{\text{Fixed cost}}{(\text{Sales revenue per unit} - \text{Variable cost per unit})}$$

$$= \frac{£500}{£14 - (£2 + £10)} = 250 \text{ baskets per month}$$

Note that the BEP must be expressed with respect to a period of time.

Real World 3.1 shows information on the BEPs of two well-known businesses.

Real World 3.1

BE at Ryanair (and BA)

Commercial airlines seem to pay a lot of attention to their BEPs and their 'load factors', that is, their actual level of activity. Figure 3.7 shows the BEPs and load factors for Ryanair, the 'no-frills' carrier.

We can see that Ryanair made operating profits in each of the six years considered. This is because the airline's load factor was consistently greater than its BEP.

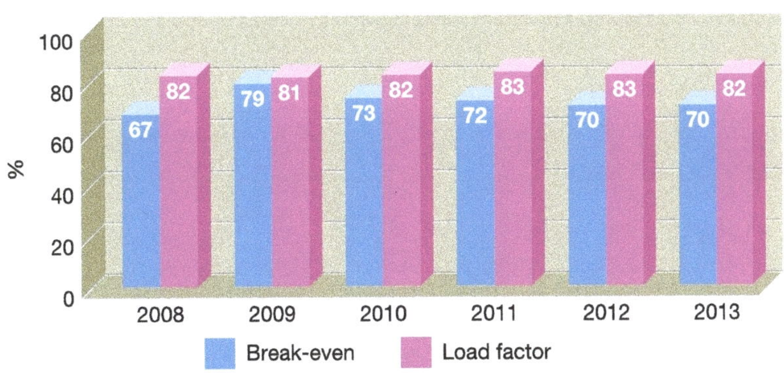

Figure 3.7 Break-even and load factors at Ryanair

Most airlines do not publish their break-even points. British Airways plc (BA) used to do so. In the most recent year that BA disclosed its BEP (2008) it was 64 per cent, with a load factor of 71 per cent. Those figures were quite typical of BA's results during previous recent years. BA is now part of International Airlines Group.

Source: Based on information contained in the Ryanair Holdings plc Annual Report 2013 and British Airways plc Annual Report 2008.

Activity 3.6

In Real World 3.1, we saw that Ryanair's break-even point varied from one year to the next. It was as low as 67 per cent in 2008, but as high as 79 per cent in 2009. Why was it not roughly the same each year?

Break-even point depends on three broad factors. These are sales revenue, variable cost and fixed cost. Each of these can vary quite noticeably from one year to another. Ryanair's sales revenue could be greatly affected by the level of disposable income among the travelling public and/or by levels of competition from other airlines. Costs can vary from one year to another, particularly the cost of aviation fuel.

[Interestingly, Ryanair's average fuel cost was €2.351 per gallon in 2009, but only €1.515 in 2010, €1.756 in 2011 and €2.075 in 2012. It seems that this major cost for the business can vary widely from one year to the next.]

Activity 3.7

Can you think of reasons why the managers of a business might find it useful to know the BEP of some activity that they are planning to undertake?

By knowing the BEP, it is possible to compare the expected, or planned, volume of activity with the BEP and so make a judgement about risk. If the volume of activity is expected to be only just above the break-even point, this may suggest that it is a risky venture. Only a small fall from the expected volume of activity could lead to a loss.

Activity 3.8

Cottage Industries Ltd (see Example 3.2) expects to sell 500 baskets a month. The business has the opportunity to rent a basket-making machine. Doing so would increase the total fixed cost of operating the workshop for a month to £3,000. Using the machine would reduce the labour time to half an hour per basket. The basket makers would still be paid £10 an hour.

(a) How much profit would the business make each month from selling baskets
- **without the machine; and**
- **with the machine?**

(b) What is the BEP if the machine is rented?

(c) What do you notice about the figures that you calculate?

(a) Estimated monthly profit from basket making:

	Without the machine		*With the machine*	
	£	£	£	£
Sales revenue (500 × £14)		7,000		7,000
Materials (500 × £2)	(1,000)		(1,000)	
Labour (500 × 1 × £10)	(5,000)			
(500 × ½ × £10)			(2,500)	
Fixed cost	(500)		(3,000)	
		(6,500)		(6,500)
Profit		500		500

(b) The BEP (in number of baskets) with the machine:

$$\text{BEP} = \frac{\text{Fixed cost}}{\text{Sales revenue per unit} - \text{Variable cost per unit}}$$

$$= \frac{\pounds 3{,}000}{\pounds 14 - (\pounds 2 + \pounds 5)} = 429 \text{ baskets a month}$$

The BEP without the machine is 250 baskets per month (see Example 3.2).

(c) There seems to be nothing to choose between the two manufacturing strategies regarding profit, at the expected sales volume. There is, however, a distinct difference between the two strategies regarding the BEP. Without the machine, the actual volume of sales could fall by a half of that which is expected (from 500 to 250) before the business would fail to make a profit. With the machine, however, a reduction in the volume of sales of just 14 per cent (from 500 to 429) would be enough to cause the business to fail to make a profit. On the other hand, for each additional basket sold above the estimated 500, an additional profit of only £2 (that is, £14 – (£2 + £10)) would be made without the machine, whereas £7 (that is, £14 – (£2 + £5)) would be made with the machine. (Note how knowledge of the BEP and the planned volume of activity gives some basis for assessing the riskiness of the activity.)

Real World 3.2 discusses the effect of low volume of activity, reduced selling prices and high fixed costs on European car-making businesses.

Real World 3.2

Cars at the crossroads

With consumer confidence waning and demand for cars falling, Europe's mass-market auto industry is in a worsening crisis that mirrors the teetering state of the continent's finances. Car sales, already in a deep decline in the southern European countries at the heart of the euro crisis, are now falling in Germany too – down 5 per cent in May, data published this week show. Plants such as Fiat's flagship Mirafiori factory in Turin and PSA Peugeot Citroën's in Aulnay, near Paris, are cutting shifts and working days to compensate for lower demand. Fiat last week began offering recession-hit Italians cheap petrol at €1 a litre to persuade them to buy its cars.

While carmakers are cutting their production schedules to keep inventories under control, there is still a glut of cars on the market, which is prompting competitive discounting to the point where some producers are thought to be losing money on every car they sell. So excess capacity is hitting European carmakers twice – in the fixed cost they pay for underutilised plants, then the higher discounts they underwrite to move unsold cars off dealership forecourts.

FT *Source*: Adapted from Reed, J. (2012) Eurozone carmakers face downsize failure, ft.com, 6 June.

We shall take a closer look at the relationship between fixed cost, variable cost and profit together with any advice that we might give the management of Cottage Industries Ltd after we have briefly considered the notion of contribution.

CONTRIBUTION

The bottom part of the break-even formula (sales revenue per unit less variable cost per unit) is known as the **contribution per unit**. Thus, for the basket-making activity, without the machine the contribution per unit is £2 and with the machine it is £7. This can be quite a useful figure to know in a decision-making context. It is called 'contribution' because it contributes to meeting the fixed cost and, if there is any excess, it then contributes to profit.

We shall see, a little later in this chapter, how knowing the amount of the contribution generated by a particular activity can be valuable in making short-term decisions of various types, as well as being useful in the BEP calculation.

Contribution margin ratio

The **contribution margin ratio** is the contribution from an activity expressed as a percentage of the sales revenue, thus:

$$\textbf{Contribution margin ratio} = \frac{\textbf{Contribution}}{\textbf{Sales revenue}} \times 100\%$$

Contribution and sales revenue can both be expressed in per-unit or total terms. For Cottage Industries Ltd (Example 3.2 and Activity 3.8), the contribution margin ratios are:

$$\text{Without the machine, } \frac{14-12}{14} \times 100\% = 14\%$$

$$\text{With the machine, } \frac{14-7}{14} \times 100\% = 50\%$$

The ratio can provide an impression of the extent to which sales revenue is eaten away by variable cost.

MARGIN OF SAFETY

The **margin of safety** is the extent to which the planned volume of output or sales lies above the BEP. To illustrate how the margin of safety is calculated, we can use the information in Activity 3.8 relating to each option.

	Without the machine (number of baskets)	*With the machine (number of baskets)*
(a) Expected volume of sales	500	500
(b) BEP	250	429
Margin of safety (the difference between (a) and (b))	250	71
Expressed as a percentage of expected volume of sales	50%	14%

The margin of safety can be used as a partial measure of risk.

Activity 3.9

What advice would you give Cottage Industries Ltd about renting the machine, on the basis of the values for margin of safety?

It is a matter of personal judgement, which in turn is related to individual attitudes to risk, as to which strategy to adopt. Most people, however, would prefer the strategy of not renting the machine, since the margin of safety between the expected volume of activity and the BEP is much greater. Thus, for the same level of return, the risk will be lower without renting the machine.

The relative margins of safety are directly linked to the relationship between the selling price per basket, the variable cost per basket and the fixed cost per month. Without the machine the contribution (selling price less variable cost) per basket is £2; with the machine it is £7. On the other hand, without the machine the fixed cost is £500 a month; with the machine it is £3,000. This means that, with the machine, the contributions have more fixed cost to 'overcome' before the activity becomes profitable. However, the rate at which the contributions can overcome fixed cost is higher with the machine, because variable cost is lower. Thus, one more, or one fewer, basket sold has a greater impact on profit than it does if the machine is not rented. The contrast between the two scenarios is shown graphically in Figure 3.8.

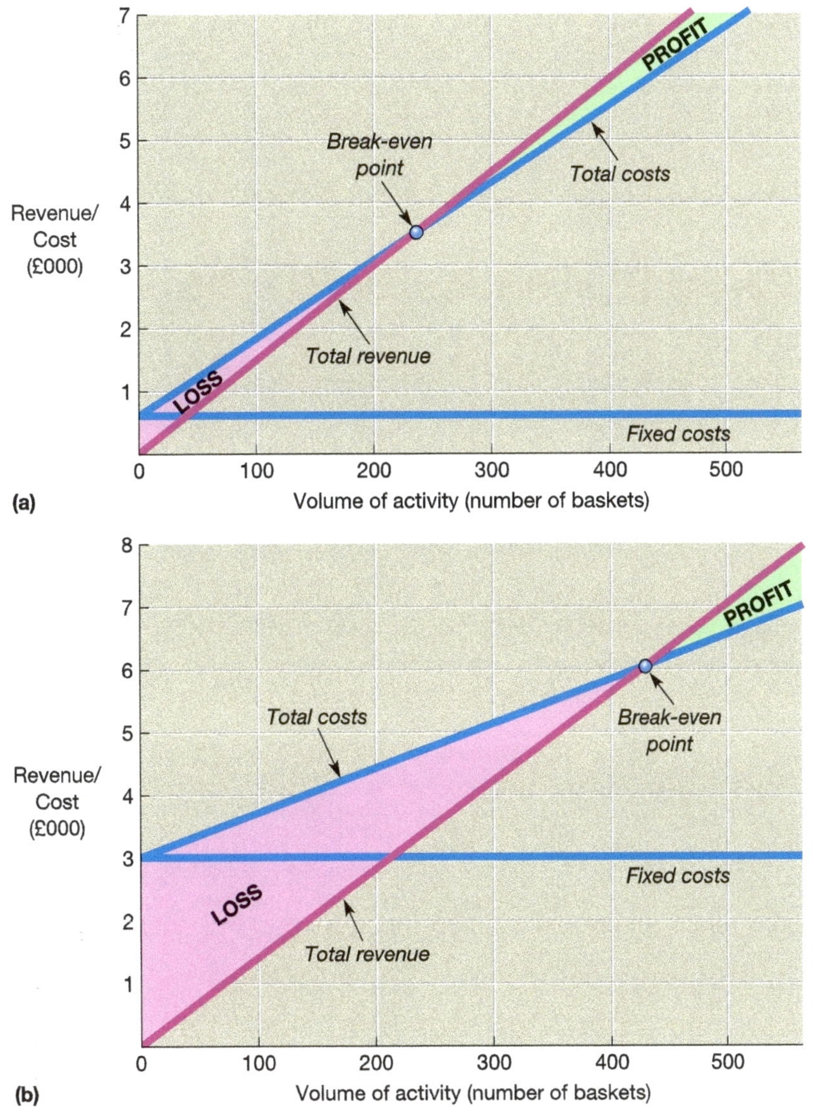

Without the machine the contribution per basket is low. Thus, each additional basket sold does not make a dramatic difference to the profit or loss. With the machine, however, the opposite is true; small increases or decreases in the sales volume will have a great effect on the profit or loss.

Figure 3.8 Break-even charts for Cottage Industries Ltd's basket-making activities (a) without the machine and (b) with the machine

Looking back to Real World 3.1 (page 69), we can see that Ryanair typically had a much larger margin of safety than BA.

Real World 3.3 goes into more detail on Ryanair's margin of safety and operating profit over recent years.

Real World 3.3

Ryanair's margin of safety

As we saw in Real World 3.1, commercial airlines pay a lot of attention to BEPs. They are also interested in their margin of safety (the difference between load factor and BEP).

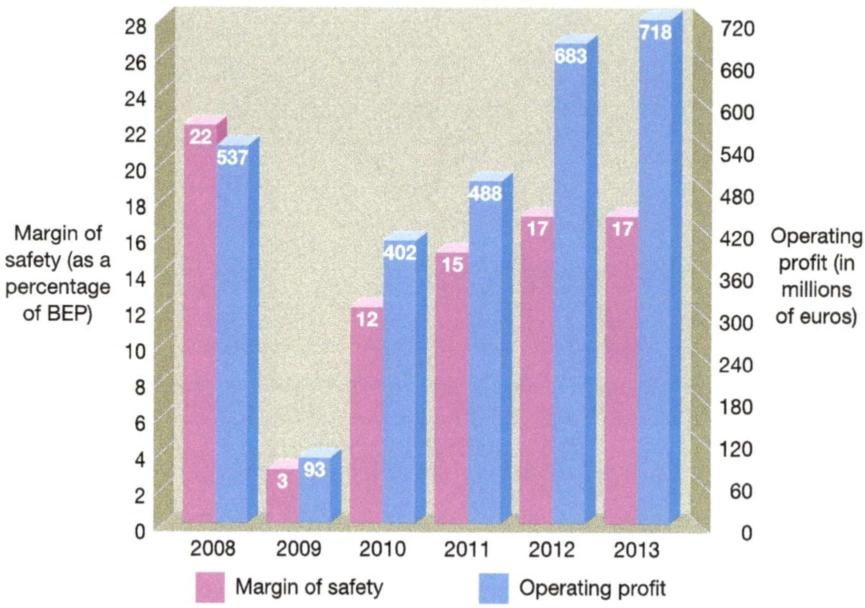

The margin of safety is expressed as the difference between the load factor and the BEP (for each year), expressed as a percentage of the BEP. Generally, the higher the margin of safety, the higher the operating profit.

Figure 3.9 Ryanair's margin of safety

Figure 3.9 shows Ryanair's margin of safety and its operating profit over a six-year period. Note that in 2009, Ryanair had a load factor that was only just above its break-even point and this led to an unusually small operating profit. In the other years, the load factors were comfortably greater than the BEP. This led to more substantial operating profits.

Source: Based on information contained in the Ryanair Holdings plc Annual Report 2013.

ACHIEVING A TARGET PROFIT

In the same way as we can derive the number of units of output necessary to break even, we can calculate the volume of activity required to achieve a particular level of profit. We can expand the equation given in the section 'Finding the break-even point' (on page 66) so that:

$$\text{Total sales revenue} = \text{Fixed cost} + \text{Total variable cost} + \text{Target profit}$$

If we let t be the required number of units of output to achieve the target profit, then

$$t \times \text{Sales revenue per unit} = \text{Fixed cost} + (t \times \text{Variable cost per unit}) + \text{Target profit}$$

so

$$(t \times \text{Sales revenue per unit}) - (t \times \text{Variable cost per unit}) = \text{Fixed cost} + \text{Target profit}$$

and

$$t \times (\text{Sales revenue per unit} - \text{Variable cost per unit}) = \text{Fixed cost} + \text{Target profit}$$

giving

$$t = \frac{\textbf{Fixed cost} + \textbf{Target profit}}{\textbf{Sales revenue per unit} - \textbf{Variable cost per unit}}$$

Activity 3.10

Cottage Industries Ltd (see Example 3.2 and Activity 3.8) has a target profit of £4,000 a month. What volume of activity is required to achieve this

(a) without the machine; and
(b) with the machine?

(a) Using the formula above, the required volume of activity without the machine:

$$\frac{\text{Fixed cost} + \text{Target profit}}{\text{Sales revenue per unit} - \text{Variable cost per unit}}$$

$$= \frac{£500 + £4{,}000}{£14 - (£2 + £10)}$$

$$= 2{,}250 \text{ baskets a month}$$

(b) The required volume of activity with the machine:

$$\frac{£3{,}000 + £4{,}000}{£14 - (£2 + £5)} = 1{,}000 \text{ baskets a month}$$

OPERATING GEARING AND ITS EFFECT ON PROFIT

The relationship between contribution and fixed cost is known as **operating gearing** (or operational gearing). An activity with a relatively high fixed cost compared with its total variable cost, at its normal level of activity, is said to have high operating gearing. Thus, Cottage Industries Ltd has higher operating gearing using the machine than it has if not using it. Renting the machine increases the level of operating gearing quite dramatically because it causes an increase in fixed cost, but at the same time it leads to a reduction in variable cost per basket.

The reason why the word 'gearing' is used in this context is that, as with intermeshing gear wheels of different circumferences, a movement in one of the factors (volume of output) causes a more-than-proportionate movement in the other (profit) as illustrated by Figure 3.10.

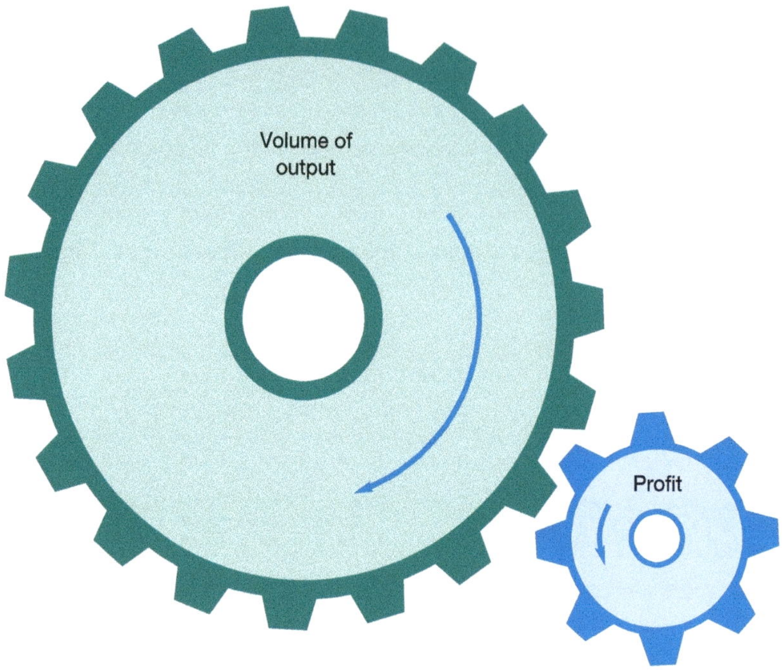

Where operating gearing is relatively high, as in the diagram, a small amount of motion in the volume wheel causes a relatively large amount of motion in the profit wheel. An increase in volume would cause a disproportionately greater increase in profit. The equivalent would also be true of a decrease in activity, however.

Figure 3.10 The effect of operating gearing

Increasing the level of operating gearing makes profit more sensitive to changes in the volume of activity. We can demonstrate operating gearing with Cottage Industries Ltd's basket-making activities as follows:

	Without the machine			*With the machine*		
Volume (number of baskets)	500	1,000	1,500	500	1,000	1,500
	£	£	£	£	£	£
Contributions*	1,000	2,000	3,000	3,500	7,000	10,500
Fixed cost	(500)	(500)	(500)	(3,000)	(3,000)	(3,000)
Profit	500	1,500	2,500	500	4,000	7,500

* £2 per basket without the machine and £7 per basket with it.

Note that, without the machine (low operating gearing), a doubling of the output from 500 to 1,000 units brings a trebling of the profit. With the machine (high operating gearing), a doubling of output from 500 units causes profit to rise by eight times. At the same time, reductions in the volume of output tend to have a more damaging effect on profit where the operating gearing is higher.

Activity 3.11

What types of business activity are likely to have high operating gearing? (*Hint*: Cottage Industries Ltd might give you some idea.)

Activities that are capital-intensive tend to have high operating gearing. This is because renting or owning capital equipment gives rise to additional fixed cost, but it can also give rise to lower variable cost.

Real World 3.4 shows how a very well-known business has benefited from high operating gearing.

Real World 3.4

Delivering profit through operating gearing

Royal Mail plc, the recently-privatised parcel and letter delivery business, believes that its high level of operating gearing is causing the rate of increases in profits to be greater than the rate of the increase in sales revenue. In its preliminary financial results statement for the year 2012/13, the business said that it is strongly affected by operating gearing. It explained that this had caused a 1 per cent increase in revenue, over the previous year, to lead to a 17 per cent increase in operating profit.

Royal Mail is exactly the type of business where a very great deal of its costs are fixed, such as premises occupancy costs, salaries and wages, plant depreciation, motor vehicle running costs and training.

Source: Royal Mail plc 2012/13 Results, 27 November 2013.

PROFIT–VOLUME CHARTS

A slight variant of the break-even chart is the **profit–volume (PV) chart**. A typical PV chart is shown in Figure 3.11.

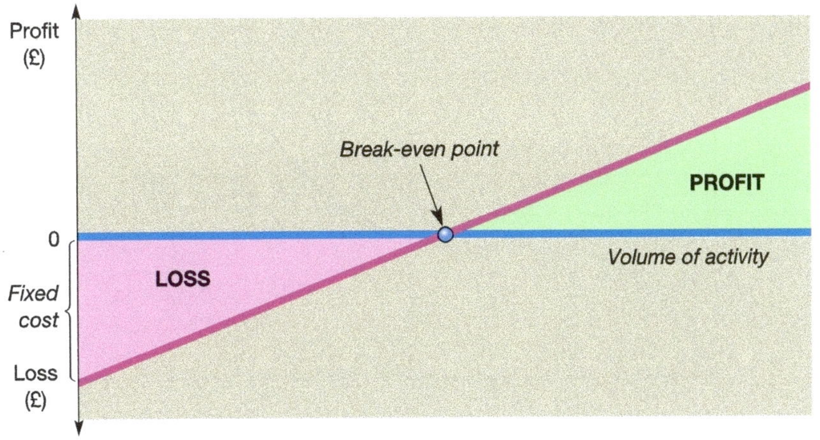

The sloping line is profit (loss) plotted against activity. As activity increases, so does total contribution (sales revenue less variable cost). At zero activity there is no contribution, so there will be a loss equal in amount to the total fixed cost.

Figure 3.11 Profit–volume chart

The PV chart is obtained by plotting loss or profit against volume of activity. The slope of the graph is equal to the contribution per unit, since each additional unit sold decreases the loss, or increases the profit, by the sales revenue per unit less the variable cost per unit. At zero volume of activity there is no contribution, so there is a loss equal to the amount of the fixed cost. As the volume of activity increases, the amount of the loss gradually decreases until BEP is reached. Beyond BEP a profit is made, which increases as activity increases.

As we can see, the PV chart does not tell us anything not shown by the break-even chart. It does, however, highlight key information concerning the profit (loss) arising at any volume of activity. The break-even chart shows this as the vertical distance between the total cost and total sales revenue lines. The PV chart, in effect, combines the total sales revenue and total variable cost lines, which means that profit (or loss) is directly readable.

THE ECONOMIST'S VIEW OF THE BREAK-EVEN CHART

So far in this chapter we have treated all the relationships as linear – that is, all of the lines in the graphs have been straight. However, this may not be strictly valid.

Consider, for example, the variable cost line in the break-even chart; accountants would normally treat this as being a straight line. In reality, however, the line may not be straight because at high levels of output economies of scale may be available to an extent not available at lower levels. For example, a raw material (a typical variable cost) may be able to be used more efficiently with higher volumes of activity. Similarly, buying large quantities of material and services may enable the business to benefit from bulk discounts and so lower the cost. On the other hand, higher volumes may lead to higher variable cost per unit of output. For instance, high usage of a particular raw material may lead to shortages, which might cause higher prices to have to be paid for supplies. In either case, the cost per unit would not be constant over all volumes of activity.

There is also a tendency for sales revenue per unit to reduce as volume is increased. To sell more of a particular product or service, it will usually be necessary to lower the price per unit.

Economists recognise that, in real life, the relationships portrayed in the break-even chart are usually non-linear. The typical economist's view of the chart is shown in Figure 3.12.

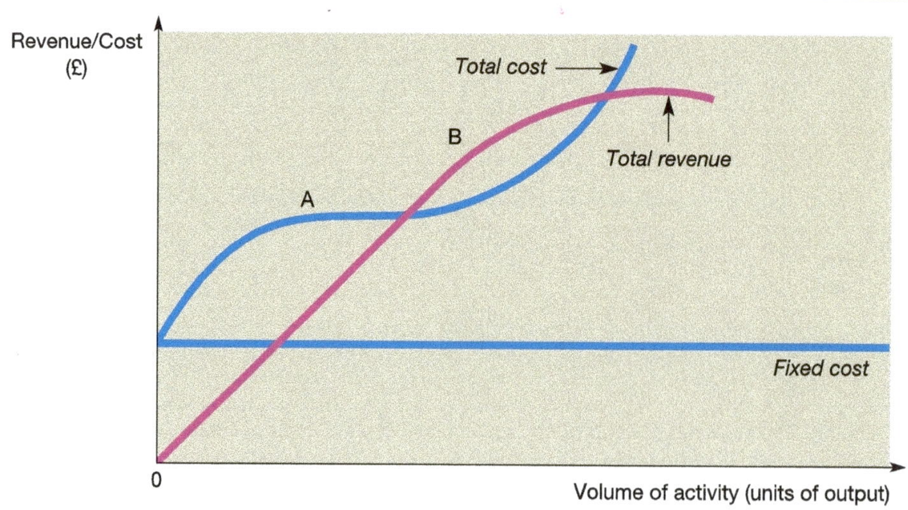

As volume increases, economies of scale have a favourable effect on variable cost, but this effect is reversed at still higher levels of output. At the same time, sales revenue per unit will tend to decrease at higher levels to encourage additional buyers.

Figure 3.12 The economist's view of the break-even chart

Note, in Figure 3.12, that the total variable cost line starts to rise quite steeply with volume but, around point A, economies of scale start to take effect. With further increases in volume, total variable cost does not rise as steeply because the variable cost *for each additional unit of output* is lowered. These economies of scale continue to have a benign effect on cost until a point is reached where the business is operating towards the end of its efficient range. Beyond this range, problems will emerge that adversely affect variable cost. For example, the business may be unable to find cheap supplies of the variable-cost elements, as mentioned above, or may suffer production difficulties, such as machine breakdowns. As a result, the total variable cost line starts to rise more steeply.

At low levels of output, sales may be made at a relatively high price per unit. To increase sales output beyond point B, however, it may be necessary to lower the average sales price per unit. This will mean that the total revenue line will not rise as steeply, and may even curve downwards. Note how this 'curvilinear' representation of the break-even chart can easily lead to the existence of more than one break-even point.

Accountants justify their approach by arguing that, although the lines may not, in practice, be perfectly straight, this defect is not usually worth taking into account. This is partly because information used in the analysis is based on estimates of the future. These estimates will, inevitably, be flawed because of our inability to predict with great accuracy. It is pointless, it can be argued, to be concerned with the minor approximation of treating total cost and total revenue lines as straight. Only where significant economies or diseconomies of scale are involved should the non-linearity of variable cost be taken into account. Furthermore, for most businesses, the range of possible volumes of activity over which they operate (the **relevant range**) is quite narrow. When dealing with short distances, it may be perfectly reasonable to treat a curved line as being straight.

FAILING TO BREAK EVEN

Where a business fails to reach its BEP, steps must be taken to remedy the problem: there must be an increase in sales revenue or a reduction in cost, or both.

Real World 3.5 discusses how the car maker Volvo failed to reach its BEP during 2013.

Real World 3.5

Not breaking China

Volvo Cars swung into a loss in the first half as a tough market in Europe continued to weigh on the Swedish premium carmaker and caused a drop in revenues. But Håkan Samuelsson, chief executive of the company owned by China's Geely, insisted that Volvo could reach its target of breaking even this year in spite of an operating loss of SKr577 million, compared with a profit of SKr349 million in the first half of 2012. Revenues fell 14 per cent to SKr56.4 billion.

Volvo has struggled in recent years as sales at the Swedish group famous for its safety standards are seen as too low to enjoy big economies of scale, while its brand has a lesser image than larger rivals such as BMW and Audi. But Mr Samuelsson, a former chief executive of German truckmaker MAN, said he was confident about breaking even for four reasons: new vehicles are being introduced this half-year; Volvo cut inventories heavily in the first six months; the sales trend in July and August was positive; and 'the lion's share' of its SKr1.5 billion cost-cutting programme had already been achieved.

→

'This is absolutely according to plan, especially as this stock [inventories] reduction has made these six months tougher. It also means that according to plan we have to turn this around. But we are confident this is possible,' Mr Samuelsson said.

FT *Source*: Milne, R. (2013) Volvo Cars swings into loss amid tough European markets, ft.com, 4 September.

WEAKNESSES OF BREAK-EVEN ANALYSIS

Although break-even analysis can provide useful insights concerning the relationship between cost, volume and profit, it does have its weaknesses. There are three general problems:

1 *Non-linear relationships*. Break-even analysis, as it is generally used, tends to assume that total variable cost and total revenue lines are perfectly straight when plotted against volume of output. In real life, this is unlikely to be the case. We saw earlier, however, that, in practice, minor variations from strict linearity are unlikely to be significant and that, over the relevant range of business operations, curved lines tend to be fairly straight.
2 *Stepped fixed cost*. Most types of fixed cost are not fixed over the whole range of activity. They tend to be 'stepped' in the way depicted in Figure 3.2. This means that, in practice, great care must be taken in making assumptions about fixed cost. The problem is heightened because many activities will involve various types of fixed cost (for example rent, supervisory salaries, administration cost), all of which are likely to have steps at different points.
3 *Multi-product businesses*. Most businesses provide more than one product (or service). This can be a problem for break-even analysis since additional sales of one product may affect sales of another of the business's products. There is also the problem of identifying the fixed cost associated with a particular product. Fixed cost may relate to more than one product – for example, production of more than one product may be carried out in the same rented accommodation. There are ways of dividing the fixed cost between products, but these tend to be arbitrary, which would undermine the value of the break-even analysis.

Activity 3.12

We saw above that, in practice, relationships between costs, revenues and volumes of activity are not necessarily straight-line ones.

Can you think of at least three reasons, with examples, why this may be the case?

We thought of the following:

- *Economies of scale with labour.* A business may operate more economically at a higher volume of activity. For example, employees may be able to increase productivity by specialising in particular tasks.
- *Economies of scale with buying goods or services.* A business may find it cheaper to buy in goods and services where it is buying in bulk as discounts are often given.
- *Diseconomies of scale.* This may mean that the per-unit cost of output is higher at higher levels of activity. For example, it may be necessary to pay higher rates of pay to workers to recruit the additional staff needed at higher volumes of activity.

- *Lower sales prices at high levels of activity.* Some consumers may only be prepared to buy the particular product or service at a lower price. Thus, it may not be possible to achieve high levels of sales activity without lowering the selling price.

Despite some practical problems, break-even analysis seems to be widely used. The media frequently refer to the BEP for businesses and activities. There is seemingly constant discussion, for example, about Eurotunnel's BEP and whether it will ever be reached. Similarly, the number of people regularly needed to pay to watch a football team so that the club breaks even is often mentioned. This is illustrated in **Real World 3.6**, which is taken from an article discussing the need for Plymouth Argyle FC, the English Football League 2 club, to increase average attendances.

Real World 3.6

Not enough Pilgrims

The Plymouth Argyle owner, James Brent, said that the attendance at home matches, which averages about 6,300, is below, but 'not a million miles away' from, the figure that enables the club to break even. He went on to say that he would need to put in some extra funds to meet the shortfall, but was happy with that situation.

Source: Information taken from Plymouth Herald (2012) James Brent: Plymouth Argyle is in good financial fettle, *Plymouth Herald*, 2 November.

Real World 3.7 describes three different situations where breaking even is considered.

Real World 3.7

Breaking even is breaking out all over

McLaren to break even

British supercar manufacturer McLaren will break even this year ahead of an expansion drive into Asia and higher-volume segments as it aims to more than double its annual sales. The carmaker, famous for its million-dollar sports cars such as the P1, quadrupled its sales last year and is betting on Chinese demand to spearhead an increase in sales to 4,000 by mid-decade.

McLaren Automotive, part of a group that includes the storied McLaren Formula 1 racing team, will launch a less expensive sports car in 2015, its chief executive said, and two new models each year from 2016 onwards. 'I expect about 1,500 [sales] this year and next year, and then after we get P13, around 4,000 cars,' said Mike Flewitt, referring to the new, lower-cost model in development.

Despite a recent slowdown in economic growth and the country's car market, mainland China has become key for rival luxury marques such as Ferrari and Lamborghini. The country is expected to overtake the US as the biggest premium car market by the end of the decade.

FT *Source*: Adapted from Foy, H. (2013) McLaren to break even ahead of expansion, ft.com, 30 September.

→

Light blues to break even

High-spending Manchester City made a net loss of £51.6 million last season, nearly halving its losses from the previous year but still risking a breach of Uefa's new break-even rules. The Abu Dhabi-owned club published its annual report showing revenues at £271 million and zero debt after all loans from its owner, Sheikh Mansour Mansour bin Zayed al Nahyan, a member of the emirate's royal family, were paid off.

The report makes no mention of Uefa's financial fair play rules and whether the club considers it is in compliance. In order to compete in Uefa competitions next season, the European football governing body allows clubs to make losses of up to €45m over the 2011/12 and 2012/13 seasons.

Manchester City's cumulative losses for the last two seasons add up to £149.5m. However, clubs are allowed certain exemptions, including infrastructure and youth development costs and wages of players signed before 2010. People with knowledge of the situation said, once these sums are taken into account, City is likely to show losses for the compliance period at around the €45m threshold.

Uefa, which can impose sanctions on clubs in breach of the rules, may also take into account the general trend of a club's finances. Without mentioning the Uefa rules, City chief executive Ferran Soriano said: 'Growing revenues and controlled expenses are bringing the club to break-even in the immediate future and profitability thereafter.'

FT *Source*: Adapted from Blitz, R. (2014) Manchester City losses almost halved, ft.com, 29 January.

Derailed Hornby will only break even

Punctuality, it seems, is just as important for toy-train companies as real ones. Hornby, maker of model rail sets, has issued its second profit warning in 18 months, blaming delays in its supply chain. In an update on trading since the beginning of October, Hornby said problems with a Chinese supplier of rail kit meant that trains would now account for only 61 per cent of sales in the UK and 68 per cent in Europe in the year to March, compared with expectations for 88 per cent and 80 per cent respectively.

Hornby, which also owns the Scalextric slot-car brand, said it expected to break even on an underlying pre-tax level in the 12 months to the end of March. However, the supply delays meant the company had suffered a decline in the value of currency held to pay its Chinese suppliers. It expects to make a £1m loss overall.

FT *Source*: Adapted from Sharman, A. (2014) Late trains to dent profit at model maker Hornby, ft.com, 24 January.

Real World 3.8 provides evidence concerning the extent to which managers use break-even analysis.

Real World 3.8

Break-even analysis in practice

A survey of management accounting practice in the United States was conducted in 2003. Nearly 2,000 businesses replied to the survey. These tended to be larger businesses, of which about 40 per cent were manufacturers and about 16 per cent financial services; the remainder were across a range of other industries.

The survey revealed that 62 per cent use break-even analysis extensively, with a further 22 per cent considering using the technique in the future.

Though the survey relates to the US, was undertaken several years ago and relates to larger businesses, in the absence of UK evidence it provides some indication of what is likely also to be current practice in the UK and elsewhere in the developed world for such businesses.

A much more recent, and UK-based, survey of the practices of 11 small and medium sized businesses found a marked tendency to use break-even analysis.

Sources: Taken from the *2003 Survey of Management Accounting* by Ernst and Young, 2003 and Lucas, M., Prowle, M. and Lowth, G. (2013) Management accounting practices of UK small-medium-sized enterprises, CIMA, July 2013.

USING CONTRIBUTION TO MAKE DECISIONS: MARGINAL ANALYSIS

In Chapter 2, where we discussed relevant costs for decision making, we saw that, when deciding between two or more possible courses of action, *only costs that vary with the decision should be included in the analysis*. This principle can be applied to the consideration of fixed cost.

For many decisions that involve

- relatively small variations from existing practice, and/or
- relatively limited periods of time,

fixed cost is not relevant. It will be the same irrespective of the decision made. This is because fixed cost elements cannot, or will not, be altered in the short term.

Activity 3.13

Ali plc owns a workshop from which it provides an IT repair and maintenance service. There has recently been a downturn in demand for the service. It would be possible for Ali plc to carry on the business from smaller, cheaper accommodation.

Can you think of any reasons why the business might not immediately move to smaller, cheaper accommodation?

We thought of broadly three reasons:

1. It is not usually possible to find a buyer for the existing accommodation at very short notice and it may be difficult to find an available alternative property quickly.
2. It may be difficult to move accommodation quickly where there is, say, delicate equipment to be moved.
3. Management may feel that the downturn might not be permanent and would, thus, be reluctant to take such a dramatic step and deny itself the opportunity to benefit from a possible revival of trade.

We shall now consider some types of decisions where fixed cost can be regarded as irrelevant. In making these decisions, we should have as our key strategic objective the enhancement of owners' (shareholders') wealth. Since these decisions are short-term in nature, wealth will normally be increased by generating as much net cash inflow as possible.

In **marginal analysis** only costs and revenues that vary with the decision are considered. This usually means that fixed cost can be ignored. This is because marginal analysis is usually applied to minor alterations in the level of activity. It tends to be true, therefore, that the variable cost per unit will be equal to the **marginal cost**, which is the additional cost of producing one more unit of output. While marginal cost normally equals variable cost, there may be times when producing one more unit will involve a step in the fixed cost. If this occurs, the marginal cost is not just the variable cost; it will include the increment, or step, in the fixed cost as well.

Marginal analysis may be used in four key areas of decision making:

- pricing/assessing opportunities to enter contracts;
- determining the most efficient use of scarce resources;
- make-or-buy decisions; and
- closing or continuation decisions.

Let us consider each of these areas in turn.

Pricing/assessing opportunities to enter contracts

To understand how marginal analysis may be used in assessing an opportunity, consider the following activity.

Activity 3.14

Cottage Industries Ltd (see Example 3.2, page 69) has spare capacity in that its basket makers have some spare time. An overseas retail chain has offered the business an order for 300 baskets at a price of £13 each.

Without considering any wider issues, should the business accept the order? (Assume that the business does not rent the machine.)

Since the fixed cost will be incurred in any case, it is not relevant to this decision. All we need to do is to see whether the price offered will yield a contribution. If it will, the business will be better off by accepting the contract than by refusing it.

	£
Additional revenue per unit	13
Additional cost per unit	(12)
Additional contribution per unit	1

For 300 units, the additional contribution will be £300 (that is, 300 × £1). Since no fixed cost increase is involved, irrespective of what else is happening to the business, it will be £300 better off by taking this contract than by refusing it.

As ever with decision making, there are other factors that are either difficult or impossible to quantify. These should be taken into account before reaching a final decision. In the case of Cottage Industries Ltd's decision concerning the overseas customer, these could include the following:

- The possibility that spare capacity will have been 'sold off' cheaply when there might be another potential customer who will offer a higher price, but, by that time, the capacity will be fully committed. It is a matter of commercial judgement as to how likely this will be.
- Selling the same product, but at different prices, could lead to a loss of customer goodwill. The fact that a different price will be set for customers in different countries (that is, in different markets) may be sufficient to avoid this potential problem.

- If the business is going to suffer continually from being unable to sell its full production potential at the 'usual' price, it might be better, in the long run, to reduce capacity and make fixed cost savings. Using the spare capacity to produce marginal benefits may lead to the business failing to address this issue.
- On a more positive note, the business may see this as a way of breaking into a different market. This is something that might be impossible to achieve if the business charges its usual price.

The marginal cost is the minimum price at which the business can offer a product or service for sale. It will result in the business being no better off as a result of making the sale than if it had not done so. Achieving more than this minimum price will generate a profit (an increase in owners' wealth).

The most efficient use of scarce resources

Normally, the output of a business is determined by customer demand for the particular goods or services. In some cases, however, output will be restricted by the productive capacity of the business. Limited productive capacity might stem from a shortage of any factor of production – labour, raw materials, space, machine capacity and so on. Such scarce factors are often known as *key* or *limiting* factors.

Where productive capacity acts as a brake on output, management must decide on how best to deploy the scarce resource. That is, it must decide which products, from the range available, should be produced and how many of each should be produced. Marginal analysis can be useful to management in such circumstances. The guiding principle is that the most profitable combination of products will occur where the *contribution per unit of the scarce factor* is maximised. Example 3.3 illustrates this point.

Example 3.3

A business provides three different services, the details of which are as follows:

Service (code name)	*AX107*	*AX109*	*AX220*
	£	£	£
Selling price per unit	50	40	65
Variable cost per unit	(25)	(20)	(35)
Contribution per unit	25	20	30
Labour time per unit	5 hours	3 hours	6 hours

Within reason, the market will take as many units of each service as can be provided, but the ability to provide the service is limited by the availability of labour, all of which needs to be skilled. Fixed cost is not affected by the choice of service provided because all three services use the same facilities.

The most profitable service is AX109 because it generates a contribution of £6.67 (£20/3) an hour. The other two generate only £5.00 each an hour (£25/5 and £30/6). So, to maximise profit, priority should be given to the production that maximises the contribution per unit of limiting factor.

Our first reaction might be that the business should provide only service AX220, as this is the one that yields the highest contribution per unit sold. If so, we would have been making the mistake of thinking that it is the ability to sell that is the limiting factor. If the above analysis is not convincing, we can take a random number of available labour hours and ask ourselves what is the maximum contribution (and, therefore, profit) that could be made by providing each service exclusively. Bear in mind that there is no shortage of anything else, including market demand, just a shortage of labour.

Activity 3.15

A business makes three different products, the details of which are as follows:

Product (code name)	*B14*	*B17*	*B22*
Selling price per unit (£)	25	20	23
Variable cost per unit (£)	10	8	12
Weekly demand (units)	25	20	30
Machine time per unit (hours)	4	3	4

Fixed cost is not affected by the choice of product because all three products use the same machine. Machine time is limited to 148 hours a week.

Which combination of products should be manufactured if the business is to produce the highest profit?

Product (code name)	*B14*	*B17*	*B22*
	£	£	£
Selling price per unit	25	20	23
Variable cost per unit	(10)	(8)	(12)
Contribution per unit	15	12	11
Machine time per unit	4 hours	3 hours	4 hours
Contribution per machine hour	£3.75	£4.00	£2.75
Order of priority	2nd	1st	3rd

Therefore produce:

20 units of product B17 using	60 hours
22 units of product B14 using	88 hours
	148 hours

This leaves unsatisfied the market demand for a further 3 units of product B14 and 30 units of product B22.

Activity 3.16

What practical steps could be taken that might lead to a higher level of contribution for the business in Activity 3.15?

The possibilities for improving matters that occurred to us are as follows:

- Consider obtaining additional machine time. This could mean obtaining a new machine, subcontracting the machining to another business or, perhaps, squeezing a few more hours a week out of the business's own machine. Perhaps a combination of two or more of these is a possibility.
- Redesign the products in a way that requires less time per unit on the machine.
- Increase the price per unit of the three products. This might well have the effect of dampening demand, but the existing demand cannot be met at present. It may, therefore, be more profitable, in the long run, to make a greater contribution on each unit sold than to take one of the other courses of action to overcome the problem.

Activity 3.17

Going back to Activity 3.15, what is the maximum price that the business concerned would logically be prepared to pay to have the remaining B14s machined by a subcontractor, assuming that no fixed or variable cost would be saved as a result of not doing the machining in-house?

Would there be a different maximum if we were considering the B22s?

If the remaining three B14s were subcontracted at no cost, the business would be able to earn a contribution of £15 a unit, which it would not otherwise be able to gain. Therefore, any price up to £15 a unit would be worth paying to a subcontractor to undertake the machining. Naturally, the business would prefer to pay as little as possible, but anything up to £15 would still make it worthwhile subcontracting the machining.

This would not be true of the B22s because they have a different contribution per unit; £11 would be the relevant figure in their case.

Make-or-buy decisions

Businesses are frequently confronted by the need to decide whether to produce the product or service that they sell themselves, or to buy it in from some other business. Thus, a producer of electrical appliances might decide to subcontract the manufacture of one of its products to another business, perhaps because there is a shortage of production capacity in the producer's own factory, or because it believes it to be cheaper to subcontract than to make the appliance itself.

It might just be part of a product or service that is subcontracted. For example, the producer may have a component for the appliance made by another manufacturer. In principle, there is hardly any limit to the scope of make-or-buy decisions. Virtually any part, component or service that is required in production of the main product or service, or the main product or service itself, could be the subject of a make-or-buy decision. So, for example, the human resources function of a business, which is normally performed in-house, could be subcontracted. At the same time, electrical power, which is typically provided by an outside electrical utility business, could be generated in-house. Obtaining services or products from a subcontractor is often called **outsourcing**.

Real World 3.9 provides an example of a major UK electricity supplier outsourcing customer service roles to India.

Real World 3.9

Npower outsources

Last month the company [RWE npower plc] unveiled deep job cuts and a major restructuring of its business that it said was aimed at improving customer service. The company will close offices and outsource work to India in a move that will see 1,460 UK staff lose their jobs.

FT *Source*: Adapted from Chazan, G. (2013) Npower pledges £1m after criticism, ft.com, 3 December.

Activity 3.18

Shah Ltd needs a component for one of its products. It can outsource production of the component to a subcontractor who will provide the components for £20 each. Shah Ltd can produce the components internally for a total variable cost of £15 per component. Shah Ltd has spare capacity.

Should the component be subcontracted or produced internally?

The answer is that Shah Ltd should produce the component internally, since the variable cost of subcontracting is greater by £5 (that is, £20 – £15) than the variable cost of internal manufacture.

Activity 3.19

Now assume that Shah Ltd (Activity 3.18) has no spare capacity, so it can only produce the component internally by reducing its output of another of its products. While it is making each component, it will lose contributions of £12 from the other product.

Should the component be subcontracted or produced internally?

The answer is to subcontract. In this case, both the variable cost of production and the opportunity cost of lost contributions must be taken into account. Thus, the relevant cost of internal production of each component is:

	£
Variable cost of production of the component	15
Opportunity cost of lost production of the other product	12
	27

This is obviously more costly than the £20 per component that will have to be paid to the subcontractor.

Activity 3.20

What factors, other than the immediately financially quantifiable, would you consider when making a make-or-buy decision?

We feel that there are two major factors:

1 The general problems of subcontracting, particularly
   (a) loss of control of quality;
   (b) potential unreliability of supply.
2 Expertise and specialisation. Generally, businesses should focus on their core competences.

Picking up on the second point in Activity 3.20, it is possible for most businesses, with sufficient determination, to do virtually everything in-house. This may, however, require a level of skill and facilities that most businesses neither have nor feel inclined to acquire. For example, though it is true that most businesses could generate their own electricity, their managements tend to take the view that this is better done by a specialist generator business. Specialists can often do things more cheaply, with less risk of things going wrong.

Real World 3.10 is an article that expands on the answer to Activity 3.20 in pointing out the limits to beneficial outsourcing.

Real World 3.10

Outsourcing can be neat, plausible and wrong

For every complicated problem, the journalist H.L. Mencken said, there is a solution that is neat, plausible, and wrong. When outsourcing first became a popular business practice two decades ago, some executives mistakenly believed they had found a neat solution that was plausible, and right.

While there were obvious 'cost arbitrage' savings to be made by taking a business unit out of a high-wage area and transporting the activity to an emerging market – the so-called 'lift and shift' approach – it turned out that life was more complicated than that. Outsourcing was not and is not an easy option. Contracts take a lot of managing. Cheaper will not necessarily mean more efficient, and more efficient will not necessarily mean more effective. The 'people factor' is significant. Service level agreements have to be monitored and maintained. And initial cost savings can be eroded as wages rise in rapidly developing economies.

In any case, intelligent outsourcing is no longer simply about cost savings. 'That's just "table stakes",' says Anoop Sagoo, senior managing director at Accenture, the consulting firm. 'We've moved on a long way from what people used to think about when they discussed outsourcing,' he says.

Another interesting aspect of current thinking on outsourcing is the way it forces (or should force) businesses to ask hard and fundamental questions about how they operate, and what sort of business they really are. If growth is the ultimate goal this matters. Jonathan Cooper-Bagnall, head of shared services and outsourcing at PA Consulting, says that intelligent outsourcing can provide businesses with the sort of flexibility they need to be able to compete successfully, and grow. 'In the wake of the financial crisis, some companies have cut their cost base very deep, and are not in a position to rebuild that cost base,' he says. 'So they have to use third parties in a smart way. Say you were a bank or a retailer setting up in a new market. Do you really need to build your own systems, hire all your own people,' he asks. Mr Cooper-Bagnall goes further. 'What is really core to your business? Do you need your own R&D team? Or are you really a branding company? Other people can handle logistics, procurement, do the product development – your job is to market it.' This is where the logic of outsourcing ultimately takes you. How and where do you create value?

But before selling a too optimistic version of outsourcing, Mr Cooper-Bagnall adds: 'The talent needed to run these [outsourced] operations is in short supply, and expensive. Business acumen, managing suppliers, and those other sorts of relationship skills, are rarely found in one individual. How do you find and develop people for these roles? It's not easy.' In order to avoid classic outsourcing pitfalls, it is worth asking what the common characteristics of successful attempts to outsource are.

Outsourcing is not the answer to everything. It can be taken too far. Companies can lose control – or 'sight' – of far-flung operations. And some activities will, or should, always remain core. But the logic of outsourcing can be hard to resist. And for those looking to grow quickly, flexibly and sustainably, it is an unavoidable option.

FT *Source*: Adapted from Stern, S. (2013) Logic of outsourcing can be hard to resist, ft.com, 20 September.

Closing or continuation decisions

It is quite common for businesses to produce separate financial statements for each department or section, to try to assess their relative performance. Example 3.4 considers how marginal analysis can help decide how to respond where it is found that a particular department underperforms.

Example 3.4

Goodsports Ltd is a retail shop that operates through three departments, all in the same accommodation. The three departments occupy roughly equal-sized areas of the accommodation. The projected trading results for next year are:

	Total	*Sports equipment*	*Sports clothes*	*General clothes*
	£000	*£000*	*£000*	*£000*
Sales revenue	534	254	183	97
Cost	(482)	(213)	(163)	(106)
Profit/(loss)	52	41	20	(9)

It would appear that if the general clothes department were to close, the business would be more profitable, by £9,000 a year.

When the cost is analysed between that part that is variable and that part that is fixed, however, the contribution of each department can be deduced and the following results obtained:

	Total	*Sports equipment*	*Sports clothes*	*General clothes*
	£000	*£000*	*£000*	*£000*
Sales revenue	534	254	183	97
Variable cost	(344)	(167)	(117)	(60)
Contribution	190	87	66	37
Fixed cost (rent and so on)	(138)	(46)	(46)	(46)
Profit/(loss)	52	41	20	(9)

Now it is obvious that closing the general clothes department, without any other developments, would make the business worse off by £37,000 (the department's contribution). The department should not be closed, because it makes a positive contribution. The fixed cost would continue whether the department was closed or not. As can be seen from the above analysis, distinguishing between variable and fixed cost, and deducing the contribution, can make the picture a great deal clearer.

Activity 3.21

In considering Goodsports Ltd (in Example 3.4), we saw that the general clothes department should not be closed 'without any other developments'.

What 'other developments' could affect this decision, making continuation either more attractive or less attractive?

The things that we could think of are as follows:

- Expansion of the other departments or replacing the general clothes department with a completely new activity. This would make sense only if the space currently occupied by the general clothes department could generate contributions totalling at least £37,000 a year.
- Subletting the space occupied by the general clothes department. Once again, this would need to generate a net rent greater than £37,000 a year to make it more financially beneficial than keeping the department open.
- Keeping the department open, even if it generated no contribution whatsoever (assuming that there is no other use for the space), may still be beneficial. If customers are attracted into the shop because it has general clothing, they may then buy something from one of the other departments. In the same way, the activity of a subtenant might attract customers into the shop. (On the other hand, it might drive them away!)

Figure 3.13 summarises the four key decision-making areas where marginal analysis tends to be used.

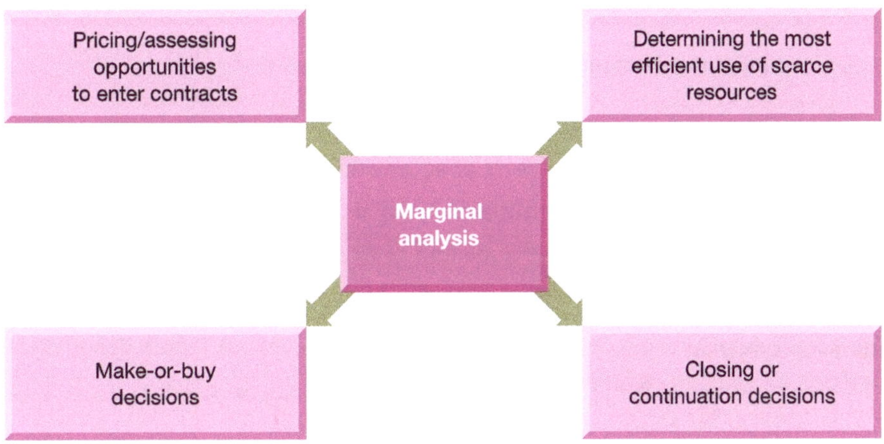

Marginal analysis tends to be used in four main decision-making areas.

Figure 3.13 The four key areas of decision making using marginal analysis

Self-assessment question 3.1

Khan Ltd can render three different types of service (Alpha, Beta and Gamma) using the same staff. Various estimates for next year have been made as follows:

Service	*Alpha*	*Beta*	*Gamma*
Selling price (£/unit)	30	39	20
Variable material cost (£/unit)	15	18	10
Other variable costs (£/unit)	6	10	5
Share of fixed cost (£/unit)	8	12	4
Staff time required (hours)	2	3	1

Fixed cost for next year is expected to total £40,000.

→

Required:

(a) If the business were to render only service Alpha next year, how many units of the service would it need to provide in order to break even? (Assume for this part of the question that there is no effective limit to market size and staffing level.)

(b) If the business has limited staff hours available next year, in which order of preference would the three services come?

(c) The maximum market for next year for the three services is as follows:

Alpha	3,000 units
Beta	2,000 units
Gamma	5,000 units

Khan Ltd has a maximum of 10,000 staff hours available next year.

What quantities of each service should the business provide next year and how much profit would this be expected to yield?

The solution to this question can be found in Appendix B.

SUMMARY

The main points of this chapter may be summarised as follows:

Cost behaviour

- Fixed cost is independent of the level of activity (for example, rent).
- Variable cost varies with the level of activity (for example, raw materials).
- Semi-fixed (semi-variable) cost is a mixture of fixed and variable costs (for example, electricity).

Break-even analysis

- The break-even point (BEP) is the level of activity (in units of output or sales revenue) at which total cost (fixed + variable) = total sales revenue.
- Calculation of BEP is as follows:

$$\text{BEP(in units of output)} = \frac{\text{Fixed cost for the period}}{\text{Contribution per unit}}$$

- Knowledge of the BEP for a particular activity can be used to help assess risk.
- Contribution per unit = sales revenue per unit less variable cost per unit.
- Contribution margin ratio = contribution/sales revenue (× 100%)
- Margin of safety = excess of planned volume (or sales revenue) of activity over volume (or sales revenue) at BEP.
- Calculation of the volume of activity (t) required to achieve a target profit is as follows:

$$t = \frac{\text{Fixed cost} + \text{Target profit}}{\text{Sales revenue per unit} - \text{Variable cost per unit}}$$

- Operating gearing is the extent to which the total cost of some activity is fixed rather than variable.

- The profit–volume (PV) chart is an alternative approach to the BE chart, which is probably easier to understand.
- Economists tend to take a different approach to BE, taking account of economies (and diseconomies) of scale and of the fact that, generally, to be able to sell large volumes, price per unit tends to fall.

Weaknesses of BE analysis

- There are non-linear relationships between cost, revenue and volume.
- There may be stepped fixed cost. Most elements of fixed cost are not fixed over all volumes of activity.
- Multi-product businesses have problems in allocating fixed cost to particular activities.

Marginal analysis (ignores fixed cost where this is not affected by the decision)

- Assessing contracts – we consider only the effect on contributions.
- Using scarce resources – the limiting factor is most effectively used by maximising its contribution per unit.
- Make-or-buy decisions – we take the action that leads to the highest total contributions.
- Closing/continuing an activity – should be assessed by net effect on total contributions.

KEY TERMS

For definitions of these terms, see Appendix A.

Fixed cost
Variable cost
Stepped fixed cost
Semi-fixed (semi-variable) cost
High-low method
Break-even analysis
Break-even chart
Break-even point (BEP)
Contribution per unit
Contribution margin ratio
Margin of safety
Operating gearing
Profit–volume (PV) chart
Economies of scale
Relevant range
Marginal analysis
Marginal cost
Outsourcing

FURTHER READING

If you would like to explore the topics covered in this chapter in more depth, we recommend the following:

Burns, J., Quinn, M., Warren, L. and Oliveira, J. (2013) *Management Accounting*, McGraw-Hill Education, Chapters 11–13.

Drury, C. (2012) *Management and Cost Accounting*, 8th edn, Cengage Learning, Chapter 8.

Hilton, R. (2011) *Managerial Accounting*, 9th edn, McGraw-Hill Higher Education, Chapter 14.

Horngren, C., Datar, S. and Rajan, M. (2012) *Cost Accounting: A Managerial Emphasis*, 14th edn, Prentice Hall International, Chapter 3.

REVIEW QUESTIONS

Solutions to these questions can be found in Appendix C.

3.1 Define the terms *fixed cost* and *variable cost*. Explain how an understanding of the distinction between fixed cost and variable cost can be useful to managers.

3.2 What is meant by the BEP for an activity? How is the BEP calculated? Why is it useful to know the BEP?

3.3 When we say that some business activity has *high operating gearing*, what do we mean? What are the implications for the business of high operating gearing?

3.4 If there is a scarce resource that is restricting sales, how will the business maximise its profit? Explain the logic of the approach that you have identified for maximising profit.

EXERCISES

Exercises 3.1 and 3.2 are basic level, 3.3 to 3.5 are intermediate level and 3.6 to 3.8 are advanced level. Those with coloured numbers have solutions given in Appendix D.

3.1 Motormusic Ltd makes a standard model of car radio, which it sells to car manufacturers for £60 each. Next year the business plans to make and sell 20,000 radios. The business's costs are as follows:

Manufacturing	
Variable materials	£20 per radio
Variable labour	£14 per radio
Other variable costs	£12 per radio
Fixed cost	£80,000 per year
Administration and selling	
Variable	£3 per radio
Fixed	£60,000 per year

Required:

(a) Calculate the break-even point for next year, expressed both in quantity of radios and sales value.

(b) Calculate the margin of safety for next year, expressed both in quantity of radios and sales value.

3.2 Lannion and Co. is engaged in providing and marketing a standard advice service. Summarised results for the past two months reveal the following:

	October	*November*
Sales (units of the service)	200	300
Sales revenue (£)	5,000	7,500
Operating profit (£)	1,000	2,200

There were no price changes of any description during these two months.

Required:

(a) Deduce the BEP (in units of the service) for Lannion and Co.

(b) State why the business might find it useful to know its BEP.

3.3 Gandhi Ltd renders a promotional service to small retailing businesses. There are three levels of service: the 'Basic', the 'Standard' and the 'Comprehensive'. The business plans next year to work at absolute full production capacity. Managers believe that the market will not accept more of any of the three services at the planned prices. The plans are:

Service	*Number of units of the service*	*Selling price*	*Variable cost per unit*
		£	£
Basic	11,000	50	25
Standard	6,000	80	65
Comprehensive	16,000	120	90

The business's fixed cost totals £660,000 a year. Each service takes about the same length of time, irrespective of the level.

One of the accounts staff has just produced a report that seems to show that the Standard service is unprofitable. The relevant extract from the report is as follows:

Standard service cost analysis

	£	
Selling price per unit	80	
Variable cost per unit	(65)	
Fixed cost per unit	(20)	(£660,000/(11,000 + 6,000 + 16,000))
Loss	(5)	

The writer of the report suggests that the business should not offer the Standard service next year. The report goes on to suggest that, if the price of the Basic service were to be lowered, the market could be expanded.

Required:

(a) Should the Standard service be offered next year, assuming that the quantity of the other services could not be expanded to use the spare capacity?

(b) Should the Standard service be offered next year, assuming that the released capacity could be used to render a new service, the 'Nova', for which customers would be charged £75 per unit, and which would have a variable cost of £50 per unit and take twice as long per unit as each the other three services?

(c) What is the minimum price that could be accepted for the Basic service, assuming that the necessary capacity to expand it will come only from not offering the Standard service?

3.4 The management of a business is concerned about its inability to obtain enough fully trained labour to enable it to meet its present budget projection.

Service:	*Alpha*	*Beta*	*Gamma*	*Total*
	£000	*£000*	*£000*	*£000*
Variable cost:				
Materials	6	4	5	15
Labour	9	6	12	27
Expenses	3	2	2	7
Allocated fixed cost	6	15	12	33
Total cost	24	27	31	82
Profit	15	2	2	19
Sales revenue	39	29	33	101

The amount of labour likely to be available amounts to £20,000. All of the variable labour is paid at the same hourly rate. You have been asked to prepare a statement of plans, ensuring that at least 50 per cent of the budgeted sales revenues are achieved for each service and the balance of labour is used to produce the greatest profit.

Required:

(a) Prepare the statement, with explanations, showing the greatest profit available from the limited amount of skilled labour available, within the constraint stated. (*Hint*: Remember that all labour is paid at the same rate.)

(b) What steps could the business take in an attempt to improve profitability, in the light of the labour shortage?

3.5 A hotel group prepares financial statements on a quarterly basis. The senior management is reviewing the performance of one hotel and making plans for next year.

The managers have in front of them the results for this year (based on some actual results and some forecasts to the end of this year):

Quarter	*Sales revenue*	*Profit/(loss)*
	£000	*£000*
1	400	(280)
2	1,200	360
3	1,600	680
4	800	40
Total	4,000	800

The total estimated number of guests (guest nights) for this year is 50,000, with each guest night being charged at the same rate. The results follow a regular pattern; there are no unexpected cost fluctuations beyond the seasonal trading pattern shown above.

For next year, management anticipates an increase in unit variable cost of 10 per cent and a profit target for the hotel of £1 million. These will be incorporated into its plans.

Required:

(a) Calculate the total variable and total fixed cost of the hotel for this year. Show the provisional annual results for this year in total, showing variable and fixed cost separately. Show also the revenue and cost per guest.

(b) 1 If there is no increase in guests for next year, what will be the required revenue rate per hotel guest to meet the profit target?

2 If the required revenue rate per guest is not raised above this year's level, how many guests will be required to meet the profit target?

(c) Outline and briefly discuss the assumptions, that are made in typical PV or break-even analysis, and assess whether they limit its usefulness.

3.6 A business makes three products, A, B and C. All three products require the use of two types of machine: cutting machines and assembling machines. Estimates for next year include the following:

Product	*A*	*B*	*C*
Selling price (£ per unit)	25	30	18
Sales demand (units)	2,500	3,400	5,100
Material cost (£ per unit)	12	13	10
Variable production cost (£ per unit)	7	4	3
Time required per unit on cutting machines (hours)	1.0	1.0	0.5
Time required per unit on assembling machines (hours)	0.5	1.0	0.5

Fixed cost for next year is expected to total £42,000.

The business has cutting machine capacity of 5,000 hours a year and assembling machine capacity of 8,000 hours a year.

Required:

(a) State, with supporting workings, which products in which quantities the business should plan to make next year on the basis of the above information. (*Hint*: First determine which machines will be a limiting factor (scarce resource).)

(b) State the maximum price per product that it would be worth the business paying to a subcontractor to carry out that part of the work that could not be done internally.

3.7 Darmor Ltd has three products, which require the same production facilities. Information about the production cost for one unit of its products is as follows:

Product	*X*	*Y*	*Z*
	£	£	£
Labour: Skilled	6	9	3
Unskilled	2	4	10
Materials	12	25	14
Other variable costs	3	7	7
Fixed cost	5	10	10

All labour and materials are variable costs. Skilled labour is paid £12 an hour and unskilled labour is paid £8 an hour. All references to labour cost above are based on basic rates of pay. Skilled labour is scarce, which means that the business could sell more than the maximum that it is able to make of any of the three products.

Product X is sold in a regulated market and the regulators have set a price of £30 per unit for it.

Required:

(a) State, with supporting workings, the price that must be charged for Products Y and Z, such that the business would find it equally profitable to make and sell any of the three products.

(b) State, with supporting workings, the maximum rate of overtime premium that the business would logically be prepared to pay its skilled workers to work beyond the basic time.

3.8 Intermediate Products Ltd produces four types of water pump. Two of these (A and B) are sold by the business. The other two (C and D) are incorporated, as components, into other products of the business. Neither C nor D is incorporated into A or B. Costings (per unit) for the products are as follows:

	A	*B*	*C*	*D*
	£	£	£	£
Variable materials	15	20	16	17
Variable labour	25	10	10	15
Other variable costs	5	3	2	2
Fixed costs	20	8	8	12
	65	41	36	46
Selling price (per unit)	70	45		

There is an outside supplier who is prepared to supply unlimited quantities of products C and D to the business, charging £40 per unit for product C and £55 per unit for product D.

Next year's estimated demand for the products, from the market (in the case of A and B) and from other production requirements (in the case of C and D) is as follows:

	Units
A	5,000
B	6,000
C	4,000
D	3,000

For strategic reasons, the business wishes to supply a minimum of 50 per cent of the above demand for products A and B.

Manufacture of all four products requires the use of a special machine. The products require time on this machine as follows:

	Hours per unit
A	0.5
B	0.4
C	0.5
D	0.3

Next year there are expected to be a maximum of 6,000 special-machine hours available. There will be no shortage of any other factor of production.

Required:

(a) State, with supporting workings and assumptions, which quantities of which products the business should plan to make next year.

(b) Explain the maximum amount that it would be worth the business paying per hour to rent a second special machine.

(c) Suggest ways, other than renting an additional special machine, that could solve the problem of the shortage of special-machine time.

Chapter 4

FULL COSTING

INTRODUCTION

Full (absorption) costing is a widely used approach that takes account of all of the cost of producing a particular product or service. In this chapter, we shall see how this approach can be used to deduce the cost of some activity, such as making a unit of product (for example, a tin of baked beans), providing a unit of service (for example, a car repair) or creating a facility (for example, building a high speed rail link from London to Birmingham).

The precise approach taken to deducing full cost will depend on whether each product or service is identical to the next or whether each job has its own individual characteristics. It will also depend on whether the business accounts for overheads on a segmental basis. We shall look at how full (or absorption) costing is carried out and we shall also consider its usefulness for management purposes.

This chapter considers the traditional, but still very widely used, form of full costing. In Chapter 5 we shall consider activity-based costing, which is a more recently developed approach.

Learning outcomes

When you have completed this chapter, you should be able to:

- Deduce the full (absorption) cost of a cost unit in a single-product and a multi-product environment.
- Discuss the problems of deducing full (absorption) cost in practice.
- Discuss the usefulness of full (absorption) cost information to managers.
- Compare and contrast the full costing and variable costing approaches.

WHAT IS FULL COSTING?

Full cost is the total amount of resources, usually measured in monetary terms, sacrificed to achieve a given objective. It takes account of all resources sacrificed to achieve that objective. Thus, if the objective were to supply a customer with a product or service, the cost of all aspects relating to the making of the product or provision of the service would be included as part of the full cost. To derive the full cost figure, we must accumulate the elements of cost incurred and then assign them to the particular product or service.

The logic of **full costing** is that the entire cost of running a facility, such as an office or factory, is part of the cost of the output that it helps to generate. Take, for example, the rent incurred in running an architect's office. Although this will not alter if the architect undertakes one more architectural job, there would be nowhere to work unless the office was available. Thus, rent of the office must be taken into account when calculating the full cost of providing each architectural job. A **cost unit** is one unit of whatever is having its cost determined. This is usually one unit of output of a particular product or service.

WHY DO MANAGERS WANT TO KNOW THE FULL COST?

We saw in Chapter 1 that the only point in providing management accounting information is to improve the quality of management decisions. There are four main areas where information relating to the full cost of the business's products or services may prove useful. These are:

- *Pricing and output decisions.* Having full cost information can help managers make decisions on the price to charge customers for the business's products or services. Full cost information, along with relevant information concerning prices, can also be used to determine the number of units of products or services to be produced. We shall consider this aspect in more detail in Chapter 9.
- *Exercising control.* Determining the full cost of a product or service is often a useful starting point for exercising cost control. Where the reported full cost figure is considered too high, for example, individual elements of full cost may then be examined to see whether there are opportunities for reduction. This may lead to re-engineering the production process, finding new sources of supply and so on. We shall pick up this point in later chapters, particularly Chapters 7 and 10.
- *Assessing relative efficiency*. Full cost information can help managers compare the cost of carrying out an activity in a particular way, or particular place, with its cost if carried out in a different way, or place. A motor car manufacturer, for example, may wish to compare the cost of building a particular model of car in one manufacturing plant, rather than in another. This could help in determining where to locate future production.
- *Assessing performance.* Profit is an important measure of business performance. To measure the profit arising from providing a particular product or service, the sales revenue that it generates should be compared with the costs consumed in generating that revenue. This can help in assessing past decisions. It can also help in guiding future decisions, such as continuing with, or abandoning, the particular product or service.

Figure 4.1 shows the four uses of full cost information.

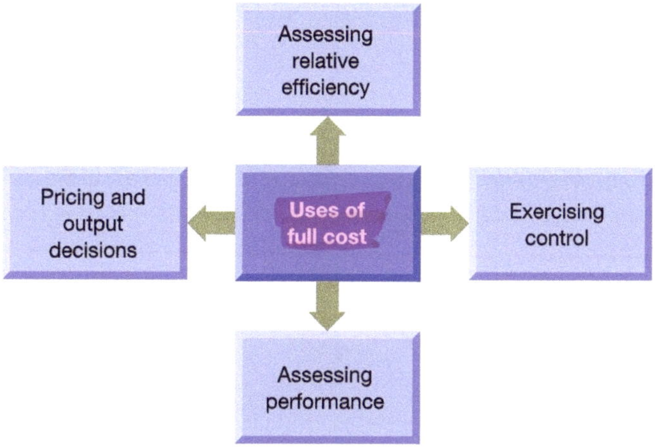

Managers use full cost information for four main purposes.

Figure 4.1 Uses of full cost by managers

Now let us consider **Real World 4.1**.

Real World 4.1

Operating cost

An interesting example of the use of full cost for pricing decisions occurs in the National Health Service (NHS). In recent years, the funding of hospitals has radically changed. A new system of Payment by Results (PBR) requires the Department of Health to produce a list of prices for an in-patient spell in hospital that covers different types of procedures. This list, which is revised annually, reflects the prices that hospitals will be paid by the government for carrying out the different procedures.

For 2013/14, the price list included the following figures:

- £8,750 for carrying out a hip replacement;
- £7,033 for carrying out a knee replacement.

(In each case the precise nature of the procedure is specified.)

These figures are based on the full cost of undertaking each type of procedure in 2010/11 (but adjusted for inflation and an efficiency discount). Full cost figures were submitted by all NHS hospitals for that year as part of their annual accounting process and an average for each type of procedure was then calculated. Figures for the many other procedures on the price list were derived in the same way.

Source: Department of Health (2013) Payment by Results tariff information for 2013/14, 25 March.

When considering the information in Real World 4.1, an important question that arises is 'what does the full cost of each type of medical procedure include?' Does it simply include the cost of the salaries earned by doctors and nurses during the time spent with the patient or does it also include the cost of other items? If the cost of other items is included, how is it determined? Would it include, for example, a charge for:

- the artificial hip or knee and drugs provided for the patient;
- equipment used in the operating theatre;

- administrative and support staff within the hospital;
- heating and lighting;
- maintaining the hospital buildings;
- laundry and cleaning?

If the cost of such items is included, how can an appropriate charge for each procedure be determined? If, on the other hand, the costs are not included, are the figures of £8,750 and £7,033 potentially misleading? Addressing questions such as these is the focus of this chapter.

In the sections that follow, we begin by considering how to calculate the full cost of a unit of output for a business providing a single product, or service. We then go on to see how the full cost of a unit of output can be calculated for a business providing a number of different products or services.

SINGLE-PRODUCT BUSINESSES

The simplest case for which to determine the full cost per unit of output is where a business produces a single product or service. Here the production process will involve a series of continuous or repetitive activities and the output will consist of identical, or near identical, items. To calculate the full cost per unit of output, we must average the total manufacturing cost over the number of units produced. It is simply a matter of adding up all of the elements of cost of production incurred in a particular period (materials, labour, rent, fuel, power and so on) and dividing this total by the total number of units of output for that period. This approach is referred to as **process costing**.

Activity 4.1

Fruitjuice Ltd began operations at the beginning of May. It has just one product, a sparkling orange drink that is marketed as 'Orange Fizz'. During May the business produced 7,300 litres of the drink. The manufacturing cost incurred was made up as follows:

	£
Ingredients (oranges, sugar, water and so on)	390
Fuel	85
Rent of factory accommodation	350
Depreciation of equipment	75
Labour	852

What is the full cost per litre of producing 'Orange Fizz' in May?

Full cost per litre = Total manufacturing costs/Number of litres produced
= £(390 + 85 + 350 + 75 + 852)/7,300
=1,752/7,300
= £0.24 per litre

Process-costing problems

Process costing tends to be fairly straightforward as it involves tracking the production of identical, or near identical, items. Nevertheless, problems can arise when measuring certain elements of manufacturing cost. In the case of Fruitjuice Ltd, for example, how is the cost of depreciation deduced? It can only be an estimate and so its reliability is open to question. The cost of raw materials may also be a problem. Should we use the 'relevant' cost of the raw materials (in this case, almost certainly the replacement cost), or the actual price paid for it (historic cost)? As the cost per litre will presumably be used for decision-making purposes, replacement cost provides the more logical choice. For some reason, however, historic cost seems to be more widely used in practice.

There can also be problems in calculating how much output was produced. If making Orange Fizz is not a very fast process, some of the product will be in the process of being made at any given moment. Partially completed Orange Fizz represents **work in progress** (or work in process) that should be taken into account when calculating the total output, and cost per unit of output, for a period. This can, however, be a little tricky. In Example 4.1 below we see why and how we deal with work in progress.

Example 4.1

Gnome Sweet Gnome Ltd began operations on 1 September. It produces a single product, which is a statue of a gnome for use in gardens and patios. During September, the business achieved the following output:

	Units
Completed gnomes	120
Partially completed gnomes at the end of September	15

How do we measure total output for September in a single figure? We cannot simply take the 120 completed gnomes as the measure of total output. To do so would ignore the fact that part of the production effort during September had been expended on partially completed gnomes. Nor can we simply add the 120 completed gnomes to the 15 gnomes that are work in progress. This would ignore the fact that some of the statues are still incomplete. Nevertheless, the partially completed statues must somehow be taken into account when calculating total output.

The approach taken is to calculate the **equivalent units of output** that the work in progress represents. This is the number of completed gnome statues that could have been produced given the material cost and other manufacturing costs incurred. To do this, we must first estimate the degree to which the work in progress has been completed.

Let us assume that the work in progress is estimated to be 80 per cent complete in terms of materials, labour and other costs. The equivalent number of completed gnome statues can then be calculated by multiplying the number of statues that are work in progress by their percentage completion. That is, 15 × 80% = 12 statues.

The total equivalent units of output for the period will, therefore, be 120 + 12 = 132 statues. This figure represents a weighted average, where the degree of completion provides the weighting.

Activity 4.2

Assume that the manufacturing cost incurred by the business in producing gnome statues during September was as follows:

	£
Materials (plastic, paint, resin and so on)	1,680
Power for equipment	140
Rent of factory space	1,050
Depreciation of equipment	230
Labour	1,920
Other manufacturing costs	260

What is the full cost per equivalent statue in September?

The costs incurred during September relate to both the completed gnomes and to the work in progress at the end of the month. To derive the full cost per equivalent statue, we must add together all of the elements of manufacturing cost incurred and then divide this amount by the number of equivalent units of completed output. Thus:

Cost per equivalent statue = Total manufacturing cost/Number of equivalent statues produced
= (1,680 + 140 + 1,050 + 230 + 1,920 + 260)/(120 + 12)
= 5,280/132
= £40.00

Total manufacturing cost can now be assigned between completed and partially completed statues in a fair way as follows:

	£
Cost of completed units (120 × £40)	4,800
Cost of partially completed units – work in progress (12* × £40).	480
Total	5,280

* Note that it is the equivalent units of output rather than the actual number of units that is being used.

It is important to be as accurate as possible when estimating the degree of completion. If an overestimate is made, the number of equivalent units of output will be overstated. This, in turn, will lead to an understatement of the full cost per unit of producing each statue during September. If an underestimate is made, the opposite will be true.

In practice, a further complication arises where work in progress exists at the beginning, as well as at the end, of the period. Another complication is concerned with assessing the degree of completion of work in progress. A product may be, say, 100 per cent complete regarding materials, but less than that as far as labour and other costs are concerned. However, Example 4.1 above gives some insight into how we deal with work in progress within a process-costing environment.

Activity 4.3

Can you think of at least two types of industry where process costing may apply?

Suitable industries are likely to include:

- paint manufacturing;
- chemical processing;
- oil extraction;
- plastic manufacturing;
- paper manufacturing;
- brick manufacturing;
- beverages;
- semiconductor chips.

You may have thought of others.

MULTI-PRODUCT BUSINESSES

Many businesses provide products or services that are distinct rather than identical. In this situation, the process-costing approach that we used with litres of 'Orange Fizz' (in Activity 4.1) and garden gnomes (in Example 4.1) would be inappropriate. While it may be appropriate to assign an average cost to each *identical* unit of output, it is not appropriate where the units of output are quite different. It would be illogical, for example, to assign the same cost to each car repair carried out by a garage, irrespective of the complexity and size of the repair.

Where a business offers distinct products or services a **job-costing** approach is normally used. This involves accumulating costs for each individual unit of output in order to determine its full cost. To understand how this can be done, we first need to understand the difference between direct and indirect cost.

Direct and indirect cost

To provide full cost information, the various elements of cost must be accumulated and then assigned to particular cost units on some reasonable basis. Where cost units are not identical, the starting point is to separate cost into two categories: direct cost and indirect cost.

- **Direct cost**. This is a cost that can be identified with specific cost units. That is to say, the cost can be traced to a particular cost unit and can be measured reliably. The main examples of a direct cost are direct materials and direct labour. Thus, in determining the cost of a car repair by a garage, both the cost of spare parts used in the repair and the cost of the mechanic's time would be part of the direct cost of that repair. Collecting elements of direct cost is a simple matter of having a cost-recording system that is capable of capturing the cost of direct materials used on each job and the cost, based on the hours worked and the rate of pay, of direct workers.
- **Indirect cost** (or **overheads**). This is all other elements of cost, that is, those items that cannot be identified with each particular cost unit (job). Thus, the amount paid to rent the garage would be an indirect cost of a particular car repair.

We shall use the terms 'indirect cost' and 'overheads' interchangeably for the remainder of this book. Indirect cost is also sometimes known as **common cost** because it is common to all of the output of the production unit (for example, factory or department) for the period.

Real World 4.2 gives some indication of the relative importance of direct and indirect costs in practice.

Real World 4.2

Counting the cost

A survey of 176 UK businesses operating in various industries, all with an annual turnover of more than £50 million, was conducted by Al-Omiri and Drury. They discovered that the full cost of the businesses' output on average is split between direct and indirect costs as shown in Figure 4.2.

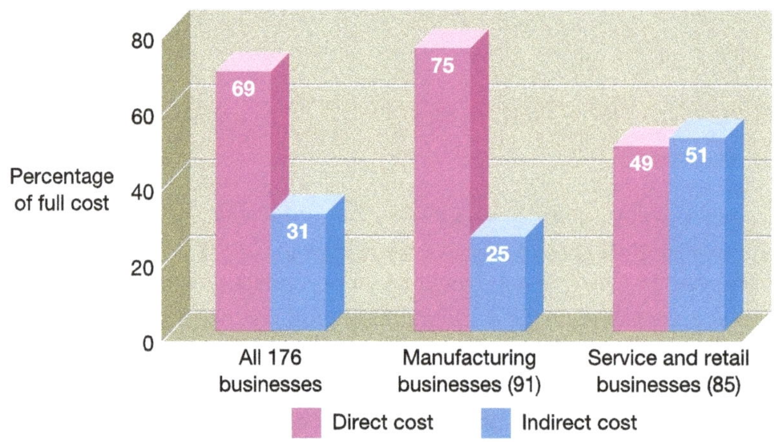

Figure 4.2 Percentage of full cost contributed by direct and indirect cost

For the manufacturers, the 75 per cent direct cost was, on average, made up as follows:

	Percentage
Direct materials	52
Direct labour	14
Other direct costs	9

Source: Al-Omiri, M. and Drury, C. (2007) A survey of factors influencing the choice of product costing systems in UK organizations, *Management Accounting Research*, December, pp. 399–424.

Activity 4.4

A garage owner wishes to know the direct cost of each job (car repair) that is carried out. How could the direct cost (labour and materials) information concerning a particular job be collected?

Usually, direct workers are required to record how long was spent on each job. Thus, the mechanic doing the job would record the length of time worked on the car. The stores staff would normally be required to keep a record of the cost of parts and materials used on each job.

A 'job sheet' will normally be prepared – probably on the computer – for each individual job. The quality of the information generated relies on staff faithfully recording all elements of direct labour and materials applied to the job.

Job costing

To deduce the full cost of a particular cost unit, we first identify the direct cost of the cost unit, which, from the definition of direct cost, is fairly straightforward. We then seek to 'charge' each cost unit with a fair share of indirect cost (overheads). Put another way, cost units will absorb overheads. This leads to full costing also being called **absorption costing**. The absorption process is shown graphically in Figure 4.3.

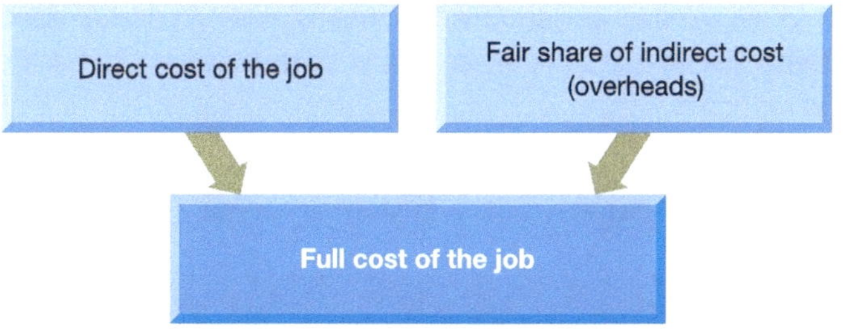

The full cost of any particular job is the sum of those cost elements that can be measured specifically in respect of the job (direct cost) and a share of the cost of creating the environment in which production (of an object or service) can take place, but which do not relate specifically to any particular job (indirect cost).

Figure 4.3 The relationship between direct cost and indirect cost

Activity 4.5

Sparky Ltd is a business that employs a number of electricians. The business undertakes a range of work for its customers, from replacing fuses to installing complete wiring systems in new houses.

In respect of a particular job done by Sparky Ltd, into which category (direct or indirect) would each of the following cost elements fall?

- **the wages of the electrician who did the job;**
- **depreciation of the tools used by the electrician;**
- **the cost of cable and other materials used on the job;**
- **rent of the building where Sparky Ltd stores its inventories of cable and other materials.**

The electrician's wages earned while working on the particular job and the cost of the materials used on the job are included in direct cost. This is because it is possible to measure how much time was spent on the particular job (and therefore its direct labour cost) and the amount of materials used (and therefore the direct material cost) in the job.

The others are included in the general cost of running the business and, as such, must form part of the indirect cost of doing the job. They cannot be directly measured in respect of the particular job, however.

It is important to note that whether a cost is direct or indirect depends on the item being costed – the cost objective. To refer to indirect cost without identifying the cost objective is incorrect.

Activity 4.6

Into which category, direct or indirect, would each of the elements of cost listed in Activity 4.5 fall, if we were seeking to find the cost of operating the entire business of Sparky Ltd for a month?

The answer is that all of them will form part of the direct cost, since they can all be related to, and measured in respect of, running the business for a month.

Broader-reaching cost objectives, such as operating Sparky Ltd for a month, tend to include a higher proportion of direct cost than do more limited ones, such as a particular job done by Sparky Ltd. As we shall see shortly, this makes costing broader cost objectives more straightforward than costing narrower ones. This is because direct cost is normally easier to deal with than indirect cost.

Full (absorption) costing and the behaviour of cost

We saw in Chapter 3 that the full cost of doing something (or total cost, as it is usually known in the context of marginal analysis) can be analysed between its fixed and variable elements. This is illustrated in Figure 4.4.

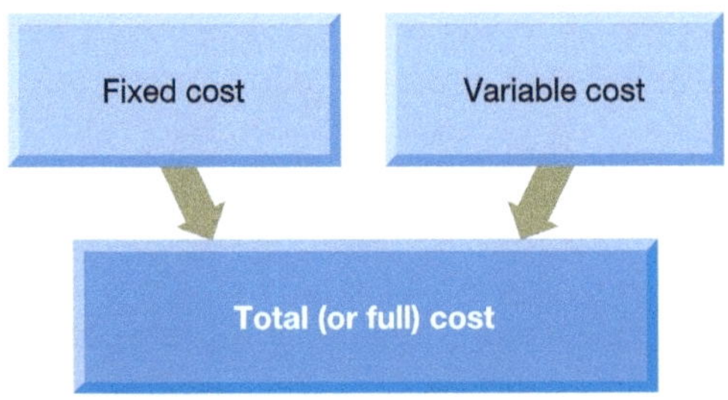

The total cost of a job is the sum of the cost that remains the same irrespective of the level of activity (fixed cost) and that which varies according to the level of activity (variable cost).

Figure 4.4 The relationship between fixed cost, variable cost and total cost

The apparent similarity of what is shown in Figure 4.4 to that shown in Figure 4.3 may create the impression that variable cost and direct cost are the same, and that fixed cost and indirect cost (overheads) are the same. This, however, is not the case.

Fixed cost and variable cost are defined in terms of **cost behaviour** in the face of changes in the volume of activity. Direct cost and indirect cost, on the other hand, are defined in terms of the extent to which they can be identified with, and measured in respect of, particular cost units (jobs). These two sets of notions are entirely different. While a fixed cost can often be an indirect cost and a variable cost can often be a direct cost, this is far from being a hard and fast rule. Take, for example, most manufactured products. They are likely to have indirect cost, such as power for machinery, which is variable, and direct cost, such as labour, which is fixed. Thus, identifying a cost as being either indirect or direct tells us nothing about whether it is fixed or variable.

The relationship between the reaction of cost to volume changes, on the one hand, and how cost elements must be gathered to deduce the full cost for a particular job, on the other, is shown in Figure 4.5.

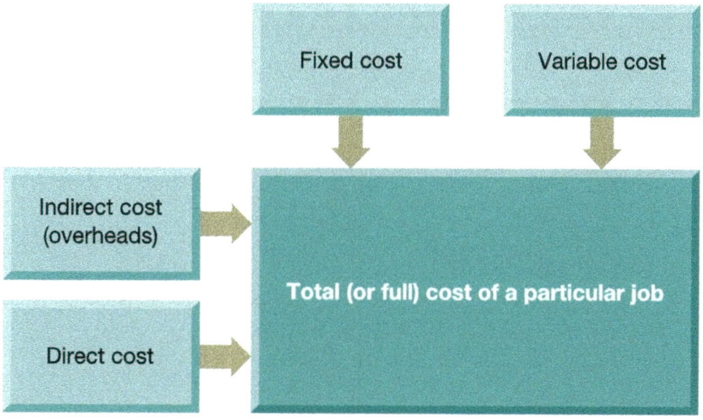

A particular job's full (or total) cost will be made up of some variable and some fixed cost elements. It will also be made up of some direct and some indirect (overhead) elements.

Figure 4.5 The relationship between direct, indirect, variable and fixed costs of a particular job

Total cost is the sum of direct and indirect costs. It is also the sum of fixed and variable costs. These two facts are not connected.

The problem of indirect cost

It is worth emphasising that the distinction between direct and indirect cost is only important in a job-costing environment, that is, where units of output differ. This distinction was of no consequence when costing a litre of 'Orange Fizz' drink (Activity 4.1) as all cost was shared equally between the individual litres of 'Orange Fizz'. Where units of output are not identical, however, this cannot be done if we wish to achieve a fair measure of the full cost of a particular job.

While indirect cost must form part of the full cost of each cost unit, it cannot, by definition, be identified directly with particular cost units. This raises a major practical issue: how can indirect cost be assigned to individual cost units?

OVERHEADS AS SERVICE RENDERERS

Indirect cost (overheads) can be viewed as rendering a service to cost units. Take, for example, a legal case undertaken by a firm of solicitors for a particular client. This case can be regarded as receiving a service from the office in which the work is done. It seems reasonable, therefore, to charge each case (cost unit) with a share of the cost of running the office (rent, lighting, heating, cleaning, building maintenance and so on). It also seems reasonable for this charge to be related to the amount of service received from the office.

The next step is the difficult one. How might the cost of running the office, which is a cost incurred for all the work undertaken by the firm, be divided between individual legal cases that differ in size and complexity?

The easiest way would be to share this overhead cost equally between each case handled by the firm within the period. This method, however, has little to commend it unless the cases were close to being identical in terms of the extent to which they received service from the office. Where they have not received identical service, we must identify something observable and measurable about the various individual cases that allows us to distinguish between them. In practice, time spent working on each individual case by direct labour tends to be used. It must be stressed, however, that this is not the 'correct' way and it is certainly not the only way.

Job costing: a worked example

To see how job costing works, let us consider Example 4.2.

Example 4.2

Johnson Ltd, a business that provides a personal computer maintenance and repair service, has overheads of £10,000 each month. Each month 1,000 direct labour hours are worked and charged to cost units (jobs carried out by the business). A particular PC repair undertaken by the business used direct materials costing £15. Direct labour worked on the repair was 3 hours and the wage rate is £16 an hour. Johnson Ltd charges overheads to jobs on a direct labour hour basis. What is the full (absorption) cost of the repair?

Solution

First, let us establish the **overhead absorption (recovery) rate**, that is, the rate at which individual repairs will be charged with overheads. This is £10 (that is, £10,000/1,000) per direct labour hour.

Thus, the full cost of the repair is:

	£
Direct materials	15
Direct labour (3 × £16)	48
	63
Overheads (3 × £10)	30
Full cost of the job	93

Note, in Example 4.2, that the number of labour hours (3 hours) appears twice in deducing the full cost: once to deduce the direct labour cost and a second time to deduce the overheads to be charged to the repair. These are really two separate issues, though they are both based on the same number of labour hours.

Note also that, if all the jobs undertaken during the month are assigned overheads in a similar manner, all £10,000 of overheads will be charged between the various jobs. Jobs that involve a lot of direct labour will be assigned a large share of overheads. Similarly, jobs that involve little direct labour will be assigned a small share of overheads.

Activity 4.7

Can you think of reasons why direct labour hours tend to be regarded as the most logical basis for sharing overheads between cost units?

The reasons that occurred to us are as follows:

- Large jobs should logically attract large amounts of overheads because they are likely to have been rendered more 'service' by the overheads than small ones. The length of time that they are worked on by direct labour may be seen as a rough way of measuring relative size, though other means of doing this may be found – for example, relative physical size, where the cost unit is a physical object, like a manufactured product.
- Most overheads are related to time. Rent, heating, lighting, non-current asset depreciation, and supervisors' and managers' salaries, which are all typical overheads, are all more or less time-based. That is to say that the overheads for one week tend to be about half of those for a similar two-week period. Thus, a basis of allotting overheads to jobs that takes account of the length of time that the units of output benefited from the 'service' rendered by the overheads seems logical.
- Direct labour hours are capable of being measured for each job. They will normally be measured to deduce the direct labour element of cost in any case. Thus, a direct labour hour basis of dealing with overheads is practical to apply in the real world.

It cannot be emphasised enough that there is no 'correct' way to allot overheads to jobs. Overheads cannot, by definition, be easily identified with individual jobs. If, nevertheless, we wish to take account of the fact that overheads are part of the full cost of all jobs, we must find some way of allotting a share of the total overheads to each job. In practice, the direct labour hour method seems to be the most popular way of doing so. Real World 4.4, which we consider later in the chapter, provides some evidence of this.

Now let us consider **Real World 4.3**, which gives an example of one well-known organisation that does not use direct labour hours to cost its output.

Real World 4.3

Recovering costs

As we saw in Real World 4.1, the UK National Health Service (NHS) seeks to ascertain the cost of various medical and surgical procedures that it undertakes for its patients. In determining the costs of a procedure that requires time in hospital as an 'in-patient', the NHS identifies the full cost of the particular procedure (for example, a hip replacement operation). To this it adds a share of the hospital overheads to cover the cost of the patient's stay in hospital. The total ward overheads are absorbed by taking this overhead total and dividing it by the number of 'bed days' throughout the hospital for the period, to establish a 'bed-day rate'. A bed day is one patient spending one day occupying a bed in the hospital. To cost the particular patient's treatment, the bed-day rate is added to the cost of the procedure according to how many bed days the particular patient had.

Note that the NHS does not use the direct labour hour basis of absorption. The bed-day rate is, however, an alternative, logical, time-based approach.

Source: NHS England (2013) *2014/15 NHS National Tariff Payments System*, NHS England, 3 October.

Activity 4.8

Marine Suppliers Ltd undertakes a range of work, including making sails for small sailing boats on a made-to-measure basis.

The business expects the following to arise during the next month:

Direct labour cost	£60,000
Direct labour time	6,000 hours
Indirect labour cost	£9,000
Depreciation of machinery	£3,000
Rent	£5,000
Heating, lighting and power	£2,000
Machine time	2,000 hours
Indirect materials	£500
Other miscellaneous indirect production cost elements (overheads)	£200
Direct materials cost	£3,000

The business has received an enquiry about a sail. It is estimated that this particular sail will take 12 direct labour hours to make and will require 20 square metres of sailcloth, which costs £2 per square metre.

The business normally uses a direct labour hour basis of charging indirect cost (overheads) to individual jobs.

What is the full (absorption) cost of making the sail?

The direct cost of making the sail can be identified as follows:

	£
Direct materials (20 × £2)	40.00
Direct labour (12 × (£60,000/6,000))	120.00
	160.00

To deduce the indirect cost (overhead) element that must be added to derive the full cost of the sail, we first need to total these cost elements as follows:

	£
Indirect labour	9,000
Depreciation	3,000
Rent	5,000
Heating, lighting and power	2,000
Indirect materials	500
Other miscellaneous indirect production cost (overhead) elements	200
Total indirect cost (overheads)	19,700

Since the business uses a direct labour hour basis of charging indirect cost to jobs, we need to deduce the indirect cost (or overhead) recovery rate per direct labour hour. This is simply:

£19,700/6,000 = £3.28 per direct labour hour

Thus, the full cost of the sail is expected to be:

	£
Direct materials (20 × £2)	40.00
Direct labour (12 × (£60,000/6,000))	120.00
Indirect cost (12 × £3.28)	39.36
Full cost	199.36

Figure 4.6 shows the process for applying indirect (overhead) and direct costs to the sail that was the subject of Activity 4.8.

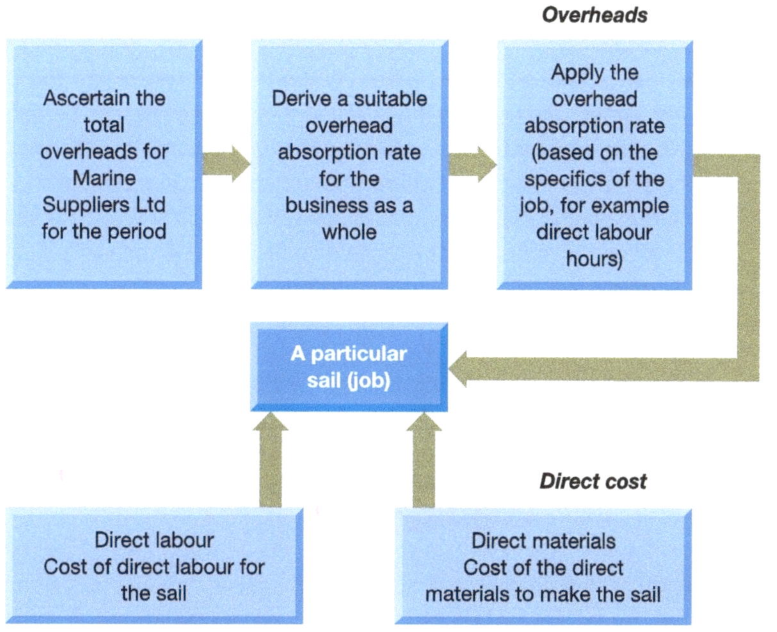

The full cost is made up of the sail's (job's) 'fair' share of the total overheads, plus the direct cost element that is measured specifically in relation to the particular sail.

Figure 4.6 How the full cost is derived for the sail by Marine Suppliers Ltd in Activity 4.8

Activity 4.9

Suppose that Marine Suppliers Ltd (see Activity 4.8) used a machine hour basis of charging overheads to jobs. What would be the cost of the particular job if it was expected to take 5 machine hours (as well as 12 direct labour hours)?

The total overheads of the business will of course be the same irrespective of the method of charging them to jobs. Thus, the overhead recovery rate, on a machine hour basis, will be:

£19,700/2,000 = £9.85 per machine hour

The full cost of the sail is, therefore, expected to be:

	£
Direct materials (20 × £2)	40.00
Direct labour (12 × (£60,000/6,000))	120.00
Indirect cost (5 × £9.85)	49.25
Full cost	209.25

Selecting a basis for charging overheads

We saw earlier that there is no single correct way of charging overheads. The final choice is a matter of judgement. It seems reasonable to say, however, that the nature of the overheads should influence the choice of the basis of charging the overheads to jobs. Where production is capital-intensive and overheads are primarily machine-based (such as depreciation, machine maintenance, power and so on), machine hours might be favoured. Otherwise direct labour hours might be preferred.

It would be irrational to choose one of these methods in preference to the other simply because it apportions either a higher or a lower amount of overheads to a particular job. The total overheads will be the same irrespective of how they are apportioned between individual jobs and so a method that gives a higher share of overheads to one particular job must give a lower share to the remaining jobs. There is one cake of fixed size: if one person receives a relatively large slice, others must on average receive relatively small slices. To illustrate further this issue of apportioning overheads, consider Example 4.3.

Example 4.3

A business, that provides a service, expects to incur overheads totalling £20,000 next month. The total direct labour time worked is expected to be 1,600 hours and machines are expected to operate for a total of 1,000 hours.

During the next month, the business expects to do just two large jobs. Information concerning each job is as follows:

	Job 1	*Job 2*
Direct labour hours	800	800
Machine hours	700	300

How much of the total overheads will be charged to each job if overheads are to be charged on:

(a) a direct labour hour basis; and
(b) a machine hour basis?

What do you notice about the two sets of figures that you calculate?

Solution

(a) Direct labour hour basis

Overhead recovery rate = £20,000/1,600 = £12.50 per direct labour hour.

Job 1	£12.50 × 800 = £10,000
Job 2	£12.50 × 800 = £10,000

(b) Machine hour basis

Overhead recovery rate = £20,000/1,000 = £20.00 per machine hour.

Job 1	£20.00 × 700 = £14,000
Job 2	£20.00 × 300 = £6,000

It is clear from these calculations that the total overheads charged to jobs is the same (that is, £20,000) whichever method is used. Whereas the machine hour basis gives Job 1 a higher share of these overheads than the direct labour hour method, the opposite is true for Job 2.

It is not feasible to charge overheads using one method for one job and using the other method for the other job. This would mean either total overheads would not be fully charged to the jobs, or the jobs would be overcharged with overheads. If, for example, the direct labour hour method was used for Job 1 (£10,000) and the machine hour basis was used for Job 2 (£6,000), only £16,000 of a total £20,000 of overheads would be charged to jobs. As a result, the objective of full (absorption) costing, which is to charge *all* overhead costs to jobs carried out during the period, would not be achieved. Furthermore, if selling prices are based on full cost, there is a risk that this particular business would not charge high enough prices to cover all its costs.

Figure 4.7 shows the effect of the two different methods of charging overheads to Jobs 1 and 2.

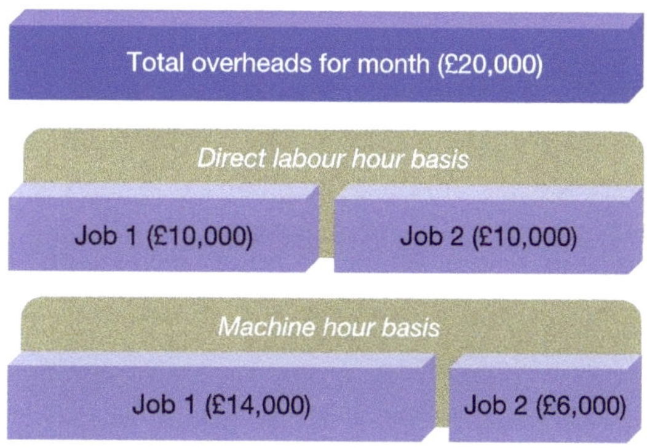

The share of the total overheads for the month charged to jobs can differ significantly depending on the basis used.

Figure 4.7 The effect of different bases of charging overheads to jobs in Example 4.3

Activity 4.10

The point was made above that it would normally be irrational to prefer one basis of charging overheads to jobs simply because it apportions either a higher or a lower amount of overheads to a particular job. This is because the total overheads are the same irrespective of the method of charging the total to individual jobs. Can you think of any circumstances where it may not be so irrational?

This might occur where a customer has agreed to pay a price for a particular job based on full cost plus an agreed fixed percentage for profit. Here it would be beneficial to the producer for the total cost of the job to be as high as possible. Public sector organisations, such as central and local government, have been known to enter into such **cost-plus pricing** contracts. They are, however, pretty rare nowadays as they are so open to abuse. Normally, contract prices are agreed in advance, typically in conjunction with competitive tendering.

Real World 4.4 provides some insight into the basis of overhead recovery in practice.

Real World 4.4

Overhead recovery rates in practice

A survey of 129 UK manufacturing businesses showed that the direct labour hour basis (or a close approximation to it) of charging indirect cost (overheads) to cost units was overwhelmingly the most popular. It was used by 72 per cent of the respondents to the survey.

15 per cent of respondents used a 'production-time based overhead rate'. This is presumably something like a machine hour rate.

Though this survey applied only to manufacturing businesses, in the absence of other information it provides some impression of what happens in practice.

Source: Based on information taken from Brierley, J., Cowton, C. and Drury, C. (2007) *Product costing practices in different manufacturing industries: a British survey*, *International Journal of Management*, December.

Segmenting the overheads

We have just seen that charging the same overheads to different jobs on different bases is not feasible. It is perfectly feasible, however, to charge one segment of the total overheads on one basis and another segment on another basis.

Activity 4.11

Taking the same business as in Example 4.3, on closer analysis we find that of the overheads totalling £20,000 next month, £8,000 relates to machines (depreciation, maintenance, rent of the space occupied by the machines and so on) and the remaining £12,000 to more general overheads. The other information about the business is exactly as it was before.

How much of the total overheads will be charged to each job if the machine-related overheads are to be charged on a machine hour basis and the remaining overheads are charged on a direct labour hour basis?

Direct labour hour basis

Overhead recovery rate = £12,000/1,600 = £7.50 per direct labour hour

Machine hour basis

Overhead recovery rate = £8,000/1,000 = £8.00 per machine hour

Overheads charged to jobs

	Job 1	*Job 2*
	£	£
Direct labour hour basis:		
£7.50 × 800	6,000	
£7.50 × 800		6,000
Machine hour basis:		
£8.00 × 700	5,600	
£8.00 × 300		2,400
Total	11,600	8,400

We can see from this that all the overheads of £20,000 have been charged.

Segmenting the overheads in this way is quite common. A business may be divided into separate areas (cost centres) for costing purposes, charging overheads differently from one area to the next, according to the nature of the work done in each.

Dealing with overheads on a cost centre basis

We saw in Chapter 1 that businesses are often divided into departments, where each department carries out a separate task. Many of these businesses charge overheads to cost units on a department-by-department basis. They do so in the belief that it will give rise to more accurate full costing information. It is probably only in a minority of cases, however, that it leads to any great improvement in accuracy. Although applying overheads on a departmental basis may not be of enormous benefit, it is probably not an expensive exercise. Cost elements are collected department by department for other purposes (particularly control) and so applying overheads on a department-by-department basis is a fairly straightforward matter.

In Example 4.4 we see how the departmental approach to deriving full cost can be applied in a service-industry context.

Example 4.4

Autosparkle Ltd offers a motor vehicle paint-respray service. The jobs that it undertakes range from painting a small part of a saloon car, usually following a minor accident, to a complete respray of a double-decker bus.

Each job starts life in the Preparation Department, where it is prepared for the Paintshop. Here, the job is worked on by direct workers, in most cases taking some direct materials from the stores with which to treat the old paintwork and, generally, to render the vehicle ready for respraying. Thus the job will be charged with direct materials, direct labour and a share of the Preparation Department's overheads. The job then passes into the Paintshop Department, already valued at the cost that it picked up in the Preparation Department.

In the Paintshop, the staff draw direct materials (mainly paint) from the stores and direct workers spend time respraying, using sophisticated spraying apparatus as well as working by hand. So, in the Paintshop, the job is charged with direct materials, direct labour and a share of that department's overheads. The job now passes into the Finishing Department, valued at the cost of the materials, labour and overheads that it accumulated in the first two departments.

In the Finishing Department, vehicles are cleaned and polished ready to go back to the customers. Further direct labour and, in some cases, materials are added. All jobs also pick up a share of that department's overheads. The job, now complete, passes back to the customer.

Figure 4.8 shows graphically how this works for a particular job.

The approach to charging overheads to jobs (for example, direct labour hours) might be the same for all three departments, or it might be different from one department to another. It is possible that cost elements relating to the spraying apparatus dominate the Paintshop overhead cost, so the Paintshop's overheads might well be charged to jobs on a machine hour basis. The other two departments are probably labour-intensive, so that direct labour hours may be seen as being appropriate there.

→

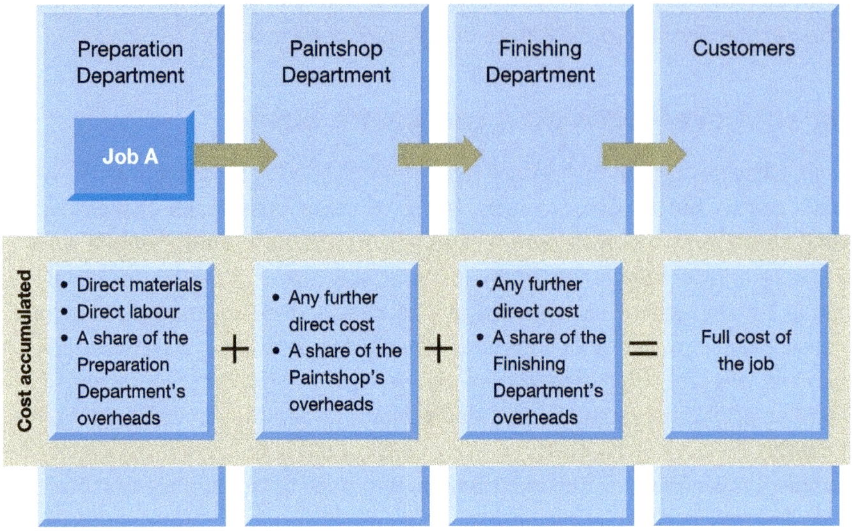

As the particular paint job passes through the three departments, where work is carried out on it, the job 'gathers' cost of various types.

Figure 4.8 A cost unit (Job A) passing through Autosparkle Ltd's process

The passage of a job through the departments, picking up cost as it goes, can be compared to a snowball being rolled across snow: as it rolls, it picks up more and more snow.

Where cost determination is dealt with departmentally, each department is known as a **cost centre**. This can be defined as a particular physical area or some activity or function for which the cost is separately identified. Charging direct cost to jobs in a departmental system is exactly the same as where the whole business is one single cost centre. It is simply a matter of keeping a record of:

- the number of hours of direct labour worked on the particular job and the grade of labour, where there are different grades with different rates of pay;
- the cost of the direct materials taken from stores and applied to the job; and
- any other direct cost elements, for example some subcontracted work, associated with the job.

This record keeping will normally be done cost centre by cost centre.

It is obviously necessary to break down the production overheads of the entire business on a cost centre basis. This means that the total overheads of the business must be divided between the cost centres, such that the sum of the overheads of all of the cost centres equals the overheads for the entire business. By charging all of their overheads to jobs, the cost centres will, between them, charge all of the overheads of the business to jobs. **Real World 4.5** provides an indication of the number of different cost centres that businesses tend to use in practice.

Real World 4.5

Cost centres in practice

It is usual for businesses to have several cost centres. A survey of 186 larger UK businesses involved in various activities by Drury and Tayles showed the following:

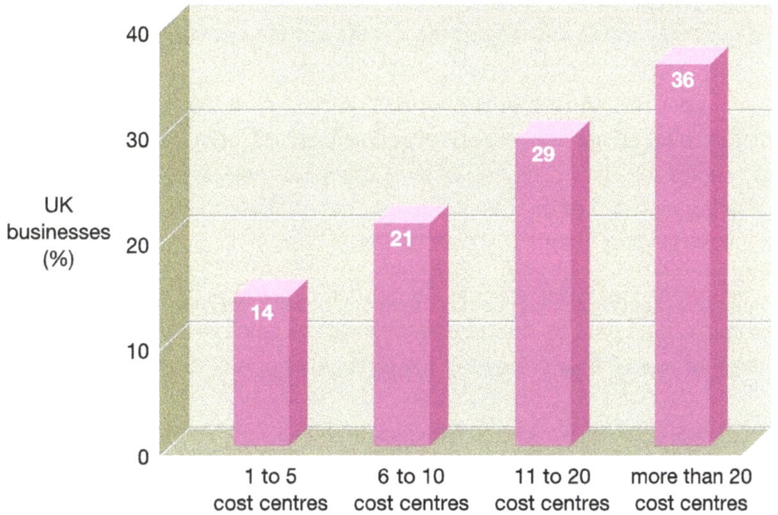

The survey of larger businesses shows, as might be expected, that they tend to have several cost centres.

Figure 4.9 Analysis of the number of cost centres within a business

We can see that 86 per cent of businesses surveyed had six or more cost centres and that 36 per cent of businesses had more than 20 cost centres. Although this is not shown in the figure, 3 per cent of businesses surveyed had a single cost centre (that is, there was a business-wide or overall overhead rate used). Clearly, businesses that deal with overheads on a business-wide basis are relatively rare.

Source: Based on information taken from Drury, C. and Tayles, M. (2006) Profitability analysis in UK organisations, *British Accounting Review*, December.

For purposes of cost assignment, we need to distinguish between **product cost centres** and **service cost centres**. Product cost centres are those in which jobs are worked on by direct workers and/or where direct materials are added. In these cost centres, jobs can be charged with a share of their overheads. The Preparation, Paintshop and Finishing Departments, discussed in Example 4.4, are all examples of product cost centres.

Activity 4.12

Can you guess what a service cost centre is? Can you think of an example of a service cost centre?

A service cost centre is one where no direct cost is involved. It renders a service to other cost centres. Examples include:

- Cleaning
- Training
- Stores
- Maintenance
- Human resources
- Catering.

All of these render services to product cost centres and, possibly, to other service cost centres.

The cost of service cost centres must be charged to product cost centres and become part of the product cost centres' overheads, so that those overheads can, in turn, be charged to jobs. As a result, all the overheads of the business will then find their way into the cost of the jobs.

Logically, the cost of a service cost centre should be charged to product cost centres on the basis of the level of service provided to the product cost centre concerned. Thus, a product cost centre that has a higher level of machine maintenance carried out should be charged with a larger share of the maintenance cost centre's (department's) cost.

The process of dividing overheads between cost centres is as follows:

- **Cost allocation**. Allocate indirect cost elements that are specific to particular cost centres. These are items that relate to, and are specifically measurable in respect of, individual cost centres. In other words, they are part of the direct cost of running the cost centre. Examples include:
  - salaries of indirect workers whose activities are wholly within the cost centre, for example the salary of the cost centre manager;
  - rent, where the cost centre is housed in a building for which rent can be separately identified;
  - electricity, where it is separately metered for each cost centre.
- **Cost apportionment**. Apportion the more general overheads to the cost centres. These are overheads that relate to more than one cost centre, perhaps to all. It would include:
  - rent, where more than one cost centre is housed in the same building;
  - electricity, where it is not separately metered;
  - salaries of cleaning staff who work in a variety of cost centres.

  These overheads would be apportioned to cost centres on the basis of the extent to which each cost centre benefits from the overheads concerned. For example, the rent cost might be apportioned on the basis of the square metres of floor area occupied by each cost centre. With electricity used to power machinery, the basis of apportionment might be the level of mechanisation of each cost centre. As with charging overheads to individual jobs, there is no correct basis of apportioning general overheads to cost centres.
- Having allocated and apportioned the cost to all cost centres, we have to apportion the total cost of service cost centres to product cost centres. Logically, the basis of apportionment should be the level of service rendered by the individual service cost centre to the individual production cost centre. With the human resources cost centre (department) cost, for example, the basis of apportionment might be the number of staff in each product cost centre. This assumes that the number of staff determines the amount of benefit received from the human resources cost centre. Where a particular product cost centre has severe personnel problems, however, it may account for a huge proportion of the human resources department's time even though it employs relatively few staff.

The final total for each product cost centre will be charged to jobs as they pass through. The process of applying overheads to cost units on a cost centre (departmental) basis is shown in Figure 4.10.

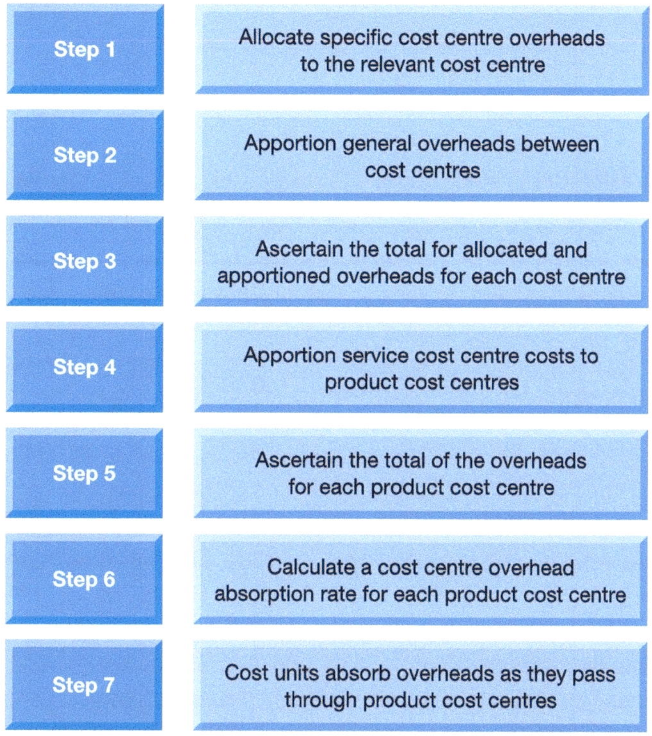

There are seven steps involved with taking the overall business overheads and transferring them to their effect on individual cost units, when dealt with on a cost centre basis.

Figure 4.10 The steps in having overheads handled on a cost centre basis

We shall now go on to consider Example 4.5, which deals with overheads on a cost centre (departmental) basis.

Example 4.5

A business consists of four cost centres:

- Preparation department
- Machining department
- Finishing department
- Human resources (HR) department.

The first three are product cost centres and the last renders a service to the other three. The level of service rendered is thought to be roughly in proportion to the number of employees in each product cost centre.

Overheads, and other data, for next month are expected to be as follows:

	£000
Rent	10,000
Electricity to power machines	3,000
Electricity for heating and lighting	800
Insurance of building	200
Cleaning	600
Depreciation of machines	2,000

→

	£000
Total monthly salaries of the indirect workers:	
Preparation department	200
Machining department	240
Finishing department	180
HR department	180

The HR department has a staff consisting of only indirect workers (including managers). The other departments have both indirect workers (including managers) and direct workers. There are 100 indirect workers within each of the four departments and none does any 'direct' work.

Each direct worker is expected to work 160 hours next month. The number of direct workers in each department is:

Preparation department	600
Machining department	900
Finishing department	500

Machining department direct workers are paid £12 an hour; other direct workers are paid £10 an hour.

All of the machinery is in the machining department. Machines are expected to operate for 120,000 hours next month.

The floor space (in square metres) occupied by the departments is as follows:

Preparation department	16,000
Machining department	20,000
Finishing department	10,000
HR department	2,000

Deducing the overheads, cost centre by cost centre, can be done, using a schedule, as follows:

	£000	*Total* £000	*Prep'n* £000	*Mach'g* £000	*Fin'g* £000	*HR* £000
Allocated cost:						
Machine power		3,000		3,000		
Machine depreciation		2,000		2,000		
Indirect salaries		800	200	240	180	180
Apportioned cost						
Rent	10,000					
Heating and lighting	800					
Insurance of buildings	200					
Cleaning	600					
Apportioned by floor area		11,600	3,867	4,833	2,417	483
Cost centre overheads		17,400	4,067	10,073	2,597	663
Reapportion HR cost by number of staff (including the indirect workers)			202	288	173	(663)
		17,400	4,269	10,361	2,770	–

Activity 4.13

Assume that the machining department overheads (in Example 4.5) are to be charged to jobs on a machine hour basis, but that the direct labour hour basis is to be used for the other two departments. What will be the full (absorption) cost of a job with the following characteristics?

	Preparation department	*Machining department*	*Finishing department*
Direct labour hours	10	7	5
Machine hours	–	6	–
Direct materials (£)	85	13	6

(*Hint*: This should be tackled as if each cost centre were a separate business, then departmental cost elements are added together for the job so as to arrive at the total full cost.)

First, we need to deduce the indirect (overhead) recovery rates for each cost centre:

Preparation department (direct labour hour based):

$$\frac{£4{,}269{,}000}{600 \times 160} = £44.47$$

Machining department (machine hour based):

$$\frac{£10{,}361{,}000}{120{,}000} = £86.34$$

Finishing department (direct labour hour based):

$$\frac{£2{,}770{,}000}{500 \times 160} = £34.63$$

The cost of the job is as follows:

	£	£
Direct labour:		
Preparation department (10 × £10)	100.00	
Machining department (7 × £12)	84.00	
Finishing department (5 × £10)	50.00	
		234.00
Direct materials:		
Preparation department	85.00	
Machining department	13.00	
Finishing department	6.00	
		104.00
Overheads:		
Preparation department (10 × £44.47)	444.70	
Machining department (6 × £86.34)	518.04	
Finishing department (5 × £34.63)	173.15	
		1,135.89
Full cost of the job		1,473.89

Activity 4.14

The manufacturing cost for Buccaneers Ltd for next year is expected to be made up as follows:

	£000
Direct materials:	
Forming department	450
Machining department	100
Finishing department	50
Direct labour:	
Forming department	180
Machining department	120
Finishing department	75
Indirect materials:	
Forming department	40
Machining department	30
Finishing department	10
Human resources department	10
Indirect labour:	
Forming department	80
Machining department	70
Finishing department	60
Human resources department	60
Maintenance cost	50
Rent	100
Heating and lighting	20
Building insurance	10
Machinery insurance	10
Depreciation of machinery	120
Total manufacturing cost	1,645

The following additional information is available:

1. **Each of the four departments is treated as a separate cost centre.**
2. **All direct labour is paid £10 an hour for all hours worked.**
3. **The human resources department renders services to all three of the production departments.**
4. **The area of the building in which the business manufactures amounts to 50,000 square metres, divided as follows:**

	Sq m
Forming department	20,000
Machining department	15,000
Finishing department	10,000
Human resources department	5,000

5. **The maintenance employees are expected to divide their time between the production departments as follows:**

	%
Forming department	15
Machining department	75
Finishing department	10

6 **Machine hours are expected to be as follows:**

	Hours
Forming department	5,000
Machining department	15,000
Finishing department	5,000

On the basis of this information:

(a) Allocate and apportion overheads to the three product cost centres.
(b) Deduce overhead recovery rates for each product cost centre using two different bases for each cost centre's overheads.
(c) Calculate the full cost of a job with the following characteristics:

Direct labour hours:	
Forming department	4 hours
Machining department	4 hours
Finishing department	1 hour
Machine hours:	
Forming department	1 hour
Machining department	2 hours
Finishing department	1 hour
Direct materials:	
Forming department	£40
Machining department	£9
Finishing department	£4

Use whichever of the two bases of overhead recovery, deduced in (b), that you consider more appropriate.

(d) Explain why you consider the basis used in (c) to be the more appropriate.

(a) Overheads can be allocated and apportioned as follows:

Cost	*Basis of apportionment*		*Total £000*	*Forming £000*	*Machining £000*	*Finishing £000*	*HR £000*
Indirect materials	Specifically allocated		90	40	30	10	10
Indirect labour	Specifically allocated		270	80	70	60	60
Maintenance	Staff time		50	7.5	37.5	5	–
Rent		100					
Heat and light		20					
Buildings insurance		10					
	Area		130	52	39	26	13
Machine insurance		10					
Machine depreciation		120					
	Machine hours		130	26	78	26	–
			670	205.5	254.5	127	83
HR	Direct labour			39.84	26.56	16.6	(83)
			670	245.34	281.06	143.6	–

Note: The direct cost is not included in the above because it is allocated *directly* to jobs.

(b) Overhead recovery rates are as follows:
Basis 1: direct labour hours

$$\text{Forming} = \frac{\pounds 245{,}340}{\pounds(180{,}000/10)} = \pounds 13.63 \text{ per direct labour hour}$$

$$\text{Machining} = \frac{\pounds281{,}060}{\pounds(120{,}000/10)} = \pounds23.42 \text{ per direct labour hour}$$

$$\text{Finishing} = \frac{\pounds143{,}600}{\pounds(75{,}000/10)} = \pounds19.15 \text{ per direct labour hour}$$

Basis 2: machine hours

$$\text{Forming} = \frac{\pounds245{,}340}{5{,}000} = \pounds49.07 \text{ per machine hour}$$

$$\text{Machining} = \frac{\pounds281{,}060}{15{,}000} = \pounds18.74 \text{ per machine hour}$$

$$\text{Finishing} = \frac{\pounds143{,}600}{5{,}000} = \pounds28.72 \text{ per machine hour}$$

(c) Full cost of job – on direct labour hour basis of overhead recovery

	£	£
Direct labour cost (9 × £10)		90.00
Direct materials (£40 + £9 + £4)		53.00
Overheads:		
Forming (4 × £13.63)	54.52	
Machining (4 × £23.42)	93.68	
Finishing (1 × £19.15)	19.15	167.35
Full cost		310.35

(d) The reason for using the direct labour hour basis rather than the machine hour basis was that labour is more important, in terms of the number of hours applied to output, than is machine time. Strong arguments could have been made for the use of the alternative basis; certainly, a machine hour basis could have been justified for the machining department.

It may be reasonable to use one basis in respect of one product cost centre's overheads and a different one for those of another. For example, machine hours could have been used for the machining department and a direct labour hours basis for the other two.

Job costing is used in a wide variety of industries such as building, civil engineering, accounting, advertising, film making, interior design, consultancy and airplane construction.

Batch costing

Many types of goods and some services are produced in a batch of identical, or nearly identical, units of output. Each batch produced, however, is distinctly different from other batches. A theatre, for example, may put on a production whose nature and cost is very different from that of other productions. On the other hand, ignoring differences in the desirability of the various types of seating, all of the individual units of output (tickets to see the production) are identical.

In these circumstances, the cost per ticket is calculated using **batch costing** and involves:

- using a job costing approach (taking account of direct and indirect costs and so on) to find the cost of mounting the production; and then
- dividing the cost of mounting the production by the expected number of tickets to be sold to find the cost per ticket.

Figure 4.11 shows the process for deriving the cost of one cost unit (product) in a batch.

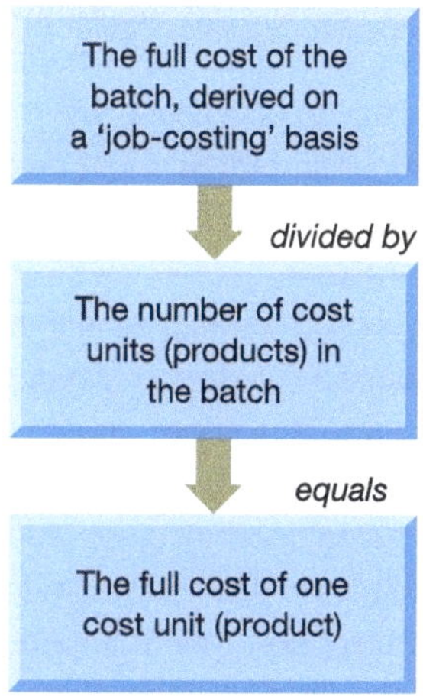

The cost for the batch is derived using a job-costing basis and this is divided by the number in the batch to determine the cost for each cost unit.

Figure 4.11 Deriving the cost of one cost unit where production is in batches

Batch costing is used in a variety of industries including clothing manufacturing, engineering component manufacturing, tyre manufacturing, bakery goods and footwear manufacturing.

Activity 4.15

Consider the following businesses:

- **a pharmaceutical manufacturer**
- **a sugar refiner**
- **a picture framer**
- **a private hospital**
- **a coal-mining business**
- **an architect's office**
- **a cement manufacturer**
- **an antique furniture restorer**

Try to identify for each business which form of full costing (process, job or batch costing) is likely to be most appropriate.

Process costing is likely to be most appropriate for the sugar refiner, the coal-mining business and the cement manufacturer. Each business is normally involved in producing identical, or near identical, items through a series of repetitive activities.

Job costing is likely to be most appropriate for the picture framer, the private hospital, the architect's office and the antique furniture restorer. Each of these businesses is normally involved in producing a customised product, or service, with each item requiring different inputs of labour, materials and so on.

Batch costing is likely to be most appropriate for the pharmaceutical manufacturer. The production process will normally involve making identical products in batches, where each batch is different.

Non-manufacturing overheads

An international accounting standard (IAS 2 *Inventories*) requires all inventories, including work in progress, to be valued at full cost. When determining full cost, only those overheads relating to the manufacturing process should be included. Non-manufacturing overheads do not form part of the full cost calculation. These overheads, normally relating to general administration, selling, marketing and distribution, must be charged to the period in which they are incurred. These rules, however, apply only for external reporting purposes. They need not be applied for internal reporting purposes.

For managerial decision making, non-manufacturing overheads are sometimes included as part of the total cost of goods produced. To do this, an appropriate basis for assigning these overheads to products must be found. This is not an easy task and inappropriate bases are often used. One basis used in practice is direct labour hours, even though its relevance for this purpose is questionable. Another basis used involves adding an amount based on the percentage of total non-manufacturing overheads to total manufacturing costs. (See reference 1 at the end of the chapter.) Thus, if total non-manufacturing overheads were £2.5 million and total manufacturing costs were £10 million, an additional 25 per cent (£2.5m/£10m) loading would be added as part of the total overhead cost.

These, and other arbitrary bases for assigning non-manufacturing overheads found in practice, are unlikely to improve the quality of management decisions. Unless a fair share of non-manufacturing overheads can be assigned to products, managers will be presented with misleading information.

Where the cost of products includes both manufacturing and non-manufacturing costs and things turn out as expected, selling the products at their full cost should cause the business to break even exactly. Thus, whatever profit (in total) is loaded onto full cost to set actual selling prices will result in that level of profit being earned for the period.

Full (absorption) costing and estimation errors

Although deducing full cost can be done after the work has been completed, it is frequently estimated in advance. This may be because some idea of full cost is needed as a basis for setting a selling price. Estimates, however, rarely turn out to be 100 per cent accurate. Where actual outcomes differ from estimated outcomes, an over-recovery or under-recovery of overheads will normally occur. Example 4.6 illustrates how this over- or under-recovery is calculated.

Example 4.6

Downham Engineering plc produces a standard valve. At the beginning of the year, it was planned that manufacturing the valves would incur £4 million in overheads and would require 400,000 direct labour hours for the year. The business, which uses the direct labour basis of absorbing overheads, set the overhead recovery rate at (£4.0m/400,000) = £10 per direct labour hour.

At the end of the year it was found that, in producing the valves, 450,000 direct labour hours were used in the production process but that the manufacturing overheads were as planned.

As 450,000 direct labour hours were used, the amount charged for overheads would have been 450,000 × £10 = £4.5 million. This means that £0.5 million (that is, £4.5m − £4.0m) of overheads were 'over-recovered'.

For external reporting purposes, any under- or over-recovery of overheads is normally adjusted in the income statement. Thus, the over-recovery in Example 4.6 would normally be deducted from the cost of goods sold figure shown in the income statement for that year.

Activity 4.16

Refer to Example 4.6 and assume that, at the end of the year, it was found that 380,000 direct labour hours were used during the year in making the valves and that manufacturing overheads incurred were £4.2 million.

What adjustment should be made to the income statement for the year?

The manufacturing overheads recovered will be 380,000 × £10 = £3.8 million. This means that £0.4 million (that is, £4.2m – £3.8m) has been under-recovered. This amount will be added to the cost of goods sold shown in the income statement for the year.

Real World 4.6 is taken from the results of a survey conducted by the UK Chartered Institute of Management Accountants (CIMA) in July 2009. Broadly the survey asked management accountants in a wide range of business types and sizes to indicate the extent to which their business used a range of management accounting techniques. 439 management accountants completed the survey. We shall be making reference to this survey on a number of occasions throughout the book. When we do, we shall refer to it as the 'CIMA survey'.

Real World 4.6

The use of full cost information

The businesses surveyed by CIMA derived full cost information to the following extent:

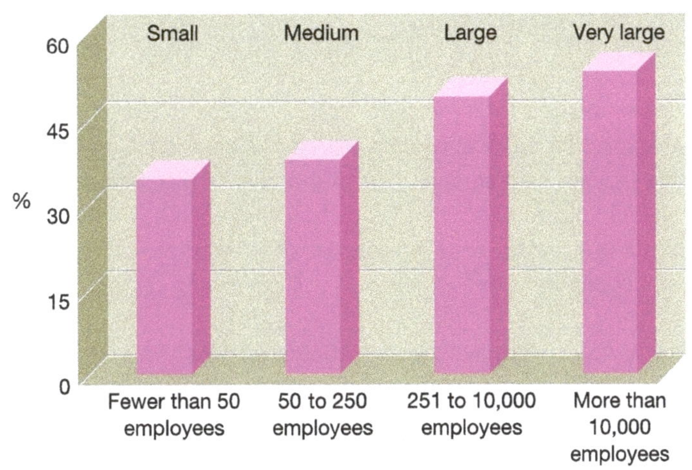

Full cost information is fairly widely used and the size of the business seems to be a factor. It is used by about 45 per cent of all of the businesses surveyed.

Figure 4.12 The use of full cost information

Source: Figure adapted from CIMA (2009) *Management Accounting Tools for Today and Tomorrow*, p. 12.

The CIMA survey reveals that full cost information is more widely used by larger businesses than by smaller ones. The reasons for this are not clear. It may be that larger businesses have greater resources and expertise than smaller ones. This may enable them to employ techniques that are simply not practical for smaller businesses. On the other hand, it may reflect the different types of business within each size category.

Full (absorption) costing and relevant costs

We saw in Chapter 2 that relevant costs for decision-making purposes are future costs that vary with the decision. Full costing, on the other hand, tends to rely on past cost. In addition, it focuses on outlay cost and ignores opportunity costs. This appears to suggest an unbridgeable gap between the relevant cost approach and the full costing approach. If so, the usefulness of full costing for decision-making purposes is called into question.

In theory, relevant cost analysis should be used when deciding to set a price for a product, to introduce a new product, or to cease to produce an existing product. In practice, however, it may not be feasible to do this. Let us assume that a business makes fifty products. Here the range of possibilities is enormous. In addition to carrying out relevant cost analysis on each product, combinations of two, three, four products and so on may also have to be carried out to identify the consequences of product decisions. To help managers cope with a tsunami of possible options, full cost information may act as a useful filter. It can direct attention to those products or services that would benefit from relevant cost analysis. By providing an indication of the long-run average cost of each product, managers have some idea of the long-term cash outflows to be incurred. They may then decide to investigate further using relevant cost analysis.

FULL (ABSORPTION) COSTING VERSUS VARIABLE COSTING

An alternative to full (absorption) costing is **variable (marginal) costing** – which we discussed in Chapter 3. We may recall that this approach distinguishes between fixed and variable costs.

A variable costing approach will measure its income in a different way to that which we came across in this chapter. Variable costing will include only variable cost, including variable direct and variable indirect elements, as part of the cost of the goods or service produced. Any fixed cost, including fixed direct and fixed indirect elements, will be treated as a cost of the period in which it is incurred. Thus, inventories of finished products, or work in progress, carried from one accounting period to the next, will be valued on the basis of their variable cost only.

As we have seen, full costing includes in product cost not only the direct cost (whether fixed or variable) but also a 'fair' share of the indirect cost (both fixed and variable) that was incurred during the period that the product is produced.

To illustrate the difference between the two approaches, let us consider Example 4.7.

Example 4.7

Lahore Ltd commenced operations on 1 June and makes a single product, which sells for £14 per unit. In the first two months of operations, the following results were achieved:

	June (*number of units*)	*July* (*number of units*)
Production output	6,000	6,000
Sales volume	4,000	5,000
Opening inventories	–	2,000
Closing inventories	2,000	3,000

Manufacturing overhead cost (all fixed) is £18,000 per month and direct manufacturing cost is £5 per unit. There is also a monthly fixed non-manufacturing overhead cost (marketing and administration) of £5,000. There was no work in progress at the end of either June or July. Lahore Ltd's direct costs are all variable and all overheads are fixed.

The operating profit for each month is calculated below, first using a variable costing approach and then a full costing approach.

Variable costing

In this case, only the variable costs are charged to the units produced and all the fixed cost (manufacturing and non-manufacturing) is charged to the period. Inventories will be carried forward at their variable cost.

	June		*July*	
	£	£	£	£
Sales revenue				
(4,000 × £14)		56,000		
(5,000 × £14)				70,000
Opening inventories				
(2,000 × £5)	–		10,000	
Cost of units produced				
(6,000 × £5)	30,000		30,000	
Closing inventories				
(2,000 × £5)	(10,000)	(20,000)		
(3,000 × £5)			(15,000)	(25,000)
Contribution margin		36,000		45,000
Fixed cost:				
Manufacturing	(18,000)		(18,000)	
Non-manufacturing	(5,000)	(23,000)	(5,000)	(23,000)
Operating profit		13,000		22,000

Full costing

In this case, the manufacturing overhead cost becomes part of the product cost and inventories are carried forward to the next period at their full cost – that is, direct (all variable) cost *plus* an appropriate manufacturing overhead (all fixed) cost element. There are 6,000 units produced in each period and the fixed manufacturing overhead cost for each period is £18,000. Hence, the manufacturing overhead cost element per unit is £3 (that is, £18,000/6,000). The full cost per unit will therefore be £8 (that is, £5 + £3).

	June		*July*	
	£	£	£	£
Sales revenue				
(4,000 × £14)		56,000		
(5,000 × £14)				70,000
Opening inventories	–			
(2,000 × £8)			16,000	
Cost of units produced				
(6,000 × £8)	48,000		48,000	
Closing inventories				
(2,000 × £8)	(16,000)	(32,000)		
(3,000 × £8)			(24,000)	(40,000)
Gross profit		24,000		30,000
Non-manufacturing cost		(5,000)		(5,000)
Operating profit		19,000		25,000

We can see that the total operating profit over the two months is £35,000 (that is, £13,000 + £22,000) when derived on a variable cost basis. On a full cost basis it is £44,000 (that is, £19,000 + £25,000). This is a difference of £9,000 (that is, £44,000 − £35,000). This is accounted for by the fact that the manufacturing overhead (all fixed) cost element of the inventories valuation at the end of July, on the full cost basis (that is, 3,000 × £3), has yet to be treated as an expense. It has already been treated as an expense on the variable cost basis, however.

It should be noted that Lahore Ltd's overheads are all fixed and that its direct costs are all variable. This would be highly unusual in practice, but was used as the assumption in this example in the interests of simplicity.

In practice, the choice of costing approach may not have such a dramatic effect on reported profit as shown in Example 4.7. Differences in operating profit revealed in this example arise from the changes in inventories levels between periods – from zero at the beginning of June, to 2,000 units at the end of June, to 3,000 units by the end of July. These are significant changes in the context of a monthly output of only 6,000 units. In practice, this would be unusual. Where similar amounts of inventories and work in progress are held at reporting-period ends and fixed cost remains unchanged from one reporting period to the next, reported profit will not vary much between the two approaches. This is because a similar amount of fixed cost will be treated as an expense each year; all of it originating from the current year in the case of variable costing, some of it originating from past years in the case of full costing.

It is important to note that, over the entire life of a particular business, total operating profit will be the same whichever costing method has been applied. This is because, ultimately, all fixed costs will be charged as expenses.

Which method is better?

A key difference between the two approaches is that, under the variable costing approach, profit is influenced only by changes in sales. Profit under the full (absorption costing) approach, on the other hand, is influenced by changes in the level of both sales and production.

Activity 4.17

Briefly explain why profit calculated under an absorption costing approach is influenced by changes in the level of production (as well as sales). Take a look at Example 4.7 to help you.

Under a variable costing approach, all fixed production costs are charged to the period in which they are incurred. Under an absorption costing approach, fixed production costs are assigned to inventories and only the fixed production costs linked to those inventories that are sold during the period are charged against that period's sales revenue. Where production exceeds sales for a period, some of the fixed production costs incurred during the period will be carried forward in inventories to the next period. The larger the amount of fixed production costs carried forward, the smaller will be the amount charged against profit for the current period. Where sales exceed production, profit for the current period will be charged with fixed production costs brought forward in inventories from the previous period.

It is claimed that, by ignoring the effect of changes in the level of production, the profit measure derived under variable costing provides a more realistic measure of overall achievement. In a multi-product environment, however, the profitability of each item cannot be determined unless each is assigned a fair share of *all* costs. After all, goods and services cannot be provided unless fixed costs are incurred in their production. This suggests that full (absorption) costing provides a fairer measure of profit, item by item.

Variable costing highlights the key relationship between costs, volume of output and profit. This can be very helpful when making a range of management decisions. Full (absorption) costing, on the other hand, tends to obscure this relationship. Under normal reporting procedures, fixed and variable costs are not separated out. It would, however, be possible to separate them.

We saw in Chapter 3 that variable costing identifies those costs that can be avoided in the short term. This again may be very helpful when making a range of management decisions. A powerful counterargument, however, is that, over the long term, all elements of cost can be avoided. For managers to focus solely on those that can be avoided over the short term (the variable costs) may be a bad idea. When making long-term planning decisions, for example, managers need to know the full cost of producing products or services.

In practice, management accountants can prepare internal financial reports using either approach. We have seen, however, that absorption costing must be used for external reporting purposes. Some businesses align their internal reporting procedures with their external reporting procedures. A potential advantage of doing so is that managers are encouraged to focus on the same numbers as those presented to shareholders and lenders.

Real World 4.7 provides some indication of the extent to which variable costing is used in practice.

Real World 4.7

Variable costing in practice

A survey of 41 UK manufacturing businesses found that 68 per cent of them used a variable costing approach to management reporting.

Many would find this surprising. The requirement is for financial statements in published annual reports to be in full-cost terms. It seemed to be widely believed that this has led those businesses to use a full-cost approach for management reporting as well. This appears not to be the case, however.

It should be added that many of those that used variable costing quite possibly misused it. For example, three-quarters of those that used it treated labour cost as variable. Possibly in some cases the cost of labour is variable (with the level of activity), but it seems likely that this is not true for most of these businesses. At the same time, most of the 68 per cent treat all overheads as a fixed cost. It seems likely that, for most businesses, overheads would have a variable element.

Source: Dugdale, D., Jones, C. and Green, S. (2005) *Contemporary Management Accounting Practices in UK Manufacturing*, CIMA Research Publication, Vol. 1, Number 13.

Self-assessment question 4.1

Hector and Co. Ltd has been invited to tender for a contract to produce 1,000 clothes hangers. The following information relates to the contract.

- *Materials*: The clothes hangers are made of metal wire covered with a padded fabric. Each hanger requires 2 metres of wire and 0.5 square metres of fabric.
- *Direct labour*: Each hanger requires 10 minutes of skilled labour and 5 minutes of unskilled labour.

The business already holds sufficient of each of the materials required to complete the contract. Information on the cost of the materials is as follows:

	Metal wire	*Fabric*
	£/m	*£/sq m*
Historic cost	2.20	1.00
Current buying-in cost	2.50	1.10
Scrap value	1.70	0.40

The metal wire is in constant use by the business for a range of its products. The fabric has no other use for the business and is scheduled to be scrapped if the present contract does not go ahead.

Unskilled labour, which is paid at the rate of £7.50 an hour, will need to be taken on specifically to undertake the contract. The business is fairly quiet at the moment, which means that a pool of skilled labour exists that will still be employed at full pay of £12.00 an hour to do nothing if the contract does not proceed. The pool of skilled labour is sufficient to complete the contract.

The business charges jobs with overheads on a direct labour hour basis. The production overheads of the entire business for the month in which the contract will be undertaken are estimated at £50,000. The estimated total direct labour hours that will be worked are 12,500. The business tends not to alter the established overhead recovery rate to reflect increases or reductions to estimated total hours arising from new contracts. The total overheads are not expected to increase as a result of undertaking the contract.

The business normally adds 12.5 per cent profit loading to the job cost to arrive at a first estimate of the tender price.

Required:

(a) Price this job on a traditional job-costing basis.

(b) Indicate the minimum price at which the contract could be undertaken such that the business would be neither better nor worse off as a result of doing it.

The solution to this question can be found in Appendix B.

SUMMARY

The main points of this chapter may be summarised as follows:

Full (absorption) cost = the total amount of resources sacrificed to achieve a particular objective

Uses of full (absorption) cost information

- Pricing and output decisions.
- Exercising control.
- Assessing relative efficiency.
- Assessing performance.

Single-product businesses – process costing

- Where all units of output are identical, the full cost can be calculated as follows:

$$\text{Cost per unit} = \frac{\text{Total cost of output}}{\text{Number of units produced}}$$

- Where there is work in progress at the end of the period, the equivalent units of output that work in progress represents must be calculated to derive total output and cost per unit of output.

Multi-product businesses – job costing

- Where units of output are not identical, it is necessary to divide the cost into two categories: direct cost and indirect cost (overheads).
- Direct cost = cost that can be identified with, and measured in respect of, specific cost units (for example, labour of a garage mechanic, in relation to a particular car repair).
- Indirect cost (overheads) = cost that cannot be identified with, and measured in respect of, a particular job (for example, the rent of a garage).
- Full (absorption) cost = direct cost + indirect cost.
- Direct/indirect cost is not linked to variable/fixed cost.
- Indirect cost is difficult to assign to individual cost units – arbitrary bases are used and there is no single correct method.

→

- Traditionally, indirect cost is seen as the cost of providing a 'service' to cost units.
- Time-based methods, such as the direct labour hour method, are often used to assign indirect cost to cost units in practice.

Dealing with indirect cost on a cost centre (departmental) basis

- Indirect cost (overheads) can be segmented – usually on a cost centre basis – each product cost centre has its own overhead recovery rate.
- Cost centres are areas, activities or functions for which costs are separately determined.
- Overheads must be allocated or apportioned to cost centres.
- Service cost centre cost must then be apportioned to product cost centre overheads.
- Product cost centre overheads must then be absorbed by cost units (jobs).

Batch costing

- A variation of job costing where each job consists of a number of identical (or near identical) cost units:

$$\text{Cost per unit} = \frac{\text{Cost of the batch (direct + indirect)}}{\text{Number of units in the batch}}$$

Full cost information and relevant cost

- Full costing has been criticised for ignoring relevant costs. It focuses on past costs and ignores opportunity costs.
- Relevant cost analysis can be difficult to apply in practice because of the range of possible options.
- Full costing can help in directing managers' attention to areas that may benefit from relevant cost analysis.

Full (absorption) costing versus variable costing

- With full costing, both fixed and variable costs are included in product cost and treated as expenses when the product is sold.
- With variable costing, only the variable product cost is linked to the products in this way. Fixed cost is treated as an expense of the period in which it was incurred.
- Variable costing tends to be more straightforward and, according to proponents, provides a more realistic measure of overall achievement.
- Proponents of full costing argue, however, that it provides a better measure of profitability, item by item. Manufacturing fixed costs are an essential ingredient of total product cost.
- Variable costing highlights the relationship between cost, volume and profit, which is obscured under a full costing system.
- Variable costing directs managers' attention to those (variable) costs that can be avoided in the short term. However, all costs can be avoided in the long term and it may be a bad idea to focus on the short term.

KEY TERMS

For definitions of these terms, see Appendix A.

Full cost
Full costing
Cost unit
Process costing
Work in progress
Equivalent units of output
Job costing
Direct cost
Indirect cost
Overheads
Common cost
Absorption costing
Cost behaviour
Overhead absorption (recovery) rate
Cost-plus pricing
Cost centre
Product cost centre
Service cost centre
Cost allocation
Cost apportionment
Batch costing
Variable (marginal) costing

REFERENCE

1 Drury, C. and Tayles, M. (1994) Product costing in UK manufacturing organisations, *European Accounting Review* 3:3, pp. 443–469.

FURTHER READING

If you would like to explore the topics covered in this chapter in more depth, we recommend the following:

Drury, C. (2012) *Management and Cost Accounting*, 8th edn, Cengage Learning, Chapters 3, 4 and 5.

Hilton, R. and Platt, D. (2014) *Managerial Accounting*, 10th edn, McGraw-Hill Higher Education, Chapters 2 and 3.

Horngren, C., Datar, S. and Rajan, M. (2012) *Cost Accounting: A Managerial Emphasis*, 14th edn, Prentice Hall International, Chapter 4.

Kaplan, R., Atkinson, A., Matsumura, E. and Young, S.M. (2011) *Management Accounting*, 6th edn, Prentice Hall, Chapter 4.

REVIEW QUESTIONS

Solutions to these questions can be found in Appendix C.

4.1 What problem does the existence of work in progress cause in process costing?

4.2 What is the point of distinguishing direct cost from indirect cost? Why is this not necessary in process-costing environments?

4.3 Are direct cost and variable cost the same thing? Explain your answer.

4.4 It is sometimes claimed that the full cost of a product or service reflects the break-even selling price. Why is this said and what does it mean?

EXERCISES

Exercises 4.1, 4.2 and 4.3 are basic level, 4.4 and 4.5 are intermediate level and 4.6, 4.7 and 4.8 are advanced level. Those with coloured numbers have solutions given in Appendix D.

4.1 Consider this statement:

'In a job costing system, it is necessary to divide up the business into departments. Fixed costs (or overheads) will be collected for each department. Where a particular fixed cost relates to the business as a whole, it must be divided between the departments. Usually this is done on the basis of area of floor space occupied by each department relative to the entire business. When the total fixed costs for each department have been identified, this will be divided by the number of hours that were worked in each department to deduce an overhead recovery rate. Each job that was worked on in a department will have a share of fixed cost allotted to it according to how long it was worked on. The total cost for each job will therefore be the sum of the variable cost of the job and its share of the fixed cost.'

Required:
Prepare a table of two columns. In the first column you should show any phrases or sentences in the above statement with which you do not agree. In the second column you should show your reason for disagreeing with each one.

4.2 Bodgers Ltd, a business that provides a market research service, operates a job costing system. Towards the end of each financial year, the overhead recovery rate (the rate at which indirect cost will be absorbed by jobs) is established for the forthcoming year.

(a) Why does the business bother to predetermine the recovery rate in the way outlined?
(b) What steps will be involved in predetermining the rate?
(c) What problems might arise with using a predetermined rate?

4.3 Pieman Products Ltd makes road trailers to the precise specifications of individual customers.

The following are predicted to occur during the forthcoming year, which is about to start:

Direct materials cost	£50,000
Direct labour cost	£160,000
Direct labour time	16,000 hours
Indirect labour cost	£25,000
Depreciation of machine	£8,000
Rent	£10,000
Heating, lighting and power	£5,000
Indirect materials	£2,000
Other indirect cost (overhead) elements	£1,000
Machine time	3,000 hours

All direct labour is paid at the same hourly rate.

A customer has asked the business to build a trailer for transporting a racing motorcycle to race meetings. It is estimated that this will require materials and components that will cost £1,150. It will take 250 direct labour hours to do the job, of which 50 will involve the use of machinery.

Required:
Deduce a logical cost for the job and explain the basis of dealing with overheads that you propose.

4.4 Promptprint Ltd, a printing business, has received an enquiry from a potential customer for the quotation of a price for a job. The pricing policy of the business is based on the plans for the next financial year shown below.

	£
Sales revenue (billings to customers)	196,000
Materials (direct)	(38,000)
Labour (direct)	(32,000)
Variable overheads	(2,400)
Maintenance	(3,000)
Depreciation	(27,600)
Rent	(36,000)
Heat and light	(8,000)
Profit	49,000

A first estimate of the direct cost for the particular job is:

	£
Direct materials	4,000
Direct labour	3,600

Required:

(a) Prepare a recommended price for the job based on the plans, commenting on your method, ignoring the information given in the Appendix (below).

(b) Incorporate the effects of the information shown in the Appendix (below) into your estimates of the direct material cost, explaining any changes you consider it necessary to make to the above direct material cost of £4,000.

Appendix to Exercise 4.4

Based on historic cost, direct material cost was computed as follows:

	£
Paper grade 1	1,200
Paper grade 2	2,000
Card (zenith grade)	500
Inks and other miscellaneous items	300
	4,000

Paper grade 1 is regularly used by the business. Enough of this paper to complete the job is currently held. Because it is imported, it is estimated that if it is used for this job, a new purchase order will have to be placed shortly. Sterling has depreciated against the foreign currency by 25 per cent since the last purchase.

Paper grade 2 is purchased from the same source as grade 1. The business holds exactly enough of it for the job, but this was bought in for a special order. This order was cancelled, although the defaulting customer was required to pay £500 towards the cost of the paper. The accountant has offset this against the original cost to arrive at the figure of £2,000 shown above. This paper is rarely used and due to its special chemical coating will be unusable if it is not used on the job in question.

The card is another specialist item currently held by the business. There is no use foreseen and it would cost £750 to replace, if required. However, the inventories controller had planned to spend £130 on overprinting to use the card as a substitute for other materials costing £640.

Inks and other items are in regular use in the print shop.

4.5 Many businesses charge overheads to jobs on a cost centre basis.

Required:

(a) What is the advantage that is claimed for charging overheads to jobs on a cost centre basis and why is it claimed?

(b) What circumstances need to exist for it to make a difference to a particular job whether overheads are charged on a business-wide basis or on a cost centre basis? (Note that the answer to this part of the question is not specifically covered in the chapter. You should, nevertheless, be able to deduce the reason from what you know.)

4.6 Shown below is an extract from next year's plans for a business manufacturing three products, A, B and C, in three product cost centres.

	A	*B*	*C*
Production	4,000 units	3,000 units	6,000 units
Direct material cost	£7 per unit	£4 per unit	£9 per unit
Direct labour requirements:			
Cutting department:			
Skilled operatives	3 hr/unit	5 hr/unit	2 hr/unit
Unskilled operatives	6 hr/unit	1 hr/unit	3 hr/unit
Machining department	1/2 hr/unit	1/4 hr/unit	1/3 hr/unit
Pressing department	2 hr/unit	3 hr/unit	4 hr/unit
Machine requirements:			
Machining department	2 hr/unit	1 1/2 hr/unit	2 1/2 hr/unit

The skilled operatives employed in the cutting department are paid £16 an hour and the unskilled operatives are paid £10 an hour. All the operatives in the machining and pressing departments are paid £12 an hour.

	Product cost centres			*Service cost centres*	
	Cutting	*Machining*	*Pressing*	*Engineering*	*Human resources*
Planned total overheads	£154,482	£64,316	£58,452	£56,000	£34,000
Service cost centre					
Cost incurred for the benefit of other cost centres, as follows:					
Engineering services	20%	45%	35%	–	
Human resources services	55%	10%	20%	15%	

The business operates a full absorption costing system.

Required:

Derive the total planned cost of:

(a) One completed unit of product A.

(b) One incomplete unit of product B, which has been processed by the cutting and machining departments but which has not yet been passed into the pressing department.

4.7 Athena Ltd is an engineering business doing work for its customers to their particular requirements and specifications. It determines the full cost of each job taking a 'job-costing' approach, accounting for overheads on a cost centre (departmental) basis. It bases its prices to customers on this full cost figure. The business has two departments (both of which are cost centres): a Machining Department, where each job starts, and a Fitting Department, which completes all of the jobs. Machining Department overheads are charged to jobs on a machine hour basis and those of the Fitting Department on a direct labour hour basis. The budgeted information for next year is as follows:

Heating and lighting	£25,000	(allocated equally between the two departments)
Machine power	£10,000	(all allocated to the Machining Department)
Direct labour	£200,000	(£150,000 allocated to the Fitting Department and £50,000 to the Machining Department; all direct workers are paid £10 an hour)
Indirect labour	£50,000	(apportioned to the departments in proportion to the direct labour cost)
Direct materials	£120,000	(all applied to jobs in the Machining Department)
Depreciation	£30,000	(all relates to the Machining Department)
Machine time	20,000 hours	(all worked in the Machining Department)

Required:

(a) Prepare a statement showing the budgeted overheads for next year, analysed between the two cost centres. This should be in the form of three columns: one for the total figure for each type of overhead and one column each for the two cost centres, where each type of overhead is analysed between the two cost centres. Each column should also show the total of overheads for the year.

(b) Derive the appropriate rate for charging the overheads of each cost centre to jobs (that is, a separate rate for each cost centre).

(c) Athena Ltd has been asked by a customer to specify the price that it will charge for a particular job that will, if the job goes ahead, be undertaken early next year. The job is expected to use direct materials costing Athena Ltd £1,200, to need 50 hours of machining time, 10 hours of Machine Department direct labour and 20 hours of Fitting Department direct labour. Athena Ltd charges a profit loading of 20 per cent to the full cost of jobs to determine the selling price.

Show workings to derive the proposed selling price for this job.

4.8 Bookdon plc manufactures three products, X, Y and Z, in two product cost centres: a machine shop and a fitting section; it also has two service cost centres: a canteen and a machine maintenance section. Shown below are next year's planned production data and manufacturing cost for the business.

	X	*Y*	*Z*
Production	4,200 units	6,900 units	1,700 units
Direct materials	£11/unit	£14/unit	£17/unit
Direct labour:			
Machine shop	£6/unit	£4/unit	£2/unit
Fitting section	£12/unit	£3/unit	£21/unit
Machine hours	6 hr/unit	3 hr/unit	4 hr/unit

Planned overheads are as follows:

	Machine shop	*Fitting section*	*Canteen*	*Machine maintenance section*	*Total*
Allocated overheads	£27,660	£19,470	£16,600	£26,650	£90,380
Rent, heat and light					£17,000
Depreciation and insurance of equipment					£25,000
Additional data:					
Gross carrying amount of equipment	£150,000	£75,000	£30,000	£45,000	
Number of employees	18	14	4	4	
Floor space occupied	3,600 sq m	1,400 sq m	1,000 sq m	800 sq m	

All machining is carried out in the machine shop. It has been estimated that approximately 70 per cent of the machine maintenance section's cost is incurred servicing the machine shop and the remainder servicing the fitting section.

Required:

(a) Calculate the following planned overhead absorption rates:

(i) A machine hour rate for the machine shop.

(ii) A rate expressed as a percentage of direct wages for the fitting section.

(b) Calculate the planned full cost per unit of product X.

Chapter 5

COSTING AND COST MANAGEMENT IN A COMPETITIVE ENVIRONMENT

INTRODUCTION

We saw in Chapter 1 that major changes have occurred in the business world in recent years. They include more demanding customers, deregulation, privatisation, growing expectations among shareholders and the impact of new technology. These changes have led to a much faster changing and more competitive environment that has radically altered the way that businesses should be managed. In this chapter we shall consider some of the accounting techniques that have been developed to help businesses maintain their competitiveness in this new era.

We begin this chapter by considering the impact of the competitive environment on the traditional full-costing approach. This approach, which was examined in Chapter 4, has been much criticised for obscuring important information needed to manage costs. Activity-based costing (ABC) is a full-costing approach that offers an alternative to the traditional one. We shall see later how it takes a much more enquiring, much less accepting attitude towards indirect cost (overheads).

To provide goods and services that meet customers' requirements for quality and price, yet deliver an acceptable financial return, businesses are creating much leaner operations. There is a relentless focus on eliminating waste and spending only on value-creating activities. We end the chapter by exploring the costing and cost management methods developed to support this focus.

Learning outcomes

When you have completed this chapter, you should be able to:

- Describe the nature of the modern product costing and pricing environment.
- Discuss the principles and practical aspects of activity-based costing.
- Describe the methods that may be used to manage costs over the life cycle of a product.
- Explain the role of value chain analysis and benchmarking in managing costs.
- Explain the importance of total quality management in the modern environment and identify the main types of quality costs that may be incurred.

COST DETERMINATION IN THE CHANGED BUSINESS ENVIRONMENT

Costing and pricing: the traditional way

The traditional, and still widely used, approach to job costing developed when the notion of trying to determine the cost of industrial production first emerged. This was around the time of the UK Industrial Revolution when industry was characterised by the following:

- *Direct-labour-intensive and direct-labour-paced production*. Labour was at the heart of production. To the extent that machinery was used, it tended to support the efforts of direct labour and the speed of production was dictated by direct labour.
- *A low level of indirect cost relative to direct cost.* Little was spent on power, personnel services, machinery (depreciation charges) and other areas typical of the indirect cost (overheads) of modern businesses.
- *A relatively uncompetitive market.* Transport difficulties, limited industrial production worldwide and a lack of knowledge by customers of competitors' prices meant that businesses could prosper without being too scientific in costing. Typically they could simply add a margin for profit to arrive at the selling price (cost-plus pricing). Customers would have tended to accept those products that the supplier had to offer, rather than demanding precisely what they wanted.

Since overheads at that time represented a pretty small element of total cost, it was acceptable and practical to deal with them in a fairly arbitrary manner. Not too much effort was devoted to trying to control overheads because the potential rewards of better control were relatively small, certainly when compared with the benefits from firmer control of direct labour and material costs. It was also reasonable to charge overheads to individual jobs on a direct labour hour basis. Most of the overheads were incurred directly in support of direct labour: providing direct workers with a place to work, heating and lighting the workplace, employing people to supervise the direct workers and so on. Direct workers, perhaps aided by machinery, carried out all production.

At that time, service industries were a relatively unimportant part of the economy and would have largely consisted of self-employed individuals. These individuals would probably have been uninterested in trying to do more than work out a rough hourly/daily rate for their time and to try to base prices on this.

Costing and pricing: the new environment

In recent years, the world of industrial production has fundamentally changed. Most of it is now characterised by:

- *Capital-intensive and machine-paced production.* Machines are at the heart of much production, including both the manufacture of goods and the rendering of services. Most labour supports the efforts of machines, for example, technically maintaining them. Also, machines often dictate the pace of production. According to evidence provided in Real World 4.2 (page 106), direct labour accounts on average for just 14 per cent of manufacturers' total cost.

- *A high level of indirect cost relative to direct costs.* Modern businesses tend to have very high depreciation, servicing and power costs. There are also high costs of personnel and staff welfare, which were scarcely envisaged in the early days of industrial production. At the same time, there are very low (sometimes no) direct labour costs. Although direct material cost often remains an important element of total cost, more efficient production methods lead to less waste and, therefore, to a lower total material cost, again tending to make indirect cost (overheads) more dominant. Again according to Real World 4.2, overheads account for 25 per cent of manufacturers' total cost and 51 per cent of service sector total cost.
- *A highly competitive international market.* Production, much of it highly sophisticated, is carried out worldwide. Transport, including fast airfreight, is relatively cheap. Fax, telephone and, particularly, the internet ensure that potential customers can quickly and cheaply find the prices of a range of suppliers. Markets now tend to be highly price-competitive. Customers increasingly demand products custom made to their own requirements. This means that businesses need to know their product costs with a greater degree of accuracy than historically has been the case. Businesses also need to take a considered and informed approach to pricing their output.

In the UK, as in many developed countries, service industries now dominate the economy, employing the great majority of the workforce and producing most of the value of productive output. Though there are still many self-employed individuals supplying services, many service providers are vast businesses.

Activity 5.1

Can you think of any service providers that are vast businesses?

Four types that we came up with are banks, restaurant chains, insurance companies and cinema operators.

For most of these larger service providers, the activities very closely resemble modern manufacturing activity. They too are characterised by high capital-intensity, overheads dominating direct costs and a competitive international market.

COST MANAGEMENT SYSTEMS

Changes in the competitive environment mean that businesses must now manage costs much more effectively than in the past. This, in turn, places an obligation on cost management systems that will provide the information that enables managers to do this. Traditional cost management systems have often proved inadequate for the task and so new systems have gained in popularity in recent years. We shall take a look at some of these systems shortly but, before doing so, we shall consider an important reason why the need for new systems has arisen.

The problem of overheads

In Chapter 4 we considered the traditional approach to job costing (deriving the full cost of output where one unit of output differs from another). We may recall that this approach involves collecting, for each job, those costs that can be clearly linked to, and measured in respect of, that particular job (direct costs). All indirect costs (overheads) are allocated or apportioned to product cost centres and then charged to individual jobs according to some formula. The evidence suggests that this formula is usually based on the number of direct labour hours worked on each particular job (see Real World 4.4, page 116).

In the past, this approach has worked reasonably well, largely because overhead recovery rates (that is, rates at which overheads are absorbed by jobs) were typically of a much lower value for each direct labour hour than the rate paid to direct workers as wages or salaries. It is now, however, becoming increasingly common for overhead recovery rates to be between five and ten times the hourly rate of pay, because overheads are now much more significant. When production is dominated by direct labour paid, say, £10 an hour, it might be reasonable to have an overhead recovery rate of, say, £1 an hour. When, however, direct labour plays a relatively small part in production, to have an overhead recovery rate of, say, £60 for each direct labour hour is likely to lead to very arbitrary product costing. Even a small change in the amount of direct labour worked on a job could massively affect the total cost deduced. This is not because the direct worker is very highly paid, but because of the effect of the direct labour hours on the overhead cost loading. A further problem is that overheads are still typically charged on a direct labour-hour basis even though the overheads may not be closely related to direct labour.

Real World 5.1 provides a rather disturbing view of costing and cost control in large banks.

Real World 5.1

Bank accounts

In a study of the cost structures of 52 international banks, the German consultancy firm, Droege, found that indirect cost (overheads) could represent as much as 85 per cent of total cost. However, while direct costs were generally under tight management control, overheads were not. The overheads, which include such items as IT development, risk control, auditing, marketing and public relations, were often not allocated between operating divisions or were allocated in a rather arbitrary manner.

Source: Based on information in Skorecki, A. (2004) Banks have not tackled indirect costs, ft.com, 7 January.

Taking a closer look

The changes in the competitive environment discussed above have led to much closer attention being paid to the issue of overheads, what causes them and how they are charged to jobs. Historically, businesses have been content to accept that overheads exist and, therefore, for job (product) costing purposes they must be dealt with in as practical a way as possible. In recent years, however, there has been increasing recognition of the fact that overheads do not just happen; something must be causing them. To illustrate this point, let us consider Example 5.1.

Example 5.1

Modern Producers Ltd has a storage area that is set aside for its inventories of finished goods. The cost of running the stores includes a share of the factory rent and other establishment costs, such as heating and lighting. It also includes the salaries of staff employed to look after the inventories and the cost of financing the inventories held in the stores.

The business has two product lines: A and B. Product A tends to be made in small batches and low levels of finished inventories are held. The business prides itself on its ability to supply Product B, in relatively large quantities, instantly. As a consequence, most of the space in the finished goods store is filled with finished Product Bs, ready to be despatched immediately an order is received.

Traditionally, the whole cost of operating the stores would have been treated as a part of general overheads and included in the total of overheads charged to jobs, probably on a direct labour hour basis. This means that, when assessing the cost of Products A and B, the cost of operating the stores has fallen on them according to the number of direct labour hours worked on manufacturing each one, a factor that has nothing to do with storage. In fact, most of the stores' cost should be charged to Product B, since this product causes (and benefits from) the stores' cost much more than Product A.

Failure to account more precisely for the cost of running the stores is masking the fact that Product B is not as profitable as it seems to be. It may even be leading to losses as a result of the relatively high stores-operating cost that it causes. However, much of this cost is charged to Product A, without regard to the fact that Product A causes little of it.

ACTIVITY-BASED COSTING

Activity-based costing (ABC) aims to overcome the kind of problem just described by directly tracing the cost of all support activities (that is, overheads) to particular products or services. For a manufacturing business, these support activities may include materials ordering, materials handling, storage, inspection and so on. The cost of the support activities makes up the total overheads cost. The outcome of this tracing exercise is to provide a more realistic, and more finely measured, account of the overhead cost element for a particular product or service.

To implement a system of ABC, managers must begin by carefully examining the business's operations. They will need to identify:

- each of the various support activities involved in the process of making products or providing services;
- the costs to be attributed to each support activity; and
- the factors that cause a change in the costs of each support activity, that is, the **cost drivers**.

Identifying the cost drivers is a vital element of a successful ABC system. They have a cause-and-effect relationship with activity costs and so are used as a basis for attaching activity costs to a particular product or service. This point is now discussed in further detail.

Attributing overheads

Once the various support activities, their costs and the factors that drive these costs have been identified, ABC requires three steps:

- Establishing an overhead **cost pool** for each activity. Thus, the business in Example 5.1 will create a cost pool for operating the finished goods store. There will be just one cost pool for each separate cost driver.
- Allocating the total cost associated with each support activity to the relevant cost pool.
- Charging the output with the total cost in each pool using the relevant cost driver. (In the case of Example 5.1, Products A and B would be the output.)

This third step involves dividing the amount in each cost pool by the estimated total usage of the cost driver to derive a cost per unit of the cost driver. This unit cost figure is then multiplied by the number of units of the cost driver used by a particular product, or service, to determine the amount of overhead cost to be attached to it (or absorbed by it). Example 5.2 should make this clear.

Example 5.2

The management accountant at Modern Producers Ltd (see Example 5.1) has estimated that the cost of running the finished goods stores for next year will be £90,000. This will be the amount allocated to the 'finished goods stores cost pool'.

It is estimated that each Product A will spend an average of one week in the stores before being sold. With Product B, the equivalent period is four weeks. Both products are of roughly similar size and have very similar storage needs. It is felt, therefore, that the period spent in the stores ('product weeks') is the cost driver.

Next year, 50,000 Product As and 25,000 Product Bs are expected to pass through the stores. The estimated total usage of the cost driver will be the total number of 'product weeks' that the products will be in store. For next year, this will be:

Product A 50,000 × 1 week =	50,000
Product B 25,000 × 4 weeks =	100,000
	150,000

The cost per unit of cost driver is the total cost of the stores divided by the number of 'product weeks', as calculated above. This is:

£90,000/150,000 = £0.60

To determine the cost to be attached to a particular unit of product, the figure of £0.60 must be multiplied by the number of 'product weeks' that a product stays in the finished goods store. Thus, each unit of Product A will be charged with £0.60 (that is, £0.60 × 1) and each Product B with £2.40 (that is, £0.60 × 4).

Benefits of ABC

Through the direct tracing of overheads to products in the way described, ABC seeks to establish a more accurate cost for each unit of product or service. This should help managers in assessing product profitability and in making decisions concerning pricing and the appropriate product mix. Other benefits, however, may also flow from adopting an ABC approach.

Activity 5.2

Can you think of any other benefits that an ABC approach to costing may provide?

By identifying the various support activities' costs and analysing what causes them to change, managers should gain a better understanding of the business. This, in turn, should help them in controlling overheads and improving efficiency. It should also help them in forward planning. They may, for example, be in a better position to assess the likely effect of new products and processes on activities and costs.

ABC versus the traditional approach

We can see that there is a basic philosophical difference between the traditional and the ABC approaches. The traditional approach views overheads as *rendering a service to cost units*, the cost of which must be charged to those units. ABC, on the other hand, views overheads as being *caused by* activities. Since it is the cost units that cause these activities, it is, therefore, the cost units that must be charged with the costs that they cause.

With the traditional approach, overheads are apportioned to product cost centres. Each product cost centre would then derive an overhead recovery rate, typically overheads per direct labour hour. Overheads would then be applied to units of output according to how many direct labour hours were worked on them.

With ABC, the overheads are analysed into cost pools, with one cost pool for each cost-driving activity. The overheads are then charged to units of output, through activity cost driver rates. These rates attempt to reflect the extent to which each cost unit is believed to cause the particular part of the overheads.

Cost pools are much the same as cost centres, except that each cost pool is linked to a particular *activity* (operating the stores in Examples 5.1 and 5.2), rather than being more general, as is the case with cost centres in traditional job (or product) costing.

The two different approaches are illustrated in Figure 5.1.

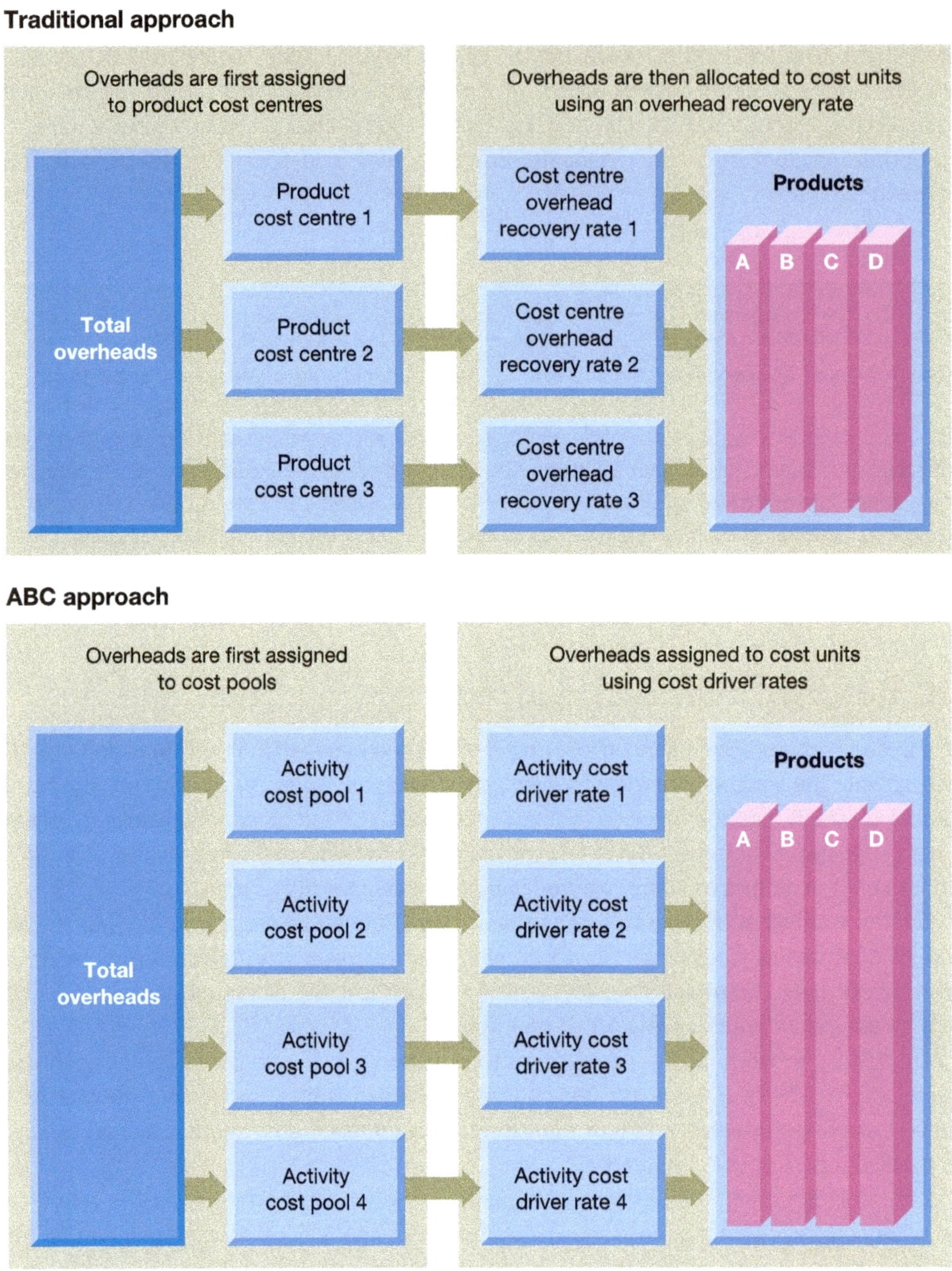

With the traditional approach, overheads are first assigned to product cost centres and then absorbed by cost units based on an overhead recovery rate (using direct labour hours worked on the cost units or some other approach) for each cost centre. With activity-based costing, overheads are assigned to cost pools and then cost units are charged with overheads to the extent that they drive the costs in the various pools.

Source: Adapted from Innes, J. and Mitchell, F. (1990) *Activity Based Costing: A Review with Case Studies*, CIMA Publishing. With kind permission of Elsevier.

Figure 5.1 Traditional versus activity-based costing

ABC and service industries

Much of our discussion of ABC has concentrated on the manufacturing industry, perhaps because early users of ABC were manufacturing businesses. In fact, ABC is possibly even more relevant to service industries because, in the absence of a direct material element, a service business's total cost is likely to be largely made up of overheads. There is certainly evidence that ABC has been adopted more readily by businesses that sell services rather than products, as we shall see later.

Activity 5.3

What is the difference in the way in which direct costs are accounted for when using ABC, relative to their treatment taking a traditional approach to full costing?

The answer is no difference at all. ABC is concerned only with the way in which overheads are charged to jobs to derive the full cost.

Example 5.3 provides an example of activity-based costing and brings together the points that have been raised so far.

Example 5.3

Comma Ltd manufactures two types of Sprizzer – Standard and Deluxe. Each product requires the incorporation of a difficult-to-handle special part (one of them for a Standard and four for a Deluxe). Both of these products are made in batches (large batches for Standards and small ones for Deluxes). Each new batch requires that the production facilities are 'set up'.

Details of the two products are:

	Standard	*Deluxe*
Annual production and sales – units	12,000	12,000
Sales price per unit	£65	£87
Batch size – units	1,000	50
Direct labour time per unit – hours	2	$2\frac{1}{2}$
Direct labour rate per hour	£8	£8
Direct material cost per unit	£22	£32
Number of special parts per unit	1	4
Number of set-ups per batch	1	3
Number of separate material issues from stores per batch	1	1
Number of sales invoices issued per year	50	240

In recent months, Comma Ltd has been trying to persuade customers who buy the Standard to purchase the Deluxe instead. An analysis of overhead costs for Comma Ltd has provided the following information:

Overhead cost analysis	£	*Cost driver*
Set-up cost	73,200	Number of set-ups
Special part handling cost	60,000	Number of special parts
Customer invoicing cost	29,000	Number of invoices
Material handling cost	63,000	Number of batches
Other overheads	108,000	Labour hours

→

Required:

(a) Calculate the profit per unit and the return on sales for Standard and Deluxe Sprizzers using both:

(i) the traditional direct-labour-hour-based absorption of overheads; and

(ii) activity-based costing methods.

(b) Comment on the managerial implications for Comma Ltd of the results in (a) above.

Solution

(a) (i) **Traditional approach**

Using the traditional full (absorption) costing approach that we considered in Chapter 4, the overheads are added together and an overheads recovery rate deduced as follows:

Overheads	£
Set-up cost	73,200
Special part handling cost	60,000
Customer invoicing cost	29,000
Material handling cost	63,000
Other overheads	108,000
	333,200

$$\text{Overhead recovery rate} = \frac{\text{Total overheads}}{\text{Number of labour hours}}$$

$$= \frac{333{,}200}{54{,}000\ [\text{that is, } (12{,}000 \times 2) + (12{,}000 \times 2\tfrac{1}{2})]}$$

$$= £6.17 \text{ per hour}$$

The total cost per unit of each type of Sprizzer is calculated by adding the direct cost to the overheads cost per unit. The overheads cost per unit is calculated by multiplying the number of direct labour hours spent on the product (2 hours for each Standard and $2^1/_2$ hours for each Deluxe) by the overheads recovery rate calculated above. Hence:

	Standard	*Deluxe*
	£	£
Direct costs		
Labour	16.00	20.00
Material	22.00	32.00
Indirect cost		
Overheads (£6.17 per hour)	12.34	15.43
Total cost per unit	50.34	67.43

The return on sales is calculated as follows:

	Standard	*Deluxe*
	£ per unit	*£ per unit*
Sales price	65.00	87.00
Total cost (see above)	50.34	67.43
Profit	14.66	19.57
Return on sales [(profit/sales) × 100%]	22.55%	22.49%

(ii) **ABC approach**

Using the ABC costing approach, the activity cost driver rates will be calculated as follows:

		(a) Standard driver volume	(b) Deluxe driver volume	(c) Total driver volume (a + b)	(d) Costs £	(e) Driver rate (d/c) £
		12	720	732	73,200	100
		12,000	48,000	60,000	60,000	1
Customer invoices	Invoices per year	50	240	290	29,000	100
Material handling	Number of batches	12	240	252	63,000	250
Other overheads	Labour hours	24,000	30,000	54,000	108,000	2

The activity-based costs are derived as follows:

Overhead	*(f) Total costs Standard (a × e)* £	*(g) Total costs Deluxe (b × e)* £	*Unit costs Standard (f/12,000)* £	*Unit costs Deluxe (g/12,000)* £
Set-up	1,200	72,000	0.10	6.00
Special part	12,000	48,000	1.00	4.00
Customer invoices	5,000	24,000	0.42	2.00
Material handling	3,000	60,000	0.25	5.00
Other overheads	48,000	60,000	4.00	5.00
Total overheads			5.77	22.00

The total cost per unit is calculated as follows:

	Standard £ per unit	*Deluxe £ per unit*
Direct costs:		
Labour	16.00	20.00
Material	22.00	32.00
Indirect costs		
See above	5.77	22.00
Total cost per unit	43.77	74.00

The return on sales is calculated as follows:

	Standard £ per unit	*Deluxe £ per unit*
Sales price	65.00	87.00
Total cost (see above)	43.77	74.00
Profit	21.23	13.00
Return on sales [(profit/sales) × 100%]	32.67%	14.94%

(b) The figures show that under the traditional approach the returns on sales for each product are broadly equal. However, the ABC approach shows that the Standard product is far more profitable. Hence, the business should reconsider its policy of trying to persuade customers to switch to the Deluxe product.

Criticisms of ABC

Although many businesses now adopt a system of ABC, its critics point out that ABC can be time-consuming and costly. Costs of setting up the ABC system, as well as costs of running and updating it, must be incurred. These costs can be very high, particularly where the business's operations are complex and involve a large number of activities and cost drivers. ABC information generated in these circumstances is also likely to be complex. If managers find ABC reports difficult to understand, the potential benefits of this costing approach may be lost.

Where a business sells products or services that all have similar levels of output and involve similar activities and processes, it is unlikely that finer measurements provided by ABC will lead to strikingly different outcomes from those obtained under the traditional approach. As a result, opportunities for better pricing, planning and cost control may not be great and may not justify the cost of switching to an ABC system.

Measurement and tracing problems can arise with ABC, which may undermine any potential benefits. Not all costs can be easily identified with a particular activity and yet all overheads have to be allocated to one cost pool or another. Failure for this to happen means that not all of the overheads are taken into account. Dealing with unallocated overheads can often be done on some sensible basis. In some cases, however, a lack of data concerning a particular cost may lead to fairly arbitrary cost allocations between activities. There is also the problem that the relationship between activity costs and their cost drivers may be difficult to determine. Identifying a cause-and-effect relationship could be particularly difficult where most activity costs are fixed and so do not vary with changes in usage.

ABC is also criticised for the same reason that traditional full costing is criticised – it does not provide relevant information for decision making.

Activity 5.4

Can you recall from Chapter 4 why traditional full costing is criticised for being irrelevant for decision making?

Traditional full costing tends to use past costs and to ignore opportunity costs. Past costs, however, are irrelevant in decision making. Opportunity costs, on the other hand, are relevant and can be significant. For these reasons, some view full costing as an expensive waste of time. ABC suffers from these same weaknesses and so would also be regarded as irrelevant by critics of full costing.

We may recall from Chapter 4, however, that advocates of full costing claim that it *is* relevant. It provides an indication of long-run average cost, which, in turn, gives managers some idea of the long-term cash flows to be incurred.

ABC in practice

Real World 5.2 shows how ABC came to be used at the Royal Mail.

Real world 5.2

Delivering ABC

Early in the 2000s the publicly owned Royal Mail adopted ABC and used it to find the cost of making postal deliveries. Royal Mail identified 340 activities that gave rise to costs, created a cost pool and identified a cost driver for each of these. The volume of mail is obviously a major driver of costs.

The Royal Mail was in the public sector until 2013, when it became a private sector business.

Source: Royal Mail Group Ltd (2013) ABC Costing manual 2013–14, September.

Real World 5.3 provides some indication of the extent to which ABC is used in practice.

Real World 5.3

ABC in practice

A survey of 176 UK businesses operating in various industries, all with annual sales revenue of more than £50 million, was conducted by Al-Omiri and Drury. This indicated that 29 per cent of larger UK businesses use ABC.

The adoption of ABC in the UK varies widely between industries, as is shown in Figure 5.2.

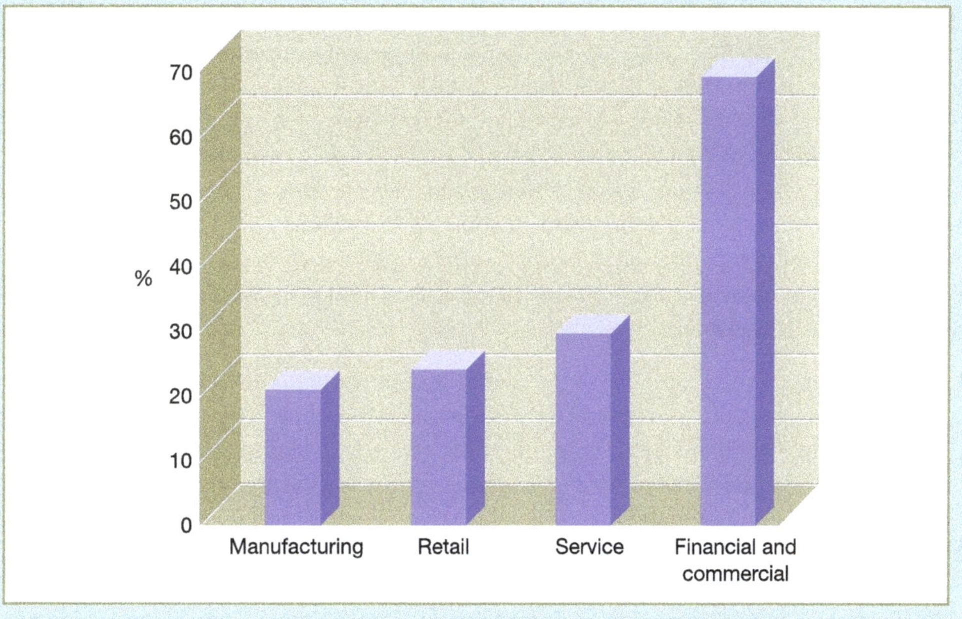

Figure 5.2 The percentage of businesses in different sectors that use ABC

Al-Omiri and Drury took their analysis a step further by looking at the factors that apparently tend to lead a particular business to adopt ABC. They found that businesses that used ABC tended to be:

→

- large;
- sophisticated, in terms of using advanced management accounting techniques generally;
- in an intensely competitive market for their products;
- operating in a service industry, particularly in the financial services.

The 2009 CIMA survey emphatically supported the finding that larger businesses tend to use ABC more than smaller ones. It showed that only 22 per cent of businesses with fewer than 50 employees use ABC, whereas 46 per cent of businesses with more than 10,000 employees use the technique.

All of these findings are broadly in line with other recent research evidence involving businesses from around the world.

Sources: Al-Omiri, M. and Drury, C. (2007) A survey of factors influencing the choice of product costing systems in UK organisations, *Management Accounting Research*, December; CIMA (2009) *Management Accounting Tools for Today and Tomorrow*, p. 12.

MANAGING COSTS OVER THE PRODUCT LIFE CYCLE

In the remainder of this chapter, we shall take a look at further methods that can be used to manage costs in a highly competitive environment. We begin by examining methods that focus on managing costs over the life cycle of a product.

Total life-cycle costing

Total life-cycle costing draws management's attention to the fact that it is not only during the production phase that costs are incurred. Costs begin to accumulate at an earlier point and continue to accumulate after production. Total life-cycle costing is concerned with tracking and reporting all costs relating to a product from the beginning to the end of its life – which could be for a period of twenty years or more. If the revenues generated over the life cycle of the product are also tracked, its profitability can be assessed. This represents a radical departure from traditional management accounting approaches, which are normally concerned with assessing performance over periods of one year or less.

Total life-cycle costing starts from the premise that the life cycle of a product or service has three phases. These are:

1. The *pre-production phase.* This is the period that precedes production of the product or service. During this phase, research and development – both of the product or service and of the market – is conducted. The product or service is designed and so is the means of production. The phase culminates with setting up the necessary production facilities and with advertising and promotion.
2. The *production phase* comes next. During this phase the product is made and sold or the service is provided to customers.
3. The *post-production phase* comes last. During this phase, costs may be incurred to correct faults that arose with products or services sold (after-sales service). Since these costs may start to be incurred before the last product or service is sold, this phase will typically overlap with the production phase. At this phase, costs may also be incurred as a result of closing production at the end of the product's or service's life. Examples include the costs incurred from decommissioning an oil rig or power station.

When undertaking total life-cycle costing, businesses often consider environmental costs alongside the more obvious financial costs involved.

The total life cycle is shown in Figure 5.3.

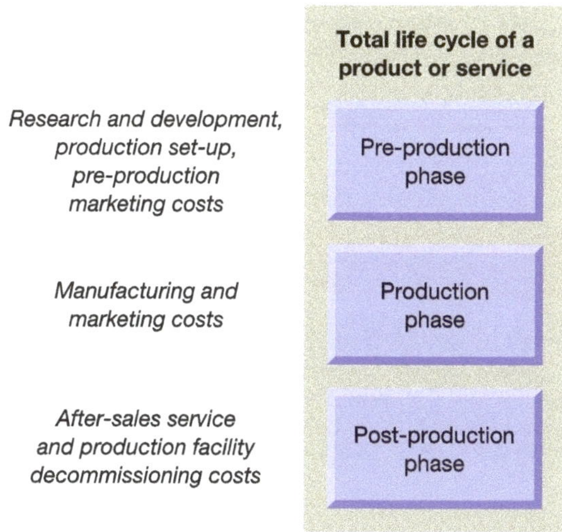

From the producer's viewpoint, the life of a product can be seen as having three distinct phases. During the first the product is developed and everything is prepared so that production and marketing can start. Next comes production and sales. Lastly, dealing with post-production activities is undertaken.

Figure 5.3 The total life cycle of a product or service

For some businesses, particularly those engaged in an advanced manufacturing environment, a very high proportion (perhaps as much as 80 per cent) of the total costs incurred over the life of a particular product are either incurred, or committed, at the pre-production phase. Let us consider the example of a car manufacturer. When designing, developing and setting up production of a new model, a significant proportion of the total life-cycle costs are incurred. In addition, a commitment to incur costs during the production phase is made. This is because the design will incorporate features that lead to particular manufacturing costs. Once the design of the car has been finalised and the manufacturing plant set up, it may be too late to 'design out' a costly feature without incurring another large cost. Decisions made at the pre-production phase can also lead to a commitment to incur costs at the post-production phase.

Activity 5.5

Can you provide an example of a decision made at the pre-production phase of a new car model that will result in costs being incurred *after* the manufacture of the product?

After-sales service costs may be incurred as a result of some design fault. Once the manufacturing facilities have been established, it may not be economic to revise the design but merely to deal with the problem through after-sales service procedures.

Where the manufacturing plant or production facilities are no longer needed when production ceases there may be decommissioning costs.

Total life-cycle costing can be used to manage costs. It was mentioned earlier that, by the start of the production phase, it may be too late to try to manage a large element of the product's or service's total life-cycle cost. With total life-cycle costing, managers will be able to see, at an early stage, the cost consequences of incorporating particular designs or particular elements into products. Where the costs are unacceptable, changes may be made. This may involve assessing the costs of alternative designs. Where a number of equally acceptable designs for a particular product are being considered, knowledge of the total life-cycle costs of each can help decide the final outcome.

Real World 5.4 provides some idea of the extent to which total life-cycle costing is used in practice.

Real World 5.4

Total (whole) life-cycle costing in practice

The 2009 CIMA survey showed that total life-cycle costing is not widely used in practice, as is shown by Figure 5.4. About 14 per cent of all of the businesses surveyed used the approach.

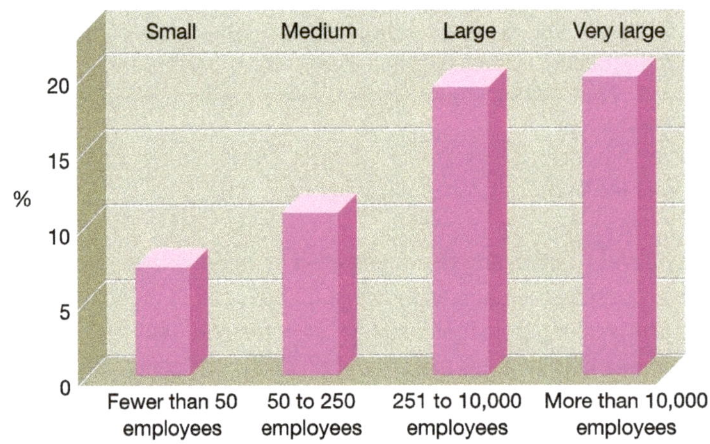

The use of total life-cycle costing is not widespread, but it tends to be much more popular with larger businesses.

Figure 5.4 The use of total life-cycle costing

Source: Adapted from CIMA (2009) *Management Accounting Tools for Today and Tomorrow*, p. 12.

Real World 5.5 shows how a well-known international car maker uses total life-cycle costing.

Real World 5.5

Total life-cycle management at Renault

According to Renault, the French motor vehicle manufacturer uses life-cycle management to promote more economic and ecological vehicles.

Renault sees the life of a particular vehicle as comprising four phases:

1 Design phase
2 Manufacturing phase
3 Use phase
4 End of life.

Renault links the life cycle to environmental as well as economic aspects of their business.

Source: Renault (2011), www.renault.com.

Note that Renault divides the *post-production phase* into two sections: use and end of life.

Target costing

We saw in Chapter 4 that businesses may adopt a cost-plus approach to pricing. This involves totalling the costs of providing a product or service and then adding a percentage for profit to derive a selling price. Cost-plus pricing, however, is not normally suitable for businesses that operate in a highly competitive market.

Activity 5.6

Why do you think this is the case?

The cost-plus price figure derived may be unacceptable to potential buyers.

Target costing approaches the pricing decision from the opposite direction. The starting point is to set a target price for a product based on market research, which will normally include an analysis of competitors' prices. The target profit, based on the financial objective of the business, is then deducted from the identified price. The resulting figure is the target cost of the product. Where the target cost is less than the current estimated cost, there will be a 'cost gap'. Efforts must then be made to bridge this gap by making the product in a way that meets the target cost.

A team of specialists, drawn from each of the main functional areas, such as design, production, purchasing and marketing, will normally be charged with achieving the target cost. Together they will examine all aspects of the product and the production process to try to eliminate anything that does not add value. This may involve revising the design, developing more efficient means of production, and negotiating with suppliers to provide goods and services more cheaply. The process is often iterative (trial and error) and will continue until total product costs are reduced in line with the target cost figure, or it is found that the target cost figure cannot be achieved. To prevent too much time and resources being consumed in this process, deadlines may be set for reaching the target cost figure.

Target costing is not so much a costing technique as a framework within which various disciplines and techniques may be applied. Thus, some of the techniques covered elsewhere in this chapter, such as activity-based costing, benchmarking and value chain analysis, may be used to help achieve the target cost figure.

The target costing process is summarised in Figure 5.5.

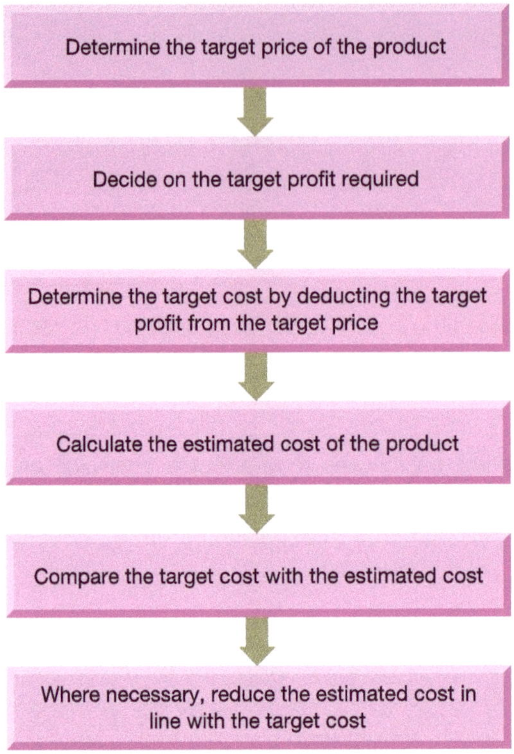

Target costing involves six main steps, which begin with determining the target price for the product.

Figure 5.5 The target costing process

Target costing can be seen as part of total life-cycle costing. As we have seen, a large proportion of the total costs of a product may well be determined at the pre-production phase. Careful planning at this phase of the product's life may prevent future manufacturing costs from becoming 'locked in'. Small changes in design, for example, may reduce the number of components required or enable the use of standard components rather than specialised components. In the end, such small changes may lead to significant cost savings.

Target costing was developed by Japanese businesses during the 1970s in response to an increasingly competitive environment. It is particularly relevant for manufacturers of products with short life cycles.

Activity 5.7

Can you think why this should be the case?

It is because cost savings are likely to be greatest where there is a need to make frequent updates to existing products and/or to develop a constant stream of new products – as in, say, the manufacture of fast-moving, electronic consumer goods.

Target costing is less relevant for businesses where product development is not such a significant issue, which will include most service businesses. Nevertheless, opportunities to use this costing approach may still arise. A firm of management consultants, for example, may consider bidding for a particular contract in the belief that a particular price would secure the contract. This price would become the target price and ways would then have to be found to deliver the service to conform to the contract specifications and to the consultancy firm's required financial returns.

Activity 5.8

Although target costing has its enthusiasts, there are potential problems with its use. Try to think of at least one of these.

There seem to be three main problem areas:

- It can lead to various conflicts – for example, between the business, its suppliers and its own staff.
- It can cause a great deal of stress for employees who are trying to meet target costs that are sometimes extremely difficult to achieve.
- Although, in the end, ways may be found to meet a target cost (through product or service redesign, negotiating lower prices with suppliers and so on), the whole process can be very time-consuming and expensive.

Real World 5.6 indicates the level of usage of target costing. This shows quite a low level of usage in the UK. In contrast, other survey evidence shows that target costing is very widely used by Japanese manufacturing businesses.

Real World 5.6

Target practice

The 2009 CIMA survey showed that target costing is not widely used in practice, as is shown by Figure 5.6.

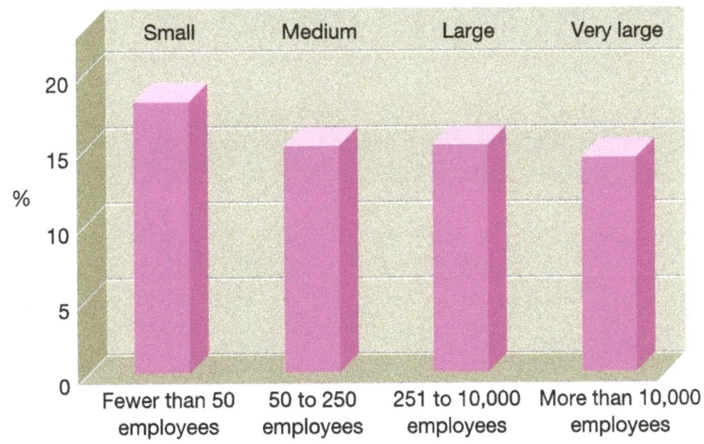

It is not obvious why the larger businesses do not use TQM as much as the smaller ones.

Figure 5.6 The use of target costing

Target costing is used by about 16 per cent of all of the businesses surveyed.

Source: Adapted from CIMA (2009) *Management Accounting Tools for Today and Tomorrow*, p. 12.

Kaizen costing

To ensure long-term competitiveness, businesses may look beyond the use of target costing at the pre-production phase of a product's life. When the production phase is reached, **kaizen costing** may be used to continue the quest for cost savings. The Japanese word 'kaizen' means 'continuous improvement', which can be accomplished through many small steps. Kaizen costing seeks to achieve cost savings through small, incremental changes on a continuous basis rather than, say, through the radical redesign of the production process on a 'one-off' basis. Since the production phase is quite late in the product life cycle (from a cost management point of view) only small cost savings can usually be made. The majority of production-phase cost savings should already have been made through target costing.

To reduce manufacturing costs, the production process should be closely scrutinised in the search for greater efficiency. Examples of the kind of improvements that may result from such scrutiny include:

- eliminating overproduction;
- reducing the number of defective products produced through changes to processes;
- synchronising manufacturing processes and eliminating bottlenecks;
- identifying and eliminating excess inventories;
- reducing waiting times for deliveries through closer links with suppliers;
- improving storage and handling processes.

The search for improvements is normally carried out through the use of teams, with membership drawn from various functions of the business.

Kaizen costing aims to reduce the manufacturing cost of a product to below that incurred during the previous period. This involves target setting. A target percentage reduction in manufacturing cost is set for a period and, at the end of each period, the actual percentage reduction is compared against this target. Any significant deviation between the target and actual percentage reduction should be investigated and action taken if the target has not been reached.

The kaizen costing process is summarised in Figure 5.7.

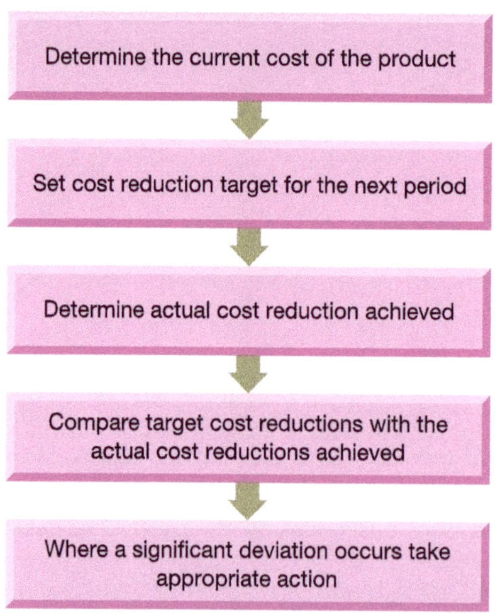

Kaizen costing involves five main steps, which begin with determining the current cost of the product.

Figure 5.7 The kaizen costing process

Kaizen costing is often part of a broader culture of continuous improvement within a business. The underlying philosophy is that no process can ever be perfect and so there is always room for improvement. It involves close scrutiny of every part of the production process with ideas being generated as to how things can be improved. Employees are seen as vital to the success of this approach and are encouraged to offer suggestions for eliminating waste and for improving processes and the quality of output. The vehicle manufacturer Toyota adopts the kaizen approach and actively promotes employee involvement. At its European production sites, around 3,000 proposals for improvements are submitted in a typical year (see reference 1 at the end of the chapter).

Activity 5.9

Which group of employees within a business may be best placed to identify the small improvements involved with kaizen costing?

Those closest to production, particularly those with 'hands-on' experience, may be in the best position to do this.

Kaizen costing is closely associated with **lean manufacturing**, which is committed to the elimination of waste through continuous improvement.

Kaizen costing can help to create a more open approach to dealing with issues and problems within a business. It can also help to create a more committed and motivated workforce through team working and employee involvement. Kaizen costing can, however, be difficult to implement. Managers may be suspicious of this new technique and may feel their territory is being threatened by the remit given to cross-functional teams. They may also recoil at the huge amount of time and effort required to bring about changes in the business culture and ways of operating. A long-term commitment by top management is, therefore, vital in order to achieve success.

Figure 5.8 shows the phases of the product life cycle covered by the three forms of costing discussed.

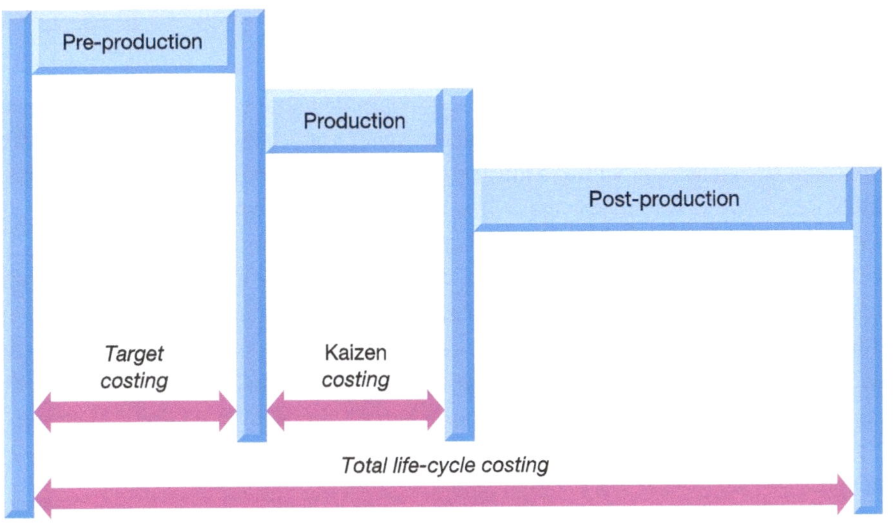

Total life-cycle costing covers all three phases of the product life cycle, whereas target costing and kaizen costing are each concerned with only a single phase.

Figure 5.8 The relationship between the three types of costing

Real World 5.7 explains how a major UK manufacturer used kaizen costing to advantage.

Real World 5.7

Kaizen costing is part of the package

Kappa Packaging is a major UK packaging business. It has a factory at Stalybridge where it makes, among other things, packaging (cardboard cartons) for glass bottles containing alcoholic drinks. In 2002, Kappa introduced a new approach to reducing the amount of waste paper and cardboard. Before this, the business wasted 14.6 per cent of its raw materials used. This figure was taken as the base against which improvements would be measured.

Improvements were made at Kappa as a result of:

- making staff more aware of the waste problem;
- requiring staff to monitor the amount of waste for which they were individually responsible; and
- establishing a kaizen team to find ways of reducing waste.

As a result of kaizen savings, Kappa was able to reduce waste from 14.6 per cent to 13.1 per cent in 2002 and 11 per cent in 2003. The business estimates that each 1 per cent waste saving was worth £110,000 a year. So by the end of 2003, Kappa was saving about £400,000 a year, relative to 2001: that is, over £2,000 per employee each year.

Source: Information taken from 'Accurate measurement of process waste leads to reduced costs', www.envirowise.gov.uk, 2003.

OTHER APPROACHES TO MANAGING COSTS IN THE MODERN ENVIRONMENT

Value chain analysis

To secure competitive advantage, a business must be able to perform key activities more successfully than its competitors. This means that it must either obtain some cost advantage over its competitors, or differentiate itself in some way from them. To help identify particular ways in which competitive advantage may be achieved, it is useful to analyse a business into a sequence of value-creating activities. This sequence is known as the value chain. **Value chain analysis** examines the potential for each link in the chain to add value.

For a manufacturing business, the value-creating sequence begins with the acquisition of inputs, such as raw materials and energy. It ends with the sale of completed goods and after-sales service. Value chain analysis applies to service-providing businesses as well as to manufacturers. Service providers also have a sequence of activities leading to provision of the service to their customers. For both types of business, analysing these activities in an attempt to identify and eliminate non-value-added activities can reap significant rewards.

Figure 5.9 sets out the main 'links' in the value chain for a manufacturing business. We can see that five primary activities are supported by four secondary activities.

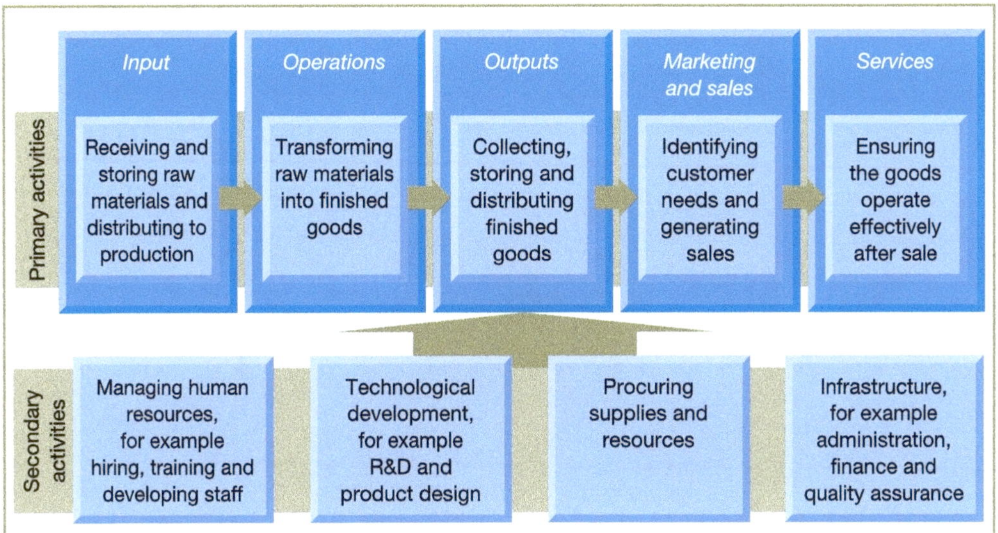

The five primary activities which form the links in the value chain are underpinned by four support activities.

Source: Adapted from Porter, M. (1985) *Competitive Advantage: Creating and Sustaining Superior Performance*, The Free Press.

Figure 5.9 The main links in the value chain of a manufacturing business

Each link in the value chain represents an activity that will incur costs and affect profits. Ideally, each will add value – that is, the customer will be prepared to pay more for the activity than it costs to carry out. If, however, a business is to outperform its rivals, it must ensure that the value chain is configured in such a way that it leads either to a cost advantage or to differentiation.

To achieve a cost advantage, the costs associated with each link in the chain must be identified and then examined to see whether they can be reduced or eliminated. For example, a non-value-added activity may be identified, such as the inspection of the completed product by a quality controller. The introduction of a 'quality' culture in the business could lead to much greater reliability in output quality. As a result, inspection would no longer be needed and this cost could be eliminated. To achieve differentiation from its rivals, a business must achieve uniqueness in at least one part of the value chain. A large baker, for example, may try to differentiate its products by moving production facilities to its retail shops to ensure that the products are freshly available to customers.

Real World 5.8 provides some impression of the use of value chain analysis in practice.

Real World 5.8

Value chain analysis

The CIMA survey, mentioned earlier, examined the extent to which value chain analysis is used by businesses of different size. The results are set out in Figure 5.10.

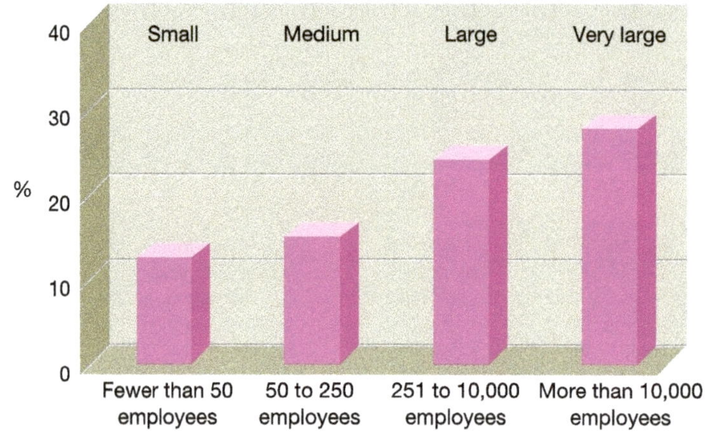

This technique is not widely used. Usage does, however, increase in line with increases in business size.

Figure 5.10 Use of value chain analysis

Source: Adapted from figure in CIMA (2009) *Management Accounting Tools for Today and Tomorrow*, p. 19.

In some cases, value chain analysis may result in significant operational changes, such as the introduction of new manufacturing or service-provision technology or the development of new sales policies. In other cases it may result in significant strategic shifts. A manufacturing business, for example, may find that it is unable to match the manufacturing costs achieved by its rivals. At the same time, it may have competitive strengths in the areas of marketing and distribution. In such circumstances, a decision may be made to focus on the business's core competencies. This may lead it to outsource the manufacturing function and to concentrate on the marketing and distribution of the goods.

Benchmarking

Benchmarking is an activity – usually a continuing one – where a business seeks to emulate a business that is 'best-in-class' in order to achieve greater success. The best-in-class business provides a standard, or benchmark, against which a business can compare its own performance. Benchmarking can also provide an insight into how performance can be improved. Studying a high-performing business, and discovering the factors that lead to success, may lead to the introduction of new ideas. These could result in improved operational efficiency and greater competitive advantage.

The benchmarking process involves a series of steps, which are set out in Figure 5.11.

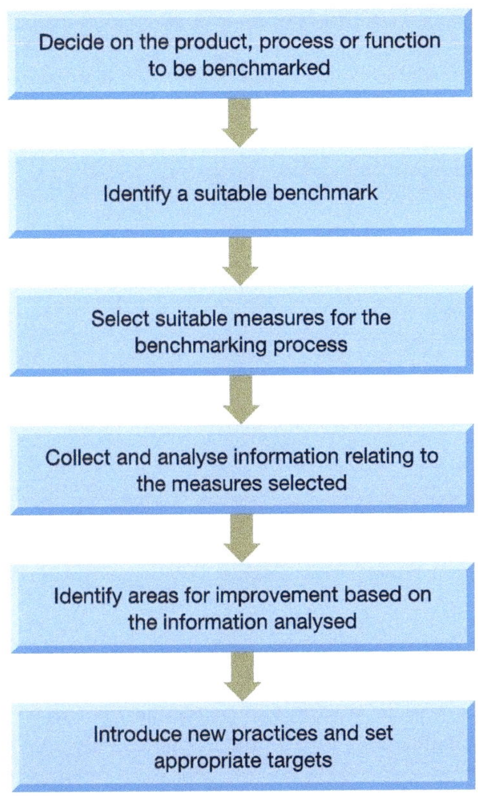

Benchmarking involves six stages as shown above.

Source: Based on information in Rigby, D. *Management Tools*, www.bain.com.

Figure 5.11 The benchmarking process

Benchmarking can be applied to any business process and so the methods for identifying and measuring performance can cover a very wide range. They include interviews and questionnaires involving managers, employees, suppliers, and customers. They also include the mapping of business processes and statistical analysis as well as the use of performance indicators relating to key factors such as time, quality, income and costs.

Businesses do not have to be benchmarked and many are understandably reluctant to divulge commercially sensitive information. Thus, a competitor business that is regarded as best-in-class is unlikely to be a willing partner in the benchmarking process. Nevertheless it may still be possible to glean a lot through an analysis of the competitor's activities using information from other sources. Where a best-in-class business is not a direct competitor, it may be prepared to share information concerning processes or functions carried out by both businesses, such as credit collection and inventories control. It may also be possible for a business to benchmark internally by using a successful division or department as the best-in-class.

In some cases, industry associations disseminate information based on performance measures submitted by participating businesses. In the report that is produced, individual businesses are not normally identified and data may be aggregated. This kind of benchmarking is not so useful when seeking to understand why some businesses perform so well.

Activity 5.10

Why is this type of benchmarking not so useful for this purpose?

It does not provide access to best-in-class businesses. A deeper understanding of their decisions and processes cannot therefore be gained.

Benchmarking in practice

Real World 5.9 provides an example of how benchmarking may be used to assess the operational efficiency of law firms.

Real World 5.9

Legal fees

The banking group NatWest plc undertook an analysis of the performance of 337 small to medium-sized law firms in the UK. The NatWest report covered law firms with a fee income of up to £27 million during 2012. A variety of measures were used to provide benchmarks against which operational efficiency could be compared. The main measures employed, as well as figures for the upper quartile of law firms for each measure, were:

Performance measure	*Calculation of measure*	*Upper quartile*
Fees per equity partner (£000)	Total fees earned/Number of equity (non-salaried) partners	676
Fees per fee earner (£000)	Total fees earned/Number of employees generating fees	193
Profit as a percentage of fees (%)	(Profit/Total fees earned) × 100%	33
Profit per equity partner (£000)	Profit/Number of equity partners	160
Chargeable hours (per year)	Number of hours charged to clients by fee earners	1,198
Recovered rate per hour (£)	Recorded rate per hour by a fee earner × the percentage of time recorded that can be billed	188
Work in progress (days)	The delay from time being recorded for work done to the bill being raised	26
Debtor days (days)	Time taken for clients to pay the bill	27
Total lock-up (days)	The delay from the time being recorded for work done to the cash being received (WIP + Debtor days)	69

For benchmarking purposes, the upper quartile figures can be used as a measure of superior performance and so provide a surrogate for best-in-class.

Source: Adapted from NatWest Bank, '2013 Financial Benchmarking Report – Law firms', nw-businesssense.com.

Activity 5.11

Try to think of two more measures that could be used as benchmarks against which law firms could measure their operational efficiency. (*Hint*: Think of measures relating to time, income and profit.)

The following measures could also be used:

- Year-on-year change in total fees earned;
- Year-on-year change in profit per equity partner;
- Fee-earning employees as a percentage of total employees;
- Percentage of time recorded by fee-earner that is billed to clients;
- Profit per employee (both fee-earners and non-fee-earners);
- Bad debts as a percentage of total fees earned.

You may have thought of others.

Real World 5.10 provides an indication of the use of and effectiveness of benchmarking among large businesses.

Real World 5.10

Benchmarking

Bain & Company, a firm of management consultants, undertakes an annual survey of key management tools. Its 2013 survey, using a database of more than 12,000 executives worldwide, found the following levels of usage and perceived effectiveness of benchmarking:

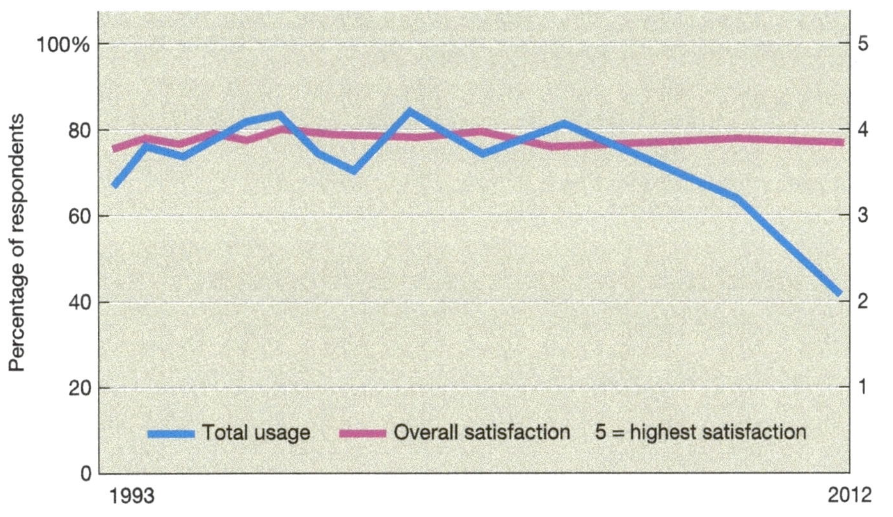

Although the level of satisfaction with benchmarking has remained consistently high, it has not been so widely used in recent years.

Figure 5.12 The use of benchmarking

The chart shows a decline in the level of usage in recent years; however, there has been no decline in its perceived effectiveness.

Source: Rigby, D. (2013) Management Tools, Bain & Company, http://www.bain.com/publications/articles/management-tools-benchmarking.aspx Used with permission from Bain & Company.

Total quality management

Quality has become a major weapon that businesses deploy when competing against their rivals. As mentioned earlier, customers increasingly demand products (both goods and services) that meet their specific requirements. One of these requirements will be that products should be of a suitable quality. This means that the products should meet customers' needs and be available at a price they are willing to pay.

This emphasis on creating quality products has led to **total quality management** (TQM). The TQM philosophy is concerned with providing products that meet, or exceed, customers' requirements all of the time. This implies that defective products should never reach the customer. Ideally, there should never be any defective production. TQM has been characterised as 'getting it right first time, every time'. It aims to create a virtuous sequence of events where quality improvements lead to reduced production problems, increased customer satisfaction and increased profits.

Employee involvement at all levels within the business is essential if a quality culture is to be developed. Managers must, therefore, take steps to bring this about.

Activity 5.12

What steps might a business take to ensure a high level of employee involvement in improving quality? Try to think of at least three.

A business may:

- Commit to a high level of communication between management and employees. This will include keeping employees fully informed of the objectives and strategy of the business as well as key changes in the external environment.
- Make employees aware of the importance of a customer focus and the role that quality plays in satisfying customer needs.
- Provide training in quality assurance procedures.
- Provide incentives that are linked to quality improvements.
- Encourage proposals for quality improvements.
- Empower employees to make changes to processes in order to improve quality.
- Demonstrate the commitment of top management to developing a quality culture.

You may have thought of others.

TQM should be seen as a continuous effort rather than a 'one-off' exercise. It requires a detailed investigation of existing processes in order to identify areas for improvement. To undertake the work needed, teams of employees may be created with members drawn from various business functions. They will be responsible for collecting and analysing data relating to existing processes and for ensuring that new processes are developed and properly monitored. In the quest for quality improvement, a wide range of methods may be used such as benchmarking, employee and customer surveys, statistical analysis and business process mapping.

A systematic approach should be adopted to delivering quality improvements. The main steps are set out in Figure 5.13.

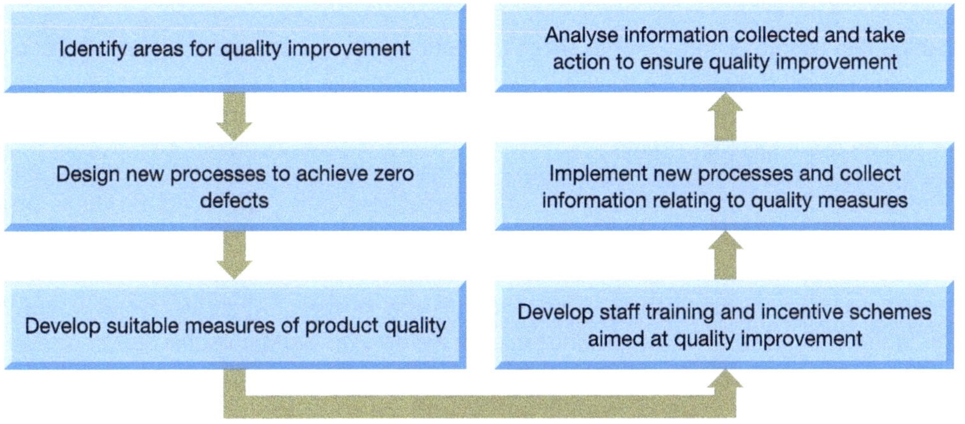

Improving quality involves six stages, as shown above.

Source: Based on information in Rigby, D. *Management Tools*, Bain & Company, http://www.bain.com/publications/articles/management-tools-benchmarking.aspx.

Figure 5.13 Delivering improvements in quality

Real World 5.11 provides some idea of the extent to which TQM is used in practice.

Real World 5.11

Quality practice

The 2009 CIMA survey showed that TQM is not widely used in practice, as is shown by Figure 5.14.

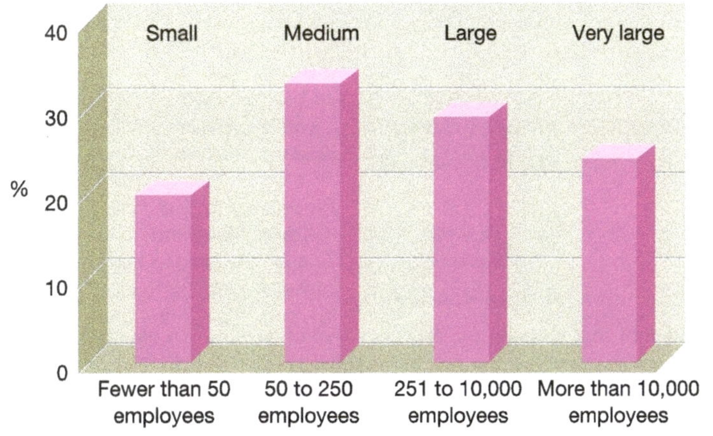

It is not obvious why the larger businesses do not use TQM as much as medium-size ones.

Figure 5.14 The use of total quality management

Total quality management was used by just over a quarter of all of the businesses surveyed.

Source: CIMA (2009) *Management Accounting Tools for Today and Tomorrow*, p. 19.

Managing quality costs

Ensuring that products and services are of the right quality will only be achieved at a cost. It has been estimated that these **quality costs** can amount to up to 30 per cent of total processing costs. They tend to be incurred during the production phase of the product life cycle and fall into four main categories:

1. *Prevention costs.* These are involved with procedures to try to prevent products being produced that are not up to the required quality. Such procedures might include staff training on quality issues and investment in new equipment. Some types of prevention costs might be incurred during the *pre-production phase* of the product life cycle, where the production process could be designed in such a way as to avoid potential quality problems with the output.
2. *Appraisal costs.* These are concerned with monitoring raw materials, work in progress and finished products to ensure that they achieve the quality standards that have been set.
3. *Internal failure costs.* These include the costs of rectifying substandard products before they reach the customer as well as the costs of scrap arising from quality failures.
4. *External failure costs.* These include the costs of rectifying quality problems with products that have been passed to the customer. They also include the cost to the business of its loss of reputation from having passed substandard products to the customer.

These four categories of cost together comprise the total quality costs incurred by a business.

Figure 5.15 summarises the main categories of total quality costs.

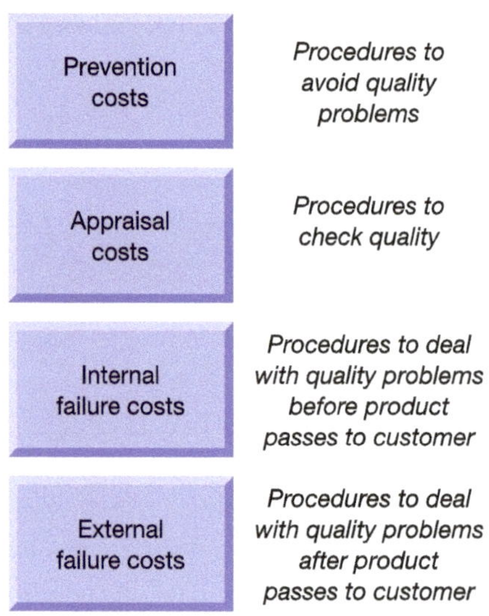

Quality costs fall into four distinct categories. The first two are mainly concerned with avoiding substandard production and the last two with dealing with it should it arise.

Figure 5.15 The main categories of quality costs

Activity 5.13

Look back at the four categories of quality costs that may be incurred and try to think of at least two examples of specific costs that may be incurred within each category.

- *Prevention costs* may include those related to quality training sessions, quality improvement meetings, investment in quality-related information systems, reviews of product design and projects aimed at product improvement.
- *Appraisal costs* may include those related to inspection and testing of the raw materials supplied, reviews of existing processes, quality audits of the final product, checking of testing equipment and reviews of performance standards.
- *Internal failure costs* may include those related to reworking materials, re-testing products, scrapping products and assigning a lower quality grade to products produced (and discounting the selling price).
- *External failure costs* may include those related to dealing with customer complaints, lost future orders, goods returned for reworking, product recalls, reputational loss and legal liability for failure to meet contract specifications.

By identifying, categorising and measuring the various quality costs, we have a basis for managing them. We can see more clearly the returns from investing in quality improvements. Let us say that a business is making products that contain a significant proportion of defects. It may well respond to this problem by increasing inspection costs. However, this may not be enough to eliminate the problem and so internal and external failure costs, such as reworking materials and dealing with customer complaints, may still be incurred. If the business invests in prevention, such as the purchase of new equipment and better staff training, appraisal costs and failure costs may be reduced. In other words, to produce higher quality products, total costs do not have to increase. Indeed, additional costs incurred in prevention may be more than offset by lower appraisal and failure costs leading to significant cost savings.

An alternative view

While the costing methods just described are used and are regarded as useful by many businesses, some believe that they fail to provide the key to successful cost management. It has been suggested that undue emphasis on costing methods, such as total life-cycle costing, is misplaced and what is really needed is for businesses to develop ways of learning and adapting to their changing environment. To manage costs successfully, businesses should continually review them in the face of new threats and pressures rather than relying on particular techniques to provide solutions.

Hopwood (see reference 2 at the end of the chapter) suggests that to transform costs over time in order to fit the strategic objectives, businesses do not need very sophisticated techniques or highly bureaucratic systems. Rather, they need to change the ways in which costs are viewed and dealt with. He suggests that the following broad principles should be adopted.

1 Spread the responsibility

Employees throughout the business should share responsibility for managing costs. Thus, design experts, engineers, store managers, sales managers and so on, should all contribute towards managing costs and should see this as part of their job. The involvement of non-accountants is, of course, a feature of target costing and kaizen costing. Thus, this point already appears to be widely accepted.

Hopwood suggests that employees should be provided with a basic understanding of costing ideas, such as fixed and variable costs, relevant costs and so on, to enable them to contribute fully. As cost-consciousness permeates the business, and non-accounting employees become more involved in costing issues, the role of accountants will change. They will often facilitate, rather than initiate, cost management proposals and will become part of the multi-skilled teams engaged in creatively managing them.

2 Spread the word

Throughout the business, costs and cost management should become everyday topics for discussion. Managers should seize every opportunity to raise these topics with employees, as talking about costs can often lead to ideas being developed and action being taken to manage costs.

3 Think local

Emphasis should be placed on managing costs within specific sites and settings. Managers of departments, product lines or local offices are more likely to become engaged in managing costs if they are allowed to take initiatives in areas over which they have control. Local managers tend to have local knowledge not possessed by managers at head office. They are more likely to be able to spot cost-saving opportunities than are their more senior colleagues. Where initiatives for cost management have been developed by senior management, and are applied across the whole business, they are unlikely to have the same beneficial effect as local initiatives.

4 Benchmark continually

Benchmarking should be a never-ending journey. There should be regular, as well as special-purpose, reporting of cost information for benchmarking purposes. The costs of competitors may provide a useful basis for comparison, as we saw earlier. In addition, costs that may be expected as a result of moving to new technology or work patterns may be helpful.

5 Focus on managing rather than reducing costs

Conventional management accounting tends to focus on cost reduction, which is, essentially, taking a short-term perspective on costs. Effective cost management, however, requires that, in some situations, costs should be increased rather than reduced.

Activity 5.14

In what kind of situations might it be a good idea to increase costs? Try to think, in broad terms, of two such situations.

This may include situations leading to:

- additional revenues being generated;
- lower costs being incurred over the longer term;
- lower costs being incurred in other areas of the business.

Hopwood argues that these principles, when used in conjunction with overall financial controls, provide the best way to manage costs.

Real World 5.12 gives an example of how local managers who are not accountants can identify potential cost savings and not resent their implementation.

Real World 5.12

Costing problem? Call a doctor

One research study contrasts the difference in approach to cost management in UK and Finnish hospitals. In the UK, cost management is seen as the domain of financial staff. This can lead to problems as financial systems that have been introduced to manage costs have led to more complex organisational structures. In addition there is often an emphasis on cost savings, which can lead to conflict between financial staff and medical staff. The latter often resent cost cuts being imposed on them by the financial staff.

In contrast, medical staff in Finnish hospitals share responsibility for cost management. Doctors and other medical professionals recognise the need to use resources in an efficient way and are committed to ensuring that resources are not wasted. Rather than fighting cost-cutting initiatives from financial staff, they see both medical knowledge and cost awareness as being necessary to successful medical practice.

Source: Based on information in Hopwood, A. (2002) Costs count in the strategic agenda, ft.com, 13 August.

Self-assessment question 5.1

Psilis Ltd makes a product in two qualities, called 'Basic' and 'Super'. The business is able to sell these products at a price that gives a standard profit mark-up of 25 per cent of full cost. Management is concerned by the lack of profit.

Full cost for one unit of a product is calculated by charging overheads to each type of product on the basis of direct labour hours. The costs are as follows:

	Basic	*Super*
	£	£
Direct labour (all £10/hour)	40	60
Direct material	15	20

The total overheads are £1,000,000.

Based on experience over recent years, in the forthcoming year the business expects to make and sell 40,000 Basics and 10,000 Supers.

Recently, the business's management accountant has undertaken an exercise to try to identify activities and cost drivers in an attempt to be able to deal with the overheads on a more precise basis than had been possible before. This exercise has revealed the following analysis of the annual overheads:

Activity (and cost driver)	*Cost*	*Annual number of activities*		
	£000	*Total*	*Basic*	*Super*
Number of machine set-ups	280	100	20	80
Number of quality-control inspections	220	2,000	500	1,500
Number of sales orders processed	240	5,000	1,500	3,500
General production (machine hours)	260	500,000	350,000	150,000
Total	1,000			

→

The management accountant explained the analysis of the £1,000,000 overheads as follows:

- The two products are made in relatively small batches, so that the amount of the finished product held in inventories is negligible. The Supers are made in very small batches because demand for them is relatively low. Each time a new batch is produced, the machines have to be reset by skilled staff. Resetting for Basic production occurs about 20 times a year and for Supers about 80 times: about 100 times in total. The cost of employing the machine-setting staff is about £280,000 a year. It is clear that the more set-ups that occur, the higher the total set-up costs; in other words, the number of set-ups is the factor that drives set-up costs.
- All production has to be inspected for quality, which costs about £220,000 a year. The higher specifications of the Supers mean that there is more chance that there will be quality problems. Thus the Supers are inspected in total 1,500 times annually, whereas the Basics only need about 500 inspections. The number of inspections is the factor that drives these costs.
- Sales order processing (dealing with customers' orders, from receiving the original order to despatching the products) costs about £240,000 a year. Despite the larger amount of Basic production, there are only 1,500 sales orders each year because the Basics are sold to wholesalers in relatively large-sized orders. The Supers are sold mainly direct to the public by mail order, usually in very small-sized orders. It is believed that the number of orders drives the costs of processing orders.

Required:

(a) Deduce the full cost of each of the two products on the basis used at present and, from these, deduce the current selling price.

(b) Deduce the full cost of each product on an ABC basis, taking account of the management accountant's recent investigations.

(c) What conclusions do you draw? What advice would you offer the management of the business?

(d) The managers of the business are concerned that sales order processing is not being carried out efficiently. They have therefore decided to benchmark this function against best practice. Produce a list of measures that might be used by the business as a basis for a benchmarking exercise. (*Hint*: In developing the measures think about the key factors of time, quality, income and cost.)

(e) The benchmarking process will be carried out by a team of staff. Set out the criteria that you feel would be appropriate to use when selecting team members.

The solution to this question can be found in Appendix B.

SUMMARY

The main points of this chapter may be summarised as follows:

Activity-based costing (ABC)

- ABC is an approach to dealing with overheads (in full costing) that treats all costs as being caused or 'driven' by activities. Advocates argue that it is more relevant to the modern commercial environment than is the traditional approach.
- It involves identifying the support activities and their costs (overheads) and then analysing these costs to see what drives them.

- The costs of each support activity are collected into a cost pool and the relevant cost driver is used to attach an amount of overheads from this pool to each unit of output.
- ABC should help provide more accurate costs for each unit of output and should help in better control of overheads.
- ABC is, however, time-consuming and costly, and can involve measurement problems. It is unlikely to suit all businesses.

Total (whole) life-cycle costing

- Total life-cycle costing is concerned with tracking and reporting all costs relating to a product from the beginning to the end of its life.
- The life cycle of a product can be broken down into three phases: pre-production, production and post-production.
- A high proportion of costs is incurred and/or committed during the pre-production phase.

Target costing

- Target costing is a market-based approach to managing costs that is used at the pre-production phase.
- It attempts to reduce costs so that an acceptable profit can be made at the target price.
- It is a framework within which various techniques may be used to reduce costs rather than a costing method.

Kaizen costing

- Kaizen costing is concerned with continual and gradual cost reduction at the production phase.
- It involves setting targets for reductions in manufacturing costs each period and then comparing actual costs reductions against the targets.
- It is often part of a broader culture of continuous improvement within a business.

Value chain analysis

- Value chain analysis involves analysing the various activities in the product life cycle to identify and try to eliminate non-value-added activities.
- Each link in the chain represents an activity that gives rise to costs. Any links in the chain that fail to add value should be examined critically and eliminated whenever possible.

Benchmarking

- Benchmarking attempts to emulate a successful aspect of, for example, another business or division.
- It is normally a continuing process aimed at gaining greater operating efficiency and competitive advantage.
- It involves identifying a suitable benchmark measure for a particular product or function, collecting and analysing information relating to the measure, identifying areas for improvement and then introducing new practices and targets.

→

Managing quality

- The total quality management (TQM) philosophy is concerned with providing products that meet or exceed customers' requirements all of the time.
- Ensuring the quality of output will incur costs, known as *quality costs.* They can be divided into four categories: prevention costs, appraisal costs, internal failure costs and external failure costs.
- If more is spent on prevention costs, cost savings may be made through the reduction of appraisal costs and failure costs.

An alternative view

- Costs may be managed without using sophisticated techniques if:
  - there is a shared responsibility for managing costs;
  - discussion of costs becomes an everyday activity;
  - costs are managed locally;
  - benchmarking is used at regular intervals;
  - the focus is on managing rather than reducing costs.

KEY TERMS

For definitions of these terms, see Appendix A.

Activity-based costing (ABC)
Cost driver
Cost pool
Total life-cycle costing
Target costing
Kaizen costing
Lean manufacturing
Value chain analysis
Benchmarking
Total quality management
Quality costs

REFERENCES

1 Toyota production system and what it means for business, www.toyota-forklifts.eu, accessed 9 April 2014.

2 Hopwood, A. (2002) Costs count in the strategic agenda, ft.com, 13 August.

FURTHER READING

If you would like to explore the topics covered in this chapter in more depth, we recommend the following:

Bhimani, A., Horngren, C., Datar, S. and Rajan, M. (2012) *Management and Cost Accounting*, 5th edn, Financial Times Prentice Hall, Chapters 11, 12 and 20.

Burns, J., Quinn, M., Warren, L. and Oliveira, J. (2013) *Management Accounting*, McGraw-Hill Education, Chapters 6 and 20.

Drury, C. (2012) *Management and Cost Accounting*, 8th edn, Cengage Learning, Chapter 10.

Hilton, R. and Platt, D. (2014) *Managerial Accounting*, 10th edn, McGraw-Hill Higher Education, Chapters 3, 5 and 15.

REVIEW QUESTIONS

Solutions to these questions can be found in Appendix C.

5.1 How does activity-based costing (ABC) differ from the traditional approach? What is the underlying difference between their philosophies?

5.2 The use of activity-based costing in helping to deduce full costs has been criticised. What has been the basis of this criticism?

5.3 What are the main categories of quality costs that a business may incur and why is it useful to categorise them?

5.4 Identify the main phases of the total life cycle of a product or service and identify the particular phase(s) for which target costing and kaizen costing are particularly appropriate.

EXERCISES

Exercises 5.1 to 5.3 are basic level, 5.4 to 5.6 are intermediate level and 5.7 and 5.8 are advanced level. Those with coloured numbers have solutions given in Appendix D.

5.1 Comment critically on the following statements that you have overheard:

(a) 'Achieving quality involves additional costs. If you want to improve the quality of products manufactured you have to increase total costs.'
(b) 'TQM and kaizen costing have striking similarities in their philosophy and approach.'
(c) 'Target costing is more relevant for manufacturing businesses than for service businesses.'

5.2 Describe the main similarities and differences in approach between target costing and kaizen costing.

5.3 Saxos plc is planning to adopt benchmarking in order to try to improve the efficiency of its inventory control procedures. It wishes to identify a willing partner that excels in this aspect of operations, wherever the business may be located.

What possible problems may be encountered by Saxos plc when setting up the benchmarking process?

5.4 Kaplan plc makes a range of suitcases of various sizes and shapes. There are ten different models of suitcase produced by the business. In order to keep inventories of finished suitcases to a minimum, each model is made in a small batch. Each batch is costed as a separate job and the cost for each suitcase is deduced by dividing the batch cost by the number of suitcases in the batch.

At present, the business derives the cost of each batch using a traditional job-costing approach. Recently, however, a new management accountant was appointed, who is advocating the use of activity-based costing (ABC) to deduce the cost of the batches. The management accountant claims that ABC leads to much more reliable and relevant costs and that it has other benefits.

Required:

(a) Explain how the business deduces the cost of each suitcase at present.

(b) Discuss the purposes to which the knowledge of the cost for each suitcase, deduced on a traditional basis, can be put and how valid the cost is for the purpose concerned.

(c) Explain how ABC could be applied to costing the suitcases, highlighting the differences between ABC and the traditional approach.

(d) Explain what advantages the new management accountant probably believes ABC to have over the traditional approach.

5.5 Jerry's Taxis Ltd operates a taxi service in a large provincial city. All of the taxis are owned by the business and all the drivers are employees rather than owner drivers. The managers wish to benchmark the operating efficiency of the business against another taxi service. A suitable taxi service has been identified and has agreed to the benchmarking exercise. It is highly successful and operates a similar business model in a nearby city of similar size.

Required:

Produce a checklist of *ten* measures of operating efficiency that could be used as the basis for the benchmarking exercise. (*Hint*: When identifying measures, think about the key factors of time, quality, income and costs.)

5.6 Comment critically on the following statements that you have overheard:

(a) 'Direct labour hours are the most appropriate basis to use to charge indirect cost (overheads) to jobs in the modern manufacturing environment where people are so important.'

(b) 'Activity-based costing is a means of more accurately accounting for direct labour cost.'

(c) 'Activity-based costing cannot really be applied to the service sector because the "activities" that it seeks to analyse tend to be related to manufacturing.'

(d) 'Kaizen costing is an approach where great efforts are made to reduce the costs of developing a new product and setting up its production processes.'

(e) 'Benchmarking is an approach to job costing where each direct worker keeps a record of the time spent on each job on his or her workbench before it is passed on to the next direct worker or into finished inventories stores.'

5.7 Moleskin Ltd manufactures a range of products used in the building industry. Manufacturing is undertaken using one of two processes: the Alpha Process and the Omega process. All of the products are manufactured in batches. The current pricing policy has been to absorb all overheads using direct labour hours to obtain total cost. Price is then calculated as total cost plus a 35 per cent mark-up.

A recent detailed analysis has examined overhead cost; the results are:

	Analysis of overhead costs per month	*Monthly volume*
	£	
Alpha Process cost	96,000	480 hours
Omega Process cost	44,800	1,280 hours
Set-up cost	42,900	260 set-ups
Handling charges	45,600	380 movements
Other overheads	50,700	(see below)
	280,000	

There are 4,000 direct labour hours available each month.

Two of Moleskin's products are a joist (JT101) and a girder (GR27). JT101s are produced by the Alpha Process in a simple operation. GR27s are manufactured by the Omega Process, a more complex operation with more production stages. Both products are sold by the metre.

Details for the two products are:

	JT101	*GR27*
Monthly volume	1,000 metres	500 metres
Batch size	1,000 metres	50 metres
Processing time per batch		
– Alpha	100 hours	–
– Omega	–	25 hours
Set-ups per batch	1	2
Handling charges per batch	1 movement	5 movements
Materials per metre	£16	£15
Direct labour per metre	$^1/_2$ hour	$^1/_2$ hour

Direct labour is paid £16 per hour.

Required:

(a) Calculate the price per metre for both JT101s and GR27s detailed above, using traditional absorption costing based on direct labour hours.

(b) Calculate the price per metre for both JT101s and GR27s using activity-based costing. Assume that 'Other overheads' are allocated using direct labour hours.

(c) Outline the points that you would raise with the management of Moleskin in the light of your answers to (a) and (b).

(d) Outline the practical problems that may be encountered in implementing activity-based techniques and comment on how they may be overcome.

5.8 A business manufactures refrigerators for domestic use. There are three models: Lo, Mid and Hi. The models, their quality and their price are aimed at different markets.

Product costs are computed on a blanket (business-wide) overhead-rate basis using a labour-hour method. Prices as a general rule are set based on cost plus 20 per cent. The following information is provided:

	Lo	*Mid*	*Hi*
Material cost (£/unit)	25	62.5	105
Direct labour hours (per unit)	$^1/_2$	1	1
Budget production/sales (units)	20,000	1,000	10,000

The budgeted overheads for the business amount to £4,410,000. Direct labour is costed at £8 an hour.

The business is currently facing increasing competition, especially from imported goods. As a result, the selling price of Lo has been reduced to a level that produces a very low profit margin. To address this problem, an activity-based costing approach has been suggested. The overheads are examined and these are grouped around main business activities of machining (£2,780,000), logistics (£590,000) and establishment (£1,040,000) costs. It is maintained that these costs could be allocated based respectively on cost drivers of machine hours, material orders and space, to reflect the use of resources in each of these areas. After analysis, the following proportionate statistics are available in relation to the total volume of products:

	Lo %	*Mid* %	*Hi* %
Machine hours	40	15	45
Material orders	47	6	47
Space	42	18	40

Required:

(a) Calculate for each product the full cost and selling price determined by:

1 the original costing method

2 the activity-based costing method.

(b) What are the implications of the two systems of costing in the situation given?

(c) What business/strategic options exist for the business in the light of the new information?

Chapter 6

BUDGETING

INTRODUCTION

In its 2013 annual report, BSkyB Group plc, the satellite television broadcaster, stated:

> There is a comprehensive budgeting and forecasting process, and the annual budget, which is regularly reviewed and updated, is approved by the board [of directors].

As we shall see, the practice at BSkyB is typical of businesses of all sizes.

What is a budget? What is it for? How is it prepared? Who prepares it? Why does the board regard it as important enough to consider? We shall be looking at the answers to each of these questions in the course of this chapter.

We shall see that budgets set out short-term plans to help managers run the business. They provide the means to assess whether actual performance was as planned and, if not, the reasons for this. Budgets do not exist in a vacuum; they are an integral part of a planning framework adopted by well-run businesses. To understand fully the nature of budgets we must, therefore, understand the strategic planning framework within which they are set.

The chapter begins with a discussion of the budgeting framework and then goes on to consider detailed aspects of the budgeting process. We shall see that preparing budgets relies on an understanding of many of the issues relating to the behaviour of costs and full costing, topics that we explored in Chapters 4 and 5.

Learning outcomes

When you have completed this chapter, you should be able to:

- Define a budget and show how budgets, strategic objectives and strategic plans are related.
- Explain the budgeting process and the interlinking of the various budgets within the business.
- Identify the uses of budgeting and construct various budgets, including the cash budget, from relevant data.
- Discuss the criticisms that are made of budgeting.

HOW BUDGETS LINK WITH STRATEGIC PLANS AND OBJECTIVES

It is vital that businesses develop plans for the future. Whatever a business is trying to achieve, it is unlikely to happen unless its managers are clear what the future direction of the business is going to be. As we discussed in Chapter 1 (pages 10 to 11), the development of plans involves five key steps:

1 *Establish mission, vision and objectives*
The mission and vision statements set out the overriding purpose of the business and what it seeks to achieve. The strategic objectives translate these into specific targets for the future and will be used as a basis for evaluating actual performance. You may recall that, in Chapter 1, we met the mission and vision statements of Aggreko plc (page 8).

2 *Undertake a position analysis*
This involves an assessment of where the business is currently placed in relation to where it wants to be, as set out in its mission, vision and strategic objectives.

3 *Identify and assess the strategic options*
The business must explore the various ways in which it might move from where it is now (identified in Step 2) to where it wants to be (identified in Step 1).

4 *Select strategic options and formulate plans*
This involves selecting what seems to be the best of the courses of action or strategies (identified in Step 3) and formulating a long-term strategic plan. This strategic plan is then normally broken down into a series of short-term plans, one for each element of the business. These plans are the budgets. Thus, a **budget** is a business plan for the short term – typically one year – and is expressed mainly in financial terms. Its role is to convert the strategic plans into actionable blueprints for the immediate future. Budgets will define precise targets concerning such things as:
- Cash receipts and payments
- Sales volumes and revenues, broken down into amounts and prices for each of the products or services provided by the business
- Detailed inventories requirements
- Detailed labour requirements
- Specific production requirements.

5 *Perform, review and control*
Here the business pursues the budgets derived in Step 4. By comparing the actual outcome with the budgets, managers can see if things are going according to plan or not. Action would be taken to exercise control where actual performance appears not to be matching the budgets.

Activity 6.1

The approach described in Step 3 suggests that managers will systematically collect information and then carefully evaluate all the options available. Do you think this is what managers really do?

In practice, managers may not be as rational and capable as implied.

To develop the point made in the answer to Activity 6.1, managers may find it difficult to handle a large amount of information relating to a wide range of options. To avoid becoming overloaded, they may restrict their range of possible options and/or discard some information. Managers may also adopt rather simple approaches to evaluating the mass of information provided. These approaches might not, however, lead to the best decisions being made.

From the description of the planning process that we have just met, we can see that the relationship between the mission, vision, strategic objectives, strategic plans and budgets can be summarised as follows:

- the mission and vision set the overall direction and, once set, this is likely to last for quite a long time – perhaps throughout the life of the business;
- the strategic objectives, which are also long-term, will translate the mission and vision into specific, often quantifiable, targets;
- the strategic plans identify how each objective will be pursued; and
- the budgets set out, in detail, the short-term plans and targets necessary to fulfil the strategic objectives.

An analogy might be found in terms of a student enrolling on a course of study. The student's mission might be to have a happy and fulfilling life. A key strategic objective flowing from this mission might be to embark on a career that will be rewarding in various ways. The particular study course might have been identified as the most effective way to work towards this objective. Successfully completing the course would then be the strategic plan. In working towards this strategic plan, passing a particular stage of the course might be identified as the target for the forthcoming year. This short-term target is analogous to the budget. Having achieved the 'budget' for the first year, the student's budget for the second year becomes passing the second stage.

Exercising control

However well planned the activities of a business might be, they will come to nothing unless steps are taken to try to achieve them in practice. The process of making planned events actually occur is known as **control**. This is part of Step 5 (above).

Control can be defined as compelling events to conform to plan. This definition is valid in any context. For example, when we talk about controlling a car, we mean making the car do what we plan that it should do.

In a business context, management accounting has an important role to play in the control process. This is because it is possible to state many plans in accounting terms (as budgets). Since it is also possible to state *actual* outcomes in the same terms, making comparison between actual and planned outcomes is a relatively simple matter. Where actual outcomes are at variance with budgets, this variance should be highlighted by accounting information. Managers can then take steps to get the business back on track towards the achievement of the budgets. We shall be looking more closely at the control aspect of budgeting in Chapter 7.

Figure 6.1 shows the planning and control process in diagrammatic form.

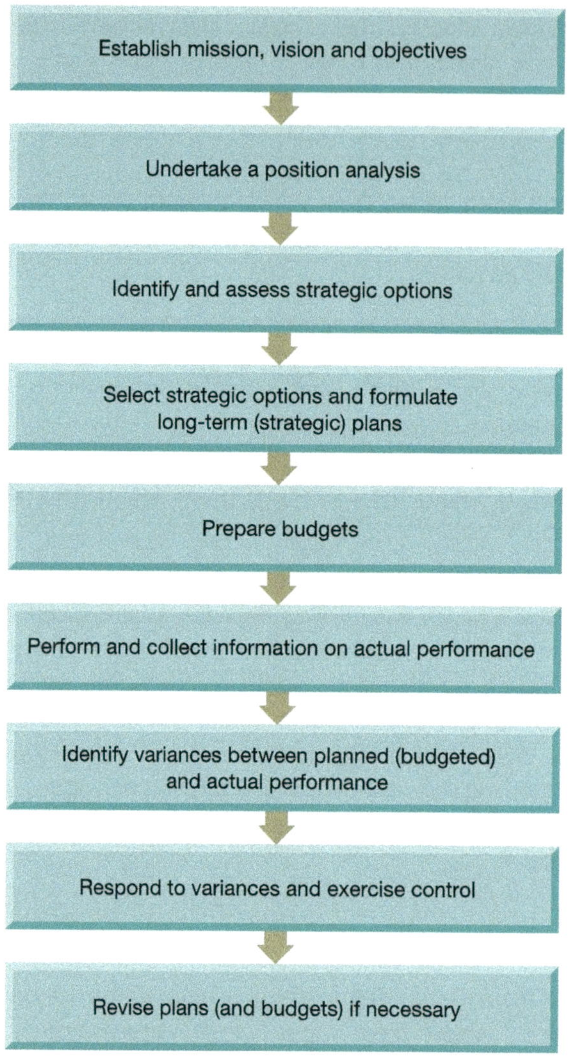

Once the mission, vision and objectives of the business have been determined, the various strategic options available must be considered and evaluated in order to derive a strategic plan. The budget is a short-term financial plan for the business that is prepared within the framework of the strategic plan. Control can be exercised through the comparison of budgeted and actual performance. Where a significant divergence emerges, some form of corrective action should be taken. If the budget figures prove to be based on incorrect assumptions about the future, it might be necessary to revise the budget.

Figure 6.1 The planning and control process

It should be emphasised that planning (including budgeting) is the responsibility of managers rather than accountants. Although accountants play a role in the planning process, by supplying relevant information to managers and by contributing to decision making as part of the management team, they should not dominate the process. In practice, however, this often seems to occur. While accountants may be adept at dealing with financial information, managers are failing in their responsibilities if they allow them to have an excessive influence in the budgeting process.

TIME HORIZON OF PLANS AND BUDGETS

Setting strategic plans is typically a major exercise performed about every five years and budgets are usually set annually for the forthcoming year. These time horizons, however, may vary according to the needs of the particular business. Those businesses involved in certain industries – say, information technology – may feel that five years is too long a planning period since new developments can, and do, occur virtually overnight. Here, a planning horizon of two or three years may be more appropriate. Similarly, a budget need not be set for one year, although this appears to be a widely used time horizon.

One business that tends to keep its strategic planning under more frequent review is J Sainsbury plc, the supermarket business. **Real World 6.1**, which is an extract from the annual report for the business, explains how strategic planning is a regular annual event.

Real World 6.1

Strategic planning at the supermarket

According to its annual report, Sainsbury's has the following approach to strategic planning:

> The Board continued to focus on strategic matters during the year. We hold a two-day Strategy Conference in the autumn, which the Operating Board Directors attend. This enables the Board to conduct an in-depth review of relevant economic factors and their likely impact on customers and the market, to evaluate key opportunities and threats, consider the corporate plan and agree the strategic goals for the short-term and longer term perspectives, and the five areas of focus: Great food, Compelling general merchandise and clothing, Complementary channels and services, Developing new business and Growing space and creating property value. The Board receives a detailed half-year update on progress against the agreed priorities and then, to complete the cycle in July, agrees the objectives and principal areas of focus for the next conference.

Source: J Sainsbury plc Annual Report 2013, p. 39. Reproduced by kind permission of J Sainsbury plc.

Activity 6.2

Can you think of any reason why most businesses prepare detailed budgets for the forthcoming year, rather than for a shorter or longer period?

The reason is probably that a year represents a long enough time for the budget preparation exercise to be worthwhile, yet short enough into the future for detailed plans to be capable of being made. As we shall see later in this chapter, the process of formulating budgets can be a time-consuming exercise, but there are economies of scale – for example, preparing the budget for the next year would not normally take twice as much time and effort as preparing the budget for the next six months.

An annual budget sets targets for the forthcoming year for all aspects of the business. It is usually broken down into monthly budgets, which define monthly targets. Indeed, in many instances, the annual budget will be built up from monthly figures. The sales staff, for example, may be required to set sales targets for each month of the budget period. These targets may well differ from month to month, particularly where there are seasonal demand variations. Other budgets will be set for each month, as we shall explain shortly.

LIMITING FACTORS

Some aspect of the business will, inevitably, stop it achieving its objectives to the maximum extent. This is often a limited ability of the business to sell its products. Sometimes, it is some production shortage (such as labour, materials or plant) that is the **limiting factor**, or, linked to these, a shortage of funds. Often, production shortages can be overcome by an increase in funds – for example, more plant can be bought or leased. This is not always a practical solution, because no amount of money will buy certain labour skills or increase the world supply of some raw material.

Easing an initial limiting factor may sometimes be possible. For example, subcontracting can eliminate a plant capacity problem. This means that some other factor, perhaps lack of sales demand, will replace the production problem, though at a higher level of output. Ultimately, however, the business will hit a ceiling; some limiting factor will prove impossible to ease.

The limiting factor must be identified. Ultimately, most, if not all, budgets will be affected by the limiting factor. If this can be identified at the outset, all managers can be informed of the restriction early in the process. When preparing the budgets, account can then be taken of the limiting factor.

BUDGETS AND FORECASTS

A budget may, as we have already seen, be defined as a business plan for the short term. Budgets are, to a great extent, expressed in financial terms. Note particularly that a budget is a *plan*, not a forecast. To talk of a plan suggests an intention or determination to achieve the targets; **forecasts** tend to be predictions of the future state of the environment.

Clearly, forecasts are very helpful to the planner/budget-setter. If, for example, a reputable forecaster has predicted the number of new cars to be purchased in the UK during next year, it will be valuable for a manager in a car manufacturing business to take account of this information when setting next year's sales budgets. However, a forecast and a budget are distinctly different.

PERIODIC AND CONTINUAL BUDGETS

Budgeting can be undertaken on a periodic or a continual basis. A **periodic budget** is prepared for a particular period (usually one year). Managers will agree the budget for the year and then allow the budget to run its course. Although it may be necessary to revise the budget on occasions, preparing the periodic budget is, in essence, a one-off exercise during each financial year. A **continual budget**, as the name suggests, is continually updated. We have seen that an annual budget will normally be broken down into smaller time intervals (usually monthly periods) to help control the activities of the business. A continual budget will add a new month to replace the month that has just passed, thereby ensuring that, at all times, there will be a budget for a full planning period. A continual budget is also referred to as a **rolling budget**.

Activity 6.3

Which method of budgeting do you think is likely to be more costly and which method is likely to be more beneficial for forward planning?

Periodic budgeting will usually take less time and effort and will, therefore, be less costly. However, as time passes, the budget period shortens and towards the end of the financial year managers will be working to a very short planning period indeed. Continual budgeting, on the other hand, will ensure that managers always have a full year's budget to help them make decisions. It is claimed that continual budgeting ensures that managers plan throughout the year rather than just once each year. In this way it encourages a perpetual forward-looking attitude.

While continual budgeting encourages a forward-looking attitude, there is a danger that budgeting will become a mechanical exercise. Managers may not have time to step back from their other tasks each month and consider the future with sufficient care. Continually taking this forward-looking attitude may be difficult, therefore, to sustain.

Continual budgets do not appear to be very popular in practice. A survey of 340 senior financial staff of small, medium and large businesses in North America revealed that only 9 per cent of businesses use them (see reference 1 at the end of the chapter).

HOW BUDGETS LINK TO ONE ANOTHER

A typical larger business will prepare more than one budget for a particular period. Each budget prepared will relate to a specific aspect of its operations. The ideal situation is probably that there should be a separate operating budget for each person who is in a managerial position, no matter how junior. The contents of all of the individual operating budgets will be summarised in **master budgets**, usually consisting of a budgeted income statement and statement of financial position (balance sheet). The cash budget is considered by some to be a third master budget.

Figure 6.2 illustrates the interrelationship and interlinking of individual operating budgets, in this particular case using a manufacturing business as an example.

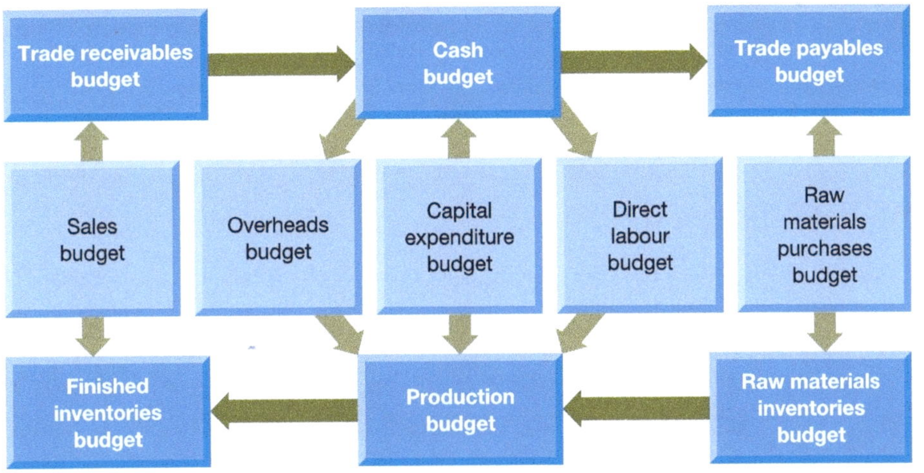

The starting point is usually the sales budget. The expected level of sales normally defines the overall level of activity for the business. The other operating budgets will be drawn up in accordance with this. Thus, the sales budget will largely define the finished inventories requirements and from this we can define the production requirements and so on. This shows the interrelationship of operating budgets for a manufacturing business.

Figure 6.2 The interrelationship of operating budgets

The sales budget is usually the first to be prepared (at the left of Figure 6.2), as the level of sales often determines the overall level of activity for the forthcoming period. This is because sales demand is probably the most common limiting factor (see page 188). The finished inventories requirement tends to be set by the level of sales, though it would also be dictated by the policy of the business on the level of the finished products inventories that it chooses to hold. The requirement for finished inventories will determine the required production levels, which will, in turn, dictate the requirements of the individual production departments or sections. The demands of manufacturing, in conjunction with the business's policy on how long it holds raw materials before they enter production, define the raw materials inventories budget. The purchases budget will be dictated by the materials inventories budget, which will, in conjunction with the policy of the business on taking credit from suppliers, dictate the trade payables budget. One of the determinants of the cash budget will be the trade payables budget; another will be the trade receivables budget, which itself derives, through the business's policy on settlement periods granted to credit customers, from the sales budget. Cash will also be affected by overheads and direct labour costs (themselves linked to production) and by capital expenditure. Cash will also be affected by new finance and redemption of existing sources. (This is not shown in Figure 6.2 because the diagram focuses only on budgets concerned with operational matters.) The factors that affect policies on matters such as inventories holding, trade receivables collection and trade payables settlement periods will be discussed in some detail in Chapter 11.

A manufacturing business has been used as the example in Figure 6.2 simply because it has all of the types of operating budgets found in practice. Service businesses have similar budgets, but may not have inventories budgets. All of the issues relating to budgets apply equally well to all types of business.

Sales demand is not necessarily the limiting factor. Assuming that the budgeting process takes the order just described, it might be found in practice that there is some constraint other than sales demand. The production capacity of the business may, for example, be incapable of meeting the necessary levels of output to match the sales budget for one or more months. Finding a practical way of overcoming the problem may be possible. As a last resort, it might be necessary to revise the sales budget to a lower level to match the production limitation.

Activity 6.4

Can you think of any ways in which a short-term shortage of production facilities of a manufacturer might be overcome?

We thought of the following:

- Higher production in previous months and increasing inventories ('stockpiling') to meet periods of higher demand.
- Increasing production capacity, perhaps by working overtime and/or acquiring (buying or leasing) additional plant.
- Subcontracting some production.
- Encouraging potential customers to change the timing of their purchases by offering discounts or other special terms during the months that have been identified as quiet.

You might well have thought of other approaches.

There will be the horizontal relationships between budgets, which we have just looked at, but there will usually be vertical ones as well. Breaking down the sales budget into a number of subsidiary budgets, perhaps one for each regional sales manager, is a common approach. The overall sales budget will be a summary of the subsidiary ones. The same may be true of virtually all of the other budgets, most particularly the production budget.

Figure 6.3 shows the vertical relationship of the sales budgets for a business. The business has four geographical sales regions, each one the responsibility of a separate manager. Each regional manager is responsible to the overall sales manager of the business. The overall sales budget is the sum of the budgets for the four sales regions.

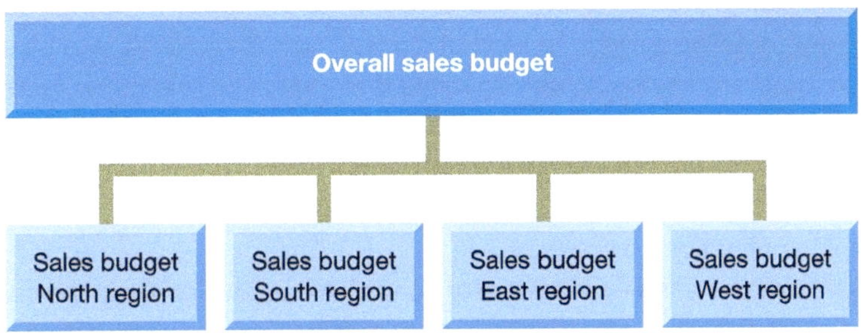

This business manages its sales through four geographical areas. The overall sales budget for the business as a whole is the sum of the four regional sales budgets.

Figure 6.3 The vertical relationship between a business's sales budgets

Although sales are often managed on a geographical basis, and so their budgets reflect this, they may be managed on some other basis. For example, a business that sells a range of products may manage sales on a product-type basis, with a specialist manager responsible for each type of product. Thus, an insurance business may have separate sales managers and, therefore, separate sales budgets, for life insurance, household insurance, motor insurance and so on. Very large businesses may even have separate product-type managers for each geographical region. Each of these managers would have a separate budget, which would combine to form the overall sales budget for the business as a whole.

All of the operating budgets that we have just reviewed must mesh with the master budgets, that is, the budgeted income statement and statement of financial position.

HOW BUDGETS HELP MANAGERS

Budgets are generally regarded as having five areas of usefulness. These are:

- *Budgets tend to promote forward thinking and the possible identification of short-term problems*. We have seen that a shortage of production capacity might be identified during the budgeting process. Making this discovery in good time could leave a number of means of overcoming the problem open to exploration. If the potential production problem is picked up early enough, all of the suggestions in the answer to Activity 6.4 and, possibly, other ways of overcoming the problem can be explored. Identifying the potential problem early gives managers time for calm and rational consideration of the best way of overcoming it. The best solution to the potential problem possibly may only be feasible if action can be taken well in advance. This would be true of all of the suggestions made in the answer to Activity 6.4.
- *Budgets can be used to help co-ordination between the various sections of the business*. It is crucially important that the activities of the various departments and sections of the

business are linked so that the activities of one are complementary to those of another. The activities of the purchasing/procurement department of a manufacturing business, for example, should dovetail with the raw materials needs of the production departments. If they do not, production could run out of raw materials, leading to expensive production stoppages. Possibly, just as undesirable, excessive amounts of raw materials could be bought, leading to large and unnecessary inventories holding costs. We shall see how this co-ordination tends to work in practice later in this chapter.

- *Budgets can motivate managers to better performance*. Having a stated task can motivate managers and staff in their performance. Simply to tell managers to do their best is not very motivating, but to define a required level of achievement is more likely to be so. Managers will be better motivated by being able to relate their particular role to the business's overall objectives. Since budgets are directly derived from strategic objectives, budgeting makes this possible. It is clearly not possible to allow managers to operate in an unconstrained environment. Having to operate in a way that matches the goals of the business is a price of working in an effective business.
- *Budgets can provide a basis for a system of control*. As we saw earlier in the chapter, control is concerned with ensuring that events conform to plans. If managers wish to control and to monitor their own performance and that of their more junior staff, they need some yardstick against which to measure and assess performance. Current performance could possibly be compared with past performance or perhaps with what happens in another business. However, planned performance is usually the most logical yardstick. If there is information available concerning the actual performance for a period, and this can be compared with the planned performance, then a basis for control will have been established. This will enable the use of **management by exception**, an approach where senior managers can spend most of their time dealing with those staff or activities that have failed to achieve the budget (the exceptions). Thus, senior managers do not have to spend too much time on those that are performing well. Effective budgets allow all managers to exercise self-control. By knowing what is expected of them and what they have actually achieved, they can assess how well they are performing and take steps to correct matters where they are failing to achieve.
- *Budgets can provide a system of authorisation for managers to spend up to a particular limit*. Some activities (for example, staff development and research and development) are allocated a fixed amount of funds at the discretion of senior management. This provides the authority to spend.

Figure 6.4 shows the benefits of budgets in diagrammatic form.

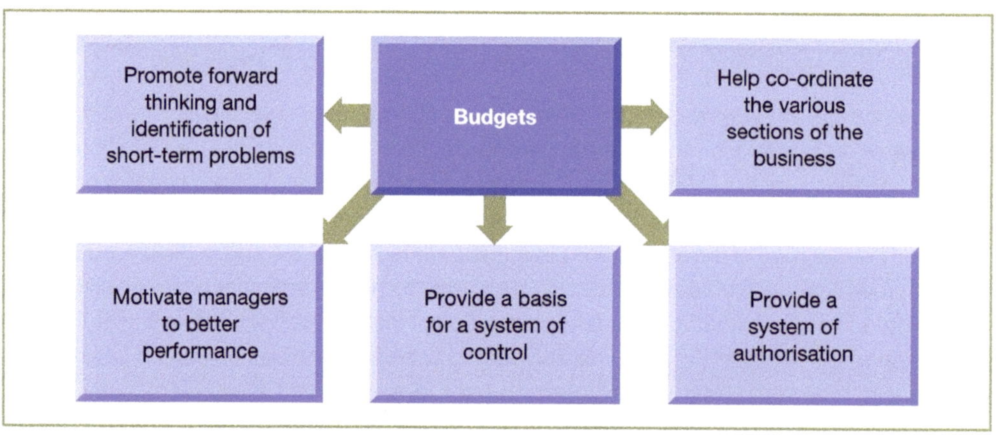

Figure 6.4 Budgets are seen as having five main benefits to the business

The following two activities pick up issues that relate to some of the uses of budgets.

Activity 6.5

The third point on the list of the uses of budgets (motivation) implies that managers are set stated tasks. Do you think there is a danger that requiring managers to work towards such predetermined targets will stifle their skill, flair and enthusiasm?

If the budgets are set in such a way as to offer challenging yet achievable targets, the manager is still required to show skill, flair and enthusiasm. There is the danger, however, that if targets are badly set (either unreasonably demanding or too easy to achieve), they could be demotivating and have a stifling effect.

Activity 6.6

The fourth point on the list of the uses of budgets (control) implies that current management performance is compared with some yardstick. What is wrong with comparing actual performance with past performance, or the performance of others, in an effort to exercise control?

What happened in the past, or is happening elsewhere, does not necessarily represent a sensible target for this year in this business. Considering what happened last year, and in other businesses, may help in the formulation of plans, but past events and the performance of others should not automatically be seen as the target.

The five identified uses of budgets can conflict with one another on occasion. Using the budget as a motivational device provides a possible example of this. Some businesses set the budget targets at a more difficult level than the managers are expected to achieve in an attempt to motivate managers to strive to reach their targets. For control purposes, however, the budget becomes less meaningful as a benchmark against which to compare actual performance. Incidentally, there is good reason to doubt the effectiveness of setting excessive targets as a motivational device, as we shall see in Chapter 7.

Conflict between the different uses will mean that managers must decide which particular uses for budgets should be given priority. Managers must be prepared, if necessary, to trade off the benefits resulting from one particular use for the benefits of another.

THE BUDGET-SETTING PROCESS

Budgeting is such an important area for businesses, and other organisations, that it tends to be approached in a fairly methodical and formal way. This usually involves a number of steps, which we shall now consider.

Step 1: Establish who will take responsibility

Those responsible for the budget-setting process must have real authority within the organisation.

Activity 6.7

Why would those responsible for the budget-setting process need to have real authority?

One of the crucial aspects of the process is establishing co-ordination between budgets so that the plans of one department match and are complementary to those of other departments. This usually requires compromise where adjustment of initial budgets must be undertaken. This in turn means that someone on the board of directors (or another senior manager) has to be closely involved; only people of this rank are likely to have the necessary moral and, if needed, formal managerial authority to force departmental managers to compromise.

A **budget committee** is usually formed to supervise and take responsibility for the budget-setting process. This committee usually includes a senior representative of most of the functional areas of the business – marketing, production, human resources and so on. Often, a **budget officer** is appointed to carry out the technical tasks of the committee, or to supervise others carrying them out. Not surprisingly, given their technical expertise, accountants are often given this role.

Step 2: Communicate budget guidelines to relevant managers

Budgets are intended to be the short-term plans that seek to work towards the achievement of strategic plans and to the overall objectives of the business. It is, therefore, important that, in drawing up budgets, managers are well aware of what the strategic plans are and how the forthcoming budget period is intended to work towards them. Managers also need to be made well aware of the commercial/economic environment in which they will be operating. This may include awareness of market trends, future rates of inflation, forecast changes in technology and so on. It is the budget committee's responsibility to see that managers have all the necessary information.

Step 3: Identify the key, or limiting, factor

There will be a limiting factor that will restrict the business from achieving its objectives to the maximum extent, as we saw earlier in the chapter (page 188). Identifying the limiting factor at the earliest stage in the budget-setting process will be helpful.

Step 4: Prepare the budget for the area of the limiting factor

The limiting factor will determine the overall level of activity for the business. The limiting-factor budget will, as we have already seen, usually be the sales budget, since the ability to sell is normally the constraint on future growth. (When discussing the interrelationship of budgets earlier in the chapter, we started with the sales budget for this reason.)

Step 5: Prepare draft budgets for all other areas

The other budgets are prepared, consistent with the budget for the area of the limiting factor. In all budget preparation, the computer has become an almost indispensable tool. Much of the work of preparing budgets is repetitive and tedious, yet the resultant budget has to be a reliable representation of the plans made. Computers are ideally suited to such tasks and human beings are not. Budgets often have to be redrafted several times because of some minor alteration; computers do this without complaint.

Setting individual budgets may be approached in one of two broad ways. The *top-down approach* is where the senior management of each budget area originates the budget targets, perhaps discussing them with lower levels of management and, as a result, refining them before the final version is produced. With the *bottom-up approach*, the targets are fed upwards from the lowest level. For example, junior sales managers will be asked to set their own sales targets, which then become incorporated into the budgets of higher levels of management until the overall sales budget emerges.

Where the bottom-up approach is adopted, it is usually necessary to haggle and negotiate at different levels of authority to achieve agreement. Perhaps the plans of some departments do not fit in with those of others or the targets set by junior managers are not acceptable to their superiors. The bottom-up approach is less popular in practice than top-down (see reference 2 at the end of the chapter).

Activity 6.8

What are the advantages and disadvantages of each type of budgeting approach (bottom-up and top-down)?

The bottom-up approach allows greater involvement among managers in the budgeting process and this, in turn, may increase the level of commitment to the targets set. It also allows the business to draw more fully on the local knowledge and expertise of its managers. However, this can be time-consuming and may result in some managers setting themselves undemanding targets in order to have an easy life.

The top-down approach enables senior management to communicate plans to employees and to co-ordinate the activities of the business more easily. It may also help in establishing more demanding targets for managers. However, the level of commitment to the budget may be lower as many of those responsible for achieving the budgets will have been excluded from the budget-setting process.

There will be further discussion of the benefits of participation in target setting in Chapter 7.

Step 6: Review and co-ordinate budgets

The budget committee must, at this stage, review the various budgets and satisfy itself that the budgets are consistent with one another. Where there is a lack of co-ordination, steps must be taken to ensure that the budgets mesh. Since this will require that at least one budget must be revised, this activity normally benefits from a diplomatic approach. Ultimately, however, the committee may be forced to assert its authority and insist that alterations are made.

Step 7: Prepare the master budgets

The master budgets are the budgeted income statement and budgeted statement of financial position – and, perhaps, a summarised cash budget. The individual operating budgets, that have already been prepared, should provide all of the information required to prepare the master budgets. The budget committee usually undertakes the task of preparing the master budgets.

Step 8: Communicate the budgets to all interested parties

The formally agreed operating budgets are now passed to the individual managers who will be responsible for their implementation. This is, in effect, senior management communicating to the other managers the targets that are expected to be achieved.

Step 9: Monitor performance relative to the budget

Much of the budget-setting activity will have been pointless unless each manager's actual performance is compared with the benchmark of planned performance, which is embodied in the budget. This issue is examined in detail in Chapter 7.

The steps in the budget-setting process are shown in diagrammatic form in Figure 6.5.

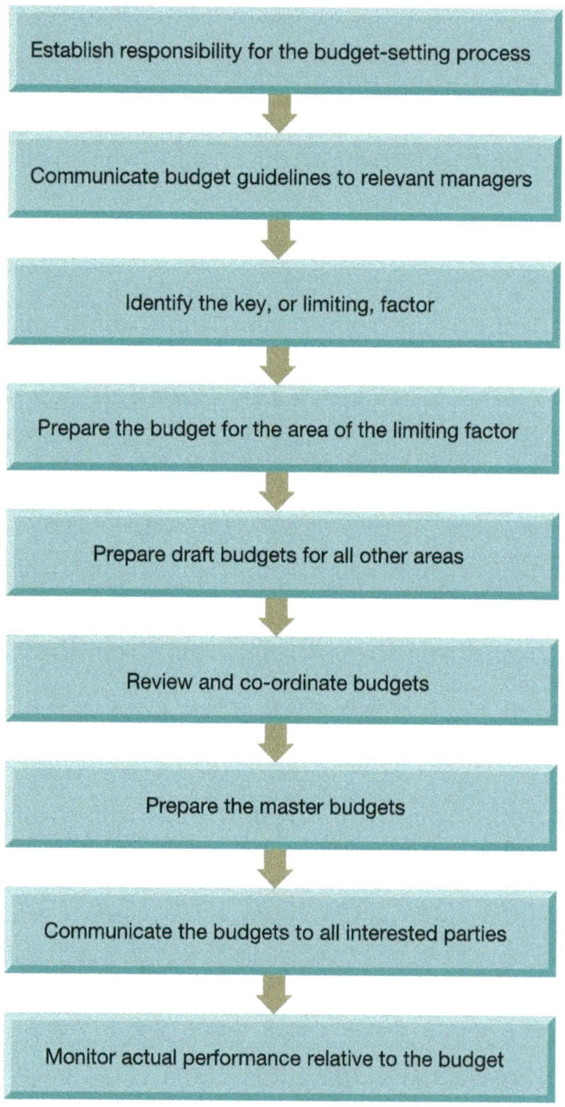

Once the budgets are prepared, they are communicated to all interested parties and, over time, actual performance is monitored in relation to the targets set out in the budgets.

Figure 6.5 Steps in the budget-setting process

Where the established budgets are proving to be unrealistic, it is usually helpful to revise them. They may be unrealistic because certain assumptions made when the budgets were first set have turned out to be incorrect. This may occur where managers (budget-setters) have made poor judgements or where the environment has changed unexpectedly from what was, quite reasonably, assumed. Unrealistic budgets are of little value and revising them may be the only logical approach to take. Nevertheless, revising budgets should be regarded as exceptional and only undertaken after careful consideration.

USING BUDGETS IN PRACTICE

This section provides an indication of how budgets are used, the extent to which they are used and their level of accuracy.

Real World 6.2 shows how the UK brewer and pub/hotel operator Greene King plc undertakes its budgeting process.

Real World 6.2

Budgeting at Greene King

According to its annual report Greene King has

- **a comprehensive planning and financial reporting procedure including annual budgets and a three-year strategic plan, both of which are reviewed and approved by the board;**
- **on-going monitoring by both the board and senior management of performance against budgets, through the periodic reporting of detailed management accounts and key performance indicators.**

Source: Greene King plc Annual Report 2013, p. 45.

There is quite a lot of survey evidence that reveals the extent to which budgeting is used by businesses in practice. **Real World 6.3** reviews some of this evidence, which shows that most businesses prepare and use budgets.

Real World 6.3

Budgeting in practice

A survey of 41 UK manufacturing businesses found that 40 of the 41 surveyed prepared budgets.

Source: Dugdale, D., Jones, C. and Green, S. (2006) *Contemporary Management Accounting Practices in UK Manufacturing*, CIMA Publication, Elsevier.

Another survey of UK businesses, but this time businesses involved in the food and drink sector, found that virtually all of them used budgets.

Source: Abdel-Kader, M. and Luther, R. (2004) *An Empirical Investigation of the Evolution of Management Accounting Practices*, Working paper No. 04/06, University of Essex, October.

A survey of the opinions of senior finance staff at 340 businesses of various sizes and operating in a wide range of industries in North America revealed that 97 per cent of those businesses had a formal budgeting process.

Source: BPM Forum (2008) Perfect how you project.

→

On the other hand, a survey of seven small and four medium-sized UK business found that not all of the small ones had a formal budgeting process, though all of the medium-sized ones did.

Source: Lucas, M., Prowle, M. and Lowth, G. (2013) Management accounting practices of UK small-medium-sized enterprises, CIMA, July 2013, p. 6.

Although these four surveys relate to UK and North American businesses, they provide some idea of what is likely also to be the practice elsewhere in the developed world.

Real World 6.4 gives some insight about the accuracy of budgets.

Real World 6.4

Budget accuracy

The survey of senior finance staff of North American businesses, mentioned in Real World 6.3, asked them to compare the actual revenues with the budgeted revenues for 2007. Figure 6.6 shows the results.

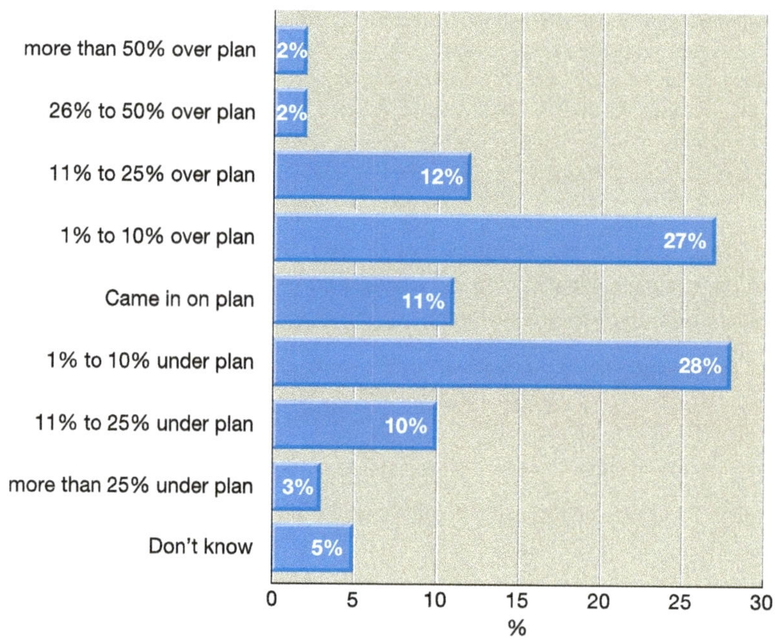

66 per cent of revenue budgets were accurate within a range of 10 per cent.

Figure 6.6 The accuracy of revenue budgets

We can see that only 66 per cent of revenue budgets were accurate within 10 per cent. The survey revealed that budgets for expenses were generally more accurate, with 74 per cent being accurate within 10 per cent.

Source: BPM Forum (2008) Perfect how you project.

INCREMENTAL AND ZERO-BASE BUDGETING

Budget setting seems often to be done on the basis of what happened last year, with some adjustment for any changes in factors that are expected to affect the forthcoming budget period (for example, inflation). This approach is known as **incremental budgeting** and is often used for **discretionary budgets**, such as research and development and staff training. With this type of budget, the **budget holder** (the manager responsible for the budget) is allocated a sum of money to be spent in the area of activity concerned. Such budgets are referred to as 'discretionary' budgets because the sum allocated is normally at the discretion of senior management. These budgets are very common in local and central government (and in other public bodies), but are also used in commercial businesses to cover the types of activity that we have just referred to.

Discretionary budgets are often found in areas where there is no clear relationship between inputs (resources applied) and outputs (benefits). Compare this with, say, a raw materials usage budget in a manufacturing business, where the amount of material used and, therefore, the amount of funds involved, are clearly related to the level of production and, ultimately, to sales volumes. Discretionary budgets can easily eat up funds, with no clear benefit being derived. It is often only the proposed periodic increases in these budgets that are closely scrutinised.

Real World 6.5 provides some idea of the extent to which incremental budgeting is used in practice.

Real World 6.5

Budgeting by increments

The 2009 CIMA survey showed that incremental budgeting is quite widely used in practice, as is shown by Figure 6.7.

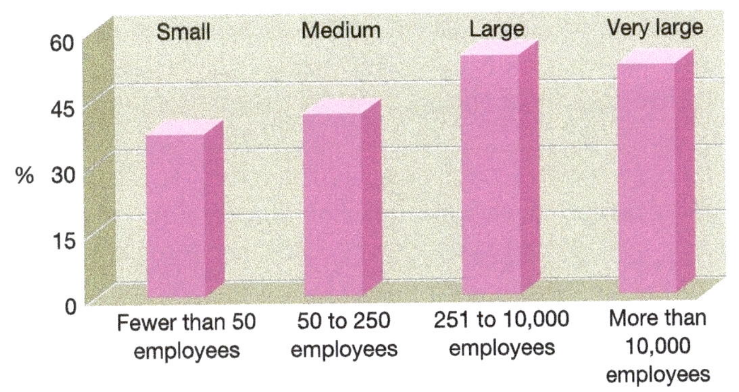

Incremental budgeting is used by about 47 per cent of all of the businesses surveyed.

Figure 6.7 The use of incremental budgeting

It seems reasonable to presume that where businesses use an incremental approach, it is in the context of discretionary budgets.

Source: CIMA (2009) *Management Accounting Tools for Today and Tomorrow*, p. 15.

Zero-base budgeting (ZBB) rests on the philosophy that all spending needs to be justified. Thus, when establishing, say, the training budget each year, it is not automatically accepted that training courses should be financed in the future simply because they were undertaken this year. The training budget will start from a zero base (that is no resources at all) and will only be increased above zero if a good case can be made for the scarce resources of the business to be allocated to this form of activity. Top management will need to be convinced that the proposed activities represent 'value for money'.

ZBB encourages managers to adopt a more questioning approach to their areas of responsibility. To justify the allocation of resources, managers are often forced to think carefully about the particular activities and the ways in which they are undertaken. This questioning approach should result in a more efficient use of business resources. An increasing portion of the total cost of most businesses is in areas where the link between outputs and inputs is not always clear. The commitment of resources is, therefore, discretionary rather than demonstrably essential to production. Thus, ZBB is increasingly relevant.

Activity 6.9

Can you think of any disadvantages of using ZBB?

The principal problems with ZBB are:

- It is time-consuming and therefore expensive to undertake.
- Managers whose sphere of responsibility is subjected to ZBB can feel threatened by it.

The benefits of a ZBB approach can be gained to some extent – perhaps at not too great a cost – by using the approach on a selective basis. For example, a particular budget area could be subjected to ZBB-type scrutiny only every third or fourth year. In any case, if ZBB is used more frequently, there is the danger that managers will use the same arguments each year to justify their activities. The process will simply become a mechanical exercise and the benefits will be lost. For a typical business, some areas are likely to benefit from ZBB more than others. As mentioned earlier, the areas most likely to benefit from ZBB involve discretionary spending, such as training, advertising and research and development.

If senior management is aware that their subordinates are likely to feel threatened by the nature of this form of budgeting, care can be taken to apply ZBB with sensitivity. However, in the quest for cost control and value for money, ZBB can result in some tough decisions being made.

Real World 6.6 gives some impression of how much ZBB is used in practice.

Real World 6.6

Too low for zero

A significant proportion of businesses use ZBB in practice, according to the 2009 CIMA survey. The detail is shown in Figure 6.8.

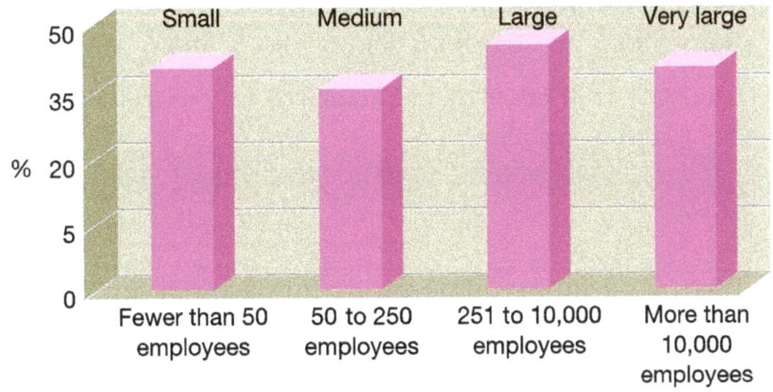

Zero-base budgeting is used by about 41 per cent of all of the businesses surveyed.

Figure 6.8 The use of zero-base budgeting

As with incremental budgeting, it is likely that ZBB is mainly used when preparing discretionary budgets.

Source: CIMA (2009) *Management Accounting Tools for Today and Tomorrow*, p. 15.

PREPARING BUDGETS

We shall now look in some detail at how the various budgets used by the typical business are prepared, starting with the cash budget and then looking at the others.

The cash budget

It is helpful for us to start with the cash budget because:

- It is a key budget (some people see it as a 'master budget' along with the budgeted income statement and budgeted statement of financial position); most economic aspects of a business are reflected in cash sooner or later. This means that, for a typical business, the cash budget reflects the whole business more comprehensively than any other single budget.
- A very small, unsophisticated business (for example, a corner shop) may feel that full-scale budgeting is not appropriate to its needs, but almost certainly it should prepare a cash budget as a minimum.

Since budgets are documents that tend to be used only internally by a business, their format is a question of management choice and will vary from one business to the next. However, since all managers, irrespective of the business, are likely to be using budgets for similar purposes, some consistency of approach tends to be found. In most businesses, the cash budget will probably possess the following features:

1. The budget period would be broken down into sub-periods, typically months.
2. The budget would be in columnar form, with one column for each month.
3. Receipts of cash would be identified under various headings and a total for each month's receipts shown.
4. Payments of cash would be identified under various headings and a total for each month's payments shown.
5. The surplus of total cash receipts over payments, or of payments over receipts, for each month would be identified.

6 The running cash balance would be identified. This would be achieved by taking the balance at the end of the previous month and adjusting it for the surplus or deficit of receipts over payments for the current month.

Typically, all of the pieces of information in points 3 to 6 in this list would be useful to management for one reason or another.

Probably the best way to deal with this topic is through an example.

Example 6.1

Vierra Popova Ltd is a wholesale business. The budgeted income statements for each of the next six months are as follows:

	Jan £000	*Feb* £000	*Mar* £000	*Apr* £000	*May* £000	*June* £000
Sales revenue	52	55	55	60	55	53
Cost of goods sold	(30)	(31)	(31)	(35)	(31)	(32)
Salaries and wages	(10)	(10)	(10)	(10)	(10)	(10)
Electricity	(5)	(5)	(4)	(3)	(3)	(3)
Depreciation	(3)	(3)	(3)	(3)	(3)	(3)
Other overheads	(2)	(2)	(2)	(2)	(2)	(2)
Total expenses	(50)	(51)	(50)	(53)	(49)	(50)
Profit for the month	2	4	5	7	6	3

The business allows all of its customers one month's credit (this means, for example, that cash from January sales will be received in February). Sales revenue during December totalled £60,000.

The business plans to maintain inventories at their existing level until March. During that month they are to be reduced by £5,000. Inventories will remain at this lower level indefinitely. Inventories purchases are made on one month's credit. December purchases totalled £30,000. Salaries, wages and 'other overheads' are paid in the month concerned. Electricity is paid quarterly in arrears in March and June. The business plans to buy and pay for a new delivery van in March. This will cost a total of £15,000, but an existing van will be traded in for £4,000 as part of the deal.

The business expects to have £12,000 in cash at the beginning of January.

The cash budget for the six months ending in June will look as follows:

	Jan £000	*Feb* £000	*Mar* £000	*Apr* £000	*May* £000	*June* £000
Receipts						
Trade receivables (Note 1)	60	52	55	55	60	55
Payments						
Trade payables (Note 2)	(30)	(30)	(31)	(26)	(35)	(31)
Salaries and wages	(10)	(10)	(10)	(10)	(10)	(10)
Electricity	–	–	(14)	–	–	(9)
Other overheads	(2)	(2)	(2)	(2)	(2)	(2)
Van purchase	–	–	(11)	–	–	–
Total payments	(42)	(42)	(68)	(38)	(47)	(52)
Cash surplus for the month	18	10	(13)	17	13	3
Opening balance (Note 3)	12	30	40	27	44	57
Closing balance	30	40	27	44	57	60

Notes:

1 The cash receipts from trade receivables lag a month behind sales because customers are given a month in which to pay for their purchases. So, December sales will be paid for in January and so on.

2 For inventories to remain constant at the end of each month, the business must replace exactly the amount that has been used. In most months, the purchases of inventories will, therefore, equal the cost of goods sold. During March, however, the business plans to reduce its inventories by £5,000. This means that inventories purchases will be lower than inventories usage in that month. The payments for inventories purchases lag a month behind purchases because the business expects to be allowed a month to pay for what it buys.

3 Each month's cash balance is the previous month's figure plus the cash surplus (or minus the cash deficit) for the current month. The balance at the start of January is £12,000 according to the information provided just before the cash budget (above).

4 Depreciation does not give rise to a cash payment. In the context of profit measurement (in the income statement), depreciation is a very important aspect. Here, however, we are interested only in cash.

Activity 6.10

Looking at the cash budget of Vierra Popova Ltd, what conclusions do you draw and what possible course of action do you recommend regarding the cash balance over the period concerned?

Given the size of the business, there is a fairly large cash balance that seems to be increasing. Management might consider:

- putting some of the cash into an income-yielding deposit;
- increasing the investment in non-current (fixed) assets;
- increasing the investment in current assets;
- paying a dividend to the owners;
- repaying borrowings.

Activity 6.11

Vierra Popova Ltd (Example 6.1) now wishes to prepare its cash budget for the second six months of the year. The budgeted income statements for each month of the second half of the year are as follows:

	July *£000*	*Aug* *£000*	*Sept* *£000*	*Oct* *£000*	*Nov* *£000*	*Dec* *£000*
Sales revenue	**57**	**59**	**62**	**57**	**53**	**51**
Cost of goods sold	**(32)**	**(33)**	**(35)**	**(32)**	**(30)**	**(29)**
Salaries and wages	**(10)**	**(10)**	**(10)**	**(10)**	**(10)**	**(10)**
Electricity	**(3)**	**(3)**	**(4)**	**(5)**	**(6)**	**(6)**
Depreciation	**(3)**	**(3)**	**(3)**	**(3)**	**(3)**	**(3)**
Other overheads	**(2)**	**(2)**	**(2)**	**(2)**	**(2)**	**(2)**
Total expenses	**(50)**	**(51)**	**(54)**	**(52)**	**(51)**	**(50)**
Profit for the month	**7**	**8**	**8**	**5**	**2**	**1**

The business will continue to allow all of its customers one month's credit.

It plans to increase inventories from the 30 June level by £1,000 during each month until, and including, September. During the following three months, inventories levels will be decreased by £1,000 each month.

→

Inventories purchases, which had been made on one month's credit until the June payment, will, starting with the purchases made in June, be made on two months' credit.

Salaries, wages and 'other overheads' will continue to be paid in the month concerned. Electricity is paid quarterly in arrears in September and December.

At the end of December, the business intends to pay off part of some borrowings. This payment is to be such that it will leave the business with a cash balance of £5,000 with which to start next year.

Prepare the cash budget for the six months ending in December. (Remember that any information you need that relates to the first six months of the year, including the cash balance that is expected to be brought forward on 1 July, is given in Example 6.1.)

The cash budget for the six months ended 31 December is:

	July £000	*Aug* £000	*Sept* £000	*Oct* £000	*Nov* £000	*Dec* £000
Receipts						
Trade receivables	53	57	59	62	57	53
Payments						
Trade payables (Note 1)	–	(32)	(33)	(34)	(36)	(31)
Salaries and wages	(10)	(10)	(10)	(10)	(10)	(10)
Electricity	–	–	(10)	–	–	(17)
Other overheads	(2)	(2)	(2)	(2)	(2)	(2)
Borrowings repayment (Note 2)	–	–	–	–	–	(131)
Total payments	(12)	(44)	(55)	(46)	(48)	(191)
Cash surplus for the month	41	13	4	16	9	(138)
Opening balance	60	101	114	118	134	143
Closing balance	101	114	118	134	143	5

Notes:

1 There will be no payment to suppliers (trade payables) in July because the June purchases will be made on two months' credit and will therefore be paid in August. The July purchases, which will equal the July cost of sales figure plus the increase in inventories made in July, will be paid for in September and so on.

2 The borrowings repayment is simply the amount that will cause the balance at 31 December to be £5,000.

Preparing other budgets

Though each one will have its own particular features, many of the other budgets will follow the same sort of pattern as the cash budget, that is, they will show inflows and outflows during each month and the opening and closing balances in each month.

Example 6.2

To illustrate some of the other budgets, we shall continue to use the example of Vierra Popova Ltd that we considered in Example 6.1. To the information given there, we need to add the fact that the inventories balance at 1 January was £30,000.

Trade receivables budget

This would normally show the planned amount owed to the business by credit customers at the beginning and at the end of each month, the planned total credit sales revenue for each month and the planned total cash receipts from credit customers (trade receivables). The layout would be something like this:

	Jan £000	*Feb* £000	*Mar* £000	*Apr* £000	*May* £000	*June* £000
Opening balance	60	52	55	55	60	55
Sales revenue	52	55	55	60	55	53
Cash receipts	(60)	(52)	(55)	(55)	(60)	(55)
Closing balance	52	55	55	60	55	53

The opening and closing balances represent the amount that the business plans to be owed (in total) by credit customers (trade receivables) at the beginning and end of each month, respectively.

Trade payables budget

Typically this shows the planned amount owed to suppliers by the business at the beginning and at the end of each month, the planned credit purchases for each month and the planned total cash payments to trade payables. The layout would be something like this:

	Jan £000	*Feb* £000	*Mar* £000	*Apr* £000	*May* £000	*June* £000
Opening balance	30	30	31	26	35	31
Purchases	30	31	26	35	31	32
Cash payment	(30)	(30)	(31)	(26)	(35)	(31)
Closing balance	30	31	26	35	31	32

The opening and closing balances represent the amount planned to be owed (in total) by the business to suppliers (trade payables), at the beginning and end of each month respectively.

Inventories budget

This would normally show the planned amount of inventories to be held by the business at the beginning and at the end of each month, the planned total inventories purchases for each month and the planned total monthly inventories usage. The layout would be something like this:

	Jan £000	*Feb* £000	*Mar* £000	*Apr* £000	*May* £000	*June* £000
Opening balance	30	30	30	25	25	25
Purchases	30	31	26	35	31	32
Inventories used	(30)	(31)	(31)	(35)	(31)	(32)
Closing balance	30	30	25	25	25	25

The opening and closing balances represent the amount of inventories, at cost, planned to be held by the business at the beginning and end of each month respectively.

A *raw materials inventories budget*, for a manufacturing business, would follow a similar pattern, with the 'inventories usage' being the cost of the inventories put into production. A *finished inventories budget* for a manufacturer would also be similar to the one shown above, except that 'inventories manufactured' would replace 'purchases'. A manufacturing business would normally prepare both a raw materials inventories budget and a finished inventories budget. Both of these would typically be based on the full cost of the inventories (that is, including overheads). There is no reason why the inventories should not be valued on the basis of either variable cost or direct costs, should managers feel that this would provide more useful information.

The inventories budget will normally be expressed in financial terms, but may also be expressed in physical terms (for example, kilograms or metres) for individual inventories items.

Note how the trade receivables, trade payables and inventories budgets in Example 6.2 link to one another, and to the cash budget for the same business shown in Example 6.1. Note particularly that:

- the purchases figures in the trade payables budget and in the inventories budget are identical;
- the cash payments figures in the trade payables budget and the trade payables figures in the cash budget are identical;
- the cash receipts figures in the trade receivables budget and the trade receivables figures in the cash budget are identical.

Other values would link different budgets in a similar way. For example, the row of sales revenue figures in the trade receivables budget would be identical to the sales revenue figures that will be found in the sales budget. This is how the linking (co-ordination), which was discussed earlier in this chapter, is achieved.

Activity 6.12

Have a go at preparing the trade receivables budget for Vierra Popova Ltd for the six months from July to December (see Activity 6.11).

The trade receivables budget for the six months ended 31 December is:

	July *£000*	*Aug* *£000*	*Sep* *£000*	*Oct* *£000*	*Nov* *£000*	*Dec* *£000*
Opening balance (Note 1)	53	57	59	62	57	53
Sales revenue (Note 2)	57	59	62	57	53	51
Cash receipts (Note 3)	(53)	(57)	(59)	(62)	(57)	(53)
Closing balance (Note 4)	57	59	62	57	53	51

Notes:

1 The opening trade receivables figure is the previous month's sales revenue figure (sales are on one month's credit).

2 The sales revenue is the current month's figure.

3 The cash received each month is equal to the previous month's sales revenue figure.

4 The closing balance is equal to the current month's sales revenue figure.

Note that if we knew any three of the four figures each month, we could deduce the fourth.

This budget could be set out in any manner that would have given the sort of information that management would require in respect of planned levels of trade receivables and associated transactions.

Activity 6.13

Have a go at preparing the trade payables budget for Vierra Popova Ltd for the six months from July to December (see Activity 6.11). (*Hint*: Remember that the trade payables settlement period alters from the June purchases onwards.)

The trade payables budget for the six months ended 31 December is:

	July £000	*Aug* £000	*Sept* £000	*Oct* £000	*Nov* £000	*Dec* £000
Opening balance	32	65	67	70	67	60
Purchases	33	34	36	31	29	28
Cash payments	–	(32)	(33)	(34)	(36)	(31)
Closing balance	65	67	70	67	60	57

This, again, could be set out in any manner that would have given the sort of information that management would require in respect of planned levels of trade payables and associated transactions.

ACTIVITY-BASED BUDGETING

Activity-based budgeting (ABB) extends the principles of activity-based costing (ABC), which we discussed in Chapter 5, to the budgeting process. Under a system of ABB, once the limiting factor has been established (whether it is sales volume or any other factor), the sales budget is determined. The activities necessary to achieve the budgeted sales are then identified. Budgets for each of the various activities are prepared by multiplying the budgeted usage of the cost driver for the particular activity (as determined by the sales budget) by the budgeted rate for the relevant cost driver. The following example should help to make the process clear.

Example 6.3

Danube Ltd produces two products, the Gamma and the Delta. The sales budget for next year shows that 60,000 units of Gamma and 80,000 units of Delta are expected to be sold. Each type of product spends time in the finished goods stores. Both products are of roughly similar size and have very similar storage needs. It is felt, therefore, that the period spent in the stores ('product weeks') is the cost driver and so a budget for this cost-driving activity is created. It is estimated that Product Gamma will spend an average of two weeks in the stores before being sold; for Product Delta, the average period is five weeks.

To calculate the activity budget for the finished goods stores, the estimated total usage of the cost driver must be calculated. This will be the total number of 'product weeks' that the products will be in store.

The budgeted rate for the cost driver has been set at £1.50 per product week.

Product		*Product weeks*
Delta	60,000 × 2 weeks =	120,000
Gamma	80,000 × 5 weeks =	400,000
		520,000

The number of product weeks will then be multiplied by the budgeted rate for the cost driver to derive the activity budget figure. That is:

520,000 × £1.50 = £780,000

The same process will be carried out for the other cost-driving activities identified.

Note that budgets are prepared according to the cost-driving activity. They are not prepared according to the function, as is the case with the traditional approach to budgeting. In other words, under ABB, there will be a separate budget for each cost pool.

Through the application of ABC principles, the factors that cause costs are known and there is a direct linking of costs with output. This means that ABB should provide a better understanding of future resource needs and more accurate budgets. It should also provide a better understanding of the effect on budgeted costs of changes in the usage of the cost driver because of the explicit relationship between cost drivers, activities and costs.

Control should be improved within an ABB environment for two reasons:

- By developing more accurate budgets, managers should be provided with demanding yet achievable targets.
- ABB should ensure that costs are closely linked to responsibilities. Managers who have control over particular cost drivers will become accountable for the costs that are caused. An important principle of effective budgeting is that those responsible for meeting a particular budget (budget holders) should have control over the events that affect performance in their area.

Real World 6.7 provides some indication of the extent to which ABB is used in practice.

Real World 6.7

Quite a lot of activity

The 2009 CIMA survey showed that ABB is used by a significant proportion of businesses in practice, as shown in Figure 6.9.

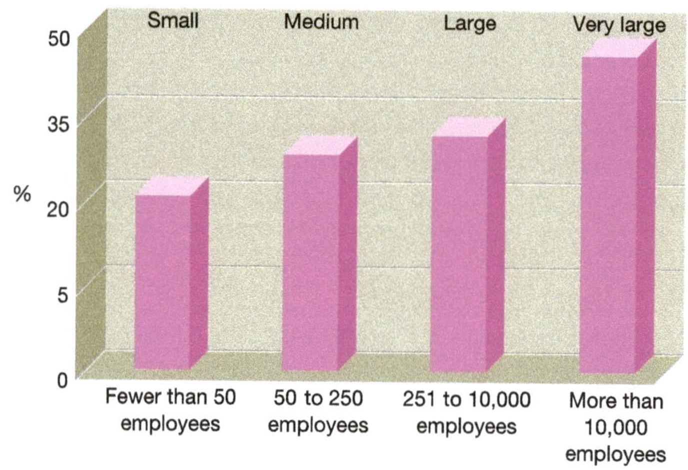

Activity-based budgeting is used by about 30 per cent of all of the businesses surveyed.

Figure 6.9 The use of activity-based budgeting

Unsurprisingly, the percentages that use ABB almost precisely match the proportion of the same survey sample that use activity-based costing. It is logical that businesses that use an activity-based approach to deriving their costs should also apply the same approach to holding managers responsible for the costs that are incurred, through the budgets.

Source: CIMA (2009) *Management Accounting Tools for Today and Tomorrow*, p. 15.

NON-FINANCIAL MEASURES IN BUDGETING

The efficiency of internal operations and customer satisfaction levels have become of critical importance to businesses striving to survive in an increasingly competitive environment. As we shall see in Chapter 9, non-financial performance indicators have an important role to play in assessing performance in such key areas as customer/supplier delivery times, set-up times, defect levels and customer satisfaction levels.

There is no reason why budgeting needs to be confined to financial targets and measures. Non-financial measures can also be used as the basis for targets and these can be brought into the budgeting process and reported alongside the financial targets for the business.

BUDGETS AND MANAGEMENT BEHAVIOUR

All accounting statements and reports are intended to affect the behaviour of one or more groups of people. Budgets are intended to affect the behaviour of managers, for example, to encourage them to work towards the business's objectives and to do this in a co-ordinated manner.

Whether budgets are effective and how they could be made more effective are crucial issues for managers. We shall examine this topic in detail in Chapter 7, after we have seen, in the earlier part of that chapter, how budgets can be used to help managers to exercise control.

WHO NEEDS BUDGETS?

Until relatively recently it would have been a heresy to suggest that budgeting was not of central importance to any business. The benefits of budgeting, mentioned earlier in this chapter, have been widely recognised and the vast majority of businesses prepare annual budgets (see Real World 6.3 on page 197). However, there is increasing concern that, in today's highly dynamic and competitive environment, budgets may actually be harmful to the achievement of business objectives. This has led a small number of businesses to abandon traditional budgets as a tool of planning and control.

Various charges have been levelled against the conventional budgeting process. It is claimed, for example, that:

- Budgets cannot deal with a fast-changing environment and they are often out of date before the start of the budget period.
- They focus too much management attention on the achievement of short-term financial targets. Instead, managers should focus on the things that create value for the business (for example, innovation, building brand loyalty, responding quickly to competitive threats and so on).
- They reinforce a 'command and control' structure that concentrates power in the hands of senior managers and prevents junior managers from exercising autonomy. This may be particularly true where a top-down approach that allocates budgets to managers is being used. Where managers feel constrained, attempts to retain and recruit able managers can be difficult.

- Budgeting takes up an enormous amount of management time that could be better used. In practice, budgeting can be a lengthy process that may involve much negotiation, reworking and updating. However, this may add little to the achievement of business objectives.
- Budgets are based around business functions (sales, marketing, production and so on). To achieve the business's objectives, however, the focus should be on business processes that cut across functional boundaries and reflect the needs of the customer.
- They encourage incremental thinking by employing a 'last year plus *x* per cent' approach to planning. This can inhibit the development of 'break out' strategies that may be necessary in a fast-changing environment.
- They can protect costs rather than lower costs, particularly in the area of discretionary budgets. In some cases, a fixed budget for an activity, such as research and development, is allocated to a manager. If the amount is not spent, the budget may be taken away and, in future periods, the budget for this activity may be either reduced or eliminated. Such a response to unused budget allocations can encourage managers to spend the whole of the budget, irrespective of need, in order to protect the allocations they receive.
- They promote 'sharp' practice among managers. In order to meet budget targets, managers may try to negotiate lower sales targets or higher cost allocations than they feel is really necessary. This helps them to build some 'slack' into the budgets and so meeting the budget becomes easier (see reference 3 at the end of the chapter).

Although some believe that many of the problems identified can be solved by better budgeting systems such as activity-based budgeting and zero-base budgeting and by taking a more flexible approach, others believe that a more radical solution is required.

Real World 6.8 is taken from a question and answer column written by John Timpson. He is the chief executive of a very successful high street shoe-repairing and key-cutting business with over 800 branches (and expanding) throughout the UK. His answer to a question about budgeting echoes some of the criticisms of conventional budgeting that we have just considered. The column appeared in the *Daily Telegraph*.

Real World 6.8

Cobblers

A long time ago I learnt that having a lot of figures doesn't mean you are better informed – it just makes life more complicated.

In the 1980s, we set budget sales figures for every shop every week, our Finance Director insisting that individual shop numbers added up to his company budget. It was a tortuous process that took weeks of area management time and although head office hoped the plan would provide the perfect incentive, it made no difference to our performance. Sales never seemed to follow our forecast – our customers clearly didn't know how much they were expected to spend! I scrapped the budgetary process and for the last 20 years we have compared branch performance with last year – it has saved us a lot of bother.

Life at Timpson has little to do with budgets and we don't have KPIs. We have bought several loss making companies and found that every one of them was monitoring minute detail from Head Office – Sketchley, the dry cleaners, were keen on keeping a count of their 'supercrease' sales; Max Spielmann, the photo chain, kept an eye on the average price of picture frames; and shoe repairers Mr Minit was controlling costs so closely that they recorded every shop's expenditure on postage stamps. While management concentrated on the detail they seemed to miss out on the big picture. Instead of studying their computers they should have visited more shops to talk to the colleagues who met their customers.

Of the few figures I receive, the most important is the bank balance compared with the same day last year. It gives me a daily health check on our business. I get a daily report on all the new shops we have opened in the last three months and a weekly sales report for the company, in total, and by department. We revise our profit forecast every week and produce management accounts every month, but I seldom look beyond the front page summary.

The only time I ask for detail is when we are introducing a new service – like our current growth in portraits, locksmith work and complicated car keys. If you know which shops are successful you can pass their secret around the rest of the business.

With little to look at it is easy to see how the company is doing and I have plenty of time left to visit our branches and discover what is really going on.

Source: John Timpson, The management column, *Daily Telegraph* Business, 6 June 2011.

BEYOND CONVENTIONAL BUDGETING

In recent years, a few businesses have abandoned budgeting, although they still recognise the need for forward planning. No one seriously doubts that there must be appropriate systems in place to steer a business towards its objectives. It is claimed, however, that the systems adopted should reflect a broader, more integrated approach to planning. The new systems that have been implemented are often based around a 'leaner' financial planning process that is more closely linked to other measurement and reward systems. Emphasis is placed on the use of rolling forecasts and key performance indicators (such as market share, customer satisfaction and innovations) that identify both monetary and non-monetary targets to be achieved both over the long term and in the short term. These are often very demanding ('stretch') targets, based on benchmarks that have been set by world-class businesses.

The new 'beyond budgeting' model promotes a more decentralised, participative approach to managing the business. It is claimed that the traditional hierarchical management structure, where decision making is concentrated at the higher levels of the hierarchy, encourages a culture of dependency where meeting the budget targets set by senior managers is the key to managerial success. This traditional structure is replaced by a network structure where decision making is devolved to 'front-line' managers. A more open, questioning attitude among employees is encouraged by the new structure. There is a sharing of knowledge and best practice; protective behaviour by managers is discouraged. In addition, rewards are linked to targets based on improvement in relative performance rather than to meeting the budget. It is claimed that this new approach allows greater adaptability to changing conditions, increases performance and increases motivation among staff.

Figure 6.10 sets out the main differences between the traditional and 'beyond budgeting' planning models.

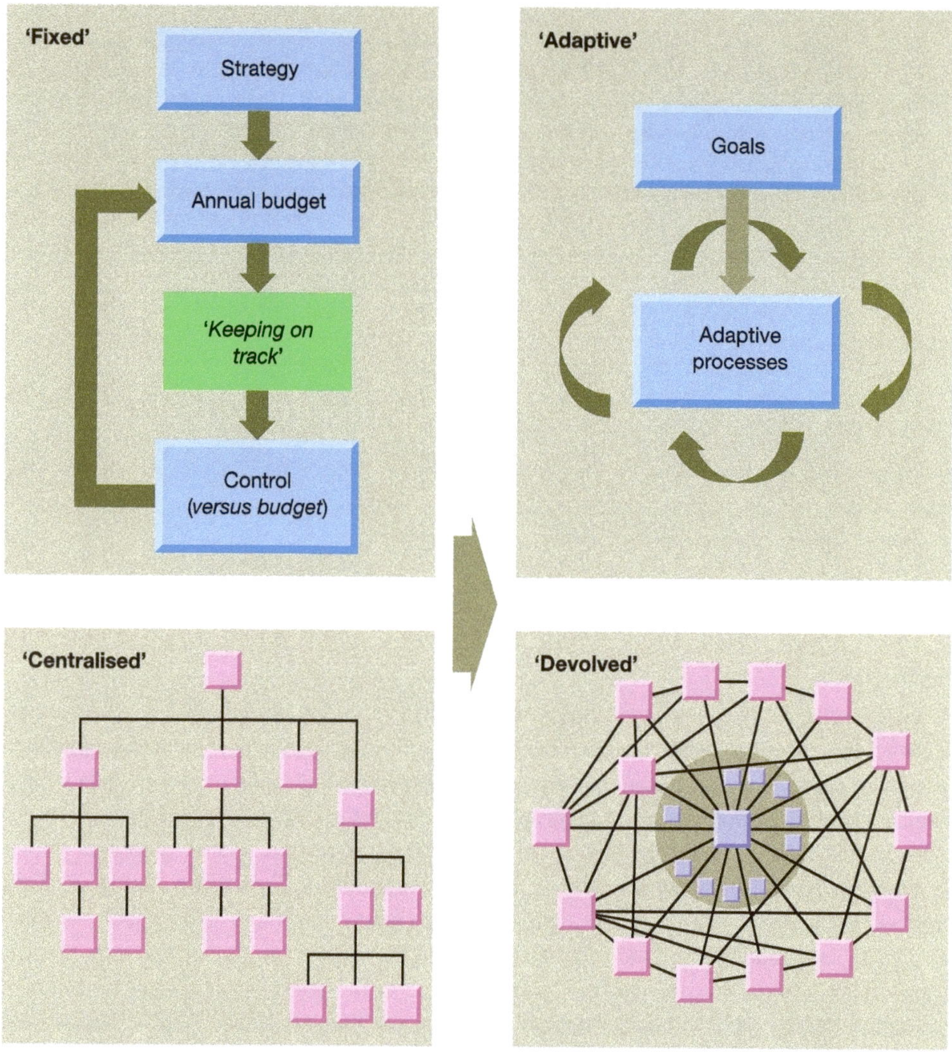

Source: Beyond budgeting, www.bbrt.org.

The traditional model is based on the use of fixed targets, which determine the future actions of managers. The 'beyond budgeting' model, on the other hand, is based on the use of stretch targets that can be adapted. The traditional hierarchical management structure is replaced by a network structure.

Figure 6.10 The traditional planning model versus the 'beyond budgeting' planning model

Real World 6.9 looks at the management planning systems at Toyota, the well-known Japanese motor vehicle business. Toyota does not use conventional budgets.

Real World 6.9

Steering Toyota

The Beyond Budgeting Institute (BBI) is at the forefront of those who argue that budgeting systems have an adverse effect on the ability of businesses to compete effectively. The following is an outline of Toyota's planning and control systems, published by BBI:

> Despite incurring its first loss in many decades (not even Toyota can make a profit when the market suddenly collapses by over 30 per cent) Toyota remains the best managed manufacturing company in the world. Its Toyota Production System is legendary and spawned the lean manufacturing movement. The management focus is on continuously improving systems and meeting internal and external customers' needs. Everyone has a voice and is expected to contribute to the continuous improvement of their work. Medium-term operational goals aimed at best practice are set at every level. Planning takes place at the plant/team level and happens monthly within a clear strategic framework (12 month rolling forecasts support capacity planning). Knowledge about current performance is visual and immediate (e.g. throughput, downtime, inventory levels). Resources are made available just-in-time to meet each customer order. There are no fixed targets, no annual budget contracts and people are trusted with information to make the right decisions.

Source: BBI, 'Toyota – A World Class manufacturing model', www.bbrt.org/beyond-budgeting, accessed 13 February 2014.

Whether the trickle of businesses that are now seeking an alternative to budgets will turn into a flood remains to be seen. However, it is clear that in today's highly competitive environment a business must be flexible and responsive to changing conditions. Management systems that in any way hinder these attributes will not survive.

LONG LIVE BUDGETS!

Despite the criticisms, budgeting remains a very widely used technique and Real World 6.3 provides supporting evidence. Furthermore, **Real World 6.10** suggests that things are unlikely to change much in the near future. This contains an account of a round table discussion at a Better Budgeting forum. Although the discussion took place some time ago, the points made still seem relevant and are well put.

Real World 6.10

Alive and kicking

A Better Budgeting forum was attended by representatives of 32 large organisations, including BAA (the airport operator), the BBC, Ford Motors, Sainsbury (the supermarket business) and Unilever (the household goods group).

The report of the forum discussions said:

> If you were to believe all that has been written in recent years, you'd be forgiven for thinking that budgeting is on its way to becoming extinct. Various research reports allude to the widespread dissatisfaction with the bureaucratic exercise in cost cutting that budgeting is accused of having become. Budgets are pilloried as being out of touch with the needs of modern business and accused of taking too long, costing too much and encouraging all sorts of perverse behaviour.
>
> Yet if there was one conclusion to emerge from the day's discussions it was that budgets are in fact alive and well. Not only did all the organisations present operate a formal budget but all

→

bar two had no interest in getting rid of it. Quite the opposite – although aware of the problems it can cause, the participants by and large regarded the budgeting system and the accompanying processes as indispensable.

Later in the report, in what could have been a reference to the use of 'rolling forecasts' among businesses that claim to have abandoned budgeting (see Real World 6.9, relating to Toyota), it said:

It quickly became obvious that, as one participant put it, 'one man's budget is another man's rolling forecast'. What people refer to when they talk about budgeting could in reality be very different things.

This presumably meant that businesses that abandon 'budgets' reintroduce them under another name.

Source: The Chartered Institute of Management Accountants and The Faculty of Finance and Management, Institute of Chartered Accountants in England and Wales (2004) *Better Budgeting*, March.

Activity 6.14

John Timpson (see Real World 6.8) denies having a budgetary process for his business. From what he says, do you agree?

Although Timpson may no longer have a full budgeting system in place, there are still benchmarks and targets. It can be argued that these constitute a rudimentary budgeting system. He compares branch performance with the previous year and the bank balance with the same day in the previous year. This is presumably because he sees last year's figures as some sort of benchmark or budget. Furthermore, he mentions 'profit forecasts', which may well suggest a target, or budget, to be achieved.

It can also be argued that Toyota's 'operational goals' and 'rolling forecasts' (Real World 6.9) are really budgeting by another name.

Real World 6.11 provides survey evidence of senior finance staff that indicates considerable support for budgets. Nevertheless, many recognised that budgeting is not always well managed and acknowledged some of the criticisms of budgets that were mentioned earlier.

Real World 6.11

Problems with budgets

The survey of the opinions of senior finance staff at 340 businesses of various sizes and operating in a wide range of industries in North America that was mentioned earlier (see Real World 6.3) showed that 86 per cent of those surveyed regarded the budget process as either 'essential' or 'very important'. However,

- 66 per cent thought that budgeting in their business was not agile or flexible enough;
- 59 per cent were not very confident that budget targets would be met in 2008;
- 67 per cent felt that their business devoted inappropriate amounts of time to budgeting (51 per cent felt it was too much and 16 per cent too little);
- 76 per cent felt that their businesses used inappropriate software in the budgeting process (generally using a spreadsheet rather than custom-designed software).

Source: BPM Forum (2008) Perfect how you project.

Despite the undoubted problems with budgeting, and the way in which it is obviously practised in some businesses, the ideas summarised as 'beyond budgeting' (that we discussed earlier) seem not to be popular in practice, as is made very clear by **Real World 6.12**.

Real World 6.12

Not going into the beyond

The 2009 CIMA survey showed that the 'beyond budgeting' philosophy is little followed in practice, as is shown by Figure 6.11.

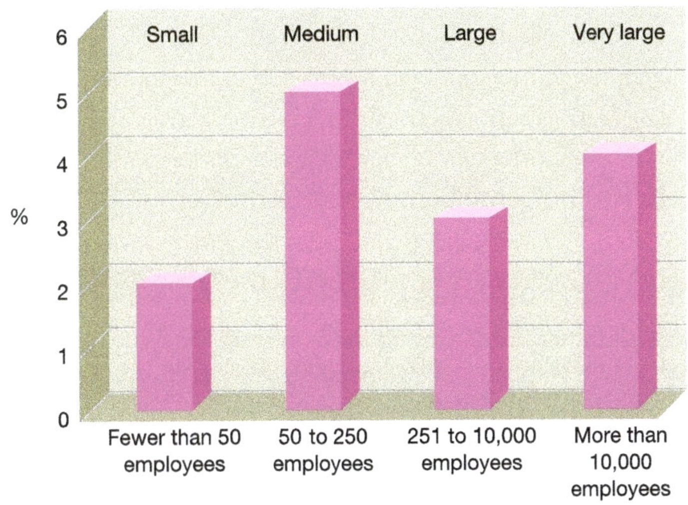

The 'beyond budgeting' philosophy is followed by only about 3 per cent of all of the businesses surveyed.

Figure 6.11 The use of the 'beyond budgeting' philosophy

Source: CIMA (2009) *Management Accounting Tools for Today and Tomorrow*, p. 15.

A survey of 588 management accountants working in Canada and the USA indicated that budgets are overwhelmingly key tools in management. Only 5 per cent of management accountants surveyed worked in organisations where managers were considering abandoning budgeting. The survey revealed that steps had recently been taken or were to be taken to overcome some of the criticisms identified by the 'beyond budgeting' advocates.

Source: Bibby, T. and Lindsay, R. (2010) Beyond budgeting or budgeting reconsidered? A survey of North-American budgeting practice, *Management Accounting Research*, Volume 21, Issue 1, March.

A survey of 40 managers in UK businesses showed that all of their businesses used budgets, with only 5 per cent expressing serious doubt about their usefulness. Like the survey of Canadian and US management accountants, this study showed that the nature of budgeting was changing to overcome perceived problems.

Source: Dugdale, D. and Lyne, S. (2010) Budgeting practice and organisational structure, Chartered Institute of Management Accountants, *Research*, Volume 6, Issue 4, April.

Self-assessment question 6.1 pulls together the points made in this chapter about preparing budgets.

Self-assessment question 6.1

Antonio Ltd, which makes and sells one standard product, has planned production and sales for the next nine months as follows:

	Production *Units*	*Sales* *Units*
May	350	350
June	400	400
July	500	400
August	600	500
September	600	600
October	700	650
November	750	700
December	750	800
January	750	750

During the period, the business plans to advertise so as to generate these increases in sales. Payments for advertising of £1,000 and £1,500 will be made in July and October respectively.

The selling price per unit will be £20 throughout the period. Forty per cent of sales are normally made on two months' credit. The other 60 per cent are settled within the month of the sale.

Raw materials will be held for one month before they are taken into production. Purchases of raw materials will be on one month's credit (buy one month, pay the next). The cost of raw materials is £8 per unit of production.

Other direct production expenses, including labour, are £6 per unit of production. These will be paid in the month concerned.

Various production overheads, which at present are £1,800 a month and are expected to continue at that level until the end of June, are expected to rise to £2,000 each month from 1 July to 31 October. They are expected to rise again from 1 November to £2,400 a month and to remain at that level for the foreseeable future. These overheads include a steady £400 each month for depreciation. Overheads are planned to be paid 80 per cent in the month of production and 20 per cent in the following month.

To help to meet the planned increased production, a new item of plant will be bought and delivered in August. The cost of this item is £6,600; the contract with the supplier will specify that this will be paid in three equal amounts in September, October and November.

The raw materials inventories level is planned to be enough for 500 units of production on 1 July. The balance at the bank on the same day is planned to be £7,500.

Required:

(a) Draw up the following for the six months ending 31 December:
   (i) A raw materials inventories budget, showing both physical quantities and financial values.
   (ii) A trade payables budget.
   (iii) A cash budget.

(b) The cash budget reveals a potential cash deficiency during October and November. Can you suggest any ways in which a modification of plans could overcome this problem?

The solution to this question can be found in Appendix B.

SUMMARY

The main points of this chapter may be summarised as follows:

A budget is a short-term business plan, expressed in financial or in physical terms.

- Budgets are the short-term means of working towards the business's objectives.
- They are usually prepared for a one-year period with sub-periods of a month.
- There is usually a separate budget for each key area.

Uses of budgets

- Promote forward thinking.
- Help co-ordinate the various aspects of the business.
- Motivate performance.
- Provide the basis of a system of control.
- Provide a system of authorisation.

The budget-setting process

- Establish who will take responsibility.
- Communicate guidelines.
- Identify key factor.
- Prepare budget for key factor area.
- Prepare draft budgets for all other areas.
- Review and co-ordinate.
- Prepare master budgets (income statement and statement of financial position).
- Communicate the budgets to interested parties.
- Monitor performance relative to budget.

Preparing budgets

- There is no standard style – practicality and usefulness are the key issues.
- They are usually prepared in columnar form, with a column for each month (or similarly short period).
- Each budget must link (co-ordinate) with others.

Criticisms of budgets

- Cannot deal with rapid change.
- Focus on short-term financial targets, rather than value creation.
- Encourage a 'top-down' management style.
- Can be time-consuming.
- Based around traditional business functions and do not cross boundaries.
- Encourage incremental thinking (last year's figure, plus *x* per cent).
- Protect rather than lower costs.
- Promote 'sharp' practice among managers.
- Budgeting is still widely regarded as useful and extensively practised despite the criticisms.
- Even businesses that claim to have abandoned budgets use planning and control devices that appear to be budgets by another name.

KEY TERMS

For definitions of these terms, see Appendix A.

Budget
Control
Limiting factor
Forecast
Periodic budget
Continual budget
Rolling budget
Master budget
Management by exception
Budget committee
Budget officer
Incremental budgeting
Discretionary budget
Budget holder
Zero-base budgeting (ZBB)
Activity-based budgeting (ABB)

REFERENCES

1 BPM Forum (2008) Perfect how you project.

2 Durfee, D. (2006) Alternative budgeting, *CFO Magazine*, June.

3 Teach, E. (2014) No time for budgets, *CFO Magazine*, 27 May.

FURTHER READING

If you would like to explore the topics covered in this chapter in more depth, we recommend the following:

Drury, C. (2012) *Management and Cost Accounting*, 8th edn, Cengage Learning, Chapter 15.

Hilton, R. (2012) Managerial Accounting, 9th edn, McGraw-Hill Higher Education, Chapter 9.

Horngren, C., Datar, S. and Rajan, M. (2011) *Cost Accounting: A Managerial Emphasis*, 14th edn, Prentice Hall International, Chapter 6.

Kaplan, R., Atkinson, A., Matsumura, E. and Young, S.M. (2011) *Management Accounting*, 6th edn, Prentice Hall, Chapter 10.

REVIEW QUESTIONS

Solutions to these questions can be found in Appendix C.

6.1 Define a budget. How is a budget different from a forecast?

6.2 What were the five uses of budgets that were identified in the chapter?

6.3 What do budgets have to do with control?

6.4 What is a budget committee? What purpose does it serve?

EXERCISES

Exercises 6.1 and 6.2 are basic level, 6.3 to 6.5 are intermediate level and 6.6 to 6.8 are advanced level. Those with coloured numbers have solutions given in Appendix D.

6.1 Prolog Ltd is a small wholesaler of high-specification personal computers. It has in recent months been selling 50 machines a month at a price of £2,000 each. These machines cost £1,600 each. A new model has just been launched and this is expected to offer greatly enhanced performance. Its selling price and cost will be the same as for the old model. From the beginning of January, sales are planned to increase at a rate of 20 machines each month until the end of June, when sales will amount to 170 units a month. Sales are planned to continue at that level thereafter. Operating costs including depreciation of £2,000 a month are planned as follows:

	Jan	*Feb*	*Mar*	*Apr*	*May*	*June*
Operating costs (£000)	6	8	10	12	12	12

Prolog expects to receive no credit for operating costs. Additional shelving for storage will be bought, installed and paid for in April, costing £12,000. Tax of £25,000 is due at the end of March. Prolog anticipates that trade receivables will amount to two months' sales revenue. To give its customers a good level of service, Prolog plans to hold enough inventories at the end of each month to fulfil anticipated demand from customers in the following month. The computer manufacturer, however, grants one month's credit to Prolog. Prolog Ltd's statement of financial position is:

Statement of financial position at 31 December

	£000
ASSETS	
Non-current assets	80
Current assets	
Inventories	112
Trade receivables	200
Cash	–
	312
Total assets	392
Equity and liabilities	
Equity	
Share capital (25p ordinary shares)	10
Retained profit	177
	187
Current liabilities	
Trade payables	112
Taxation	25
Overdraft	68
	205
Total equity and liabilities	392

Required:

(a) Prepare a cash budget for Prolog Ltd showing the cash balance or required overdraft for the six months ending 30 June.

(b) State briefly what further information a banker would require from Prolog Ltd before granting additional overdraft facilities for the anticipated expansion of sales.

6.2 You have overheard the following statements:

(a) 'A budget is a forecast of what is expected to happen in a business during the next year.'
(b) 'Monthly budgets must be prepared with a column for each month so that you can see the whole year at a glance, month by month.'
(c) 'Budgets are OK but they stifle all initiative. No manager worth employing would work for a business that seeks to control through budgets.'
(d) 'Activity-based budgeting is an approach that takes account of the planned volume of activity in order to deduce the figures to go into the budget.'
(e) 'Any sensible person would start with the sales budget and build up the other budgets from there.'

Required:
Critically discuss these statements, explaining any technical terms.

6.3 A nursing home, which is linked to a large hospital, has been examining its budgetary control procedures, with particular reference to overhead costs.

The level of activity in the facility is measured by the number of patients treated in the budget period. For the current year, the budget stands at 6,000 patients and this is expected to be met.

For months 1 to 6 of this year (assume 12 months of equal length), 2,700 patients were treated. The actual variable overhead costs incurred during this six-month period are as follows:

Expense	£
Staffing	59,400
Power	27,000
Supplies	54,000
Other	8,100
Total	148,500

The hospital accountant believes that the variable overhead costs will be incurred at the same rate during months 7 to 12 of the year.

Fixed overheads are budgeted for the whole year as follows:

Expense	£
Supervision	120,000
Depreciation/financing	187,200
Other	64,800
Total	372,000

Required:
(a) Present an overheads budget for the six-month period ending the year (one budget). You should show each expense. What is the total overhead cost for each patient that would be incorporated into any statistics?
(b) The nursing home actually treated 3,800 patients during months 7 to 12, the actual variable overheads were £203,300 and the actual fixed overheads were £190,000. In summary form, examine how well the home exercised control over its overheads.
(c) Interpret your analysis and point out any limitations or assumptions.

6.4 Linpet Ltd is to be incorporated on 1 June. The opening statement of financial position of the business will then be as follows:

	£
Assets	
Cash at bank	60,000
Share capital	
£1 ordinary shares	60,000

During June, the business intends to make payments of £40,000 for a leasehold property, £10,000 for equipment and £6,000 for a motor vehicle. The business will also purchase initial trading inventories costing £22,000 on credit.

The business has produced the following estimates:

1. Sales revenue for June will be £8,000 and will increase at the rate of £3,000 a month until, and including, September. In October, sales revenue will rise to £22,000, and in subsequent months it will be maintained at this figure.
2. The gross profit percentage (that is, (gross profit/sales) × 100) on goods sold will be 25 per cent.
3. There is a risk that supplies of trading inventories will be interrupted towards the end of the accounting year. The business therefore intends to build up its initial level of inventories (£22,000) by purchasing £1,000 of inventories each month in addition to the monthly purchases necessary to satisfy monthly sales requirements. All purchases of inventories (including the initial inventories) will be on one month's credit.
4. Sales revenue will be divided equally between cash and credit sales. Credit customers are expected to pay two months after the sale is agreed.
5. Wages and salaries will be £900 a month. Other overheads will be £500 a month for the first four months and £650 a month thereafter. Both types of expense will be payable when incurred.
6. 80 per cent of sales revenue will be generated by salespeople who will receive 5 per cent commission on sales revenue. The commission is payable one month after the sale is agreed.
7. The business intends to purchase further equipment in November for £7,000 cash.
8. Depreciation will be provided at the rate of 5 per cent a year on property and 20 per cent a year on equipment. (Depreciation has not been included in the overheads mentioned in point 5 above.)

Required:

(a) State why a cash budget is required for a business.

(b) Prepare a cash budget for Linpet Ltd for the six-month period to 30 November.

6.5 Lewisham Ltd manufactures one product line – the Zenith. Plans over the next few months are as follows:

1 *Sales demand*

	Units
July	180,000
August	240,000
September	200,000
October	180,000

Each Zenith will sell for £3.

2 *Receipts from sales*. Payments from credit customers are expected to be 70 per cent during the month of sale, and 28 per cent during the following month. The remaining trade receivables are expected to go bad (that is, to be uncollectable).

Credit customers who pay in the month of sale are entitled to deduct a 2 per cent discount from the invoice price.

3 *Finished goods inventories*. These are expected to be 40,000 units at 1 July. The business's policy is that, in future, the inventories at the end of each month should equal 20 per cent of the following month's planned sales requirements.

4 *Raw materials inventories*. These are expected to be 40,000 kg on 1 July. The business's policy is that, in future, the inventories at the end of each month should equal 50 per cent of the following month's planned production requirements. Each Zenith requires 0.5 kg of the raw material, which costs £1.50/kg. Raw materials purchases are paid in the month after purchase.

5 *Labour and overheads*. The direct labour cost of each Zenith is £0.50. The variable overhead element of each Zenith is £0.30. Fixed overheads, including depreciation of £25,000, total £47,000 a month. All labour and overheads are paid during the month in which they arise.

6 *Cash in hand*. At 1 August the business plans to have a bank balance (in funds) of £20,000.

Required:

Prepare the following budgets:

(a) Finished inventories budget (expressed in units of Zenith) for each of the three months July, August and September.

(b) Raw materials inventories budget (expressed in kilograms of the raw material) for the two months July and August.

(c) Cash budget for August and September.

6.6 Daniel Chu Ltd, a new business, will start production on 1 April, but sales will not start until 1 May. Planned sales for the next nine months are as follows:

	Sales Units
May	500
June	600
July	700
August	800
September	900
October	900
November	900
December	800
January	700

The selling price of a unit will be a consistent £100 and all sales will be made on one month's credit. It is planned that sufficient finished goods inventories for each month's sales should be available at the end of the previous month.

Raw materials purchases will be such that there will be sufficient raw materials inventories available at the end of each month precisely to meet the following month's planned production. This planned policy will operate from the end of April. Purchases of raw materials will be on one month's credit. The cost of raw material is £40 a unit of finished product.

The direct labour cost, which is variable with the level of production, is planned to be £20 a unit of finished production. Production overheads are planned to be £20,000 each month, including £3,000 for depreciation. Non-production overheads are planned to be £11,000 a month, of which £1,000 will be depreciation.

Various non-current (fixed) assets costing £250,000 will be bought and paid for during April.

Except where specified, assume that all payments take place in the same month as the cost is incurred.

The business will raise £300,000 in cash from a share issue in April.

Required:
Draw up the following for the six months ending 30 September:

(a) A finished inventories budget, showing just physical quantities.
(b) A raw materials inventories budget showing both physical quantities and financial values.
(c) A trade payables budget.
(d) A trade receivables budget.
(e) A cash budget.

6.7 Newtake Records Ltd owns a chain of 14 shops selling compact discs. At the beginning of June the business had an overdraft of £35,000 and the bank had asked for this to be eliminated by the end of November. As a result, the directors have recently decided to review their plans for the next six months.

The following plans were prepared for the business some months earlier:

	May £000	*June £000*	*July £000*	*Aug £000*	*Sept £000*	*Oct £000*	*Nov £000*
Sales revenue	180	230	320	250	140	120	110
Purchases	135	180	142	94	75	66	57
Administration expenses	52	55	56	53	48	46	45
Selling expenses	22	24	28	26	21	19	18
Taxation payment	–	–	–	22	–	–	–
Finance payments	5	5	5	5	5	5	5
Shop refurbishment	–	–	14	18	6	–	–

Notes:

1 The inventories level at 1 June was £112,000. The business believes it is preferable to maintain a minimum inventories level of £40,000 of goods over the period to 30 November.
2 Suppliers allow one month's credit. The first three months' purchases are subject to a contractual agreement, which must be honoured.
3 The gross profit margin, that is (gross profit/sales) × 100%, is 40 per cent.
4 Cash from all sales is received in the month of sale. However, 50 per cent of customers pay with a credit card. The charge made by the credit card business to Newtake Records Ltd is 3 per cent of the sales revenue value. These charges are in addition to the selling expenses identified in the table immediately preceding these notes. The credit card business pays Newtake Records Ltd in the month of sale.
5 The business has a bank loan, which it is paying off in monthly instalments of £5,000. The interest element represents 20 per cent of each instalment.
6 Administration expenses are paid when incurred. This item includes a charge of £15,000 each month in respect of depreciation.
7 Selling expenses are payable in the following month.

Required (working to the nearest £1,000):

(a) Prepare a cash budget for the six months ending 30 November which shows the cash balance at the end of each month.

(b) Prepare the inventories budget for the six months to 30 November which shows the inventories position at the end of each month.

(c) Prepare a budgeted income statement for the whole of the six-month period ending 30 November. (A monthly breakdown of profit is *not* required.)

(d) What problems is Newtake Records Ltd likely to face in the next six months? Can you suggest how the business might deal with these problems?

6.8 Brown and Jeffreys, a West Midlands business, makes one standard product for use in the motor trade. The product, known as the Fuel Miser, for which the business holds the patent, when fitted to the fuel system of production model cars has the effect of reducing petrol consumption.

Part of the production is sold direct to a local car manufacturer, which fits the Fuel Miser as an optional extra to several of its models. The rest of the production is sold through various retail outlets, garages and so on.

Brown and Jeffreys assemble the Fuel Miser, but all three components are manufactured by local engineering businesses. The three components are codenamed A, B and C. One Fuel Miser consists of one of each component.

The planned sales for the first seven months of the forthcoming accounting period, by channels of distribution and in terms of Fuel Miser units, are as follows:

	Jan	*Feb*	*Mar*	*Apr*	*May*	*June*	*July*
Manufacturers	4,000	4,000	4,500	4,500	4,500	4,500	4,500
Retail and so on	2,000	2,700	3,200	3,000	2,700	2,500	2,400
	6,000	6,700	7,700	7,500	7,200	7,000	6,900

The following further information is available:

1 There will be inventories of finished units at 1 January of 7,000 Fuel Misers.

2 The inventories of raw materials at 1 January will be:
A 10,000 units
B 16,500 units
C 7,200 units

3 The selling price of Fuel Misers is to be £10 each to the motor manufacturer and £12 each to retail outlets.

4 The maximum production capacity of the business is 7,000 units a month. There is no possibility of increasing this.

5 Assembly of each Fuel Miser will take 10 minutes of direct labour. Direct labour is paid at the rate of £7.20 an hour during the month of production.

6 The components are each expected to cost the following:
A £2.50
B £1.30
C £0.80

7 Indirect costs are to be paid at a regular rate of £32,000 each month.

8 The cash at the bank at 1 January will be £2,620.

The planned sales volumes must be met and the business intends to pursue the following policies for as many months as possible, consistent with meeting the sales targets:

- Finished inventories at the end of each month are to equal the following month's total sales to retail outlets and half the total of the following month's sales to the motor manufacturer.
- Raw materials at the end of each month are to be sufficient to cover production requirements for the following month. The production for July will be 6,800 units.
- Suppliers of raw materials are to be paid during the month following purchase. The payment for January will be £21,250.
- Customers will pay in the month of sale, in the case of sales to the motor manufacturer, and the month after sale, in the case of retail sales. Retail sales during December were 2,000 units at £12 each.

Required:
Prepare the following budgets in monthly columnar form, both in terms of money and units (where relevant), for the six months of January to June inclusive:

(a) Sales budget.*
(b) Finished inventories budget (valued at direct cost).†
(c) Raw materials inventories budget (one budget for each component).†
(d) Production budget (direct costs only).*
(e) Trade receivables budget.†
(f) Trade payables budget.†
(g) Cash budget.†

Notes:
* The sales and production budgets should merely state each month's sales or production in units and in money terms.
† The other budgets should all seek to reconcile the opening balance of inventories, trade receivables, trade payables or cash with the closing balance through movements of the relevant factors over the month.

Chapter 7

ACCOUNTING FOR CONTROL

INTRODUCTION

Associated British Foods Group plc, the food processor, states in its 2013 annual report (p. 55):

> All operations prepare annual operating plans and budgets which are updated regularly. Performance against budget is monitored at operational level and centrally, with variances being reported promptly.

This raises important issues such as the way in which performance is monitored, the nature of variances, why the business should identify them, how they should be reported and what action the business should take where variances occur. These issues provide the focus for the chapter. We shall see that the procedures at Associated British Foods are widely adopted throughout the business world.

This chapter develops some of the themes that were discussed in Chapter 6. We shall see how a budget can be used to help control a business and how, by collecting information on actual performance and comparing it with a revised budget, it is possible to identify those activities that are in control and those that are not.

Budgets are designed to influence the behaviour of managers and so we shall explore their value as a motivational device. We shall also consider the ways in which managers may use budgets in practice. Finally, we shall take a look at standard costing and its relationship with budgeting. We shall see that standards can provide the building blocks for budgets.

Learning outcomes

When you have completed this chapter, you should be able to:

- Discuss the role and limitations of budgets for performance evaluation and control.
- Undertake variance analysis and discuss possible reasons for the variances calculated.
- Discuss the issues that should be taken into account when designing an effective system of budgetary control.
- Explain the nature, role and limitations of standard costing.

BUDGETING FOR CONTROL

In Chapter 6, we saw that budgets provide a useful basis for exercising control over a business. Control involves making events conform to a plan and, since the budget is a short-term plan, making events conform to it is an obvious way to try to control the business. We also saw that, for most businesses, the routine is as shown in Figure 7.1.

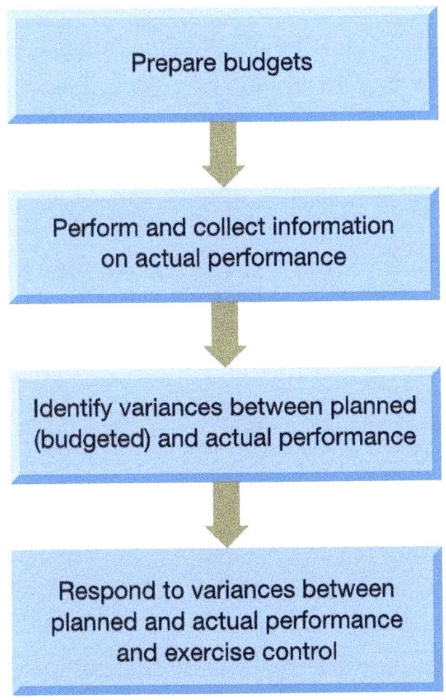

Budgets, once set, provide the yardstick for assessing whether things are going to plan. Variances between budgeted and actual performance can be identified and reacted to.

Figure 7.1 The budgetary control process

If plans are drawn up sensibly, we have a basis for exercising control over the business. We must, however, measure actual performance in the same terms as those in which the budget is stated. If they are not in the same terms, proper comparison will not be possible.

Exercising control involves finding out where and why things did not go according to plan and then seeking ways to put them right for the future. One reason why things may not have gone according to plan is that the budget targets were unachievable. In this case, it may be necessary to revise the budgets for future periods so that targets become achievable.

This last point should not be taken to mean that budget targets can simply be ignored if the going gets tough, but that they should be adaptable. Unrealistic budgets cannot form a basis for exercising control and little can be gained by sticking with them.

Real World 7.1 discusses how one budget was looking very unrealistic.

Real World 7.1

Student loans budget fails examination

Ministerial miscalculations over student loan repayments have resulted in the potential loss of £5 billion taxpayer-funded debt for which the government has no tracking records, according to research by the public spending watchdog. The National Audit Office estimates that around 368,000 students who have borrowed money are unlikely to pay it back because the Department for Business, Innovation and Skills does not have their employment records. These individuals could be unemployed students living in the UK, European Union students who have returned home or Britons who have moved overseas.

Amyas Morse, NAO chief, said that, given the expanding size of the student loan book, the business department needed to take a 'more energetic and considered approach' to maximising taxpayer value and achieving a high level of collections. Ministers had initially assumed that 35 per cent of new student loans would never be repaid but, according to the spending watchdog's calculations, the correct figure is more than 40 per cent.

Liam Byrne, shadow minister for higher education, said the miscalculation would cost an extra £600 million a year from 2015/16, blowing a 'huge hole' in the department's budget. 'We need to know fast how ministers got it so wrong, and how they're going to fix it without putting Britain's scientists, students and colleges under threat,' Mr Byrne said. 'This is industrial scale incompetence in the department for industry.'

FT *Source*: Adapted from Warrell, H. (2013) Miscalculation on student loans poses £5bn loss risk, ft.com, 28 November.

Provided that there is an adequate system of budgetary control, decision making and responsibility can be delegated to junior management, yet senior management can still retain control. This is because senior managers can use the system to discover which junior managers are meeting budget targets and therefore working towards achieving the objectives of the business. (We should remember that budgets are the short-term plans for achieving the business's objectives.) This enables a *management-by-exception* environment to be created where senior management can focus on areas where things are *not* going according to plan (the exceptions – it is to be hoped). Junior managers who are performing to budget can be left to get on with their jobs.

TYPES OF CONTROL

The control process just outlined is known as **feedback control**. Its main feature is that steps are taken to get operations back on track as soon as there is a signal that they have gone wrong. This is similar to the thermostatic control that is a feature of most central heating systems. The thermostat incorporates a thermometer that senses when the temperature has fallen below a pre-set level (analogous to the budget). The thermostat then takes action to correct matters by activating the heating device that restores the required minimum temperature. Figure 7.2 depicts the stages in a feedback control system using budgets.

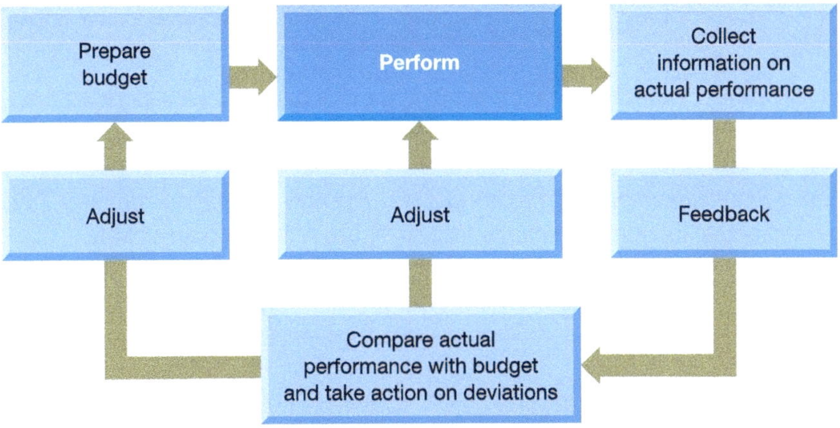

When a comparison of budgeted and actual performance shows a divergence, steps can be taken to get performance back on track. If the budget needs revising, this can be done.

Figure 7.2 Feedback control

There is an alternative type of control, known as **feedforward control**. Here predictions are made as to what can go wrong and steps are then taken to avoid any undesirable outcome. Budgets can also be used to exert this type of control. It involves preparing a budget and then comparing it with a forecast of actual outcomes in order to identify potential problems. For example, a cash budget may be compared with a forecast of actual cash flows. Where significant deviations from budget are revealed, corrective action may be taken before the problems arise. Figure 7.3 depicts the stages in a feedforward control system using budgets.

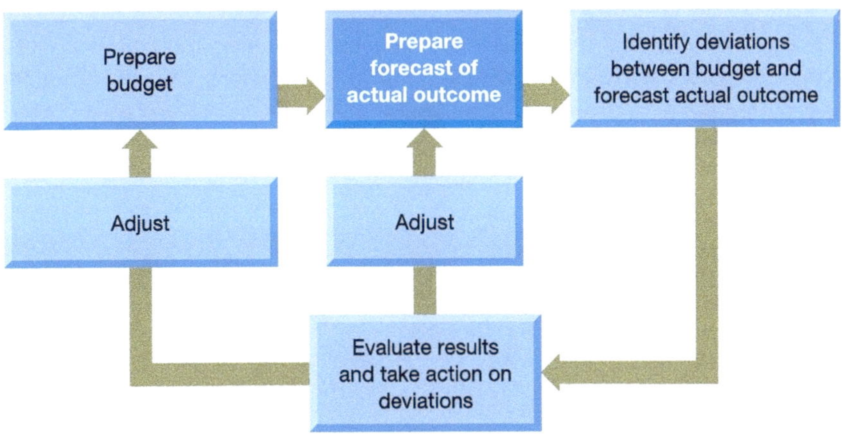

When a comparison of budgeted performance and forecast actual outcomes shows a divergence, preventative measures can be taken. If the budget needs revising, this can be done.

Figure 7.3 Feedforward control

Feedforward controls are proactive and try to anticipate problems beforehand, whereas feedback controls react to existing problems. To put it another way, feedforward controls are preventative, whereas feedback controls are remedial. As it is better to avoid problems rather than have to solve them, feedforward controls are preferable. However, they require timely and accurate predictions of actual outcomes, which are not always available.

VARIANCES FROM BUDGET

We saw in Chapter 1 that the key financial objective of a business is to increase the wealth of its owners (shareholders). Since profit is the net increase in wealth from business operations, the most important budget target to meet is the profit target. We shall therefore take this as our starting point when comparing the budget with the actual results. Example 7.1 shows the budgeted and actual income statements for Baxter Ltd for the month of May.

Example 7.1

The following are the budgeted and actual outcomes for Baxter Ltd, a manufacturing business, for the month of May:

	Budget		*Actual*	
Output (production and sales)	1,000 units		900 units	
	£		£	
Sales revenue	100,000		92,000	
Raw materials	(40,000)	(40,000 metres)	(36,900)	(37,000 metres)
Labour	(20,000)	(2,500 hours)	(17,500)	(2,150 hours)
Fixed overheads	(20,000)		(20,700)	
Operating profit	20,000		16,900	

From these figures, it is clear that the budgeted profit was not achieved. As far as May is concerned, this is a matter of history. However, the business (or one or more aspects of it) is out of control. Senior management must discover where things went wrong during May and try to ensure that these mistakes are not repeated in later months. It is not enough to know that things went wrong overall. We need to know where and why. To achieve this we must compare the budgeted and actual figures for the various items (sales revenue, raw materials and so on) in the statement shown above.

Activity 7.1

Can you see any problems in comparing the various items (sales revenue, raw materials and so on) for the budget with the actual performance of Baxter Ltd in an attempt to draw conclusions as to which aspects were out of control?

The problem is that the actual level of output was not as budgeted. In fact it was 10 per cent lower than budget. This means that we cannot, for example, say that there was a labour cost saving of £2,500 (that is, £20,000 – £17,500) and conclude that all is well in that area.

Flexing the budget

One practical way to overcome our difficulty is to 'flex' the budget to what it would have been had the planned level of output been 900 units rather than 1,000 units. **Flexing a budget** simply means revising it, assuming a different volume of output.

To flex the budget, we need to know which revenues and costs are fixed and which are variable relative to the volume of output. Once we know this, flexing is a simple operation. We shall assume that sales revenue, materials cost and labour cost vary strictly with volume. Fixed overheads, by definition, will not. Whether, in real life, labour cost does vary with the volume of output is not so certain, but it will serve well enough as an assumption for our purposes. If labour cost is actually fixed, we can simply take this into account in the flexing process.

On the basis of our assumptions regarding the behaviour of revenues and costs, the flexed budget would be as follows:

	Flexed budget
Output (production and sales)	900 units
	£
Sales revenue	90,000
Raw materials	(36,000) (36,000 metres)
Labour	(18,000) (2,250 hours)
Fixed overheads	(20,000)
Operating profit	16,000

This is simply the original budget, with the sales revenue, raw materials and labour cost figures scaled down by 10 per cent (the same factor as the actual output fell short of the budgeted one).

Putting the original budget, the flexed budget and the actual outcome for May together gives us the following:

	Original budget	*Flexed budget*	*Actual*
Output (production and sales)	1,000 units	900 units	900 units
	£	£	£
Sales revenue	100,000	90,000	92,000
Raw materials	(40,000)	(36,000) (36,000 m)	(36,900) (37,000 m)
Labour	(20,000)	(18,000) (2,250 hr)	(17,500) (2,150 hr)
Fixed overheads	(20,000)	(20,000)	(20,700)
Operating profit	20,000	16,000	16,900

Flexible budgets allow us to make a more valid comparison between the budget (using the flexed figures) and the actual results. Key differences, or variances, between budgeted and actual results for each aspect of the business's activities can then be calculated. In the rest of this section we consider some of the variances that may be calculated.

Sales volume variance

Let us begin by dealing with the shortfall in sales volume. By flexing the budget, as we just did, it may seem as if we are saying that it does not matter that the business failed to achieve the budgeted sales volume, because we just revise the budget and carry on as if all is well. It is clearly not true that losing sales volume does not matter because a sales volume shortfall normally means losing profit. The first point we must pick up, therefore, is the profit shortfall arising from the loss of sales of 100 units of the product.

Activity 7.2

What will be the loss of profit arising from the sales volume shortfall, assuming that everything except sales volume was as planned?

→

The answer is simply the difference between the original and flexed budget profit figures. The only difference between these two profit figures is the volume of sales; everything else was the same. (That is to say that the flexing was carried out assuming that the per-unit sales revenue, raw material cost and labour cost were all as originally budgeted.) This means that the figure for the loss of profit due to the volume shortfall, taken alone, is £4,000 (that is, £20,000 – £16,000).

When we considered the relationship between cost, volume and profit in Chapter 3, we saw that selling one unit less will result in one less unit contribution to profit. The contribution is sales revenue less variable cost. We can see from the original budget that the unit sales revenue is £100 (that is, £100,000/1,000), raw material cost is £40 a unit (that is, £40,000/1,000) and labour cost is £20 a unit (that is, £20,000/1,000). Thus the contribution is £40 a unit (that is, £100 – (£40 + £20)).

If 100 units of sales are lost, £4,000 (that is, 100 × £40) of contributions and, therefore, profit are forgone. Incidentally, this would be an alternative means of finding the sales volume variance, instead of taking the difference between the original and flexed budget profit figures. Once we have produced the flexed budget, however, it is generally easier to compare the two profit figures.

The difference between the original and flexed budget profit figures is called the **sales volume variance**.

In this case, it is an **adverse variance** because, taken alone, it has the effect of making the actual profit lower than the budgeted profit. A variance that has the effect of increasing profit beyond the budgeted profit is known as a **favourable variance**. We can therefore say that a **variance** is the effect of one factor (taken alone) on the budgeted profit. Later we shall consider other forms of variance, some of which may be favourable and some adverse. The difference between the sum of all the various favourable and adverse variances will represent the difference between the budgeted and actual profit. This is shown in Figure 7.4.

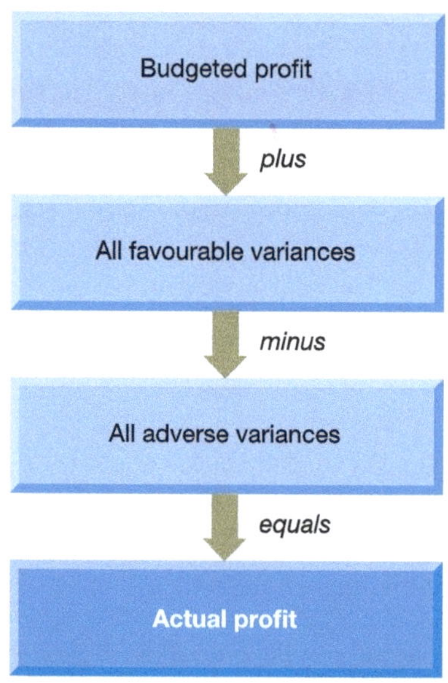

The variances represent the differences between the budgeted and actual profit and so can be used to reconcile the two profit figures.

Figure 7.4 Relationship between the budgeted and actual profit

When calculating a particular variance, such as that for sales volume, we assume that all other factors went according to plan.

Activity 7.3

What else do the relevant managers of Baxter Ltd need to know about the May sales volume variance?

They need to know why the volume of sales fell below the budgeted figure. Only by discovering this information will they be in a position to try to ensure that it does not occur again.

Who should be held accountable for this sales volume variance? The answer is probably the sales manager, who should know precisely why this has occurred. This is not the same as saying, however, that it was the sales manager's fault. The problem may have been that the business failed to produce the budgeted quantities so that not enough items were available to sell. Nevertheless, the sales manager should know the reason for the problem.

The budget and actual figures for Baxter Ltd for *June* are given in Activity 7.4 and will be used as the basis for a series of activities that provide an opportunity to calculate and assess the variances. We shall continue to use the *May* figures for explaining the variances.

Note that the business had budgeted for a higher level of output for *June* than it did for *May*.

Activity 7.4

	Budget for June		*Actual for June*	
Output (production and sales)	1,100 units		1,150 units	
	£		£	
Sales revenue	110,000		113,500	
Raw materials	(44,000)	(44,000 metres)	(46,300)	(46,300 metres)
Labour	(22,000)	(2,750 hours)	(23,200)	(2,960 hours)
Fixed overheads	(20,000)		(19,300)	
Operating profit	24,000		24,700	

Try flexing the June budget, comparing it with the original June budget and so find the sales volume variance.

	Flexed budget	
Output (production and sales)	1,150 units	
	£	
Sales revenue	115,000	
Raw materials	(46,000)	(46,000 metres)
Labour	(23,000)	(2,875 hours)
Fixed overheads	(20,000)	
Operating profit	26,000	

The sales volume variance is £2,000 (favourable) (that is, £26,000 – £24,000). It is favourable because the original budget profit was lower than the flexed budget profit. This arises from more sales actually being made than were budgeted.

For the month of May, we have already identified one reason why the budgeted profit of £20,000 was not achieved and that the actual profit was only £16,900. This was the £4,000 loss of profit (adverse variance) that arose from the sales volume shortfall. Now that the budget is flexed, we can compare like with like and reach further conclusions about May's trading.

The fact that the sales revenue, raw materials, labour and fixed overheads figures differ between the flexed budget and the actual results suggests that the adverse sales volume variance was not the only problem area. To identify those relating to each of the revenue and cost items mentioned, we need to calculate further variances. We shall now do this.

Sales price variance

Starting with the sales revenue figure, we can see that, for *May*, there is a difference of £2,000 (favourable) between the flexed budget and the actual figures. This can only arise from higher prices being charged than were envisaged in the original budget, because any variance arising from the volume difference has already been 'stripped out' in the flexing process. This price difference is known as the **sales price variance**. Higher sales prices will, all other things being equal, mean more profit. So there is a favourable variance.

When senior management is trying to identify the reason for a sales price variance, it would normally be the sales manager who should be able to offer an explanation. As we shall see later in the chapter, favourable variances of significant size will normally be investigated.

Activity 7.5

Using the figures in Activity 7.4, what is the sales price variance for June?

The sales price variance for *June* is £1,500 (adverse) (that is, £115,000 – £113,500). Actual sales prices, on average, must have been lower than those budgeted. The actual price averaged £98.70 (that is, £113,500/1,150) whereas the budgeted price was £100. Selling output at a lower price than that budgeted will have an adverse effect on profit, hence an adverse variance.

The sales variances are summarised in Figure 7.5.

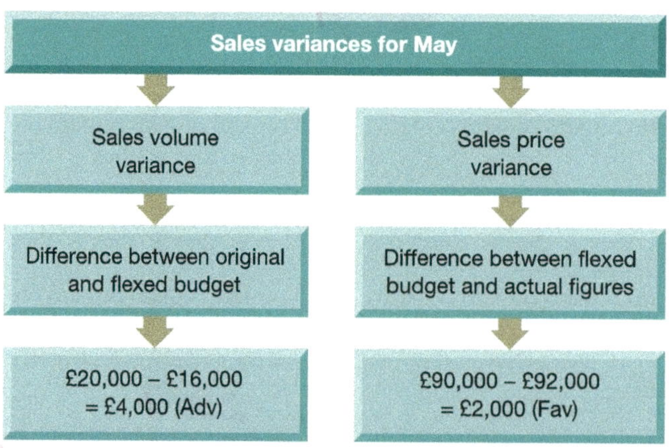

The sales volume variance and the sales price variance are the two main sales variances.

Figure 7.5 Sales variances

Let us now move on to look at the cost variances, starting with materials variances.

Materials variances

In *May*, there was an overall or **total direct materials variance** of £900 (adverse) (that is, £36,900 – £36,000). It is adverse because the actual material cost was higher than the budgeted one, which has an adverse effect on operating profit.

Who should be held accountable for this variance? The answer depends on whether the difference arises from excess usage of the raw material, in which case it is the production manager, or whether it is a higher-than-budgeted cost per metre being paid, in which case it is the responsibility of the buying manager. Fortunately, we can go beyond this total variance to examine the effect of changes in both usage and cost. We can see from the figures that in *May* there was a 1,000 metre excess usage of the raw material (that is, 37,000 metres – 36,000 metres). All other things being equal, this alone would have led to a profit shortfall of £1,000, since clearly the budgeted cost per metre is £1. The £1,000 (adverse) variance is known as the **direct materials usage variance**. Normally, this variance would be the responsibility of the production manager.

Activity 7.6

Using the figures in Activity 7.4, what was the direct material usage variance for June?

The direct material usage variance for *June* was £300 (adverse) (that is, (46,300 metres – 46,000 metres) × £1). It is adverse because more material was used than was budgeted, for an output of 1,150 units. Excess usage of material will tend to reduce profit.

The other aspect of direct materials is their cost. The **direct materials price variance** simply takes the actual cost of materials used and compares it with the cost that was allowed (according to the budget), given the quantity used. In *May* the actual cost of direct materials used was £36,900, whereas the allowed cost of the 37,000 metres was £37,000. Thus we have a favourable variance of £100. Paying less than the budgeted cost will have a favourable effect on profit, hence a favourable variance.

Activity 7.7

Using the figures in Activity 7.4, what was the direct materials price variance for June?

The direct materials price variance for *June* was zero (that is, £46,300 – (46,300 × £1)).

As we have just seen, the total direct materials variance is the sum of the usage variance and the price variance. The relationship between the direct materials variances for May is shown in Figure 7.6.

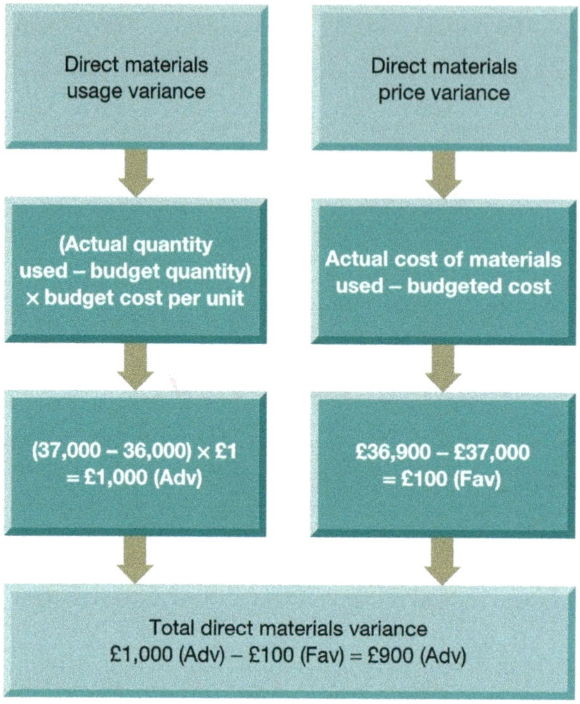

The total direct materials variance is the sum of the direct materials usage variance and the price variance. It can be analysed into those two.

Figure 7.6 Total, usage and price variances for direct materials for May

Labour variances

Direct labour variances are similar in form to those for direct materials. The **total direct labour variance** for *May* was £500 (favourable) (that is, £18,000 – £17,500). It is favourable because £500 less was spent on labour than was budgeted for the actual level of output achieved.

Again, this total variance is not particularly helpful and needs to be analysed further into its usage and cost elements. We should bear in mind that the number of hours used to complete a particular quantity of output is the responsibility of the production manager, whereas the responsibility for the rate of pay lies primarily with the human resources manager.

The **direct labour efficiency variance** compares the number of hours that would be allowed for the achieved level of production with the actual number of hours taken. It then costs this difference at the allowed hourly rate. Thus, for *May*, it was (2,250 hours – 2,150 hours) × £8 = £800 (favourable). We know that the budgeted hourly rate is £8 because the original budget shows that 2,500 hours were budgeted to cost £20,000. The variance is favourable because fewer hours were used than would have been allowed for the actual level of output. Working more quickly would tend to lead to higher profit.

Activity 7.8

Using the figures in Activity 7.4, what was the direct labour efficiency variance for June?

The direct labour efficiency variance for *June* was £680 (adverse) (that is, (2,960 hours – 2,875 hours) × £8). It is adverse because the work took longer than the budget allowed and so will have an adverse effect on profit.

The **direct labour rate variance** compares the actual cost of the hours worked with the allowed cost. For 2,150 hours worked in *May*, the allowed cost would be £17,200 (that is, 2,150 × £8). So, the direct labour rate variance is £300 (adverse) (that is, £17,500 – £17,200).

The relationship between the direct labour variances for May is shown in Figure 7.7.

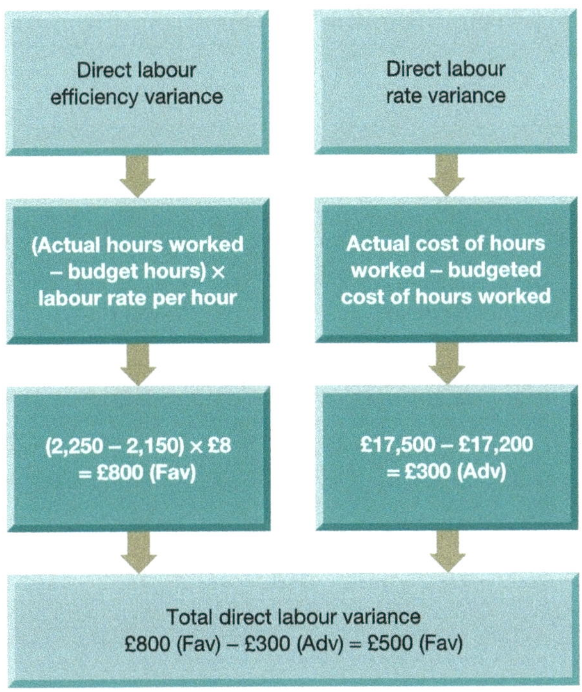

The total direct labour variance is the sum of the direct labour efficiency variance and the rate variance. It can be analysed into those two.

Figure 7.7 Total, efficiency and rate variances for direct labour for May

Activity 7.9

Using the figures in Activity 7.4, what was the direct labour rate variance for June?

The direct labour rate variance for *June* was £480 (favourable) (that is, (2,960 × £8) – £23,200). It is favourable because a lower rate was paid than the budgeted one. Paying a lower wage rate will have a favourable effect on profit.

Fixed overhead variance

The final area is that of overheads. In our example, we have assumed that all of the overheads are fixed. Variable overheads certainly exist in practice, but they have been omitted here simply to restrict the amount of detail. Variances involving variable overheads are similar in style to labour and material variances.

The **fixed overhead spending variance** is simply the difference between the flexed (or original – they will be the same) budget and the actual figures. For *May*, this was £700 (adverse) (that is, £20,700 – £20,000). It is adverse because more overheads cost was actually incurred than was budgeted. This would tend to lead to less profit. In theory, this is the responsibility of whoever controls overheads expenditure.

In practice, overheads tend to be a very slippery area. It is one that is notoriously difficult to control. Of course, fixed overheads (and variable ones) are usually made up of more than one type of cost. Typically, they would include such things as rent, administrative costs, management salaries, cleaning, electricity and so on. These items could be separately budgeted and the actual figures recorded. Individual spending variances could then be identified for each overhead item. This should reveal any problem areas.

Activity 7.10

Using the figures in Activity 7.4, what was the fixed overhead spending variance for June?

The fixed overhead spending variance for *June* was £700 (favourable) (that is, £20,000 – £19,300). It was favourable because less was spent on overheads than was budgeted, thereby having a favourable effect on profit.

RECONCILING THE BUDGETED PROFIT WITH THE ACTUAL PROFIT

We are now in a position to reconcile the original *May* budgeted operating profit with the actual operating profit, as follows:

	£	£
Budgeted operating profit		20,000
Favourable variances		
Sales price	2,000	
Direct materials price	100	
Direct labour efficiency	800	2,900
Adverse variances		
Sales volume	(4,000)	
Direct materials usage	(1,000)	
Direct labour rate	(300)	
Fixed overhead spending	(700)	(6,000)
Actual operating profit		16,900

Activity 7.11

If you were the chief executive of Baxter Ltd, what attitude would you take to the overall difference between the budgeted profit and the actual one?

How would you react to the individual variances that are the outcome of the analysis shown above?

You would probably be concerned about how large the variances are and their direction (favourable or adverse). In particular you may have thought of the following:

- The overall adverse profit variance is £3,100 (that is £20,000 – £16,900). This represents 15.5 per cent of the budgeted profit (that is £3,100/£20,000 × 100%) and you (as chief executive) would almost certainly see it as significant and worrying.
- The £4,000 adverse sales volume variance represents 20 per cent of budgeted profit and would be a particular cause of concern.
- The £2,000 favourable sales price variance represents 10 per cent of budgeted profit. Since this is favourable it might be seen as a cause for celebration rather than concern. On the other hand it means that Baxter Ltd's output was, on average, sold at prices 10 per cent above the planned price. This could have been the cause of the worrying adverse sales volume variance. The business may have sold fewer units because it charged higher prices.
- The £100 favourable direct materials price variance is very small in relation to budgeted profit – only 0.5 per cent. It would be unrealistic to expect the actual figures to hit the precise budgeted figures each month and so this is unlikely to be regarded as significant. The direct materials usage variance, however, represents 5 per cent of the budgeted profit. The chief executive may feel this is cause for concern.
- The £800 favourable direct labour efficiency variance represents 4 per cent of budgeted profit. Although it is a favourable variance, the reasons for it may be worth investigating. The £300 adverse direct labour rate variance represents only 1.5 per cent of the budgeted profit and may not be regarded as significant.
- The £700 fixed overhead adverse variance represents 3.5 per cent of budgeted profit. The chief executive may feel that this is too low to cause real concern.

The chief executive will now need to ask some questions as to why things went so badly wrong in several areas and what can be done to improve future performance.

We shall shortly come back to the dilemma as to which variances to investigate and which to accept.

Activity 7.12

Using the figures in Activity 7.4, try reconciling the original operating profit figure for June with the actual June figure.

	£	£
Budgeted operating profit		24,000
Favourable variances		
Sales volume	2,000	
Direct labour rate	480	
Fixed overhead spending	700	3,180
Adverse variances		
Sales price	(1,500)	
Direct materials usage	(300)	
Direct labour efficiency	(680)	(2,480)
Actual operating profit		24,700

Activity 7.13

The following are the budgeted and actual income statements for Baxter Ltd for the month of July:

	Budget		*Actual*	
Output (production and sales)	1,000 units		1,050 units	
	£		£	
Sales revenue	100,000		104,300	
Raw materials	(40,000)	(40,000 metres)	(41,200)	(40,500 metres)
Labour	(20,000)	(2,500 hours)	(21,300)	(2,600 hours)
Fixed overheads	(20,000)		(19,400)	
Operating profit	20,000		22,400	

Produce a reconciliation of the budgeted and actual operating profit, going into as much detail as possible with the variance analysis.

The original budget, the flexed budget and the actual outcome are as follows:

	Original budget	*Flexed budget*		*Actual*	
Output (production and sales)	1,000 units	1,050 units		1,050 units	
	£	£		£	
Sales revenue	100,000	105,000		104,300	
Raw materials	(40,000)	(42,000)	(42,000 m)	(41,200)	(40,500 m)
Labour	(20,000)	(21,000)	(2,625 hr)	(21,300)	(2,600 hr)
Fixed overheads	(20,000)	(20,000)		(19,400)	
Operating profit	20,000	22,000		22,400	

Reconciliation of the budgeted and actual operating profits for July

	£	£
Budgeted operating profit		20,000
Favourable variances:		
Sales volume (22,000 – 20,000)	2,000	
Direct materials usage ((42,000 – 40,500) × £1)	1,500	
Direct labour efficiency ((2,625 – 2,600) × £8)	200	
Fixed overhead spending (20,000 – 19,400)	600	4,300
Adverse variances:		
Sales price (105,000 – 104,300)	(700)	
Direct materials price ((40,500 × £1) – 41,200)	(700)	
Direct labour rate ((2,600 × £8) – 21,300)	(500)	(1,900)
Actual operating profit		22,400

Real World 7.2 shows how two UK-based businesses, the retailer Next plc and the food ingredients business Tate & Lyle PLC, use variance analysis to exercise control over their operations. Many businesses explain in their annual reports how they operate systems of budgetary control.

Real World 7.2

What Next?

In its 2013 annual report, Next plc states:

> **The Board is responsible for approving semi-annual Group budgets. Performance against budget is reported to the Board monthly and any substantial variances are explained.**

Refined controls

Tate & Lyle PLC makes it clear that it too uses budgets and variance analysis to help keep control over its activities. The 2013 annual report states that there is

> **A comprehensive planning and budgeting system for all items of expenditure with an annual budget approved by the Board. Performance is reported monthly against budget and prior year results; significant variances are investigated.**

The boards of directors of these businesses will not seek explanations of variances arising at each branch/department, but they will be looking at figures for the businesses as a whole or the results for major divisions of them.

Equally certainly, branch/department managers will receive a monthly (or perhaps more frequent) report of variances arising within their area of responsibility alone.

Sources: Next plc Annual Report 2013, p. 29; Tate & Lyle PLC Annual Report 2013, p. 44.

Real World 7.3 gives some indication of the importance of flexible budgeting in practice.

Real World 7.3

Flexing the budgets

A survey of the UK food and drinks industry provides us with an indication of the importance attached by management accountants to flexible budgeting. The survey asked those in charge of the management accounting function to rate the importance of flexible budgeting by selecting one of three possible categories – 'not important', 'moderately important' or 'important'. Figure 7.8 sets out the results, from the sample of 117 respondents.

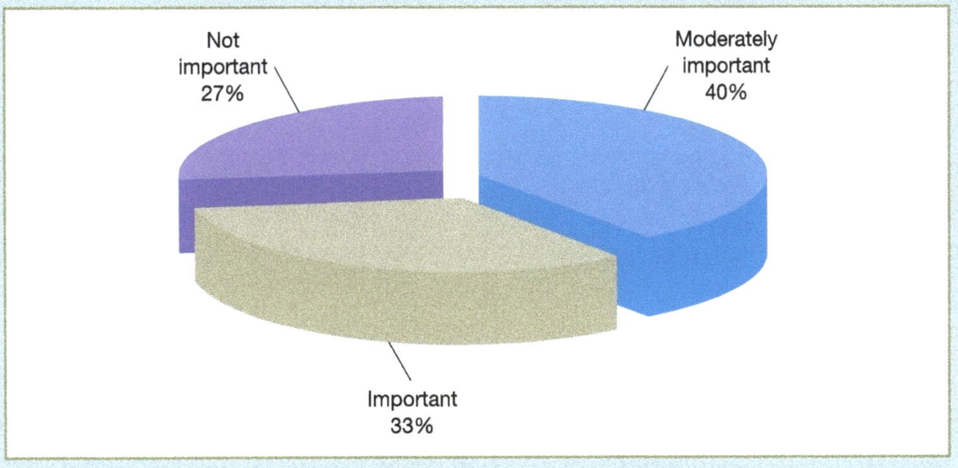

Figure 7.8 Degree of importance attached to flexible budgeting

→

Respondents were also asked to state the frequency with which flexible budgeting was used within the business, using a five-point scale ranging from 1 (never) through to 5 (very often). Figure 7.9 sets out these results.

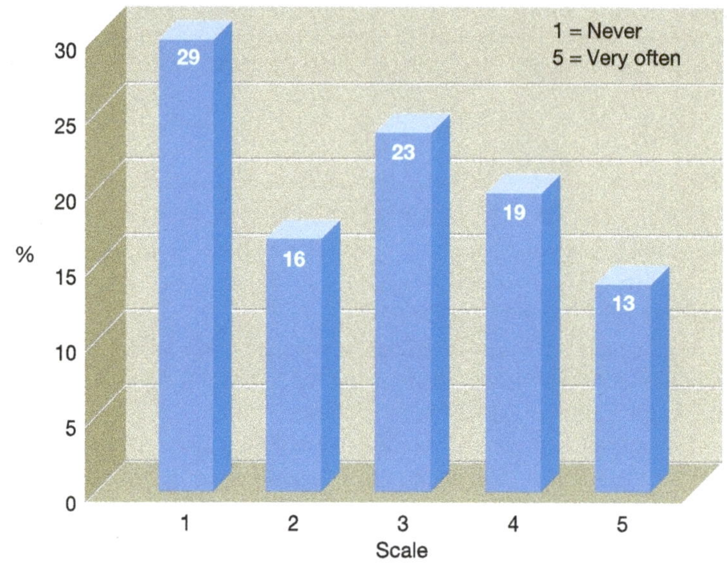

Figure 7.9 Frequency of use of flexible budgets

We can see that, while flexible budgeting is regarded as important by a significant proportion of management accountants and is being used in practice, not all businesses use it.

Source: Taken from information appearing in Abdel-Kader, M. and Luther, R. (2004) *An Empirical Investigation of the Evolution of Management Accounting Practices*, Working paper No. 04/06, University of Essex, October.

REASONS FOR ADVERSE VARIANCES

Adverse variances may occur simply because the budgets against which performance is being measured are unachievable. If this is the case, budgets will not provide a useful means of exercising control. There are other reasons, however, that may lead to actual performance deviating from budgeted performance.

Activity 7.14

The variances that we have considered are:

- **sales volume**
- **sales price**
- **direct materials usage**
- **direct materials price**
- **direct labour efficiency**
- **direct labour rate**
- **fixed overhead spending.**

Assuming that the budget targets are reasonable, jot down some possible reasons for *adverse* variances for each of the above occurring.

The reasons that we thought of included the following:

Sales volume

- Poor performance by sales staff.
- Deterioration in market conditions between the time when the budget was set and the actual event.
- Lack of goods or services to sell as a result of some production problem.

Sales price

- Poor performance by sales staff.
- Deterioration in market conditions between the time of setting the budget and the actual event.

Direct materials usage

- Poor performance by production department staff, leading to high rates of scrap.
- Substandard materials, leading to high rates of scrap.
- Faulty machinery, causing high rates of scrap.

Direct materials price

- Poor performance by the buying department staff.
- Using higher quality material than was planned.
- Change in market conditions between the time when the budget was set and the actual event.

Labour efficiency

- Poor supervision.
- A low skill grade of worker taking longer to do the work than was envisaged for the correct skill grade.
- Low-grade materials, leading to high levels of scrap and wasted labour time.
- Problems with a customer for whom a service is being rendered.
- Problems with machinery, leading to labour time being wasted.
- Dislocation of materials supply, leading to workers being unable to proceed with production.

Labour rate

- Poor performance by the human resources department.
- Using a higher grade of worker than was planned.
- Change in labour market conditions between the time of setting the budget and the actual event.

Fixed overheads

- Poor supervision of overheads.
- General increase in costs of overheads not taken into account in the budget.

Note that different variances may have the same underlying cause. For example, the purchase of low quality, cheaper materials may result in an unfavourable direct materials usage variance, a favourable direct materials price variance and an unfavourable direct labour efficiency variance.

VARIANCE ANALYSIS IN SERVICE INDUSTRIES

Although we have tended to use the example of a manufacturing business to explain variance analysis, this should not be taken to imply that variance analysis is not relevant and useful to service sector businesses. It is simply that manufacturing businesses tend to have all of the variances found in practice. Service businesses, for example, may not have material variances.

Real World 7.2 revealed that Next plc, a well-known retailer, uses budgets and variance analysis to help manage its complex business. It is probably fair to say that nearly all major service-providing businesses use some form of variance reporting to help them manage their affairs.

NON-OPERATING-PROFIT VARIANCES

There are many areas of business that have a budget but where a failure to meet it will not have a direct effect on operating profit. It will often, however, have an indirect effect and, sometimes, a profound one. The cash budget, for example, sets out planned receipts, payments and the resultant cash balance for the period. If this budget turns out to be wrong, for example, because of unforeseen expenditures, there may be unplanned cash shortages and accompanying costs. These costs may be limited to interest incurred on borrowing. If, however, the cash shortage cannot be covered by borrowing, the consequences could be more serious, such as lost profits from projects that were abandoned because of a lack of funds.

Control must, therefore, be exercised over areas such as cash management, to try to avoid adverse **non-operating-profit variances**.

INVESTIGATING VARIANCES

It is unreasonable to expect budget targets to be met precisely each month and so variances will usually arise. Discovering the reasons for these variances can be costly. Information will usually have to be produced and examined and discussions with appropriate members of staff carried out. Sometimes, activities may have to be stopped to discover what went wrong. Since small variances are almost inevitable, and investigating variances can be expensive, managers need some guiding principle concerning which variances to investigate and which to accept.

Activity 7.15

What principle do you feel should guide managers when deciding whether to spend money investigating a particular variance? (*Hint*: Think back to Chapter 1)

When deciding whether to produce accounting information, there should be a consideration of both benefit and cost. The benefit likely to be gained from knowing why a variance arose needs to be weighed against the cost of obtaining that knowledge.

There are difficulties in implementing this principle, however, as both the value of the benefit and the cost of investigation may be difficult to assess in advance of the investigation.

The following practical guidelines for investigating variances, which try to take some account of benefit and cost, may be adopted by managers:

- Significant *adverse* variances should normally be investigated as a continuation of the underlying problem could be very costly. Managers must decide what 'significant' means and, ultimately, this will be a matter of managerial judgement. It may be decided, for example, that variances above a threshold of a percentage of the budgeted figure (say, 5 per cent) or a fixed financial amount (say, £1,000) are considered significant.
- Significant *favourable* variances should probably be investigated. Although they may not cause such immediate concern as adverse variances, they still indicate that things are not going according to plan. If actual performance is significantly better than planned, it may mean that the budget target is unrealistically low.
- Insignificant variances, though not triggering immediate investigation, should be kept under review. For each aspect of operations, the cumulative sum of variances, over a series of control periods, should be zero, with small adverse variances in some periods being compensated for by small favourable ones in others. This is because small variances caused by random factors will not necessarily recur and they are as likely to be favourable as adverse.

While these guidelines may be of some help, managers must be flexible. They may, for example, decide against investigating a significant variance where the cost of correcting the potential causes is expected to be very high. They may calculate that it would be cheaper to live with the problem and so adjust the budget.

Where a variance is caused by systemic (non-random) factors, which will recur over time, the cumulative sum of the periodic variances will not be zero but an increasing figure. Even though the individual variances may be insignificant, the cumulative effect of these variances may not. Thus, an investigation may well be worthwhile, particularly if the variances are adverse.

To illustrate the cumulative effect of relatively small systemic variances, let us consider Example 7.2.

Example 7.2

Indisurers Ltd finds that the variances for direct labour efficiency for processing motor insurance claims, since the beginning of the year, are as follows:

	£		£
January	25 (adverse)	July	20 (adverse)
February	15 (favourable)	August	15 (favourable)
March	5 (favourable)	September	23 (adverse)
April	20 (adverse)	October	15 (favourable)
May	22 (adverse)	November	5 (favourable)
June	8 (favourable)	December	26 (adverse)

The average total cost of labour performing this task is about £1,200 a month. Management believes that none of these variances, taken alone, is significant given the monthly labour cost. The question is, are they significant when taken together? If we add them together, taking account of the signs, we find that we have a net adverse variance for the year of £73. Of itself this, too, is probably not significant, but we should expect the cumulative total to be close to zero where the variances are random. We might feel that a pattern is developing and, given long enough, a net adverse variance of significant size might build up.

Investigating the labour efficiency might be worth doing. Finding the cause of the variance would put management in a position to correct a systemic fault, which could lead to future cost savings. (Note that 12 periods are probably not enough to reach a statistically sound conclusion on whether the variances are random or not, but it provides an illustration of the point.)

Plotting the cumulative variances, from month to month, as in Figure 7.10, makes it clear what is happening as time proceeds.

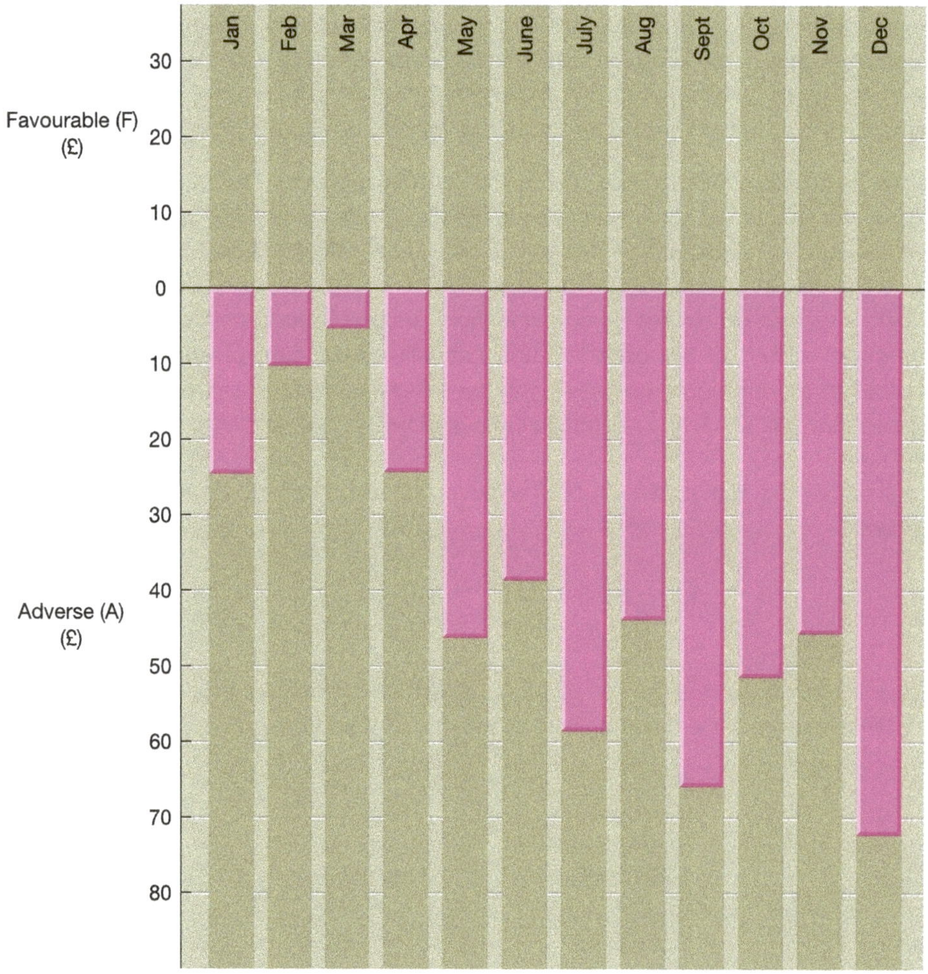

Starting at zero at the beginning of January, each month the cumulative variance is plotted. This is the sum taking account of positive and negative signs. The January figure is £25 (A). The February one is £10 (A) (that is £25 (A) plus £15 (F)) and so on. The graph seems to show an overall trend of adverse variances, but with several favourable variances involved.

Figure 7.10 The cumulative variances for labour efficiency in motor insurance claim handling at Indisurers Ltd

VARIANCE ANALYSIS IN PRACTICE

Real World 7.4 provides some evidence concerning the use of variance analysis.

Real World 7.4

Using variance analysis

The CIMA survey, mentioned in previous chapters, examined the extent to which the use of variance analysis varies with business size. Figure 7.11 shows the results.

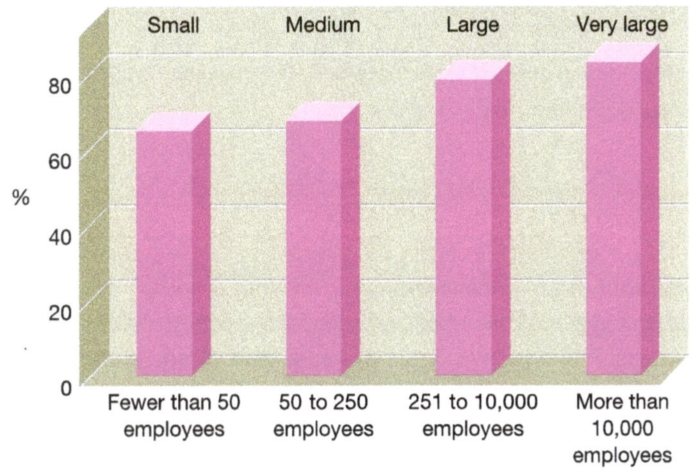

The use of this approach increases in line with the size of the business.

Figure 7.11 Variance analysis and business size

The survey also indicated that variance analysis was the most widely used of a variety of costing tools examined (which included the techniques covered in previous chapters). Overall, more than 70 per cent of respondents used this technique.

Source: Figure adapted from CIMA (2009) *Management Accounting Tools for Today and Tomorrow*, p. 12.

The CIMA survey indicated that there is a tendency for smaller businesses to be less likely to use variance analysis. This was emphasised by the survey of seven small and four medium sized UK business, that we met earlier in the chapter, which found that none of these eleven businesses used variance analysis.

Source: Lucas, M., Prowle, M. and Lowth, G. (2013) Management accounting practices of UK small-medium-sized enterprises, CIMA, July, p. 7.

COMPENSATING VARIANCES

There may be superficial appeal in the idea of **compensating variances**. These are linked favourable and adverse variances, which are traded off against each other. A sales manager, for example, may suggest that more of a particular service could be sold if prices were lowered, as this would result in increased profits. This suggestion would lead to a favourable sales volume variance, but also to an adverse sales price variance. On the face of it, provided that the former is greater than the latter, all would be well.

Activity 7.16

Can you think of a reason why the sales manager should not go ahead with the price reduction?

The change in policy will have ramifications for other areas of the business, including

- the need to supply more of the service: staff and other resources may not be available to accommodate this increase;
- the need to provide more finance: increased levels of activity will lead to an increased need for funds to pay, for example, additional staff costs.

Trading off variances in this way is, therefore, not normally acceptable without a more far-reaching consultation and revision of plans.

MAKING BUDGETARY CONTROL EFFECTIVE

It should be clear from what we have seen of **budgetary control** that a system, or a set of routines, must be put in place to enable the potential benefits to be gained. Most businesses that operate successful budgetary control systems tend to share some common features. These include the following:

- *A serious attitude taken to the system*. This should apply to all levels of management, right from the very top. For example, senior managers need to make clear to junior managers that they take notice of the monthly variance reports and base some of their actions and decisions upon them.
- *Clear demarcation between areas of managerial responsibility*. It needs to be clear which manager is responsible for each business area so that accountability can more easily be ascribed for any area that seems to be going out of control.
- *Budget targets that are challenging yet achievable*. Setting unachievable targets is likely to have a demotivating effect. Managers may be invited to participate in establishing their own targets to help create a sense of ownership. This, in turn, may increase levels of commitment and motivation. We shall consider this in more detail shortly.
- *Established data collection, analysis and reporting routines*. These should take the actual results and the budget figures and use them to calculate and report the variances. This should be part of the business's regular accounting information system, so that the required reports are automatically produced each month.
- *Reports aimed at individual managers, rather than general-purpose documents*. This avoids managers having to read through many pages of reports to find the part that is relevant to them.
- *Fairly short reporting periods*. These would typically be one month long, so that things cannot go too far wrong before they are picked up.
- *Timely variance reports*. Reports should be produced and made available to managers shortly after the end of the relevant reporting period. If it is not until the end of June that a manager is informed that the performance in May was below the budgeted level, it is quite likely that the performance for June will be below target as well. Reports on the performance in May ideally need to emerge in early June.

- *Action being taken to get operations back under control if they are shown to be out of control.* The report will not change things by itself. Managers need to take action to try to ensure that the reporting of significant adverse variances leads to action to put things right for the future.

BEHAVIOURAL ISSUES

Budgets are prepared with the objective of affecting the attitudes and behaviour of managers. The point was made in Chapter 6 that budgets are intended to motivate managers; research evidence generally shows that budgets can be effective in achieving this. More specifically, the research shows:

- The existence of budgets can improve job satisfaction and performance. Where a manager's role might otherwise be ill-defined or ambiguous, budgets can bring structure and certainty. Budgets provide clear, quantifiable, targets that must be pursued. This can be reassuring to managers and can increase their level of commitment.
- Demanding, yet achievable, budget targets tend to motivate better than less demanding targets. It seems that setting the most demanding targets that are acceptable to managers is a very effective way to motivate them.
- Unrealistically demanding targets tend to have an adverse effect on managers' performance. Once managers begin to view the budget targets as being too difficult to achieve, their level of motivation and performance declines. The relationship between the level of performance and the perceived degree of budget difficulty is shown in Figure 7.12.

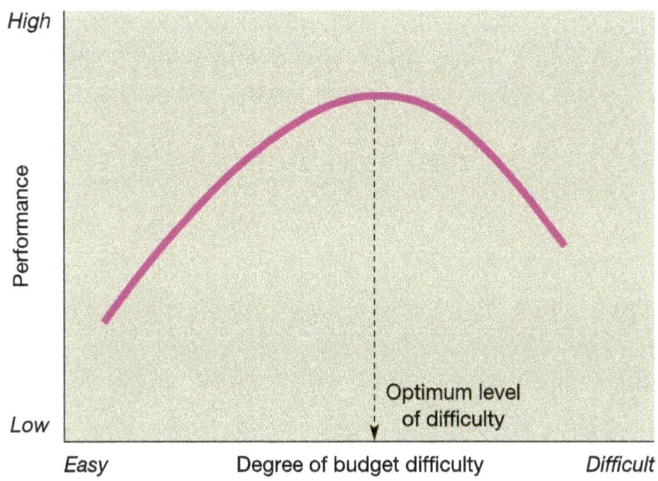

At a low level of budget difficulty, performance also tends to be low as managers do not find the targets sufficiently motivating. However, as the degree of difficulty starts to increase, managers rise to the challenge and improve their performance. Beyond a certain point, managers see the budgets as being too difficult to achieve and so motivation and performance decline.

Figure 7.12 Relationship between the level of performance and the perceived degree of budget difficulty

- The participation of managers in setting their targets tends to improve motivation and performance. This is probably because those managers feel a sense of commitment to the targets and a moral obligation to achieve them.

It has been suggested that allowing managers to set their own targets will lead to slack (that is, easily achievable) targets being introduced. This would make achievement of the target that much easier. On the other hand, in an effort to impress, a manager may select a target that is not really achievable. These points imply that care must be taken in the extent to which managers have unfettered choice of their own targets.

Conflict can occur in the budget-setting process, as different groups may well have different agendas. For example, junior managers may be keen to build slack into their budgets while their senior managers may seek to impose unrealistically demanding budget targets. Sometimes, such conflict can be constructive and can result in better decisions being made. To resolve the conflict over budget targets, negotiations may have to take place and other options may have to be explored. This may lead to a better understanding by all parties of the issues involved and final agreement may result in demanding, yet achievable, targets.

The impact of management style

There has been a great deal of discussion among experts on the way in which managers use information generated by the budgeting system and the impact of its use on the attitudes and behaviour of subordinates (that is, the staff). A pioneering study by Hopwood (see reference 1 at the end of the chapter) examined the way that managers, working within a manufacturing environment, used budget information to evaluate the performance of subordinates. He argued that three distinct styles of management could be observed. These are:

- *Budget-constrained style*. This management style focuses rigidly on the ability of subordinates to meet the budget. Other factors relating to the performance of subordinates are not given serious consideration even though they might include improving the long-term effectiveness of the area for which the subordinate has responsibility,
- *Profit-conscious style*. This management style uses budget information in a more flexible way and often in conjunction with other data. The main focus is on the ability of each subordinate to improve long-term effectiveness.
- *Non-accounting style*. In this case, budget information plays no significant role in the evaluation of a subordinate's performance.

Activity 7.17

How might a manager respond to information that indicates a subordinate has not met the budget targets for the period, assuming the manager adopts

(a) a budget-constrained style?
(b) a profit-conscious style?
(c) a non-accounting style?

(a) A manager adopting a budget-constrained style is likely to take the budget information very seriously. This may result in criticism of the subordinate and, perhaps, some form of sanction.
(b) A manager adopting a profit-conscious style is likely to take a broader view when examining the budget information and so will take other factors into consideration (for example, factors that could not have been anticipated at the time of preparing the budgets), before deciding whether criticism or punishment is justified.
(c) A manager adopting a non-accounting style will regard the failure to meet the budget as being relatively unimportant and so no action may be taken.

Hopwood found that subordinates working for a manager who adopts a budget-constrained style had unfortunate experiences. They suffered higher levels of job-related stress and had poorer working relationships, with both their colleagues and their manager, than those subordinates whose manager adopted one of the other two styles. Hopwood also found that the subordinates of a budget-constrained style of manager were more likely to manipulate the budget figures, or to take other undesirable actions, to ensure the budgets were met.

Reservations about the Hopwood study

Though Hopwood's findings are interesting, subsequent studies have cast doubt on their universal applicability. Later studies confirm that human attitudes and behaviour are complex and can vary according to the particular situation. For example, it has been found that the impact of different management styles on such factors as job-related stress and the manipulation of budget figures seems to vary. The impact is likely to depend on such factors as the level of independence enjoyed by the subordinates and the level of uncertainty associated with the tasks to be undertaken.

It seems that where there is a high level of interdependence between business divisions, subordinate managers are more likely to feel that they have less control over their performance. This is because the performance of staff in other divisions could be an important influence on the final outcome. In such a situation, rigid application of the budget could be viewed as being unfair and may lead to undesirable behaviour. However, where managers have a high degree of independence, the application of budgets as a measure of performance is likely to be more acceptable. In this case, the managers are likely to feel that the final outcome is much less dependent on the performance of others.

Later studies have also shown that where a subordinate is undertaking a task that has a high degree of uncertainty concerning the outcome (for example, developing a new product), budget targets are unlikely to be an adequate measure of performance. In such a situation, other factors and measures should be taken into account in order to derive a more complete assessment of performance. However, where a task has a low degree of uncertainty concerning the outcome (for example, producing a standard product using standard equipment and an experienced workforce), budget measures may be regarded as more reliable indicators of performance. Thus, it appears that a budget-constrained style is more likely to work where subordinates enjoy a fair amount of independence and where the tasks set have a low level of uncertainty concerning their outcomes.

Failing to meet the budget

The existence of budgets gives senior managers a ready means to assess the performance of their subordinates (that is, junior managers). If a junior manager fails to meet a budget, this must be handled carefully by the relevant senior manager. Adverse variances may imply that the manager needs help. If this is the case, a harsh, critical approach would have a demotivating effect and would be counterproductive.

Real World 7.5 gives some indication of the effects of the **behavioural aspects of budgetary control** in practice.

Real World 7.5

Behavioural problems

A survey indicated that there is a large degree of participation in setting budgets by those who will be expected to perform to the budget (the budget holders).

The survey also showed that senior managers have greater influence in setting the targets than their junior manager budget holders. Where there is a conflict between the cost estimates submitted by the budget holders and their senior managers, in 40 per cent of respondent businesses the senior manager's view would prevail without negotiation. In nearly 60 per cent of cases, however, a reduction would be negotiated between the budget holder and the senior manager. The general philosophy of the businesses that responded to the survey, regarding budget holders influencing the setting of their own budgets, is:

- 23 per cent of respondents believe that budget holders should not have too much influence since they will seek to obtain easy budgets (build in slack) if they do;
- 69 per cent of respondents take an opposite view.

The general view on how senior managers should judge their subordinates is:

- 46 per cent of respondent businesses think that senior managers should judge junior managers mainly on their ability to achieve the budget;
- 40 per cent think otherwise.

Though this research is not very recent (1993), in the absence of more recent evidence it provides some feel for budget setting in practice.

Source: Drury, C., Braund, S., Osborne, P. and Tayles, M. (1993) *A Survey of Management Accounting Practices in UK Manufacturing Companies*, Chartered Association of Certified Accountants.

Budgets and innovation

We saw in the previous chapter that budgets are often criticised for reinforcing a 'command and control' structure that concentrates power in the hands of senior managers and prevents junior managers from exercising autonomy. It has been argued that this can deter innovation and can leave junior managers feeling constrained and frustrated. There is not compelling evidence, however, to support this view. **Real World 7.6** discusses some research that explored the possible tension between budgetary control and innovative behaviour.

Real World 7.6

Not guilty

A research project was carried out within a large multinational business, which is referred to as 'Astoria' by researchers to preserve its anonymity. The business employs a broadly traditional budgeting system even though it is subject to rapid technological change and operates within a highly competitive environment. Interviews with 25 managers, drawn from different functional areas, were conducted to see whether the budgeting process stifled innovation in any way. The researchers concluded:

> **. . . we found little evidence to suggest that managers at Astoria were deterred from engaging in innovative activities simply because they had budget responsibilities. Of course, the amount of resources available to them may have presented a sort of boundary, but they didn't see the**

presence of budgetary targets as a constraint. The closest we came to finding any suggestion that budgets might inhibit innovation was a comment from one manager who remarked that 'everybody has a sandpit to play in. My sandpit financially is my control plan. If I stay within it, I'm free to play.' More generally, managers considered that, if they felt restricted in pursuing innovation, it was the degree of general empowerment they had that mattered. One manager went so far as to say that he felt 'constrained in some ways by not having enough hours in the day'. Our findings suggest that, although much of the accounting literature argues that budgets may deter innovation, this seems far from the truth.

Source: Marginson, D. and Ogden, S. (2005) Budgeting and innovation, *Financial Management*, April, pp. 29–31.

STANDARD QUANTITIES AND COSTS

We have already seen that a budget is a business plan for the short term – typically one year – that is expressed mainly in financial terms. A budget is typically constructed from standards. **Standard quantities and costs** (or revenues) are those planned for an individual unit of input or output and provide the building blocks for budgets.

We can say about Baxter Ltd's operations (see Example 7.1 on page 000) that:

- the standard selling price is £100 for one unit of output;
- the standard marginal cost for one manufactured unit is £60;
- the standard raw materials cost is £40 for one unit of output;
- the standard raw materials usage is 40 metres for one unit of output;
- the standard raw materials price is £1 a metre (that is, for one unit of input);
- the standard labour cost is £20 for one unit of output;
- the standard labour time is 2.50 hours for one unit of output;
- the standard labour rate is £8 an hour (that is, for one unit of input).

Standards, like the budgets to which they are linked, represent targets against which actual performance is measured. They also provide the basis for variance analysis, which, as we have seen, helps managers to identify where deviations from planned, or standard, performance have occurred and the extent of those deviations. To maintain their usefulness for planning and control purposes, they should be subject to frequent review and, where necessary, revision. **Real World 7.7** provides some evidence on the frequency of updating standards in practice.

Real World 7.7

Keeping up standards

KPMG, the accountancy firm, conducted interviews with senior financial officers of 12 large international manufacturing businesses covering pharmaceuticals, industrials and consumer goods. A key finding was that increasing economic volatility was leading to more frequent updates of standards. Most of the businesses updated standards annually. However, one updated on a quarterly basis and one had not updated for two years because of the costs and time involved.

Source: KPMG (2010) Standard costing: insights from leading companies, February.

Standards may be applied to a wide variety of products or services. A firm of accountants, for example, may set standard costs per hour for each grade of staff (audit manager, audit senior, trainee and so on). When planning a particular audit of a client business, it can decide the standard hours that each grade of staff should spend on the audit and, using the standard cost per hour for each grade, it can derive a standard cost or 'budget' for the job as a whole. These standards can subsequently be compared with the actual hours and hourly rates.

SETTING STANDARDS

When setting standards various points have to be considered. We shall now explore some of the more important of these.

Who sets the standards?

Standards often result from the collective effort of various individuals including management accountants, industrial engineers, human resource managers, production managers and other employees. The manager responsible for achieving a particular standard will usually have some involvement and may provide specialised knowledge. This provides the opportunity to influence the final decision, with the consequent risk that 'slack' may be built into the standard in order to make it easier to achieve. The same problem was mentioned earlier in relation to budgets.

How is information gathered?

Setting standards involves gathering information concerning how much material should be used, how much machine time should be required, how much direct labour time should be spent and so on. Two possible ways of collecting information for standard setting are available.

Activity 7.18

Can you think what these might be?

The first is to examine the particular processes and tasks involved in producing the product or service and to develop suitable estimates. Standards concerning material usage, machine time and direct labour hours may be established by carrying out dummy production runs, time-and-motion studies and so on. This will require close collaboration between the management accountant, industrial engineers and those involved in the production process.

The second approach is to collect information relating to past costs, times and usage for the same, or similar, products and to use this information as a basis for predicting the future. This information may have to be adjusted to reflect changes in price, changes in the production process and so on.

Where the product or service is entirely new or involves entirely new processes, the first approach will probably have to be used, even though it is usually more costly.

What kind of standards should be used?

There are basically two types of standards that may be used: **ideal standards** and **practical standards**. Ideal standards, as the name suggests, assume perfect operating conditions where there is no inefficiency due to lost production time, defects and so on. The objective of setting ideal standards, which are attainable in theory at least, is to encourage employees to strive towards excellence. Practical standards, also as the name suggests, do not assume ideal operating conditions. Although they demand a high level of efficiency, account is taken of possible lost production time, defects and so on. They are designed to be challenging yet achievable.

There are two major difficulties with using ideal standards.

- They do not provide a useful basis for exercising control. Unless the standards set are realistic, any variances computed are extremely difficult to interpret.
- They may not achieve their intended purpose of motivating managers: indeed, the opposite may occur. We saw earlier that the evidence suggests that where managers regard a target as beyond their grasp, it is likely to have a demotivating effect.

Given these problems, it is not surprising that practical standards seem to enjoy more widespread support than ideal standards. Nevertheless, by taking account of wastage, lost production time and so on, there is a risk that they will entrench operating inefficiencies.

THE LEARNING-CURVE EFFECT

Where an activity undertaken by direct workers has been unchanged for some time, and the workers are experienced at performing it, the standard labour time will normally stay unchanged. However, where a new activity is introduced, or new workers are involved with performing an existing activity, a **learning-curve** effect will normally occur. This is shown in Figure 7.13.

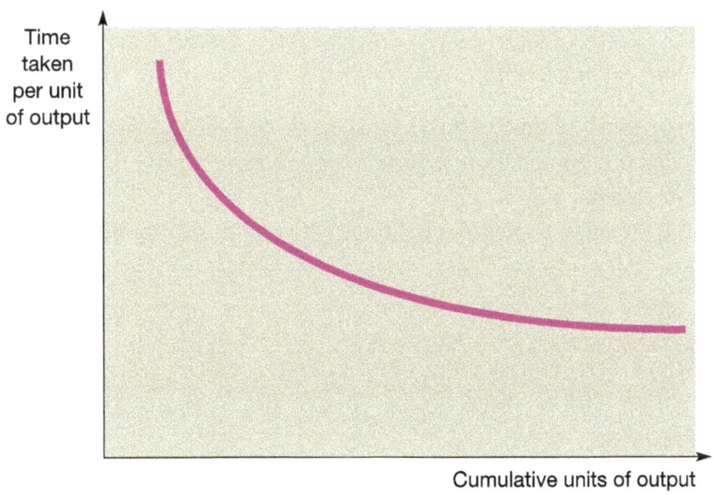

Each time a particular task is performed, people become quicker at it. This learning-curve effect becomes less and less significant until, after performing the task a number of times, no further learning occurs.

Figure 7.13 The learning-curve effect

The first unit of output takes a relatively long time to produce. As experience is gained, the worker takes less time to produce each successive unit of output. The rate of reduction in the time taken will, however, decrease as experience is gained. Thus, for example, the reduction in time taken between the first and second unit produced will be much bigger than the reduction between, say, the ninth and the tenth. Eventually, the rate of reduction in time taken will reduce to zero so that each unit will take as long as the preceding one. At this point, the point where the curve in Figure 7.13 becomes horizontal (the bottom right of the graph), the learning-curve effect will have been eliminated and a steady, long-term standard time for the activity will have been established.

The learning-curve effect seems to have little to do with whether workers are skilled or unskilled; if they are unfamiliar with the task, the learning-curve effect will arise. Practical experience shows that learning curves show remarkable regularity and, therefore, predictability from one activity to another.

The learning-curve effect applies equally well to activities involved with providing a service (such as dealing with an insurance claim, in an insurance business) as to manufacturing-type activities (like upholstering an armchair by hand, in a furniture-making business).

Clearly, the learning-curve effect must be taken into account when setting standards, and when interpreting any adverse labour efficiency variances, where a new process and/or new staff are involved.

OTHER USES FOR STANDARD COSTING

We have already seen that standards can play a valuable role in performance evaluation and control. However, standards relating to costs, usages, selling prices and so on may also be used for other purposes such as

- measuring operating efficiency
- product-sourcing decisions
- determining the cost of inventories and work in progress for income measurement purposes
- determining the cost of items for use in pricing decisions.

This does not mean that standards should be seen as the primary measure in all cases. When making decisions about operating efficiency, product sourcing or pricing, they may be used as a secondary measure.

Real World 7.8 provides some information on the use of standards for decision making.

Real World 7.8

Standard practice

The KPMG survey, mentioned in Real World 7.7 (page 253), found that some of the twelve manufacturing businesses in the study had moved away from using standard costing as the key measure of operating effectiveness and for product-sourcing decisions. Instead, they relied on other operating and financial measures.

Source: KPMG (2010) Standard costing: insights from leading companies, February.

SOME PROBLEMS . . .

Although standards and variances may be useful for decision-making purposes, they have limited application. Many business and commercial activities do not have direct relationships between inputs and outputs, as is the case with, say, the number of direct labour hours worked and the number of products manufactured. Many expenses of modern business are in areas such as human resource development, advertising, maintenance of equipment and research and development, where the expense is discretionary and there is no direct link to the level of output.

There are also potential problems when applying standard costing techniques. These include the following:

- Standards can quickly become out of date as a result of both changes in the production process and price changes. When standards become outdated, performance can be adversely affected. For example, a human resources manager who recognises that it is impossible to meet targets on rates of pay for labour, because of general labour cost rises, may have less incentive to minimise costs.
- Factors may affect a variance for which a particular manager is accountable but over which the manager has no control. When assessing the manager's performance, these uncontrollable factors should be taken into account but there is always a risk that they will not.
- In practice, creating clear lines of demarcation between the areas of responsibility of various managers may be difficult. In this case, one of the prerequisites of effective standard costing is lost.
- Once a standard has been met, there is no incentive for employees to improve the quality or quantity of output further. There are usually no additional rewards for doing so, only additional work. Indeed, employees may have a disincentive for exceeding a standard as it may then be viewed by managers as too loose and therefore in need of tightening. However, simply achieving a standard, and no more, may not be enough in highly competitive and fast-changing markets. To compete effectively, a business may need to strive for continuous improvement and standard costing techniques may impede this process.
- Standard costing may create incentives for managers and employees to act in undesirable ways. It may, for example, encourage the build-up of excess inventories, leading to significant storage and financing costs. This problem can arise where there are opportunities for discounts on bulk purchases of materials, which the purchasing manager then exploits to achieve a favourable direct materials price variance. One way to avoid this problem might be to impose limits on the level of inventories held.

Activity 7.19

Can you think of another example of how a manager may achieve a favourable direct materials price variance but in doing so would create problems for a business?

A manager may buy cheaper, but lower quality, materials. Although this may lead to a favourable price variance, it may also lead to additional inspection and reworking costs and, perhaps, lost sales.

To avoid this problem, the manager may be required to buy material of a particular quality or from particular sources.

A final example of the perverse incentives created by standard costing relates to labour efficiency variances. Where these variances are calculated for individual employees, and form the basis for their rewards, there is little incentive for them to work co-operatively. Co-operative working may be in the best interests of the business, however. To avoid this problem, some businesses calculate labour efficiency variances for groups of employees rather than individual employees. This, however, creates the risk that some individuals will become 'free riders' and will rely on the more conscientious employees to carry the load.

Activity 7.20

How might the business try to eliminate the 'free-rider' problem just mentioned?

One way would be to carry out an evaluation, perhaps by the group members themselves, of individual contributions to group output, as well as evaluating group output as a whole.

Real World 7.9 indicates that, despite the problems mentioned above, standard costing is used by businesses.

Real World 7.9

Standard usage

The CIMA survey, mentioned previously, examined the extent to which the use of standard costing varies with business size. Figure 7.14 shows the results.

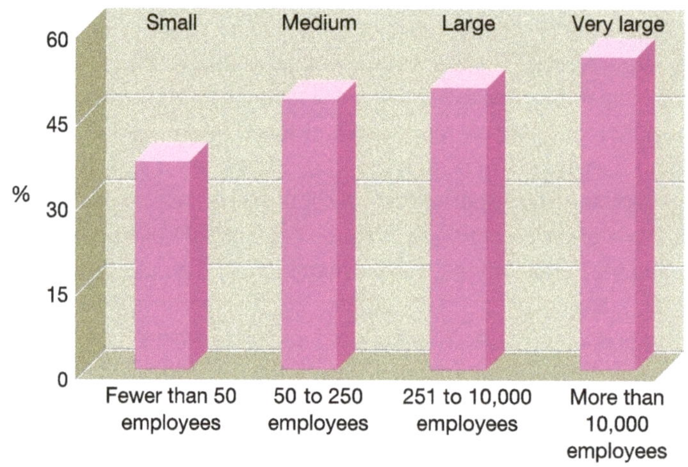

The use of this technique increases in line with the size of the business.

Figure 7.14 Standard costing and business size

Source: Figure adapted from CIMA (2009) *Management Accounting Tools for Today and Tomorrow*, p. 12.

THE NEW BUSINESS ENVIRONMENT

The traditional standard costing approach was developed during an era when business operations were characterised by few product lines, long production runs and heavy reliance on direct labour. More recently, the increasingly competitive environment and the onward march of technology have changed the business landscape. Now, many business operations are characterised by a wide range of different products, shorter product life cycles (leading to shorter production runs) and automated production processes. The effect of these changes has resulted in

- a need for more frequent development of standards to deal with frequent changes to the product range;
- a change in the focus for control – where manufacturing systems are automated, for example, direct labour becomes less important than direct materials;
- a decline in the importance of monitoring from cost and usage variances – where manufacturing systems are automated, deviations from standards relating to costs and usage become less frequent and less significant.

Thus, where a business has highly automated production systems, traditional standard costing, with its emphasis on costs and usage, is likely to take on less importance. Other elements of the production process such as quality, production levels, product cycle times, delivery times and the need for continuous improvement become the focus of attention. This does not mean, however, that a standards-based approach is not useful for the new manufacturing environment. It can still provide valuable control information and there is no reason why standard costing systems cannot be redesigned to reflect a concern for some of the elements mentioned earlier. Nevertheless, other measures, including non-financial ones, may help to augment the information provided by the standard costing system.

Real World 7.10 indicates the extent to which particular standard costing variances are calculated.

Real World 7.10

Maintaining standards

Senior financial managers of 33 UK businesses were asked about their costing systems. It emerged that standard costing was used by 30 of the businesses concerned, which represented most of the businesses that might be expected to use this method. The popularity among these businesses of standards for each of the main cost items is set out in Figure 7.15.

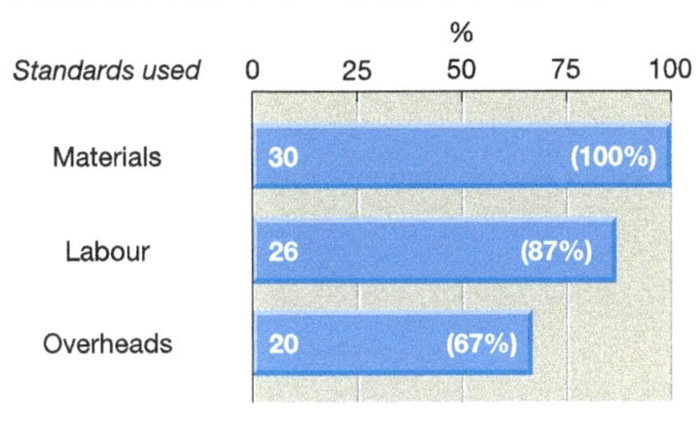

Standards for materials were used by all businesses in the survey that used standard costing. Standards for labour were used by nearly all businesses.

Figure 7.15 The popularity of standards in practice

Despite the popularity of materials standards, the study found that four businesses calculated the total direct materials variance only and that only two-thirds of businesses calculated both the direct materials price and usage variances. For labour standards, the variance analysis is even less complete. The study found that 15 businesses calculated the total direct labour variance only and only one-third of businesses calculated both the direct labour and efficiency variances. It seems, therefore, that standard costing was not extensively employed by the businesses.

Source: Figure based on information in Dugdale, D., Jones, C. and Green, S. (2006) *Contemporary Management Accounting Practices in UK Manufacturing*, CIMA Publication, Elsevier.

Self-assessment question 7.1

Toscanini Ltd makes a standard product, which is budgeted to sell at £4.00 a unit, in a competitive market. It is made by taking a budgeted 0.4 kg of material, budgeted to cost £2.40/kg, and having it worked on by hand by an employee, paid a budgeted £8.00/hour, for a budgeted 6 minutes. Monthly fixed overheads are budgeted at £4,800. The output for May was budgeted at 4,000 units.

The actual results for May were as follows:

	£
Sales revenue (3,500 units)	13,820
Materials (1,425 kg)	(3,420)
Labour (345 hours)	(2,690)
Fixed overheads	(4,900)
Actual operating profit	2,810

No inventories of any description existed at the beginning or end of the month.

Required:

(a) Deduce the budgeted profit for May and reconcile it, through variances, with the actual profit in as much detail as the information provided will allow.

(b) State which manager should be held accountable, in the first instance, for each variance calculated.

(c) Assuming that the budget was well set and achievable, suggest at least one feasible reason for each of the variances that you identified in (a), given what you know about the business's performance for May.

(d) If it were discovered that the actual total world market demand for the business's product was 10 per cent lower than estimated when the May budget was set, explain how and why the variances that you identified in (a) could be revised to provide information that would be potentially more useful.

The solution to this question can be found in Appendix B.

SUMMARY

The main points of this chapter may be summarised as follows:

Controlling through budgets

- Budgets can act as a system of both feedback and feedforward control.
- To exercise control, budgets can be flexed to match actual volume of output.

Variance analysis

- Variances may be favourable or adverse according to whether they result in an increase to, or a decrease from, the budgeted profit figure.
- Budgeted profit plus all favourable variances less all adverse variances equals actual profit.
- Commonly calculated variances:
  - Sales volume variance = difference between the original budget and the flexed budget profit figures.
  - Sales price variance = difference between actual sales revenue and actual volume at the standard sales price.
  - Total direct materials variance = difference between the actual direct materials cost and the direct materials cost according to the flexed budget.
  - Direct materials usage variance = difference between actual usage and budgeted usage, for the actual volume of output, multiplied by the standard materials cost.
  - Direct materials price variance = difference between the actual materials cost and the actual usage multiplied by the standard materials cost.
  - Total direct labour variance = difference between the actual direct labour cost and the direct labour cost according to the flexed budget.
  - Direct labour efficiency variance = difference between actual labour time and budgeted time, for the actual volume of output, multiplied by the standard labour rate.
  - Direct labour rate variance = difference between the actual labour cost and the actual labour time multiplied by the standard labour rate.
  - Fixed overhead spending variance = difference between the actual and budgeted spending on fixed overheads.
- Significant and/or persistent variances should normally be investigated to establish their cause. However, the costs and benefits of investigating variances must be considered.
- Trading off favourable variances against linked adverse variances should not be automatically acceptable.
- Not all activities can usefully be controlled through traditional variance analysis.

Effective budgetary control

- Good budgetary control requires establishing systems and routines to ensure such things as a clear distinction between individual managers' areas of responsibility; prompt, frequent and relevant variance reporting; and senior management commitment.
- There are behavioural aspects of control relating to management style, participation in budget setting and the failure to meet budget targets that should be taken into account by senior managers.
- The view that budgetary control stifles initiative is not well supported by the evidence.

→

Standard costing

- Standards are budgeted physical quantities and financial values for one unit of inputs and outputs.
- There are two types of standards: ideal standards and practical standards.
- Information necessary for developing standards can be gathered by analysing the task or by using past data.
- There tends to be a learning-curve effect: routine tasks are performed more quickly with experience.
- Standards can be useful in providing data for income measurement, pricing decisions, product sourcing and efficiency measurement.
- Standards have their limitations, particularly in modern manufacturing environments; however, they are still widely used.

KEY TERMS

For definitions of these terms, see Appendix A.

Feedback control
Feedforward control
Flexing a budget
Flexible budget
Sales volume variance
Adverse variance
Favourable variance
Variance
Sales price variance
Total direct materials variance
Direct materials usage variance
Direct materials price variance
Total direct labour variance
Direct labour efficiency variance
Direct labour rate variance
Fixed overhead spending variance
Non-operating-profit variances
Compensating variances
Budgetary control
Behavioural aspects of budgetary control
Standard quantities and costs
Ideal standards
Practical standards
Learning curve

REFERENCE

1 Hopwood, A.G. (1972) An empirical study of the role of accounting data in performance evaluation, *Empirical Research in Accounting*, a supplement to the *Journal of Accounting Research*, pp. 15–82.

FURTHER READING

If you would like to explore the topics covered in this chapter in more depth, we recommend the following:

Atkinson, A., Kaplan, R., Matsamura, E. and Young, S.M. (2011) *Management Accounting: Information for Decision Making and Strategy Execution*, 6th edn, Pearson, Chapter 12.

Bhimani, A., Horngren, C., Datar, S. and Rajan, M. (2012) *Management and Cost Accounting*, 5th edn, Financial Times Prentice Hall, Chapters 14 to 16.

Drury, C. (2012) *Management and Cost Accounting*, 8th edn, Cengage Learning, Chapters 16 to 18.

Hilton, R. (2011) *Managerial Accounting*, 9th edn, McGraw-Hill Higher Education, Chapter 10.

REVIEW QUESTIONS

Solutions to these questions can be found in Appendix C.

7.1 Explain what is meant by feedforward control and distinguish it from feedback control.

7.2 What is meant by a variance? What is the point in analysing variances?

7.3 What is the point in flexing the budget in the context of variance analysis? Does flexing imply that differences between budget and actual in the volume of output are ignored in variance analysis?

7.4 Should all variances be investigated to find their cause? Explain your answer.

EXERCISES

Exercises 7.1 and 7.2 are basic level, 7.3 and 7.4 are intermediate level and 7.5 to 7.8 are advanced level. Those with coloured numbers have solutions given in Appendix D.

7.1 You have recently overheard the following remarks:

(a) 'A favourable direct labour rate variance can only be caused by staff working more efficiently than budgeted.'
(b) 'Selling more units than budgeted, because the units were sold at less than standard price, automatically leads to a favourable sales volume variance.'
(c) 'Using below-standard materials will tend to lead to adverse materials usage variances but cannot affect labour variances.'
(d) 'Higher-than-budgeted sales could not possibly affect the labour rate variance.'
(e) 'An adverse sales price variance can only arise from selling a product at less than standard price.'

Required:
Critically assess these remarks, explaining any technical terms.

7.2 You have recently overheard the following remarks:

(a) 'When calculating variances, we ignore differences of volume of output, between original budget and actual, by flexing the budget. If there were a volume difference, it is water under the bridge by the time that the variances come to be calculated.'
(b) 'It is very valuable to calculate variances because they will tell you what went wrong.'
(c) 'All variances should be investigated to find their cause.'
(d) 'Research evidence shows that the more demanding the target, the more motivated the manager.'
(e) 'Most businesses do not have feedforward controls of any type, just feedback controls through budgets.'

Required:
Critically assess these remarks, explaining any technical terms.

7.3 Pilot Ltd makes a standard product, which is budgeted to sell at £5.00 a unit. It is made by taking a budgeted 0.5 kg of material, budgeted to cost £3.00 a kilogram, and having it worked on by hand by an employee, paid a budgeted £10.00 an hour, for a budgeted $7^1/_2$ minutes. Monthly fixed overheads are budgeted at £6,000. The output for March was budgeted at 5,000 units.

The actual results for March were as follows:

	£
Sales revenue (5,400 units)	26,460
Materials (2,830 kg)	(8,770)
Labour (650 hours)	(6,885)
Fixed overheads	(6,350)
Actual operating profit	4,455

No inventories existed at the start or end of March.

Required:

(a) Deduce the budgeted profit for March and reconcile it with the actual profit in as much detail as the information provided will allow.

(b) State which manager should be held accountable, in the first instance, for each variance calculated.

7.4 Antonio plc makes Product X, the standard costs of which are:

	£
Sales revenue	31
Direct labour (1 hour)	(11)
Direct materials (1 kg)	(10)
Fixed overheads	(3)
Standard profit	7

The budgeted output for March was 1,000 units of Product X; the actual output was 1,100 units, which was sold for £34,950. There were no inventories at the start or end of March.

The actual production costs were:

	£
Direct labour (1,075 hours)	12,210
Direct materials (1,170 kg)	11,630
Fixed overheads	3,200

Required:

Calculate the variances for March as fully as you are able from the available information and use them to reconcile the budgeted and actual profit figures.

7.5 Bradley-Allen Ltd makes one standard product. Its budgeted operating statement for May is as follows:

		£	£
Sales (volume and revenue):	800 units		64,000
Direct materials:	Type A	(12,000)	
	Type B	(16,000)	
Direct labour:	Skilled	(4,000)	
	Unskilled	(10,000)	
Fixed overheads:		(12,000)	
			(54,000)
Budgeted operating profit			10,000

The standard costs were as follows:

Direct materials:	Type A	£50/kg
	Type B	£20/m
Direct labour:	Skilled	£10/hour
	Unskilled	£8/hour

During May, the following occurred:

1 950 units were sold for a total of £73,000.
2 310 kg (costing £15,200) of type A material were used in production.
3 920 metres (costing £18,900) of type B material were used in production.
4 Skilled workers were paid £4,628 for 445 hours.
5 Unskilled workers were paid £11,275 for 1,375 hours.
6 Fixed overheads cost £11,960.

There were no inventories of finished production or of work in progress at either the beginning or end of May.

Required:

(a) Prepare a statement that reconciles the budgeted to the actual profit of the business for May, through variances. Your statement should analyse the difference between the two profit figures in as much detail as possible.

(b) Explain how the statement in (a) might be helpful to managers.

7.6 Mowbray Ltd makes and sells one product, the standard costs of which are as follows:

	£
Direct materials (3 kg at £2.50/kg)	(7.50)
Direct labour (15 minutes at £9.00/hr)	(2.25)
Fixed overheads	(3.60)
	(13.35)
Selling price	20.00
Standard profit margin	6.65

The monthly production and sales are planned to be 1,200 units.

The actual results for May were as follows:

	£	
Sales revenue	18,000	
Direct materials	(7,400)	(2,800 kg)
Direct labour	(2,300)	(255 hr)
Fixed overheads	(4,100)	
Operating profit	4,200	

There were no inventories at the start or end of May. As a result of poor sales demand during May, the business reduced the price of all sales by 10 per cent.

Required:

Calculate the budgeted profit for May and reconcile it to the actual profit through variances, going into as much detail as is possible from the information available.

7.7 Brive plc has the following standards for its only product:

Selling price:	£110/unit
Direct labour:	1 hour at £10.50/hour
Direct material:	3 kg at £14.00/kg
Fixed overheads:	£27.00/unit, based on a budgeted output of 800 units/month

During May, there was an actual output of 850 units and the operating statement for the month was as follows:

	£
Sales revenue	92,930
Direct labour (890 hours)	(9,665)
Direct materials (2,410 kg)	(33,258)
Fixed overheads	(21,365)
Operating profit	28,642

There were no inventories of any description at the beginning and end of May.

Required:

Prepare the original budget and a budget flexed to the actual volume. Use these to compare the budgeted and actual profits of the business for the month, going into as much detail with your analysis as the information given will allow.

7.8 Varne Chemprocessors is a business that specialises in plastics. It uses a standard costing system to monitor and report its purchases and usage of materials. During the most recent month, accounting period six, the purchase and usage of chemical UK194 were as follows:

Purchases/usage:	28,100 litres
Total price:	£51,704

Because of fire risk and the danger to health, no inventories are held by the business.

UK194 is used solely in the manufacture of a product called Varnelyne. The standard cost specification shows that, for the production of 5,000 litres of Varnelyne, 200 litres of UK194 are needed at a total standard cost of £392. During period six, 637,500 litres of Varnelyne were produced.

Price variances, over recent periods, for two other raw materials used by the business are:

Period	*UK500*		*UK800*	
	£		£	
1	301	F	298	F
2	251	A	203	F
3	102	F	52	A
4	202	A	98	A
5	153	F	150	A
6	103	A	201	A

where F = favourable variance and A = adverse variance.

Required:

(a) Calculate the price and usage variances for UK194 for period six.

(b) The following comment was made by the production manager:

'I knew at the beginning of period six that UK194 would be cheaper than the standard cost specification, so I used rather more of it than normal; this saved £4,900 on other chemicals.' What changes do you need to make in your analysis for (a) as a result of this comment?

(c) Calculate, for both UK500 and UK800, the cumulative price variances and comment briefly on the results.

Chapter 8

MAKING CAPITAL INVESTMENT DECISIONS

INTRODUCTION

This chapter looks at how businesses should assess proposed investments in new plant, machinery, buildings and other long-term assets. This is a very important area; expensive and far-reaching consequences can flow from bad investment decisions.

We shall also consider the problem of risk and how this may be taken into account when evaluating investment proposals. Finally, we shall discuss the ways that managers can oversee capital investment projects and how control may be exercised throughout the life of a project.

Learning outcomes

When you have completed this chapter, you should be able to:

- Explain the nature and importance of investment decision making.
- Identify the four main investment appraisal methods found in practice.
- Discuss the strengths and weaknesses of various techniques for dealing with risk in investment appraisal.
- Explain the methods used to monitor and control investment projects.

THE NATURE OF INVESTMENT DECISIONS

The essential feature of investment decisions is *time*. Investment involves making an outlay of something of economic value, usually cash, at one point in time, which is expected to yield economic benefits to the investor at some other point in time. Usually, the outlay precedes the benefits. Furthermore, the outlay is typically a single large amount while the benefits arrive as a series of smaller amounts over a fairly protracted period.

Investment decisions tend to be of profound importance to the business because:

- *Large amounts of resources are often involved*. Many investments made by businesses involve laying out a significant proportion of their total resources (see Real World 8.2). If mistakes are made with the decision, the effects on the businesses could be significant, if not catastrophic.
- *It is often difficult and/or expensive to bail out of an investment once it has been undertaken*. Investments made by businesses are often specific to their needs. A hotel business, for example, may invest in a new, custom-designed hotel complex. If the business found, after having made the investment, that room occupancy rates were too low, the only course of action might be to sell the complex. The specialist nature of the complex may, however, lead to it having a rather limited resale value. This could mean that the amount recouped from the investment is much less than it had originally cost.

Real World 8.1 gives an illustration of a major investment by a well-known business operating in the UK.

Real World 8.1

Brittany Ferries launches an investment

Brittany Ferries, the cross-Channel ferry operator, is having an additional ship built. The ship is costing the business £225 million and will be used on the Portsmouth to Santander route from 2017. Although Brittany Ferries is a substantial business, this level of expenditure is significant. Clearly, the business believes that acquiring the new ship will be profitable for it, but how would it have reached this conclusion? Presumably the anticipated future benefits from carrying passengers and freight will have been major inputs to the decision.

Source: www.brittany-ferries.co.uk.

The issues raised by Brittany Ferries' investment will be the main subject of this chapter.

Real World 8.2 indicates the level of annual net investment for a number of randomly selected, well-known UK businesses. We can see that the scale of investment varies from one business to another. (It also tends to vary from one year to another for a particular business.) In nearly all of these businesses the scale of investment was significant, despite the fact that many businesses were cutting back on investment during the economic recession.

Real World 8.2

The scale of investment by UK businesses

	Expenditure on additional non-current assets as a percentage of:	
	Annual sales revenue	*End-of-year non-current assets*
British Sky Broadcasting plc (television)	9.0	17.8
Ryanair Holdings plc (airline)	6.4	6.0
Go-Ahead Group plc (transport)	2.3	10.6
J D Wetherspoon (pub operator)	7.9	10.2
Marks and Spencer plc (stores)	8.3	13.2
Severn Trent Water Ltd (water and sewerage)	24.4	6.3
Vodafone plc (telecommunications)	32.4	12.0
Wm Morrison Supermarkets plc (supermarkets)	5.6	11.1

Sources: Annual reports of the businesses concerned for the financial year ending in 2013.

Real World 8.2 considers only expenditure on non-current assets, but this type of investment often requires a significant outlay on current assets to support it (additional inventories, for example). This suggests that the real scale of investment is even greater than indicated above.

Activity 8.1

When managers are making decisions involving capital investments, what should they seek to achieve with the decision?

Investment decisions must be consistent with the objectives of the particular organisation. For a private sector business, maximising the wealth of the owners (shareholders) is normally assumed to be the key financial objective.

INVESTMENT APPRAISAL METHODS

Given the importance of investment decisions, it is essential that proper screening of investment proposals takes place. An important part of this screening process is to ensure that appropriate methods of evaluation are used.

Research shows that there are basically four methods used by businesses to evaluate investment opportunities. They are:

- accounting rate of return (ARR),
- payback period (PP),
- net present value (NPV), and
- internal rate of return (IRR).

It is possible to find businesses that use variants of these four methods. It is also possible to find businesses, particularly smaller ones, that do not use any formal appraisal method but rely instead on the 'gut feeling' of their managers. Most businesses, however, seem to use one (or more) of these four methods. All four of the methods are fairly widely used, as we shall see later in the chapter.

We are going to assess the effectiveness of each of these methods, but we shall see that only one of them (NPV) is a wholly logical approach. The other three all have flaws. To help in examining each of the methods, it might be useful to see how each of them would cope with a particular investment opportunity. Let us consider the following example.

Example 8.1

Billingsgate Battery Company has carried out some research that shows there to be a market for a standard service that it has recently developed.

Provision of the service would require investment in a machine that would cost £100,000, payable immediately. Sales of the service would take place throughout the next five years. At the end of that time, it is estimated that the machine could be sold for £20,000.

Inflows and outflows from sales of the service would be expected to be:

Time		*£000*
Immediately	Cost of machine	(100)
1 year's time	Operating profit before depreciation	20
2 years' time	Operating profit before depreciation	40
3 years' time	Operating profit before depreciation	60
4 years' time	Operating profit before depreciation	60
5 years' time	Operating profit before depreciation	20
5 years' time	Disposal proceeds from the machine	20

Note that, broadly speaking, the operating profit before deducting depreciation (that is, before non-cash items) equals the net amount of cash flowing into the business. Broadly, apart from depreciation, all of this business's expenses cause cash to flow out of the business. Sales revenues tend to lead to cash flowing in. Expenses tend to lead to it flowing out. For the time being, we shall assume that working capital – which is made up of inventories, trade receivables and trade payables – remains constant. This means that operating profit before depreciation will tend to equal the net cash inflow.

To simplify matters, we shall assume that the cash from sales and for the expenses of providing the service are received and paid, respectively, at the end of each year. This is clearly unlikely to be true in real life. Money will have to be paid to employees (for salaries and wages) on a weekly or a monthly basis. Customers will pay within a month or two of buying the service. On the other hand, making the assumption probably does not lead to a serious distortion. It is a simplifying assumption, that is often made in real life, and it will make things more straightforward for us now. We should be clear, however, that there is nothing about any of the four methods that *demands* that this assumption is made.

Having set up the example, we shall now go on to consider how each of the appraisal methods works.

ACCOUNTING RATE OF RETURN (ARR)

The first of the four methods that we shall consider is the **accounting rate of return (ARR)**. This method takes the average accounting operating profit that the investment will generate and expresses it as a percentage of the average investment made over the life of the project. In other words:

$$\text{ARR} = \frac{\textbf{Average annual operating profit}}{\textbf{Average investment to earn that profit}} \times 100\%$$

We can see from the equation that, to calculate the ARR, we need to deduce two pieces of information about the particular project:

- the annual average operating profit; and
- the average investment.

In our example, the average annual operating profit *before depreciation* over the five years is £40,000 (that is, £000(20 + 40 + 60 + 60 + 20)/5). Assuming 'straight-line' depreciation (that is, equal annual amounts), the annual depreciation charge will be £16,000 (that is, £(100,000 − 20,000)/5). Therefore, the average annual operating profit *after depreciation* is £24,000 (that is, £40,000 − £16,000).

The average investment over the five years can be calculated as follows:

$$\text{Average investment} = \frac{\text{Cost of machine} + \text{Disposal value*}}{2}$$

$$= \frac{£100{,}000 + 20{,}000}{2}$$

$$= £60{,}000$$

*Note: To find the average investment we are simply adding the value of the amount invested at the beginning and end of the investment period together and dividing by two.

The ARR of the investment, therefore, is:

$$\text{ARR} = \frac{£24{,}000}{£60{,}000} \times 100\% = 40\%$$

The following decision rules apply when using ARR:

- For any project to be acceptable, it must achieve a target ARR as a minimum.
- Where there are competing projects that all seem capable of exceeding this minimum rate (that is, where the business must choose between more than one project), the one with the higher (or highest) ARR should be selected.

To decide whether the 40 per cent return is acceptable, we need to compare this percentage return with the minimum rate required by the business.

Activity 8.2

Chaotic Industries is considering an investment in a fleet of ten delivery vans to take its products to customers. The vans will cost £15,000 each to buy, payable immediately. The annual running costs are expected to total £50,000 for each van (including the driver's salary). The vans are expected to operate successfully for six years, at the end of which period they will all have to be sold, with disposal proceeds expected to be about £3,000 a van. At present, the business outsources transport, for all of its deliveries, to a commercial carrier. It is expected that this carrier will charge a total of £530,000 each year for the next six years to undertake the deliveries.

What is the ARR of buying the vans? (Note that cost savings are as relevant a benefit from an investment as are net cash inflows.)

The vans will save the business £30,000 a year (that is, £530,000 – (£50,000 × 10)), before depreciation, in total. Therefore, the inflows and outflows will be:

Time		*000*
Immediately	Cost of vans (10 × £15,000)	(150)
1 year's time	Saving before depreciation	30
2 years' time	Saving before depreciation	30
3 years' time	Saving before depreciation	30
4 years' time	Saving before depreciation	30
5 years' time	Saving before depreciation	30
6 years' time	Saving before depreciation	30
6 years' time	Disposal proceeds from the vans (10 × £3,000)	30

The total annual depreciation expense (assuming a straight-line method) will be £20,000 (that is, (£150,000 – £30,000)/6). Therefore, the average annual saving, *after depreciation*, is £10,000 (that is, £30,000 – £20,000).

The average investment will be

$$\text{Average investment} = \frac{£150{,}000 + £30{,}000}{2}$$

$$= £90{,}000$$

and the ARR of the investment is

$$\text{ARR} = \frac{£10{,}000}{£90{,}000} \times 100\%$$

$$= 11.1\%$$

ARR and ROCE

In essence, ARR and the return on capital employed (ROCE) ratio take the same approach to measuring business performance. Both relate operating profit to the cost of assets used to generate that profit. ROCE, however, assesses the performance of the entire business *after* it has performed, while ARR assesses the potential performance of a particular investment *before* it has performed.

We saw that investments are required to achieve a minimum target ARR. Given the link between ARR and ROCE, this target could be based on overall rates of returns previously achieved – as measured by ROCE. It could also be based on the industry-average ROCE.

The link between ARR and ROCE strengthens the case for adopting ARR as the appropriate method of investment appraisal. ROCE is a widely-used measure of profitability and some businesses express their financial objective in terms of a target ROCE. It seems sensible, therefore, to use a method of investment appraisal that is consistent with this overall measure of business performance. A secondary point in favour of ARR is that it provides a result expressed in percentage terms, which many managers seem to prefer.

Problems with ARR

Activity 8.3

ARR suffers from a major defect as a means of assessing investment opportunities. Can you reason out what this is? Consider the three competing projects whose profits are shown below. All three involve investment in a machine that is expected to have no residual value at the end of the five years. Note that all of the projects have the same total operating profits after depreciation over the five years.

Time		*Project A* £000	*Project B* £000	*Project C* £000
Immediately	Cost of machine	(160)	(160)	(160)
1 year's time	Operating profit after depreciation	20	10	160
2 years' time	Operating profit after depreciation	40	10	10
3 years' time	Operating profit after depreciation	60	10	10
4 years' time	Operating profit after depreciation	60	10	10
5 years' time	Operating profit after depreciation	20	160	10

(*Hint*: The defect is not concerned with the ability of the decision maker to forecast future events, though this too can be a problem. Try to remember the essential feature of investment decisions, which we identified at the beginning of this chapter.)

The problem with ARR is that it ignores the time factor. In this example, exactly the same ARR would have been computed for each of the three projects.

Since the same total operating profit over the five years (£200,000) arises in all three of these projects, and the average investment in each project is £80,000 (that is, £160,000/2), each project will give rise to the same ARR of 50 per cent (that is, £40,000/£80,000).

To maximise the wealth of the owners, a manager faced with a choice between the three projects set out in Activity 8.3 should select Project C. This is because most of the benefits arise within twelve months of making the initial investment. Project A would rank second and Project B would come a poor third. Any appraisal technique that is not capable of distinguishing between these three situations is seriously flawed. We shall look at why timing is so important later in the chapter.

There are further problems associated with the ARR method, which we shall now discuss.

Use of average investment

Using the average investment in calculating ARR can lead to daft results. Example 8.2 illustrates the kind of problem that can arise.

Example 8.2

George put forward an investment proposal to his boss. The business uses ARR to assess investment proposals using a minimum 'hurdle' rate of 27 per cent. Details of the proposal were:

Cost of equipment	£200,000
Estimated residual value of equipment	£40,000
Average annual operating profit before depreciation	£48,000
Estimated life of project	10 years
Annual straight-line depreciation charge	£16,000 (that is, (£200,000 – £40,000)/10)

The ARR of the project will be:

$$\text{ARR} = \frac{48{,}000 - 16{,}000}{(200{,}000 + 40{,}000)/2} \times 100\% = 26.7\%$$

The boss rejected George's proposal because it failed to achieve an ARR of at least 27 per cent. Although George was disappointed, he realised that there was still hope. In fact, all that the business had to do was to give away the piece of equipment at the end of its useful life rather than sell it. The residual value of the equipment then became zero and the annual depreciation charge became ((£200,000 – £0)/10) = £20,000 a year. The revised ARR calculation was then:

$$\text{ARR} = \frac{48{,}000 - 20{,}000}{(200{,}000 + 0)/2} \times 100\% = 28\%$$

Use of accounting profit

We have seen that ARR is based on accounting profit. When measuring performance over the whole life of a project, however, it is cash flows rather than accounting profits that are important. Cash is the ultimate measure of the economic wealth generated by an investment. This is because it is cash that is used to acquire resources and for distribution to owners. Accounting profit is more appropriate for reporting achievement on a periodic basis. It is a useful measure of productive effort for a relatively short period, such as a year or half year. It is really a question of 'horses for courses'. Accounting profit is extrememly useful for measuring performance over a short period but cash is the appropriate measure when considering performance over the life of a project.

Competing investments

The ARR method can create problems when considering competing investments of different size. Consider Activity 8.4.

Activity 8.4

Sinclair Wholesalers plc is currently considering opening a new sales outlet in Coventry. Two possible sites have been identified for the new outlet. Site A has an area of 30,000 square metres. It will require an average investment of £6 million and will produce an average operating profit of £600,000 a year. Site B has an area of 20,000 square metres. It will require an average investment of £4 million and will produce an average operating profit of £500,000 a year.

What is the ARR of each investment opportunity? Which site would you select and why?

The ARR of Site A is £600,000/£6m = 10 per cent. The ARR of Site B is £500,000/£4m = 12.5 per cent. Site B, therefore has the higher ARR. In terms of the absolute operating profit generated, however, Site A is the more attractive. If the ultimate objective is to increase the wealth of the shareholders of Sinclair Wholesalers plc, it would be better to choose Site A even though the percentage return is lower. It is the absolute size of the return rather than the relative (percentage) size that is important. This is a general problem of using comparative measures, such as percentages, when the objective is measured in absolute terms, like an amount of money.

Real World 8.3 illustrates how using percentage measures can lead to confusion.

Real World 8.3

Increasing road capacity by sleight of hand

During the 1970s, the Mexican government wanted to increase the capacity of a major four-lane road. It came up with the idea of repainting the lane markings so that there were six narrower lanes occupying the same space as four wider ones had previously done. This increased the capacity of the road by 50 per cent (that is, $^2/_4 \times 100$). A tragic outcome of the narrower lanes was an increase in deaths from road accidents. A year later the Mexican government had the six narrower lanes changed back to the original four wider ones. This reduced the capacity of the road by 33 per cent (that is, $^2/_6 \times 100$). The Mexican government reported that, overall, it had increased the capacity of the road by 17 per cent (that is, 50% − 33%), despite the fact that its real capacity was identical to that which it had been originally. The confusion arose because each of the two percentages (50 per cent and 33 per cent) is based on different bases (four and six).

Source: Gigerenzer, G. (2002) *Reckoning with Risk*, Penguin.

PAYBACK PERIOD (PP)

Another approach to appraising possible investments is the **payback period (PP)**. This is the time taken for an initial investment to be repaid out of the net cash inflows from a project. As the PP method takes time into account and it deals with cash, rather than accounting profit, it appears, at first glance, to overcome two key weaknesses of the ARR method.

Let us consider PP in the context of the Billingsgate Battery example (see Example 8.1). We should recall that the project's cash flows are:

Time		*£000*
Immediately	Cost of machine	(100)
1 year's time	Operating profit before depreciation	20
2 years' time	Operating profit before depreciation	40
3 years' time	Operating profit before depreciation	60
4 years' time	Operating profit before depreciation	60
5 years' time	Operating profit before depreciation	20
5 years' time	Disposal proceeds	20

Note that all of these figures are amounts of cash to be paid or received (we saw earlier that operating profit before depreciation is a rough measure of the cash flows from the project).

We can see that this investment will take three years before the £100,000 outlay is covered by the inflows. (This is still assuming that the cash flows occur at year ends.) Derivation of the payback period can be shown by calculating the cumulative cash flows as follows:

Time		*Net cash flows £000*	*Cumulative cash flows £000*	
Immediately	Cost of machine	(100)	(100)	
1 year's time	Operating profit before depreciation	20	(80)	(–100 + 20)
2 years' time	Operating profit before depreciation	40	(40)	(–80 + 40)
3 years' time	Operating profit before depreciation	60	20	(–40 + 60)
4 years' time	Operating profit before depreciation	60	80	(20 + 60)
5 years' time	Operating profit before depreciation	20	100	(80 + 20)
5 years' time	Disposal proceeds	20	120	(100 + 20)

We can see that the cumulative cash flows become positive at the end of the third year. Had we assumed that the cash flows arise evenly over the year, the precise payback period would be:

$$2 \text{ years} + (^{40}/_{60}) \text{ years} = 2^2/_3 \text{ years}$$

where 40 represents the cash flow still required at the beginning of the third year to repay the initial outlay and 60 is the projected cash flow during the third year.

The following decision rules apply when using PP:

- For a project to be acceptable it should have a payback period no longer than a maximum payback period set by the business.
- If there were two (or more) competing projects whose payback periods were all shorter than the maximum payback period requirement, the project with the shorter (or shortest) payback period should be selected.

If, for example, Billingsgate Battery had a maximum acceptable payback period of four years, the project would be undertaken. A project with a longer payback period would not be acceptable.

Activity 8.5

What is the payback period of the Chaotic Industries project from Activity 8.2?

The inflows and outflows are expected to be:

Time		*Net cash flows £000*	*Cumulative net cash flows £000*	
Immediately	Cost of vans	(150)	(150)	
1 year's time	Saving before depreciation	30	(120)	(−150 + 30)
2 years' time	Saving before depreciation	30	(90)	(−120 + 30)
3 years' time	Saving before depreciation	30	(60)	(−90 + 30)
4 years' time	Saving before depreciation	30	(30)	(−60 + 30)
5 years' time	Saving before depreciation	30	0	(−30 + 30)
6 years' time	Saving before depreciation	30	30	(0 + 30)
6 years' time	Disposal proceeds from the vans	30	60	(30 + 30)

The payback period here is five years; that is, it is not until the end of the fifth year that the vans will pay for themselves out of the savings that they are expected to generate.

The logic of using PP is that projects that can recoup their cost quickly are economically more attractive than those with longer payback periods. In other words, it emphasises liquidity.

The PP method has certain advantages. It is quick and easy to calculate. Also, it can easily be understood by managers. PP is an improvement on ARR in respect of timing and of the use of cash flows (rather than accounting flows). It is not, however, a complete answer to the problem.

Problems with PP

Activity 8.6

In what respect is PP not a complete answer as a means of assessing investment opportunities? Consider the cash flows arising from three competing projects:

Time		*Project 1 £000*	*Project 2 £000*	*Project 3 £000*
Immediately	Cost of machine	(200)	(200)	(200)
1 year's time	Operating profit before depreciation	70	20	70
2 years' time	Operating profit before depreciation	60	20	100
3 years' time	Operating profit before depreciation	70	160	30
4 years' time	Operating profit before depreciation	80	30	200
5 years' time	Operating profit before depreciation	50	20	440
5 years' time	Disposal proceeds	40	10	20

(*Hint*: Again, the defect is not concerned with the ability of the manager to forecast future events. This is a problem, but it is a problem whatever approach we take.)

→

The PP for each project is three years and so the PP method would regard the projects as being equally acceptable. It cannot distinguish between those projects that pay back a significant amount early within the three-year payback period and those that do not.

In addition, this method ignores cash flows after the payback period. A decision maker concerned with increasing owners' wealth would greatly prefer Project 3 because the cash inflows are received earlier. In fact, most of the initial cost of making the investment has been repaid by the end of the second year. Furthermore, the cash inflows are greater in total.

The cumulative cash flows of each project in Activity 8.6 are set out in Figure 8.1.

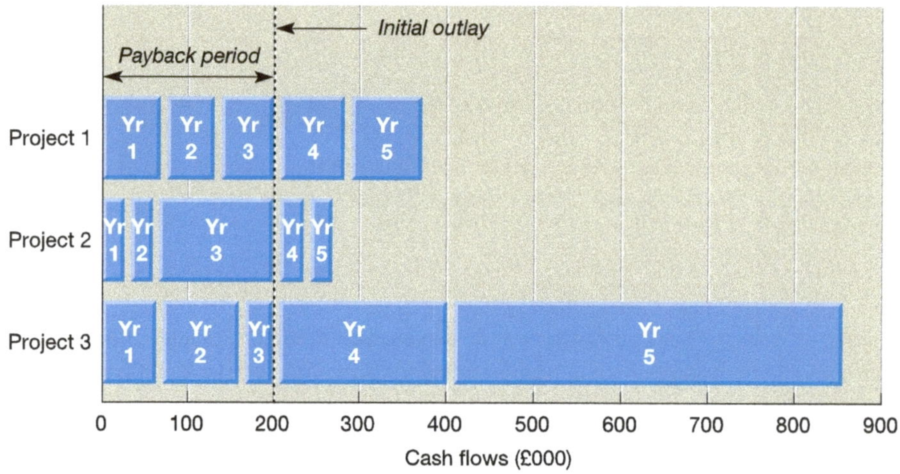

The payback method of investment appraisal would view Projects 1, 2 and 3 as being equally attractive. In doing so, the method completely ignores the fact that Project 3 provides most of the payback cash earlier in the three-year period and goes on to generate large benefits in later years.

Figure 8.1 The cumulative cash flows of each project in Activity 8.6

We shall now consider some additional points concerning the PP method.

Relevant information

We saw earlier that the PP method is simply concerned with how quickly the initial investment can be recouped. Cash flows arising beyond the payback period are ignored. While this neatly avoids the practical problems of forecasting cash flows over a long period, it means that not all relevant information may be taken into account.

Risk

By favouring projects with a short payback period, the PP method appears to provide a means of dealing with the problem of risk. This is, however, a fairly crude approach to assessing risk. It looks only at the risk that the project will end earlier than expected. This is only one of many risk areas. What, for example, about the risk that the demand for the product may be less than expected? There are more systematic approaches to dealing with risk that can be used, which we shall look at later in the chapter.

Wealth maximisation

Although the PP method takes some note of the timing of project costs and benefits, it is not concerned with maximising the wealth of the business owners. Instead, it favours projects that pay for themselves quickly.

Required payback period

Managers must select a maximum acceptable payback period. As this cannot be objectively determined, it is really a matter of judgement. The maximum period can, therefore, vary from one business to the next.

Real World 8.4 explains that the well-known fashion and household retailer Next plc uses the payback period approach to assessing the opening of new stores. It also seems to use ARR.

Real World 8.4

The Next investment

Next plc has identified 'five core operational objectives'. One of these is to 'Invest in profitable new space' (stores and so on). More specifically it plans to:

> **Open profitable new retail space, maintaining the Company's strict payback and profitability hurdles of 15% net store profit (before central overheads) and payback on net capital invested in 24 months.**

Later in the annual report, Next says that new space opened during the year ended on 26 January 2013 is expected to achieve a profitability of 23 per cent and a payback period of 23 months.

Source: Next plc Annual Report 2013, pp. 5 and 7.

NET PRESENT VALUE (NPV)

From what we have seen so far, it seems that to make sensible investment decisions, we need a method of appraisal that both:

- considers *all* of the costs and benefits of each investment opportunity; and
- makes a logical allowance for the *timing* of those costs and benefits.

The **net present value (NPV)** method of investment appraisal provides us with this.

Consider the Billingsgate Battery example's cash flows, which we should recall are:

Time		*£000*
Immediately	Cost of machine	(100)
1 year's time	Operating profit before depreciation	20
2 years' time	Operating profit before depreciation	40
3 years' time	Operating profit before depreciation	60
4 years' time	Operating profit before depreciation	60
5 years' time	Operating profit before depreciation	20
5 years' time	Disposal proceeds	20

Given a financial objective of maximising owners' wealth, it would be easy to assess this investment if all cash inflows and outflows were to occur immediately. It would then simply be a matter of adding up the cash inflows (total £220,000) and comparing them with the cash outflows (£100,000). This would lead us to conclude that the project should go ahead because the owners would be better off by £120,000. Of course, it is not as easy as this because time is involved. The cash outflow will occur immediately, whereas the cash inflows will arise at different times.

Time is an important issue because people do not normally see an amount paid out now as equivalent in value to the same amount being received in a year's time. Therefore, if we were offered £100 in one year's time in exchange for paying out £100 now, we would not be interested, unless we wished to do someone a favour.

Activity 8.7

Why would you see £100 to be received in a year's time as not equal in value to £100 to be paid immediately? (There are basically three reasons.)

The reasons are:

- interest lost
- risk
- inflation.

We shall now take a closer look at these three reasons in turn.

Interest lost

If we are to be deprived of the opportunity to spend our money for a year, we could equally well be deprived of its use by placing it on deposit in a bank or building society. By doing this, we could have our money back at the end of the year along with some interest earned. This interest, which is forgone if we do not place our money on deposit, represents an *opportunity cost*. As we saw in Chapter 2, an opportunity cost occurs where one course of action deprives us of the opportunity to derive some benefit from an alternative action.

An investment must exceed the opportunity cost of the funds invested if it is to be worthwhile. Therefore, if Billingsgate Battery Company sees putting the money in the bank on deposit as the alternative to investment in the machine, the return from investing in the machine must be better than that from investing in the bank. If this is not the case, there is no reason to buy the machine.

Risk

All investments expose their investors to **risk**. Hence buying a machine, on the strength of estimates made before its purchase, exposes a business to risk. Things may not turn out as expected.

Activity 8.8

Can you suggest some areas where things could go other than according to plan in the Billingsgate Battery Company example (basically, buying a machine and using it to render a service for five years)?

We have come up with the following:

- The machine might not work as well as expected; it might break down, leading to loss of the business's ability to provide the service.
- Sales of the service may not be as buoyant as expected.
- Labour costs may prove to be higher than expected.
- The sale proceeds of the machine could prove to be less than were estimated.

It is important to remember that the purchase decision must be taken *before* any of these things are known. It is only after the machine has been purchased that we find out whether, say, the forecast level of sales is going to be achieved. We can study reports and analyses of the market. We can commission sophisticated market surveys and advertise widely to promote sales. All these may give us more confidence in the likely outcome. Ultimately, however, we must decide whether to accept the risk that things will not turn out as expected in exchange for the opportunity to generate wealth.

We saw in Chapter 1 that people normally expect greater returns in exchange for taking on greater risk. Examples of this in real life are not difficult to find. One such example is that banks tend to charge higher rates of interest to borrowers whom the bank perceives as more risky. Those who can offer good security for a loan and who can point to a regular source of income, tend to be charged lower rates of interest.

Going back to Billingsgate Battery Company's investment opportunity, it is not enough to say that we should buy the machine providing the expected returns are higher than those from investing in a bank deposit. We should expect much greater returns than the bank deposit interest rate because of the much greater risk involved. The logical equivalent of investing in the machine would be an investment that is of similar risk. Determining how risky a particular project is and, therefore, how large the **risk premium** should be, is a difficult task. We shall consider this in more detail later in the chapter.

Inflation

If we are to be deprived of £100 for a year, when we come to spend that money it will not buy the same amount of goods and services as it would have done a year earlier. Generally, we shall not be able to buy as many tins of baked beans or loaves of bread or bus tickets as before. This is because of the loss in the purchasing power of money, or **inflation**, which tends to occur over time. Investors will expect to be compensated for this loss of purchasing power. This will be on top of a return that takes account of what could be gained from an alternative investment of similar risk.

In practice, interest rates observable in the market tend to take inflation into account. This means that rates offered to building society and bank depositors normally include an allowance for the expected rate of inflation.

What will logical investors do?

To summarise, logical investors seeking to increase their wealth will only invest when they believe they will be adequately compensated for the loss of interest, for the loss in the purchasing power of money invested and for the risk that the expected returns may not materialise. This normally involves checking to see whether the proposed investment will yield a return greater than the basic rate of interest (which will normally include an allowance for inflation) plus an appropriate risk premium.

These three factors (interest lost, risk and inflation) are set out in Figure 8.2.

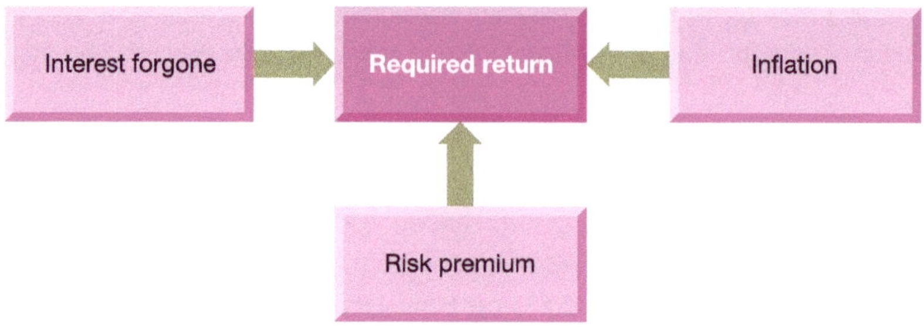

There are three factors that influence the required return to investors (opportunity cost of finance).

Figure 8.2 Factors influencing the return required by investors from a project

Let us now return to the Billingsgate Battery Company example. We should recall that the cash flows expected from this investment are:

Time		*£000*
Immediately	Cost of machine	(100)
1 year's time	Operating profit before depreciation	20
2 years' time	Operating profit before depreciation	40
3 years' time	Operating profit before depreciation	60
4 years' time	Operating profit before depreciation	60
5 years' time	Operating profit before depreciation	20
5 years' time	Disposal proceeds	20

We have already seen that it is not enough simply to compare the basic cash inflows and outflows for the investment. Each of these cash flows must be expressed in similar terms, so that a direct comparison can be made between the sum of the inflows over time and the immediate £100,000 investment. Fortunately, we can do this.

Let us assume that, instead of making this investment, the business could make an alternative investment with similar risk and obtain a return of 20 per cent a year.

Activity 8.9

We know that Billingsgate Battery Company could alternatively invest its money at a rate of 20 per cent a year. How much do you judge the present (immediate) value of the expected first year receipt of £20,000 to be? In other words, if instead of having to wait a year for the £20,000, and being deprived of the opportunity to invest it at 20 per cent, you could have some money now, what sum to be received now would you regard as exactly equivalent to getting £20,000 but having to wait a year for it?

We should obviously be happy to accept a lower amount if we could get it immediately than if we had to wait a year. This is because we could invest it at 20 per cent (in the alternative project). Logically, we should be prepared to accept the amount that, with a year's income, will grow to £20,000. If we call this amount PV (for present value) we can say:

$$PV + (PV \times 20\%) = £20,000$$

– that is, the amount plus income from investing the amount for the year equals the £20,000.

If we rearrange this equation we find:

$$PV \times (1 + 0.2) = £20,000$$

(Note that 0.2 is the same as 20 per cent, but expressed as a decimal.) Further rearranging gives:

$$PV = £20,000/(1 + 0.2) = £16,667$$

Therefore, logical investors who have the opportunity to invest at 20 per cent a year would not mind whether they have £16,667 now or £20,000 in a year's time. In this sense we can say that, given a 20 per cent alternative investment opportunity, the present value of £20,000 to be received in one year's time is £16,667.

If we derive the present value (PV) of each of the cash flows associated with Billingsgate's machine investment, we could easily make the direct comparison between the cost of making the investment (£100,000) and the various benefits that will derive from it during years 1 to 5.

Using the same logic as was used to derive the PV of a cash flow expected after one year, it can be shown that:

PV of the cash flow of year n = actual cash flow of year n divided by $(1 + r)^n$

where n is the year of the cash flow (that is, how many years into the future) and r is the opportunity financing cost expressed as a decimal (instead of as a percentage).

We have already seen how this works for the £20,000 inflow for year 1 for the Billingsgate project. For year 2 the calculation would be:

$$\text{PV of year 2 cash flow (that is, £40,000)} = £40,000/(1 + 0.2)^2 = £40,000/(1.2)^2$$
$$= £40,000/1.44 = £27,778$$

This means that the present value of the £40,000 to be received in two years' time is £27,778.

Activity 8.10

See if you can show that an investor would find £27,778, receivable now, as equally acceptable to receiving £40,000 in two years' time, assuming that there is a 20 per cent investment opportunity.

The reasoning goes like this:

	£
Amount available for immediate investment	27,778
Income for year 1 (20% × 27,778)	5,556
	33,334
Income for year 2 (20% × 33,334)	6,667
	40,001

(The extra £1 is only a rounding error.)

This is to say that since the investor can turn £27,778 into £40,000 in two years, these amounts are equivalent. We can say that £27,778 is the present value of £40,000 receivable after two years (given a 20 per cent cost of finance).

Now let us calculate the present values of all of the cash flows associated with the Billingsgate machine project and, from them, the *net present value (NPV)* of the project as a whole.

The relevant cash flows and calculations are:

Time	*Cash flow* £000	*Calculation of PV*	*PV* £000
Immediately (time 0)	(100)	$(100)/(1 + 0.2)^0$	(100.00)
1 year's time	20	$20/(1 + 0.2)^1$	16.67
2 years' time	40	$40/(1 + 0.2)^2$	27.78
3 years' time	60	$60/(1 + 0.2)^3$	34.72
4 years' time	60	$60/(1 + 0.2)^4$	28.94
5 years' time	20	$20/(1 + 0.2)^5$	8.04
5 years' time	20	$20/(1 + 0.2)^5$	8.04
Net present value (NPV)			24.19

Note that $(1 + 0.2)^0 = 1$.

Once again, we must decide whether the machine project is acceptable to the business. To help us, the following decision rules for NPV should be applied:

- If the NPV is positive the project should be accepted; if it is negative the project should be rejected.
- If there are two (or more) competing projects that have positive NPVs, the project with the higher (or highest) NPV should be selected.

In this case, the NPV is positive, so we should accept the project and buy the machine. The reasoning behind this decision rule is quite straightforward. Investing in the machine will make the business, and its owners, £24,190 better off than they would be by taking up the next best available opportunity. The total benefits from investing in this machine are worth a total of £124,190 today. Since the business can 'buy' these benefits for just £100,000 today, the investment should be made. If, however, the present value of the benefits were below £100,000, it would be less than the cost of 'buying' those benefits and the opportunity should, therefore, be rejected.

Activity 8.11

What is the *maximum* the Billingsgate Battery Company should be prepared to pay for the machine, given the potential benefits of owning it?

The business would logically be prepared to pay up to £124,190 since the wealth of the owners of the business would be increased up to this price – although the business would prefer to pay as little as possible.

Using present value tables

To deduce each PV in the Billingsgate Battery Company project, we took the relevant cash flow and multiplied it by $1/(1 + r)^n$. There is a slightly different way to do this. Tables exist that show values of this **discount factor** for a range of values of *r* and *n*. Such a table appears in Appendix E on page 539. Take a look at it.

Look at the column for 20 per cent and the row for one year. We find that the factor is 0.833. This means that the PV of a cash flow of £1 receivable in one year is £0.833. So the present value of a cash flow of £20,000 receivable in one year's time is £16,660 (that is, 0.833 × £20,000). This is the same result, ignoring rounding errors, as we found earlier by using the equation.

Activity 8.12

What is the NPV of the Chaotic Industries project from Activity 8.2, assuming a 15 per cent opportunity cost of finance (discount rate)? (Use the present value table in Appendix E, page 539.)

Remember that the inflows and outflow are expected to be:

Time		*£000*
Immediately	Cost of vans	(150)
1 year's time	Saving before depreciation	30
2 years' time	Saving before depreciation	30
3 years' time	Saving before depreciation	30
4 years' time	Saving before depreciation	30
5 years' time	Saving before depreciation	30
6 years' time	Saving before depreciation	30
6 years' time	Disposal proceeds from the vans	30

The calculation of the NPV of the project is as follows:

Time	*Cash flows* *£000*	*Discount factor* *(15%)*	*Present value* *£000*
Immediately	(150)	1.000	(150.00)
1 year's time	30	0.870	26.10
2 years' time	30	0.756	22.68
3 years' time	30	0.658	19.74
4 years' time	30	0.572	17.16
5 years' time	30	0.497	14.91
6 years' time	30	0.432	12.96
6 years' time	30	0.`432	12.96
			NPV (23.49)

Activity 8.13

How would you interpret this result?

The fact that the project has a negative NPV means that the present values of the benefits from the investment are worth less than they cost. Any cost up to £126,510 (the present value of the benefits) would be worth paying, but not £150,000.

The present value table in Appendix E shows how the value of £1 diminishes as its receipt goes further into the future. Assuming an opportunity cost of finance of 20 per cent a year, £1 to be received immediately, obviously, has a present value of £1. However, as the time before it is to be received increases, the present value diminishes significantly, as is shown in Figure 8.3.

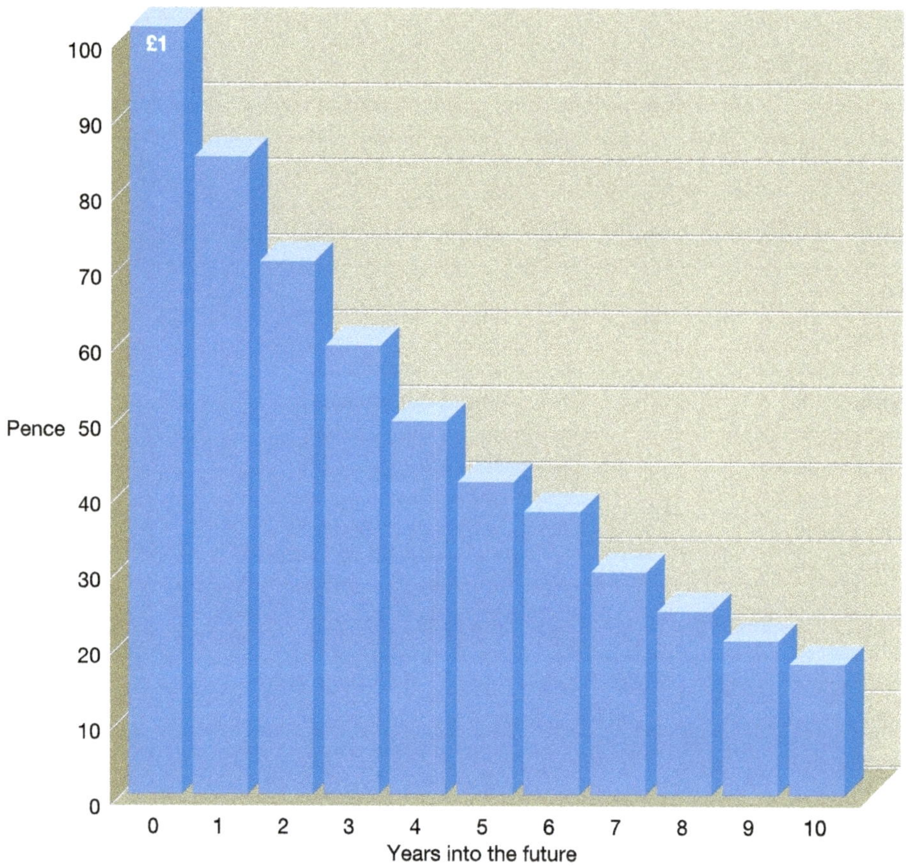

The present value of a future receipt (or payment) of £1 depends on how far in the future it will occur. Those that occur in the near future will have a larger present value than those occurring at a more distant point in time.

Figure 8.3 Present value of £1 receivable at various times in the future, assuming an annual financing cost of 20 per cent

The discount rate and the cost of capital

We have seen that the appropriate discount rate to use in NPV assessments is the opportunity cost of finance. This is, in effect, the cost to the business of the finance needed to fund the investment, given its level of risk and so on. It will normally be the cost of a mixture of funds (shareholders' funds and borrowings) employed by the business and is often referred to as the **cost of capital**. We shall refer to it as cost of capital from now on.

WHY NPV IS BETTER

From what we have seen, NPV offers a better approach to appraising investment opportunities than either ARR or PP. This is because it fully takes account of each of the following:

- *The timing of the cash flows.* By discounting the various cash flows associated with each project according to when they are expected to arise, NPV takes account of the time value of money. Furthermore, as the discounting process incorporates the opportunity cost of capital, the net benefit *after* financing costs have been met is identified (as the NPV of the project).
- *The whole of the relevant cash flows.* NPV includes *all* of the relevant cash flows. They are treated differently according to their date of occurrence, but they are all taken into account. In this way, they can all have an influence on the decision.
- *The objectives of the business.* NPV is the only method of appraisal in which the output of the analysis has a direct bearing on the wealth of the owners of the business. Positive NPVs enhance wealth; negative ones reduce it. Since we assume that private sector businesses seek to increase owners' wealth, NPV is superior to the other two methods (ARR and PP) that we have discussed so far.

NPV's wider application

NPV is the most logical approach to making business decisions about investments in productive assets. It also provides the basis for valuing any economic asset, that is, any asset capable of yielding financial benefits. This definition will include such things as equity shares and loans. In fact, when we talk of *economic value*, we mean the value derived by adding together the discounted (present) values of all future cash flows from the asset concerned.

Real World 8.5 describes a mining project where the NPV has been used to assess its financial viability.

Real World 8.5

Fully charged

The Fleur-El Sauz mining project in northern Mexico is being undertaken to produce lithium carbonate. This is an important industrial chemical that is used, among other things, for the production of battery cathodes. The project is 30 per cent owned by Rare Earth Minerals plc and 70 per cent owned by Bacanora Minerals Ltd. On 25 January 2013 it was announced that the net present value (NPV) of the mining project, at an 8% discount rate, is estimated to be $US848 million. The NPV calculation assumes an output of 35,000 tonnes of battery-grade lithium carbonate over a 20-year open pit life. It also assumes an average lithium carbonate price of $US6,000/tonne for the life of the mine.

Source: Based on information in www.rareearthmineralsplc.com, accessed 2 December 2013.

INTERNAL RATE OF RETURN (IRR)

This is the last of the four major methods of investment appraisal found in practice. It is closely related to the NPV method in that both involve discounting future cash flows. The **internal rate of return (IRR)** of an investment is the discount rate that, when applied to its future cash flows, will produce an NPV of precisely zero. In essence, it represents the yield from an investment opportunity.

Activity 8.14

We should recall that, when we discounted the cash flows of the Billingsgate Battery Company machine project at 20 per cent, we found that the NPV was a positive figure of £24,190 (see page 284). What does the NPV of the machine project tell us about the rate of return that the investment will yield for the business (that is, the project's IRR)?

The fact that the NPV is positive when discounting at 20 per cent implies that the rate of return that the project generates is more than 20 per cent. The fact that the NPV is a pretty large figure implies that the actual rate of return is quite a lot above 20 per cent. We should expect increasing the size of the discount rate to reduce NPV, because a higher discount rate gives a lower discounted figure.

IRR cannot usually be calculated directly. Iteration (trial and error) is the approach normally adopted. Doing this manually, however, is fairly laborious. Fortunately, computer spreadsheet packages can do this with ease.

Despite it being labourious, we shall now go on and derive the IRR for the Billingsgate project manually, to show how it works.

Let us try a higher rate, say 30 per cent, and see what happens.

Time	*Cash flow*	*Discount factor*	*PV*
	£000	*30%*	*£000*
Immediately (time 0)	(100)	1.000	(100.00)
1 year's time	20	0.769	15.38
2 years' time	40	0.592	23.68
3 years' time	60	0.455	27.30
4 years' time	60	0.350	21.00
5 years' time	20	0.269	5.38
5 years' time	20	0.269	5.38
			NPV (1.88)

By increasing the discount rate from 20 per cent to 30 per cent, we have reduced the NPV from £24,190 (positive) to £1,880 (negative). Since the IRR is the discount rate that will give us an NPV of exactly zero, we can conclude that the IRR of Billingsgate Battery Company's machine project is very slightly below 30 per cent. Further trials could lead us to the exact rate, but there is probably not much point, given the likely inaccuracy of the cash flow estimates. For most practical purposes, it is good enough to say that the IRR is about 30 per cent.

The relationship between the NPV and the IRR is shown graphically in Figure 8.4 using the information relating to the Billingsgate Battery Company.

In Figure 8.4, if the discount rate is equal to zero, the NPV will be the sum of the net cash flows. In other words, no account is taken of the time value of money. However, as the discount rate increases there is a corresponding decrease in the NPV of the project. When the NPV line crosses the horizontal axis there will be a zero NPV. That point represents the IRR.

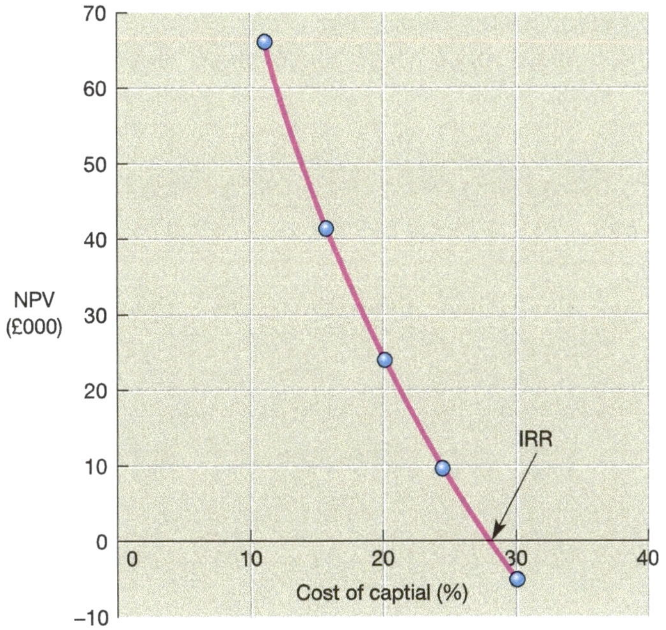

When the NPV line crosses the horizontal axis there will be a zero NPV. That point indicates the IRR.

Figure 8.4 The relationship between the NPV and IRR methods

Activity 8.15

What is the internal rate of return of the Chaotic Industries project from Activity 8.2?

(*Hint*: Remember that you already know the NPV of this project at 15 per cent (from Activity 8.12).)

Since we know that, at a 15 per cent discount rate, the NPV is a relatively large negative figure, our next trial should use a lower discount rate, say 10 per cent.

Time	*Cash flows £000*	*Discount factor (10% – from the table)*	*Present value £000*
Immediately	(150)	1.000	(150.00)
1 year's time	30	0.909	27.27
2 years' time	30	0.826	24.78
3 years' time	30	0.751	22.53
4 years' time	30	0.683	20.49
5 years' time	30	0.621	18.63
6 years' time	30	0.564	16.92
6 years' time	30	0.564	16.92
			NPV (2.46)

This figure is close to zero NPV. However, the NPV is still negative and so the precise IRR will be a little below 10 per cent.

We could undertake further trials to derive the precise IRR. If, however, we have to do this manually, further trials can be time-consuming.

We can get an acceptable approximation to the answer fairly quickly by first calculating the change in NPV arising from a 1 per cent change in the discount rate. This can be done by taking the difference between the two trials (that is, 15 per cent and 10 per cent) that have already been carried out (in Activities 8.12 and 8.15):

Trial	*Discount factor*	*Net present value*
	%	*£000*
1	15	(23.49)
2	10	(2.46)
Difference	5	21.03

The change in NPV for every 1 per cent change in the discount rate will be:

$$(21.03/5) = 4.21$$

The amount by which the IRR would need to fall below the 10% discount rate in order to achieve a zero NPV would therefore be:

$$(2.46/4.21) \times 1\% = 0.58\%$$

The IRR is therefore

$$(10.00 - 0.58) = 9.42\%$$

To say that the IRR is about 9 or 10 per cent, however, is near enough for most purposes.

Note that this approach to obtaining a more accurate figure for IRR assumes a straight-line relationship between the discount rate and NPV. We can see from Figure 8.4 that this assumption is not strictly correct. Over a relatively short range, however, this simplifying assumption is not usually a problem and so we can still arrive at a reasonable approximation using the approach that we took.

In practice, most businesses would use a computer spreadsheet, which will derive a project's IRR very quickly. In practice, therefore, it is not usually necessary either to make a series of trial discount rates manually or to make the approximation just described.

The following decision rules are applied when using IRR:

- For any project to be acceptable, it must meet a minimum IRR requirement. This is often referred to as the *hurdle rate* and, logically, this should be the opportunity cost of capital.
- Where there are competing projects, the one with the higher (or highest) IRR should be selected.

Real World 8.6 illustrates how IRR is used to assess the economic effectiveness of research and development activities of pharmaceutical development and manufacturing businesses.

Real World 8.6

IRR from R&D

For most of their history, pharmaceutical companies' core mission has consisted of developing new drugs to advance medical care. But over the past several years, drug companies' return at this central task has steadily declined, which has put pressure on them to reduce research and development funding, and enter partnerships that don't require the fixed costs of their own laboratories and employees.

The latest annual study of R&D productivity by Deloitte and Thomson Reuters found that the number of new drug approvals increased by around 30 per cent, yet the expected revenue from these medicines actually fell by a similar amount.

In total, the world's top 12 research-based pharmaceutical companies had 41 new drugs approved in 2012, with combined forecast revenues of $211 billion, compared with 32 products with expected revenues of $309 billion a year ago.

With an average internal rate of return (IRR) from R&D in 2012 of 7.2 per cent – against 7.7 per cent and 10.5 per cent in the two preceding years – drug makers are barely covering their average cost of capital, estimated at around 7 per cent.

For the 12 companies, the average cost of developing a new medicine between 2010 and 2012 has increased by 4 per cent, from $1,089 million in 2010, to $1,137 million in 2012.

There is wide variation between the 12 companies. The most successful company in the group spent just $315 million to develop a new drug, while at the other extreme one firm spent $2.8 billion.

Industry observers expect market conditions for pharmaceutical companies to continue to be challenging. Dynamics such as the US fiscal cliff, the potential that some countries might exit the euro zone, changing patterns of demand and continuing downward pressure on healthcare budgets present the industry with a volatile and highly uncertain economic environment in which to operate, let alone drive productivity improvements.

The companies analysed in the study were Pfizer Inc., Roche Holding Ltd., Novartis AG, Sanofi SA, GlaxoSmithKline plc, Johnson & Johnson, AstraZeneca plc, Merck & Co. Inc., Eli Lilly & Company, Bristol-Myers Squibb Co., Takeda Pharmaceutical Company Limited and Amgen, Inc.

Source: Extracts from Zhang, M. (2012) Big Pharma Facing Patent Cliff And Declining R&D Returns, *International Business Times*, 5 December.

Real World 8.7 gives some examples of IRRs sought in practice.

Real World 8.7

Rates of return

IRRs for investment projects can vary considerably. Here are a few examples of the expected or target returns from investment projects of large businesses.

- The leading pharmaceuticals business GlaxoSmithKline plc is aiming to increase its annual IRR from investments in new products from 11 per cent to 14 per cent.
- The fashion retailer Next plc requires an annual IRR of 20 per cent when appraising new stores.
- Apache Capital Partners, a property investment fund, has a target annual IRR of more than 20 per cent.

→

- Forth Ports plc, a port operator, concentrates on projects that generate an IRR of at least 15 per cent.
- The stores chain Marks and Spencer plc has targeted a 'hurdle' internal rate of return of 12 to 15 per cent on a new investment programme.
- The pensions and life assurance business Standard Life plc requires a 15 per cent internal rate of return from new products.

These values seem surprisingly large. A study of returns made by all of the businesses listed on the London Stock Exchange between 1900 and 2012 showed an average annual return of 5.2 per cent. This figure is the *real* return (that is, ignoring inflation). It would probably be fair to add at least 3 per cent to it to compare it with the targets for the businesses listed above. Also, the targets for the six businesses are probably pre-tax (the businesses do not specify). In that case it is probably reasonable to add about a third to the average Stock Exchange returns. This would give us around 12 per cent per year. This would be roughly in line with the GlaxoSmithKline and Marks and Spencer targets. The targets for the other businesses, however, seem rather ambitious.

Sources: UPDATE 1 – GSK's R&D engine cranks up investment returns, Reuters.com, 7 February 2012; Next plc, Results for the half-year to 31 July 2012; Thomas, D. (2009) Vultures need to pick time to swoop, ft.com, 12 June; Forth Ports plc, FAQs, www.forthports.co.uk, accessed 9 February 2010; Marks and Spencer plc, Press release on 2012 annual results, 22 May 2012; Standard Life flags 'step up in performance', ft.com, 10 March 2011; Dimson, E., Marsh, P. and Staunton, M. (2013) *Credit Suisse Global Investments Returns Yearbook*, p. 56.

Problems with IRR

IRR has certain key attributes in common with NPV. All cash flows are taken into account and their timing is logically handled. The main problem of IRR, however, is that it does not directly address the question of wealth generation. It can therefore lead to the wrong decision being made. This is because the IRR approach will always rank a project with, for example, an IRR of 25 per cent above a project with an IRR of 20 per cent. Although accepting the project with the higher percentage return will often generate more wealth, this may not always be the case. This is because IRR completely ignores the *scale of investment*.

With a 15 per cent cost of capital, £15 million invested at 20 per cent for one year will make us wealthier by £0.75 million (that is, $15 \times (20 - 15)\% = 0.75$). With the same cost of capital, £5 million invested at 25 per cent for one year will make us only £0.5 million (that is, $5 \times (25 - 15)\% = 0.50$). IRR does not recognise this.

Competing projects do not usually show such large differences in scale and so IRR and NPV normally give the same signal. However, as NPV will always give the correct signal, it is difficult to see why any other method should be used.

Activity 8.16

Which other investment appraisal method ignores the scale of investment?

We saw earlier that the ARR method suffers from this problem.

That ARR and IRR both suffer from the same problem is not coincidence. Their problem stems from the fact that they are both relative rates of return. Given the wealth-generating objective of most businesses, absolute returns measured in monetary terms are much more relevant than relative returns measured as percentages.

A further problem with the IRR method is that it has difficulty handling projects with unconventional cash flows. In the examples studied so far, each project has a negative cash flow arising at the start of its life and then positive cash flows thereafter. In practice, however, a project may have both positive and negative cash flows at future points in its life. Such a pattern of cash flows can result in there being more than one IRR, or even no IRR at all. This would make the IRR method difficult to use, although it should be said that this problem is also quite rare in practice. This is never a problem for NPV, however.

SOME PRACTICAL POINTS

When undertaking an investment appraisal, there are several practical points to bear in mind:

- *Past costs*. As with all decisions, we should take account only of *relevant costs* in our analysis. Only costs that vary with the decision should be considered, as we discussed at length in Chapter 2. This means that all past costs should be ignored as they cannot vary with the decision. A business may incur costs (such as development costs and market research costs) *before* the evaluation of an opportunity to launch a new product. As those costs have already been incurred, they should be disregarded, even though the amounts may be substantial and relate directly to the project. Costs that have already been committed but not yet paid should also be disregarded. Where a business has entered into a binding contract to incur a particular cost, it becomes in effect a past cost even though payment may not be due until some point in the future.
- *Common future costs*. It is not only past costs that do not vary with the decision; some future costs may also be the same. For example, the cost of raw materials may not vary with the decision whether to invest in a new piece of manufacturing plant or to continue to use existing plant.
- *Opportunity costs*. Opportunity costs arising from benefits forgone must be taken into account. For example, when considering a decision concerning whether or not to continue to use a machine already owned by the business, the realisable value of the machine might be an important opportunity cost.
- *Taxation*. Owners will be interested in the after-tax returns generated from the business. As a result, taxation will usually be an important consideration when making an investment decision. The profits from the project will be taxed, the capital investment may attract tax relief and so on. Tax is levied at significant rates. This means that, in real life, unless tax is formally taken into account, the wrong decision could easily be made. The timing of the tax outflow should also be taken into account when preparing the cash flows for the project.
- *Cash flows not profit flows*. We have seen that for the NPV, IRR and PP methods, it is cash flows rather than profit flows that are relevant to the assessment of investment projects. In an investment appraisal requiring the application of any of these methods, details of the profits for the investment period may be given. These need to be adjusted in order to derive the cash flows. We should remember that the operating profit *before* non-cash items (such as depreciation) is an approximation to the cash flows for the period. We should, therefore, work back to this figure.

  When the data are expressed in profit rather than cash flow terms, an adjustment in respect of working capital may also be necessary. Some adjustment should be made to take account of changes in working capital. For example, launching a new product may give rise to an increase in the net investment made in trade receivables and inventories less trade payables. This working capital investment would normally require an immediate outlay of cash. This outlay for additional working capital should be shown in the NPV calculations as an initial cash outflow. However, at the end of the life of the project, the additional working capital will be released. This divestment results in an effective inflow of cash at the end of the project. It should also be taken into account at the point at which it is received.

- *Year-end assumption*. In the examples and activities considered so far, we have assumed that cash flows arise at the end of the relevant year. This simplifying assumption is used to make the calculations easier. As we saw earlier, this assumption is clearly unrealistic, as money will have to be paid to employees on a weekly or monthly basis, credit customers will pay within a month or two of buying the product or service and so on. It is probably not a serious distortion, however. We should be clear that there is nothing about any of the four appraisal methods that demands that this assumption be made. It is perfectly possible to deal more precisely with the timing of the cash flows.
- *Interest payments*. When using discounted cash flow techniques (NPV and IRR), interest payments should not be taken into account in deriving cash flows for the period. Discounting already takes account of the costs of financing. To include interest charges in deriving cash flows for the period would therefore be double counting.
- *Other factors*. Investment decision making must not be viewed as simply a mechanical exercise. The results derived from a particular investment appraisal method will be only one input to the decision-making process. There may be broader issues connected to the decision that have to be taken into account but which may be difficult or impossible to quantify.

The reliability of the forecasts and the validity of the assumptions used in the evaluation will also have a bearing on the final decision.

Activity 8.17

The directors of Manuff (Steel) Ltd are considering closing one of the business's factories. There has been a reduction in the demand for the products made at the factory in recent years. The directors are not optimistic about the long-term prospects for these products. The factory is situated in an area where unemployment is high.

The factory is leased, with four years of the lease remaining. The directors are uncertain whether the factory should be closed immediately or at the end of the period of the lease. Another business has offered to sublease the premises from Manuff (Steel) Ltd at a rental of £40,000 a year for the remainder of the lease period.

The machinery and equipment at the factory cost £1,500,000. The value at which they appear in the statement of financial position is £400,000. In the event of immediate closure, the machinery and equipment could be sold for £220,000. The working capital at the factory is £420,000. It could be liquidated for that amount immediately, if required. Alternatively, the working capital can be liquidated in full at the end of the lease period. Immediate closure would result in redundancy payments to employees of £180,000.

If the factory continues in operation until the end of the lease period, the following operating profits (losses) are expected:

	Year 1	*Year 2*	*Year 3*	*Year 4*
	£000	*£000*	*£000*	*£000*
Operating profit (loss)	160	(40)	30	20

These figures are derived after deducting a charge of £90,000 a year for depreciation of machinery and equipment. The residual value of the machinery and equipment at the end of the lease period is estimated at £40,000.

Redundancy payments are expected to be £150,000 at the end of the lease period if the factory continues in operation. The business has an annual cost of capital of 12 per cent. Ignoring taxation,

(a) Determine the relevant cash flows arising from a decision to continue operations until the end of the lease period rather than to close immediately.
(b) Calculate the net present value of continuing operations until the end of the lease period, rather than closing immediately.
(c) What other factors might the directors take into account before making a final decision on the timing of the factory closure?
(d) State, with reasons, whether or not the business should continue to operate the factory until the end of the lease period.

Your answer should be:

(a) Relevant cash flows

	Years				
	0	*1*	*2*	*3*	*4*
	£000	*£000*	*£000*	*£000*	*£000*
Operating cash flows (Note 1)	–	250	50	120	110
Sale of machinery (Note 2)	(220)	–	–	–	40
Redundancy costs (Note 3)	180	–	–	–	(150)
Sublease rentals (Note 4)	–	(40)	(40)	(40)	(40)
Working capital invested (Note 5)	(420)	–	–	–	420
	(460)	210	10	80	380

Notes:

1 Each year's operating cash flows are calculated by adding back the depreciation charge for the year to the operating profit for the year. In the case of the operating loss, the depreciation charge is deducted.
2 In the event of closure, machinery could be sold immediately. As a result, an opportunity cost of £220,000 is incurred if operations continue.
3 If operations continue, there will be a saving in immediate redundancy costs of £180,000. However, redundancy costs of £150,000 will be paid in four years' time.
4 If operations continue, the opportunity to sublease the factory will be forgone.
5 Immediate closure would mean that working capital could be liquidated. By continuing operations this opportunity is forgone. However, working capital can be liquidated in four years' time.

(b)

	Years				
	0	*1*	*2*	*3*	*4*
Discount rate 12 per cent	1.000	0.893	0.797	0.712	0.636
Present value	(460)	187.5	8.0	57.0	241.7
Net present value	34.2				

(c) Other factors that may influence the decision include:

- *The overall strategy of the business*. The business may need to set the decision within a broader context. It may be necessary to manufacture the products at the factory because they are an integral part of the business's product range. The business may wish to avoid redundancies in an area of high unemployment for as long as possible.

- *Flexibility*. A decision to close the factory is probably irreversible. If the factory continues, however, there may be a chance that the prospects for the factory will brighten in the future.
- *Creditworthiness of sub-lessee*. The business should investigate the creditworthiness of the sub-lessee. Failure to receive the expected sublease payments would make the closure option far less attractive.
- *Accuracy of forecasts*. The forecasts made by the business should be examined carefully. Inaccuracies in the forecasts or any underlying assumptions may change the expected outcomes.

(d) The NPV of the decision to continue operations rather than close immediately is positive. Hence, shareholders would be better off if the directors took this course of action. The factory should therefore continue in operation rather than close down. This decision is likely to be welcomed by employees and would allow the business to maintain its flexibility.

The main methods of investment appraisal are summarised in Figure 8.5.

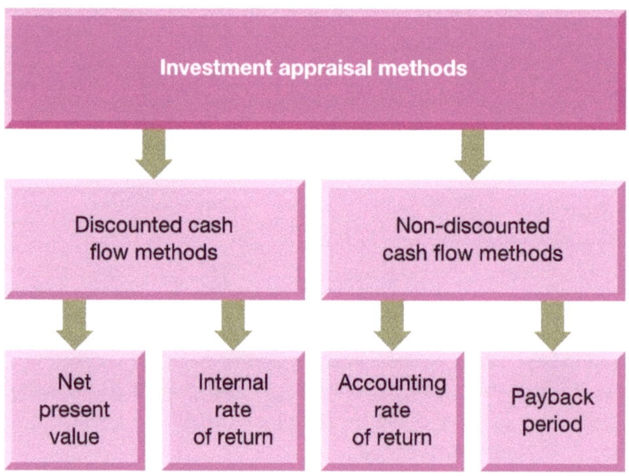

The figure shows the four investment appraisal methods discussed in the chapter.

Figure 8.5 The main investment appraisal methods

INVESTMENT APPRAISAL IN PRACTICE

Many surveys have been conducted in the UK, and elsewhere in the world, into the methods of investment appraisal used by businesses. They have shown the following features:

- Businesses tend to use more than one method to assess each investment decision.
- The discounting methods (NPV and IRR) have become increasingly popular over time. NPV and IRR are now the most popular of the four methods.
- PP continues to be popular and, to a lesser extent, so does ARR. This is despite the theoretical shortcomings of both of these methods.
- Larger businesses tend to rely more heavily on discounting methods than smaller businesses.

Real World 8.8 shows the results of a survey of a number of UK manufacturing businesses concerning their use of investment appraisal methods.

Real World 8.8

A survey of UK business practice

Senior financial managers at 83 of the UK's largest manufacturing businesses were asked about the investment appraisal methods used to evaluate both strategic and non-strategic projects. Strategic projects usually aim to increase or change the competitive capabilities of a business, for example by introducing a new manufacturing process.

Method	*Non-strategic projects* *Mean score*	*Strategic projects* *Mean score*
Net present value	3.6829	3.9759
Payback	3.4268	3.6098
Internal rate of return	3.3293	3.7073
Accounting rate of return	1.9867	2.2667

Response scale: 1= never, 2 = rarely, 3 = often, 4 = mostly, 5 = always

We can see that, for both non-strategic and for strategic investments, the NPV method is the most popular. As the sample consists of large businesses (nearly all with annual total sales revenue in excess of £100 million), a fairly sophisticated approach to evaluation might be expected. Nevertheless, for non-strategic investments, the payback method comes second in popularity. It drops to third place for strategic projects.

The survey also found that 98 per cent of respondents used more than one method and 88 per cent used more than three methods of investment appraisal.

Source: Based on information in Alkaraan, F. and Northcott, D. (2006) Strategic capital investment decision-making: a role for emergent analysis tools? A study of practice in large UK manufacturing companies, *The British Accounting Review*, 38, p. 159.

A survey of large businesses in five leading industrialised countries, including the UK, also shows considerable support for the NPV and IRR methods. There is less support for the payback method but, nevertheless, it still seems to be fairly widely used. **Real World 8.9** sets out some key findings.

Real world 8.9

A multinational survey of business practice

A survey of investment and financing practices in five different countries was carried out by Cohen and Yagil. This survey, based on a sample of the largest 300 businesses in each country, revealed the following concerning the popularity of three of the investment appraisal methods discussed in this chapter.

Frequency of the use of investment appraisal techniques

	USA	*UK*	*Germany*	*Canada*	*Japan*	*Average*
IRR	4.00	4.16	4.08	4.15	3.29	3.93
NPV	3.88	4.00	3.50	4.09	3.57	3.80
PP	3.46	3.89	3.33	3.57	3.52	3.55

Response scale: 1 = never, 5 = always.

→

Key findings of the survey include the following:

- IRR is more popular than NPV in all countries except Japan. The difference between the two methods, however, is not statistically significant.
- Managers of UK businesses use investment appraisal techniques the most, while managers of Japanese businesses use them the least. This may be related to business traditions within each country.
- There is a positive relationship between business size and the popularity of the IRR and NPV methods. This may be related to the greater experience and understanding of financial theory of managers of larger businesses. A more recent survey (by Lucas, Prowle and Lowth) of some much smaller UK businesses indicated that none of them carried out any investment appraisal. This adds emphasis to the size/sophistication relationship in this context.

Sources: Cohen, G. and Yagil, J. (2007) A multinational survey of corporate financial policies, Working Paper, Haifa University; Lucas, M., Prowle, M. and Lowth, G. (2013) Management accounting practices of UK small-medium-sized enterprises, CIMA, July.

Activity 8.18

Earlier in the chapter, we discussed the limitations of the PP method. Can you suggest reasons that might explain why it is still a reasonably popular method of investment appraisal among managers?

There seem to be several possible reasons:

- PP is easy to understand and use.
- It can avoid the problems of forecasting far into the future.
- It gives emphasis to the early cash flows when there is greater certainty concerning the accuracy of their predicted value.
- It emphasises the importance of liquidity. Where a business has liquidity problems, a short payback period for a project is likely to appear attractive.

The popularity of PP may suggest a lack of sophistication by managers concerning investment appraisal. This criticism is most often made against managers of smaller businesses. This point is borne out by both of the surveys discussed in Real World 8.9, which have found that smaller businesses are much less likely to use discounted cash flow methods (NPV and IRR) than are larger ones. Other surveys have tended to reach a similar conclusion.

IRR may be popular because it expresses outcomes in percentage terms rather than in absolute terms. This form of expression seems to be preferred by managers, despite the problems of percentage measures that we discussed earlier. This may be because managers are used to using percentage figures as targets (for example, return on capital employed).

Real World 8.10 shows extracts from the 2013 annual report of a well-known business: Rolls-Royce plc, the builder of engines for aircraft and other purposes.

Real World 8.10

The use of NPV at Rolls-Royce

In its 2013 annual report and accounts, Rolls-Royce plc stated that

> **The Group subjects all investments and capital expenditure to a rigorous examination of risks and future cash flows to ensure that they create shareholder value. All major investments require Board approval.**
>
> **The Group has a portfolio of projects at different stages of their life cycles. Discounted cash flow analysis of the remaining life of projects is performed on a regular basis.**

Source: Rolls-Royce Holdings plc Annual Report 2013, p. 137.

Rolls-Royce makes clear that it uses NPV (the report refers to creating shareholder value and to discounted cash flow, which strongly imply NPV). It is interesting to note that Rolls-Royce not only assesses new projects but also reassesses existing ones. This must be a sensible commercial approach. Businesses should not continue with existing projects unless those projects have a positive NPV based on future cash flows. Just because a project seemed to have a positive NPV before it started does not mean that this will persist in the light of changing circumstances. Activity 8.17 (pages 294–296) considered a decision to close down a project.

INVESTMENT APPRAISAL AND STRATEGIC PLANNING

So far, we have tended to view investment opportunities as unconnected, independent projects. In practice, however, successful businesses are those that set out a clear strategic framework for the selection of investment projects in the way that was described in Chapter 1. Unless this framework is in place, it may be difficult to identify those projects that are likely to generate a positive NPV. The best investment projects are usually those that match the business's internal strengths (for example, skills, experience, access to finance) with the opportunities available. In areas where this match does not exist, other businesses, for which the match does exist, are likely to have a distinct competitive advantage. This means that they will be able to provide the product or service at a better price and/or quality.

Setting out the framework just described is an essential part of *strategic planning*. In practice, strategic plans often have a time span of around five years. It involves asking 'where do we want our business to be in five years' time and how can we get there?' It will set the appropriate direction in terms of products, markets, financing and so on, to ensure that the business is best placed to generate profitable investment opportunities.

Real World 8.11 shows how Schneider Electric made an investment that fitted its strategic objectives.

Real World 8.11

Electrical fittings

The French electrical distributor and power equipment manufacturer Schneider Electric SA bought the UK engineering and IT business Invensys plc for £3.4 billion in July 2013. Analysts at HSBC though that the acquisition would represent 'an excellent strategic fit' for Schneider. Schneider claimed that the acquisition would generate annual synergy benefits of about €400 by 2018. The business felt that acquiring Invensys would give it access to new markets.

For a business other than Schneider, the lack of strategic fit might well have meant that buying Invensys for exactly the same price of £3.4 billion would not have been a good investment.

Source: Based on Thompson, A. and Wembridge, M. (2013) Schneider Electric to acquire Invensys for £3.4bn, ft.com, 31 July.

DEALING WITH RISK

All business activities are risky. This means that consideration of risk is an important aspect of financial decision making. Risk, in this context, is the extent and likelihood that what is projected to occur will not actually happen. Although we are discussing risk in the chapter on investment decision making, its importance is just as great when making shorter-term decisions of the type that we considered in Chapters 2 and 3. The approaches to dealing with risk that we are about to consider are equally applicable to shorter-term decisions. Risk is, however, a particularly important issue in the context of investment decisions, because of:

1 *The relatively long timescales involved*. There tends to be more time for things to go wrong between the decision being made and the end of the project, in comparison with many business decisions.
2 *The scale of funds involved*. Many investment projects involve very large amounts of finance. If things go wrong, the impact can be both significant and lasting.

Various approaches to dealing with risk have been proposed. These fall into two categories: assessing the level of risk and reacting to the level of risk. We now consider formal methods of dealing with risk that fall within each category.

Assessing the level of risk

Sensitivity analysis

One popular way of attempting to assess the level of risk is to carry out a **sensitivity analysis** on the proposed project. This involves an examination of the key input values affecting the project to see how changes in each input might influence the viability of the project.

Firstly, the investment is appraised, using the best estimates for each of the input factors (for example, labour cost, material cost, discount rate and so on). Assuming that the NPV is positive, each input value is then examined to see how far the estimated figure could be changed before the project becomes unviable for that reason alone. Let us suppose that the NPV for an investment in a machine to provide a particular service is a positive value. If we were to carry out a sensitivity analysis on this project, we should consider each of the key input factors, in turn:

- initial outlay for the machine;
- sales volume and selling price;
- relevant operating costs;
- life of the project; and
- financing costs (to be used as the discount rate).

We should seek to find the value that each of them could have before the NPV figure would become negative (that is, the value for the factor at which NPV would be zero). The difference between the value for that factor at which the NPV would equal zero and the estimated value represents the margin of safety for that particular input. The process is set out in Figure 8.6.

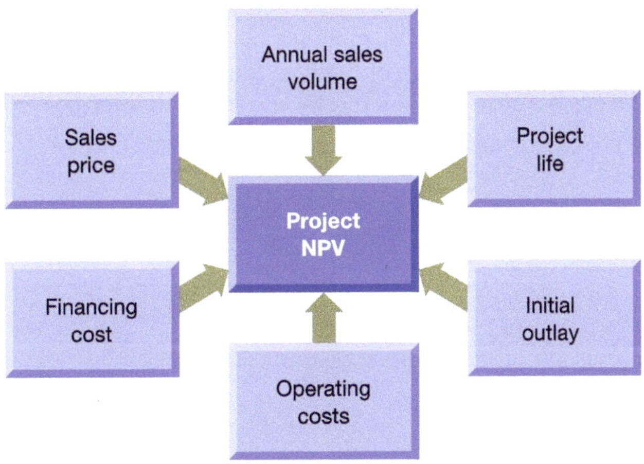

Sensitivity analysis involves identifying the key factors that affect the project. In the figure, six factors have been identified for the particular project. (In practice, the key factors are likely to vary between projects.) Once identified, each factor will be examined in turn to find the value it should have for the project to have a zero NPV.

Figure 8.6 Factors affecting the sensitivity of NPV calculations

A computer spreadsheet model of the project can be extremely valuable for this exercise because it then becomes a very simple matter to try various values for the input data and to see the effect of each. As a result of carrying out a sensitivity analysis, the decision maker is able to get a 'feel' for the project, which otherwise might not be possible. Example 8.3 is, however, straightforward, and we shall carry out a sensitivity analysis manually, to demonstrate how it is done.

Example 8.3

S. Saluja (Property Developers) Ltd intends to bid at an auction, to be held today, for a manor house that has fallen into disrepair. The auctioneer believes that the house will be sold for about £450,000. The business wishes to renovate the property and to divide it into flats, to be sold for £150,000 each. The renovation will be in two stages and will cover a two-year period. Stage 1 will cover the first year of the project. It will cost £500,000 and the six flats completed during this stage are expected to be sold for a total of £900,000 at the end of the first year. Stage 2 will cover the second year of the project. It will cost £300,000 and the three remaining flats are expected to be sold at the end of the second year for a total of £450,000. The cost of renovation will be the subject of a binding contract with local builders, were the property to be bought. There is, however, some uncertainty over the remaining input values. The business estimates its cost of capital at 12 per cent a year.

(a) What is the NPV of the proposed project?

(b) Assuming none of the other inputs deviates from the best estimates provided:

(i) What auction price would have to be paid for the manor house to cause the project to have a zero NPV?

(ii) What cost of capital would cause the project to have a zero NPV?

(iii) What is the sale price of each of the flats that would cause the project to have a zero NPV? (Each flat is projected to be sold for the same price: £150,000.)

(c) Comment on your calculations carried out in answering (b) above.

Solution

(a) The NPV of the proposed project is as follows:

	Cash flows £	*Discount factor* 12%	*Present value* £
Year 1 (£900,000 – £500,000)	400,000	0.893	357,200
Year 2 (£450,000 – £300,000)	150,000	0.797	119,550
Initial outlay			(450,000)
Net present value			26,750

(b) (i) To lead to a zero NPV, the auction price would have to be £26,750 higher than the current estimate – that is, a total price of £476,750. This is about 6 per cent above the current estimated price.

(ii) As there is a positive NPV, the cost of capital that would cause the project to have a zero NPV must be higher than 12 per cent. Let us try 20 per cent.

	Cash flows £	*Discount factor* 20%	*Present value* £
Year 1 (£900,000 – £500,000)	400,000	0.833	333,200
Year 2 (£450,000 – £300,000)	150,000	0.694	104,100
Initial outlay			(450,000)
Net present value			(12,700)

As the NPV using a 20 per cent discount rate is negative, the 'break-even' cost of capital lies somewhere between 12 per cent and 20 per cent. A reasonable approximation is obtained as follows:

	Discount rate	*Net present value*
	%	£
	12	26,750
	20	(12,700)
Difference	8	39,450

The change in NPV for every 1 per cent change in the discount rate will be:

39,450/8 = £4,931

The reduction in the 20 per cent discount rate required to achieve a zero NPV would therefore be:

12,700/4,931 = 2.6%

The cost of capital (that is, the discount rate) would, therefore, have to be 17.4 per cent (20.0 − 2.6) for the project to have a zero NPV.

This calculation is, of course, the same as that used earlier in the chapter, when calculating the IRR of the project. In other words, 17.4 per cent is the IRR of the project.

(iii) To obtain a zero NPV, the sale price of each flat must be reduced so that the NPV is reduced by £26,750. In year 1, six flats are sold (in year 2, three flats are sold). The discount factor at the 12 per cent rate for year 1 is 0.893 and that for year 2 is 0.797. We can derive the fall in price per flat (Y) to give a zero NPV by using the equation

$$(6Y \times 0.893) + (3Y \times 0.797) = £26,750$$
$$Y = £3,452$$

The sale price of each flat necessary to obtain a zero NPV is therefore:

£150,000 − £3,452 = £146,548

This represents a fall in the estimated price of 2.3 per cent.

(c) These calculations indicate that the auction price would have to be about 6 per cent above the estimated price before a zero NPV is obtained. The margin of safety is, therefore, not very high for this factor. In practice this should not represent a real risk because the business could withdraw from the bidding if the price rises to an unacceptable level.

The other two factors represent more real risks. Only after the project is at a very late stage can the business be sure as to what actual price per flat will prevail. The same may be true for the cost of capital, though it may be possible to raise finance for the project at a rate fixed before the auction of the house. It would be unusual to be able to have fixed contracts for sale of all of the flats before the auction. The calculations reveal that the price of the flats would only have to fall by 2.3 per cent from the estimated price before the NPV is reduced to zero. Hence, the margin of safety for this factor is very small. However, even if the funding cost cannot be fixed in advance, the cost of capital is less sensitive to changes and there would have to be an increase from 12 per cent to 17.4 per cent before the project produced a zero NPV. It seems from the calculations that the sale price of the flats is the key sensitive factor to consider. A careful re-examination of the market value of the flats seems appropriate before a final decision is made.

A slightly different form of sensitivity analysis than that just described is to pose a series of 'what if?' questions. This can help to see how possible changes to each input factor will affect the viability of the investment project. When considering sales, for example, the following 'what if?' questions may be asked:

- What if sales volume is 5 per cent higher than expected?
- What if sales volume is 10 per cent lower than expected?
- What if sales price is reduced by 15 per cent?
- What if sales price could be increased by 20 per cent?

While this form of sensitivity analysis also examines the effect of changes in each key factor, it does not seek to find the point at which a change makes the project no longer viable. Real World 8.12, which we shall consider very shortly, gives a real example of this approach.

There are three major drawbacks with the use of sensitivity analysis:

- It does not give managers clear decision rules concerning acceptance or rejection of the project and so they must rely on their own judgement.
- It does not provide any indication of the likelihood that a particular change to an input factor will actually occur.
- It is a static form of analysis. Only one input is considered at a time, while the rest are held constant. In practice, however, it is likely that more than one input value will differ from the best estimates provided. Even so, it would be possible to deal with changes in various inputs simultaneously, were the project data put onto a spreadsheet model. This approach, where more than one variable is altered at a time, is known as **scenario building**.

Real World 8.12 describes the evaluation of a mining project that incorporated sensitivity analysis to test the robustness of the findings.

Real World 8.12

Golden opportunity

In a news release, Amara Mining plc (a business listed on the London Stock Exchange Alternative Investment Market) announced positive results from a feasibility study of its Baomahun project in Sierra Leone. The project involves drilling for gold in an open pit operation. The business provided calculations based on a range of key variables. These variables were the estimated prices for gold and the discount rate to be applied. The following results were obtained:

Boamahun project sensitivity analysis:

Gold price (US $/ounce)	1,150	1,250	1,350	1,500
Cash flow (US $m)	92	138	184	245
IRR (%)	12	17	22	28
NPV (US$m) assuming a:				
5% discount rate	42	77	111	157
8% discount rate	20	50	80	119
10% discount rate	9	36	62	98

Source: Amara Mining plc (2014) Result of first phase of Boamahun optimization work, www.amaramining.com, 30 January.

Expected net present value

Another means of assessing risk is through the use of statistical probabilities. It may be possible to identify a range of feasible values for each of the items of input data and to assign a probability of occurrence to each of these values. Using this information, we can derive an **expected net present value (ENPV)**, which is, in effect, a weighted average of the possible outcomes where the probabilities are used as weights. To illustrate this method, let us consider Example 8.4.

Example 8.4

C. Piperis (Properties) Ltd has the opportunity to acquire a lease on a block of flats that has only two years remaining before it expires. The cost of the lease would be £100,000. The occupancy rate of the block of flats is currently around 70 per cent and the flats are let almost exclusively to naval personnel. There is a large naval base located nearby, but there is little other demand for the flats. The occupancy rate of the flats will change in the remaining two years of the lease, depending on the outcome of a defence review. The navy is currently considering three options for the naval base. These are:

- *Option 1*. Increase the size of the base by closing one in another region and transferring the personnel to the one located near the flats.
- *Option 2*. Close the naval base near to the flats and leave only a skeleton staff there for maintenance purposes. The personnel would be moved to a base in another region.
- *Option 3*. Leave the base open but reduce staffing levels by 20 per cent.

The directors of Piperis have estimated the following net cash flows for each of the two years under each option and the probability of their occurrence:

	£	*Probability*
Option 1	80,000	0.6
Option 2	12,000	0.1
Option 3	40,000	0.3
		1.0

Note that the sum of the probabilities is 1.0 (in other words it is certain that one of the possible options will arise). The business has a cost of capital of 10 per cent.

Should the business purchase the lease on the block of flats?

Solution

To calculate the expected NPV of the proposed investment, we must first calculate the weighted average of the expected outcomes for each year where the probabilities are used as weights, by multiplying each cash flow by its probability of occurrence. Thus, the expected annual net cash flows will be:

	Cash flows £ (a)	*Probability* (b)	*Expected cash flows* £ (a × b)
Option 1	80,000	0.6	48,000
Option 2	12,000	0.1	1,200
Option 3	40,000	0.3	12,000
Expected cash flows in each year			61,200

→

Having derived the expected annual cash flows, we can now discount these using a rate of 10 per cent to reflect the cost of capital:

Year	*Expected cash flows* £	*Discount factor at 10%*	*Expected present value* £
1	61,200	0.909	55,631
2	61,200	0.826	50,551
			106,182
Initial investment			(100,000)
Expected NPV			6,182

We can see that the expected NPV is positive. Hence, the wealth of shareholders is expected to increase by purchasing the lease.

The expected NPV approach has the advantage of producing a single numerical outcome and of having a clear decision rule to apply. If the expected NPV is positive, we should invest; if it is negative, we should not.

However, the approach produces an average figure, and this may be one that cannot actually occur. This point was illustrated in Example 8.4 where the expected annual cash flow (£61,200) does not correspond to any of the stated options.

Perhaps more importantly, using an average figure can obscure the underlying risk associated with the project. Simply deriving the ENPV, as in Example 8.4, can be misleading. Without some idea of the individual possible outcomes and their probability of occurring, the decision maker is in the dark. In Example 8.4, were either Option 2 or Option 3 to occur, the investment would be adverse (wealth-destroying). It is 40 per cent probable that one of these two options will occur, so this is a significant risk. Only should Option 1 arise (60 per cent probable) would investing in the flats represent a good decision. Of course, in advance of making the investment, which option will actually occur is not known.

None of this should be taken to mean that the investment in the flats should not be made, simply that the decision maker is better placed to make a judgement where information on the possible outcomes is available. Activity 8.19 further illustrates this point.

Activity 8.19

Qingdao Manufacturing Ltd is considering two competing projects. Details are as follows:

- **Project A has a 0.9 probability of producing a negative NPV of £200,000 and a 0.1 probability of producing a positive NPV of £3.8m.**
- **Project B has a 0.6 probability of producing a positive NPV of £100,000 and a 0.4 probability of producing a positive NPV of £350,000.**

What is the expected net present value of each project?

The expected NPV of Project A is

$$((0.1 \times £3.8m) - (0.9 \times £200,000)) = £200,000$$

The expected NPV of Project B is

$$((0.6 \times £100,000) + (0.4 \times £350,000)) = £200,000$$

Although the expected NPV of each project in Activity 8.19 is identical, this does not mean that the business will be indifferent about which project to undertake. We can see from the information provided that Project A has a high probability of making a loss whereas Project B is not expected to make a loss under either possible outcome. If we assume that the shareholders dislike risk – which is usually the case – they will prefer the directors to take on Project B as this provides the same level of expected return as Project A but for a lower level of risk.

It can be argued that the problem identified above may not be significant where the business is engaged in several similar projects. This is because a worse than expected outcome on one project may well be balanced by a better than expected outcome on another project. However, in practice, investment projects may be unique events and this argument will not then apply. Also, where the project is large in relation to other projects undertaken, the argument loses its force. There is also the problem that a factor that might cause one project to have an adverse outcome could also have adverse effects on other projects. For example, a large, unexpected increase in the price of oil may have a simultaneous adverse effect on all of the investment projects of a particular business.

Where the expected NPV approach is being used, it is probably a good idea to make known to managers the different possible outcomes and the probability attached to each outcome. By so doing, the managers will be able to gain an insight into the *downside risk* attached to the project. The information relating to each outcome can be presented in the form of a diagram if required. The construction of such a diagram is illustrated in Example 8.5.

Example 8.5

Zeta Computing Services Ltd has recently produced some software for a client organisation. The software has a life of two years and will then become obsolete. The cost of producing the software was £10,000. The client has agreed to pay a licence fee of £8,000 a year for the software if it is used in only one of its two divisions, or £12,000 a year if it is used in both of its divisions. The client may use the software for either one or two years in either division but will definitely use it in at least one division in each of the two years.

Zeta believes there is a 0.6 chance that the licence fee received in any one year will be £8,000 and a 0.4 chance that it will be £12,000. There are, therefore, four possible outcomes attached to this project (where p denotes probability):

- *Outcome 1*. Year 1 cash flow £8,000 ($p = 0.6$) and Year 2 cash flow £8,000 ($p = 0.6$). The probability of both years having cash flows of £8,000 will be:

$$0.6 \times 0.6 = 0.36$$

- *Outcome 2*. Year 1 cash flow £12,000 ($p = 0.4$) and Year 2 cash flow £12,000 ($p = 0.4$). The probability of both years having cash flows of £12,000 will be:

$$0.4 \times 0.4 = 0.16$$

- *Outcome 3*. Year 1 cash flow £12,000 ($p = 0.4$) and Year 2 cash flow £8,000 ($p = 0.6$). The probability of this sequence of cash flows occurring will be:

$$0.4 \times 0.6 = 0.24$$

- *Outcome 4*. Year 1 cash flow £8,000 ($p = 0.6$) and Year 2 cash flow £12,000 ($p = 0.4$). The probability of this sequence of cash flows occurring will be:

$$0.6 \times 0.4 = 0.24$$

The information in Example 8.5 can be displayed in the form of a diagram (Figure 8.7).

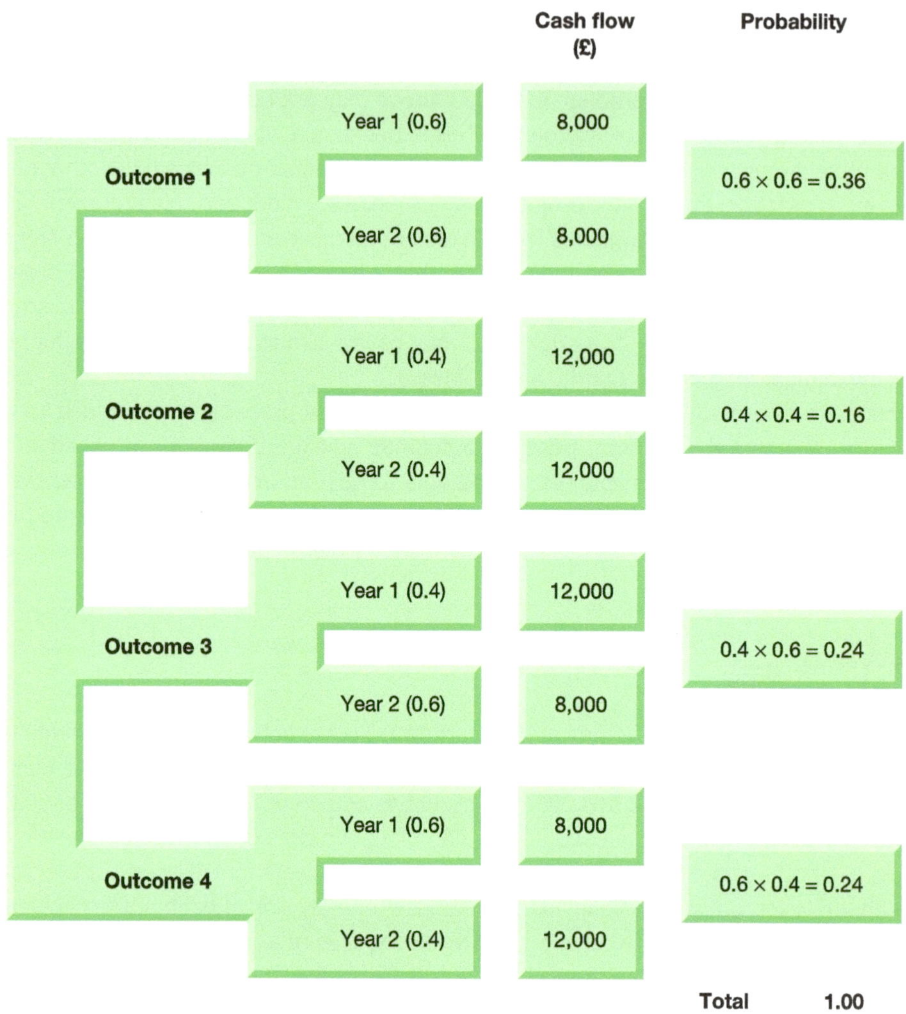

There are four different possible outcomes associated with the project, each with its own probability of occurence. The sum of the probabilities attached to each outcome must equal 1.00, in other words it is certain that one of the possible outcomes will occur. For example, outcome 1 would occur where only one division uses the software in each year.

Figure 8.7 The different possible project outcomes for the Zeta project (Example 8.5)

The source of probabilities

As we might expect, assigning probabilities to possible outcomes can often be a problem. There may be many possible outcomes arising from a particular investment project. To identify each outcome and then assign a probability to it may prove to be an impossible task. When assigning probabilities to possible outcomes, an objective or a subjective approach may be used. **Objective probabilities** are based on verifiable evidence, usually information gathered from past experience. Thus, for example, the transport manager of a business operating a fleet of motor vans may be able to provide information concerning the possible life of a new motor van purchased based on the record of similar vans acquired in the past. From the information available, probabilities may be developed for different possible life-spans. However, the past may not always be a reliable guide to the future, particularly during a period of rapid change. With motor vans, for example, changes in design and technology or changes in the purpose for which the vans are being used may undermine the validity of past data.

Subjective probabilities are based on opinion and will be used where past data are either inappropriate or unavailable. The opinions of independent experts may provide a useful basis for developing subjective probabilities, though even these may contain bias, which will affect the reliability of the judgements made.

Despite these problems, we should not be dismissive of the use of probabilities. Assigning probabilities can help to make explicit some of the risks associated with a project and should help decision makers to appreciate the uncertainties that have to be faced.

Activity 8.20

Devonia (Laboratories) Ltd has recently carried out successful clinical trials on a new type of skin cream that has been developed to reduce the effects of ageing. Research and development costs incurred relating to the new product amounted to £160,000. In order to gauge the market potential of the new product, independent market research consultants were hired at a cost of £15,000. The market research report submitted by the consultants indicates that the skin cream is likely to have a product life of four years and could be sold to retail chemists and large department stores at a price of £20 per 100 ml container. For each of the four years of the new product's life, sales demand has been estimated as follows:

Number of 100 ml containers sold	*Probability of occurrence*
11,000	0.3
14,000	0.6
16,000	0.1

If the business decides to launch the new product, it is possible for production to begin at once. The equipment necessary to produce it is already owned by the business and originally cost £150,000. At the end of the new product's life, it is estimated that the equipment could be sold for £35,000. If the business decides against launching the new product, the equipment will be sold immediately for £85,000, as it will be of no further use.

The new product will require one hour's labour for each 100 ml container produced. The cost of labour is £8.00 an hour. Additional workers will have to be recruited to produce the new product. At the end of the product's life, the workers are unlikely to be offered further work with the business and total redundancy costs of £10,000 are expected. The cost of the ingredients for each 100 ml container is £6.00. Additional overheads arising from production of the new product are expected to be £15,000 a year.

The new skin cream has attracted the interest of the business's competitors. If the business decides not to produce and sell the skin cream, it can sell the patent rights to a major competitor immediately for £125,000.

Devonia has a cost of capital of 12 per cent. Ignore taxation.

(a) Calculate the expected net present value (ENPV) of the new product.
(b) State, with reasons, whether or not Devonia should launch the new product.

→

Your answer should be as follows:

(a) Expected sales volume per year = (11,000 × 0.3) + (14,000 × 0.6) + (16,000 × 0.1)
= 13,300 units

Expected annual sales revenue = 13,300 × £20
= £266,000

Annual labour = 13,300 × £8
= £106,400

Annual ingredient costs = 13,300 × £6
= £79,800

Incremental cash flows:

	Years				
	0	*1*	*2*	*3*	*4*
	£	£	£	£	£
Sale of patent rights	(125.0)	–	–	–	–
Sale of equipment	(85.0)	–	–	–	35.0
Sales revenue	–	266.0	266.0	266.0	266.0
Cost of ingredients	–	(79.8)	(79.8)	(79.8)	(79.8)
Labour costs	–	(106.4)	(106.4)	(106.4)	(106.4)
Redundancy	–	–	–	–	(10.0)
Additional overheads	–	(15.0)	(15.0)	(15.0)	(15.0)
	(210.0)	64.8	64.8	64.8	89.8
Discount factor (12%)	1.000	0.893	0.797	0.712	0.636
	(210.0)	57.9	51.6	46.1	57.1
ENPV	2.7				

(b) The ENPV of the project is positive. This may be seen as a signal that the project should be undertaken. However, the ENPV is very low in relation to the size of the project and careful checking of the key estimates and assumptions would be advisable. A relatively small downward revision of sales (volume and/or price) or upward revision of costs could make the project ENPV negative.

It would be helpful to derive the NPV for each of the three possible outcomes regarding sales levels. This would enable the decision maker to have a clearer view of the risk involved with the investment.

Reacting to the level of risk

Demanding a higher rate of return is the logical reaction to a risky project. Clear, observable evidence shows that there is a relationship between risk and the return required by investors. It was mentioned earlier, for example, that a bank would normally ask for a higher rate of interest on a loan where it perceives the borrower to be less likely to be able to repay the amount borrowed.

When assessing investment projects, it is normal to increase the NPV discount rate in the face of increased risk – that is, to demand a risk premium: the higher the level of risk, the higher the risk premium that will be demanded. The risk premium is added to the 'risk-free' rate of return to derive the total return required (the **risk-adjusted discount rate**). The risk-free rate is normally taken to be equivalent to the rate of return from government loan notes. In practice, a business may divide projects into low-, medium- and high-risk categories and then assign a risk premium to each category. The cash flows from a particular project will then be discounted using a rate based on the risk-free rate plus the appropriate risk premium. Since all investments are risky to some extent, all projects will have a risk premium linked to them.

The relationship between risk and return is illustrated in Figure 8.8.

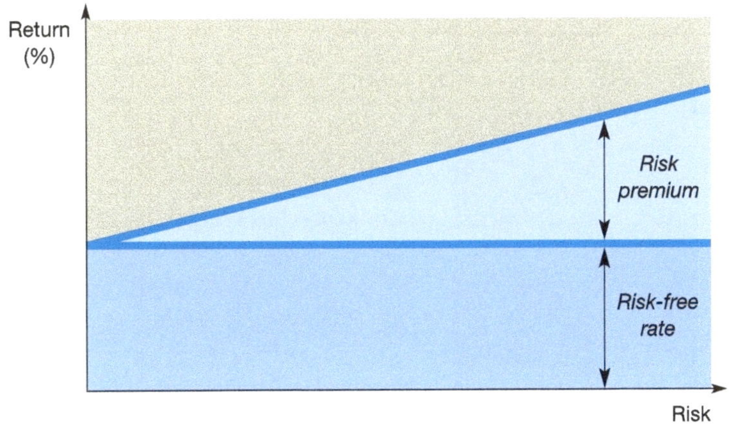

It is logical to take account of the riskiness of projects by changing the discount rate. A risk premium is added to the risk-free rate to derive the appropriate discount rate. A higher return will normally be expected from projects where the risks are higher; thus, the riskier the project, the higher the risk premium.

Figure 8.8 Relationship between risk and return

Activity 8.21

Can you think of any practical problems with estimating an appropriate value for the risk premium for a particular project?

Subjective judgement tends to be required when assigning an investment project to a particular risk category and then in assigning a risk premium to each category. The choices made will reflect the personal views of the managers responsible and this may differ from the views of the shareholders they represent. The choices made can, nevertheless, make the difference between accepting and rejecting a particular project.

MANAGING INVESTMENT PROJECTS

So far, we have been concerned with the process of carrying out the necessary calculations that enable managers to select among already identified investment opportunities. Though the assessment of projects is undoubtedly important, we must bear in mind that it is only *part* of the process of investment decision making. There are other important aspects that managers must also consider.

It is possible to see the investment process as a sequence of five stages, each of which managers must consider. The five stages are set out in Figure 8.9. We shall now consider these.

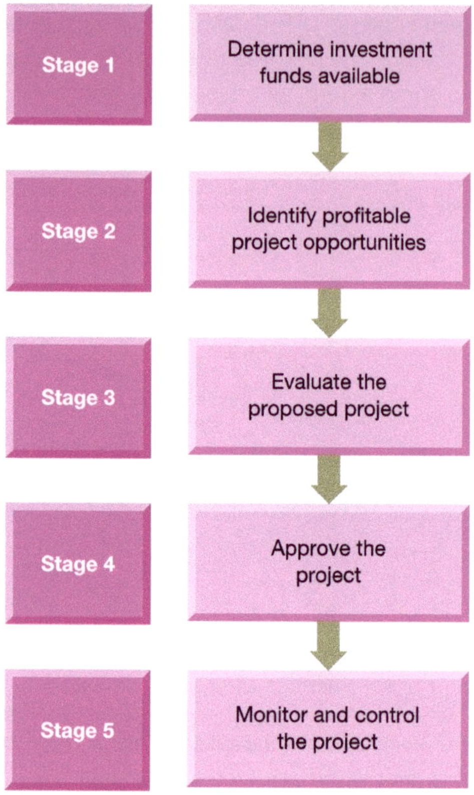

The management of an investment project involves a sequence of five key stages. The evaluation of projects using the appraisal techniques discussed earlier represents only one of these stages.

Figure 8.9 Managing the investment decision

Stage 1: Determine investment funds available

The amount of funds available for investment may be limited by the external market for funds or by internal management. In practice, it is often the business's own senior managers that restrict the amount available, perhaps because they lack confidence in the business's ability to handle higher levels of investment. In either case, it may mean that the funds will not be sufficient to finance all of the apparently profitable investment opportunities available. This shortage of investment funds is known as **capital rationing**. When it arises managers are faced with the task of deciding on the most profitable use of those funds available.

Stage 2: Identify profitable project opportunities

A vital part of the investment process is the search for profitable investment opportunities. The business should carry out methodical routines for identifying feasible projects. This may be done through a research and development department or by some other means. Failure to do this will inevitably lead to the business losing its competitive position with respect to product development, production methods or market penetration. To help identify good investment opportunities, some businesses provide financial incentives to members of staff who come forward with good investment proposals. The search process will, however, usually involve looking outside the business to identify changes in technology, customer demand, market conditions and so on. Information will need to be gathered and this may take some time, particularly for unusual or non-routine investment opportunities.

Activity 8.22

It has been argued that the sequence of these first two stages can be reversed. Can you figure out why this should be the case?

In theory, finance can always be found for profitable investment opportunities.

Stage 3: Evaluate the proposed project

If management is to agree to the investment of funds in a project, that project's proposal must be rigorously screened. For larger projects, this will involve providing answers to a number of questions, including:

- What are the nature and purpose of the project?
- Does the project align with the overall strategy and objectives of the business?
- How much finance is required?
- What other resources (such as expertise, work space and so on) are required for successful completion of the project?
- How long will the project last and what are its key stages?
- What is the expected pattern of cash flows?
- What are the major problems associated with the project and how can they be overcome?
- What is the NPV of the project? If capital is rationed, how does the NPV of this project compare with that of other opportunities available?
- Have risk and inflation been taken into account in the appraisal process and, if so, what are the results?

The ability and commitment of those responsible for proposing and managing the project will be vital to its success. This means that, when evaluating a new project, one consideration will be the quality of those proposing it. Senior managers may decide not to support a project that appears profitable on paper if they lack confidence in the ability of key managers to see it through to completion.

Stage 4: Approve the project

Once the managers responsible for investment decision making are satisfied that the project should be undertaken, formal approval can be given. However, a decision on a project may be postponed if senior managers need more information from those proposing the project, or if revisions to the proposal are required. Proposals may be rejected if they are considered unprofitable or likely to fail. Before a proposal is rejected, however, the implications of not pursuing the project must be carefully considered. Failure to pursue a particular project may impact such areas as market share, staff morale and existing business operations.

Stage 5: Monitor and control the project

Making a decision to invest in, say, the plant needed to provide a new service does not automatically cause the investment to be made and provision of the service to go smoothly ahead.

Managers will need to manage the project actively through to completion. This, in turn, will require further information-gathering exercises.

Much of the control of a project would be through the routine budgetary control procedures that we met in Chapter 7. Management should also receive progress reports at regular intervals concerning the project. These reports should provide information relating to the actual cash flows for each stage of the project, which can then be compared against the forecast figures provided when the proposal was submitted for approval. The reasons for significant variations should be ascertained and corrective action taken where possible. Any changes in the expected completion date of the project or any expected variations in future cash flows from budget should be reported immediately; in extreme cases, managers may even abandon the project if circumstances appear to have changed dramatically for the worse.

Project management techniques (for example, critical path analysis) should be employed wherever possible and their effectiveness reported to senior management.

An important part of the control process is a **post-completion audit** of the project. This is, in essence, a review of the project performance to see if it lived up to expectations and whether any lessons can be learned from the way that the investment process was carried out. In addition to an evaluation of financial costs and benefits, non-financial measures of performance such as the ability to meet deadlines and levels of quality achieved should also be reported.

The fact that a post-completion audit is an integral part of the management of the project should also encourage those who submit projects to use realistic estimates. **Real World 8.13** provides some evidence of a need for greater realism.

Real World 8.13

Looking on the bright side

McKinsey and Co, the management consultants, surveyed 2,500 senior managers worldwide during the spring of 2007. The managers were asked their opinions on investments made by their businesses in the previous three years. The general opinion is that estimates for the investment decision inputs had been too optimistic. For example sales levels had been overestimated in about 50 per cent of cases, but underestimated in fewer than 20 per cent of cases. It is not clear whether the estimates were sufficiently inaccurate to call into question the decision that had been made.

The survey goes on to ask about the extent that investments made seemed, in the light of the actual outcomes, to have been mistakes. Managers felt that 19 per cent of investments that had been made should not have gone ahead. On the other hand, they felt that 31 per cent of rejected projects should have been taken up. Managers also felt that 'good money was thrown after bad' in that existing investments that were not performing well were continuing to be supported in a significant number of cases.

Source: Based on information in 'How companies spend their money', a McKinsey Global Survey, www.theglobalmarketer.com, 2007.

Other studies confirm a tendency among managers to use over-optimistic estimates when preparing investment proposals. (See reference 1 at the end of the chapter.) It seems that sometimes this is done deliberately in an attempt to secure project approval. Where over-optimistic estimates are used, the managers responsible may well find themselves accountable at the post-completion audit stage. Such audits, however, can be difficult and time-consuming to carry out. The likely benefits must, therefore, be weighed against the costs involved. Senior management may feel, therefore, that only projects above a certain size should be subject to a post-completion audit.

Real World 8.14 provides some indication of the extent to whch post-completion audits are used by businesses.

Real World 8.14

Looking back

The CIMA survey, mentioned in earlier chapters, examined the extent to which post-completion audits are used in practice. The results for all businesses surveyed, as well as for very large businesses (that is, ones with more than 10,000 employees), are set out in Figure 8.10.

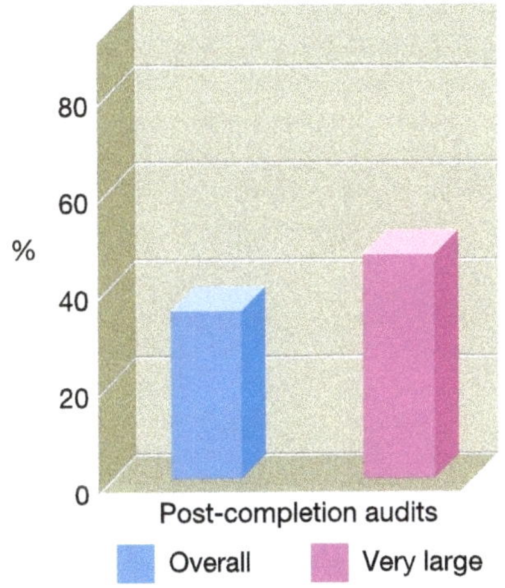

The results show that around half of very large businesses, and considerably less than half of businesses overall, use post-completion audits.

Figure 8.10 Post-completion audits

We can see that larger businesses are more likely to use this technique. These businesses are likely to undertake more and bigger investment projects and have more finance staff to monitor business performance and so the results are not surprising.

Source: Adapted from figure in CIMA (2009) *Management Accounting Tools for Today and Tomorrow*, p. 18.

Real World 8.15 describes how one large retailer, Kingfisher plc, goes about monitoring and controlling its investment projects. Kingfisher sells do-it-yourself goods, notably through the B&Q chain of stores.

Real World 8.15

Getting a grip

The 2013 annual report of Kingfisher plc reveals that the business invested £316 million during the year 2012/13. To monitor and control this vast level of expenditure, the following procedures are adopted:

- **An annual strategic planning process based on detailed medium term plans for all businesses for the next four years. This process drives the key strategic capital allocation decisions and the output is reviewed by the Board;**
- **A capital approval process through a capital expenditure committee, attended by the Group Chief Executive, Group Finance Director, CEO Group Productivity and Development, Group Property Director, Group General Counsel. The committee is delegated to review all projects above £0.75 million and to sign off the projects between £0.75 million and £15.0 million (including the capitalised value of lease commitments);**
- **Projects above £15.0 million are required to be approved by the Board although all projects above £0.75 million are also notified to the Board;**
- **Clear investment criteria including KEP [Kingfisher economic profit*] and NPV and challenging hurdle rates for IRR and DPB (discounted payback);**
- **An annual post-investment review process to undertake a full assessment of all projects above £0.75 million which were completed in the last two to four years. The findings of this exercise are considered by both the capital expenditure committee and the Board and used to inform the assumptions for similar project proposals going forward; and**
- **An annual review of KEP by store is performed which drives plans to improve the returns of weaker stores.**

* 'Kingfisher economic profit' is a measure of economic profit generated that is particular to Kingfisher.

Source: Kingfisher plc Annual Report 2012/13, www.kingfisher.com, p. 22.

Self-assessment question 8.1

Beacon Chemicals plc is considering buying some equipment to produce a chemical named X14. The new equipment's capital cost is estimated at £100 million. If its purchase is approved now, the equipment can be bought and production can commence by the end of this year. £50 million has already been spent on research and development work. Estimates of revenues and costs arising from the operation of the new equipment are:

	Year 1	*Year 2*	*Year 3*	*Year 4*	*Year 5*
Sales price (£/litre)	100	120	120	100	80
Sales volume (million litres)	0.8	1.0	1.2	1.0	0.8
Variable cost (£/litre)	50	50	40	30	40
Fixed cost (£m)	30	30	30	30	30

If the equipment is bought, sales of some existing products will be lost resulting in a loss of contribution of £15 million a year, over the life of the equipment.

The accountant has informed you that the fixed cost includes depreciation of £20 million a year on the new equipment. It also includes an allocation of £10 million for fixed overheads. A separate study has indicated that if the new equipment were bought, additional overheads, excluding depreciation, arising from producing the chemical would be £8 million a year. Production would require additional working capital of £30 million.

For the purposes of your initial calculations ignore taxation.

Required:

(a) Deduce the relevant annual cash flows associated with buying the equipment.

(b) Deduce the payback period.

(c) Calculate the net present value using a discount rate of 8 per cent.

(d) How sensitive is the NPV calculated in (c) to the estimate of the annual loss of contribution from the existing products? Comment on the sensitivity.

(*Hint*: You should deal with the investment in working capital by treating it as a cash outflow at the start of the project and an inflow at the end.)

The solution to this question can be found in Appendix B.

SUMMARY

The main points of this chapter may be summarised as follows:

Accounting rate of return (APP)

- Accounting rate of return (ARR) is the average accounting profit from the project expressed as a percentage of the average investment.
- Decision rule – projects with an ARR above a defined minimum are acceptable; the greater the ARR, the more attractive the project becomes.
- Conclusion on ARR:
  - does not relate directly to shareholders' wealth – can lead to illogical conclusions;
  - takes almost no account of the timing of cash flows;
  - ignores some relevant information and may take account of some that is irrelevant;
  - relatively simple to use;
  - much inferior to NPV.

Payback period (PP)

- Payback period (PP) is the length of time that it takes for the cash outflow for the initial investment to be repaid out of resulting cash inflows.
- Decision rule – projects with a PP up to a defined maximum period are acceptable; the shorter the PP, the more attractive the project.
- Conclusion on PP:
  - does not relate to shareholders' wealth;
  - ignores inflows after the payback date;
  - takes little account of the timing of cash flows;
  - ignores much relevant information;
  - does not always provide clear signals and can be impractical to use;
  - much inferior to NPV, but it is easy to understand and can offer a liquidity insight, which might be the reason for its widespread use.

Net present value (NPV)

- Net present value (NPV) is the sum of the discounted values of the net cash flows from the investment.
- Money has a time value.

→

- Decision rule – all positive NPV investments enhance shareholders' wealth; the greater the NPV, the greater the enhancement and the greater the attractiveness of the project.
- PV of a cash flow = cash flow × $1/(1 + r)^n$, assuming a constant discount rate.
- Discounting brings cash flows at different points in time to a common valuation basis (their present value), which enables them to be directly compared.
- Conclusion on NPV:
  - relates directly to shareholders' wealth objective;
  - takes account of the timing of cash flows;
  - takes all relevant information into account;
  - provides clear signals and is practical to use.

Internal rate of return (IRR)

- Internal rate of return (IRR) is the discount rate that, when applied to the cash flows of a project, causes it to have a zero NPV.
- Represents the average percentage return on the investment, taking account of the fact that cash may be flowing in and out of the project at various points in its life.
- Decision rule – projects that have an IRR greater than the cost of capital are acceptable; the greater the IRR, the more attractive the project.
- Cannot normally be calculated directly; a trial-and-error approach is usually necessary.
- Conclusion on IRR:
  - does not relate directly to shareholders' wealth. Usually gives the same signals as NPV but can mislead where there are competing projects of different size;
  - takes account of the timing of cash flows;
  - takes all relevant information into account;
  - problems of multiple IRRs when there are unconventional cash flows;
  - inferior to NPV.

Use of appraisal methods in practice

- All four methods identified are widely used.
- The discounting methods (NPV and IRR) show a steady increase in usage over time.
- Many businesses use more than one method.
- Larger businesses seem to be more sophisticated in their choice and use of appraisal methods than smaller ones.

Investment appraisal and strategic planning

- It is important that businesses invest in a strategic way so as to play to their strengths.

Dealing with risk

- Sensitivity analysis is an assessment, taking each input factor in turn, of how much each one can vary from estimate before a project is not viable.
  - It provides useful insights to projects.
  - It does not give a clear decision rule, but provides an impression.
  - It can be rather static, but scenario building solves this problem.

- Expected net present value (ENPV) is the weighted average of the possible outcomes for a project, based on probabilities for each of the inputs.
  - It provides a single value and a clear decision rule.
  - The single ENPV figure can hide the real risk.
  - It is useful for the ENPV figure to be supported by information on the range and dispersion of possible outcomes.
  - Probabilities may be subjective (based on opinion) or objective (based on evidence).
- Reacting to the level of risk:
  - Logically, high risk should lead to high returns.
  - Using a risk-adjusted discount rate, where a risk premium is added to the risk-free rate, is a logical response to risk.

Managing investment projects

- Determine investment funds available – dealing, if necessary, with capital rationing problems.
- Identify profitable project opportunities.
- Evaluate the proposed project.
- Approve the project.
- Monitor and control the project – using a post-completion audit approach.

KEY TERMS

For definitions of these terms, see Appendix A.

Accounting rate of return (ARR)
Payback period (PP)
Net present value (NPV)
Risk
Risk premium
Inflation
Discount factor
Cost of capital
Internal rate of return (IRR)
Sensitivity analysis
Scenario building
Expected net present value (ENPV)
Objective probabilities
Subjective probabilities
Risk-adjusted discount rate
Capital rationing
Post-completion audit

REFERENCE

1 Linder, S. (2005) *Fifty Years of Research on Accuracy of Capital Expenditure Project Estimates: A Review of the Findings and Their Validity*, Otto Beisheim Graduate School of Management, April.

FURTHER READING

If you would like to explore the topics covered in this chapter in more depth, we recommend the following:

Arnold, G. (2012) *Corporate Financial Management*, 5th edn, Pearson, Chapters 2, 3 and 4.

Drury, C. (2012) *Management and Cost Accounting*, 8th edn, Cengage Learning, Chapters 13 and 14.

McLaney, E. (2014) *Business Finance: Theory and Practice*, 10th edn, Financial Times Prentice Hall, Chapters 4, 5 and 6.

Pike, R., Neale, B. and Linsley, P. (2012) *Corporate Finance and Investment*, 7th edn, Pearson, Chapters 3 to 7.

REVIEW QUESTIONS

Solutions to these questions can be found in Appendix C.

8.1 Why is the net present value method of investment appraisal considered to be theoretically superior to other methods that are found in practice?

8.2 The payback period method has been criticised for not taking the time value of money into account. Could this limitation be overcome? If so, would this method then be preferable to the NPV method?

8.3 Research indicates that the IRR method is extremely popular even though it has shortcomings when compared to the NPV method. Why might managers prefer to use IRR rather than NPV when carrying out discounted cash flow evaluations?

8.4 Why are cash flows rather than profit flows used in the IRR, NPV and PP methods of investment appraisal?

EXERCISES

Exercises 8.1 and 8.2 are basic level, 8.3 and 8.4 are intermediate level and 8.5 to 8.8 are advanced level. Those with coloured numbers have solutions given in Appendix D.

8.1 The directors of Mylo Ltd are currently considering two mutually exclusive investment projects. Both projects are concerned with the purchase of new plant. The following data are available for each project:

	Project 1 £000	*Project 2* £000
Cost (immediate outlay)	100	60
Expected annual operating profit (loss):		
Year 1	29	18
2	(1)	(2)
3	2	4
Estimated residual value of the plant after 3 years	7	6

The business has an estimated cost of capital of 10 per cent. It uses the straight-line method of depreciation for all non-current (fixed) assets when calculating operating profit. Neither project would increase the working capital of the business. The business has sufficient funds to meet all investment expenditure requirements.

Required:

(a) Calculate for each project:

(i) the net present value;

(ii) the approximate internal rate of return;

(iii) the payback period.

(b) State, with reasons, which, if any, of the two investment projects the directors of Mylo Ltd should accept.

8.2 Arkwright Mills plc is considering expanding its production of a new yarn, code name X15. The plant is expected to cost £1 million and have a life of five years and a nil residual value. It will be bought, paid for and ready for operation on 31 December Year 0. £500,000 has already been spent on development costs of the product; this has been charged in the income statement in the year it was incurred.

The following results are projected for the new yarn:

	Year 1	*Year 2*	*Year 3*	*Year 4*	*Year 5*
	£m	*£m*	*£m*	*£m*	*£m*
Sales revenue	1.2	1.4	1.4	1.4	1.4
Costs, including depreciation	(1.0)	(1.1)	(1.1)	(1.1)	(1.1)
Profit before tax	0.2	0.3	0.3	0.3	0.3

Tax is charged at 50 per cent on annual profits (before tax and after depreciation) and paid one year in arrears. Depreciation of the plant has been calculated on a straight-line basis. Additional working capital of £0.6 million will be required at the beginning of the project and released at the end of Year 5. You should assume that all cash flows occur at the end of the year in which they arise.

Required:

(a) Prepare a statement showing the incremental cash flows of the project relevant to a decision concerning whether or not to proceed with the construction of the new plant.

(b) Compute the net present value of the project using a 10 per cent discount rate.

(c) Compute the payback period to the nearest year. Explain the meaning of this term.

8.3 Newton Electronics Ltd has incurred expenditure of £5 million over the past three years researching and developing a miniature hearing aid. The hearing aid is now fully developed. The directors are considering which of three mutually exclusive options should be taken to exploit the potential of the new product. The options are:

1 The business could manufacture the hearing aid itself. This would be a new departure, since the business has so far concentrated on research and development projects. However, the business has manufacturing space available that it currently rents to another business for £100,000 a year. This space will not continue to be leased if the decision is not to manufacture. The business would have to purchase plant and equipment costing £9 million and invest £3 million in working capital immediately for production to begin.

A market research report, for which the business paid £50,000, indicates that the new product has an expected life of five years. Sales of the product during this period are predicted as:

	Predicted sales for the year ended 30 November				
	Year 1	*Year 2*	*Year 3*	*Year 4*	*Year 5*
Number of units (000s)	800	1,400	1,800	1,200	500

The selling price per unit will be £30 in the first year but will fall to £22 in the following three years. In the final year of the product's life, the selling price will fall to £20. Variable production costs are predicted to be £14 a unit. Fixed production costs (including depreciation) will be £2.4 million a year. Marketing costs will be £2 million a year.

The business intends to depreciate the plant and equipment using the straight-line method and based on an estimated residual value at the end of the five years of £1 million. The business has a cost of capital of 10 per cent a year.

2 Newton Electronics Ltd could agree to another business manufacturing and marketing the product under licence. A multinational business, Faraday Electricals plc, has offered to undertake the manufacture and marketing of the product. In return it will make a royalty payment to Newton Electronics Ltd of £5 per unit. It has been estimated that the annual number of sales of the hearing aid will be 10 per cent higher if the multinational business, rather than Newton Electronics Ltd, manufactures and markets the product.

3 Newton Electronics Ltd could sell the patent rights to Faraday Electricals plc for £24 million, payable in two equal instalments. The first instalment would be payable immediately and the second at the end of two years. This option would give Faraday Electricals the exclusive right to manufacture and market the new product.

Required:

Ignoring taxation,

(a) Calculate the net present value (as at the beginning of Year 1) of each of the options available to Newton Electronics Ltd.

(b) Identify and discuss any other factors that Newton Electronics Ltd should consider before arriving at a decision.

(c) State, with reasons, what you consider to be the most suitable option.

8.4 C. George (Controls) Ltd manufactures a thermostat that can be used in a range of kitchen appliances. The manufacturing process is, at present, semi-automated. The equipment used cost £540,000 and has a carrying amount (as shown on the statement of financial position) of £300,000. Demand for the product has been fairly stable at 50,000 units a year in recent years.

The following data, based on the current level of output, have been prepared in respect of the product:

	Per unit	
	£	£
Selling price		12.40
Labour	(3.30)	
Materials	(3.65)	
Overheads: Variable	(1.58)	
Fixed	(1.60)	
		(10.13)
Operating profit		2.27

Although the existing equipment is expected to last for a further four years before it is sold for an estimated £40,000, the business has recently been considering purchasing new equipment that would completely automate much of the production process. The new equipment would cost £670,000 and would have an expected life of four years, at the end of which it would be sold for an estimated £70,000. If the new equipment is purchased, the old equipment could be sold for £150,000 immediately.

The assistant to the business's accountant has prepared a report to help assess the viability of the proposed change, which includes the following data:

	Per unit	
	£	£
Selling price		12.40
Labour	(1.20)	
Materials	(3.20)	
Overheads: Variable	(1.40)	
Fixed	(3.30)	
		(9.10)
Operating profit		3.30

Depreciation charges will increase by £85,000 a year as a result of purchasing the new machinery; however, other fixed costs are not expected to change.

In the report the assistant wrote:

> The figures shown above that relate to the proposed change are based on the current level of output and take account of a depreciation charge of £150,000 a year in respect of the new equipment. The effect of purchasing the new equipment will be to increase the operating profit to sales revenue ratio from 18.3 per cent to 26.6 per cent. In addition, the purchase of the new equipment will enable us to reduce our inventories level immediately by £130,000.
>
> In view of these facts, I recommend purchase of the new equipment.

The business has a cost of capital of 12 per cent. Ignore taxation.

Required:

(a) Prepare a statement of the incremental cash flows arising from the purchase of the new equipment.

(b) Calculate the net present value of the proposed purchase of new equipment.

(c) State, with reasons, whether the business should purchase the new equipment.

(d) Explain why cash flow, rather than profit, projections are used to assess the viability of proposed capital expenditure projects.

8.5 The accountant of your business has recently been taken ill through overwork. In his absence his assistant has prepared some calculations of the profitability of a project, which are to be discussed soon at the board meeting of your business. His workings, which are set out below, include some errors of principle. You can assume that there are no arithmetical errors.

Year	*0*	*1*	*2*	*3*	*4*	*5*
	£000	*£000*	*£000*	*£000*	*£000*	*£000*
Sales revenue		450	470	470	470	470
Less costs						
Materials		126	132	132	132	132
Labour		90	94	94	94	94
Overheads		45	47	47	47	47
Depreciation		120	120	120	120	120
Working capital	180					
Interest on working capital		27	27	27	27	27
Write-off of development costs	–	30	30	30	–	–
Total costs	180	438	450	450	420	420
Operating profit/(loss)	(180)	12	20	20	50	50

$$\frac{\text{Total profit (loss)}}{\text{Cost of equipment}} = \frac{(£28{,}000)}{£600{,}000} = \text{Return on investment (4.7\%)}$$

You ascertain the following additional information:

1 The cost of equipment includes £100,000, being the carrying value of an old machine. If it were not used for this project it would be scrapped with a zero net realisable value. New equipment costing £500,000 will be purchased on 31 December year 0. You should assume that all other cash flows occur at the end of the year to which they relate.
2 The development costs of £90,000 have already been spent.
3 Overheads have been costed at 50 per cent of direct labour, which is the business's normal practice. An independent assessment has suggested that incremental overheads are likely to amount to £30,000 a year.
4 The business's cost of capital is 12 per cent.

Required:
Ignoring taxation,

(a) Prepare a corrected statement of the incremental cash flows arising from the project. Where you have altered the assistant's figures you should attach a brief note explaining your alterations.
(b) Calculate:
   (i) The project's payback period.
   (ii) The project's net present value as at 31 December year 0.
(c) Write a memo to the board advising on the acceptance or rejection of the project.

8.6 Simtex Ltd has invested £120,000 to date in developing a new type of shaving foam. The shaving foam is now ready for production and it has been estimated that the business will sell 160,000 cans a year of the new product over the next four years. At the end of four years, the product will be discontinued and probably replaced by a new product.

The shaving foam is expected to sell at £6 a can and the variable cost is estimated at £4 per can. Fixed cost (excluding depreciation) is expected to be £300,000 a year. (This figure includes £130,000 of the existing general overheads of the business that will be apportioned to this new product.)

To manufacture and package the new product, equipment costing £480,000 must be acquired immediately. The estimated value of this equipment in four years' time is £100,000. The business calculates depreciation using the straight-line method (equal amounts each year). It has an estimated cost of capital of 12 per cent.

Required:
(a) Deduce the net present value of the new product.
(b) Calculate by how much each of the following must change before the new product is no longer profitable:
   (i) the discount rate;
   (ii) the initial outlay on new equipment;
   (iii) the net operating cash flows;
   (iv) the residual value of the equipment.
(c) Should the business produce the new product?

8.7 Chesterfield Wanderers is a professional football club that has enjoyed considerable success in both national and European competitions in recent years. As a result, the club has accumulated £10 million to spend on its further development. The board of directors is currently considering two mutually exclusive options for spending the funds available.

The first option is to acquire another player. The team manager has expressed a keen interest in acquiring Basil ('Bazza') Ramsey, a central defender, who currently plays for a rival club. The rival club has agreed to release the player immediately for £10 million if required. A decision to acquire 'Bazza' Ramsey would mean that the existing central defender, Vinnie Smith, could be sold to another club. Chesterfield Wanderers has recently received an offer of £2.2 million for this player. This offer is still open but will only be accepted if 'Bazza' Ramsey joins Chesterfield Wanderers. If this does not happen, Vinnie Smith will be expected to stay on with the club until the end of his playing career in five years' time. During this period, Vinnie will receive an annual salary of £400,000 and a loyalty bonus of £200,000 at the end of his five-year period with the club.

Assuming 'Bazza' Ramsey is acquired, the team manager estimates that gate receipts will increase by £2.5 million in the first year and £1.3 million in each of the four following years. There will also be an increase in advertising and sponsorship revenues of £1.2 million for each of the next five years if the player is acquired. At the end of five years, the player can be sold to a club in a lower division and Chesterfield Wanderers will expect to receive £1 million as a transfer fee. During his period at the club, 'Bazza' will receive an annual salary of £800,000 and a loyalty bonus of £400,000 after five years.

The second option is for the club to improve its ground facilities. The west stand could be extended and executive boxes could be built for businesses wishing to offer corporate hospitality to clients. These improvements would also cost £10 million and would take one year to complete. During this period, the west stand would be closed, resulting in a reduction of gate receipts of £1.8 million. However, gate receipts for each of the following four years would be £4.4 million higher than current receipts. In five years' time, the club has plans to sell the existing grounds and to move to a new stadium nearby. Improving the ground facilities is not expected to affect the ground's value when it comes to be sold. Payment for the improvements will be made when the work has been completed at the end of the first year. Whichever option is chosen, the board of directors has decided to take on additional ground staff. The additional wages bill is expected to be £350,000 a year over the next five years.

The club has a cost of capital of 10 per cent.

Required:

Ignoring taxation,

(a) Calculate the incremental cash flows arising from each of the options available to the club, and the net present value of each of the options.

(b) On the basis of the calculations made in (a) above, which of the two options would you choose and why?

(c) Discuss the validity of using the net present value method in making investment decisions for a professional football club.

8.8 Kernow Cleaning Services Ltd provides street-cleaning services for local councils in the far south west of England. The work is currently labour-intensive and few machines are used. However, the business has recently been considering the purchase of a fleet of street-cleaning vehicles at a total cost of £540,000. The vehicles have a life of four years and are likely to result in a considerable saving of labour costs. Estimates of the likely labour savings and their probability of occurrence are set out below:

	Estimated savings £	*Probability of occurrence*
Year 1	80,000	0.3
	160,000	0.5
	200,000	0.2
Year 2	140,000	0.4
	220,000	0.4
	250,000	0.2
Year 3	140,000	0.4
	200,000	0.3
	230,000	0.3
Year 4	100,000	0.3
	170,000	0.6
	200,000	0.1

Estimates for each year are independent of other years. The business has a cost of capital of 10 per cent.

Required:

(a) Calculate the expected net present value (ENPV) of the street-cleaning machines.

(b) Calculate the net present value (NPV) of the worst possible outcome and the probability of its occurrence.

Appendix D
SOLUTIONS TO SELECTED EXERCISES

Chapter 1

1.1 Strategic management involves five steps:

1. *Establish mission, vision and objectives.* The mission statement is usually a brief statement of the overriding purpose of the business. The vision statement sets out the aspirations of the business. The objectives are rather more specific than the mission and need to be consistent with the mission and vision. These objectives are often quantified.
2. *Undertake a position analysis.* Here the business is seeking to establish how it is placed relative to its environment (competitors, markets, technology, the economy, political climate and so on), given the business's mission and objectives. This is often approached within the framework of an analysis of the business's strengths, weaknesses, opportunities and threats (a SWOT analysis). Strengths and weaknesses are internal factors that are attributes of the business itself, whereas opportunities and threats are factors expected to be present in the environment in which the business operates. The SWOT framework is not the only possible approach to undertaking a position analysis, but it seems to be a very popular one.
3. *Identify and assess the strategic options.* This involves attempting to identify possible courses of action that will enable the business to reach its objectives in the light of the position analysis undertaken in Step 2.
4. *Select strategic options and formulate plans.* Here the business will select what seems to be the best of the courses of action or strategies (identified in Step 3) and will formulate a plan to implement the strategies.
5. *Perform, review and control.* Here the business pursues the plans derived in Step 4, using the traditional approach to compare actual performance against budgets, seeking to control where actual performance appears not to be matching plans.

1.2 **SWOT analysis of Jones Dairy Ltd**

Strengths

- A portfolio of identifiable customers who show some loyalty to the business.
- Good cash flow profile. Though credit will be given, a week is the normal credit period.
- An apparently sound distribution system.
- A monopoly of doorstep delivery in the area.
- Barriers to entry. There are probably relatively high entry costs to the market, which implies a 'critical mass' of volume is necessary.
- Good employees and ease of recruitment.
- Differentiated product; clearly different from what is supplied by the supermarket in that it is delivered to the door.
- Apparently good marketing, since the decline in business is less than the national average.
- Good knowledge of the local market.
- Tendency for people to shop infrequently means that doorstep delivery may be the only practical means of having fresh milk.

Weaknesses

- Ageing managers.
- Success might be dependent on the present management continuing to manage.
- Narrow product range.
- High price necessary to generate acceptable level of profit.

- Available substitute – that is, non-delivered milk.
- Single supplier.

Opportunities

- Possibility of extending the product range to include other dairy and non-dairy products to existing customers.
- Possible geographical expansion to cover other local towns and villages.
- Possibly move to act as a wholesaler to local stores at differentiated prices. It is probable that the bottlers would supply Jones more cheaply than they would supply individual small stores.
- Using plant for some other purpose, such as leasing cold store facilities.

Threats

- Apparently strong trend against doorstep delivery driven by price differential.
- Trend away from dairy products for health/cultural reasons.
- The probability that Jones is entirely dependent on the only local bottler. More geographically remote bottlers may not be prepared to supply at an acceptable price.
- Increasing strength of supermarket buying power.

Chapter 2

2.1 Lombard Ltd

Relevant costs of undertaking the contract are:

	£
Equipment costs	200,000
Component X (20,000 × 4 × £5) Any of these components used will need to be replaced.	400,000
Component Y (20,000 × 3 × £8) All of the required units will come from inventories and this will be an effective cost of the net realisable value.	480,000
Additional costs (20,000 × £8)	160,000
	1,240,000
Revenue from the contract (20,000 × £80)	1,600,000

Thus, from a purely financial point of view the project is acceptable. (Note that there is no relevant labour cost since the staff concerned will be paid irrespective of whether the contract is undertaken.)

2.2 The local authority

(a) Net benefit of accepting the touring company proposal:

		£
Net reduction in ticket revenues (see workings below)		(20,000)
Savings on:	Costumes	5,600
	Scenery	3,300
	Casual staff	3,520
Net deficit		(7,580)

Since there is a net deficit, on financial grounds, the touring company's proposal should be rejected.

Note that all of the following are irrelevant, because they will occur irrespective of the decision:

- non-performing staff salaries
- artistes' salaries
- heating and lighting
- administration costs
- refreshment revenues and costs
- programme advertising.

Workings

Normal ticket sales revenue:

	£
200 @ £24 =	4,800
500 @ £16 =	8,000
300 @ £12 =	3,600
	16,400

Ticket revenue at 50 per cent capacity for 20 performances:

(£16,400 × 50% × 20) = £164,000

Touring company ticket sales:

Total revenue for each performance for a full house:

	£
200 @ £22 =	4,400
500 @ £14 =	7,000
300 @ £10 =	3,000
	14,400

		£
Ticket revenues	(£14,400 × 10 × 50%)	72,000
	(£14,400 × 15 × $^2/_3$ × 50%)	72,000
		144,000
Net loss of revenue (£164,000 – £144,000) =		£20,000

(b) Other possible factors to consider include:

- The reliability of the estimations, including the assumption that the level of occupancy will not alter programme and refreshment sales revenue.
- A desire to offer theatregoers the opportunity to see another group of players.
- Dangers of loss of morale of staff not employed, or employed to do other than their usual work.

2.3 Andrews and Co. Ltd

Minimum contract price

			£
Materials	Steel core:	10,000 × £2.10	21,000
	Plastic:	10,000 × 0.10 × £0.10	100
Labour	Skilled:		–
	Unskilled:	10,000 × $^5/_{60}$ × £7.50	6,250
Minimum tender price			27,350

2.6 The local education authority

(a) One-off financial net benefits of closing:

	D only	*A and B*	*A and C*
Capacity reduction	800	700	800
	£m	*£m*	*£m*
Property developer (A)	–	14.0	14.0
Shopping complex (B)	–	8.0	–
Property developer (D)	9.0	–	–
Safety (C)	–	–	3.0
Adapt facilities	(1.8)	–	–
Total	7.2	22.0	17.0
Ranking based on total one-off benefits	3	1	2

(Note that all past costs of buying and improving the schools are irrelevant.)

Recurrent financial net benefits of closing:

	D only	*A and B*	*A and C*
	£m	*£m*	*£m*
Rent (C)	–	–	0.3
Administrators	0.2	0.4	0.4
Total	0.2	0.4	0.7
Ranking based on total of recurrent benefits	3	2	1

On the basis of the financial figures alone, closure of either A and B or A and C looks best. It is not possible to add the one-off and the recurring costs directly, but the large one-off cost saving associated with closing schools A and B makes this option look attractive. (In Chapter 8 we shall see that it is possible to add one-off and recurring costs in a way that should lead to sensible conclusions.)

(b) The costs of acquiring and improving the schools in the past are past costs or sunk costs and, therefore, irrelevant. The costs of employing the chief education officer is a future cost, but irrelevant because it is not dependent on outcomes, it is a common cost.

(c) There are many other factors, some of a non-quantifiable nature. These include:

- Accuracy of projections of capacity requirements.
- Locality of existing schools relative to where potential pupils live.
- Political acceptability of selling schools to property developers.
- Importance of purely financial issues in making the final decision.
- The quality of the replacement sporting facilities compared with those at school D.
- Political acceptability of staff redundancies.
- Possible savings/costs of employing fewer teachers, which might be relevant if economies of scale are available by having fewer schools.
- Staff morale.

2.7 Rob Otics Ltd

(a) The minimum price for the proposed contract would be:

	£
Materials	
Component X (2 × 8 × £180)	2,880
This inventories item is in constant use by the business. This means that the 10 units held will ultimately need to be replaced, as well as a further 6 units needing to be purchased. All of these will need to be bought at the new price.	
Component Y	0
The history of the components held in inventories is irrelevant because it applies irrespective of the decision made on this contract. Since the alternative to using the units on this contract is to scrap them, the relevant cost is zero.	
Component Z [(75 + 32) × £20] – (75 × £25)	265
The relevant cost here is how much extra the business will pay the supplier as a result of undertaking the contract.	
Other miscellaneous items	250
Labour	
Assembly (25 + 24 + 23 + 22 + 21 + 20 + 19 + 18) × £48	8,256
The assembly labour cost is irrelevant because it will be incurred irrespective of which work the members of staff do. The relevant cost is based on the sales revenue per hour lost if the other orders are lost less the material cost per hour saved; that is £60 – £12 = £48.	
Inspection (8 × 6 × £12 × 150%)	864
Total	12,515

Thus the minimum price is £12,515.

(b) Other factors include:

- Competitive state of the market.
- The fact that the above figure is unique to the particular circumstances at the time – for example, having Component Y available but having no use for it. Any subsequent order might have to take account of an outlay cost.
- Breaking even (that is, just covering the costs) on a contract will not fulfil the business's objective.
- Charging a low price may cause marketing problems. Other customers may resent the low price for this contract. The current enquirer may expect a similar price in future.

Chapter 3

3.1 Motormusic Ltd

(a) Break-even point = fixed costs/contribution per unit = (80,000 + 60,000)/[60 − (20 + 14 + 12 + 3)] = 12,727 radios.

These would have a sales value of £763,620 (that is, 12,727 × £60).

(b) The margin of safety is 7,273 radios (that is, 20,000 − 12,727). This margin would have a sales value of £436,380 (that is, 7,273 × £60).

3.3 Gandhi Ltd

(a) Given that the spare capacity could not be used by other services, the Standard service should continue to be offered. This is because it renders a positive contribution.

(b) The Standard service renders a contribution per unit of £15 (that is, £80 − £65), or £30 during the time it would take to render one unit of the Nova service. The Nova service would provide a contribution of only £25 (that is, £75 − £50).

The Nova service should, therefore, not replace the Standard service.

(c) Under the original plans, the following contributions would be rendered by the basic and standard services:

		£
Basic	11,000 × (£50 − £25) =	275,000
Standard	6,000 × (£80 − £65) =	90,000
		365,000

If the Basic were to take the Standard's place, 17,000 units (that is, 11,000 + 6,000) of them could be produced in total. To generate the same total contribution, each unit of the Standard service would need to provide £21.47 (that is, £365,000/17,000) of contribution. Given the basic's variable cost of £25, this would mean a selling price of £46.47 each (that is, £21.47 + £25.00).

3.6 Products A, B and C

(a) Total time required on cutting machines is:

(2,500 × 1.0) + (3,400 × 1.0) + (5,100 × 0.5) = 8,450 hours

Total time available on cutting machines is 5,000 hours. Therefore, this is a limiting factor.

Total time required on assembling machines is:

(2,500 × 0.5) + (3,400 × 1.0) + (5,100 × 0.5) = 7,200 hours

Total time available on assembling machines is 8,000 hours. Therefore, this is not a limiting factor.

	A (per unit) £	B (per unit) £	C (per unit) £
Selling price	25	30	18
Variable materials	(12)	(13)	(10)
Variable production costs	(7)	(4)	(3)
Contribution	6	13	5
Time on cutting machines	1.0 hour	1.0 hour	0.5 hour
Contribution per hour on cutting machines	£6	£13	£10
Order of priority	3rd	1st	2nd

Therefore, produce:

3,400 product B using	3,400 hours
3,200 product C using	1,600 hours
	5,000 hours

(b) Assuming that the business would make no saving in variable production costs by subcontracting, it would be worth paying up to the contribution per unit (£5) for product C, which would therefore be £5 × (5,100 – 3,200) = £9,500 in total.

Similarly it would be worth paying up to £6 per unit for product A – that is, £6 × 2,500 = £15,000 in total.

3.7 Darmor Ltd

(a) Contribution per hour of skilled labour of Product X is

$$\frac{£(30 - 6 - 2 - 12 - 3)}{(6/12)} = £14$$

Given the scarcity of skilled labour, if the management is to be indifferent between the products, the contribution per skilled labour hour must be the same. Thus for Product Y the selling price must be

$$(£(14 \times (9/12)) + 9 + 4 + 25 + 7) = £55.50$$

(that is, the contribution plus the variable costs), and for Product Z the selling price must be

$$(£(14 \times (3/12)) + 3 + 10 + 14 + 7) = £37.50$$

(b) The business could pay up to £26 an hour (£12 + £14) for additional hours of skilled labour. This is the potential contribution per hour, before taking account of the labour rate of £12 an hour.

3.8 Intermediate Products Ltd

(a)

	A	B	C	D
Total costs per unit (£)	(65)	(41)	(36)	(46)
Less Fixed cost (£)	20	8	8	12
Variable cost per unit (£)	(45)	(33)	(28)	(34)
Buying/selling price per unit (£)	70	45	40	55
Contribution per unit (£)	25	12	12	21
Hours on special machine	0.5	0.4	0.5	0.3
Contribution per hour (£)	50	30	24	70
Order of preference	2nd	3rd	4th	1st

Optimum use of hours on special machine		*Balance of hours*
D	3,000 × 0.3 = 900	5,100 (that is, 6,000 – 900)
A	5,000 × 0.5 = 2,500	2,600 (that is, 5,100 – 2,500)
B	6,000 × 0.4 = 2,400	200 (that is, 2,600 – 2,400)
C	400 × 0.5 = 200	
	6,000	

Therefore, make all of the demand for Ds, As and Bs plus 400 (of 4,000) Cs.

(b) The contribution per hour from Cs is £24, and so this is the maximum amount per hour that it would be worth paying to rent the machine, for a maximum of 1,800 hours (that is, 3,600 × 0.5, the time necessary to make the remaining demand for Cs).

(c) Other possible actions to overcome the shortage of machine time include the following:

- Alter the design of the products to avoid the use of the special machine.
- Increase the selling price of the product so that the demand will fall, making the available machine time sufficient but making production more profitable.

Chapter 4

4.1 Offending phrases and explanations

Offending phrase	*Explanation*
'Necessary to divide up the business into departments'	This can be done but it will not always be of much benefit. Only in quite restricted circumstances will it give a significantly different job cost.
'Fixed costs (or overheads)'	This implies that fixed cost and overheads are the same thing. They are not really connected with one another. 'Fixed' is to do with how cost behaves as the level of output is raised or lowered; 'overheads' are to do with the extent to which cost can be directly measured in respect of a particular unit of output. Though it is true that many overheads are fixed, not all are. Also, direct labour is usually a fixed cost. All of the other references to fixed and variable costs are wrong. The person should have referred to indirect and direct costs.
'Usually this is done on the basis of area'	Where overheads are apportioned to departments, they will be apportioned on some logical basis. For certain elements of cost – for example, rent – the floor area may be the most logical; for others, such as machine maintenance cost, the floor area would be totally inappropriate.
'When the total fixed costs for each department have been identified, this will be divided by the number of hours that were worked'	Where overheads are dealt with on a departmental basis, they may be divided by the number of direct labour hours to deduce a recovery rate. However, this is only one basis of applying overheads to jobs. For example, machine hours or some other basis may be more appropriate to the particular circumstances involved.

4.4 Promptprint Ltd

(a) The plan (budget) may be summarised as:

	£	
Sales revenue	196,000	
Direct materials	(38,000)	
Direct labour	(32,000)	
Total indirect cost	(77,000)	(2,400 + 3,000 + 27,600 + 36,000 + 8,000)
Profit	49,000	

The job may be priced on the basis that both indirect cost and profit should be apportioned to it on the basis of direct labour cost, as follows:

	£	
Direct materials	4,000	
Direct labour	3,600	
Overheads	8,663	(£77,000 × 3,600/32,000)
Profit	5,513	(£49,000 × 3,600/32,000)
	21,776	

This answer assumes that variable overheads vary in proportion to direct labour cost.

Various other bases of charging overheads and profit loading the job could have been adopted. For example, materials cost could have been included (with direct labour) as the basis for profit loading, or even apportioning overheads.

(b) This part of the question is, in effect, asking for comments on the validity of 'full cost-plus' pricing. This approach can be useful as an indicator of the effective long-run cost of doing the job. On the other hand, it fails to take account of relevant opportunity cost as well as the state of the market and other external factors. For example, it ignores the price that a competitor printing business may quote.

Revised estimates of direct material cost for the job:

	£	
Paper grade 1	1,500	(£1,200 × 125%) (this item of inventories needs to be replaced)
Paper grade 2	0	(it has no opportunity cost value)
Card	510	(£640 – £130: using the card on another job would save £640, but cost £130 to achieve that saving)
Inks and so on	300	(this item of inventories needs to be replaced)
	2,310	

4.5 **(a)** Charging overheads to jobs on a departmental basis means that overheads are collected 'product' cost centre (department) by 'product' cost centre. This involves picking up the overheads that are direct to each department and adding to them a share of overheads that are general to the business as a whole. The overheads of 'service' cost centres must then be apportioned to the product cost centres. At this point, all of the overheads for the whole business are divided between the 'product' cost centres, such that the sum of the 'product' cost centre overheads equals those for the whole business.

Dealing with overheads departmentally is believed to provide more accurate and useful information to decision makers, because different departments may have rather different overheads, and applying overheads departmentally can take account of that and reflect it in the job costs derived.

In theory, dealing with overheads on a departmental basis is more costly than on a business-wide basis. In practice, it possibly does not make too much difference to the cost of collecting the information. This is because, normally, businesses are divided into departments, and the costs are collected departmentally, as part of the normal routine for exercising control over the business.

(b) In order to make any difference to the job cost that will emerge as a result of dealing with overheads departmentally, as compared with a business-wide basis, the following *both* need to be the case:

- the overheads per unit of the basis of charging (for example direct labour hours) need to be different from one department to the next; and
- the proportion (but not the actual amounts) of total overheads that are charged to jobs must differ from one job to the next.

Assume, for the sake of argument, that direct labour hours are used as the basis of charging overheads in all departments. Also assume that there are three departments, A, B and C.

There will be no difference to the overheads charged to a particular job if the rate of overheads per direct labour hour is the same for all departments. Obviously, if the charging rate is the same in all departments, that same rate must also apply to the business taken as a whole.

Also, even where overheads per direct labour hour differ significantly from one department to another – if all jobs spend, say, about 20 per cent of their time in Department A, 50 per cent in Department B and 30 per cent in Department C – it will not make any difference whether overheads are charged departmentally or overall.

These conclusions are not in any way dependent on the basis of charging overheads or even whether overheads are charged on the same basis in each department.

The statements above combine to mean that, probably in many cases in practice, departmentalising overheads does not provide information that is significantly different from that which would be provided by charging overheads to jobs on a business-wide basis.

4.6 Products A, B and C

Allocation and apportionment of overheads to product cost centres:

	Basis of apportionment	*Department*								
		Cutting		*Machining*		*Pressing*		*Engineering*		*Human resources*
		£		£		£		£		£
Total		154,482		64,316		58,452		56,000		34,000
Human resources	Specified	18,700	(55%)	3,400	(10%)	6,800	(20%)	5,100	(15%)	(34,000)
		173,182		67,716		65,252		61,100		–
Engineering	Specified	12,220	(20%)	27,495	(45%)	21,385	(35%)	(61,100)		
		185,402		95,211		86,637		–		–

Note that the human resources services overheads were reapportioned to the other cost centres first because human resources renders a service to the engineering services department, but does not receive a service from it.

Calculation of the overhead absorption (recovery) rates

In both the cutting and pressing departments, no machines seem to be used, and so a direct labour hour basis of overhead absorption seems reasonable.

In the machining department, machine hours are far in excess of labour hours and the overheads are probably machine-related. In this department, machine hours seem a fair basis for cost units to absorb overheads.

Total planned direct labour hours for the cutting department are thus:

Product A	4,000 × (3 + 6) =	36,000
Product B	3,000 × (5 + 1) =	18,000
Product C	6,000 × (2 + 3) =	30,000
		84,000

The overhead absorption rate for the cutting department is £185,402/84,000 = £2.21 per direct labour hour.

Total planned machine hours for the machining department are thus:

Product A	4,000 × 2.0 =	8,000
Product B	3,000 × 1.5 =	4,500
Product C	6,000 × 2.5 =	15,000
		27,500

The overhead absorption rate for the machining department is £95,211/27,500 = £3.46 per machine hour.

Total planned direct labour hours for the pressing department are:

Product A	4,000 × 2 =	8,000
Product B	3,000 × 3 =	9,000
Product C	6,000 × 4 =	24,000
		41,000

The overhead absorption rate for the cutting department = £86,637/41,000 = £2.11 per direct labour hour.

(a) Cost of one completed unit of product A:

		£
Direct materials		7.00
Direct labour		
Cutting department – skilled	(3 × £16)	48.00
– unskilled	(6 × £10)	60.00
Machining department	(0.5 × £12)	6.00
Pressing department	(2 × £12)	24.00
Overheads		
Cutting department	(9 × £2.21)	19.89
Machining department	(2 × £3.46)	6.92
Pressing department	(2 × £2.11)	4.22
		176.03

(b) Cost of one uncompleted unit of product B:

		£
Direct materials		4.00*
Direct labour		
Cutting department – skilled	(5 × £16)	80.00
– unskilled	(1 × £10)	10.00
Machining department	(0.25 × £12)	3.00
Overheads		
Cutting department	(6 × £2.21)	13.26
Machining department	(1.5 × £3.46)	5.19
		115.45

* This assumes that all of the materials are added in the cutting or machining departments.

4.8 Bookdon plc

(a) To answer this question, we need first to allocate and apportion the overheads to product cost centres, as follows:

Cost	*Basis of apportionment*	*Total*	*Department*			
			Machine shop	*Fitting section*	*Canteen*	*Machine main'ce section*
		£	£	£	£	£
Allocated items:	Specific	90,380	27,660	19,470	16,600	26,650
Rent, rates, heat, light	Floor area	17,000	9,000	3,500	2,500	2,000
			(3,600/ 6,800)	*(1,400/ 6,800)*	*(1,000/ 6,800)*	*(800/ 6,800)*
Depreciation and insurance	Book value	25,000	12,500	6,250	2,500	3,750
			(150/300)	*(75/300)*	*(30/300)*	*(45/300)*
Canteen	Number of employees	–	10,800	8,400	(21,600)	2,400
			(18/36)	*(14/36)*		*(4/36)*
					–	34,800
Machine maintenance section	Specified %	–	24,360	10,440	–	(34,800)
			(70%)	*(30%)*		
		132,380	84,320	48,060	–	–

Note that the canteen overheads were reapportioned to the other cost centres first because the canteen renders a service to the machine maintenance section but does not receive a service from it.

Calculation of the overhead absorption (recovery) rates can now proceed:

(i) Total budgeted machine hours are:

	Hours
Product X (4,200 × 6)	25,200
Product Y (6,900 × 3)	20,700
Product Z (1,700 × 4)	6,800
	52,700

Overhead absorption rate for the machine shop is

$$\frac{£84{,}320}{52{,}700} = £1.60\text{/machine hour}$$

(ii) Total budgeted direct labour cost for the fitting section is:

	£
Product X (4,200 × £12)	50,400
Product Y (6,900 × £3)	20,700
Product Z (1,700 × £21)	35,700
	106,800

Overhead absorption rate for the fitting section is

$$\frac{£48{,}060}{£106{,}800} \times £100\% = 45\%$$

or £0.45 per £ of direct labour cost.

(b) The cost of one unit of product X is calculated as follows:

	£
Direct materials	11.00
Direct labour:	
Machine shop	6.00
Fitting section	12.00
Overheads:	
Machine shop (6 × £1.60)	9.60
Fitting section (£12 × 45%)	5.40
	44.00

Therefore, the cost of one unit of product X is £44.00.

Chapter 5

5.1 Comments

(a) It does not necessarily follow that, in order to improve the quality of output, total costs must increase. Quality costs may be divided into four categories: prevention, appraisal, internal failure and external failure. By investing resources into the prevention of faults and errors, through staff training, more advanced equipment and so forth, it may be possible to reduce costs relating to appraisal (such as inspection), internal failure (such as reworking products) and external failure (such as after-sales service). This means that the additional prevention costs incurred may be offset by the decrease in other quality-related costs.

(b) The TQM approach is concerned with improving quality, while kaizen costing is concerned with cost reduction; nevertheless, there are similarities in the approaches used. They include

- a commitment to continuous improvement;
- recognition of the importance of continuous improvement in a competitive environment;
- the involvement of employees in the quest for improvements;
- detailed investigations of existing processes in order to identify areas for improvement;
- the use of a range of possible methods to achieve the required improvements.

(c) Target costing is particularly useful for manufacturers that produce goods with short life cycles. This is because cost savings are likely to be greatest where there is a need to make frequent updates to existing products and/or to develop a constant stream of new products.

It is less relevant for businesses where product development is not such a significant issue, which will include most service businesses. Nevertheless, opportunities to use this costing approach may still arise. An example was given in the chapter of a firm of management consultants bidding for a contract. Other service providers such as IT specialists, auditors and lawyers may find themselves in a similar position.

5.2 Target costing versus kaizen costing

The main similarities between the two methods are as follows:

- Both methods involve the setting of targets and the comparison of actual performance against target performance.
- Both methods are aimed at reducing costs of production.
- Both can be linked to the concept of total life-cycle costing.
- They were both developed by Japanese businesses in response to an increasingly competitive environment.
- They both employ cross-functional work teams as a means of identifying and reducing costs.
- Neither is a cost measurement method but rather each is a framework within which various cost reduction methods can be employed.

The main differences between the two methods are:

- Target costing is most suitable for the pre-production phase of a product's life whereas kaizen costing is most suitable for the production phase.

- Target costing normally has the potential for much greater cost savings than kaizen costing.
- Kaizen costing involves making many small changes whereas target costing may make significant changes.
- Kaizen costing is concerned with continuous improvement and so extends over a longer time period than target costing.
- Target costing is less relevant to manufacturers where product development is not a significant issue. Kaizen costing can be highly relevant to all manufacturers operating within a competitive environment.

5.3 The main problems that may be encountered include:

- Introducing benchmarking can be time-consuming and costly.
- Finding a suitable successful business against which to benchmark may be difficult.
- Even if a successful business can be found, it may be reluctant to engage in the exercise because it may consider that it has little to gain, or it fears the loss of confidential information.
- An inappropriate business may be used for benchmarking purposes, due to differences in process or culture.
- The benchmarks developed may be poorly defined leading to wasted effort.
- The benchmarks chosen may not capture the key aspects of operating efficiency.

5.4 Kaplan plc

(a) The business makes each model of suitcase in a batch. The direct materials and labour costs will be recorded in respect of each batch. To these costs will be added a share of the overheads of the business for the period in which production of the batch takes place. The basis of the batch absorbing overheads is a matter of managerial judgement. Direct labour hours spent working on the batch, relative to total direct labour hours worked during the period, is a popular method. This is not the 'correct' way, however. There is no correct way. If the activity is capital-intensive, some machine hour basis of dealing with overheads might be more appropriate, though still not 'correct'. Overheads might be collected, cost centre by cost centre (department by department), and charged to the batch as it passes through each product cost centre. Alternatively, all of the overheads for the entire production facility might be totalled and the overheads dealt with more globally. It is only in restricted circumstances that overheads charged to batches will be affected by a decision to deal with them by cost centres, rather than globally.

Once the 'full cost' (direct costs plus a share of indirect costs) has been ascertained for the batch, the cost per suitcase can be established by dividing the batch cost by the number in the batch.

(b) The uses to which full cost information can be put have been identified as:

- *For pricing purposes.* In some industries and circumstances, full costs are used as the basis of pricing. Here the full cost is deduced and a percentage is added on for profit. This is known as cost-plus pricing. A solicitor handling a case for a client probably provides an example of this.

  In many circumstances, however, suppliers are not in a position to deduce prices on a cost-plus basis. Where there is a competitive market, a supplier will probably need to accept the price that the market offers – that is, most suppliers are 'price takers' not 'price makers'.
- *For income-measurement purposes.* To provide a valid means of measuring a business's income, it is necessary to match expenses with the revenue realised in the same accounting period. Where manufactured products are made or partially made in one period but sold in the next, or where a service is partially rendered in one accounting period but the revenue is realised in the next, the full cost (including an appropriate share of overheads) must be carried from one accounting period to the next. Unless we are able to identify the full cost of work done in one period, which is the subject of a sale in the next, the profit figures of the periods concerned will become meaningless.

Unless all related production costs are charged in the same accounting period as the sale is recognised in the income statement, distortions will occur that will render the income statement much less useful. Thus it is necessary to deduce the full cost of any production undertaken completely or partially in one accounting period but sold in a subsequent one.

- *For budgetary planning and control.* Often budgets are set in terms of full costs. If budgets are to be used as the yardsticks by which actual performance is to be assessed, the information on actual performance must also be expressed in the same full-cost terms. Knowing the full cost of the suitcases could be helpful in these activities.
- *General decision making.* Knowing the full cost of the suitcases might be helpful in making a decision as to whether to continue to make all or some of the models. It is argued, however, that relevant costs, which might be just the variable costs, would provide a more helpful basis for the decision.

(c) Whereas the traditional approach to dealing with overheads is just to accept that they exist and deal with them in a fairly broad manner, ABC takes a much more enquiring approach. ABC takes the view that overheads do not just 'occur', but that they are caused or 'driven' by 'activities'. It is a question of discovering which activities are driving the costs and how much cost they are driving.

For example, a significant part of the costs of making suitcases of different sizes might be resetting machinery to cope with a batch of a different size from its predecessor batch. Where a particular model is made in very small batches, because it has only a small market, ABC would advocate that this model is charged directly with its machine-setting costs. The traditional approach would be to treat machine setting as a general overhead that the individual suitcases (irrespective of the model) might bear equally. ABC, it is claimed, leads to more accurate product costing and thus to more accurate assessment of profitability.

(d) The other advantage of pursuing an ABC philosophy and identifying cost drivers is that, once the drivers have been identified, they are likely to become much more susceptible to being controlled. Thus, assessment by management of the benefit of certain activities against their cost becomes more feasible.

5.7 Moleskin Ltd

(a) Price using absorption costing

Overhead absorption rate = total overheads/total direct labour hours = £280,000/4,000 = £70 per direct labour hour.

	JT101	*GR27*
	£	£
Direct materials	16.00	15.00
Direct labour	8.00	8.00
Overheads: ½ × £70	35.00	35.00
Total cost	59.00	58.00
Mark-up at 35%	20.65	20.30
Price per metre	79.65	78.30

(b) Price using activity-based costing

Cost driver rates:

Alpha Process	£96,000/480	=	£200 per hour
Omega Process	£44,800/1,280	=	£35 per hour
Set-ups	£42,900/260	=	£165 per set up
Handling	£45,600/380	=	£120 per movement
Other overheads	£50,700/4,000	=	£12.68 per direct labour hour

Prices for the two products:

		JT101		*GR27*
		£		£
Direct materials		16.00		16.00
Direct labour		8.00		8.00
Alpha Process	(100 × £200)/1,000	20.00		–
Omega Process			(25 × £35)/50	17.50
Set-ups	£165/1,000	0.17	(2 × £165)/50	6.60
Ordering		–	(3 × £90)/50	5.40
Handling	£120/1,000	0.12	(5 × £120)/50	12.00
Other overheads	½ × £12.68	6.34	½ × £12.68	6.34
Total cost		50.63		71.84
35% mark-up		17.72		25.14
Price per metre		68.35		96.98

(c) Points for the management

- Under the traditional approach, the prices of the two products are quite similar because the direct costs are quite similar, which also leads to a similar allocation of overheads (because these are absorbed on the basis of direct labour hours).
- With ABC the prices are quite different between the products. This is because the GR27s cause much more overhead cost than the JT101s and ABC reflects this fact.
- Management must seriously consider its pricing policy. If the traditionally based price is, in fact, the current selling price, the GR27s are earning only a small margin on the ABC cost.
- If the market will not bear a higher price for the GR27s, management may consider dropping them and concentrating its efforts on the JT101s. Projected market demand for the two products will obviously have a major bearing on these considerations.

(d) Practical problems of using ABC

- Identifying the cost driving activities and determining cost driver rates can be difficult and expensive. It is sometimes necessary to use arbitrary approaches to certain parts of the overheads, as with 'other overheads' in the Joists/Girders example above.
- The costs of introducing ABC may outweigh the benefits.
- Changing the culture necessary to introduce ABC may pose difficulties. There may be resistance to a new approach.
- On a positive note, ABC may have benefits beyond cost determination and pricing. Careful analysis of costs and what drives them can provide a basis for exercising better control over them.

Chapter 6

6.1 Prolog Ltd

(a) Cash budget for the six months to 30 June:

	Jan £000	*Feb* £000	*Mar* £000	*Apr* £000	*May* £000	*June* £000
Receipts						
Credit sales revenue (Note 1)	100	100	140	180	220	260
Payments						
Trade payables (Note 2)	112	144	176	208	240	272
Operating expenses	4	6	8	10	10	10
Shelving	–	–	–	12	–	–
Taxation	–	–	25	–	–	–
	116	150	209	230	250	282
Cash flow	(16)	(50)	(69)	(50)	(30)	(22)
Opening balance	(68)	(84)	(134)	(203)	(253)	(283)
Closing balance	(84)	(134)	(203)	(253)	(283)	(305)

Notes:

1 Sales receipts will equal the month's sales revenue, but be received two months later. For example, the January sales revenue = £2,000 × (50 + 20) = £140,000, to be received in March.

2 Payments to suppliers will equal the next month's sales requirements, payable the next month. For example, January purchases = £1,600 × (50 + 40) = £144,000, payable in February.

(b) A banker may require various pieces of information before granting additional overdraft facilities. These may include:

- Security available for the loan.
- Details of past profit performance.
- Profit projections for the next twelve months.
- Cash projections beyond the next six months to help assess the prospects of repayment.
- Details of the assumptions underlying projected figures supplied.
- Details of the contractual commitment between Prolog Ltd and its supplier.
- Details of management expertise. Can they manage the expansion programme?
- Details of the new machine and its performance in relation to competing models.
- Details of funds available from owners to finance the expansion.

6.3 Nursing home

(a) The rates per patient for the variable overheads, on the basis of experience during months 1 to 6, are as follows:

Expense	*Amount for 2,700 patients* £	*Amount per patient* £
Staffing	59,400	22
Power	27,000	10
Supplies	54,000	20
Other	8,100	3
	148,500	55

Since the expected level of activity for the full year is 6,000, the expected level of activity for the second six months is 3,300 (that is, 6,000 – 2,700).

Thus the budget for the second six months will be:

	£	
Variable element:		
Staffing	72,600	(3,300 × £22)
Power	33,000	(3,300 × £10)
Supplies	66,000	(3,300 × £20)
Other	9,900	(3,300 × £3)
	181,500	(3,300 × £55)
Fixed element:		
Supervision	60,000	6/12 of the annual figure
Depreciation/finance	93,600	ditto
Other	32,400	ditto
	186,000	(per patient = £56.36 (that is, £186,000/3,300))
Total (second six months)	367,500	(per patient = £111.36 (that is, £56.36 + £55.00))

(b) For the second six months the actual activity was 3,800 patients. For a valid comparison with the actual outcome, the budget will need to be revised to reflect this activity.

	Actual costs	*Budget (3,800 patients)*	*Difference*
	£	£	£
Variable element	203,300	209,000 (3,800 × £55)	5,700 (saving)
Fixed element	190,000	186,000	4,000 (overspend)
Total	393,300	395,000	1,700 (saving)

(c) Relative to the budget, there was a saving of nearly 3 per cent on the variable element and an overspend of about 2 per cent on fixed costs. Without further information, it is impossible to deduce much more than this.

The differences between the budget and the actual may be caused by some assumptions made in framing the budget for 3,300 patients in the second part of the year. There may be some element of economies of scale in the variable costs; that is, the costs may not be strictly linear. If this were the case, basing a relatively large activity budget on the experience of a relatively small activity period would tend to overstate the large activity budget. The fixed-cost budget was deduced by dividing the budget for 12 months by two. In fact, there could be seasonal factors or inflationary pressures at work that might make such a crude division of the fixed cost element unfair.

6.4 Linpet Ltd

(a) Cash budgets are extremely useful for decision-making purposes. They allow managers to see the likely effect on the cash balance of the plans that they have set in place. Cash is an important asset and it is necessary to ensure that it is properly managed. Failure to do so can have disastrous consequences for the business. Where the cash budget indicates a surplus balance, managers must decide whether this balance should be reinvested in the business or distributed to the owners. Where the cash budget indicates a deficit balance, managers must decide how this deficit should be financed or how it might be avoided.

(b) Cash budget for the six months to 30 November:

	June £	*July* £	*Aug* £	*Sept* £	*Oct* £	*Nov* £
Receipts						
Cash sales revenue (Note 1)	4,000	5,500	7,000	8,500	11,000	11,000
Credit sales revenue (Note 2)	–	–	4,000	5,500	7,000	8,500
	4,000	5,500	11,000	14,000	18,000	19,500
Payments						
Purchases (Note 3)	–	29,000	9,250	11,500	13,750	17,500
Overheads	500	500	500	500	650	650
Wages	900	900	900	900	900	900
Commission (Note 4)	–	320	440	560	680	880
Equipment	10,000	–	–	–	–	7,000
Motor vehicle	6,000	–	–	–	–	–
Leasehold	40,000	–	–	–	–	–
	57,400	30,720	11,090	13,460	15,980	26,930
Cash flow	(53,400)	(25,220)	(90)	540	2,020	(7,430)
Opening balance	60,000	6,600	(18,620)	(18,710)	(18,170)	(16,150)
Closing balance	6,600	(18,620)	(18,710)	(18,170)	(16,150)	(23,580)

Notes:

1 50 per cent of the current month's sales revenue.

2 50 per cent of the sales revenue of the previous two months.

3 To have sufficient inventories to meet each month's sales will require purchases of 75 per cent of the month's sales inventories figures (25 per cent is profit). In addition, each month the business will buy £1,000 more inventories than it will sell. In June, the business will also buy its initial inventories of £22,000. This will be paid for in the following month. For example, June's purchases will be ((75% × £8,000) + £1,000 + £22,000) = £29,000, paid for in July.

4 This is 5 per cent of 80 per cent of the month's sales revenue, paid in the following month. For example, June's commission will be (5% × 80% × £8,000) = £320, payable in July.

6.5 Lewisham Ltd

(a) The finished goods inventories budget for the three months ending 30 September (in units of production) is:

	July '000 units	*Aug* '000 units	*Sept* '000 units
Opening inventories (Note 1)	40	48	40
Production (Note 2)	188	232	196
	228	280	236
Inventories sold (Note 3)	(180)	(240)	(200)
Closing inventories	48	40	36

(b) The raw materials inventories budget for the two months ending 31 August (in kg) is:

	July '000 kg	*Aug* '000 kg
Opening inventories (Note 1)	40	58
Purchases (Note 2)	112	107
	152	165
Production (Note 4)	(94)	(116)
Closing inventories	58	49

(c) The cash budget for the two months ending 30 September is:

	Aug £	Sept £
Inflows		
Receivables – current month (Note 5)	493,920	411,600
– preceding month (Note 6)	151,200	201,600
Total inflows	645,120	613,200
Outflows		
Payments to trade payables (Note 7)	168,000	160,500
Labour and overheads (Note 8)	185,600	156,800
Fixed overheads	22,000	22,000
Total outflows	375,600	339,300
Net inflows/(outflows)	269,520	273,900
Balance carried forward	289,520	563,420

Notes:

1 The opening balance is the same as the closing balance from the previous month.

2 This is a balancing figure.

3 This figure is given in the question.

4 This figure derives from the finished inventories budget (July, 188,000 × 0.5 = 94,000).

5 This is 98 per cent of 70 per cent of the current month's sales revenue.

6 This is 28 per cent of the previous month's sales revenue.

7 This figure derives from the raw materials inventories budget (July, 112,000 × £1.50 = £168,000).

8 This figure derives from the finished inventories budget (August, £232,000 × £0.80 = £185,600).

6.7 Newtake Records

(a) The cash budget for the period to 30 November is:

	June £000	July £000	Aug £000	Sept £000	Oct £000	Nov £000
Cash receipts						
Sales revenue (Note 1)	227	315	246	138	118	108
Cash payments						
Administration (Note 2)	(40)	(41)	(38)	(33)	(31)	(30)
Goods purchased	(135)	(180)	(142)	(94)	(75)	(66)
Repayments of borrowings	(5)	(5)	(5)	(5)	(5)	(5)
Selling expenses	(22)	(24)	(28)	(26)	(21)	(19)
Tax paid	–	–	(22)	–	–	–
Shop refurbishment	–	(14)	(18)	(6)	–	–
	(202)	(264)	(253)	(164)	(132)	(120)
Cash surplus (deficit)	25	51	(7)	(26)	(14)	(12)
Opening balance	(35)	(10)	41	34	8	(6)
Closing balance	(10)	41	34	8	(6)	(18)

Notes:

1 (50% of the current month's sales revenue) + (97% × 50% of that sales revenue). For example, the June cash receipts will be ((50% × £230,000) + (97% × 50% × £230,000)) = £226,550.

2 The administration expenses figure for the month *less* £15,000 for depreciation (a non-cash expense).

(b) The inventories budget for the six months to 30 November is:

	June £000	July £000	Aug £000	Sept £000	Oct £000	Nov £000
Opening balance	112	154	104	48	39	33
Inventories purchased	180	142	94	75	66	57
	292	296	198	123	105	90
Cost of inventories sold (60% of sales revenue)	(138)	(192)	(150)	(84)	(72)	(66)
Closing balance	154	104	48	39	33	24

(c) The budgeted income statement for the six months ending 30 November is:

	£000
Sales revenue	1,170
Cost of goods sold	(702)
Gross profit (40%)	468
Selling expenses	(136)
Admin expenses	(303)
Credit card charges	(18)
Interest charges	(6)
Profit for the period	5

(d) We are told that the business is required to eliminate the bank overdraft by the end of November. However, the cash budget shows that this will not be achieved. There is a decline in the overdraft of nearly 50 per cent over the period, but this is not enough and ways must be found to comply with the bank's requirements. It may be possible to delay the refurbishment programme that is included in the plans, or to obtain an injection of funds from the owners or other investors. It may also be possible to stimulate sales in some way. However, there has been a decline in the sales revenue since the end of July and the November sales revenue is approximately one-third of the July sales revenue. The reasons for this decline should be sought.

The inventories levels will fall below the preferred minimum level for each of the last three months. However, to rectify this situation it will be necessary to purchase more inventories, which will, in turn, exacerbate the cash flow problems of the business.

The budgeted income statement reveals a very low net profit for the period. For every £1 of sales revenue, the business is only managing to generate 0.4p in profit. The business should look carefully at its pricing policies and its overhead expenses. The administration expenses, for example, absorb more than one-quarter of the total sales revenue. Any reduction in overhead expenses will have a beneficial effect on cash flows.

Chapter 7

7.1 True or false

(a) A favourable direct labour rate variance can only be caused by something that leads to the rate per hour paid being less than standard. Normally, this would not be linked to efficient working. Where, however, the standard envisaged some overtime working, at premium rates, the actual labour rate may be below standard if efficiency has removed the need for the overtime.

(b) The statement is true. The action will lead to an adverse sales price variance and may well lead to problems elsewhere, but the sales volume variance must be favourable.

(c) It is true that below-standard materials could lead to adverse materials usage variances because there may be more than a standard amount of scrap. This could also cause adverse labour efficiency variances because working on materials that would not form part of the output would waste labour time.

(d) Higher-than-budgeted sales revenue could well lead to an adverse labour rate variance because producing the additional work may require overtime working at premium rates.

(e) The statement is true. Nothing else could cause such a variance.

7.2 Overheard remarks

(a) Flexing the budget identifies what the profit would have been, had the only difference between the original budget and the actual figures been concerned with the difference in volume of output. Comparing the original budget profit figure with that in the flexed budget reveals the profit difference (variance) arising solely from the volume difference (sales volume variance). Thus, flexing the budget does not mean at all that volume differences do not matter. Flexing the budget is the means of discovering the effect on profit of the volume difference.

In one sense, all variances are 'water under the bridge', to the extent that the past cannot be undone, and so it is impossible to go back to the last control period and put in a better performance. Identifying variances can, however, be useful in identifying where things went wrong, which should enable management to take steps to ensure that the same things do *not* go wrong in the future.

(b) Variances will not tell you what went wrong. They should, however, be a great help in identifying the manager within whose sphere of responsibility things went wrong. That manager should know why it went wrong. In this sense, variances identify relevant questions, but not answers.

(c) Identifying the reason for variances may well cost money, usually in terms of staff time. It is a matter of judgement in any particular situation, of balancing the cost of investigation against the potential benefits. As is usual in such judgements, it is difficult, before undertaking the investigation, to know either the cost or the likely benefit.

In general, significant variances, particularly adverse ones, should be investigated. Persistent (over a period of months) smaller variances should also be investigated. It should not automatically be assumed that favourable variances can be ignored. They indicate that things are not going according to plan, possibly because the plans (budgets) are flawed.

(d) Research evidence does not show this. It seems to show that managers tend to be most motivated by having as a target the most difficult goals that they find acceptable.

(e) Budgets normally provide the basis of feedforward and feedback control. During a budget preparation period, potential problems (for example, an inventories shortage) might be revealed. Steps can then be taken to revise the plans in order to avoid the potential problem. This is an example of a feedforward control: potential problems are anticipated and eliminated before they can occur.

Budgetary control is a very good example of feedback control, where a signal that something is going wrong triggers steps to take corrective action for the future.

7.3 Pilot Ltd

(a)

	Budget				
	Original	*Flexed*		*Actual*	
Output (units) (production and sales)	5,000	5,400		5,400	
	£	£		£	
Sales revenue	25,000	27,000		26,460	
Raw materials	(7,500)	(8,100)	(2,700 kg)	(8,770)	(2,830 kg)
Labour	(6,250)	(6,750)	(675 hr)	(6,885)	(650 hr)
Fixed overheads	(6,000)	(6,000)		(6,350)	
Operating profit	5,250	6,150		4,455	

	£	
Sales volume variance (5,250 – 6,150)	900	(F)
Sales price variance (27,000 – 26,460)	(540)	(A)
Materials price variance (2,830 × 3) – 8,770	(280)	(A)
Materials usage variance ((5,400 × 0.5) – 2,830) × £3)	(390)	(A)
Labour rate variance ((650 × £10) – 6,885)	(385)	(A)
Labour efficiency variance ((5,400 × 7.5/60) – 650) × £10)	250	(F)
Fixed overhead spending variance (6,000 – 6,350)	(350)	(A)
Total net variances	(795)	(A)

	£
Budgeted profit	5,250
Less Total net variance	(795)
Actual profit	4,455

(b) Sales volume variance: sales manager; sales price variance: sales manager; materials price variance: buyer; materials usage variance: production manager; labour rate variance: human resources manager; labour efficiency variance: production manager; fixed overhead spending variance: various, depending on the nature of the overheads.

7.5 Bradley-Allen Ltd

(a)

	Budget				
	Original	*Flexed*		*Actual*	
Output (units) (production and sales)	800	950		950	
	£	£		£	
Sales revenue	64,000	76,000		73,000	
Raw materials – A	(12,000)	(14,250)	(285 kg)	(15,200)	(310 kg)
– B	(16,000)	(19,000)	(950 m)	(18,900)	(920 m)
Labour – skilled	(4,000)	(4,750)	(475 hr)	(4,628)	(445 hr)
– unskilled	(10,000)	(11,875)	(1,484 hr)	(11,275)	(1,375 hr)
Fixed overheads	(12,000)	(12,000)		(11,960)	
Operating profit	10,000	14,125		11,037	

Sales variances		
Volume:	10,000 – 14,125 = £4,125	(F)
Price:	76,000 – 73,000 = £3,000	(A)
Direct materials A variances		
Usage:	[(950 × 0.3) – 310] × £50 = £1,250	(A)
Price:	(310 × £50) – £15,200 = £300	(F)
Direct materials B variances		
Usage:	[(950 × 1) – 920] × £20 = £600	(F)
Price:	(920 × £20) – £18,900 = £500	(A)
Skilled direct labour variances		
Efficiency:	[(950 × 0.5) – 445] × £10 = £300	(F)
Rate:	(445 × £10) – £4,628 = £178	(A)
Unskilled direct labour variances		
Efficiency:	[(950 × 1.5625) – 1,375] × £8 = £875	(F)
Rate:	(1,375 × £8) – £11,275 = £275	(A)
Fixed overhead variances		
Spending:	(12,000 – 11,960) = £40	(F)

Budgeted profit				£10,000
Sales:	Volume	4,125	(F)	
	Price	(3,000)	(A)	1,125
Direct material A:	Usage	(1,250)	(A)	
	Price	300	(F)	(950)
Direct material B:	Usage	600	(F)	
	Price	(500)	(A)	100
Skilled labour:	Efficiency	300	(F)	
	Rate	(178)	(A)	122
Unskilled labour:	Efficiency	875	(F)	
	Rate	(275)	(A)	600
Fixed overheads:	Expenditure			40
Actual profit				£11,037

(b) The statement in (a) is useful to management because it enables them to see where there have been failures to meet the original budget and to quantify the extent of such failures. This means that junior managers can be held accountable for the performance of their particular area of responsibility.

7.8 Varne Chemprocessors

(a) The standard usage rate of UK194 per litre of Varnelyne is 200/5,000 = 0.04. The standard price is £392/200 = £1.96 per litre of UK194.

Materials usage variance (UK194) is

$$((637{,}500 \times 0.04) - 28{,}100) \times £1.96 = £5{,}096 \text{ (A)}$$

Materials price variance is

$$(28{,}100 \times £1.96) - £51{,}704 = £3{,}372 \text{ (F)}$$

(b) The net variance on UK194 was, from the calculations in (a), £1,724 (A) (that is, £5,096 – £3,372). This seems to have led directly to savings elsewhere of £4,900, giving a net cost saving of over £3,000 for the month.

Unfortunately things may not be quite as simple as the numbers suggest. The non-standard mix to make the Varnelyne might lead to a substandard product, which could have very wide-ranging ramifications in terms of potential loss of market goodwill.

There is also the possibility that the material for which the UK194 was used as a substitute was already held in inventories. If this were the case, is there any danger that this material may deteriorate and, ultimately, prove to be unusable?

Other possible adverse outcomes of the non-standard mix could also arise.

The question is raised by the analysis in part (a) (and by the production manager's comment) of why the cost standard for UK194 had not been revised to take account of the lower price prevailing in the market.

(c) The variances, period by period and cumulatively, for each of the two materials are given as follows:

Period	*UK500*		*UK800*	
	Period £	*Cumulative* £	*Period* £	*Cumulative* £
1	301 (F)	301 (F)	298 (F)	298 (F)
2	(251) (A)	50 (F)	203 (F)	501 (F)
3	102 (F)	152 (F)	(52) (A)	449 (F)
4	(202) (A)	(50) (A)	(98) (A)	351 (F)
5	153 (F)	103 (F)	(150) (A)	201 (F)
6	(103) (A)	zero	(201) (A)	zero

Without knowing the scale of these variances relative to the actual costs involved, it is not possible to be too dogmatic about how to interpret the above information.

UK500 appears to show a fairly random set of data, with the period variances fluctuating from positive to negative and giving a net variance of zero. This is what would be expected from a situation that is basically under control, but with small variances occurring.

UK800 also shows a zero cumulative figure over the six periods, *but* there seems to be a more systematic train of events, particularly the four consecutive adverse variances from period 3 onwards. This looks as if it may be out of control and worthy of investigation.

Chapter 8

8.1 Mylo Ltd

(a) The annual depreciation of the two projects is:

$$\text{Project 1: } \frac{(£100,000 - £7,000)}{3} = £31,000$$

$$\text{Project 2: } \frac{(£60,000 - £6,000)}{3} = £18,000$$

Project 1

(i)

	Year 0	*Year 1*	*Year 2*	*Year 3*
	£000	*£000*	*£000*	*£000*
Operating profit/(loss) before depreciation		60	30	33
Capital cost	(100)			
Residual value	—	—	—	7
Net cash flows	(100)	60	30	40
10% discount factor	1.000	0.909	0.826	0.751
Present value	(100.00)	54.54	24.78	30.04
Net present value	9.36			

(ii) Clearly the IRR lies above 10%. Try 15%:

15% discount factor	1.000	0.870	0.756	0.658
Present value	(100.00)	52.20	22.68	26.32
Net present value	1.20			

Thus the IRR lies a little above 15%, perhaps around 16%.

(iii) To find the payback period, the cumulative cash flows are calculated:

Cumulative cash flows	(100)	(40)	(10)	30

Thus the payback will occur after three years if we assume year-end cash flows.

Project 2

(i)

	Year 0	*Year 1*	*Year 2*	*Year 3*
	£000	*£000*	*£000*	*£000*
Operating profit/(loss) before depreciation		36	16	22
Capital cost	(60)			
Residual value	—	—	—	6
Net cash flows	(60)	36	16	28
10% discount factor	1.000	0.909	0.826	0.751
Present value	(60.00)	32.72	13.22	21.03
Net present value	6.97			

(ii) Clearly the IRR lies above 10%. Try 15%:

15% discount factor	1.000	0.870	0.756	0.658
Present value	(60.00)	31.32	12.10	18.42
Net present value	1.84			

Thus the IRR lies a little above 15%, perhaps around 17%.

(iii) The cumulative cash flows are:

Cumulative cash flows	(60)	(24)	(8)	20

Thus, the payback will occur after three years (assuming year-end cash flows).

(b) Assuming that Mylo Ltd is pursuing a wealth-enhancement objective, Project 1 is preferable since it has the higher net present value. The difference between the two net present values is not significant, however.

8.3 Newton Electronics Ltd

(a) Option 1

	Year 0 £m	Year 1 £m	Year 2 £m	Year 3 £m	Year 4 £m	Year 5 £m
Plant and equipment	(9.0)					1.0
Sales revenue		24.0	30.8	39.6	26.4	10.0
Variable cost		(11.2)	(19.6)	(25.2)	(16.8)	(7.0)
Fixed cost (excluding depreciation)		(0.8)	(0.8)	(0.8)	(0.8)	(0.8)
Working capital	(3.0)					3.0
Marketing cost		(2.0)	(2.0)	(2.0)	(2.0)	(2.0)
Lease		(0.1)	(0.1)	(0.1)	(0.1)	(0.1)
	(12.0)	9.9	8.3	11.5	6.7	4.1
Discount factor 10%	1.000	0.909	0.826	0.751	0.683	0.621
Present value	(12.0)	9.0	6.9	8.6	4.6	2.5
Net present value	19.6					

Option 2

	Year 0 £m	Year 1 £m	Year 2 £m	Year 3 £m	Year 4 £m	Year 5 £m
Royalties	–	4.4	7.7	9.9	6.6	2.8
Discount factor 10%	1.000	0.909	0.826	0.751	0.683	0.621
Present value	–	4.0	6.4	7.4	4.5	1.7
Net present value	24.0					

Option 3

	Year 0	Year 2
Instalments	12.0	12.0
Discount factor 10%	1.000	0.826
Present value	12.0	9.9
Net present value	21.9	

(b) Before making a final decision, the board should consider the following factors:

- The long-term competitiveness of the business may be affected by the sale of the patents.
- At present, the business is not involved in manufacturing and marketing products. Would a change in direction be desirable?
- The business will probably have to buy in the skills necessary to produce the product itself. This will involve costs and problems may be encountered. Has this been taken into account?
- How accurate are the forecasts made and how valid are the assumptions on which they are based?

(c) Option 2 has the highest net present value and is therefore the most attractive to shareholders. However, the accuracy of the forecasts should be checked before a final decision is made.

8.6 Simtex Ltd

(a) Net operating cash flows each year will be:

	£000
Sales revenue (160 × £6)	960
Variable cost (160 × £4)	(640)
Relevant fixed costs	(170)
	150

The estimated net present value of the new product can then be calculated:

	£000
Annual cash flows (150 × 3.038*)	456
Residual value of equipment (100 × 0.636)	64
	520
Initial outlay	(480)
Net present value	40

* This is the sum of the discount factors over four years (that is 0.893 + 0.797 + 0.712 + 0.636 = 3.038). Where the cash flows are constant, it is a quicker procedure than working out the present value of cash flows for each year and then adding them together.

(b) (i) Assume the discount rate is 18%. The net present value of the project would be:

	£000
Annual cash flows (150 × 2.690*)	404
Residual value of equipment (100 × 0.516)	52
	456
Initial outlay	(480)
Net present value	(24)

* That is, 0.847 + 0.718 + 0.609 + 0.516 = 2.690.

Thus an increase of 6%, from 12% to 18%, in the discount rate causes a fall from +40 to –24 in the net present value: a fall of 64, or 10.67 (that is, 64/6) for each 1% rise in the discount rate. So a zero net present value will occur with a discount rate approximately equal to 12 + (40/10.67) = 15.75%. (This is, of course, the internal rate of return.)

This higher discount rate represents an increase of about 31% on the existing cost of capital figure.

(ii) The initial outlay on equipment is already expressed in present-value terms and so, to make the project no longer viable, the outlay will have to increase by an amount equal to the net present value of the project (that is, £40,000) – an increase of 8.3% on the stated initial outlay.

(iii) The change necessary in the annual net cash flows to make the project no longer profitable can be calculated as follows.

Let Y = change in the annual operating cash flows. Then (Y × cumulative discount rates for a four-year period) – NPV = 0. This can be rearranged as:

$$Y \times \text{cumulative discount rates for a four-year period} = \text{NPV}$$

$$Y \times 3.038 = £40{,}000$$
$$Y = £40{,}000/3.038$$
$$= £13{,}167$$

In percentage terms, this is a decrease of 8.8% on the estimated cash flows.

(iv) The change in the residual value required to make the new product no longer profitable can be calculated as follows:

Let V = change in the residual value. Then (V × discount factor at end of four years) – NPV of product = 0. This can be rearranged as:

$$V \times \text{discount factor at end of four years} = \text{NPV of product}$$

$$V \times 0.636 = £40{,}000$$
$$V = £40{,}000/0.636$$
$$= £62{,}893$$

This is a decrease of 62.9% in the residual value of the equipment.

(c) The net present value of the product is positive and so it will increase shareholder wealth. Thus, it should be produced. The sensitivity analysis suggests the initial outlay and the annual cash flows are the most sensitive variables for managers to consider.

8.7 Chesterfield Wanderers

(a) Player option

	Year 0	*Year 1*	*Year 2*	*Year 3*	*Year 4*	*Year 5*
	£000	*£000*	*£000*	*£000*	*£000*	*£000*
Sale of player	2,200					1,000
Purchase of Bazza	(10,000)					
Sponsorship and so on		1,200	1,200	1,200	1,200	1,200
Gate receipts		2,500	1,300	1,300	1,300	1,300
Salaries paid		(800)	(800)	(800)	(800)	(1,200)
Salaries saved		400	400	400	400	600
	(7,800)	3,300	2,100	2,100	2,100	2,900
Discount factor 10%	1.000	0.909	0.826	0.751	0.683	0.621
Present values	(7,800)	3,000	1,735	1,577	1,434	1,801
Net present value	1,747					

Ground improvement option

	Year 1	*Year 2*	*Year 3*	*Year 4*	*Year 5*
	£000	*£000*	*£000*	*£000*	*£000*
Ground improvements	(10,000)				
Increased gate receipts	(1,800)	4,400	4,400	4,400	4,400
	(11,800)	4,400	4,400	4,400	4,400
Discount factor 10%	0.909	0.826	0.751	0.683	0.621
Present values	(10,726)	3,634	3,304	3,005	2,732
Net present value	1,949				

(b) The ground improvement option provides the higher net present value and is therefore the preferable option, based on the objective of shareholder wealth enhancement.

(c) A professional football club may not wish to pursue an objective of shareholder wealth enhancement. It may prefer to invest in quality players in an attempt to enjoy future sporting success. If this is the case, the net present value approach will be less appropriate because the club is not pursuing a strict wealth-related objective.

8.8 Kernow Cleaning Services Ltd

(a) The first step is to calculate the expected annual cash flows:

Year 1	£	*Year 2*	£
£80,000 × 0.3	24,000	£140,000 × 0.4	56,000
£160,000 × 0.5	80,000	£220,000 × 0.4	88,000
£200,000 × 0.2	40,000	£250,000 × 0.2	50,000
	144,000		194,000

Year 3	£	*Year 4*	£
£140,000 × 0.4	56,000	£100,000 × 0.3	30,000
£200,000 × 0.3	60,000	£170,000 × 0.6	102,000
£230,000 × 0.3	69,000	£200,000 × 0.1	20,000
	185,000		152,000

The expected net present value (ENPV) can now be calculated as follows:

Period	*Expected cash flow*	*Discount rate 10%*	*Expected PV*
	£		£
0	(540,000)	1.000	(540,000)
1	144,000	0.909	130,896
2	194,000	0.826	160,244
3	185,000	0.751	138,935
4	152,000	0.683	103,816
ENPV			(6,109)

(b) The *worst possible outcome* can be calculated by taking the lowest values of savings each year, as follows:

Period	*Cash flow*	*Discount rate 10%*	*PV*
	£		£
0	(540,000)	1.000	(540,000)
1	80,000	0.909	72,720
2	140,000	0.826	115,640
3	140,000	0.751	105,140
4	100,000	0.683	68,300
NPV			(178,200)

The probability of occurrence can be obtained by multiplying together the probability of *each* of the worst outcomes above, that is $0.3 \times 0.4 \times 0.4 \times 0.3 = 0.014$.

Thus, the probability of occurrence is 1.4%, which is very low.

Part Two

Chapter 6

FINANCING A BUSINESS 1: SOURCES OF FINANCE

INTRODUCTION

This is the first of two chapters that examine the financing of businesses. In this chapter, we identify the main sources of finance available to businesses and discuss the main features of each source. We also consider the factors to be taken into account when choosing between the various sources of finance available.

In the following chapter, we go on to examine capital markets. We shall discuss the role and efficiency of the London Stock Exchange and the ways in which share capital can be issued. We shall also discuss how smaller businesses, which do not have access to the London Stock Exchange, may raise finance.

Learning outcomes

When you have completed this chapter, you should be able to:

- Identify the main sources of external finance available to a business and explain their main features.
- Identify the main sources of internal finance available to a business and explain their main features.
- Outline the advantages and disadvantages of each source of finance.
- Discuss the factors to be taken into account when choosing an appropriate source of finance.

SOURCES OF FINANCE

When considering the various sources of finance available, it is useful to distinguish between *external* and *internal* sources of finance. By external sources we mean those that require the agreement of other parties beyond the directors of the business. Thus, finance from an issue of new shares is an external source because the agreement of potential shareholders is required. Internal sources of finance, on the other hand, arise from management decisions that do not require agreement from other parties. Thus, retained earnings are a source of internal finance because directors have the power to retain earnings without the agreement of shareholders, whose earnings they are.

Within each of these categories, we can further distinguish between *long-term* and *short-term* finance. There is no agreed definition concerning each of these terms, but for the purpose of this chapter, a source of long-term finance will be defined as one that is expected to provide finance for at least one year. Sources of short-term finance, therefore, provide finance for a shorter period. As we shall see, sources that are seen as short term when first used by the business may end up being used for quite long periods.

We begin by considering the external sources of finance available and then go on to consider the internal sources.

EXTERNAL SOURCES OF FINANCE

Figure 6.1 summarises the main external sources of long-term and short-term finance.

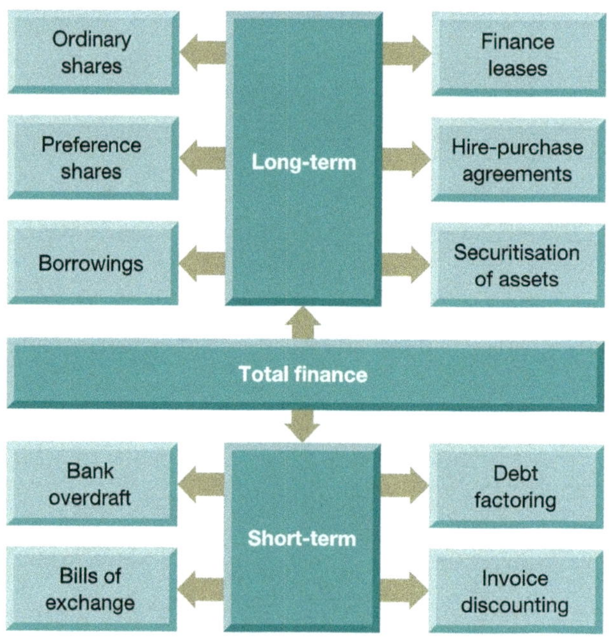

The figure shows the various external sources of long-term and short-term finance available to a business.

Figure 6.1 The major external sources of finance

EXTERNAL SOURCES OF LONG-TERM FINANCE

As Figure 6.1 reveals, the major external sources of long-term finance are:

- ordinary shares
- preference shares
- borrowings
- finance leases, including sale-and-leaseback arrangements
- hire purchase
- securitisation of assets.

We shall now look at each of these sources in turn.

Ordinary shares

Ordinary (equity) shares represent the risk capital of a business and form the backbone of a business's financial structure. There is no fixed rate of dividend and ordinary shareholders will receive a dividend only if earnings available for distribution remain after other investors (preference shareholders and lenders) have received their dividend or interest payments. If the business is wound up, the ordinary shareholders will receive any proceeds from asset disposals only after lenders and creditors, and, in some cases, preference shareholders, have received their entitlements. Because of the high risks associated with this form of investment, ordinary shareholders will normally expect a relatively high rate of return.

Although ordinary shareholders' potential losses are limited to the amount that they have invested or agreed to invest, the potential returns from their investment are unlimited. After preference shareholders and lenders have received their returns, all the remaining earnings will accrue to the ordinary shareholders. Thus, while their 'downside' risk is limited, their 'upside' potential is not. Ordinary shareholders control the business through their voting rights, which give them the power to elect the directors and to remove them from office.

From the business's perspective, ordinary shares can be a useful source of financing when compared with borrowing. It may be possible to avoid paying a dividend, whereas it is not usually possible to avoid interest payments.

Activity 6.1

Under what circumstances might a business wish to avoid paying a dividend?

Two possible circumstances are where a business is:

- expanding and wishes to retain funds in order to fuel future growth
- in difficulties and needs the funds to meet its operating costs and debt obligations.

It is worth pointing out that a business does not obtain tax relief on dividends paid to shareholders, whereas interest on borrowings is tax deductible. This makes it more expensive for a business to pay £1 of dividend than £1 of interest.

Preference shares

Preference shares offer investors a lower level of risk than ordinary shares. Provided there are sufficient earnings available, preference shares will normally be given a fixed rate of dividend each year and preference dividends will be the first slice of any dividend paid. If the business is wound up, preference shareholders may be given priority over the claims of ordinary shareholders. (The business's own particular documents of incorporation will state the precise rights of preference shareholders in this respect.)

Activity 6.2

Would you expect the returns from preference shares to be higher or lower than those from ordinary shares?

Preference shareholders will be offered a lower level of return than ordinary shareholders. This is because of the lower level of risk associated with this form of investment. Preference shareholders have priority over ordinary shareholders regarding dividends, and perhaps capital repayment.

Preference shareholders are not usually given voting rights, although these may be granted where the preference dividend is in arrears. Both preference shares and ordinary shares are, in effect, redeemable. The business is allowed to buy back the shares from shareholders at any time.

Activity 6.3

Would you expect the market price of ordinary shares or of preference shares to be the more volatile? Why?

The share price, which reflects the expected future returns from the share, will normally be less volatile for preference shares than for ordinary shares. The dividends of preference shares tend to be fairly stable over time, and there is usually an upper limit on the returns that can be received.

Preference shares are no longer an important source of new finance. A major reason for this is that dividends paid to preference shareholders, like those paid to ordinary shareholders, are not allowable against taxable profits. Loan interest, on the other hand, is an allowable expense. From the business's point of view, preference shares and loans are often seen as fulfilling a similar function. The tax benefits of loan interest can, therefore, tip the balance in favour of borrowing. In addition, interest rates on borrowing have been at historically low levels in recent years.

Borrowings

Most businesses rely on borrowings (loans) as well as share capital to finance operations. Lenders enter into a contract with the business in which the interest (coupon) rate, dates of interest payments, capital repayments and security for the loan are clearly stated. If a business is successful, lenders will not benefit beyond the fact that their claim will become more secure. If, however, the business experiences financial difficulties, there is a risk that the agreed interest payments and capital repayments will not be paid. To protect themselves against this risk, lenders often seek some form of **security** from the business. This may take the form of assets pledged either by a **fixed charge** on particular assets held by the business, or by a **floating charge**, which 'floats' over the whole of the business's assets. A floating charge will only fix on particular assets in the event that the business defaults on its obligations.

Activity 6.4

What do you think is the advantage for the business of having a floating charge rather than a fixed charge on its assets?

A floating charge on assets will allow the managers of the business greater flexibility in their day-to-day operations than a fixed charge. Individual assets can be sold without reference to the lenders.

Not all assets are acceptable to lenders as security. They must normally be non-perishable, easy to sell and of high value relative to their size. (Property normally meets these criteria and so is often favoured by lenders.) In the event of default, lenders have the right to seize the assets pledged and to sell them. Any surplus from the sale, after lenders have been paid, will be passed to the business. In some cases, security offered may take the form of a personal guarantee by the owners of the business or, perhaps, some third party. This most often occurs with small businesses.

Lenders may seek further protection through the use of **loan covenants**. These are obligations, or restrictions, on the business that form part of the loan contract. Covenants may impose:

- the right of lenders to receive regular financial reports concerning the business
- an obligation to insure the assets being offered as security
- a restriction on the right to issue further loan capital without prior permission of the existing lenders
- a restriction on the right to sell certain assets held
- a restriction on dividend payments and/or payments made to directors
- minimum levels of liquidity and/or maximum levels of gearing.

Any breach of these covenants can have serious consequences. Lenders may demand immediate repayment of the loan in the event of a material breach.

Real World 6.1 describes the financial covenants attached to the borrowings of one well-known business.

Real World 6.1

Borrowing with strings attached

Rentokil-Initial plc, a leader in business services, states on its website that its borrowing facilities have financial covenants:

> **requiring that EBITDA: Interest should be at least 4.0:1.0 and that Net Debt: Adjusted EBITDA* should be no greater than 3.5:1.0 at each semi-annual reporting date.**
>
> *EBITDA means earnings before interest, taxation, depreciation and amortisation.

The business also states that it is compliant with these covenants.

Note that the covenants focus on two gearing ratios of the business. The first is a coverage ratio, which is similar to the interest coverage ratio discussed in Chapter 3. The second ratio compares the level of borrowing to the earnings, or profits, generated.

Source: www.rentokil-initial.com Accessed 12 October 2016.

Loan covenants and the offer of security help lower the risk to which lenders are exposed. This can make the difference between a successful and an unsuccessful issue of loan capital. It can also lower the cost of loan capital to the business. The rate of return that lenders require will depend on the perceived level of risk to which they are exposed.

It is possible for a business to issue loan capital that is subordinated to (that is, ranked below) other loan capital already in issue. Holders of subordinated loan capital will not receive interest payments or capital repayments until the claims of more senior loan holders (that is, lenders ranked above them) are met. Any restrictive covenants imposed by senior loan holders concerning the issue of further loan capital often ignore the issue of **subordinated loans** as it poses no real threat to their claims. Subordinated loan holders normally expect to receive a higher return than senior loan holders because of the higher risks.

Activity 6.5

Would you expect the returns from loans to be higher or lower than those from preference shares?

Investors are usually prepared to accept a lower rate of return from loans. This is because they normally view loans as being less risky than preference shares. Lenders have priority over any claims from preference shareholders, and will usually have security for their loans.

The risk/return characteristics of loan, preference share and ordinary share finance, *from an investor's viewpoint,* are shown graphically in Figure 6.2. Note that from the viewpoint of the business (the existing shareholders), the level of risk associated with each form of finance is in reverse order. Thus, borrowing is the most risky because it exposes shareholders to the legally enforceable obligation to make regular interest payments and, usually, repayment of the amount borrowed.

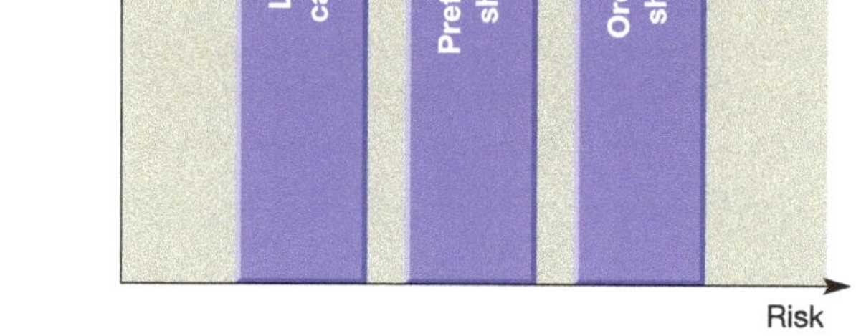

The higher the level of risk associated with a particular form of long-term finance, the higher will be the expected returns from investors. Ordinary shares are the most risky and have the highest expected return and, as a general rule, loan capital is the least risky and has the lowest expected return.

Figure 6.2 The risk/return characteristics of sources of long-term finance

Activity 6.6

What factors might a business take into account when deciding between preference shares and loans as a means of raising new finance? Try to think of at least two.

The main factors are as follows:

- Preference shares have a higher rate of return than loans. From the investor's point of view, preference shares are more risky. The amount invested cannot be secured and the return is paid after the returns paid to lenders.
- A business has a legal obligation to pay interest and make capital repayments on loans at the agreed dates. It will usually make every effort to meet its obligations, as failure to do so can have serious consequences. Failure to pay a preference dividend, meanwhile, is less important. There is no legal obligation to pay if profits are not available for distribution. Failure to pay a preference dividend may therefore prove to be an embarrassment and nothing more. It may, however, make it difficult to persuade investors to take up future preference share issues.
- Interest on loans can be deducted from profits for taxation purposes, whereas preference dividends cannot. As a result, the cost of servicing loans is, £ for £, usually much less for a business than the cost of servicing preference shares.
- Borrowing may result in managers having to accept some restrictions on their freedom of action. Loan agreements often contain covenants that can be onerous. However, no such restrictions can be imposed by preference shareholders.

A further point is that any preference shares issued form part of the permanent capital base of the business. If they are redeemed, UK law requires that they be replaced, either by a new issue of shares or by a transfer from revenue reserves. By doing this, the business's capital base stays intact. Loans, however, are not viewed in the same way and there is no legal requirement to replace those that have been redeemed.

We end this section by considering the wisdom of Warren Buffett, one of the world's richest individuals. He is chairman and chief executive officer of Berkshire Hathaway, a diversified business that has generated spectacular returns over many years. He warns of the dangers of borrowing in **Real World 6.2** below.

Real World 6.2

Life and debt

Companies with large debts often assume that these obligations can be refinanced as they mature. That assumption is usually valid. Occasionally, though, either because of company-specific problems or a worldwide shortage of credit, maturities must actually be met by payment. For that, only cash will do the job. Borrowers then learn that credit is like oxygen. When either is abundant, its presence goes unnoticed. When either is missing, that's *all* that is noticed. Even a short absence of credit can bring a company to its knees.

Source: W. Buffett (2011) Shareholder letter, Berkshire Hathaway Inc, www.berkshirehathaway.com, 26 February, p. 22.

Forms of borrowing

Borrowings may take various forms and we shall now consider some of the more important of these.

Term loans

A **term loan** is a type of loan offered by banks and other financial institutions that can be tailored to the needs of the client business. The amount of the loan, time period, repayment terms and interest rate are all open to negotiation and agreement – which can be very useful. Where, for example, the whole amount borrowed is not required immediately, a business may agree with the lender that sums are drawn only when required. This means that interest will be paid only on amounts actually drawn and there is no need to pay interest on amounts borrowed that are not yet needed. Term loans tend to be cheap to set up (from the borrower's perspective) and can be quite flexible as to conditions. For these reasons, they tend to be popular in practice.

Loan notes (or loan stock)

Loan notes (or *loan stocks*) are another form of long-term loan finance. Loan notes are frequently divided into units (rather like share capital) and investors are invited to purchase the number of units they require. Loan notes may be redeemable or irredeemable. The loan notes of listed businesses are often traded on the Stock Exchange, and their listed value will fluctuate according to the fortunes of the business, movements in interest rates and so on.

Loan notes are usually referred to as **bonds** in the USA and, increasingly, in the UK.

Real World 6.3 describes how, in 2015, Manchester United redeemed its relatively high interest, secured bonds. It financed this through an issue of lower interest-bearing bonds. This resulted in a substantial net saving in annual interest payments. The article concluded by making the point that the estimated £10 million annual interest cost saving would pay Wayne Rooney's salary for a few months.

Real World 6.3

Manchester United win

Football can be a brutal business. Top assets are prone to lose form, get hurt or break contracts. A club can miss out on huge prizes by the thickness of a goalpost, or a hashed clearance from defence. And yet lenders seem very keen to back the beautiful game. Last week Manchester United told holders of its senior secured bonds – paying interest of 8.375 per cent a year – that it wanted to buy them all back by the end of this month, two years ahead of schedule. To raise the cash to redeem the $269 million outstanding, it will issue $425 million in 12-year notes paying just 3.79 per cent.

At the same time, the club said it would replace a two year old bank loan with one about a quarter smaller ($225 million), while cutting the interest-rate range and extending the term six years to 2025. In exchange, the bank gets another covenant – a promise that earnings before interest, tax, depreciation and amortisation will not drop below £65 million a year. The closest United came to that in recent years was £91 million in 2012, so it is hardly an imposition.

FT *Source*: McLannahan, B. (2015) 'Manchester United is calling the shots', ft.com, 4 June.

Activity 6.7

Would you expect the market price of ordinary shares or of loan notes to be the more volatile? Why?

Price movements will normally be much less volatile for loan notes than for ordinary shares. The price of loan notes and ordinary shares will reflect the expected future returns from each. Interest from loan notes is fixed by contract over time. Returns from ordinary shares, on the other hand, are less certain.

Activity 6.8

Would you expect the returns on loan notes to be higher or lower than those of ordinary shares? Why?

Loan note holders will expect to receive a lower level of return than ordinary shareholders. This is because of the lower level of risk associated with this form of investment.

Eurobonds

Eurobonds are unsecured loan notes denominated in a currency other than the home currency of the business that issued them. They are issued by listed businesses (and other large organisations) in various countries and the finance is raised on an international basis. They are often denominated in US dollars, but many are issued in other major currencies. They are bearer bonds (that is, the owner of the bond is not registered and the holder of the bond certificate is regarded as the owner) and interest is normally paid, without deduction of tax, on an annual basis.

Eurobonds are part of an international capital market that is not restricted by regulations imposed by authorities in particular countries. This partly explains why the cost of servicing eurobonds is usually lower than the cost of similar domestic bonds. Eurobonds are made available to financial institutions, which may retain them as an investment or sell them to clients. Various banks and other financial institutions throughout the world have created a market for eurobonds. Nevertheless, some eurobonds are held for a long time and are not frequently traded.

The extent of borrowing by UK businesses in currencies other than sterling has expanded greatly in recent years. Businesses are often attracted to eurobonds because of the size of the international capital market. Access to a wider pool of potential investors can increase the chances of a successful issue.

Real World 6.4 provides an example of eurobond financing by a well-known business.

Real World 6.4

Something worth watching?

On a number of occasions in recent years, ITV plc, the broadcasting and online business, has raised money from eurobonds. In September 2015, it announced a further €600m eurobond issue.

The bonds are for a 7-year period and are due for repayment in 2022. They attract a fixed rate of interest of 2.125%. The proceeds of the bond will be used mainly to repay borrowing following the acquisition of Talpa Media B.V. in April 2015.

Source: 'ITV plc announces €600m Euro Bond issue', itvplc.com/media, 11 September 2015.

Deep discount bonds

A business may issue redeemable loan notes that offer a rate of interest below the market rate. In some cases, the loan notes may have a zero rate of interest. These loans are issued at a discount to their redeemable value and are referred to as **deep discount bonds**. Thus, loan notes may be issued at, say, £80 for every £100 of nominal value. Although lenders will receive little or no interest during the period of the loan, they will receive a £20 gain when it is finally redeemed at the full £100. The effective rate of return over the life of their loan (known as the redemption yield) can be quite high and often better than returns from other forms of lending with the same level of risk.

Deep discount bonds may have particular appeal to businesses with short-term cash flow problems. They receive an immediate injection of cash and there are no significant cash outflows associated with the loan notes until the maturity date. From an investment perspective, the situation is reversed. Deep discount bonds are likely to appeal to investors that do not have short-term cash flow needs since a large part of the return is received on maturity of the loan. However, deep discount bonds can often be traded on the London Stock Exchange, which will not affect the borrower but will enable the lender to obtain cash.

Convertible loan notes

Convertible loan notes (or *convertible bonds*) give investors the right to convert loan notes into ordinary shares at a specified price at a given future date (or range of dates). The share price specified, which is known as the exercise price, will normally be higher than the market price of the ordinary shares at the time of the loan notes issue. In effect, the investor swaps the loan notes for a particular number of shares. The investor remains a lender to the business, and will receive interest on the amount of the loan notes, until such time as the conversion takes place. There is no obligation to convert to ordinary shares. This will be done only if the market price of the shares at the conversion date exceeds the agreed conversion price.

An investor may find this form of investment a useful 'hedge' against risk (that is, it can reduce the level of risk). It may be particularly useful when investment in a new business is being considered. Initially, the investment will be in the form of loan notes and regular interest payments will be received. If the business is successful, the investor can then convert the investment into ordinary shares.

A business may also find this form of financing useful. If the business is successful, the loan notes become self-liquidating (that is, no cash outlay is required to redeem them) as investors will exercise their option to convert. It may also be possible to offer a lower rate of interest on the loan notes because of the expected future benefits arising from conversion. However, there will be some dilution of control and possibly a dilution of earnings for existing shareholders if holders of convertible loan notes exercise their option to convert. (Dilution of earnings available to shareholders will not automatically occur as a result of the conversion of loan capital to share capital. There will be a saving in interest charges that will have an offsetting effect.)

Loan capital and default risk

A number of credit-rating agencies, including Moody's Investor Services and Standard & Poor's Corporation (S&P), categorise loan capital issued by businesses according to their perceived default risk. The lower the risk of default, the higher will be the rating category assigned to the loan. To arrive at an appropriate loan rating, an agency may rely on various sources of information, including published and unpublished reports, interviews with directors and visits to the business's offices and factories. The ratings used by the two leading agencies are very similar.

Real World 6.5 sets out the main debt-rating categories for Standard & Poor.

Real World 6.5

The main debt-rating categories for Standard & Poor

AAA	The lowest risk category. The capacity of the business to pay interest and repay the principal is extremely strong.
AA	High-quality debt. The capacity to pay interest and repay the principal differs only to a small degree from those in the AAA category.
A	A strong capacity to pay interest and repay the principal but the business is more susceptible to adverse effects of changing circumstances and economic conditions.
BBB	Medium-quality debt. There is adequate capacity to pay the interest and repay the principal.
BB, B, CCC, CC and C	These categories are more speculative forms of debt. Although likely to have some qualities, these may be outweighed by large uncertainties or major exposure to adverse conditions.
BB	Less vulnerable to non-payment than other speculative forms of debt but still facing major uncertainties or exposure to adverse economic conditions.
B	More vulnerable to non-payment than those rated 'BB', but the business currently maintains the capacity to meet its financial commitments
CCC	Vulnerable to non-payment, and dependent upon favourable business, financial and economic conditions to meet commitments.
CC	Currently highly vulnerable to non-payment. Although default has not yet occurred, default is expected to be a virtual certainty.
C	Currently highly vulnerable to non-payment and expected to have lower ultimate recovery than those in the previous category.

It should be mentioned that the track record of the credit rating agencies has been far from flawless. Some years ago, they provided good ratings for bonds backed by US sub-prime residential mortgages. These ratings helped to ensure their successful take up by institutional investors. In 2006, the US housing boom ended abruptly and the initial bond debt ratings proved to be excessively optimistic, with many sub-prime mortgage owners defaulting. The consequences were disastrous for the financial institutions holding the bonds and provoked the 2007-2008 financial crisis.

Source: Table adapted from *Standard & Poor's Ratings Definitions*, www.standardandpoors.com, 20 November 2014.

Loan capital falling within any of the first four categories identified in Real World 6.5 is considered to be of high quality and is referred to as *investment grade*. Some institutional investors are restricted by their rules to investing only in investment-grade loans. For this reason, many businesses are concerned with maintaining investment-grade status.

Once loan capital has been assigned to a particular category, it will tend to remain in that category unless there is a significant change in circumstances.

Junk (high-yield) bonds

Loan notes rated below the first four categories identified in Real World 6.5 are often given the rather disparaging name of **junk bonds**. In some cases, loan notes with a junk bond rating began life with an investment-grade rating but, because of a decline in the business's fortunes, have been downgraded. (This type of bond is known as a 'fallen angel'.)

Activity 6.9

Does it really matter if the loan notes of a business are downgraded to a lower category?

A downgrade is usually regarded as serious as it will normally increase the cost of borrowing. Investors are likely to seek higher returns to compensate for the perceived increase in default risk.

In addition to increasing the cost of borrowing, a downgrade to junk bond status may cast doubt over the financial viability of the business. This may, in turn, affect its relationship with existing, or potential, customers. For example, a business that is bidding for a long-term government contract may find itself at a disadvantage when competing with other, better-capitalised businesses.

Not all junk bonds start life with an investment-grade rating. Since the 1980s, loan notes with an initial low rating have been issued by US businesses. This type of borrowing provides investors with high interest rates to compensate for the high level of default risk (hence their alternative name, high-yield bonds). Businesses that issue junk bonds, or high-yield bonds, are usually less financially stable than those offering investment-grade bonds. The junk bonds issued may also provide lower levels of security and weaker loan covenants than those normally associated with standard loan agreements.

Junk bonds became popular in the USA as they allowed some businesses to raise finance that was not available from other sources. Within a fairly short space of time, a market for this form of borrowing developed. Normally, businesses use junk bonds to finance everyday needs such as investment in inventories, receivables and non-current assets; however, they came to public attention through their use in financing hostile takeovers. There have been cases where a small business borrows heavily, through the use of junk bonds, to finance a takeover of a much larger business. Following the takeover, non-core assets of the larger business are then sold to repay the junk bond holders.

The junk bond market in the USA has enjoyed a brief but turbulent history. It has suffered allegations of market manipulation, the collapse of a leading market maker and periods when default levels on junk bonds have been very high. While these events have shaken investor confidence, the market has proved more resilient than many had expected. Nevertheless, there is always the risk that, in a difficult economic climate, investors will make a 'flight to quality' and the junk bond market will become illiquid.

Real World 6.6 contains extracts from an article that discusses the most recent turbulence in the junk bond market. This has largely been caused by falls in commodity prices.

Real World 6.6

A lot of junk

In the US energy sector record low oil prices have placed extreme strain on the finances of shale oil drillers. Chesapeake Energy was one of the largest shale oil drilling companies in the US and the second-biggest issuer of junk bonds in the sector, raising $11bn from investors. Drilling for shale oil is a loss making enterprise as oil prices have fallen below $40 a barrel. Chesapeake bonds collapsed to 48 cents last week as investors face being completely wiped out. The cost of insurance on Chesapeake bonds – or credit default swaps – soared as holders of the bonds desperately try and cover their losses.

The shale oil drillers are by no means the only companies in trouble. Many conventional oil production companies from the North Sea to the Gulf of Mexico rely on an assessment of the value of their oil reserves, or reserves based lending, to determine how much they can borrow.

The energy sector may be in serious trouble, but the problem can still be contained as it only represents about 15 per cent of the wider junk bond market. The bigger issue is in emerging market debt. Commodity focused corporates in Brazil, Russia, India and China that have borrowed in US dollars will face ruin next year. The rising value of the US dollar and collapse of emerging market currencies will make repayments unaffordable for many.

The crisis has already spread from energy to pharmaceuticals. Valeant was one of the largest ever junk issuers when it issued $10bn in bonds to buy Salix in March this year. The Canadian drug group has seen its shares collapse and bonds fall sharply after a report by Citron Research, which questioned the aggressive expansion and accuracy of sales numbers through its network of pharmacies. Valeant strongly denies the allegations but the damage has been done.

Stepping back from the specific allegations at Valeant the wider issue here is a company that has been allowed to grow incredibly quickly through acquisitions fuelled by cheap debt. A situation that could only exist with borrowing as cheap as it is.

The collapse of the junk bond market will reach far and wide. In the past, the junk bond market has only really been used by professional investors or those with a higher risk appetite. As interest rates were cut from 2009 onwards retail investors, pension funds and insurance companies alike have all ploughed billions into high-yield bonds.

Source: J. Ficenec (2015), 'Six big risks facing global markets in 2016', *Daily Telegraph*, 22 November.

Historically, European investors have shown less interest in junk bonds than their US counterparts. Perhaps this is because they tend to view ordinary shares as a high-risk/high-return investment and view loan capital as a form of low-risk/low-return investment. Junk bonds are a hybrid form of investment lying somewhere between ordinary shares and conventional loan notes. It can be argued that the same results as from junk bonds can be achieved through holding a balanced portfolio of ordinary shares and conventional loan notes.

Mortgages

A **mortgage** is a form of loan that is secured on an asset, frequently property. Financial institutions such as banks, insurance businesses and pension funds are often prepared to lend to businesses on this basis. The mortgage may be over a long period (20 years or more).

Real World 6.7 describes the extent to which one well-known business uses mortgages to finance its main assets.

Real World 6.7

Flying with a heavy load

At 31 March 2015 Ryanair, the budget airline, reported aircraft held at a carrying amount (that is cost less depreciation) of €5,410.4m. It also reported that aircraft with a carrying amount of €5,138.8m were mortgaged to lenders as security for loans. Under the financial security arrangements for the newly-acquired Boeing 737-800 next generation aircraft, Ryanair does not hold the legal title to these aircraft while the loan amounts remain outstanding.

Source: Ryanair Holdings plc, Annual Report 2015, www.ryanair.com, pp.173–174.

Borrowing and interest payments

Floating and fixed rates of interest

Interest rates on loan notes may be either floating or fixed. A **floating interest rate** means that the rate of return will rise and fall with market rates of interest. (But it is possible for a floating rate loan note to be issued that sets a maximum rate of interest and/or a minimum rate of interest payable.) The market value of the loan notes, however, is likely to remain fairly stable over time.

The converse will normally be true for loans with **fixed interest rates**. Interest payments will remain unchanged with rises and falls in market rates of interest, but the value of the loan notes will fall when interest rates rise, and will rise when interest rates fall.

Activity 6.10

Why do you think the value of fixed-interest loan notes will rise and fall with rises and falls in interest rates?

It is because investors will be prepared to pay less for loan notes that pay a rate of interest below the market rate of interest and will be prepared to pay more for loan notes that pay a rate of interest above the market rate of interest.

Managing interest rate risk

Movements in interest rates can be a significant issue for businesses with high levels of borrowing. A business with a floating rate of interest may find that rate rises place huge strains on cash flows and profitability. Conversely, a business that has a fixed rate of interest will find that, when rates are falling, it will not enjoy the benefits of lower interest charges. To reduce or eliminate these risks, a business may enter into a **hedging arrangement**.

To hedge against the risk of interest rate movements, various devices may be employed. One popular device is the **interest rate swap**. This is an arrangement between two businesses whereby each business assumes responsibility for the other's interest payments. Typically, it involves a business with a floating-interest-rate loan note swapping interest payment obligations with a business with a fixed-interest-rate loan note. A swap agreement can be undertaken through direct negotiations with another business, but it is usually easier to negotiate through a bank or other financial intermediary. Although there is an agreement to swap interest payments, the legal responsibility for these payments will still rest with the business that entered into the original loan note agreement. Thus, the borrowing business may continue to make interest payments to the lender in line with the loan note agreement. However, at the end of an agreed period, a compensating cash adjustment between the two parties to the swap agreement will be made.

A swap agreement can be a useful hedging device where there are different views concerning future movements in interest rates. For example, a business with a floating-rate agreement may believe that interest rates are going to rise, whereas a business with a fixed-rate agreement may believe that interest rates are going to fall.

Real World 6.8 sets out the policies of two large businesses for dealing with interest rate risk.

Real World 6.8

Hedging interest rate risk

Wolseley plc, a major distributor of plumbing and heating products, states its hedging policy as follows:

> To manage the Group's exposure to interest rate fluctuations, the Group's policy is to keep between 0 per cent and 50 per cent of projected borrowings required during the next two years at fixed rates. This percentage is regularly reviewed by the board. At 31 July 2015, 52 per cent of loans were at fixed rates. This has been approved. The Group borrows in the desired currencies principally at rates determined by reference to short-term benchmark rates applicable to the relevant currency or market, such as LIBOR. Rates which reset at least every 12 months are regarded as floating rates and the Group then, if appropriate, considers interest rate swaps to generate the desired interest rate profile.[1]

Barratt Developments plc is a major UK builder. In its annual report for 2015, the business states:

> The Group has a conservative treasury risk management strategy and the group's interest rates are fixed using both swaps and fixed rate debt instruments. The Group's policy target is for 0–40% of average borrowings over the 3 year plan period to be at fixed rates of interest. Due to the seasonality of the Group's funding requirements, 105.4% (2014: 87.2%) of the Group's gross borrowings were fixed as at 30 June 2015 and the average over the 3 year plan period is 43.2%. Group interest rates are fixed using both swaps and fixed rate debt instruments.[2]

At 30 June 2015, £137m of the £188m of its floating rate debt had been converted to fixed rate debt through the use of swap arrangements.

Sources: (1) Wolseley plc, Annual Report and Accounts 2015, www.wolseley.com p. 155; (2) Barratt Developments plc, Annual Report and Accounts 2015, www.barrattdevelopments.co.uk, p.145.

Swap agreements may also be used to exploit imperfections in the capital markets. It may be the case that one business has an advantage over another when negotiating interest rates for a fixed loan note agreement, but would prefer a floating loan note agreement, whereas the other business is in the opposite position. When this occurs, both businesses can benefit from a swap agreement.

Islamic finance and the payment of interest

The increasing economic importance of those who follow the Islamic faith has led to greater attention being paid to their needs concerning the financing of businesses. Many of these individuals are citizens of Islamic states, but many others are nationals of the USA and Western European countries, particularly the UK and France.

A key feature of Islamic finance is the belief, based on the teachings of the Islamic holy book (the Quran), that charging pure interest is wrong. This stems from the notion that it is immoral to gain income (in the form of interest) merely because money has been lent. Sharia law, which guides Islamic practice, is not against free enterprise capitalism; it is the lack of risk taking that is the problem. Sharia is, however, also hostile to pure speculation. It is probably fair to say that Sharia looks favourably on profits earned through hard work and enterprise, but shuns gains from pure financing and speculation.

We can see that normal interest-bearing loans to businesses, such as term loans and loan notes, are contrary to Sharia law. All investors, not just equity investors, are required to bear part of the risk associated with operating the business. In recent years, special types of bonds have emerged to meet this requirement. This enabled Tesco plc, the supermarket business, to make an issue of Sharia-compliant bonds in Malaysia.

Borrowing and share warrants

Holders of **warrants** have the right, but not the obligation, to buy ordinary shares in a business at a given price (the 'exercise' price). As with convertible loan notes, the price at which shares may eventually be bought is usually higher than the market price of those shares at the time of the issue of the warrants. The warrant will usually state the number of shares that the holder may buy and the time limit within which the option to buy them can be exercised. Occasionally, perpetual warrants are issued that have no set time limits. Warrants do not confer voting rights or entitle the holders to make any claims on the assets of the business.

Share warrants may be sold to investors by the business concerned. When this occurs, they can be a valuable source of finance. Often, however, they are given away 'free' as a 'sweetener' to accompany the issue of loan notes. That is, they are used as an incentive to potential lenders. The issue of warrants in this way may enable the business to offer lower rates of interest on the loan notes or to negotiate less restrictive loan conditions.

Warrants enable investors to benefit from any future increases in the business's ordinary share price, without having to buy the shares themselves. But if the share price remains below the exercise price, the warrant will not be used and the investor will lose out.

Activity 6.11

Under what circumstances will the holders of share warrants exercise their option to purchase?

Holders will exercise this option only if the market price of the shares exceeds the exercise price within the specified time period. If the exercise price is higher than the market price, it will be cheaper for the investor to buy the shares in the market.

Share warrants may be detachable, which means that they can be sold separately from the loan notes. The warrants of businesses whose shares are listed on the Stock Exchange are often also listed, providing a ready market for buying and selling the warrants.

Issuing warrants to lenders can be particularly useful for businesses investing in risky projects. Potential lenders may feel that such projects provide them with an opportunity for loss but no opportunity for gain. By attaching share warrants to the loan issue, they are given the opportunity to participate in future gains. This should increase their appetite for risk and, by doing so, make the issue more attractive.

Share warrants are a speculative form of investment. They have a gearing element, which means that changes in the value of the underlying shares can lead to a disproportionate change in value of the warrants. To illustrate this gearing element, let us suppose that a share has a current market price of £2.50 and that an investor is able to exercise an immediate option to purchase a single share for £2.00. In theory, the value of the warrant is £0.50 (that is, £2.50 − £2.00). Let us further suppose that the price of the share rises by 10 per cent, to £2.75, before the warrant option is exercised. The value of the warrant should now rise to £0.75 (that is, £2.75 − £2.00), which represents a 50 per cent increase in value. This gearing effect can, of course, operate in the opposite direction as well.

It is worth noting the difference in status within a business between holders of convertible loan notes and holders of loan notes with share warrants attached, where both groups decide to exercise their right to convert. Convertible loan note holders will become ordinary shareholders and will no longer be lenders to the business. The value of their loan notes will be converted into shares. Loan note holders with warrants attached will, by converting their warrants, also become shareholders. However, their status as lenders is unaffected. They will be both ordinary shareholders and lenders to the business.

Both convertible loans and share warrants are examples of **financial derivatives**. These are any form of financial instrument, based on share or loan capital, which can be used by investors to increase their returns or reduce risk.

ATTITUDES TOWARDS THE LEVEL OF BORROWING

In practice, the level of borrowing adopted by a business will be determined by the attitude of owners, managers and lenders. The factors that influence the attitude of each of these groups are considered below.

Owners

The attitude of owners (shareholders) is likely to be influenced by the following:

- *Risk.* Risk-averse investors will be prepared to take on more risk only where there is the opportunity for higher rates of return. Higher gearing must therefore offer the prospect of higher returns.
- *Returns.* Where investors are receiving relatively poor returns, they may be reluctant to provide additional share capital. Instead, they may encourage managers to try to increase their returns by exploiting the benefits of higher financial gearing.
- *Control.* Owners may be reluctant to issue more ordinary shares where it results in a dilution of control. Loan capital may therefore be viewed as a better option.
- *Flexibility.* This refers to the ability to implement decisions without delay. Loan capital can often be raised more quickly than share capital. This can be important where a business operates in a fast-changing environment.
- *Debt capacity.* Too high a level of borrowing may eliminate the capacity for future borrowing.
- *Exerting financial discipline* Investors may view higher levels of borrowing as a way of ensuring that managers do not waste resources. Where a business is highly geared, the obligation to make substantial interest payments and capital repayments can exert a powerful financial discipline over managers.

Activity 6.12

What might managers have to do in order to meet the borrowing commitments?

They will probably have to ensure that the business is run efficiently. Costs may have to be tightly controlled, outstanding receivables collected quickly and any underutilised assets sold.

The factors influencing the attitude of owners are summarised in Figure 6.3.

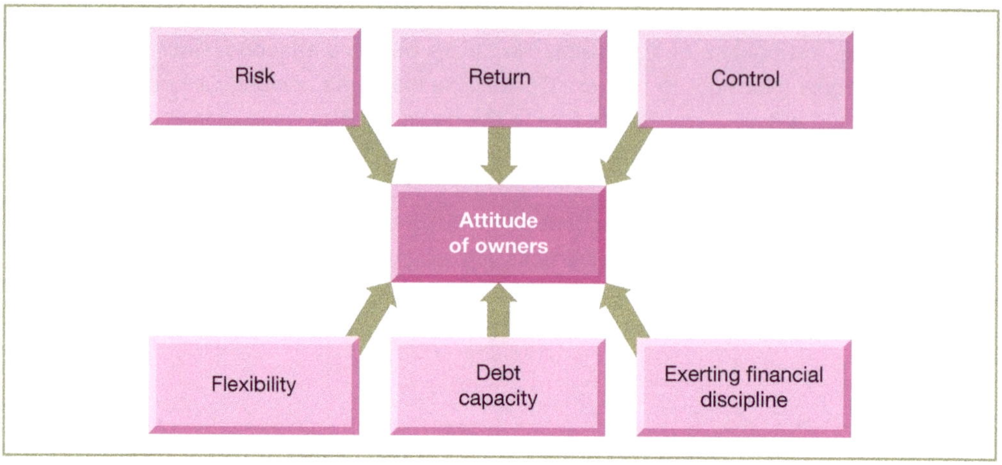

Figure 6.3 Factors influencing the attitude of owners towards borrowing

Managers

Managers may resist high levels of borrowing if they feel that it places their income and jobs at risk. They make a huge investment of 'human capital' in the business and become dependent on its continuing financial health. They cannot diversify this 'human capital' risk in the way that investors can diversify their financial capital risk.

Managers may also object to the tight financial discipline that loan capital imposes on them. They may feel under constant pressure to ensure that cash is available to cover interest payments and capital repayments. They may also feel that this pressure prevents them from investing in value-creating projects. Incentives may have to be offered to encourage them to take on these additional risks and pressures.

Borrowing can, however, benefit managers struggling to achieve the returns required by shareholders. Increasing the level of gearing may be employed as a means of boosting profits. When this gearing effect is no longer needed to achieve the required returns, borrowings can be reduced.

Lenders

When deciding whether to provide loan finance, lenders will be concerned with the ability of the business to repay the amount borrowed and to pay interest at the due dates. Various factors will have a bearing on these issues.

Activity 6.13

What factors are likely to influence the ability of a business to repay the amount borrowed and to pay interest at due dates? Try to think of at least two.

The following factors are likely to be important:

- *Profitability.* Where a business has a stable level of profits, lenders may feel that there is less risk to their investment than where profits are volatile. Profit stability will depend on such factors as the nature of the products sold, the competitive structure of the industry and so on.
- *Cash-generating ability.* Where a business is able to generate strong, predictable cash flows, lenders may feel there is less risk to their investment.

- *Security for the loan.* The nature and quality of assets held by a business will determine whether there is adequate security for a loan.
- *Fixed costs.* We saw in Chapter 2 that fixed costs, such as rents, increase risk as they have to be paid irrespective of the profits generated. Where a business has high fixed costs, a commitment to make interest payments may increase risk to unacceptable levels.

This is not an exhaustive list: you may have thought of other factors.

Borrowing and industry characteristics

Levels of borrowing can vary significantly between industries. Generally speaking, they are higher in industries where profits are stable (which lenders tend to prefer). Thus, higher borrowing is quite common in utilities such as electricity, gas and water businesses, which are less affected by economic recession, changes in consumer tastes and so forth.

High levels of borrowing may also be found in industries where the level of competition is not high. In a highly competitive environment, highly-geared businesses are more vulnerable to lower-geared businesses temporarily reducing prices in order to eliminate competitors.

Other forms of long-term financing

Let us now take a look at other forms of long-term financing from external sources.

Finance leases

When a business needs a particular asset, such as a piece of equipment, instead of buying it direct from a supplier, the business may arrange for a bank (or other business) to buy it and then lease it to the business. The bank that owns the asset, and then leases it to the business, is known as a 'lessor'. The business that leases the asset from the bank and then uses it is known as the 'lessee'.

A **finance lease**, as such an arrangement is known, is in essence a form of lending. This is because, had the lessee borrowed the funds and then used them to buy the asset itself, the effect would be much the same. The lessee would have use of the asset but would also have a financial obligation to the lender – just as with a leasing arrangement.

With finance leasing, legal ownership of the asset remains with the lessor; however, the lease agreement transfers to the lessee virtually all the rewards and risks associated with the item being leased. The finance lease agreement will cover a substantial part of the life of the leased item, and often cannot be cancelled.

Real World 6.9 provides some impression of the importance of finance leasing over recent years.

Real World 6.9

Finance leasing in the UK

Figure 6.4 charts the amount of new finance leasing employed by businesses to acquire core assets such as machinery, equipment and purchased software.

→

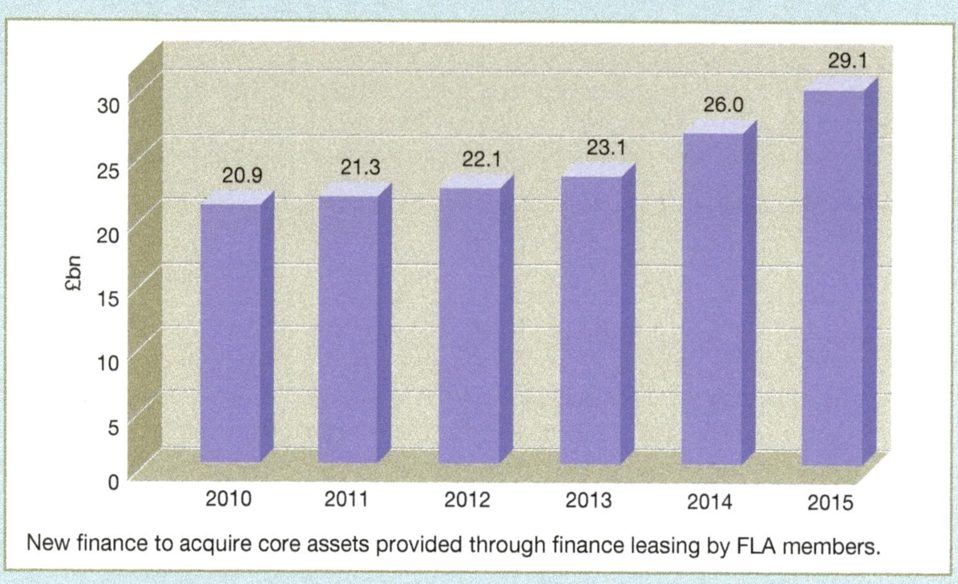

Figure 6.4 Asset finance 2010–2014

Asset finance to businesses provided through finance leasing suffered a significant decline as a result of the economic recession. Business investment fell significantly between 2008 and 2010. This decline, however, seems to have been reversed with four consecutive years of growth. Finance leasing now provides around 31.5 per cent of finance for UK machinery, equipment and purchased software.

Source: Annual Review 2016, The Finance and Leasing Association, www.fla.org.uk, p.17.

Over the years, some important benefits associated with finance leasing have disappeared. Changes in the tax laws make it no longer such a tax-efficient form of financing, and changes in accounting disclosure requirements make it no longer possible to conceal this form of 'borrowing' from investors. Nevertheless, the popularity of finance leases has continued. Other reasons must, therefore, exist for businesses to adopt this form of financing. These reasons are said to include the following:

- *Ease of borrowing.* Leasing may be obtained more easily than other forms of long-term finance. Lenders normally require some form of security and a profitable track record before making advances to a business. However, a lessor may be prepared to lease assets to a new business without a track record and to use the leased assets as security for the amounts owing.
- *Cost.* Leasing agreements may be offered at reasonable cost. As the asset leased is used as security, standard lease arrangements can be applied and detailed credit checking of lessees may be unnecessary. This can reduce administration costs for the lessor and thereby help in providing competitive lease rentals.
- *Flexibility.* Leasing can help provide flexibility where there are rapid changes in technology. If an option to cancel can be incorporated into the lease, the business may be able to exercise this option and invest in new technology as it becomes available. This will help the business to avoid the risk of obsolescence. Avoiding this risk will come at a cost to the lessee, however, because the risk is passed to the lessor.

- *Cash flows.* Leasing, rather than buying an asset outright, means that large cash outflows can be avoided. The leasing option allows cash outflows to be smoothed out over the asset's life. In some cases, it is possible to arrange for low lease payments to be made in the early years of the asset's life, when cash inflows may be low, and for these to increase over time as the asset generates positive cash flows.

These benefits are summarised in diagrammatic form in Figure 6.5.

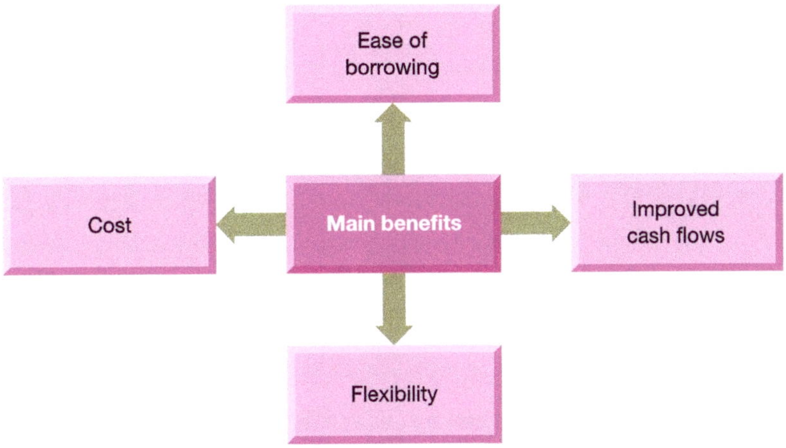

The four main benefits shown are discussed in this chapter.

Figure 6.5 Benefits of finance leasing

A finance lease should not be confused with an **operating lease**. The latter is a form of rental agreement rather than a form of lending. The rewards and risks of ownership stay with the owner and the lease period is shorter than the life of the asset. An operating lease provides greater flexibility than a finance lease but is normally more expensive.

Operating leases can be found in many industries, including the airline industry. The operating lease period for an aircraft is often 3–5 years whereas the life of the leased aircraft may be 20 years or more. **Real World 6.10** gives an example of the use of finance and operating leases by a well-known airline.

Real World 6.10

Leased assets take off

easyJet plc, the budget airline, employs both finance leases and operating leases to acquire its fleet of aircraft. At 30 September 2015, the business had 11 aircraft that were acquired through finance leases and 67 aircraft that were acquired through operating leases. At the end of September 2015, finance and operating lease liabilities for these aircraft were £188 million and £384 million respectively.

During the year to 30 September 2015, an average of 241 aircraft were either owned or leased by the business.

Source: Based on information in easyJet Annual Report and Accounts 2015, pp. 115–116.

Sale-and-leaseback arrangements

A **sale-and-leaseback** arrangement involves a business raising finance by selling an asset to a financial institution. The sale is accompanied by an agreement to lease the asset back to the business to allow it to continue to use the asset. The lease rental payment is a business expense that is allowable against profits for taxation purposes.

There are usually rental reviews at regular intervals throughout the period of the lease, and the amounts payable in future years may be difficult to predict. At the end of the lease agreement, the business must either try to renew the lease or find an alternative asset. Although the sale of the asset will result in an immediate injection of cash for the business, it will lose benefits from any future capital appreciation on the asset. Where a capital gain arises on the sale of the asset to the financial institution, a liability for taxation may also arise.

Activity 6.14

Can you think which type of asset is often subject to a sale-and-leaseback arrangement?

Property is often the asset subject to such an arrangement.

Sale-and-leaseback arrangements can be used to help a business focus on its core areas of competence. In recent years, many hotel businesses have entered into sale-and-leaseback arrangements to enable them to become hotel operators rather than a combination of hotel operators and owners. Similarly, many UK high-street retailers (for example, Boots, Debenhams, Marks and Spencer, Tesco and Sainsbury) have sold off their store sites under sale-and-leaseback arrangements.

Real World 6.11 explains how a leading European mobile 'phone operator is considering raising funds through the sale-and-leaseback of some of its mobile masts.

Real World 6.11

The future of sale-and-leaseback is Orange

Orange has opened discussions with infrastructure groups about a sale of its mobile masts in Spain as it looks to cut costs in European markets. The French telecoms group could sell about 9,400 towers, or 53 per cent of its Spanish network, according to *Expansion,* the Spanish newspaper that first reported the sale.

Such deals are typically structured as a sale and leaseback arrangement where Orange would become a tenant that uses the masts. Telecoms groups in markets in the US and Africa have been active in selling their mast network, although the trend is not as prevalent in Europe.

Orange has spoken to tower operators to gauge interest in the sale, although no firm decision has been taken to sell the infrastructure. A decision will depend on the level of interest, according to a person familiar with the situation.

The value of tower deals can be difficult to estimate, although in a comparable deal in 2013 Albertis acquired 4,227 mobile telephone towers for €385 million from Telefonica and Yoigo in Spain. Orange declined to comment.

FT *Source*: Thomas, D. (2014) 'Orange looks to offload Spanish mobile masts to cut costs', *Financial Times*, 14 August.

Hire purchase

Hire purchase (HP) is a form of credit used to acquire an asset. Under the terms of a hire purchase agreement a customer pays for an asset by instalments over an agreed period. Normally, the customer will pay an initial deposit (down payment) and then make instalment payments at regular intervals, perhaps monthly, until the balance outstanding has been paid. The customer will usually take possession of the asset after payment of the initial deposit, although legal ownership of the asset will not be transferred until the final instalment has been paid.

HP agreements will often involve three parties:

- the supplier
- the customer
- a financial institution.

Although the supplier will deliver the asset to the customer, the financial institution will buy the asset from the supplier and then enter into an HP agreement with the customer. This intermediary role played by the financial institution enables the supplier to receive immediate payment for the asset but allows the customer a period of extended credit. Figure 6.6 sets out the main steps in the hire purchase process.

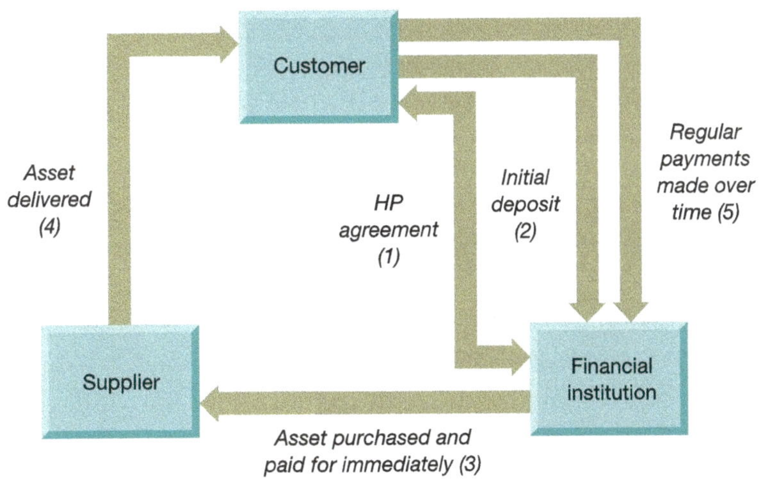

There are usually three parties to a hire purchase agreement. The financial institution will buy the asset from the supplier, who will then deliver it to the customer. The customer will pay an initial deposit and will agree to pay the balance to the financial institution through a series of regular instalments.

Figure 6.6 The hire purchase process

Activity 6.15

In what way is an HP agreement:

(a) similar to
(b) different from

a finance lease?

HP agreements are similar to finance leases in so far as they allow a customer to obtain immediate possession of the asset without paying its full cost. HP agreements differ from finance leases because, under the terms of an HP agreement, the customer will eventually become the legal owner of the asset, whereas under the terms of a finance lease, ownership will stay with the lessor.

Real World 6.12 shows the extent to which one large UK business depends on hire purchase to finance its main assets.

Real World 6.12

Getting there by instalments

Stagecoach Group plc, the transport business, reported in its 2015 annual report, passenger service vehicles with a carrying amount of £776.6 million, of which £90.5 million related to assets purchased under HP agreements. This amounts to around 12 per cent of the total.

Source: Stagecoach Group plc, Annual Report 2015, p. 81.

Securitisation

Securitisation involves bundling together illiquid financial or physical assets of the same type so as to provide backing for an issue of bonds. This financing method was first used by US banks, which bundled together residential mortgage loans to provide asset backing for bonds issued to investors. (Mortgage loans held by a bank are financial assets that provide future cash flows in the form of interest receivable.)

Securitisation has spread beyond the banking industry and has now become an important source of finance for businesses in a wide range of industries. Future cash flows from a variety of illiquid assets are now used as backing for bond issues, including:

- credit card receipts
- water industry charges
- rental income from university accommodation
- ticket sales for football matches
- royalties from music copyright
- consumer instalment contracts
- beer sales to pub tenants.

The effect of securitisation is to capitalise future cash flows arising from illiquid assets. This capitalised amount is sold to investors, through the financial markets, to raise finance for the business holding these assets.

Securitisation usually involves setting up a special-purpose vehicle (SPV) to acquire the assets from the business wishing to raise finance. This SPV will then arrange the issue of bonds to investors. Income generated from the securitised assets is received by the SPV and used to meet the interest payable on the bonds. When the bonds mature, they may be repaid from receipts arising from one or more of the following:

- the securitised assets (so long as the maturity dates coincide)
- the issue of new bonds
- surplus income generated by the securitised assets.

To reassure investors about the quality of the bonds, the securitised assets may be of a higher value than the value of the bonds (this is known as *overcollateralisation*). Alternatively, some form of credit insurance can be available from a third party, such as a bank.

The main elements of the securitisation process are set out in Figure 6.7.

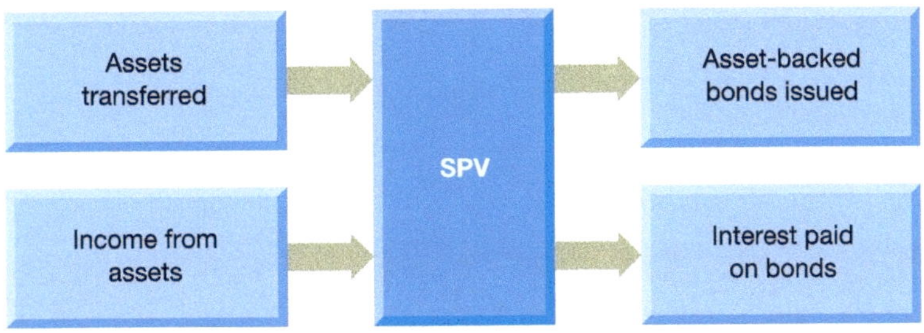

A business will transfer assets to a special-purpose vehicle, which will then arrange for the issue of bonds to investors. Interest paid on the bonds will be met from income generated by the securitised assets.

Figure 6.7 The securitisation process

Securitisation may also be used to help manage risk. Where, for example, a bank has lent heavily to a particular industry, its industry exposure can be reduced by bundling together some of the outstanding loan contracts and making a securitisation issue.

Securitisation and the financial crisis

Securitising mortgage loan repayments became popular among US mortgage lenders during the early 2000s. Monthly repayments due from mortgage borrowers were 'securitised' and sold to major banks. Unfortunately, many of the mortgage loans were made to people on low incomes who were not good credit risks (sub-prime loans). When they began to default on their obligations, it became clear that the securitised mortgages, now owned by the banks, were worth much less than they had paid to the mortgage lenders. This led to the so-called 'sub-prime' crisis, which then triggered the worldwide economic problems during 2008. There is, however, no inherent reason why securitisation should be a problem and it is unfortunate that it is linked to the sub-prime crisis. It can be a legitimate and practical method of raising finance. It is not surprising, therefore, that securitisation is slowly regaining popularity.

Real World 6.13 describes an unusual securitisation issue and then goes on to discuss how the market for this form of finance has changed over the years.

Real World 6.13

The man who sold the bonds

In 1997, a securitisation issue was undertaken on behalf of the musician David Bowie. It was a groundbreaking event as it represented one of the first bond issues that used intellectual

→

property as asset backing. The 'Bowie Bonds' as they became known, securitised future revenues from albums that he produced before 1990. The bonds raised $55 million and had a life of 10 years.

Kevin Ingram, a partner of leading law firm, Clifford Chance points out:

> There was a period of time before the financial crisis when securitisation was a fashionable area for esoteric financing. The Bowie Bonds were a kind of hybrid form of secured finance and were high profile, being very much a sign of the excitement of the securitisation market at the time. But the popularity of different types of financing goes in cycles and during the financial crisis there were well documented concerns about securitisation – not least esoterics – and issuance dropped.
>
> To bring things up to date, the securitisation market has been re-establishing itself, first through a focus on core products such as residential mortgages and auto loans but now people are looking again at securitisation as an alternative way of financing a range of assets including aspects of intellectual property, such as patents.

Source: Adapted from R. Simmons (2016), 'David Bowie's contribution to securitisation', *Lawyer2B*, l2b.thelawyer.com, 11 January.

EXTERNAL SOURCES OF SHORT-TERM FINANCE

Short term, in this context, is usually taken to mean up to one year. Figure 6.1 reveals that the major external sources of short-term finance are:

- bank overdrafts
- bills of exchange
- debt factoring
- invoice discounting.

Each of these sources is discussed below.

Bank overdrafts

A **bank overdraft** enables a business to maintain a negative balance on its bank account. It represents a very flexible form of borrowing as the size of an overdraft can (subject to bank approval) be increased or decreased more or less instantaneously. It is relatively inexpensive to arrange and interest rates are often very competitive, though normally higher than those for a term loan. As with all loans, the rate of interest charged will vary according to how creditworthy the customer is perceived to be by the bank. An overdraft is fairly easy to arrange – sometimes it can be agreed by a telephone call to the bank. In view of these advantages, it is not surprising that an overdraft is an extremely popular form of short-term finance.

Banks prefer to grant overdrafts that are self-liquidating, that is, the funds are used in such a way as to extinguish the overdraft balance by generating cash inflows. The banks may ask for projected cash flow statements from the business to see when the overdraft will be repaid and how much finance is required. They may also require some form of security on amounts advanced.

One potential drawback with this form of finance is that it is repayable on demand. This may pose problems for a business that is illiquid. However, many businesses operate for many years using an overdraft, simply because the bank remains confident of their ability to repay and the arrangement suits the business. Thus, bank overdrafts, though in theory regarded as short term, can, in practice, become a source of long-term finance.

Bills of exchange

A **bill of exchange** is similar, in some respects, to an IOU. It is a written agreement that is addressed by one person to another, requiring the person to whom it is addressed to pay a particular amount at some future date. Bills of exchange, which carry no interest, are used in trading transactions. They are offered by a buyer to a supplier in exchange for goods. The supplier who accepts the bill of exchange may either keep the bill until the date the payment is due (this is usually between 60 and 180 days after the bill is first drawn up) or present it to a bank for payment. The bank will often be prepared to pay the supplier the face value of the bill, less a discount, and will then collect the full amount of the bill from the buyer at the specified payment date.

Activity 6.16

What advantages do you see from a buyer drawing up a bill of exchange?

By drawing up a bill of exchange, a buyer is able to delay payment for goods purchased. It therefore provides a period of credit. The supplier, however, can receive immediate payment by discounting the bill with a bank.

Nowadays, bills of exchange are rarely used for trading transactions within the UK, but they are still used for international trading.

Debt factoring

Debt factoring is a service offered by a financial institution (known as a factor). Many of the large factors are subsidiaries of commercial banks. Debt factoring involves the factor taking over the trade receivables collection for a business. In addition to operating normal credit control procedures, a factor may offer to undertake credit investigations and advise on the creditworthiness of customers. It may also offer protection for approved credit sales.

Two main forms of factoring agreement exist:

- *recourse factoring,* where the factor assumes no responsibility for bad debts arising from credit sales
- *non-recourse factoring,* where, for an additional fee, the factor assumes responsibility for bad debts up to an agreed amount.

Under both forms of factoring any goods returned by a customer becomes the responsibility of the business rather than the factor.

The factor is usually prepared to make an advance to the business of between 80 and 85 per cent of approved trade receivables (although it can sometimes be as high as 95 per cent). This advance is usually paid immediately after the goods have been supplied to the customer. The balance of the debt, less any deductions for fees and interest, will be paid after an agreed period or when the debt is collected. The charge made for the factoring service is based on total sales revenue and is often between 0.5 and 3.0 per cent of sales revenue. Any advances made to the business by the factor will attract a rate of interest similar to the rate charged on bank overdrafts.

Debt factoring is, in effect, outsourcing trade receivables collection to a specialist subcontractor. Many businesses find a factoring arrangement very convenient. It can result in savings in credit management and can create more certain cash flows. It can also release the time of key personnel for more profitable ends. This may be extremely important for smaller businesses that rely on the talent and skills of a few key individuals. In addition, the level of finance available will rise 'spontaneously' with the level of sales. The business can decide how much of the finance available is required and can use only that which it needs. There is a possibility that some will see a factoring arrangement as an indication that the business is experiencing financial difficulties. This may have an adverse effect on the confidence of customers, suppliers and staff. For this reason, some businesses try to conceal the factoring arrangement by collecting outstanding debts on behalf of the factor.

Businesses operating in certain sectors where trade disputes are part of the business culture, such as building contractors, may find that factoring arrangements are not available. Small businesses may also find themselves in the same position. While some factors are prepared to consider start-up businesses, a minimum sales revenue of £50,000 per year is often required. This is normally because of the set up costs involved.

Figure 6.8 shows the factoring process diagrammatically.

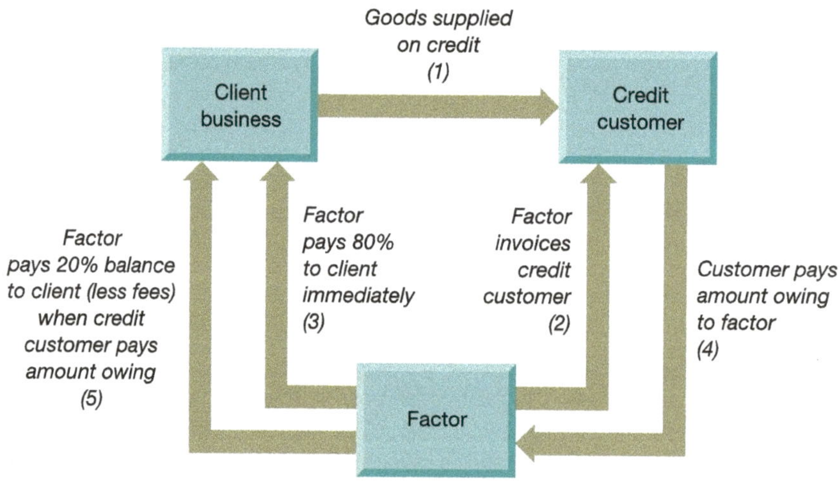

There are three main parties to the factoring agreement. The client business will sell goods on credit and the factor will take responsibility for invoicing the customer and collecting the amount owing. The factor will then pay the client business the invoice amount, less fees and interest, in two stages. The first stage typically represents 80 per cent of the invoice value and will be paid immediately after the goods have been delivered to the customer. The second stage will represent the balance outstanding and will usually be paid when the customer has paid the factor the amount owing.

Figure 6.8 The factoring process

When considering a factoring agreement, we need to carefully weigh the likely costs and benefits. Example 6.1 illustrates how this may be done.

Example 6.1

Balkan Ltd has annual credit sales revenue of £50 million, of which bad debts account for £0.2 million. The average settlement period for trade receivables is 80 days, which is causing some strain on the liquidity of the business.

Balkan Ltd is considering whether to use a factoring business to improve its liquidity position. The factor will advance an equivalent to 80 per cent of trade receivables (where the trade receivables figure is based on an average settlement period of 30 days) at an interest rate of 10 per cent. In addition, the factor will collect the trade receivables and will charge a fee of 3 per cent of total sales revenue for doing so. The remaining 20 per cent of the trade receivables will be paid to Balkan Ltd, when the factor receives the cash. If the factor service is used, it is expected that the average settlement period for trade receivables will be reduced to 30 days, bad debts will be eliminated and credit administration savings of £320,000 will be gained.

The business currently has an overdraft of £10.0 million at an interest rate of 11 per cent a year.

In evaluating the factoring arrangement, it is useful to begin by considering the cost of the existing arrangements:

Existing arrangements

	£000
Bad debts written off each year	200
Interest cost of average receivables outstanding [(£50m × 80/365) × 11%]	1,205
Total cost of existing arrangement	1,405

The cost of the factoring arrangement can now be compared with this:

Factoring arrangement

	£000
Factoring fee (£50m × 3%)	1,500
Interest on factor loan (assuming 80% advance and reduction in average credit period) [(£40m × 30/365) × 10%]	329
Interest on overdraft (remaining 20% of receivables financed in this way) [(£10m × 30/365) × 11%]	90
	1,919
Savings in credit administration	(320)
Total cost of factoring	1,599

The net additional cost for the business from factoring would be £194,000 (that is, £1,599,000 less £1,405,000). Obviously, all other things being equal, the business would continue with the existing arrangements.

Invoice discounting

Invoice discounting involves a factor or other financial institution providing a loan based on a proportion of the face value of a business's credit sales outstanding. The amount advanced is usually around 80–85 per cent of the value of the approved sales invoices outstanding and is secured by a fixed charge over the trade receivables of the business. The business must agree to repay the advance within a relatively short period – perhaps 60 or 90 days. Responsibility for collecting the trade receivables outstanding remains with the business and repayment of the advance is not dependent on the trade receivables being collected. Invoice discounters prefer to deal with larger, well-run businesses. Thus, a client business will normally be expected to generate sales revenue in excess of £250,000 per year and have efficient credit control procedures in place.

Invoice discounting will not result in such a close relationship developing between the business and the financial institution as occurs with factoring. It may be a short-term arrangement, whereas debt factoring usually involves a longer-term arrangement. Businesses can, however, become reliant on the improved cash flows under invoice discounting and so become locked into a longer-term arrangement. Invoice discounters prefer to lend on the basis of commercial invoices. A business selling to the public on credit may, therefore, find it difficult to use this form of finance.

Nowadays, invoice discounting is a much more important source of funds to businesses than factoring. There are three main reasons for this:

- It is a confidential form of financing which the business's customers will know nothing about.
- The service charge for invoice discounting is around 0.2–0.5 per cent of sales revenue compared with around 0.5–3.0 per cent for factoring.
- A debt factor may upset customers by setting tough credit limits or by the way in which it collects debts. This may damage the relationship between the business and its customers.

Real World 6.14 shows the relative importance of invoice discounting and factoring.

Real World 6.14

The popularity of invoice discounting and factoring

Figure 6.9 charts the relative importance of invoice discounting and factoring in terms of the value of client sales revenue.

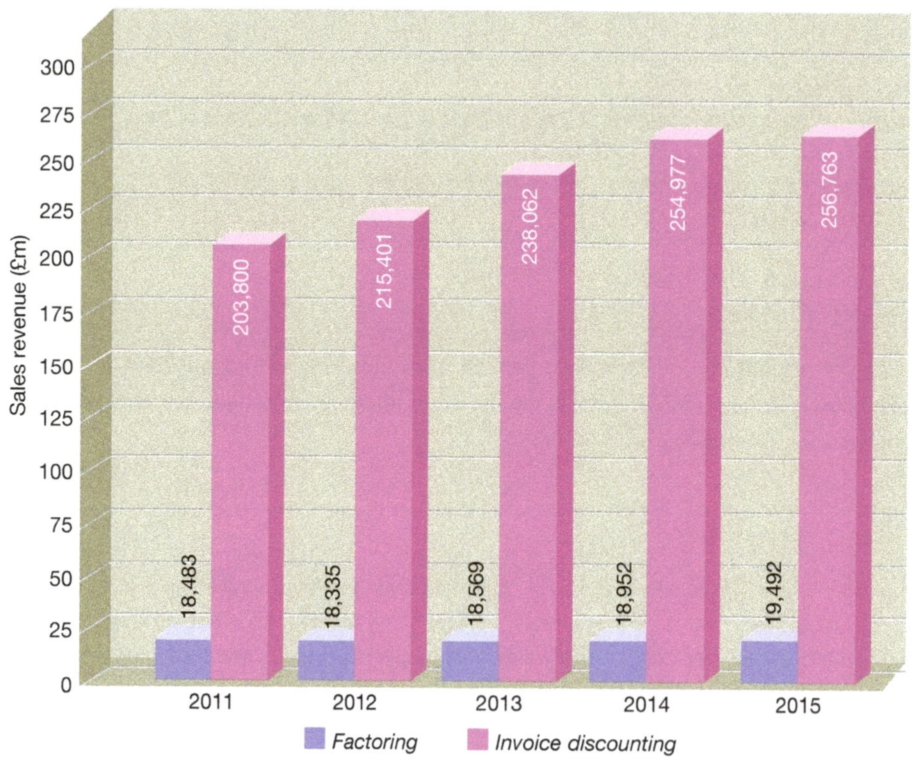

In recent years, client sales revenue from invoice discounting has risen much more sharply than client sales revenue for factoring.

Figure 6.9 Client sales revenue: domestic invoice discounting and factoring, 2011–2015

Source: Chart constructed from data published by the Asset Based Finance Association, 2011–2015, www.abfa.org.uk.

Factoring and invoice discounting are forms of **asset-based finance** as the assets of receivables are, in effect, used as security for the cash advances received by the business.

LONG-TERM VERSUS SHORT-TERM BORROWING

Where it is clear that some form of borrowing is required to finance the business, a decision must be made as to whether long-term or short-term borrowing is more appropriate. There are various issues to be taken into account, which include the following:

- *Matching.* The business may attempt to match the type of borrowing with the nature of the assets held. Thus, long-term borrowing may be used to finance assets that form part of the permanent operating base of the business. These normally include non-current assets and a certain level of current assets. This leaves assets held for a short period, such as current assets used to meet seasonal increases in demand, to be financed by short-term borrowing, which tends to be more flexible in that funds can be raised and repaid at short notice. Figure 6.10 shows this funding division graphically. A business may wish to match the period of borrowing exactly with the asset life. This may not be possible, however, because of the difficulty of predicting the life of many assets.

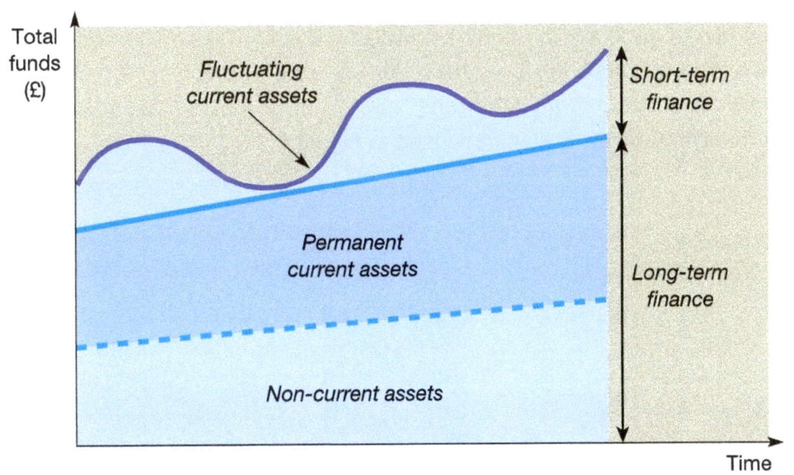

The broad consensus on financing seems to be that all of the permanent financial needs of the business should come from long-term sources. Only that part of current assets that fluctuates in the short term, probably on a seasonal basis, should be financed from short-term sources.

Figure 6.10 Short-term and long-term financing requirements

- *Flexibility.* Short-term borrowing may be used as a means of postponing a commitment to long-term borrowing. This may be desirable if interest rates are high but are forecast to fall in the future. Short-term borrowing does not usually incur a financial penalty for early repayment, whereas a penalty may arise if long-term borrowing is repaid early.
- *Refunding risk.* Short-term borrowing has to be renewed more frequently than long-term borrowing. This may create problems for the business if it is in financial difficulties or if there is a shortage of funds available for lending.

- *Interest rates.* Interest payable on long-term borrowing is often higher than that for short-term borrowing, as lenders require a higher return where their funds are locked up for a long period. This fact may make short-term borrowing a more attractive source of finance for a business. However, there may be other costs associated with borrowing (arrangement fees, for example) to be taken into account. The more frequently borrowings are renewed, the higher these costs will be.

Activity 6.17

Some businesses may take up a less cautious financing position than that shown in Figure 6.10 and others may take up a more cautious one. How would the diagram differ under each of these options?

A less cautious position would mean relying on short-term finance to help fund part of the permanent asset base. A more cautious position would mean relying on long-term finance to help finance the fluctuating assets of the business.

INTERNAL SOURCES OF FINANCE

In addition to external sources of finance, there are certain internal sources of finance that a business may use to generate funds for particular activities. These sources usually have the advantage that they are flexible. They may also be obtained quickly – particularly working capital sources – and do not require the compliance of other parties. The main internal sources of funds are described below and summarised in Figure 6.11.

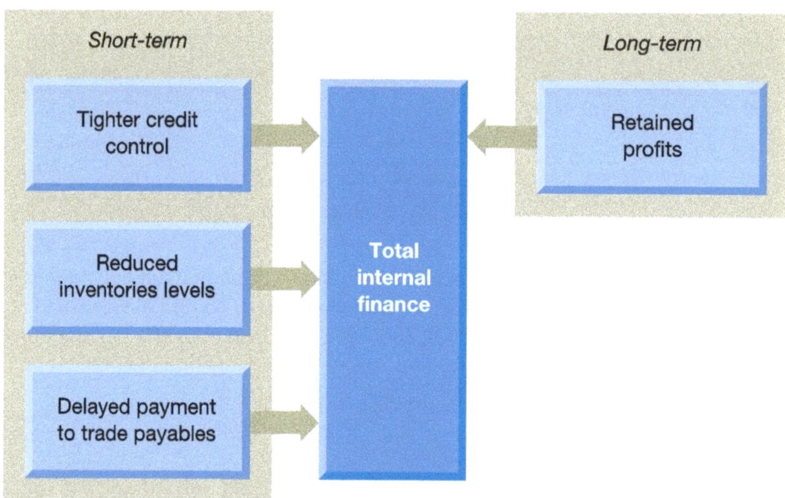

The major internal source of long-term finance is the profits that are retained rather than distributed to shareholders. The major internal sources of short-term finance involve reducing the level of trade receivables and inventories and increasing the level of trade payables.

Figure 6.11 The major internal sources of finance

INTERNAL SOURCES OF LONG-TERM FINANCE

Retained earnings

Earnings that are retained within the business, rather than distributed to shareholders in the form of dividends, represent by far the most important source of new finance for UK businesses in terms of value of funds raised.

Activity 6.18

Are retained earnings a free source of finance for the business? Explain.

No. This is because they have an opportunity cost to shareholders. If shareholders receive a dividend, they can use the cash to make other income-yielding investments. If the business retains the cash, shareholders are deprived of this potential income.

In view of the opportunity cost involved, shareholders will expect a rate of return from retained earnings that is equivalent to what they would receive had the funds been invested in another opportunity with the same level of risk.

Even though the reinvestment of earnings incurs a cost to the business, it may be preferable to raise finance from equity (ordinary share) investors in this way rather than by an issue of shares. There are a number of reasons why this may be so. No issue costs are incurred and the amount raised is certain, once the earnings have been generated. Where new shares are issued, issue costs may be substantial and the success of the issue may be uncertain. In addition, any new shares issued to outside investors will result in existing shareholders suffering some dilution of control.

Retaining earnings may be an easier option than asking investors to subscribe to a new share issue. These earnings are already held by the business and so there is no delay in receiving the funds. Moreover, there is often less scrutiny when earnings are retained for reinvestment purposes than when new shares are issued. Investors tend to examine closely the reasons for any new share issue. One problem with the use of earnings, however, is that their timing and amount may be difficult to determine. Thus, relying on earnings generated in the future to fund the business may prove to be unwise.

Some shareholders may prefer earnings to be retained by the business rather than distributed in the form of dividends. Where a business reinvests its earnings, it will expand and share values may well increase as a result. Receiving increases in wealth in the form of increased share value rather than in the form of dividends may suit some shareholders. In the UK, dividends are treated as income for tax purposes and therefore attract income tax. Gains on the sale of shares attract capital gains tax. Generally speaking, capital gains tax bites less hard than income tax. (For example, the UK maximum capital gains tax rate for 2016/17 is 28 per cent compared to 45 per cent for income tax.) Furthermore, shareholders have a choice as to when to sell the shares and so realise the capital gain. (In the UK, it is only when the gain is realised that capital gains tax comes into play.) Investors may be attracted to particular businesses according to the dividend/retention policies that they adopt. This point is considered in more detail in Chapter 9.

Retained earnings and 'pecking order' theory

It has been suggested that businesses have a 'pecking order' when taking on long-term finance. This pecking order can be summarised as follows:

- Retained earnings will be used to finance the business if possible.
- Where retained earnings are insufficient, or unavailable, loan capital will be used.
- Where loan capital is insufficient, or unavailable, share capital will be used.

One explanation for such a pecking order is that the managers of the business have access to information that investors do not. Suppose that managers have reliable information indicating that the prospects for the business are better than predicted by the market. This would mean that the shares are currently undervalued. To raise finance by a further issue of shares will, therefore, involve selling them below their true worth. The result would be a transfer of wealth from existing shareholders to those who take up the new share issue. Consequently, managers, who are employed to act in the best interests of existing shareholders, may prefer to rely on retained earnings, followed by loan capital, instead.

Activity 6.19

Why shouldn't the managers simply release any inside information to the market to allow the share price to rise and so make it possible to issue shares at a fair price?

There are at least two reasons why this may not be a good idea:

- It may be time-consuming and costly to persuade the market that the prospects of the business are better than current estimates. Investors may not believe what the managers tell them.
- It may provide useful information to competitors about future developments.

Now suppose the managers of a business have access to bad news about the future. If investors know that managers rely on retained earnings and loan capital when in possession of good news, they will assume that the issue of share capital means that managers are in possession of bad news. This may lead investors to believe that the shares are currently overvalued and so they will not be interested in subscribing to a new issue. (There is some evidence to show that the value of shares will fall when a share issue is announced.) Hence, managers will again be inclined to favour retained earnings followed by loan capital, with share capital as a last resort.

Pecking order theory may partly explain the heavy reliance of businesses on retained earnings. It does not, however, provide a complete explanation. Why, for example, do some businesses issue new equity shares even though they have the opportunity to issue loan capital? Clearly, there are other influences that come into play when making a financing decision. We shall pursue this point further in Chapter 8, where we consider the capital structure of businesses in some detail.

INTERNAL SOURCES OF SHORT-TERM FINANCE

Figure 6.11 reveals that the major internal forms of short-term finance are:

- tighter credit control
- reducing inventories levels
- delaying payments to trade payables.

We saw in Chapter 2, in the context of projected cash flow statements, that increases and decreases in these working capital items will have a direct and immediate effect on cash. This effectively raises finance that can be used elsewhere in the business.

Tighter credit control

By exerting tighter control over amounts owed by credit customers a business may be able to reduce the proportion of assets held in this form and so release funds for other purposes. Having funds tied up in trade receivables represents an opportunity cost in that those funds could be used for profit-generating activities. It is important, however, to weigh the benefits of tighter credit control against the likely costs in the form of lost customer goodwill and lost sales. To remain competitive, a business must take account of the needs of its customers and the credit policies adopted by rival businesses within the industry. We consider this further in Chapter 10.

Activity 6.21 involves weighing the costs of tighter credit control against likely future benefits.

Activity 6.20

Rusli Ltd provides a car valet service for car-hire businesses when their cars are returned from hire. Details of the service costs are as follows:

	Per car	
	£	£
Car valet charge		20
Less Variable costs	14	
Fixed costs	4	18
Profit		2

Sales revenue is £10 million a year and is all on credit. The average credit period taken by Rusli Ltd's customers is 45 days, although the terms of credit require payment within 30 days. Bad debts are currently £100,000 a year. Trade receivables are financed by a bank overdraft with an interest cost of 10 per cent a year.

The credit control department of Rusli Ltd believes it can eliminate bad debts and can reduce the average credit period to 30 days if new credit control procedures are implemented. These procedures will cost £50,000 a year and are likely to result in a reduction in sales of 5 per cent a year.

Should the business implement the new credit control procedures?

(*Hint:* To answer this activity it is useful to compare the current cost of trade credit with the costs under the proposed approach.)

The current cost of trade credit is:

	£
Bad debts	100,000
Overdraft interest ((£10m × 45/365) × 10%)	123,288
	223,288

→

The annual cost of trade credit under the new policy will be:

	£
Overdraft interest ((95% × £10m) × (30/365) × 10%))	78,082
Cost of control procedures	50,000
Net cost of lost sales ((£10m/£20 × 5%) × (20 − 14*))	150,000
	278,082

* The loss will be the contribution from valeting the car, that is, the difference between the valet charge and the variable costs. The fixed costs are ignored as they do not vary with the decision.

The above figures reveal that the business will be worse off if the new policies are adopted.

Reducing inventories levels

This internal source of funds may prove attractive to a business. As with trade receivables, holding inventories imposes an opportunity cost on a business as the funds tied up cannot be used for other purposes. If inventories are reduced, funds become available for those purposes. However, a business must ensure there are sufficient inventories available to meet likely future sales demand. Failure to do so will result in lost customer goodwill and lost sales revenue.

The nature and condition of the inventories held will determine whether it is possible to exploit this form of finance. A business may have excessive inventories as a result of poor buying decisions. This may mean that a significant proportion of inventories held is slow-moving or obsolete and therefore cannot be liquidated easily. These issues are picked up again in Chapter 10.

Delaying payment to trade payables

By providing a period of credit, suppliers are in effect offering a business an interest-free loan. If the business delays payment, the period of the 'loan' is extended and funds are retained within the business. This can be a cheap form of finance for a business, although this is not always the case. If a business fails to pay within the agreed credit period, there may be significant costs: for example, the business may find it difficult to buy on credit when it has a reputation as a slow payer.

Where a very large business fails to pay its trade payables on time, however, any costs arising are likely to be borne by its smaller suppliers. **Real World 6.15** describes how the government-appointed Groceries Code Adjudicator condemned the payment practices of one large supermarket towards its suppliers.

Real World 6.15

Every little helps

Tesco was guilty of serious breaches of industry rules as it deliberately withheld cash from suppliers to flatter its financial performance, the supermarket ombudsman has found. An investigation by the Groceries Code Adjudicator has ruled that the supermarket broke the legally-binding industry code of practice as it 'prioritised its own finances over treating suppliers fairly'.

Christine Tacon, the adjudicator, ordered Tesco to introduce significant changes to its treatment of suppliers and its procurement and payment systems after she found evidence of 'unacceptable and unreasonable' delays to supplier payments. She found that the supermarket group had 'knowingly delayed paying money to suppliers in order to improve its own financial position.'

Dave Lewis, the chief executive of Tesco, said that the company had addressed 'virtually all' of the issues raised in the GCA report. He said that Tesco was 'a very different company' from the one that the investigation describes.

Ms Tacon's highly critical report revealed internal Tesco emails, which advised that 'payments should not be made to suppliers before a certain date in order to avoid underperformance against a forecasted margin.' Ms Tacon ordered the supermarket to report back within four weeks on how it planned to implement improvements to its treatment of its supply chain. She said: 'The length of the delays [in payment], their widespread nature and the range of Tesco's unreasonable practices and behaviours towards suppliers concerned me. The most shocking thing I found was how widespread it was, how many instances I came across. In every sector, practically every supplier I spoke to had evidence of delays in payment.' The investigation also revealed that in some cases Tesco took months or even years to repay sums it charged in error.

Mark Johnson, associate professor of operations management at Warwick Business School, said that other retailers were likely to have delayed supplier payments in a similar way to flatter their financial results: 'Firms in different sectors have long known that they can manipulate payment terms and order dates to make their accounts look healthier than they are. Some retailers are sharper with it than others.'

Source: J. Hurley (2016), 'Tesco delayed payments to suppliers and boosted profits', *The Times*, www.thetimes.co.uk, 27 January.

Activity 6.22 is concerned with the cash flow benefit of more efficient management of the working capital elements.

Activity 6.21

Trader Ltd is a wholesaler of imported washing machines. The business is partly funded by a bank overdraft and the bank is putting pressure on Trader Ltd to reduce this as soon as possible.

Sales revenue is £14.6 million a year and is all on credit. Purchases and cost of sales are roughly equal at £7.3 million a year. Current investment in the relevant working capital elements are:

	£m
Inventories	1.5
Trade receivables	3.8
Trade payables	0.7

Trader Ltd's accountant believes that much of the overdraft could be eliminated through better control of working capital. As a result, she has investigated several successful businesses that are similar to Trader Ltd and found the following averages:

Average inventories turnover period	22
Average settlement period for trade receivables	57
Average settlement period for trade payables	55

How much cash could Trader Ltd generate if it were able to bring its ratios into line with those of similar businesses?

→

The cash that could be generated is as follows:

	£m	£m
Inventories		
Current level	1.5	
Target level: $^{7.3}/_{365} \times 22 =$	0.4	1.1
Trade receivables		
Current level	3.8	
Target level: $^{14.6}/_{365} \times 57 =$	2.3	1.5
Trade payables		
Current level	0.7	
Target level: $^{7.3}/_{365} \times 55 =$	1.1	0.4
Total		3.0

Some final points

The so-called short-term sources just described are short term to the extent that they can be reversed at short notice. For example, a reduction in the level of trade receivables can be reversed within a couple of weeks. Typically, however, once a business has established a reduced receivables settlement period, a reduced inventories holding period and/or an expanded payables settlement period, it will tend to maintain these new levels.

In Chapter 10, we shall see how these three elements of working capital may be managed. We shall also see that, for many businesses, the funds invested in working capital items are vast. By exercising tighter control of trade receivables and inventories and by exploiting opportunities to delay payment to trade payables, it may be possible to release substantial amounts for other purposes.

Self-assessment question 6.1

Helsim Ltd is a wholesaler and distributor of electrical components. The most recent draft financial statements of the business revealed the following:

Income statement for the year

	£m	£m
Sales revenue		14.2
Opening inventories	3.2	
Purchases	8.4	
	11.6	
Closing inventories	(3.8)	(7.8)
Gross profit		6.4
Administration expenses		(3.0)
Distribution expenses		(2.1)
Operating profit		1.3
Finance costs		(0.8)
Profit before taxation		0.5
Tax		(0.2)
Profit for the period		0.3

Statement of financial position as at the end of the year

	£m
ASSETS	
Non-current assets	
Property, plant and equipment	
Land and buildings	3.8
Equipment	0.9
Motor vehicles	0.5
	5.2
Current assets	
Inventories	3.8
Trade receivables	3.6
Cash at bank	0.1
	7.5
Total assets	12.7
EQUITY AND LIABILITIES	
Equity	
Share capital	2.0
Retained earnings	1.8
	3.8
Non-current liabilities	
Loan notes (secured on property)	3.5
Current liabilities	
Trade payables	1.8
Short-term borrowings	3.6
	5.4
Total equity and liabilities	12.7

Notes:

1 Land and buildings are shown at their current market value. Equipment and motor vehicles are shown at their written-down values (that is, cost less accumulated depreciation).

2 No dividends have been paid to ordinary shareholders for the past three years.

In recent months, trade payables have been pressing for payment. The managing director has therefore decided to reduce the level of trade payables to an average of 40 days outstanding. To achieve this, he has decided to approach the bank with a view to increasing the overdraft (the short-term borrowings comprise only a bank overdraft). The business is currently paying 10 per cent a year interest on the overdraft.

Required:

(a) Comment on the liquidity position of the business.

(b) Calculate the amount of finance required to reduce trade payables, from the level shown on the statement of financial position, to an average of 40 days outstanding.

(c) State, with reasons, how you consider the bank would react to the proposal to grant an additional overdraft facility.

(d) Identify four sources of finance (internal or external, but excluding a bank overdraft) that may be suitable to finance the reduction in trade payables and state, with reasons, which of these you consider the most appropriate.

The solution to this question can be found at the back of the book on pp. 584–585.

SUMMARY

The main points of this chapter may be summarised as follows:

Sources of finance

- Long-term finance is for at least one year whereas short-term finance is for a shorter period.
- External sources of finance require the agreement of outside parties, whereas internal sources do not.
- The higher the risk associated with a source of finance, the higher the expected return from investors.

External sources of long-term finance

- Include ordinary shares, preference shares, borrowings, leases, hire purchase agreements and securitisation.
- From an investor's perspective, ordinary shares are normally the most risky form of investment and provide the highest expected returns to investors.
- Preference shares offer investors a lower level of risk than ordinary shares. They are given the first slice of any dividend paid.
- Borrowings (loans) are normally the least risky and provide the lowest expected returns to investors.
- Loans are relatively low risk because lenders usually have security for their loan. Loan covenants can further protect lenders.
- Types of loan capital include convertible loan notes, term loans, mortgages, eurobonds, deep discount bonds and junk bonds.
- Credit-rating agencies categorise loans issued by businesses according to estimated default risk.
- Convertible loan notes offer the right of conversion to ordinary shares at a specified date and a specified price.
- Junk bonds are relatively high risk and fall outside the investment-grade categories established by credit-rating agencies.
- Warrants give holders the right, but not the obligation, to buy ordinary shares at a given price and are often used as a 'sweetener' to accompany a loan issue.
- Interest rates may be floating or fixed.
- Interest rate risk may be reduced, or eliminated, through the use of hedging arrangements such as interest rate swaps.
- Islamic law rejects the idea of charging interest and instead insists that all investors should bear some of the risk of a business venture.

Attitudes towards the level of borrowing

- The level of borrowing will be determined by the attitudes of:
  - shareholders
  - managers
  - lenders.
- These attitudes are influenced by a variety of factors.

Other forms of external long-term finance

- A finance lease is really a form of lending that gives the lessee the use of an asset over most of its useful life in return for regular payments.
- A sale-and-leaseback arrangement involves the sale of an asset to a financial institution accompanied by an agreement to lease the asset back to the business.
- Hire purchase is a form of credit used to acquire an asset. Under the terms of a hire purchase (HP) agreement a customer pays for an asset by instalments over an agreed period.
- Securitisation involves bundling together similar, illiquid assets to provide backing for the issue of bonds.

External sources of short-term finance

- Include bank overdrafts, bills of exchange, debt factoring and invoice discounting.
- Bank overdrafts are flexible and cheap but are repayable on demand.
- Bills of exchange are similar to IOUs.
- Debt factoring and invoice discounting use trade receivables as a basis for borrowing, with the latter more popular because of cost and flexibility.

Choosing between long-term and short-term borrowing

- Important factors include matching the type of borrowing to the type of assets, flexibility, refunding risk and interest rates.

Internal sources of finance

- Include retained earnings, tighter control of trade receivables, reducing inventories levels and delaying payments to trade payables.
- Retained earnings are by far the most important source of new long-term finance (internal or external) for UK businesses.
- They are not a free source of finance, as investors will require returns similar to those from ordinary shares.

KEY TERMS

Security
Fixed charge
Floating charge
Loan covenants
Subordinated loans
Term loan
Loan note
Bonds
Eurobonds
Deep discount bonds
Convertible loan notes
Junk (high-yield) bonds
Mortgage
Floating interest rate
Fixed interest rate
Hedging arrangement
Interest rate swap
Warrant
Financial derivative
Finance lease

→

Operating lease
Sale and leaseback
Hire purchase
Securitisation
Bank overdraft
Bill of exchange
Debt factoring
Invoice discounting
Asset-based finance

For definitions of these terms, see the Glossary, pp. 625–633.

FURTHER READING

If you wish to explore the topics discussed in this chapter in more depth, try the following books:

Arnold, G. (2013) *Corporate Financial Management,* 5th edn, Pearson, Chapters 11 and 12.

Brealey, R., Myers, S., Allen, F. and Mohanty, P. (2014) *Principles of Corporate Finance,* 11th edn, Irwin/McGraw-Hill, Chapters 14, 25 and 26.

Hillier, D., Ross, S., Westerfield, R., Jaffe, J. and Jordan, B. (2013) *Corporate Finance,* 2nd European edn, McGraw-Hill Higher Education, Chapters 19–21.

Pike, R., Neale, B. and Linsley, P. (2015) *Corporate Finance and Investment,* 8th edn, Pearson, Chapters 15 and 16.

REVIEW QUESTIONS

Solutions to these questions can be found at the back of the book on pp. 594–595.

6.1 What are share warrants and what are the benefits to a business of issuing share warrants?

6.2 'Convertible loan notes are really a form of delayed equity.' Do you agree? Discuss.

6.3 What are the benefits of an interest swap agreement and how does it work?

6.4 Distinguish between invoice discounting and debt factoring.

EXERCISES

Exercises 6.4 to 6.7 are more advanced than 6.1 to 6.3. Those with coloured numbers have solutions at the back of the book, starting on p. 611.

If you wish to try more exercises, visit the students' side of this book's companion website.

6.1 Answer *all* parts below.

Required:
Provide reasons why a business may decide to:

(a) lease rather than buy an asset which is to be held for long-term use
(b) use retained earnings to finance growth rather than issue new shares
(c) repay long-term loan capital earlier than the specified repayment date.

6.2 H. Brown (Portsmouth) Ltd produces a range of central heating systems for sale to builders' merchants. As a result of increasing demand for the business's products, the directors have decided to expand production. The cost of acquiring new plant and machinery and the increase in working capital requirements are planned to be financed by a mixture of long-term and short-term borrowing.

Required:

(a) Discuss the major factors that should be taken into account when deciding on the appropriate mix of long-term and short-term borrowing necessary to finance the expansion programme.
(b) Discuss the major factors that a lender should take into account when deciding whether to grant a long-term loan to the business.
(c) Identify three conditions that might be included in a long-term loan agreement and state the purpose of each.

6.3 Securitisation is now used in a variety of industries. In the music industry, for example, rock stars such as David Bowie and Iron Maiden have used this form of financing to their benefit.

Required:

(a) Explain the term 'securitisation'.
(b) Discuss the main features of this form of financing and the benefits of using securitisation.

6.4 Raphael Ltd is a small engineering business that has annual credit sales revenue of £2.4 million. In recent years, the business has experienced credit control problems. The average collection period for sales has risen to 50 days even though the stated policy of the business is for payment to be made within 30 days. In addition, 1.5 per cent of sales are written off as bad debts each year.

The business has recently been in talks with a factor that is prepared to make an advance to the business equivalent to 80 per cent of trade receivables, based on the assumption that customers will, in future, adhere to a 30-day payment period. The interest rate for the advance will be 11 per cent a year. The trade receivables are currently financed through a bank overdraft, which has an interest rate of 12 per cent a year. The factor will take over the credit control procedures of the business and this will result in a saving to the business of £18,000 a year; however, the factor will make a charge of 2 per cent of sales revenue for this service. The use of the factoring service is expected to eliminate the bad debts incurred by the business.

Required:
Calculate the net cost of the factor agreement to the business and state whether or not the business should take advantage of the opportunity to factor its trade receivables.

6.5 Cybele Technology Ltd is a software business that is owned and managed by two computer software specialists. Although sales have remained stable at £4 million per year in recent years, the level of trade receivables has increased significantly. A recent financial report submitted to the owners indicates an average settlement period for trade receivables of 60 days compared with an industry average of 40 days. The level of bad debts has also increased in recent years and the business now writes off approximately £20,000 of bad debts each year.

The recent problems experienced in controlling credit have led to a liquidity crisis for the business. At present, the business finances its trade receivables by a bank overdraft bearing an interest rate of 14 per cent a year. However, the overdraft limit has been exceeded on several occasions in recent months and the bank is now demanding a significant decrease in the size of the overdraft. To comply with this demand, the owners of the business have approached a factor who has offered to make an advance equivalent to 85 per cent of trade receivables, based on the assumption that the level of receivables will be in line with the industry average. The factor will charge a rate of interest of 12 per cent a year for this advance. The factor will take over the sales records of the business and, for this service, will charge a fee based on 2 per cent of sales. The business believes that the services offered by the factor should eliminate bad debts and should lead to administrative cost savings of £26,000 per year.

Required:

(a) Calculate the effect on the profit of Cybele Technology Ltd of employing a debt factor. Discuss your findings.

(b) Discuss the potential advantages and disadvantages for a business that employs the services of a debt factor.

6.6 Telford Engineers plc, a medium-sized manufacturer of automobile components, has decided to modernise its factory by introducing a number of robots. These will cost £20 million and will reduce operating costs by £6 million a year for their estimated useful life of 10 years starting next year (Year 10). To finance this scheme, the business can raise £20 million either by issuing:

(i) 20 million ordinary shares at 100p, or

(ii) loan notes at 7 per cent interest a year with capital repayments of £3 million a year commencing at the end of Year 11.

Telford Engineers' summarised financial statements appear below.

Summary of statements of financial position at 31 December

	Year 6	*Year 7*	*Year 8*	*Year 9*
	£m	*£m*	*£m*	*£m*
ASSETS				
Non-current assets	48	51	65	64
Current assets	55	67	57	55
Total assets	103	118	122	119
EQUITY AND LIABILITIES				
Equity	48	61	61	63
Non-current liabilities	30	30	30	30
Current liabilities				
Trade payables	20	27	25	18
Short-term borrowings	5	–	6	8
	25	27	31	26
Total equity and liabilities	103	118	122	119
Number of issued 25p shares	80m	80m	80m	80m
Share price	150p	200p	100p	145p

Note that the short-term borrowings consisted entirely of bank overdrafts.

Summary of income statements for years ended 31 December

	Year 6	*Year 7*	*Year 8*	*Year 9*
	£m	*£m*	*£m*	*£m*
Sales revenue	152	170	110	145
Operating profit	28	40	7	15
Interest payable	(4)	(3)	(4)	(5)
Profit before taxation	24	37	3	10

	Year 6	Year 7	Year 8	Year 9
	£m	£m	£m	£m
Tax	(12)	(16)	(0)	(4)
Profit for the year	12	21	3	6
Dividends paid during each year	6	8	3	4

You should assume that the tax rate for Year 10 is 30 per cent, that sales revenue and operating profit will be unchanged except for the £6 million cost saving arising from the introduction of the robots, and that Telford Engineers will pay the same dividend per share in Year 10 as in Year 9.

Required:

(a) Prepare, for each financing arrangement, Telford Engineers' projected income statement for the year ending 31 December Year 10 and a statement of its share capital, reserves and loans on that date.

(b) Calculate Telford's projected earnings per share for Year 10 for both schemes.

(c) Which scheme would you advise the business to adopt? You should give your reasons and state what additional information you would require.

6.7 Gainsborough Fashions Ltd operates a chain of fashion shops. In recent months the business has been under pressure from its suppliers to reduce the average credit period taken from three months to one month. As a result, the directors have approached the bank to ask for an increase in the existing overdraft for one year to be able to comply with the suppliers' demands. The most recent financial statements of the business are as follows:

Statement of financial position as at 31 May

	£m
ASSETS	
Non-current assets	
Property, plant and equipment at cost less depreciation	
Fixtures and fittings	67.0
Motor vehicles	7.0
	74.0
Current assets	
Inventories	198.0
Trade receivables	3.0
	201.0
Total assets	275.0
EQUITY AND LIABILITIES	
Equity	
£1 ordinary shares	20.0
General reserve	4.0
Retained earnings	17.0
	41.0
Non-current liabilities	
Borrowings – loan notes repayable in just over one year's time	40.0
Current liabilities	
Trade payables	162.0
Accrued expenses	10.0

	£m
Borrowings – bank overdraft	17.0
Tax due	5.0
	194.0
Total equity and liabilities	275.0

Abbreviated income statement for the year ended 31 May

	£m
Sales revenue	740.0
Operating profit	38.0
Interest charges	(5.0)
Profit before taxation	33.0
Tax	(10.0)
Profit for the year	23.0

A dividend of £23 million for the year was made.

Notes:

1 The loan notes are secured by personal guarantees from the directors.

2 The current overdraft bears an interest rate of 12 per cent a year.

Required:

(a) Identify and discuss the major factors that a bank would take into account before deciding whether or not to grant an increase in the overdraft of a business.

(b) State whether, in your opinion, the bank should grant the required increase in the overdraft for Gainsborough Fashions Ltd. You should provide reasoned arguments and supporting calculations where necessary.

Chapter 7

FINANCING A BUSINESS 2: RAISING LONG-TERM FINANCE

INTRODUCTION

We begin this chapter by looking at the role of the London Stock Exchange (which we shall refer to as simply the Stock Exchange) in raising finance for large businesses. We then go on to consider whether shares listed on the Stock Exchange are efficiently priced. If so, there are far reaching implications for both managers and investors. We shall see that share price efficiency has been the subject of much research and debate.

Share capital may be issued in various ways and the most important of these will be explored in the chapter. Some involve direct appeals to investors, whereas others involve the use of financial intermediaries. Smaller businesses do not have access to the Stock Exchange and so must look elsewhere to raise long-term finance. We conclude this chapter by considering some of the main providers of long-term finance for these businesses.

Learning outcomes

When you have completed this chapter, you should be able to:

- Discuss the role and nature of the Stock Exchange.
- Discuss the nature and implications of stock market efficiency.
- Outline the main methods by which share capital may be issued.
- Identify the problems that smaller businesses experience in raising finance and describe the ways in which they may gain access to long-term finance.

THE STOCK EXCHANGE

The **Stock Exchange** acts as a *primary* and *secondary* capital market for large businesses. As a primary market, its main function is to enable these businesses to raise new capital. Thus, businesses may use the Stock Exchange to raise capital by issuing shares or loan notes. To issue either through the Stock Exchange, however, a business must be 'listed'. This means that it must meet fairly stringent Stock Exchange requirements concerning size, profit history, information disclosure and so on.

Share issues arising from the initial listing of the business on the Stock Exchange are known as *initial public offerings* (IPOs). Share issues undertaken by businesses that are already listed and seeking additional finance are known as *seasoned equity offerings* (SEOs). There is convincing evidence, from both the USA and the UK, to suggest that investing in IPOs is usually a bad idea. One comprehensive study of 2,499 IPOs floated on the Stock Exchange between 1975 and 2004 found that they underperformed the market by 12.6 per cent after three years and 31.6 per cent after five years (see reference 1 at the end of the chapter).

Real World 7.1 provides some interesting comments on the wisdom of investing in IPOs from two leading figures in the investment world.

Real World 7.1

Issues become problems

Benjamin Graham, an economist and successful investor, warned against investing in IPOs. He also expressed despair at the failure of investors to learn from their mistakes. In his famous book, *The Intelligent Investor,* he wrote

> In every case, investors have burned themselves on IPOs, have stayed away for at least two years, but have always returned for another scalding. For as long as stock markets have existed, investors have gone through this manic-depressive cycle.
>
> In America's first great IPO boom back in 1825, a man was said to have been squeezed to death in the stampede of speculators trying to buy shares in the new Bank of Southwark. The wealthiest buyers hired thugs to punch their way to the front of the line. Sure enough, by 1829, stocks had lost roughly 25% of their value.

Warren Buffett, a disciple of Graham, has speculated on why IPOs are often overpriced (and so underperform the market). He points out:

> It's almost a mathematical impossibility to imagine that, out of the thousands of things for sale on a given day, the most attractively priced is the one being sold by a knowledgeable seller (company insiders) to a less-knowledgeable buyer (investors).

Source: B. Graham (2003) *The Intelligent Investor*, HarperBusiness p.141; Warren Buffett.

The role of the Stock Exchange in raising equity has decreased over the years. IPOs and SEOs no longer represent an important source of finance for many modern businesses. This is partly because many do not incur large outlays on physical assets, such as plant and machinery. They also become cash generative earlier in their development and so become less reliant on outside finance.

The function of the Stock Exchange as a secondary market is to help investors transfer their securities (that is, shares and loan notes) with ease. It provides a 'second-hand' market where shares and loan notes already in issue may be bought and sold.

Activity 7.1

Could listed businesses also benefit by the Stock Exchange making it easier for investors to sell their securities? If so, how?

Investors are more likely to invest if they know their investment can be turned into cash whenever required. Listed businesses are, therefore, likely to find it easier to raise long-term finance and to do so at lower cost.

Although investors are not obliged to use the Stock Exchange as the means of transferring shares in a listed business, it is usually the most convenient way of buying or selling shares.

Listed businesses

Businesses listed on the Stock Exchange vary considerably in size, with market capitalisations ranging from below £2 million to more than £2,000 million. **Real World 7.2** provides some impression of the distribution of businesses across this wide range.

Real World 7.2

UK listed businesses by equity market value

The distribution of UK listed businesses by equity market value at the end of February 2016 is shown in Figure 7.1.

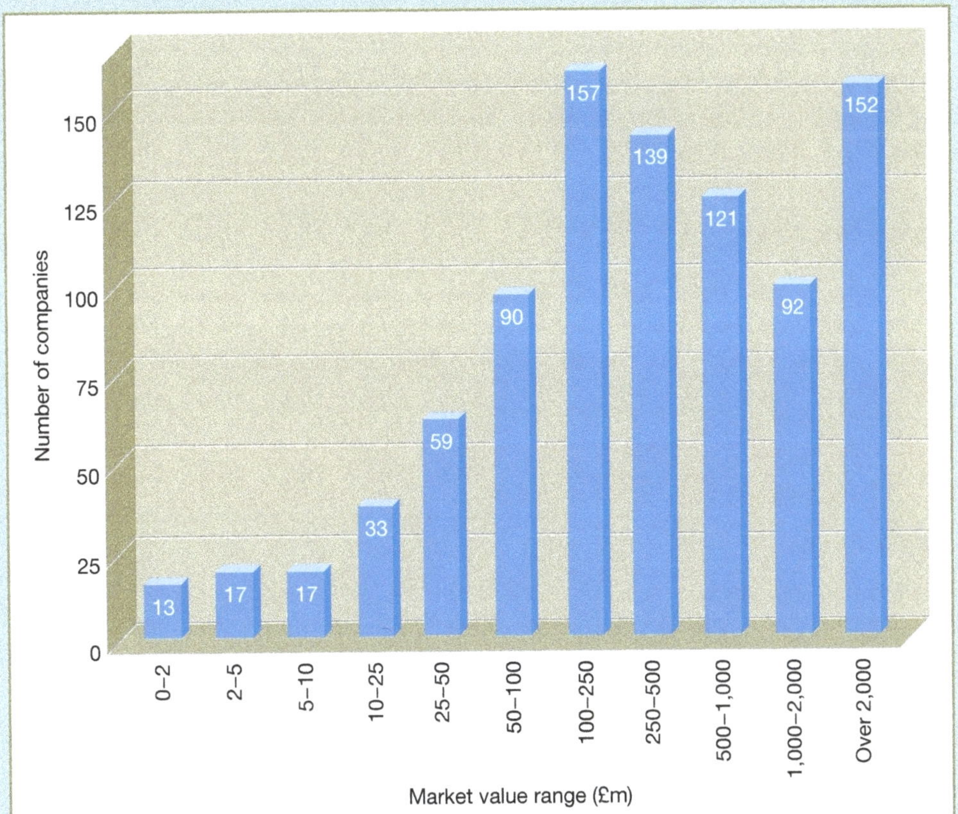

Figure 7.1 Distribution of UK listed businesses by equity market value

→

The chart shows that 13 businesses have a market capitalisation of less than £2 million. However, 152 businesses have a market capitalisation of more than £2,000 million.

Source: Chart compiled from information in 'Primary Market Fact Sheet', London Stock Exchange, www.londonstockexchange.com, February 2016.

Share price indices

There are various indices available to help monitor trends in overall share price movements of Stock Exchange listed businesses. **FTSE (Footsie) indices**, as they are called, derive their name from the organisations behind them: the *Financial Times* (FT) and the Stock Exchange (SE). The most common indices are:

- *FTSE 100.* This is probably the best-known share price index. It is based on the share price movements of the 100 largest businesses, by **market capitalisation**, listed on the Stock Exchange. (Market capitalisation is the total market value of the shares issued by a business.) Businesses within this index are often referred to as 'large cap' businesses.
- *FTSE Mid 250.* An index based on the share price movements of the next 250 largest businesses, by market capitalisation, listed on the Stock Exchange.
- *FTSE A 350.* This index combines businesses in the FTSE 100 and FTSE Mid 250 indices.
- *FTSE Actuaries All Share Index.* An index based on the share price movements of more than 800 shares, which account for more than 90 per cent of the market capitalisation of all listed businesses.

Each index is constructed using a base date and a base value (the FTSE 100 index, for example, was constructed in 1984 with a base of 1,000). Each index is updated throughout each trading day and reviewed on a quarterly basis. Changes in the relative size of businesses during a particular quarter will usually lead to some businesses within an index being replaced by others.

Raising finance

The amount of finance raised by Stock Exchange businesses each year varies according to economic conditions. **Real World 7.3** gives an indication of the amounts raised in recent years from equity issues by listed businesses (including those that are newly listed).

Real World 7.3

Equity issues

The following amounts were raised from new equity issues by listed businesses through the main market of the London Stock Exchange over the ten-year period 2006–2015.

	Number of businesses	*Total amount raised (£m)*
2015	566	28,260
2014	579	26,217
2013	477	23,788
2012	532	11,449
2011	688	17,790
2010	510	23,915

	Number of businesses	*Total amount raised (£m)*
2009	454	77,047
2008	527	66,472
2007	653	28,494
2006	822	33,448

We can see that the amounts raised vary significantly over the period.

Source: Compiled from 'Main Market Fact Sheets', December 2006 to December 2015, London Stock Exchange, www.londonstockexchange.com.

The Stock Exchange can be a useful vehicle for entrepreneurs to realise value from their business.

Activity 7.2

How can the Stock Exchange help entrepreneurs to do this?

By listing their businesses on the Stock Exchange, the shares become more easily available to other investors. Entrepreneurs can then convert the value of their stake in the business into cash by selling all, or some, of their shares.

Real World 7.4 describes how one group of entrepreneurs was poised to benefit enormously from an IPO.

Real World 7.4

A sweet moment

Makers of viral game sensation Candy Crush Saga will instantly rack up mega-fortunes when their London firm floats on the New York Stock Exchange tomorrow valued at nearly £5 billion.

Leading the pack will be Mel Morris, a former flooring salesman from Derbyshire, who can expect a paper windfall of some £530 million. Banking only slightly less than Mr Morris is the Italian entrepreneur Riccardo Zacconi, 47, who has stake of around 10 per cent – worth around £452 million. Other founders will also make hundreds of millions from the sale.

Candy Crush has gripped British mobile users with its highly-addictive task of moving matching candies to make lines disappear, and was the most downloaded free app and the top revenue-grossing app in 2013.

The game accounts for nearly three-quarters of revenue at King Digital Entertainment, which will debut on Wall Street priced at $21–24 a share – up to £14.50 each.

That sky-high valuation makes it bigger than toy giant Hasbro, the 90-year-old maker of favourites like Monopoly and Scrabble.

Source: T. Jefferies and M. Duell (2014) 'What a saga! Candy Crush founding trio to rake in up to £530m EACH as tech firm behind mobile game sensation hits Wall Street', www.thisismoney.co.uk, 25 March.

Advantages and disadvantages of a listing

In addition to the advantages already mentioned, a Stock Exchange listing may help a business by:

- raising its profile, which may be useful in dealings with customers and suppliers
- ensuring that its shares are valued in an efficient manner (a point to which we return later)
- broadening its investor base
- acquiring other businesses by using its own shares as payment rather than cash
- attracting and retaining employees by offering incentives based on share ownership schemes.

Before a decision is made to float (that is, to list), however, the advantages must be weighed against the possible disadvantages of a listing.

Raising finance through the Stock Exchange can be a costly process. To make an initial public offering, a business will rely on the help of various specialists such as lawyers, accountants and bankers. Their services, however, do not come cheap. Typically, between 4 per cent and 8 per cent of the total proceeds from a sale will be absorbed in professional fees (see reference 2 at the end of the chapter). In addition to these out-of-pocket expenses, a huge amount of management time is usually required, which can lead to missed business opportunities.

Another important disadvantage is the regulatory burden placed on listed businesses. Once a business is listed, there are continuing requirements to be met, covering issues such as:

- disclosure of financial information
- informing shareholders of significant developments
- the rights of shareholders and lenders
- the obligations of directors.

These requirements can be onerous and can also involve substantial costs for the business.

The activities of listed businesses are closely monitored by financial analysts, financial journalists and other businesses. Such scrutiny can be unwelcome, particularly if the business is dealing with sensitive issues or is experiencing operational problems. Furthermore, if investors become disenchanted with the business and the price of its shares falls, this may make it vulnerable to a takeover bid from another business.

Real World 7.5 describes plans for one well-known business to avoid the spotlight and to protect itself by de-listing and then turning into a private company.

Real World 7.5

It's a private matter

American entrepreneur Michael Dell is taking the PC maker he founded private for $24.4bn (£15.6bn), in a deal that marks the end of an era for the computer industry. The billionaire, who already owns about 16 pc of the company, is combining with private-equity firm Silver Lake and Microsoft to buy the company he founded as a student. Having floated in New York in 1988 as PCs were becoming a staple in homes, Dell has struggled to adapt as consumers increasingly prefer tablet devices such as Apple's iPad.

Taking the company private will allow Mr Dell to more easily alter the company's direction as he will no longer face shareholder scrutiny. 'Under a new private company structure, we will have the time and flexibility to really pursue and realise [our strategy],' said Brian Gladden, Dell's chief financial officer.

Dell shareholders will receive $13.65 a share in cash, just over a 25 per cent premium to the share price before rumours about the acquisition surfaced last month.

Source: R. Blackden (2013) 'Dell to go private in $24.4bn deal', *Daily Telegraph*, 6 February.

Stock Exchange investors are often accused of taking a short-term view, which puts pressure on managers to produce quick results. If managers judge that shareholders are focused on the forthcoming quarterly, or half-yearly, profit announcements, they may strive to produce results that meet expectations. This may prevent managers from undertaking projects that are likely to only yield benefits over the longer term. Instead, they will opt for investments that perform well over the short term, even though the long-term prospects may be poor. This is a serious criticism of the way in which the Stock Exchange operates, which we shall explore a little later in the chapter.

STOCK MARKET EFFICIENCY

We mentioned above that the Stock Exchange helps share prices to be efficiently priced. The term 'efficiency' in this context does not relate to the way in which the Stock Exchange is administered but rather to the way in which information is processed. An **efficient stock market** is one in which information is processed quickly and accurately and so share prices faithfully reflect all relevant information available. In other words, prices are determined in a rational manner and represent the best estimate of the 'true worth' of the shares.

Activity 7.3

How would you define the 'true worth' of a share? (*Hint*: Think back to Chapter 3)

The value of an economic asset can be defined in terms of its future benefits. In the case of a share, it is the discounted cash inflows from future dividends.

The term 'efficiency' does not imply that investors have perfect knowledge concerning a business and its future prospects and that this knowledge is reflected in the share price. Information may come to light concerning the business that investors did not previously know about and which may indicate that the current share price is higher or lower than its 'true worth'. However, in an efficient market, new information will be quickly absorbed by investors and this will lead to an appropriate share price adjustment.

We can see that the term 'efficiency' in relation to the Stock Exchange is not the same as the economists' concept of perfect markets, which you may have come across in your previous studies. The definition of an efficient capital market does not rest on a set of restrictive assumptions regarding the operation of the market (for example, no taxes, no transaction costs, no entry or exit barriers and so on). In reality, such assumptions will not hold. The term 'efficient market' is a narrower concept that has been developed by studying how stock markets behave in the real world. It simply describes the situation where relevant information is *quickly* and *accurately* reflected in share prices. The speed at which new information is absorbed in share prices will mean that not even nimble-footed investors will have time to make superior gains by buying or selling shares when new information becomes available.

To understand why the Stock Exchange may be efficient, it is important to bear in mind that shares listed on the Stock Exchange are scrutinised by many individuals, including skilled analysts, who are constantly seeking to make gains from identifying shares that are inefficiently priced. They are alert to new information and will react quickly when new opportunities arise. If, for example, shares can be identified as being below their 'true worth', investors would immediately exploit this information by buying those shares. When this is done on a large scale, the effect will be to drive up the price of the shares, thereby eliminating any inefficiency within the market. Thus, as a result of the efforts to make gains from inefficiently priced shares, investors will, paradoxically, promote the efficiency of the market.

Three levels of efficiency have been identified concerning the operation of stock markets. These are as follows.

Weak form of efficiency

The weak form reflects the situation where past market information, such as the sequence of share prices, rates of return and trading volumes and so on, is fully reflected in current share prices and so should have no bearing on future share prices. In other words, future share price movements are independent of past share price movements. Movements in share prices will follow a random path and, as a result, any attempt to study past prices in order to detect a pattern of price movements will fail. It is not possible, therefore, to make gains from simply studying past price movements. Investors and analysts who draw up charts of share price changes (known as technical analysis) in order to predict future price movements will thus be wasting their time.

Semi-strong form of efficiency

The semi-strong form takes the notion of efficiency a little further and describes the situation where all publicly available information, including past share prices, is fully reflected in the current share price. Other publicly available forms of information will include published financial statements, business announcements, newspaper reports, economic forecasts and so on. These forms of information, which become available at random intervals, are quickly absorbed by the market and so investors who study relevant reports and announcements (this is known as fundamental analysis), in an attempt to make above-average returns on a consistent basis, will be disappointed. The information will already be incorporated into share prices.

Strong form of efficiency

The strong form is the ultimate form of efficiency and describes the situation where share prices fully reflect all available information, whether public or private. This means that the share price will be a good approximation to the 'true' value of the share. As all relevant information is absorbed in share prices, even those who have 'inside' information concerning a business, such as unpublished reports or confidential management decisions, will not be able to make superior returns, on a consistent basis, from using this information.

The various forms of efficiency described above can be viewed as a progression where each higher form of efficiency incorporates the previous form(s). Thus, if a stock market is efficient in the semi-strong form it will also be efficient in the weak form. Similarly, if a stock market is efficient in the strong form, it will also be efficient in the semi-strong and weak forms (see Figure 7.2).

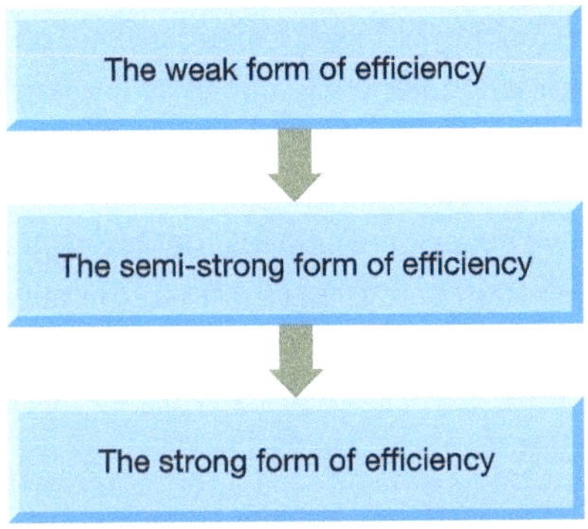

The figure shows the three levels of efficiency that have been identified for stock markets. These forms of efficiency represent a progression where each level incorporates the previous level(s).

Figure 7.2 Three levels of market efficiency

Activity 7.4

Can you explain why the relationship between the various forms of market efficiency described above should be the case?

If a stock market is efficient in the semi-strong form it will reflect all publicly available information. This will include past share prices. Thus, the semi-strong form will incorporate the weak form. If the stock market is efficient in the strong form, it will reflect all available information; this includes publicly available information. Thus, it will incorporate the semi-strong and weak forms.

Activity 7.5 below tests your understanding of how share prices might react to a public announcement under two different levels of market efficiency.

Activity 7.5

Dornier plc is a large civil engineering business that is listed on the Stock Exchange. On *1 May* it received a confidential letter stating that it had won a large building contract from an overseas government. The new contract is expected to increase the profits of the business by a substantial amount over the next five years. The news of the contract was announced publicly on *4 May*.

How would the shares of the business react to the formal announcement on 4 May assuming (a) a semi-strong, and (b) a strong form of market efficiency?

Under the semi-strong form, the formal announcement is new information to the market and should lead to an increase in share price. Under the strong form of efficiency, however, there should be no market reaction as the information would have already been incorporated into the share price.

Evidence on stock market efficiency

You may wonder what evidence exists to support each of the above forms of efficiency. For the weak form there is now a large body of evidence that spans many countries and many time periods. Much of this evidence has involved checking to see whether share price movements follow a random pattern: that is, finding out whether successive price changes were independent of each other. The research evidence generally confirms the existence of a random pattern of share prices.

Research has also been carried out to assess the value of trading rules used by some investors. These rules seek to achieve superior returns by identifying trend-like patterns to determine the point at which to buy or sell shares. The research has produced mixed results but tends to demonstrate that trading rules are not worthwhile. However, the value of these rules is difficult to assess, partly because of their sheer number and partly because of the subjective judgement involved in interpreting trends.

Activity 7.6

If share prices follow a random pattern, does this not mean that the market is acting in an irrational (and inefficient) manner?

No. New information concerning a business is likely to arise at random intervals and so share price adjustments to the new information will arise at those random intervals. The randomness of share price movements is therefore to be expected if markets are efficient.

Although the weight of research evidence offers little support for the belief that share prices exhibit repetitive patterns of behaviour, some analysts (known as technical analysts) continue to search for such patterns. **Real World 7.6** illustrates one of the techniques used to help predict future price movements.

Real World 7.6

Reading the signs

According to technical analysts, charts indicate the direction in which share prices are moving and so help investors decide whether to buy or sell. They believe that share prices exhibit trends and so past price movements can offer a clue to future price movements. Detecting a trend and its future direction is, therefore, the key to profitable trading.

The following is an extract from a paper produced by Recognia Inc., a leader in technical analysis. In this paper, various chart patterns are explained and the head and shoulders pattern described below is, perhaps, the most well known of these.

> **. . . the classic head and shoulders top looks like a human head with shoulders on either side of the head. A perfect example of the pattern has three sharp high points, created by three successive rallies in the price of the share.**

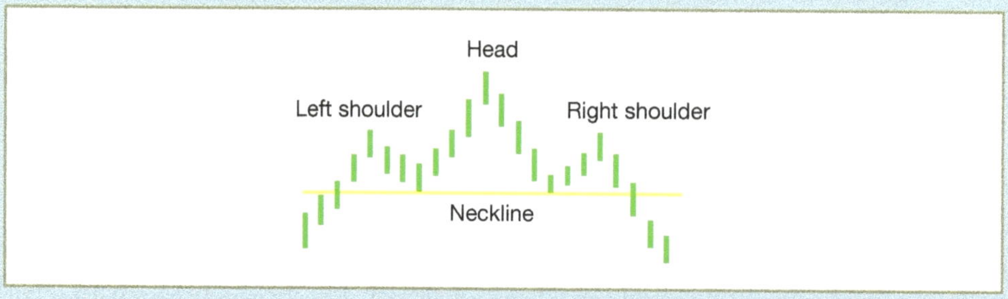

Figure 7.3 Head and shoulders pattern

The first point – the left shoulder – occurs as the price of the share in a rising market hits a high and then falls back. The second point – the head – happens when prices rise to an even higher high and then fall back again. The third point – the right shoulder – occurs when prices rise again but don't hit the high of the head. Prices then fall back again once they have hit the high of the right shoulder. The shoulders are definitely lower than the head and, in a classic formation, are often roughly equal to one another.

A key element of the pattern is the neckline. The neckline is formed by drawing a line connecting two low price points of the formation. The first low point occurs at the end of the left shoulder and the beginning of the uptrend to the head. The second marks the end of the head and the beginning of the upturn to the right shoulder. The neckline can be horizontal or it can slope up or down. However, as Elaine Yager, Director of Technical Analysis at Investec Ernst and Company in New York points out, a head and shoulders top neckline that is sloping downwards is highly unusual and demonstrates extreme weakness.

The pattern is complete when the support provided by the neckline is 'broken'. This occurs when the price of the share, falling from the high point of the right shoulder, moves below the neckline. Technical analysts will often say that the pattern is not confirmed until the price closes below the neckline – it is not enough for it to trade below the neckline.

Source: *Understanding Classic Chart Patterns*, Recognia Inc. 2009, www.recognia.com, pp. 5–6.

Research to test the semi-strong form of efficiency has usually involved monitoring the reaction of the share price to new information, such as profit announcements. This is done to see whether the market reacts to new information in an appropriate manner. The results usually show that share prices readjust quickly and accurately to any new information that affects the value of the business. This implies that investors cannot make superior returns by reacting quickly to new information. The results also show that investors are able to distinguish between new information that affects the value of the underlying business and new information that does not.

Other semi-strong tests have assessed whether it is possible to predict future returns by using available public information. These tests have produced more mixed results. One test involves the use of P/E ratios. We saw in Chapter 3 that the P/E ratio reflects the market's view of the growth prospects of a particular share: the higher the P/E ratio, the greater the growth prospects. Tests have shown, however, that shares with low P/E ratios outperform those with high P/E ratios. The market overestimates the growth prospects of businesses with high P/E ratios and underestimates the growth prospects of those with low P/E ratios. In other words, the market gets it wrong. We shall return to this point a little later.

Research to test the strong form of efficiency has often involved an examination of the performance of investment fund managers. These managers are highly skilled and have access to a wide range of information, not all of which may be in the public domain. If, despite their advantage over private investors, fund managers were unable to generate consistently superior performance over time compared to the market, it would provide some support for the view that markets are strong-form efficient. The results, alas, are mixed. Although earlier studies often supported the view that fund managers cannot outperform the market, more recent studies have suggested that some can.

Implications for managers

If stock markets are efficient, what should managers do? It seems that they must learn six important lessons.

Lesson 1: Timing doesn't matter

Managers considering a new share issue may feel that timing is important. In an inefficient stock market, the share price may fall below its 'true worth' and making a new issue at this point could be costly. In an efficient stock market, however, the share price will faithfully reflect the available information. This implies that the timing of issues will not be critical as there is no optimal point for making a new issue. Even if the market is depressed and share prices are low, it cannot be assumed that things will improve. The prevailing share price still reflects the market's estimate of future returns from the share.

Activity 7.7

Why might managers who accept that the market is efficient, at least in the semi-strong form, be justified in delaying the issue of new shares until what they believe will be a more appropriate time?

They may believe the market has underpriced the shares because it does not have access to all relevant information. They may have access to inside information which, when made available to the market, will lead to an upwards adjustment in share prices.

Lesson 2: Don't search for undervalued businesses

If the stock market accurately absorbs publicly available information, share prices will represent the best estimates available of their 'true worth'. This means that investors should not spend time trying to find undervalued shares in order to make gains. Unless they have access to information which the market does not have, they will not be able to 'beat the market' on a consistent basis. To look for undervalued shares will only result in time being spent and transaction costs being incurred to no avail. Similarly, managers should not try to identify undervalued shares in other businesses with the intention of identifying possible takeover targets. While there may be a number of valid and compelling reasons for taking over another business, the argument that shares of the target business are undervalued by the stock market is not one of them.

Lesson 3: Take note of market reaction

The investment plans and decisions of managers will be quickly and accurately reflected in the share price. Where these plans and decisions result in a fall in share price, managers may find it useful to review them. In effect, the market provides managers with a 'second opinion', which is both objective and informed. This opinion should not go unheeded.

Lesson 4: You can't fool the market

Managers may believe that form is as important as substance when communicating information to investors. This may induce them to 'window dress' the financial statements to provide a better picture of financial health than is warranted by the facts. The evidence suggests, however, that the market will see through any cosmetic attempts to improve the financial picture. It quickly and accurately assesses the economic substance of a business and prices the shares accordingly. Thus, accounting policy changes (such as switching depreciation methods, or switching inventories valuation methods, to boost profits in the current year) will be a waste of time.

Lesson 5: The market, not the business, decides the level of risk

Investors will correctly assess the level of risk associated with an investment and will impose an appropriate rate of return. Moreover, this rate of return will apply to whichever business undertakes that investment. Managers will not be able to influence this rate of return by adopting particular financing strategies. This means, for example, that the issue of certain types of security, or combinations of securities, will not reduce investors' required rate of return.

Lesson 6: Champion the interests of shareholders

The primary objective of a business is the maximisation of shareholder wealth. If managers take decisions and actions that are consistent with this objective, it will be reflected in the share price. This is likely to benefit the managers of the business as well as the shareholders.

ARE THE STOCK MARKETS REALLY EFFICIENT?

The idea that stock markets are efficient, at least in major industrialised countries, reached its high water mark during the 1970s. In 1978, Professor Michael Jensen, a leading proponent of market efficiency, confidently claimed 'there is no other proposition in economics which has more solid empirical evidence supporting it than the efficient market hypothesis.' Since then, however, a growing body of evidence has risen to challenge the hypothesis and its far-reaching conclusions. Although the notion of efficient markets is still held in respect, many now believe that it does not provide a complete explanation of how markets behave. This revised position should not, perhaps, come as a great surprise. The world is usually much richer and more complex than the theories and models we employ to explain it.

Below we consider some stock market 'anomalies' that challenge the efficient market hypothesis.

The problem of short termism

We saw earlier that stock market investors are often accused of adopting a short-term focus. This is difficult to square with the efficient market hypothesis. The value of a share is represented by the future discounted cash flows that it generates. In a stock market where shares are efficiently priced, investors should therefore be concerned with the ability of a business to generate long-term cash flows rather than its ability to meet short-term profit targets. In other words, if a stock market is efficient, a critical mass of investors will not adopt a short-term view when making share investment decisions. The evidence, however, does not always support this position.

One important study (see reference 3 at the end of the chapter) examined 624 businesses listed on the UK FTSE and US S&P indices over the period 1980–2009 to see whether the pricing of shares was affected by short termism. If so, it should be apparent by the excessive discounting of future cash flows from shares over and above the risk-free rate. The findings of the study suggest that short termism does exist and that it is prevalent across all industry sectors. According to the study:

> In the UK and US, cash-flows five years ahead are discounted at rates more appropriate eight or more years hence; ten-year ahead cash-flows are valued as if sixteen or more years ahead; and cash-flows more than thirty years ahead are scarcely valued at all.

Interestingly, there was much greater evidence of short termism among the sample businesses in the final decade of the study. It seems, therefore, that short termism is on the rise.

The behaviour of investors does appear to have changed over time. In the UK, shares of listed businesses are now held for around six months compared with eight years in 1960 (see reference 4 at the end of the chapter). It seems that investors are acting increasingly like share traders and less like owners. They may, therefore, become less concerned with the future stream of dividends and more concerned with short-term share price movements (which, in turn, may be influenced by short-term profit performance). Why such a change in behaviour has occurred among investors is not clear. One suggestion is that it can be traced back to the short-term focus of institutional investors. Fund managers often have their performance subjected to quarterly review, thereby increasing pressure to produce short-term returns.

Other stock market anomalies

Researchers have unearthed other 'anomalies' in major stock markets. Once again, these may be exploited by investors to achieve superior returns. Some of the more important are:

- *Business size.* A substantial body of evidence suggests that, other things being equal, small businesses yield higher returns than large businesses. It is not clear why this should be the case and various explanations exist. Some argue that it is because institutional investors tend to shun small businesses even though they may offer high returns. For such large investors, the size of the investment would be fairly modest and any benefits would be outweighed by the costs of evaluation and monitoring.
- *Price/earnings (P/E) ratio.* We mentioned earlier that research has shown that a portfolio of shares held in businesses with a low P/E ratio will outperform a portfolio of shares held in businesses with a high P/E ratio. This suggests that investors can make superior returns from investing in businesses with low P/E ratios.
- *Market overreaction.* Studies have shown that stock markets often overreact to new information. Where, for example, a business announces bad news, the fall in share price can be excessive and some time can elapse before the share price adjusts correctly to the news. In other words, the market does not react both quickly and accurately to new information.

Activity 7.8

How might an investor exploit this anomaly?

An investor could make an abnormal gain by buying shares immediately after the announcement and then selling them when their price has correctly adjusted.

- *Investment timing.* Various studies indicate that superior returns may be gained by timing investment decisions appropriately. There is evidence, for example, that higher returns can be achieved by buying shares at the beginning of April, in the UK, and then selling them later in the month, than similar trading in other months. There is also evidence that on Mondays there is an above-average fall in share prices. This may be because investors review their share portfolio at the weekend and sell unwanted shares when the market opens on Monday, thereby depressing prices. This means it is better to buy rather than sell shares on a Monday. There is also evidence that the particular time of the day in which shares are traded can lead to superior returns.

Activity 7.9

Can you suggest why, in the UK, April may provide better returns than other months of the year?

A new tax year begins in April. Investors may sell loss-making shares in March to offset any capital gains tax on shares sold at a profit during the tax year. As a result, share prices will become depressed. At the start of the new tax year, however, investors will start to buy shares again and so share prices will rise.

A fervent disciple of efficient markets may argue that market anomalies are of only minor importance and that, on the whole, the markets are efficient for most of the time. In the real world, there may well be inefficiencies but these are short-term, chance events. Where investors discover share price anomalies, they will exploit them in order to make gains. By doing so, they will eliminate the anomalies and thereby make the markets more efficient.

This sort of reasoning, however, cannot explain why some 'super investors', such as Warren Buffett, have managed to outperform the stock market over many years. Their success suggests that there may be significant 'pockets of inefficiency' within the market. Thus, while the market may display some features of efficiency, it should not be viewed simply through the lens of efficient markets.

Bubbles, bull markets and behavioural finance

In recent years, a new discipline called **behavioural finance** has emerged, which tries to provide a more complete understanding of the way in which stock markets behave. In particular, it seeks to explain why and how markets may be inefficient. This new discipline takes account of the psychological traits of individuals when seeking to explain market behaviour. It does not accept that individuals always behave in a rational manner, and there is a plethora of research evidence in psychology to support this view. Many studies have shown, for example, that individuals make systematic errors when processing information.

Activity 7.10

What will be the effect of investors making systematic errors when buying and selling shares?

It will result in the mispricing of shares. This suggests that profitable opportunities can be exploited.

A detailed study of these systematic errors, or biases, is beyond the scope of this book. However, it is worth providing an example to illustrate the challenge they pose to the notion of efficient markets.

One well-documented bias is the *overconfidence* that individuals place in their own analytical skills and judgement. They tend to display a persistent bias towards overestimating their understanding and their ability to control events. They also underestimate the risks they face. (Researchers have found that men are more likely to suffer from overconfidence than women—but no prizes for guessing that!) This bias towards overconfidence can lead to a variety of errors when making investment decisions, including:

- making poor choices by failing to appreciate that others have better information
- an under-reaction to new share price information, arising from a tendency to place more emphasis on new information confirming an original share valuation than new information challenging this valuation
- a reluctance to sell shares that have incurred losses because this involves admitting to past mistakes
- incorrectly assessing the riskiness of future returns
- a tendency to buy and sell shares more frequently than is prudent.

These errors may help to explain share price 'bubbles' and overextended 'bull' markets, where investor demand keeps share prices buoyant despite evidence suggesting that share prices are too high.

Share price bubbles, which inflate and then burst, appear in stock markets from time to time. When they inflate there is a period of high prices and high trading volumes, which is sustained by the enthusiasm of investors rather than by the fundamentals affecting the shares. During a bubble, investors appear to place too much faith in their optimistic views of future share price movements and, for a while at least, ignore warning signals concerning future growth prospects. However, as the warning signals become stronger, the disparity between investors' views and reality eventually becomes too great and a correction occurs, bringing investors' views more into line with fundamental values. This realignment of investors' views, leading to a sharp correction in share prices, means that the bubble has burst.

Share price bubbles are unusual and may be limited to particular industries or even particular businesses. **Real World 7.7** below reveals concern over an impending US stock market bubble.

Real World 7.7

Bubble trouble

A growing number of investors believe that US stocks are overvalued, creating the risk of a significant bear (sellers) market, according to research by Yale University market scholar Robert Shiller. The Nobel economics laureate told the Financial Times that his valuation confidence indices, based on investor surveys, showed greater fear that the market was overvalued than at any time since the peak of the dotcom bubble in 2000. He said, 'It looks to me a bit like a bubble again with essentially a tripling of stock prices since 2009 in just six years and at the same time people losing confidence in the valuation of the market'.

He said the recent bout of volatility 'shows that people are thinking something, worried thoughts. It suggests to me that many people are re-evaluating their exposure to the stock market. I'm not being very helpful about market timing but I can easily see aftershocks coming'.

FT *Source*: Authers, J. (2015) 'Fears grow over US stock market bubble', *Financial Times*, 13 June.

How should managers act?

The debate over the efficiency of stock markets has yet to run its course and further research is needed before a clear picture emerges. Although this situation may suit researchers, it may not suit managers confronted with an increasingly mixed set of messages concerning stock market behaviour. Probably the best thing for managers to do is to assume that well-developed markets, such as those in the UK and the USA, are efficient for much of the time, at least in the semi-strong form. The weight of evidence still supports this view. Although it may be possible to 'beat the market', it is not easy to do so and failure to recognise this may prove costly. Where it is clear, however, that market inefficiency exists, managers should exploit this.

SHARE ISSUES

A business may issue shares in a number of ways. These may involve direct appeals to investors or may involve financial intermediaries. The most common methods of share issue are set out in Figure 7.4.

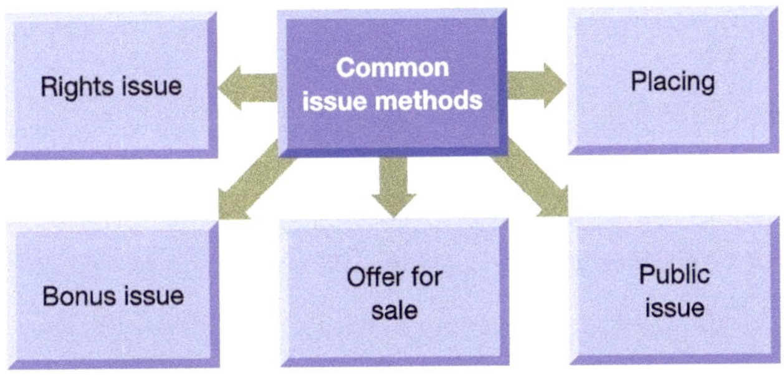

The figure sets out five methods of issuing shares. As explained in the chapter, bonus issues differ from the other methods in that they do not lead to an injection of cash for the business.

Figure 7.4 Common methods of share issue

Each of the methods identified above will now be examined in turn.

Rights issues

Rights issues can be made by established businesses seeking to raise finance by issuing additional shares for cash. UK company law gives existing shareholders the right of first refusal on these new shares, which are offered to them in proportion to their existing shareholding. Only where they waive their right would the shares then be offered to the investing public.

The business (in effect, the existing shareholders) would typically prefer that existing shareholders buy the shares through a rights issue, irrespective of the legal position. This is for two reasons:

- Ownership (and, therefore, control) of the business remains in the same hands; there is no 'dilution' of control.
- The costs of making the issue (advertising; complying with various company law requirements) tend to be less if the shares are to be offered to existing shareholders.

Rights issues are a fairly common form of share issue. During 2015, they accounted for approximately 40 per cent of all finance raised from shares issued by Stock Exchange listed businesses (see reference 5 at the end of the chapter).

To encourage existing shareholders to take up their 'rights' to buy new shares, they are always offered at a price below the current market price of the existing ones. The evidence shows that shares are offered at an average discount of 31 per cent below the current pre-rights price (see reference 6 at the end of the chapter). The size of discounts offered appears to have increased in recent years.

As shareholders can acquire shares at a price below the current market price, the entitlement to participate in a rights offer has a cash value. Those shareholders not wishing to take up the rights offer can sell their rights to others. Calculating the cash value of the rights entitlement is quite straightforward. Example 7.1 can be used to illustrate how this is done.

Example 7.1

Shaw Holdings plc has 20 million ordinary shares of 50p in issue. These shares are currently valued on the Stock Exchange at £1.60 per share. The directors of Shaw Holdings plc believe the business requires additional long-term capital and have decided to make a one-for-four issue (that is, one new share for every four shares held) at £1.30 per share. What is the value of the rights per new share?

Solution

The first step in the valuation process is to calculate the price of a share following the rights issue. This is known as the *ex-rights price* and is simply a weighted average of the price of shares before the issue of rights and the price of the rights shares. In the above example we have a one-for-four rights issue. The theoretical ex-rights price is therefore calculated as follows:

		£
Price of four shares before the rights issue (4 × £1.60)		6.40
Price of taking up one rights share		1.30
		7.70
Theoretical ex-rights price	(£7.70/5)	£1.54

As the price of each share, in theory, should be £1.54 following the rights issue and the price of a rights share is £1.30, the value of the rights offer will be the difference between the two:

$$£1.54 - £1.30 = £0.24 \text{ per new share}$$

Market forces will usually ensure that the actual price of rights and the theoretical price will be fairly close.

Activity 7.11

An investor with 2,000 shares in Shaw Holdings plc (see Example 7.1) has contacted you for investment advice. She is undecided whether to take up the rights issue, sell the rights or allow the rights offer to lapse.

Calculate the effect on the net wealth of the investor of each of the options being considered.

Before the rights issue, the position of the investor was:

	£
Value of shares (2,000 × £1.60)	3,200

If she takes up the rights issue, she will be in the following position:

	£
Value of holding after rights issue ((2,000 + 500) × £1.54)	3,850
Less Cost of buying the rights shares (500 × £1.30)	(650)
	3,200

If she sells the rights, she will be in the following position:

	£
Value of holding after rights issue (2,000 × £1.54)	3,080
Sale of rights (500 × £0.24)	120
	3,200

If she lets the rights offer lapse, she will be in the following position:

	£
Value of holding after rights issue (2,000 × £1.54)	3,080

As we can see, the first two options should leave her in the same position concerning net wealth as she was in before the rights issue. Before the rights issue she had 2,000 shares worth £1.60 each, or £3,200. However, she will be worse off if she allows the rights offer to lapse than under the other two options. In practice, the business may sell the rights offer on behalf of the investor and pass on the proceeds in order to ensure that she is not worse off as a result of the issue.

When making a rights issue, the total funds needed must first be determined. This will depend on the future plans of the business. A decision on the issue price of the rights shares must then be made. Generally speaking, this decision is not critical. In the example above, the business made a one-for-four issue with the price of the rights shares set at £1.30. However, it could have raised the same amount by making a one-for-two issue and setting the rights price at £0.65, or a one-for-one issue and setting the price at £0.325, and so on. The issue price that is finally decided upon will not affect the value of the underlying assets of the business or the proportion of the underlying assets and earnings of the business to which the shareholder is entitled. Nevertheless, it is important to ensure that the issue price is not *above* the current market price of the shares.

Activity 7.12

Why is this important?

If the issue price is above the current market price, it would be cheaper for the investor to buy shares in the open market (assuming transaction costs are not significant) than to take up the rights offer. This would mean that the share issue would fail.

It was mentioned earlier that rights shares will usually be priced at a discount to the market price of shares at the date of the rights announcement. By the date that the rights shares have to be taken up, there is a risk that the market price will have fallen below the rights price. If this occurs, the rights issue will fail for the same reasons as mentioned in Activity 7.12.

The higher the discount offered, the lower the risk of such failure. Not surprisingly, discounts tend to be higher when markets are either volatile or falling. There is a danger, however, that offering a very high discount will convey an impression that there is little enthusiasm for the issue among shareholders.

Despite the benefits of giving pre-emptive rights to shareholders, it does result in less competition for new shares. This may increase the costs of raising finance, as other forms of share issue may be able to raise the amount more cheaply.

Real World 7.8 describes how one large business made a rights issue to strengthen its financial position following a number of setbacks.

Real World 7.8

When wrongs lead to rights

Serco slumped to a pre-tax loss of more than £1bn last year following a crisis with several large public sector contracts, including a loss making deal providing housing for asylum seekers. Shares in the outsourcing group fell 11 per cent on Thursday after Serco warned there would be no final dividend for 2014 and refused to provide financial guidance beyond this year.

The company, which employs 122,000 staff in 20 countries, swung from a pre-tax profit of £108.3m in 2013 to a loss of £1.4bn last year. Revenue fell almost 8 per cent to £4bn – its first sales decline in the 25 years since it joined the stock market.

Serco was plunged into turmoil in July 2013 when it admitted overcharging the British government for tagging thousands of offenders, some of whom were dead. But it subsequently emerged that the group had also bungled several other public sector contracts, mainly in the UK and Australia.

The group outlined a £1.3bn provision against its loss making contracts on Thursday, as it confirmed plans for a £555m rights issue to strengthen its balance sheet [statement of financial position].

Rupert Soames, the chief executive hired last year to turnround Serco, said he would decline a £908,000 bonus and instead tried to draw a line under the group's difficulties. 'There is a real sense that, having confessed our sins and in taking the punishment, we are now ready to start on the path to recovery,' he said.

Serco has overhauled its management and a revised strategy involves focusing on providing defence, healthcare, justice and welfare services to governments worldwide.

Stephen Rawlinson, analyst at Whitman Howard, said: 'Serco has reassured the market on all of the major issues. With a fair wind on trading and good disposal prices the company may be giving cash back to shareholders by 2018.'

The rights issue was flagged to investors last year and is fully underwritten by Bank of America, Merrill Lynch and JPMorgan Cazenove.

Serco will issue new ordinary shares at 101p, representing a discount of 51.1 per cent to the closing price on March 11. Serco's shares closed down 11 per cent at 183.70p.

FT *Source*: Plimmer, G. (2015) 'Serco shares tumble after final dividend is scrapped', ft.com 12 March.

Bonus issues

A **bonus issue** should not be confused with a rights issue of shares. A bonus, or **scrip**, issue also involves the issue of new shares to existing shareholders in proportion to their existing shareholdings. However, shareholders do not have to pay for the new shares issued. The bonus issue is achieved by transferring a sum from the reserves to the paid-up share capital of the business and then issuing shares, equivalent in value to the sum transferred, to existing shareholders. As the reserves are already owned by the shareholders, they do not have to pay for the shares issued. In effect, a bonus issue will simply convert reserves into paid-up capital. To understand this conversion process, and its effect on the financial position of the business, let us consider Example 7.2.

Example 7.2

Wickham plc has the following abbreviated statement of financial position as at 31 March:

	£m
Net assets	20
Financed by	
Share capital (£1 ordinary shares)	10
Reserves	10
	20

The directors decide to convert £5 million of the reserves to paid-up capital. As a result, it was decided that a one-for-two bonus issue should be made. Following the bonus issue, the statement of financial position of Wickham plc will be as follows:

	£m
Net assets	20
Financed by	
Share capital (£1 ordinary shares)	15
Reserves	5
	20

We can see in Example 7.2 that, following the bonus issue, share capital has increased but there has also been a corresponding decrease in reserves. Net assets of the business remain unchanged. More shares are now in issue but the proportion of the total number of shares held by each shareholder will remain unchanged. Thus, bonus issues do not, of themselves, result in an increase in shareholder wealth. They will simply switch part of the owners' claim from reserves to share capital.

Activity 7.13

Assume that the market price per share in Wickham plc (see Example 7.2) before the bonus issue was £2.10. What will be the market price per share following the share issue?

The business has made a one-for-two issue. A holder of two shares would therefore be in the following position before the bonus issue:

$$2 \text{ shares held at £2.10 market price} = £4.20$$

As the wealth of the shareholder has not increased as a result of the issue, the total value of the shareholding will remain the same. This means that, as the shareholder holds one more share following the issue, the market value per share will now be:

$$\frac{£4.20}{3} = £1.40$$

You may wonder from the calculations above why bonus issues are made. Various reasons have been put forward to explain this type of share issue, which include:

- *Share price.* The share price may be very high and, as a result, shares of a business may become difficult to trade on the Stock Exchange. It seems that shares trading within a certain price range generate more investor interest. If the number of shares in issue is increased, the market price of each share will be reduced, which may make the shares more marketable.
- *Lender confidence.* Making a transfer from distributable reserves to paid-up share capital will increase the permanent capital base of the business. This may increase confidence among lenders. In effect, it will lower the risk of ordinary shareholders withdrawing their investment through dividend distributions, thereby leaving lenders in an exposed position.
- *Market signals.* A bonus issue offers managers an opportunity to signal to shareholders their confidence in the future. The issue may be accompanied by the announcement of good news concerning the business (for example, securing a large contract or achieving an increase in profits). Under these circumstances, the share price may rise in the expectation that earnings/dividends per share will be maintained. Shareholders would, therefore, be better off following the issue. However, it is the *information content* of the bonus issue, rather than the issue itself, that will create this increase in wealth.

Offer for sale

An **offer for sale** may involve a public limited company selling a new issue of shares to a financial institution known as an issuing house. It may also involve shares already held by existing shareholders being sold to an issuing house. The issuing house will, in turn, sell the shares purchased from the business, or its shareholders, to the public. To do this, it will publish a prospectus setting out details of the business and the type of shares to be sold, and investors will be invited to apply for shares.

The advantage of this type of issue, from the business's viewpoint, is that the sale proceeds of the shares are certain. It is the issuing house that will take on the risk of selling the shares to investors. Any unsold shares will remain with the issuing house. An offer for sale is most often used when a business seeks a listing on the Stock Exchange and wishes to raise a large amount of funds.

Public issue

A **public issue** involves a public limited company making a direct invitation to the public to buy its shares. Typically, this is done through a newspaper advertisement, and the invitation will be accompanied by the publication of a prospectus. The shares may, once again, be a new issue or shares already in issue. An issuing house may be asked by the business to help administer the issue of the shares to the public and to offer advice concerning an appropriate selling price. However, the business rather than the issuing house will take on the risk of selling the shares. Both an offer for sale and a public issue result in a widening of share ownership in the business.

Setting a share price

When making an issue, the business, or issuing house, will usually set a fixed price for the shares. However, establishing a price may not be an easy task, particularly where the market is volatile or where the business has unique characteristics.

Activity 7.14

What are the risks involved for the business of selling shares at a fixed price?

If the share price is set too high, the issue will be undersubscribed and the anticipated amount will not be received. If the share price is set too low, the issue will be oversubscribed and the amount received will be less than could have been achieved.

One way of dealing with the pricing problem is to make a **tender issue** of shares. This involves the investors determining the price at which the shares are issued. Although a reserve price may be set to help guide investors, it is up to each individual investor to decide on the number of shares to be purchased and the price to be paid. Once the offers from investors have been received, a price at which all the shares can be sold will be established (known as the *striking price*). Investors who have made offers at, or above, the striking price will be issued shares at the striking price and offers received below the striking price will be rejected. Note that all of the shares will be issued at the same price, irrespective of the prices actually offered by individual investors.

Example 7.3 illustrates the way in which a striking price is achieved.

Example 7.3

Celibes plc made a tender offer of shares and the following offers were received by investors:

Share price	*Number of shares tendered at this particular price*	*Cumulative number of shares tendered*
	000s	*000s*
£2.80	300	300
£2.40	590	890
£1.90	780	1,670
£1.20	830	2,500

The directors of Celibes plc wish to issue 2,000,000 shares, at a minimum price of £1.20.

The striking price would have to be £1.20 as, above this price, there would be insufficient interest to issue 2,000,000 shares. At the price of £1.20, the total number of shares tendered exceeds the number of shares available and so a partial allotment would be made. Normally, each investor would receive 4 shares for every 5 shares tendered (that is 2,000/2,500).

Activity 7.15

Assume that, instead of issuing a fixed number of shares, the directors of Celibes plc (see Example 7.3) wish to maximise the amount raised from the share issue. What would be the appropriate striking price?

The price at which the amount raised from the issue can be maximised is calculated as follows:

Share price	*Cumulative number of shares*	*Share sale proceeds*
	000s	*£000*
£2.80	300	840
£2.40	890	2,136
£1.90	1,670	**3,173**
£1.20	2,500	3,000

The table shows that the striking price should be £1.90 to maximise the share sale proceeds.

Tender issues are not popular with investors and therefore are not in widespread use.

Placing

A **placing** does not involve an invitation to the public to subscribe to shares. Instead, the shares are 'placed' with selected investors, such as large financial institutions. These shares are normally offered at a small discount to the current market price. The maximum discount that can be offered under current listing rules is 10 per cent.

A placing can be a quick and relatively cheap method of raising funds because savings can be made in advertising and legal costs. It can, however, result in the ownership of the business being concentrated in a few hands and may prevent small investors from participating in the new issue of shares. Businesses seeking relatively small amounts of cash will often employ this form of issue.

Real World 7.9 describes how a placing was used by a well-known toy manufacturer to finance more efficient inventories management.

Real World 7.9

Placed on the right track

During 2015, Hornby plc, which owns the model railway, Scalextric, Airfix and Corgi car brands, made a share placing that raised £15 million. Hornby used the funds raised to establish a new warehouse in Canterbury, with a new inventories control, sales and distribution system.

Hornby used to manufacture its products at a factory in Margate, but moved production to China in the 1990s.

FT *Source*: Information taken from Murray Brown, J. (2015) 'Hornby signals third profit warning in three years', *Financial Times*, 10 November.

A placing is sometimes used in conjunction with a rights issue. Where a planned rights issue is unlikely to raise all the funds needed, a placing may also be made to fill the funding gap.

Placings have become an extremely popular way of issuing shares among listed businesses. During 2015, they accounted for around 86 per cent of the total amount raised from shares issued by newly-listed businesses (see reference 7) at the end of the chapter. **Real World 7.10** indicates that they also account for a significant proportion of the total amount raised from shares issued by already-listed businesses.

Real World 7.10

Raising the issue

The table below reveals the percentage of the total amount raised from issuing shares, according to issuing method, by businesses already listed on the Stock Exchange.

Percentage of total funds raised through different issuing methods by already-listed businesses 2010–2015

	2015	*2014*	*2013*	*2012*	*2011*	*2010*
	%	%	%	%	%	%
Public offer	3.7	2.1	1.0	8.2	1.0	4.1
Placing	46.5	46.7	31.5	45.2	82.5	27.3

	2015	2014	2013	2012	2011	2010
	%	%	%	%	%	%
Public offer and placing	9.5	13.6	10.3	18.3	9.5	1.7
Rights issue	40.3	37.6	57.2	28.3	7.0	66.9
	100.0	100.0	100.0	100.0	100.0	100.0

We can see that, together, placings and rights issues account for a vast proportion of the total amount raised each year.

Source: Based on figures in Table 3 of Main Market Statistics covering the five-year period ending 31 December 2015, London Stock Exchange, www.londonstockexchange.com.

LONG-TERM FINANCE FOR THE SMALLER BUSINESS

Although the Stock Exchange provides an important source of long-term finance for large businesses, it is not really suitable for smaller businesses. The total market value of shares to be listed on the Stock Exchange must be at least £700,000 and in practice the amounts are much higher because of the listing costs identified earlier. Thus, smaller businesses must look elsewhere for help in raising long-term finance. Reports and studies over several decades, however, have highlighted the problems that they encounter in doing so. These problems can be a major obstacle to growth and include:

- a lack of financial management skills (leading to difficulties in developing credible business plans that will satisfy lenders)
- a lack of knowledge concerning the availability of sources of long-term finance
- insufficient security for loan capital
- failure to meet rigorous assessment criteria (for example, a good financial track record over five years)
- an excessively bureaucratic screening process for loan applications (see reference 8 at the end of the chapter).

In addition, the cost of finance is often higher for smaller businesses than for larger businesses because of the higher risks involved.

Not all financing constraints are externally imposed. Small business owners often refuse to raise new finance through ordinary share issues.

Activity 7.16

Can you think why this should be so?

It is often because they do not wish to dilute their control of the business.

Some small business owners also refuse to consider loan finance as they do not believe in borrowing (see reference 9 at the end of the chapter).

Although obtaining long-term finance for smaller businesses is not always easy (and one consequence may be excessive reliance on short-term sources of finance, such as bank overdrafts), things have improved over recent years. Some important ways in which small businesses can gain access to long-term finance are set out in Figure 7.5 and considered below.

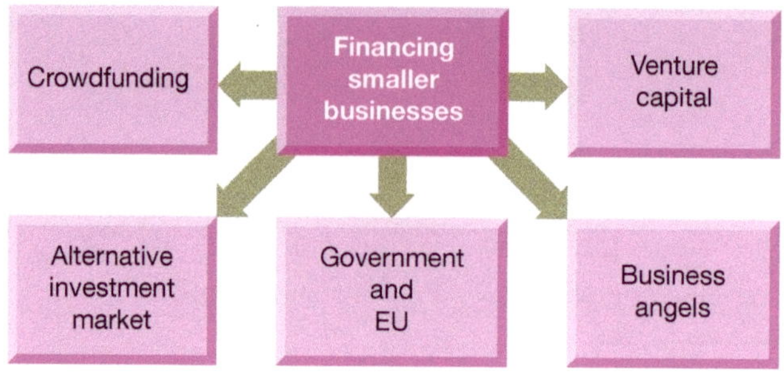

Each of the methods of obtaining long-term finance for smaller businesses is described below.

Figure 7.5 Long-term finance for smaller businesses

Private-equity firms

Private-equity firms provide long-term capital to small and medium-sized businesses wishing to grow but that do not have ready access to stock markets. The supply of **private equity** has increased rapidly in the UK over recent years since both government and corporate financiers have shown greater commitment to entrepreneurial activity.

It is possible to distinguish between private equity and **venture capital** based on the investment focus. In broad terms, private equity focuses on investments in established businesses whereas venture capital focuses on investments in start-up, or early-stage, businesses. In the sections that follow, however, we shall treat private equity as encompassing investments that are sometimes described as being financed by venture capital.

Types of investment

Private-equity firms are interested in investing in small and medium-sized businesses with good growth potential. These businesses must also have owners with the ambition and determination to realise this potential. Although private-equity-backed businesses usually have higher levels of risk than would be acceptable to other providers of finance, they also have the potential for higher returns. The investment period will usually be between three and seven years, and during that period private equity firms seek to increase the value of the business in order to realise gains from the selling price.

Private equity is used to fund different types of business needs and provides:

- *Venture capital.* Start-up capital is provided to businesses that are still at the concept stage of development through to those that are ready to commence trading. It may be used to help design, develop and market new products and services. Venture capital is also available for businesses that have undertaken their development work and are ready to begin operations.
- *Expansion (development) capital.* This provides funding for established businesses needing additional working capital, new equipment, product development investment and so on.
- *Replacement capital.* This includes the refinancing of bank borrowings to reduce the level of gearing. It also includes capital for the buyout of part of the ownership of a business or the buyout of another private-equity firm.
- *Buyout and buyin capital.* This is capital available to finance the acquisition of an existing business. A *management buyout* (MBO) is where an existing management team acquires

the business, and an *institutional buyout* (IBO) is where the private-equity firm acquires the business and instals a management team of its choice. A *management buyin* (MBI) is where an outside management team acquires an existing business. Buyouts and buyins often occur where a large business wishes to divest itself of one of its operating units or where the owners of a family business wish to sell because of succession problems.

- *Rescue capital.* This is used to turn around a business after a period of poor performance.

Venture capital investments, which were mentioned above, can be particularly challenging for private-equity firms for two reasons. First, they are very high risk: investing in existing businesses with a good track record is a much safer bet. Second, start-ups and early-stage businesses often require fairly small amounts of finance. Unless a significant amount of finance is required, it is difficult to justify the high cost of investigating and monitoring the investment.

Real World 7.11 provides an impression of private-equity investment in UK businesses.

Real World 7.11

Nothing ventured, nothing gained

Figure 7.6 shows the main private-equity investments made in UK businesses during 2013 and 2014, according to financing stage.

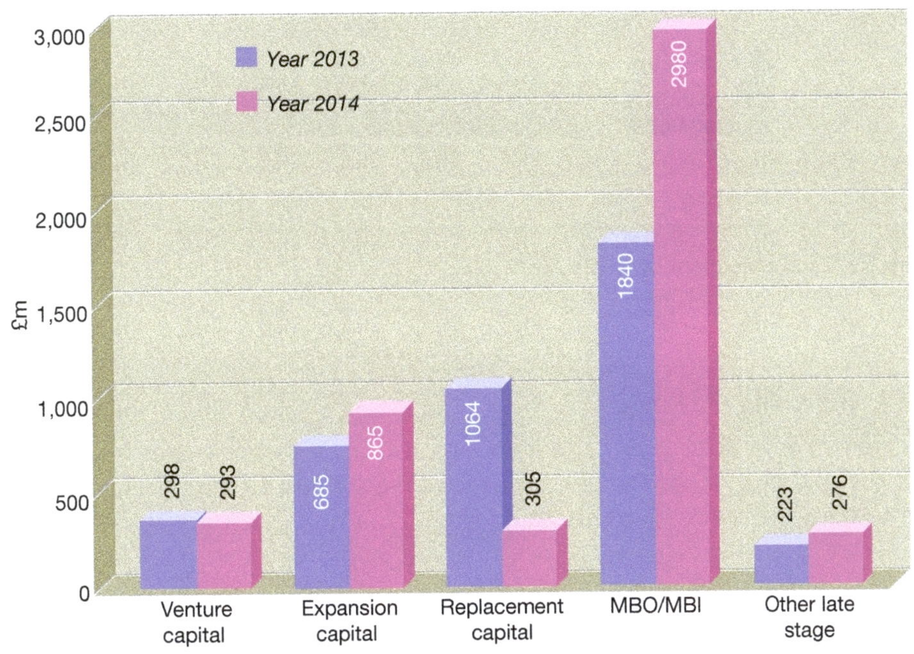

MBOs and MBIs were, by far, the most significant form of investment during 2013 and 2014.

Figure 7.6 Investment of private-equity firms in UK businesses by financing stage, 2013 and 2014

Source: Chart compiled from information in British Private Equity and Venture Capital Association, 'Report on investment activity 2014', www.bvca.co.uk, Table 4, p. 5.

The private-equity investment process

Private-equity investment involves a five-step process that is similar to the investment process undertaken within a business. The five steps are set out in Figure 7.7 and below we consider each in turn.

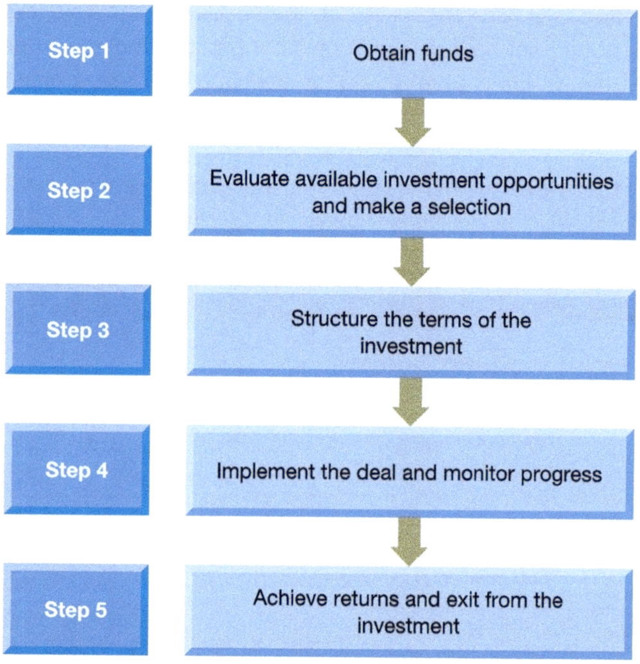

The figure shows the five steps that a private-equity firm will go through when making an investment in a business.

Figure 7.7 The investment process

Source: M. Van der Wayer (1995) 'The venture capital vacuum', *Management Today*, July, pp. 60–64, Figure 7.9.

Step 1: Obtaining the funds

Private-equity firms obtain their funds from various sources, including large financial institutions, government agencies and private investors. **Real World 7.12** provides an insight into the main sources of funds for private-equity firms.

Real World 7.12

Funding private equity

Figure 7.8 reveals the main sources of finance employed by private-equity firms during 2014 for investment purposes.

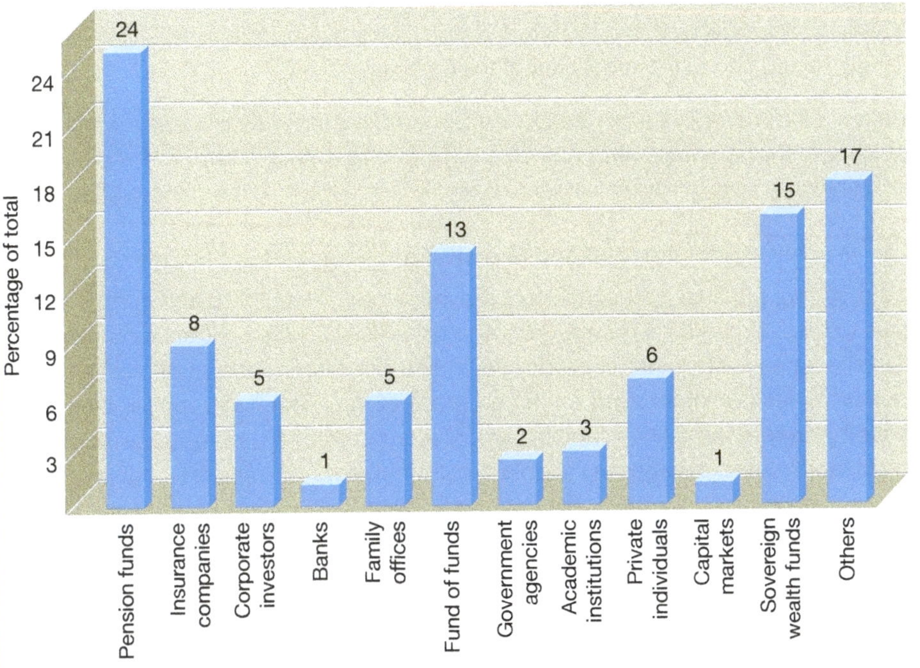

Contributions from each source vary over time. Over the three-year period ending in 2014, pension funds were the largest private-equity contributors.

Figure 7.8 Finance raised by private-equity firms by source, 2012–2014

Source: Chart compiled from information in British Private Equity and Venture Capital Association, 'Report on Investment Activity 2014', www.bvca.co.uk, Table 18, p. 12.

Once obtained, there can be a two or three-year time lag before the funds are invested in suitable businesses.

Activity 7.17

Can you think of reasons why there may be such a delay?

Suitable businesses take time to identify and, once found, they require careful investigation. There may also be lengthy negotiations with owners over the terms of the investment.

Step 2: Evaluating investment opportunities and making a selection

When a suitable business is identified, the management plans will be reviewed and an assessment made of the investment potential, including the potential for growth. This will involve an examination of:

- the market for the products
- the business processes and the ways in which they can be managed

- the ambition and quality of the management team
- the opportunities for improving performance
- the types of risks involved and the ways in which they can be managed
- the track record and future prospects of the business.

Private-equity firms will also be interested to see whether the likely financial returns are commensurate with the risks that have to be taken. The internal rate of return (IRR) method is often used in helping to make this assessment and an IRR in excess of 20 per cent is often required.

Step 3: Structuring the terms of the investment

When structuring the financing agreement, private-equity firms try to ensure that their own exposure to risk is properly managed. This will involve establishing control mechanisms within the financing agreements to protect their investment. One important control mechanism is the requirement to receive information on the progress of the business at regular intervals. The information provided, as well as information collected from other sources, will then be used as a basis for providing a staged injection of funds. In this way, progress is regularly reviewed and where serious problems arise, the option of abandoning further investments in order to contain any losses is retained.

In some cases, the private-equity firm may reduce the amount of finance at risk by establishing a financing syndicate with other private-equity firms. However, this will reduce the potential returns. It will also increase the possibility of disputes between syndicate members, particularly when things do not go according to plan.

Private-equity firms usually expect the owner/managers to demonstrate their commitment by investing in the business. Although the amounts they invest may be small in relation to the total investment, they should be large in relation to their personal wealth.

Step 4: Implementing the deal and monitoring progress

Private-equity firms usually work closely with client businesses throughout the investment period. It is quite common for them to have a representative on the board of directors to keep an eye on things. They may also provide a form of consultancy service by offering advice on technical and marketing matters.

Business plans that were prepared at the time of the initial investment will be monitored to see whether they are achieved. Those businesses that meet their key targets are likely to find the presence of the private-equity firms less intrusive than those that do not. Monitoring is likely to be much closer at the early stages of the investment until certain problems, such as the quality of management and cost overruns, become less of a risk (see reference 10 at the end of the chapter).

Step 5: Achieving returns and exiting from the investment

A major part of the total returns from the investment is usually achieved through the final sale of the investment. The particular method of divestment is therefore of great concern to the private-equity firm. The most common forms of divestment are through:

- a trade sale (that is, where the investment is sold to another business)
- flotation of the business on the Stock Exchange, or sale of the quoted equity
- sale of the investment to the management team (buyback)
- sale of the investment to another private-equity firm or financial institution.

In some cases, there will be an 'involuntary exit' when the business fails, in which case the investment must be written off.

Private equity and borrowing

A private-equity firm will often require a business to borrow a significant proportion of its needs from a bank or other financial institution. In this way, the business reaps the benefit of financial gearing. It also reduces the amount of equity that the private-equity firm needs to invest. Cash flows generated by the business during the investment period are used to reduce or eliminate the outstanding loans.

Example 7.4 provides a simple illustration of how a private-equity firm may structure and then evaluate its investment in a business.

Example 7.4

Ippo Ltd is a private-equity firm that has recently purchased Andante Ltd for £80 million. The business requires an immediate injection of £60 million to meet its needs and Ippo Ltd has insisted that this be raised by a 10 per cent bank loan. Ippo Ltd intends to float Andante Ltd in four years' time to exit from the investment and then expects to receive £160 million on the sale of its shares. During the next four years, the cash flows generated by Andante Ltd (after interest has been paid) will be used to eliminate the outstanding loan.

The net cash flows (before interest) of the business, over the four years leading up to the flotation, are predicted to be as follows:

Year 1	*Year 2*	*Year 3*	*Year 4*
£m	*£m*	*£m*	*£m*
20.0	20.0	20.1	15.0

Ippo Ltd has a cost of capital of 18 per cent and uses the IRR method to evaluate investment projects.

The following calculations reveal that the loan can be entirely repaid over the next four years.

	Year 1	*Year 2*	*Year 3*	*Year 4*
	£m	*£m*	*£m*	*£m*
Net cash flows	20.0	20.0	20.1	15.0
Loan interest (10%)	(6.0)	(4.6)	(3.1)	(1.4)
Cash available to repay loan	14.0	15.4	17.0	13.6
Loan at start of year	60.0	46.0	30.6	13.6
Cash available to repay loan	14.0	15.4	17.0	13.6
Loan at end of year	46.0	30.6	13.6	–

There are no cash flows remaining after the loan is repaid and so Ippo Ltd will receive nothing until the end of the fourth year, when the shares are sold.

The IRR of the investment will be the discount rate which, when applied to the net cash inflows, will provide an NPV of zero. Thus,

$$(£160\text{m} \times \text{discount factor}) - £80\text{m} = 0$$

$$\text{Discount factor} = 0.50$$

A discount rate of approximately 19 per cent will give a discount factor of 0.5 in four years' time.

Thus, the IRR of the investment is approximately 19 per cent. This is higher than the cost of capital of Ippo Ltd and so the investment will increase the wealth of its shareholders.

To illustrate the benefits for the private-equity firm of gearing, Activity 7.18 requires you to rework the above example. This time, on the assumption that the investee business relies on equity finance rather than borrowing.

Activity 7.18

Assume that:

(a) Ippo Ltd (see Example 7.4) provides additional ordinary share capital at the beginning of the investment period of £60 million, thereby eliminating the need for Andante Ltd to take on a bank loan

(b) any cash flows generated by Andante Ltd would be received by Ippo Ltd in the form of annual dividends.

What would be the IRR of the total investment in Andante Ltd for Ippo Ltd? (*Hint:* Start with a discount rate of 10 per cent.)

The IRR can be calculated using the trial and error method as follows. At discount rates of 10 per cent and 16 per cent, the NPV of the investment proposal is:

		Trial 1		*Trial 2*	
Year	*Cash flows*	*Discount rate*	*Present value*	*Discount rate*	*Present value*
	£m	*10%*	*£m*	*16%*	*£m*
0	(140.0)	1.00	(140.0)	1.00	(140.0)
1	20.0	0.91	18.2	0.86	17.2
2	20.0	0.83	16.6	0.74	14.8
3	20.1	0.75	15.1	0.64	12.9
4	175.0	0.68	119.0	0.55	96.3
		NPV	28.9	**NPV**	1.2

The calculations reveal that, at a discount rate of 16 per cent, the NPV is close to zero. Thus, the IRR of the investment is approximately 16 per cent, which is lower than the cost of capital. In other words, the investment would reduce the wealth of shareholders in Ippo Ltd, when the benefit of gearing is not employed.

A further advantage of requiring a business to take on large borrowing is that it imposes a tight financial discipline on managers. There must always be enough cash available to make interest payments and capital repayments. This should encourage managers to be aggressive in chasing sales and to bear down on costs.

Self-assessment question 7.1

Ceres plc is a large conglomerate which, following a recent strategic review, has decided to sell its agricultural foodstuffs division. The managers of this operating division believe that it could be run as a separate business and are considering a management buyout. The division has made an operating profit of £10 million for the year to 31 May Year 6 and the board of Ceres plc has indicated that it would be prepared to sell the division to the managers for a price based on a multiple of 12 times the operating profit for the most recent year.

The managers of the operating division have £5 million of the finance necessary to acquire the division and have approached Vesta Ltd, a private-equity firm, to see whether it would be prepared to assist in financing the proposed management buyout. The divisional managers have produced the following forecast of operating profits for the next four years:

Year to 31 May	*Year 7*	*Year 8*	*Year 9*	*Year 10*
	£m	*£m*	*£m*	*£m*
Operating profit	10.0	11.0	10.5	13.5

To achieve the profit forecasts shown above, the division will have to invest a further £1 million in working capital during the year to 31 May Year 8. The division has premises costing £40 million and plant and machinery costing £20 million. In calculating operating profit for the division, these assets are depreciated, using the straight-line method, at the rate of 2.5 per cent on cost and 15 per cent on cost, respectively.

Vesta Ltd has been asked to invest £45 million in return for 90 per cent of the ordinary shares in a new business specifically created to run the operating division. The divisional managers would receive the remaining 10 per cent of the ordinary shares in return for their £5 million investment. The managers believe that a bank would be prepared to provide a 10 per cent loan for any additional finance necessary to acquire the division. (The properties of the division are currently valued at £80 million and so there would be adequate security for a loan up to this amount.) All net cash flows generated by the new business during each financial year will be applied to reducing the balance of the loan and no dividends will be paid to shareholders until the loan is repaid. (There are no other cash flows apart from those mentioned above.) The loan agreement will be for a period of eight years. However, if the business is sold during this period, the loan must be repaid in full by the shareholders.

Vesta Ltd intends to realise its investment after four years when the non-current assets and working capital (excluding the bank loan) of the business are expected to be sold to a rival at a price based on a multiple of 12 times the most recent annual operating profit. Out of these proceeds, the bank loan will have to be repaid by existing shareholders before they receive their returns. Vesta Ltd has a cost of capital of 25 per cent and employs the internal rate of return method to evaluate investment proposals.

Ignore taxation.

Workings should be in £ millions and should be made to one decimal place.

Required:

(a) Calculate:

(i) The amount of the loan outstanding at 31 May Year 10 immediately prior to the sale of the business.

(ii) The approximate internal rate of return for Vesta Ltd of the investment proposal described above.

(b) State, with reasons, whether or not Vesta Ltd should invest in this proposal.

The solution to this question can be found at the back of the book on p. 586.

Cause for concern?

In recent years, private-equity firms have extended their reach by acquiring listed businesses. Following acquisition, the business is usually de-listed and then restructured, perhaps with the intention of re-flotation at some future date. This development has placed private-equity firms and their business methods in the spotlight. Critics have raised concerns over the:

- job losses that usually accompany restructuring
- very high levels of gearing employed, which greatly increase financial risk

- lack of transparency in business dealings
- lack of accountability to employees and the communities in which they operate
- adverse effect on the Stock Exchange's role, resulting from the acquisition and de- listing of large businesses
- tax benefits received by private-equity firms.

While some changes to levels of transparency and tax benefits have been made, critics of private-equity firms remain largely unappeased.

It should be noted that the methods employed by private-equity firms have produced echoes elsewhere. Some businesses, particularly those vulnerable to a takeover from a private-equity firm, have adopted methods such as job losses and high gearing, to remain viable and independent.

BUSINESS ANGELS

Business angels are often wealthy individuals who have been successful in business. Most are entrepreneurs who have sold their businesses while others tend to be former senior executives of a large business, or business professionals such as accountants, lawyers and management consultants. Although they may be willing to invest £250,000 or more to acquire a minority equity stake in a business, the typical investment is below £100,000. Loan capital may also be provided as part of a financing package. Typically, business angels make one or two investments over a three-year period and will usually be prepared to invest for a period of between three and five years.

Business angels invest with the primary motive of making a financial return, but non-financial motives also play an important part. They often enjoy being involved in growing a business and may also harbour altruistic motives such as wishing to help budding entrepreneurs or to make a contribution to the local economy (see reference 11 at the end of the chapter).

Business angels play an important financing role because the size and/or nature of their investments rarely appeal to private-equity firms. They tend to invest in start-ups and early-stage businesses, although they may also invest in more mature businesses. They are generally acknowledged to be a significant source of finance for small businesses; however, the exact scale of their investment is difficult to determine. This is because they are under no obligation to disclose how much they have invested. It has been estimated, however, that in the UK, business angels invest eight times as much in start-up businesses as do private-equity firms (see reference 12 at the end of the chapter).

Business angels can be an attractive source of finance because they are not encumbered by bureaucracy. They can make investment decisions quickly, particularly if they are familiar with the industry in which the business operates. They may also accept lower financial returns than are demanded by private-equity firms in order to have the opportunity to become involved in an interesting project.

Business angels often seek an active role within the business, which is usually welcomed by business owners as their skills, knowledge and experience can frequently be put to good use. The forms of involvement will typically include providing advice and moral support, providing business contacts and helping to make strategic decisions. However, the active involvement of a business angel may not simply be for the satisfaction gained from helping a business to grow.

Activity 7.19

What other motive may a business angel have for becoming actively involved?

By having a greater understanding of what is going on, and by exerting some influence over decision making, business angels are better placed to increase their financial rewards and/or reduce their level of investment risk.

Business angels tend to invest in businesses within their own locality. This may be because active involvement in the business may be feasible only if the business is within easy reach. Unsurprisingly, business angels also tend to invest in industries with which they have personal experience. One study revealed that around a third of business angels invest solely in industries with which they have had work experience. Around two-thirds of business angels, however, have made at least one investment within an industry with which they were unfamiliar (see reference 11 at the end of the chapter).

Angel syndicates

Where a large investment is required, a syndicate of business angels may be formed to raise the money. The syndicate may then take a majority equity stake in the business. Several advantages may spring from syndication.

Activity 7.20

Can you think of at least two advantages of syndication for a business angel?

The advantages include:

- sharing of risk
- pooling of expertise leading to better evaluation of investment opportunities
- access to larger-scale investment opportunities
- an increased capacity to provide follow-up funding
- sharing of transaction and monitoring costs
- increased opportunity to hold a diversified portfolio of investments.

You may have thought of others.

Business angels are often enthusiastic about syndication and there is a growing trend towards this form of financing. There are, however, potential disadvantages.

Activity 7.21

Can you think of at least two possible disadvantages of syndication for a business angel?

The possible disadvantages are:

- greater complexity of deal structures
- peer pressure
- disputes within the syndicate
- domination of the group by a single individual
- the need to comply with group decisions.

You may have thought of others.

From the perspective of an investee business, an angel syndicate can unlock access to a deeper pool of finance. However, dealing with a syndicate, rather than an individual, can lead to more drawn out and complex negotiations. It also means that more individuals have to be persuaded by the attractiveness of the deal.

The investment process

It was mentioned earlier that business angels can make decisions quickly. This does not mean, however, that finance is made available to a business overnight. A period of 4–6 months may be needed between the initial introduction and the provision of the finance. There is usually a thorough review of the business plan and financial forecasts. This may be followed by a series of meetings to help the business angel gain a deeper insight into the business and to deal with any concerns and issues that may arise.

Assuming these meetings go well and the business angel wishes to proceed, negotiations over the terms of the investment will then be undertaken. This can be the trickiest part of the process as agreement has to be reached over key issues such as the value of the business, the equity stake to be offered to the business angel and the price to be paid. Failure to reach agreement with the owners over a suitable price, and the post-investment role to be played by a business angel, are the two most common 'deal killers'. One study revealed that business angels may make four offers for every offer that is finally accepted (see reference 13 at the end of the chapter).

If agreement can be reached between the parties, **due diligence** can then be carried out. This will involve an investigation of all material information relating to the financial, technical and legal aspects of the business. Even at this early stage, the business angel should be considering the likely exit route from the investment. The available routes are broadly the same as those identified earlier for private-equity firms.

Angel networks

Business angels offer an informal source of share finance and it is not always easy for owners of small businesses to identify a suitable angel. However, business angel networks have developed to help owners of small businesses find their 'perfect partner'. These networks will offer various services, including:

- publishing investor bulletins and organising meetings to promote the investment opportunities available
- registering the investment interests of business angels and matching them with emerging opportunities
- screening investment proposals and advising owners of small businesses on how to present their proposal to interested angels.

The British Business Angels Association (BBAA) is the trade association for the business angel networks. In addition to being a major source of information about the business angel industry, it can help direct small businesses to their local network.

The UK government has increased tax reliefs for business angels in the hope of encouraging greater investment from this source. **Real World 7.13**, however, which is written by a leading business angel researcher, argues that this is not what is needed.

Real World 7.13

Tempting angels

Under the Seed Enterprise Investment Scheme (SEIS), which came into effect on April 6 2012, investors are given 50 per cent income tax relief on investments of up to £100,000 in young businesses, plus a one year capital gains tax holiday. At the same time, the limit for investments through the Enterprise Investment Scheme (EIS), upon which SEIS is based, was doubled and a wider range of companies became eligible. But are tax incentives for angel investors effective?

Proponents argue that it increases the amount of money that angels have available to invest, encourages new people to become business angels, and enables companies to attract investment to create new jobs. But critics say that tax incentives rarely, if ever, entice an investor to make an investment that they would otherwise not have made. There are also reasons to believe tax incentives are not enough to maintain a thriving business angel community.

First, the role of business angels is not simply to provide risk capital to businesses deemed too small or unattractive to attract venture capital or bank funding. Equally important is the hands-on role that angels play in their investee companies, by offering expertise to the entrepreneurs they back. Tax incentives arguably attract 'dumb' investors who cannot add any value. Second, angel investing has been described as 'a giant game of hide-and-seek with everyone blindfolded'. Potential investors need help to find entrepreneurs seeking finance and vice versa. Tax incentives do nothing to help with this. Third, tax incentives do not enhance the quality of the opportunities that angels come across. Indeed, the most frequent complaint of angels is that the businesses they see are not investment ready. Fourth, tax incentives put the emphasis on making the investment rather than enhancing returns. A tax incentive is ineffective if there is no 'harvest event'. Many business angels are stuck in investments that are unlikely to produce an exit but which need more money. Greater consideration of the exit at the time of the investment could have avoided some of these problems.

We used to have an effective infrastructure of business angel networks – mostly funded by the public sector, latterly regional development agencies – which addressed these issues. They enabled angels and entrepreneurs seeking finance to connect with one another. Several ran investment-ready courses for entrepreneurs. Some ran training programmes for angels. But, having lost their funding, most have now closed – and a huge amount of learning has been lost.

Some commercially orientated networks continue to operate, performing an important role. However, to be viable, they typically focus on larger deals of more than £500,000, and their geographical coverage is patchy. Angel networks supported by public sector funding focused on businesses seeking smaller amounts.

FT *Source*: Mason, C. (2012) 'Does tax relief tempt angels?', *Financial Times*, 20 April.

GOVERNMENT AND EU ASSISTANCE

The UK government offers tax incentives for investment in small businesses, such as the Seed Enterprise Investment Scheme mentioned above. Grants may also be awarded through regional and central government. However, one of the most effective ways in which the UK government assists small businesses is through the Enterprise Finance Guarantee Scheme. This helps small businesses that have viable business plans but lack the security, or suitable track record, to borrow. The scheme guarantees:

- 75 per cent of the amount borrowed, for which the borrower pays a premium of 2 per cent per year on the outstanding borrowing
- loans ranging from £1,000 to £1 million for a maximum period of 10 years.

The scheme is available for businesses that have annual sales revenue of up to £41 million.

In 2013, the UK government set up the British Business Bank. Its aim is to support economic growth by increasing access to finance and markets to smaller businesses. As well as developing new initiatives, the bank has taken over existing government commitments, such as the Enterprise Finance Guarantee Scheme. The bank does not lend or invest directly. Instead, it works through various financial institutions such as banks, leasing businesses and venture capital funds. To support smaller businesses, the bank also produces a guide which explains the various types and sources of finance available.

The EU provides assistance to smaller businesses in various forms. In addition to cash grants, the EU, through the European Investment Fund, offers loans. These loans are made through local financial institutions and are often on preferential terms. There are also specific EU funding programmes such as Cosme (Competitiveness of Enterprises and Small and Medium-Sized Enterprises). This programme helps small businesses gain access to financial markets through guarantees or by providing risk capital to private equity funds. A further funding programme, Horizon 2020, supports projects relating to innovation, advanced technology and the environment.

THE ALTERNATIVE INVESTMENT MARKET (AIM)

There are now a number of stock markets throughout the world that specialise in the shares of smaller businesses. These include the **Alternative Investment Market (AIM)**, which is the largest and most successful. AIM is a second-tier market of the London Stock Exchange. It was created in 1995 and grew rapidly for many years. It now includes a significant proportion of non-UK businesses, reflecting the international ambitions of the market. AIM offers smaller businesses a stepping stone to the main market – though not all AIM-listed businesses wish to make this step – and offers private-equity firms a useful exit route from their investments.

The regulatory framework

AIM provides businesses with many of the benefits of a listing on the main market without the cost or burdensome regulatory environment. Obtaining an AIM listing and raising funds costs the typical business about £500,000. Differences in the regulatory environment between the main market and AIM can be summarised as follows:

Main market	*AIM*
Minimum 25 per cent of shares in public hands	No minimum of shares to be in public hands
Normally, 3-year trading record required	No trading record requirement

Main market	*AIM*
Prior shareholder approval required for substantial acquisitions and disposals	No prior shareholder approval required for such transactions
Pre-vetting of admission documents by the UK Listing Authority	Admission documents not pre-vetted by the Stock Exchange or the UK Listing Authority
Minimum market capitalisation	No minimum market capitalisation

Source: Adapted from information on London Stock Exchange website, www.londonstockexchange.com.

A key element of the regulatory regime is that each business must appoint a Nominated Adviser (NOMAD) before joining AIM and then retain its services throughout the period of a listing. The NOMAD's role, which is undertaken by corporate financiers and investment bankers, involves the dual responsibilities of corporate adviser and regulator. It includes assessing the suitability of a business for joining AIM, bringing a business to market and monitoring its share trading. A NOMAD must also help AIM-listed businesses to strike the right balance between fostering an entrepreneurial culture and public accountability. It will therefore advise on matters such as corporate governance structures and the timing of public announcements.

To retain its role and status in the market, a NOMAD must jealously guard its reputation. It will, therefore, not act for businesses that it considers unsuitable for any reason. If a NOMAD ceases to act for a business, its shares are suspended until a new NOMAD is appointed. The continuing support of a NOMAD is therefore important, which helps it to wield influence over the business. This should help create a smooth functioning market and pre-empt the need for a large number of prescriptive rules.

This lighter regulatory touch has led some to accuse it of being little more than a casino. This criticism, however, often emanates from competitor markets. To date, the flexibility and cost-effectiveness of AIM have proved difficult to match.

AIM-listed businesses

AIM-listed businesses vary considerably in size, with equity market values ranging from less than £2 million to more than £1 billion. A majority, however, has an equity market value of less than £25 million. In recent years, the London Stock Exchange has tried to encourage larger AIM-listed businesses to transfer to the main market. However, as they can raise money easily and cheaply without enduring a heavy regulatory burden, there is little incentive to do so. AIM-listed businesses include Majestic Wine plc and Millwall Football Club.

Real World 7.14 below provides some impression of the size distribution of AIM-listed businesses.

Real World 7.14

Distribution of AIM-listed businesses by equity market value

The distribution of businesses by equity market value at the end of February 2016 is shown in Figure 7.9.

→

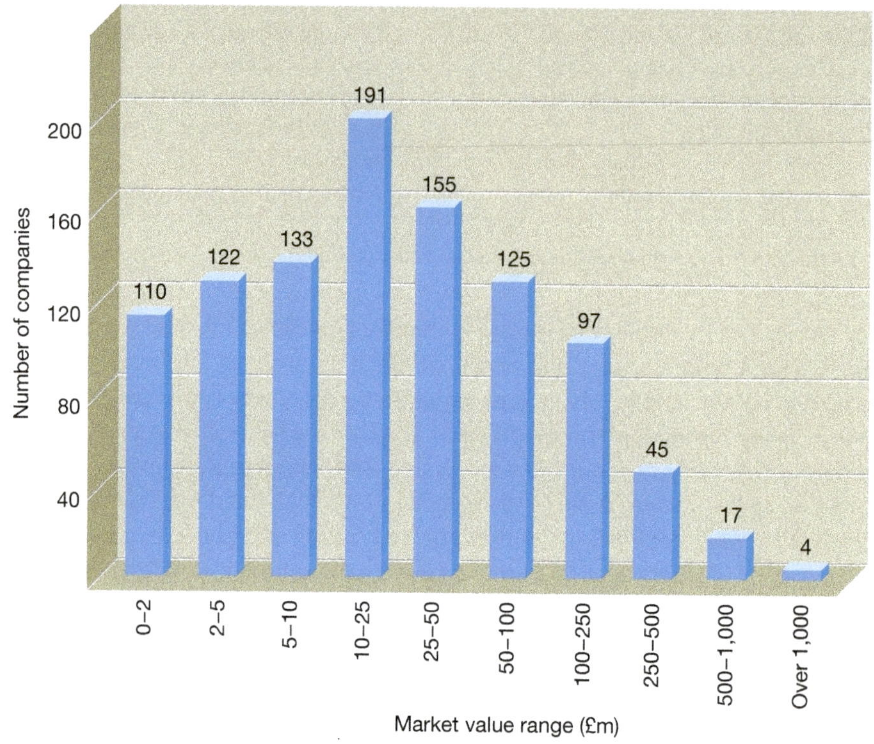

The chart shows that 110 businesses have a market capitalisation of less than £2 million. However, four businesses have a market capitalisation of more than £1,000 million.

Figure 7.9 Distribution of AIM-listed businesses by equity market value

Source: Chart compiled from information in AIM market statistics, London Stock Exchange, www.londonstockexchange.com, February 2016.

Investing in AIM-listed businesses

AIM has proved to be successful in attracting both private and institutional investors. However, AIM-listed businesses are 'usually smaller, and younger, companies with less diversified businesses that are often heavily dependent on relatively small sectors of the economy. They are, therefore, more susceptible to economic shocks than larger, more established companies' (see reference 14 at the end of the chapter). This means there is always a risk that, during difficult economic times, share prices will fall sharply as investors make a 'flight to quality'. Share price weakness during periods of uncertainty may be increased by a lack of media coverage or analysts' reports to help investors understand what is going on.

Although market liquidity has improved in recent years, it can still be a problem. This is particularly true for businesses that are too small to attract institutional investors, or where the shares are tightly held by directors, or where investors lack confidence in the business. If, for whatever reason, shares are infrequently traded, market makers may significantly adjust buying and selling prices, leading to sharp price changes. This can also mean that relatively small share trades will lead to a huge change in share price.

A broad range of industry sectors are represented in the market. However, financial businesses and resource-based businesses, such as mining, oil and gas businesses, are easily the most important. The market might be more attractive to investors if a more balanced portfolio of businesses could be achieved.

Real World 7.15 reveals that, since its inception, returns to investors from AIM-listed businesses have been disappointing.

Real World 7.15

Aiming to lose money

. . . Aim provides a lower-cost alternative for growth companies seeking investment. Yet it has been dogged by poor returns and a host of corporate failures – including some high-profile fraud cases. Investing in small, unproven companies is inherently riskier than backing larger, more predictable ones, and Aim's annualised total return of −1.6 per cent a year when measured over the past two decades is hardly cause for celebration. The fact that average returns from small-cap UK companies outside Aim have been much stronger, by comparison, is a further worry.

Over the past 20 years, investors would have lost money in 72 per cent of all the companies ever to have listed on Aim, according to Professors Dimson and Marsh of London Business School. Analysing data on the 2,877 companies which have listed on Aim, they calculate that in more than 30 per cent of cases, shareholders lost at least 95 per cent of their investment. By contrast, there are 39 companies – just 1.4 per cent of the historic total – that have given investors multi-year returns in excess of 1,000 per cent. 'While these have been superb performers, there have simply not been enough of them for Aim as a whole to generate a decent return for investors,' says Prof Dimson.

Five of the top ten best-performing Aim shares of all time have since moved to a main market listing – a hoped-for rite of passage since the junior market was created – and the professors argue that to exclude them from any 'best of' index would skew the overall picture. However, their subsequent level of success has been mixed – separate research by Numis Securities shows that the 100 or so Aim alumni have generally performed poorly since transferring.

Aim's two decades of underperformance are variously blamed on its high weighting of resources stocks (currently around one-third of companies listed), a high level of IPOs from 'unseasoned' companies, and a tendency towards fads. Aim's lower cost of listing often results in several small opportunist companies chasing the same market trend – and not all of them will survive. Investors bold enough to buy shares in oil explorers, biotech or tech companies will often pick a 'basket' of stocks, but this is clearly a high-risk investment strategy.

Another problem is the number of 'lobster pots' – one fund manager's nickname for the hundreds of small and illiquid companies at the lower echelons of Aim where it has been easy for investors to put their money in, but nigh on impossible to get it out again.

FT *Source*: Barrett, C. (2015) 'AIM – 20 years of a few winners and many losers', *Financial Times*, 19 June.

Crowdfunding

Crowdfunding has become an increasingly popular method of raising finance for small businesses. It involves connecting a business directly to a large pool of potential investors (the crowd) through an internet-based platform. Crowdfunding can be used to raise both equity and debt. In the latter case, it is provided through various methods such as peer-to-peer lending, mini-bonds and invoice financing.

Businesses wishing to raise equity finance by crowdfunding will make a pitch through an internet platform. Before doing so, however, they must demonstrate that they represent a viable investment. The platform provider will, therefore, carry out due diligence on each applicant, which normally leads to a high rejection rate. Businesses that are admitted to the platform will receive the funds raised from investors when the target amount is reached. If the target is not reached, the money is returned to investors.

In most cases, the money required by businesses is for start-up (seed) capital and so this form of financing offers an alternative to business angels. Most pitches made by businesses for equity funding are for less than £500,000 (see reference 15 at the end of the chapter). In this fast-moving area, however, pitches seem to be increasing in size. Individual investors can usually invest small amounts (from as little as £10) and are charged a success fee based on profits arising from their equity investment.

One drawback for investors is that they hold an illiquid investment as there is no secondary market for the shares acquired.

Activity 7.22

Can you think how the equity investment of investors may eventually be liquidated?

The most likely opportunities are where a business is eventually floated on the stock exchange or where it is acquired by another business.

Crowdfunding is an innovative and rapidly evolving form of alternative finance. It is also a disruptive force as it bypasses traditional financial institutions. However, financial institutions are adapting to this new world by investing through crowdfunding platforms, particularly with respect to debt financing. At present, the UK dominates the crowdfunding market in Europe. It boasts the most sophisticated trading platforms as well as a regulatory framework designed for this emerging market. This latter feature, however, raises difficulties. Regulators must somehow strike the right balance between investor protection and allowing this new form of financing to develop.

Crowdfunding offers the prospect of high rewards for equity investors but also carries high risks. Investing seed capital is always a risky business and high failure rates among fledgling businesses are the norm. The problem is that crowdfunding attracts many unsophisticated investors who may not fully appreciate the risks involved. Furthermore, the opportunities on offer do not always provide sufficient transparency or high-quality information. This increases the difficulties of making informed judgements as well as the chances of fraud by businesses and internet platform providers.

SUMMARY

The main points of this chapter may be summarised as follows:

The Stock Exchange

- It provides a primary and secondary market in capital for large businesses.
- Obtaining a Stock Exchange listing can help a business to raise finance and help to raise its profile, but obtaining a listing can be costly and the regulatory burden can be onerous.

Capital market efficiency

- A stock market is efficient if information is processed by investors quickly and accurately so that prices faithfully reflect all relevant information.
- Three forms of efficiency have been suggested: the weak form, the semi-strong form and the strong form.
- If a stock market is efficient, managers of a listed business should learn six important lessons:
  - Timing doesn't matter.
  - Don't search for undervalued businesses.
  - Take note of market reaction.
  - You can't fool the market.
  - The market decides the level of risk.
  - Champion the interests of shareholders.
- Stock market anomalies and behavioural research provide a challenge to the notion of market efficiency.

Share issues

- Share issues that involve the payment of cash by investors include rights issues, public issues, offers for sale and placings.
- A rights issue is made to existing shareholders. The law requires that shares to be issued for cash must first be offered to existing shareholders.
- A public issue involves a direct issue to the public and an offer for sale involves an indirect issue to the public.
- A placing is an issue of shares to selected investors.
- A bonus (scrip) issue involves issuing shares to existing shareholders. No payment is required as the issue is achieved by transferring a sum from reserves to the share capital.
- A tender issue allows investors to determine the price at which the shares are issued.

Smaller businesses

- Do not have access to the Stock Exchange main market and so must look elsewhere for funds.
- Private equity (venture capital) is long-term capital for small or medium-sized businesses not listed on the Stock Exchange. These businesses often have high levels of risk but provide the private-equity firm with the prospect of high levels of return.
- Private-equity firms are interested in businesses with good growth prospects and offer finance for start-ups, business expansions and buyouts.
- The investment period is usually five years or more and the private-equity firms may exit by a trade sale, flotation, buyback or sale to another financial institution.
- Business angels are often wealthy individuals who are willing to invest in businesses at an early stage of development.
- They can usually make quick decisions and will often become actively involved in the business.

→

- Various business angel networks exist to help small business owners find an angel.
- The EU and UK government assists small businesses through a variety of measures such as guaranteeing or providing loans, providing grants and tax incentives.
- The Alternative Investment Market (AIM) specialises in the shares of smaller businesses.
- AIM is a second-tier market of the Stock Exchange, which offers many of the benefits of a main market listing without the same cost or regulatory burden.
- AIM has proved popular with investors but could benefit from greater market liquidity and a more balanced portfolio of listed businesses.
- Crowdfunding involves connecting a business directly to a large pool of potential investors. Businesses wishing to raise equity or debt in this way use an internet platform to make their pitch.

KEY TERMS

Stock Exchange
FTSE (Footsie) indices
Market capitalisation
Efficient stock market
Behavioural finance
Rights issue
Bonus issue (scrip issue)
Offer for sale
Public issue
Tender issue
Placing
Private equity
Venture capital
Business angels
Due diligence
Alternative Investment Market (AIM)
Crowdfunding

For definitions of these terms, see the Glossary, pp. 625–633.

REFERENCES

1 Gregory A., Guermat C. and Al-Shawawreh (2009) *UK:IPOs: Long-run returns, behavioural timing and pseudo timing.* Discussion paper No 08/06, Centre for Finance and Investment, University of Exeter, September.

2 London Stock Exchange, *Practical Guide to Listing,* www.londonstockexchange.com, p. 24.

3 Haldane, A. and Davies, R. (2011) The short long Speech given at 29th Société Universitaire Europèene de Recherches Financières Colloquium: New Paradigms in Money and Finance? Brussels, May, p. 1.

4 Wighton, D. (2011) 'We must end short termism. And it won't wait', *The Times,* 17 May, www.thetimes.co.uk.

5 London Stock Exchange, Main Market Statistics, December 2015, Table 3.

6 Armitage, S. (2000) 'The direct costs of UK rights issues and open offers', *European Financial Management,* Vol. 6, pp. 57–68.

7 London Stock Exchange, Main Market Statistics, December 2015.

8 Institute of Chartered Accountants in England and Wales (2000) *SME Finance and Regulation.*

9 *Report of the Committee of Inquiry on Small Firms* (Bolton Committee), Cmnd 4811, HMSO, 1971; British Private Equity and Venture Capital Association, *A Guide to Private Equity,* www.bvca.co.uk.

10 Norton, E. (1995) 'Venture capital as an alternative means to allocate capital: an agency-theoretic view', *Entrepreneurship,* Winter, pp. 19–30.

11 Macht, S. (2007) 'The post-investment period of business angels: Impact and involvement', www.eban.org, July, pp. 14–15.

12 Mason, C.M. and Harrison, R.T. (2000) 'The size of the informal venture capital market in the United Kingdom', *Small Business Economics*, Vol. 15, pp. 137–148.

13 Mason, C.M. and Harrison, R.T. (2002) quoted in Carriere, S. (2006) 'Best practice in angel groups and angel syndication', www.eban.org, January, p. 7.

14 Moore, J. (2008) 'The acid test – how the market has performed', *AIM: The growth market of the world*, London Stock Exchange, p. 93.

15 *Equity Crowdfunding in the UK: Evidence from the Equity Tracker*, British Business Bank, 2014, p. 22.

FURTHER READING

If you wish to explore the topics discussed in this chapter in more depth, try the following books:

Arnold, G. (2013) *Corporate Financial Management*, 5th edn, Pearson, Chapters 9 and 10.

Pike, R. Neale, B. and Linsley P. (2015) *Corporate Finance and Investment*, 8th edn, Pearson, Chapters 2 and 16.

Sulphey M. (2014) *Behavioral Finance*, PHI Learning, Chapters 3–6.

Sun, L. (2012) *Capital Market Efficiency and Stock Price Anomalies: Theories and evidence*, LAP Lambert Academic Publishing.

REVIEW QUESTIONS

Solutions to these questions can be found at the back of the book on pp. 595–596.

7.1 UK private-equity firms have been criticised for the low level of funding invested in business start-ups by comparison with the levels invested by their US counterparts. Can you think of possible reasons why such a difference may exist?

7.2 Why might a listed business revert to being an unlisted business?

7.3 Distinguish between an offer for sale and a public issue of shares.

7.4 What kind of attributes should the owners and managers of a business possess to attract private equity finance?

EXERCISES

Exercises 7.5 to 7.7 are more advanced than 7.1 to 7.4. Those with coloured numbers have solutions at the back of the book, starting on p. 612.

If you wish to try more exercises, visit the students' side of this book's companion website.

7.1 Comment on each of the following statements.

(a) A stock market that is efficient in the strong form is one in which investors cannot make any gains from their investment.

(b) Private-equity firms are not interested in investing in business start-ups.

(c) Short-term behaviour by investors is difficult to reconcile with the notion of stock market efficiency.

7.2 Consider each of the following.

1 An investor expects to make abnormal gains on her stock market investments by analysing published annual reports, relevant newspaper articles, industry reports and published share prices.
2 Dorsal plc, a business listed on the London Stock Exchange, received a confidential letter from a rival business on 30 July 2016 offering to buy all its shares at a premium of 20 per cent on their current market value. At a private meeting, convened on the same day, the directors of Dorsal plc agreed to accept the offer and made a public announcement of this decision on 3 August 2016.
3 Juniper plc is an airport operator that is listed on the London Stock Exchange. Recently, the board of directors agreed to change the company's depreciation policy concerning airport runways. In future, these assets will be written off over 100 years rather than 50 years. This change, which will reduce the annual depreciation charge over the next 50 years, is solely designed to increase reported profits over that period and thereby create a better impression to investors of business performance.

Required:

(a) What is the maximum level of market efficiency that the investor is assuming in (1) above? Briefly explain your answer.
(b) What would be the share price reaction to the announcement in (2) above under the strong form of market efficiency and why?
(c) What is the maximum level of market efficiency that the board of directors is assuming in (3) above that is consistent with such behaviour? Briefly explain your answer.

7.3 Provide *two* reasons why:

(a) Tax incentives may have only limited value in stimulating greater investment by business angels.
(b) Business angels can be an attractive source of finance to entrepreneurs.
(c) Business angels may find it difficult being part of an angel syndicate in order to finance a business.

7.4 Pizza Shack plc operates a chain of pizza restaurants. The business started operations five years ago and has enjoyed uninterrupted and rapid growth. The directors, however, believe that future growth can be achieved only if the business seeks a listing on the London Stock Exchange. If the directors go ahead with a listing, the financial advisers to the business have suggested that an issue of ordinary shares by tender at a minimum price of £2.20 would be an appropriate method of floating the business. The advisers have suggested that 3 million ordinary shares should be issued in the first instance, although the directors of the business are keen to raise the maximum amount of funds possible.

Initial research carried out by the financial advisers suggests that the following demand for shares at different market prices is likely:

Share price	*Number of shares tendered at each share price*
£	*000s*
3.60	850
3.20	1,190
2.80	1,380
2.40	1,490
2.00	1,540
1.60	1,560
	8,010

Required:

(a) Discuss the advantages and disadvantages of making a tender issue of shares.

(b) Calculate the expected proceeds from the tender issue, assuming the business

(i) issues 3 million shares

(ii) wishes to raise the maximum amount of funds possible.

7.5 The board of directors of Wicklow plc is considering an expansion of production capacity following an increase in sales over the past two years. The most recent financial statements for the business are set out below.

Statement of financial position as at 30 November Year 5

	£m
ASSETS	
Non-current assets	
Property, plant and equipment	
Land and buildings	22.0
Machinery and equipment	11.0
Fixtures and fittings	8.0
	41.0
Current assets	
Inventories	14.0
Trade receivables	22.0
Cash at bank	2.0
	38.0
Total assets	79.0
EQUITY AND LIABILITIES	
Equity	
£0.50 ordinary shares	20.0
Retained earnings	19.0
	39.0
Non-current liabilities	
Borrowings – 12% loan	20.0
Current liabilities	
Trade payables	20.0
Total equity and liabilities	79.0

Income statement for the year ended 30 November Year 5

	£m
Sales revenue	95.0
Operating profit	8.0
Interest charges	(2.4)
Profit before taxation	5.6
Tax (30%)	(1.7)
Profit for the year	3.9

A dividend of £1.2 million was proposed and paid during the year.

The business plans to invest a further £15 million in machinery and equipment and is considering two possible financing options. The first option is to make a one-for-four rights issue. The current market price per share is £2.00 and the rights shares would be issued at a discount of 25 per cent on this market price. The second option is to take a further loan that will have an initial annual rate of interest of 10 per cent. This is a variable rate and while interest rates have been stable for a number of years, there has been speculation recently that interest rates will begin to rise in the near future.

The outcome of the expansion is not certain. The management team involved in developing and implementing the expansion plans has provided three possible outcomes concerning operating profit (profit before interest and tax) for the following year:

	Change in profits before interest and tax from previous year
Optimistic	+30%
Most likely	+10%
Pessimistic	−20%

The dividend per share for the forthcoming year is expected to remain the same as for the year ended 30 November Year 5.

Wicklow plc has a lower level of gearing than most of its competitors. This has been in accordance with the wishes of the Wicklow family, which has a large shareholding in the business. The share price of the business has shown rapid growth in recent years and the P/E ratio for the business is 20.4 times, which is much higher than the industry average of 14.3 times.

Costs of raising finance should be ignored.

Required:

(a) Prepare calculations that show the effect of each of the possible outcomes of the expansion programme on:
 (i) earnings per share
 (ii) the gearing ratio (based on year-end figures), and
 (iii) the interest cover ratio of Wicklow plc, under both of the financing options.

(b) Assess each of the financing options available to Wicklow plc from the point of view of an existing shareholder and compare the possible future outcomes with the existing situation.

7.6 Devonian plc has the following long-term capital structure as at 30 November Year 4:

	£m
Ordinary shares 25p fully paid	50.0
General reserve	22.5
Retained earnings	25.5
	98.0

The business has no long-term loans.

In the year to 30 November Year 4, the operating profit (profit before interest and taxation) was £40 million and it is expected that this will increase by 25 per cent during the forthcoming year. The business is listed on the London Stock Exchange and the share price as at 30 November Year 4 was £2.10.

The business wishes to raise £72 million in order to re-equip one of its factories and is considering two possible financing options. The first option is to make a one-for-five rights issue at a discount price of £1.80 per share. The second option is to take out a long-term loan at an interest rate of 10 per cent a year. If the first option is taken, it is expected that the price/earnings (P/E) ratio will remain the same for the forthcoming year. If the second option is taken, it is estimated that the P/E ratio will fall by 10 per cent by the end of the forthcoming year.

Assume a tax rate of 30 per cent.

Required:

(a) Assuming a rights issue of shares is made, calculate:
  (i) the theoretical ex-rights price of an ordinary share in Devonian plc
  (ii) the value of the rights for each original ordinary share.

(b) Calculate the price of an ordinary share in Devonian plc in one year's time assuming:
  (i) a rights issue is made
  (ii) a loan issue is made.
  Comment on your findings.

(c) Explain why rights issues are usually made at a discount.

(d) From the business's viewpoint, how critical is the pricing of a rights issue likely to be?

7.7 Carpets Direct plc wishes to increase the number of its retail outlets. The board of directors has decided to finance this expansion programme by raising the funds from existing shareholders through a one-for-four rights issue. The most recent income statement of the business is as follows:

Income statement for the year ended 30 April

	£m
Sales revenue	164.5
Operating profit	12.6
Interest	(6.2)
Profit before taxation	6.4
Tax	(1.9)
Profit for the year	4.5

An ordinary dividend of £2.0 million was proposed and paid during the year.

The share capital of the business consists of 120 million ordinary shares with a nominal value of £0.50 per share. The shares of the business are currently being traded on the Stock Exchange at a price/earnings ratio of 22 times and the board of directors has decided to issue the new shares at a discount of 20 per cent on the current market value.

Required:

(a) Calculate the theoretical ex-rights price of an ordinary share in Carpets Direct plc.

(b) Calculate the price at which the rights in Carpets Direct plc are likely to be traded.

(c) Identify and evaluate, at the time of the rights issue, each of the options arising from the rights issue to an investor who holds 4,000 ordinary shares before the rights announcement.